Anthology of Magazine Verse

&

Yearbook of American Poetry
1981 Edition

YEARBOOK RESEARCH & COMPILATION:

JASON R. PATER

ANTHOLOGY OF MAGAZINE VERSE

AND YEARBOOK OF AMERICAN POETRY

1981 EDITION

Edited by

ALAN F. PATER

Introduction by

KENNETH J. ATCHITY

BEVERLY HILLS
MONITOR BOOK COMPANY, INC.

COPYRIGHT © 1981 BY MONITOR BOOK COMPANY, INC.

SECOND ANNUAL EDITION

Printed in the United States of America

ISBN number: 0-917734-05-X

ISSN number: 0196-2221

Library of Congress catalogue card No. 80-645223

The Anthology of Magazine Verse & Yearbook of American Poetry is published annually by Monitor Book Company, Inc., 195 South Beverly Drive, Beverly Hills, CA 90212.

Preface to the First Edition (1980)

Much of thé world's finest and most prolific poetry has first appeared in periodical literature: poetry monthlies and quarterlies, general literary magazines, college journals, etc.

Regrettably, most of those publications have limited circulations, and once an issue has been read—and the next one arrives—it is filed away and rarely opened again. But the wealth of excellent work contained in their pages—by both talented, promising new poets and well-known, established writers—should be kept alive, distributed more widely and be readily available. That is the *raison d'etre* of the *Anthology of Magazine Verse*.

After William Stanley Braithwaite ended his much respected annual surveys of magazine poetry in 1929, there was a lamentable gap in the important business of selecting and preserving in book form the verse of the day. That pause was temporarily filled with the re-emergence of the *Anthology of Magazine Verse* in the mid-1930's through the early 1940's by the editor of this current volume, but World War II then interrupted the continuation of the series.

Now, this new series of annual collections is aimed at re-establishing the purpose and spirit of the Braithwaite books on a continuing basis, and thereby providing a yearly barometer of the trends of poetry in the United States and Canada.

An effort has been made to include poems of various lengths, forms and styles, as well as a multiplicity of subjects and geographical originations. And the spread of magazine sources chosen reflects these criteria.

It should be noted that the sources included in any given volume of the Anthology constitute only a portion of the total number of periodicals regularly received by the editor and considered for suitable material. Since the quality of the individual poem is the main criterion for acceptance, the specific magazines represented in each edition of the Anthology will necessarily vary from year to year.

Magazine poetry best represents the era in which it is written—it is current, abundant, as varied in style and content as the numberless journals in which it is published. Its topics are today's issues and events, as well as the perennial ones. New poets, who, because of the current realities of the book world, find it difficult to have their work published in hardcover, fortunately have an outlet in the increasing volume of magazines that print new and original poetry. It is from their ranks that the future major poets will emerge.

Also part of this volume is the *Yearbook of American Poetry*—the first and only annual gathering of factual material in this burgeoning field. The *Yearbook*'s directories, bibliographies and listings (to be updated with each succeeding edition) will provide a yearly record of information and reference material for the world of poetry—an area heretofore lacking a comprehensive information sourcebook of its own.

Together, the *Anthology of Magazine Verse and Yearbook of American Poetry* will, hopefully, be inspiring, stimulating, informative, and an accurate reflection of the state of the poetic form today.

Beverly Hills,
California   A.F.P.

Table of Contents

PART ONE

Anthology
of Magazine Verse

Introduction

by
KENNETH JOHN ATCHITY

*Associate Professor of Comparative Literature,
Occidental College; senior editor,* Contemporary Quarterly,
co-editor, Dreamworks

The vitality of vision in American letters today shows in the diversity and professionalism of this anthology. We are in the midst of a poetic pentecost: The Muse descends among her apostles and teaches them to sing in as many voices as there are neighborhoods and nations, natural wonders and horrors, personal and social agonies and triumphs, nightmares and dreams.

Poets complain that no one is listening, that their voices cry in a wilderness of philistines and videots. But, as with most religions, the best disciples are the priests. Like a clerical directory, this volume suggests—as much by its omissions and exclusions as by the names it includes—how considerable the audience of poets, and therefore the audience for poetry, already is. If only poets read poetry, that is a goodly number of elect. What better audience? And when was it ever different? The public addressed in all these poems is the poetic public of those whose sensitivities are sufficient to comprehend and to care.

Poetry rings unreasonable bells. It doesn't explain—it causes: an emotion, an insight, a new vision of the world or of life. If you're not sure the poem has worked this way, it hasn't worked poetically. Poetic certainty is immediate, touching the chill within us, before understanding comes along to explain what happened, before analysis with its flashing lights arrives on the scene to investigate how what happened happened.

Contemporary poetry is different from classical poetry in only one respect. Classical poetry has worked its miracles through time; contemporary poetry is still a risk. This volume allows us to participate in the risk, to further the sorting process already begun by the editor. When we recognize our involvement with poetry this way, we accept our responsibility to judge as well as to create. Judgment leads to new creation just as surely as creation leads to judgment. While poetry is an intensely personal craft, poets are made through publication. As Rainer Maria Rilke puts it in "The Knight" (translated by John N. Miller), the poet's pen is "The strange emancipating sword/Which draws me from my place of lurking/Where I spend so many bored, stoop-shouldered days—/That I might finally stretch my wings/And play/And sing."

The net is cast in all directions, "involving the four corners of the sky," and its catch laid out for sorting. The universality of the Muse's modern presence is manifested by the internationalism of these selections. Umberto Saba's voice speaks clearly in Christopher Millis' translation of "Woman": ". . . Behind/the darkest hair that I wind/in my fingers, I'm no longer afraid/of the little white pointed demon ear." Marie Takvan's vision is brought from Norway by Harold P. Hansen in "The Deepest Bow": "I want to dance a young dance/to a song within me/and to the notes from my taut strings." Lynn C. Jacox gives us Jorge Luis Borges' haunting "Ode Written in 1966" in a self-effacing English that allows the Argentinian poet's light to shine through the darkness of his vision:

> . . . No one is the homeland. Not even time
> Charged with battles, with swords and with exodus
> And with the slow population of regions
> That border the rising of the sun and the setting of a star
> . . . The homeland, friends, is a perpetual act
> Like the perpetual world. (If the Eternal

> Spectator were to cease dreaming us
> For a single instant, he would hurl
> Blunt, white lightning, His forgetfulness.)
> No one is the homeland, but we all must
> Be worthy of the ancient oath . . .

Other welcome voices that join here with the American muse include those of Pablo Neruda and Carlos Montemayor, Pier Paolo Pasolini, Salvatore Quasimodo, and Dino Campana; Stefan George, Aleksandr Pushkin, Gevorg Emin (Armenian), Leah Goldberg (Hebrew), Edvard Kocbek (Slovanian), Par Langerkvist (Swedish), Kadia Molodowski (Yiddish), and Wislawa Szymborska (Polish).

The American poets represent Walt Whitman's "multitudes within" one culture, their variety evident in both style and theme. Styles range from elegance to explosion. Samuel Hazo's "Maps for a Son Are Drawn as You Go" is all lyrical precision and easy familiarity with the American language: "By then/you'll learn that all you know/will help you less than how/you think./The rest is memory,/and memory's the graveyard of the mind/as surely as tomorrow is its myth." The undemanding classicism of Merle Molofsky's "Reflections" achieves its chill through personal metaphor and confessional rhythms. The other end of the stylistic spectrum, dramatic and insistent, shows in David James' "The Famous Outlaw Stops in for a Drink": "I ride into town./The moon splatters above the buildings/like a bullet/hitting sand." Both extremes are traditional—and contemporary—American.

Self-reflexive poetry (art about art) has often, in our tradition, been awkward in its introspection. Here, in many fine examples like John Koethe's "Picture of Little Letters," Nicholas Rinaldi's "Teahouse," and Joyce Carol Oates' "The Present Tense," a new strain of unselfconscious self-consciousness reveals itself. In Albert Goldbarth's "Note from an Exhibition," art is accepted easily as a familiar metaphor for the accelerating world of images we live in today: "It's/not that easy really: You don't whip a star/in on taut black fishline. You don't nail sun to the/cross in your lens. It will rise/without your faith. And behind the perpendicular/weave of nylon, the heat of you that's/calling me sexually defies measurement."

By making the unbearable appear contained, art has become a primary method of control in this century. We create our own worlds in order to resist those infinite worlds not our own with which the mechanisms of global communication surround us. One example of this genre is John Hay's "Music by the Waters," which condenses Wallace Stevens' mystery-invoking "The Idea of Order at Key West" to the familiar pragmatics of the peripatetic craftsman who assembles a self-image from materials daily at hand—in order to make it through the day:

> Out of the marbled underwaters,
> artifacts of surf, comes the shining
> of bubble and frog-green weed; the salivated
> quartz egg; purple dye of greater storms
> in minor shells; all things touched by tides;
> patterns of water not of water;
> castoffs, like speckled eyes from deeper sight,
> tones on the mind. I pick them and they sing.

The Belgian Maurice Careme, translated by Norma Farber in *Poetry Now*, illustrates the new intimacy of art and nature in "You Can Get Despondent":

> You can get despondent over not being a poet,
> over your genius being just a bird in your head,
>
> a bird that can only repeat endlessly
> the same song causing the fir-trees to embrace,

when there might be so many things to say
about the clouds, the prairies, the smile,

like a fresh cherry, of very young girls,
about the horses round which the wasps are glittering,

about dawn which uses the weirs of wheat
to rescue its pearly fish from obscurity,

about the angels you see sometimes high overhead
in a triangle—and you think they're birds;

about God himself, God who is everything at once:
man, blade of grass, pebble, squirrel and great forest.

Satire and skepticism are also present in force, from the allegorical-philosophical of Howard Nemerov's "The Three Towns" to the droll confessional of Ronald Koertge's "The Magic Words": "are not Abracadabra . . . /The real magic words are these: I love myself/more than I love you." Nature continues to compel poetic vision, as in Ann Stanford's "The Deserted Garden," Diane Wakoski's "Aging," or "Life's Evil," by Eugenio Montale (translated by Jan Pallister. The natural and individual come together in Kathleen Spivack's "Shining": " . . . I am walking toward the sea./The grass is shining with just-rain./I want to say/so much and yet say nothing, . . . /I am trampling/wild strawberries, the scarlet hidden ones,/in my haste, in my haste."

Alienation is the key through which aging is shown in Paul Lake's "An Old Folks Home." The violence of contemporary life moves from the personal of Ruth Daigon's "Like an Ideal Tenant" ("the bullet fits precisely in the wound,/closer than . . . / . . . a lover") to the social-political of Virginia Brady Young's "Taught to Be Polite": "The guns at Dong Ha boomed/when he died. A farmer cursed/the mess his body made."

Whether apocalyptical or ameliorative, these poems reveal the dreams of our culture—and of the visionaries who offer their own visions as ours. The old associations of poetry with folly, of poets with children whose license to play makes them our prophets, still link poetry with truth. Not philosophical truth, which strives vainly to prove the unprovable—but the truth of experience which needs only the agony of expression to be shared. Poets accept their role today as self-importantly and as humbly as they always have. The narrator in Charles Bukowski's "My Style" confesses: "I became a writer but when I was a boy/I used to dream of becoming the village idiot;/I used to lie in bed and imagine myself that idiot,/planning ways to get food easily and sympathy easily,/a planned confusion of not too much love or effort./some would claim that I have succeeded/in this." Art is the playhouse of the mind, and poets are congratulated for saying things that madmen are incarcerated for saying. "The difference," said Salvador Dali, "between myself and a madman is that I am not mad."

The poet's dream has always been to make his return to the all-licensed freedom of dream. We accompany him as far as we can imagine. If we allow it, his eyes see for us; they become our own. His dreams are conjugal, joining him and us, as in David Wagoner's "Under the Sign of Moth": "My wife is already sleeping, not knowing/We will spread our dreams under the Sign of Moth,/A constellation presiding over us/ . . . by clinging/Somehow to the plaster heaven we trusted/To see us safely . . . through the night."

Poetry is, as Wagoner suggests, "a dream of becoming/A shape that wants to leave old forms behind." Robert Penn Warren's "Commuter's Entry in a Connecticut Diary" can't decide whether the dream or the day "is the world." A similar disorientation, based on the narrator's diminishing awareness of his own failure to hold the parts of experience apart, concludes "A Small Elegy" by the Czech poet Jiri Orten (translated by Lyn Coffin):

   . . .   How
dark it is outside! What was I going to say?
Oh, yes, now I remember. Because

of all those hours I slept soundly, through calm
nights, because of all the loved ones who are deep
in dreams—now, when everything's running short, I
        can't stand
being here by myself.   The lamplight's too strong.
I am sowing grain on the headland.
I will not live long.

The poet, in his dreamwork, flies into that "undiscover'd country" from which no traveler returns. He is our soul who leaves our body when we sleep. But he returns, in that extraordinary waking act known as poetry—to tell us what he saw in his visionary flight. From the image factory of his visionary mind he reconstructs his vision, brings it to us: a gift of new life. "Myths are public dreams," says Joseph Campbell, "dreams are private myths." The dreamwork of contemporary poetry, as we partake of its energy in this anthology, is the shaping of tomorrow's myth, the making of the human future. The shaping transcends the shape, as making is preferred by poets over having made. We keep moving because we see clearly where we have been and envision, in our dreams and art, where we might go. We survive this way; we evolve. As Unamuno says, "Dream abides. It is the only thing that abides. Vision abides."

Index of Poets

Index of Translators

(Due to publishing deadline requirements, poems for the Anthology are selected from magazines with cover dates during the 12-month period ending October 31 of each year. Poems for this edition of the Anthology were selected from magazines with cover dates during the 12 months ending October 31, 1980.)

HE SAYS HE WROTE BY MOONLIGHT

He says he wrote by moonlight
in the box in Attica
when the bulb went dark at nine.
They let him have a pencil stub
and papers, laughing or not
thinking much about it.
He says there was a tiny window
and for fifteen nights
he watched his piece of moon
grow larger while the graphite dwindled,
turned into words and lines of poems.
Every hour he was not asleep
he wrote— "to keep from going crazy,"
he says. And now in Elmira,
where the doors clang green and hard
and the yard is another torture
of gray pavement beneath angry feet,
he says, "Sometimes I think
that's what I miss most
being inside—my rec hour's early
and my window's wrong—
I haven't seen the moon in two years."

The Greenfield Review   *Katharyn Machan Aal*

OUT OF MOURNING

Spring again,
and I sit in the green chair reading.
The yellow dog noses among the neighbor's
daffodils. Over my book I watch for you
to come, waiting as I have all the nights
of my days for that moment beyond time
when April sorrows will be stilled by
the white flower in the moist red earth.

Did you know, my deep eyed dove, did you
know even then that August afternoon
as you danced in the willow's shade
that I who had been gone was standing
by the corner of the house watching
your whispered dreams?

Did you know
as you turned and looked and flowed
into my arms, locking your legs around
my waist, that you had hooked the very
marrow of my soul?

And did you know
that Easter morning as you cradled
the neighbor's child in your arms,
leaning your head against my knees
while I read in the April sun, that
the wind would blow over your grave
before another dawn?

Were these your gifts?
Waking or sleeping, I keep these images
inviolate, like mottled sunbeams through
winter windows or leaves long buried
in the beds of streams, kicked to the
surface by spring storms.

You grow
through the years. You are older
and the color in your cheeks runs
to red. Stand by my chair and put
your arms around my neck. Good.
I would feel that touch before another night.

Laurel Review   *Anthony S. Abbott*

THE BERKELEY PIER

A dancer dips and holds. The sun
lights on her hand, a yellow finch,
and on the reel of her man's fishing pole.
Their child has caught a crab
small and brown as his father's hand.

Near sundown, a mile out the bay,
the beak of a boat opens its wake.
Now a gull lifts and balances
like a thought I had in childhood.

Alone, in Idaho, my shadow played guitar
across a photo of San Francisco
taped to the wall. Colossal, it soared
from Buena Vista Park through Haight Ashbury,
a cathedral, and the forest of the Presidio.
And a cowboy song my father murmured
twenty years earlier surfaced that night.
He kept clearing his throat to make room
in the darkness around my bed. What I thought was:

men are more afraid than women. A bolt of water
unravels and winds around the pilings.
What I thought was: something lucent and airborne,
music, the wind feathering my hair
at pier's end, might hold us aloft this night.

Rocky Mountain Review   *John Addiego*

ULSTER

Men worked, men loafed, men sired.
Men drank oblivion in the "Olde Inn Ephemeral."
Men listened to cathedral hush.
A pleasure waned, an anguish grew.
A calendar grinned gloomily,
A hymnbook withered in the dead man's pew.

A little girl chased butterflies
While Aunt Susan checked her eyelids
For the customary sties.
What else?
A jovial drunk smacked and resmacked his lips,
Admiring the elastic hips
Of Aimee Kells.

A young nun looped
Some colored yarn for Uncle Moe
In Chillicothe, USA.
She aimed to make a scarf,
Showing a spunky David Crockett,
Reloading at the Alamo.

A bombed-out laundry
Kept on smoldering.
The hawks spat angry words at doves
While surgeons rinsed their bitter gloves.

The Christian Century   *Hans Adler*

TO A CAPTAIN IN SINAI

Five times I howled
before the dawn appeared,
the restless bed
creaked in fear
beneath my banging shoulder,
while the gulp in my throat
grew and grew
like a yawning crater.

Since you were clutched away
to the Judgment Day War,
the sun is black sand,
and missiles in black sackcloth
float under my breath
exploding it,
making a choking icicle
of me.

Before the night dies again
on my lips,
flash a sign from the desert,
my love,
make a sign of life
so that I can live,
ending howls in sounds
of peace.

Midstream   *Ada Aharoni*

WINTER IN ANOTHER COUNTRY

I was born in Cologne.
That word again: Cologne.
I let my mouth fill with it
as my mother did
when the pains began
and that word was black currant jam
on her tongue.
The sweetness filled her,
as the iron bed painted gold gleamed,
as the cottage began to spin,
as she herself spun
on the sharp end of nothingness
until even her brunette hair had become blonde,
her skin, her irises blonde,
and she became her own memory.

I wake beside the wicker basket
I slept in years ago.
Did it happen,
or did I dream it all, Mother?—you,
the dove flying into my forehead
the moment I woke,
and pain as the beak broke through skin

and then the smell of roses.
And petals falling to the floor
from the wound in my head
as I bent to touch them,
as they disappeared
into petals and late snow
as I stood beside your grave, Mother,
when I was twenty.
I was an orphan.
Why couldn't I accept that?
Didn't I have everything?—
that freedom from past
people had died for.

I stand back from my desk
and stare out the window.
I put my hands against the glass.
Cold. Snow. Winter in another country.
I blow on the glass and watch it fog up,
then I draw a cross on it
and circle it with my finger. The world.
One red line intersected by one black line.
Two roads,
and where they meet, a grave
and in that grave
bones wrapped in a coverlet of rose-red light—
you, Mother.
Just bones and a name and words:
Eulalie Mornais, who loved to dance.
Born 1882, died 1913.
God carry her to Paradise
and dance there with her immortal soul.

Poetry   AI

EACH DAY IS ANXIOUS

Each day is anxious all over again,
Stronger and stronger the smell of ripe rye.
If you are placed at my feet, just lie there
Tender one, just lie.

In the wide maples, orioles cry,
And nothing but darkness will calm them.
How pleasant it is for me to chase
The mischievous wasps from your green eyes.

Coach bells jingle on the highway—
We will remember this gentle sound.
To keep you from crying, I'll sing for you,
A little evening parting song.

The Nantucket Review   *Anna Akhmatova*
                                       —Translated from the Russian
                                        by Judith Hemschemeyer and
                                              Anne Wilkinson

THIS FALL

this fall the japanese maple turned coral red
last fall it turned the color of pumpkins
if I were a photographer
I would take a picture at its height each year
when every leaf was done
before a rainstorm blew it into a skeleton

trees turn first in valleys, along creeks
up their streams, fingers
on the hand of a watershed: then
the fire spreads out between those veins
across the map to the ridgetops
up the altitude lines like stairs

if I were a photographer
I would hang out of a small plane each afternoon
take pictures of the stream valley
every day through fall, make them frames of a film
watch color move: I would choose one leaf
see every morning after the dew dried
a few more cells turned red or brown

I would take pictures of that leaf, its veins
the same as the valley, run their films
side by side on the screen: then pick one frame
from each, hang them together on a wall
call it autumn.

Quarry West   *Jody Aliesan*

MIME

You remember that whitefaced actor
on the Green last summer, doing a mime
of staring through a window—how he made
us feel that window existed, how his hands
went flat against it and he carefully laid
his cheek against the window; then how he reared
back, his fist in a ball, and we cringed
as he smashed it through, the hand
limp and bleeding on the other side,
then carefully snaked it back through shards
of glass and we applauded? And how
all day, as we walked, I kept feeling
that just to my right there was a wall
with a window—the way you sometimes feel
at the border of two western states, stopping
the car to have a picture taken of yourself
slouching beside a sign on the desert highway,
a little excited, expecting to see a curtain
of rain across the border, or a vast
rectangle of sunshine if you've come through rain

hours to there? I was almost convinced
there *is* a wall and a window. It pressed
against my shoulder and I was a blind
man walking along the college streets of New Haven,
guided by how my shoulder or hip or elbow
carefully brushed the wall of brick and stone,
and then a pane of glass. I stood
blindly before it: how I wanted to look
into something but darkness with a few
flecks of light like fireflies which I take to be
saints in the distance, or the small lit lamps
of a future village down in an alpine valley,
or spaceships vanishing among the stars, or just
something I have imagined that is real
as the band that played last summer on the Green
with the men in their bowler hats, the mime
shaping with soft hands the tangible,
the broken—and with two blinks, our eyes.

The Hampden-Sydney Poetry Review   *Dick Allen*

COCK

At dawn crowed the cock
and near-by tolled the bell
a tremor ripples your flesh
            —and rebounds

At dawn a cock crowed
a cock
and nearby a bell tolled
a bell
and your body would answer aloud
clamor aloud
            —quake

Love-time, a cock proclaimed
a cock
fingers fumbling on pillow
fumbling
and elbows extend to embrace
desiring chase
            —mute

Wind stalks through the corn
the corn
clouds in the realms of the sky
clouds
rivers go lapping their course
between hillocks kissing
            —their source

In the window the morning stands pat
stands pat
and on your bed the sun is again

```
                        laid out
                        but without the crow
                          —of the cock
```

Poetry Now   *Aharon Amir*
                                          — Translated from the Hebrew
                                                   by Bernhard Frank

THE FINAL FALL

There are things
you could have said
in calmer countries.

Autumn came from the woods,
invaded the garden. Look,
it falls now on the patio
as it did last year
when this wine was grape.

The sun sets clouds on fire,
the wind blows the ashes away
and trees move their tired arms
—old dancers outplayed by the tempo.

That was the fall you knew,
snowless as a dream-world should be;
these lines file it for a while.

Canadian Literature   *Alexandre L. Amprimoz*

WITH THE NUNS AT CAPE MAY POINT

(for Kristin)

Yesterday a shark was reported cruising
    just beyond the jetty and so tonight
    I scan the distance, watching and waiting
For my child, to learn she is alive.
    Tonight only the black line of a ferry,
    shapeless in the distance, bears on.
Given shore and ocean, at evening
    there is no climate, the bay
    dissolving in the butter of the setting sun.
A procession of nuns, on vacation or retreat,
    approach the receding tide, carol
    the water. We felt their voices advancing;
The vacationers fell back, dumb. Both ways
    the form is older than any of us,
    each coming and going clumsy.
The tide returns, running over sleep. My wife
    is a nun, processing; my child a shark, waiting;
    and I, a ship melting in the night.

The Christian Century   *David Earle Anderson*

COMMANDING A TELEPHONE TO RING

You must never take your eyes off it.
You must stare at it,
repeating all the while
your number like a litany.

You must see how thoroughly black it is,
and how its black may be covered by a fine layer of dust.
Then you must study its white as well as its black,
the white of its numerals and letters,
the white space with your own black number in the center,
the number you are whispering to yourself as you stare.

You must count the twists and turns of the cord.
You must observe the receiver as it rests in repose
and the shine of the prong
that stops your finger when dialing.
And those circles,
those circles.

Notice how much of it is made up of circles.
Here go the numbers and letters in a circle.
Here is the circle of the dial itself.
Here is the circular panel on which your number is written.
The holes for the fingers are circular holes
and inside each hole is a circular white dot.
When you listen, you place a circle to your ear.
When you talk, you speak into a circular mouthpiece
filled with circles of circular perforations.

Having seen all this, keep staring at it further,
murmuring your number over and over.

If you are patient, it will ring.
And if you are wise,
you will know not to answer it.

The Chariton Review   *Jack Anderson*

WHAT HAS HAPPENED

What has happened
to spring, it doesn't leap
and cavort and roll and
tumble anymore?

What has happened
to summer, it doesn't
soothe and comfort and
bring infinity nearer?

What has happened
to autumn with its memories
and the sweet odors of
falling leaves and the
sorrow of tired grass?

What has happened
to winter and its recall
of endless time and the
sturdy indifference of whatever
there is that rules us all?

Bitterroot   *Charles Angoff*

RED WING HAWK

Now when I drove to the sand pit, the horizon
Through currents of mirage would gleam like an illusion,
A curtain which might open. The red wing hawk
Seemed especially for me, his appearance a sign.
I walked across furrows, which crumbled into ashes
In the heat, and prayed to see a hawk:
Swimming and flying in the liquid air,
Metallic as museums' bronze statues in the sun.
And one was there spiraling, tiny as a leaf
In a whirlpool, spinning as we used to on the grass;
He slanted with wings fixed open and motionless
And passed over me speechless in the dust, my arms raised
High and fingers spread wide for his wing tips,
While his face looked as fierce as Egyptian carvings,
A glinting from inside me expressed in the sky,
As if yellow eyes in sunlight were answering prayer.

The Poetry Miscellany   *James Applewhite*

FLIES LOVE ME

Flies love me.
They follow me up the long ascent
from the beach, up each mossy step,
nittering and twitching
a dark halo around my head,
jealous of the attention
given to silver gulls
as they swoop burning
fish from the sun.

They call to their friends
and soon I am surrounded
by a cordon of curious maroon eyes,
a purgatory of fuzzy bodies.
Through their mica wings I see
my skin slide like a rose-colored amoeba.

Into the darkest corners
of my sandals they trace
the blue rivers of my instep.
They crawl into craters of warts
and canyons between toes.

They compare my nails,
bending their flexible heads,
peering and wondering at the possession
of so many moons rising simultaneously
out of such a small geography.

Through the grassland of my arms
they stalk freckles. Cautiously
they circle them, feeling
for the slightest vibration.
Their feet tingle, their antennae probe.

Baffled, they jump into air and hold
a whining caucus, dive through space,
wind a blue helix of argument
before landing on another expedition.

Poem   *Nuala Archer*

AT 85

a photograph of you at the edge
of the porch would remember a hundred times
you stood there, pinching
a chesterfield, surveying distances
with an absent gaze. i recall
a line by yeats ("a tattered coat
upon a stick") that doesn't apply to you.
you still swim at 85
and william butler's dead besides.

memory dissipates in a swirling puff.
europe is in flames again: radios
goose-step into living rooms,
words blacken with obsessions,
youth folds shut in a cardboard suitcase
among things you thought you'd keep, forgets you
on a train station platform and goes elsewhere.

another wincing drag.

at 85 you are content to breathe the air,
to have a smoke, to savor a shot
of four roses, and lean against
another autumn wind.

RiverSedge   *Richard Ardinger*

SUN SET

Sun set
through the window I see
grey surrendering to night
and shadows singing
in the diapason of black

A somber fountain
darkens and bathes me
with large wet rays
speaking words
I dazzle in blackness

Denver Quarterly   *Umberto Aridjis*
— Translated from the Spanish
by Eliot Weinberger

POSSIBLE LOVE POEM TO THE USURER

My house also has
an oversized room.
The door is made of water.
It swells constantly.
The only chair is far away,
as if it were still a tree.

There is nothing of mine here.
The mirror does not return my face.
If there are walls they are the neighbor's
and a cold wind pierces them
only to fall, little by little, in my lungs.
The air is always stale.

I am the other wall.
I breathe and hum old songs.
Don't you hear me? Close to your house
is my house, with this enormous room
full of missing things,
and I'm here, close by, in a tree.
Only the leaves come between us.

New Orleans Review   *Octavio Armand*
— Translated from the Spanish
by Carol Maier

WINDFALL

I found my son fallen
asleep on a stepping-stone
to the house,
curled with such care

just a kid hauled down
to story hour telling
of Saint Joan, his mother
or King Thunderhead who wept
on his cloud throne

and suddenly he seemed no longer
the first draft of my flesh
or the last staff of my age
no longer a thing to sing to

vulcanized, braised, tempered
by love's industries

but just a leaf's own windfall   ·
gusted up from a cellar hole
or blown down from some lesser limb
in the lacy heart of the maples
and marbled by shadows
clocking around his face.

Yankee   *Joel Arsenault*

CONCERT

That night when October played
the strings in our blood,
crickets did not notice us
as they chanted their star elegies.

I turned to you
when dawn ripened the hills,
but the sun was already there.
Below, a flock of pigeons
swirled into the black oaks
and everywhere was leaf and tongue,
scratch and stroke,
cells that whirled wind and air.
We did not speak much of the heavens
or of eclipses to come,
both knowing blood will always sing
back into the silence,
sweetened by the orchards of the earth.

Sou'wester   *Michael Arvey*

THE ROAD THE CROWS OWN

Between the turnpike and the avenue
There is a road the crows still own,
Paved with the flesh of scarecrows,
A path not even Frost would take.

The crows walk slowly there,
Sure of the land, and therefore
Sure of everything.
They are not frivolous.
They do not sing.

They take their seats above us,
Formal in their black,
And fix their eyes on us severely.
Their mouths are hinged for reprimand.

These are the eagles
That we dare not tame.
We do not nail *them* to our doorways or our lamps.

We do not press *their* heads into our coins.
Huge muscles gleam under their feathers.

One crow stands guard
Across the entrance of the road.
Dark settler, the holdout of a nation,
He waves the fraying emblems of his wings
And warns us off.

Outerbridge   *Susan Astor*

DUFFERIN, SIMCOE, GREY

This year we are making
nothing but elegies.
Do what you are good at,
our parents always told us,
make what you know.

This is what we are making,
these songs for the dying.
You have to celebrate something.
The nets rot, the boats rot, the farms
revert to thistle, foreigners
and summer people admire the weeds
and the piles of stones dredged from the fields
by men whose teeth were gone by thirty.

But the elegies are new and yellow,
they are not even made, they grow,
they come out everywhere,
in swamps, at the edges of puddles,
all over the acres
of parked cars; they are mournful
but sweet, like flowered hats
in attics we never knew we had.

We gather them, keep them in vases,
water them while our houses wither.

The American Poetry Review   *Margaret Atwood*

GENERATIONS

See how he loves me.
Sunlight racing
Down the front porch steps,
He leaps into my arms,
Engulfing me like summer.
In a small boy's eyes—joy,
A joy I father.
His head nests on my shoulder,
Dusksoft,
Darkening my vision.
I could die for him.

He hangs on tight
As if I might.

Forms   *Joseph Awad*

BOOKS

"Pictures *are* my friends—
I have none others,"
wrote Ruskin,
who also worshipped little girls,
overlooking the empty-headedness
for the beauty

And Music also keeps very good company,
but as Dr. Johnson has pointed out,
it gave him
no new
ideas

But surely
People make the worst friends
of all, refusing
to be decent—
So Books are my friends,
I embrace their words,
and lend my volumes
to no one

And when I am away
I often dream of Alexandria
or the Fascist bookburnings
and grow fearful,
having believed in the
story of the book that
was shot
and slowly bled
to death

And once I gave a party
and some of the people who should have come, didn't,
but all of my books were there,
enjoying themselves immensely,
murmuring lightly,
and discussing so many things
from so many different and interesting
points of view

Poetry   *William Baer*

THE QUESTION, IS IT?

We the People
of the great North American
societal provenience

await with hope
the hazard of high endeavour
with a good deal of uncertainty,
not to say misgiving.
Especially when we recall
that James Abbott McNeill Whistler,
to whom so many were in the habit of deferring
in the declining decades of the last century,
said that art happens,
and how could we tell
whether it would happen to us?
"Some of you folks,"
pronounced the learned sociologist,
speaking, at this year's annual
            meeting of the Society,
with all the assurance
of an Egyptian soothsayer
at the court of Rameses the Second,
"may find yourselves
in the way of attaining the maximum."
All of us, say the nihilists
who go to the taverns
to practice their wit on the waiters
and proclaim in voices, artificially loud,
their voluble contraries.
The question arises, therefore,
whether the dogmatism of the nihilists
is or is not preferable to the persistent
            ambiguities of the learned academics.
If enlightenment could not be found
in having recourse to the habits of the ant
            and the beetle,
or even in the voluminous monographs
of the celebrated anthropologist, Claude Lévi-Strauss,
then one might take what comfort one could
from the contemplation of Raphael
copying the works of his mentors with the frenzy
of a divinity in the act of making himself visible.
Well, you know, you know, you know,
no matter what age you were born in,
nor how carefully instructed in the
            principles of the dialectics,
simple recognition, even belated,
of the inadequacies of the biological analogy,
might start cogitations
that it would not be well to abandon,
(let us say)
for a trip to the woods in Spring
to admire the skill of the trailing arbutus
in decanting its fragrance.

Canadian Literature   *Alfred G. Bailey*

PERSIMMON TREES, SHE REMEMBERS, NOT FAR AWAY

Your father's farm was lovely that October. The black barn
leaned like an animal in the sweet field, and the smell
of hay, of smoke,
                          more like a cloud, rose from the land
you said you loved. You'd take me there often,
teach me *foal* and *loft* and *fallow,* though the trees,

the deeper we walked into them, were what you liked most,
their leaves lit with color, their words, you'd say,
as soft and timid as wind.
                                    One place in particular, twenty
minutes from the house, a small patch of persimmon
trees clustered tight as a nest in the middle

of a grass clearing, was your favorite, their leaves
the first to brown and fall. You'd shake their trunks,
laughing,
                      and collect the tiny fruits in the sagging
skin of your clothes, or pull down from their limbs
the more stubborn ones as the soft pulp of those fallen

seeped like cider into the earth beneath your feet.
Then, as we walked back to the house, you'd stop to taste
the sweet-sour kiss of persimmons
                                            on my lips, or closer in,
tell me you heard the barn moaning like the old trees
that it had been, before our own parents touched that way.

The Seattle Review   *David Baker*

INCIDENT AT MOSSEL BAY

Three days of ocean riding
and my body, sister to mussel and conch,
tastes of sea.

One I love enters me.
I become the white coast of a blue bay;
its tides cleanse and alter me.
Far-off waters gather,
their incoming tug and tow
pulling at my waist and thighs.
The beads of my spine are worked loose

until in the crash and foam of a wave's breaking,
spray spills over my shores.
Subsiding waters hiss.

Rinsed, I shine like a rainbowed shell.
The ocean's harvest, I smell of brine and weeds.
No matter the water's salty sting.
I am an open beach.
I let the whole sea
wash in.

Green River Review   *Mary Balazs*

AUTOBIOGRAPHY, CHAPTER XII: HEARING MONTANA

(for Bob Conley)

The distance drums your words into my ears; it's good
    to hear your voice backed by the force of snow.

I speak of things small enough to ride the wires and
    the Dakota winds. I try to find a certain power of
    words to make the distance thin.

And growing in my ears are the sounds I think we know:
    the flight of low geese, the awesome scream of
    owls, the sudden fall of skree.

I name these things with my weaker words, but feel a
    need to chant until the magic of my voice
    strikes me dumb as stone.

Words are sacred, friend, you remind me once again.
    I hear the cadence dancing on the wires and
    some other voices dimly cutting in

humming the weather, ways to know the snow, something
    with love in it, god knows what, as if these
    other voices are also somehow dimly you.

Denver Quarterly   *Jim Barnes*

ACCIDENT AT THREE MILE ISLAND

(". . . how everything turns away/Quite leisurely . . . "
                      —W. H. Auden*)*

The island steams under the opening sky.
All around the narrow length of land
the river flows as it always has, and late

birds heading north to Canada notice
nothing unusual about the air.
There may, or may not, have been a disaster

among the undergrowth: what birds may tell
is augured late at best, and fish homing
upstream are mainly interested in falls.

Who knows? At any rate, the land was calm.
Nothing surprised farmers off their tractors
or knocked the rheumy cattle off their hoofs.

though something surely must disappear every
time the earth shakes or the sky moves an inch
or two to right or left. Still, there will always

be a boy fishing from some river bank
who doesn't especially want anything to happen
except summer and a dog scratching at his side.

New Letters   *Jim Barnes*

THE DOG IN US

When a man sweats
Inside his clothes, not having changed
For two days or a week—
Depending on how long it takes—
He knows humanity, the stuff of self;
So a shirt becomes a second skin,
A part of him,
Not something for a fancy ball.

But no one likes
The animal smell, the sourness
Gone stale. Who hasn't sniffed
Another's clothes, sensing the interest,
The deep disgust, and the hairs
Like hackles rising on the arm? Deodorants
Make us neutral, clean; deny
The dog in us, the everyman.

The Literary Review   *John Barnie*

MATING THE GOATS

On some Vermont road
three of us are riding
in the truck, smoking Camel straights,
with Elly goat in back.
The curved trees, smoke and snow
are like being under a wave
as it breaks.
He drives skillfully
and they talk about goats
while I try to see snow.
We arrive on a frozen plateau where
miraculously,
like a city discovered on the North Pole,
there is a house
and the other goat.
The goats are luminous,
moving in the dark on footless legs.
He bites her neck,
her stupid eyes are gold spheres,
the people lean on the fence,
speaking with expertise.
I watch,
breathing in loops of white air,
and I wish I could live an unfamiliar landscape
or be a goat.

Chicago Review   *Aliki Barnstone*

STAINED GLASS

Standing uptight in books against the wall,
my poets want to shine like jonquils or
apocalyptic John, and one night crawl
into my hunger, each a minotaur
dining on virgins in its labyrinth
of ink. For me they're rays of horny song,
night widows of the sun, a hyacinth
of hope. I am their only friend along
the shelf. If I crawl in with them, the dust
will make me bald and poor, my face will flake
like Alexandrian tomb masks, with dead eyes
growing huge, black and cracked. And so my lust
for poets is like pilgrims at the fake
shrine of old saints, a stained glass of surprise.

The North American Review   *Willis Barnstone*

WAKING EARLY

(to Susan)

I wake before the clock begins the day,
Surprised by brightness and my stranger shadow
On the headboard like a bas-relief, yet stay

The momentary start, and walk to the window.
Snow scrabbles randy patterns on the air
And dulls the angular outlines in the meadow . . .

But snow recedes to self, and self, aware,
To the icy glass and soft swish of the cover
Pulled tightly to your chin. I briefly stare

Then leave the room to you, my sleeping lover.

Southern Poetry Review   *R. L. Barth*

IN DAYS OF NEW

Because he was armored,
a refined, gentle knight

Who kneeled to his lady
and pledged his devotion

She unbuckled his sword
and slowly undressed him

Wanting to free his love
from the old rigid ways.

Then recoiled from the beast
who growled and showed his claws

His eyes now charged with fire
ready to strangle her.

The Malahat Review   *Elizabeth Bartlett*

SOLUTIONS

The guilty have fewer dreams
than the innocent. You can spot them
as they sleep: they are immune
to darkness; they lie in their houses,
cold, undisturbed,
like mirrors in an empty room.
When they do have dreams,
the heart hangs back
and they dream of childhood gothic:
a burgomaster and his town
of witchburners, a dwarf
with filthy fingers, a troll
singing of hatchets
in the Black Forest of their hearts.
Fish spring from their veins.
The dew gathers on their tongues.
And somewhere, horsemen
ride toward a sea of rattling ships
and waves like herded wart-hogs
in a book by the Brothers Grimm.
Few understand their dreams.
Few of the guilty
remember what their dreams intended.
They listen to the little taproots
probing their souls,
and wait for nothing to happen,
as nothing will.

Carolina Quarterly   *David Barton*

SEAL ROCK

My sister writes, "Come out, I need you."

On a morning swept clear of fog,
we drive up northern California coast.
Light ripples across wheat-colored hills,
reveals the sea's blue edge.

I talk of friends, my work, the sea.
Words break against her, fall away.
Newly divorced, she endures
with a bitter calm,
her eyes dark as the shore.

We reach Seal Rock at noon.
Digging our soles in wet sand,
we breathe the salt air.

Our lungs fill with light.
Thunderous waves shake the rocks beyond us, and
foam, like white birds, flies above each crest.

I reach for her hand,
her thin, nervous fingers
warm in my palm.

What can be said between one wave and the next?

Black Maria   *Sue Baugh*

ANY APRIL

At the instant—
the very moment you
read these words,
a doe is dropping her fawn
somewhere in a dark wood.
Her tongue licks the new deer
as it untangles its legs
to find her milk—
then lies in the cool leaf shade
to hide and quiet its heart pound.
Where were you when this happened?
What were you thinking
before these words told you of the miracle?
Come June, perhaps at twilight,
you will hear eight hooves
bolt from the undergrowth.
You will know then
that life has taken hold.
Be still now, and think of April,
and the soft light thud.

The Beloit Poetry Journal   *Cathy Beard*

THE PHOTOGRAPHER'S WIFE

He posed her, naked,
her hands holding her breasts
and a shadow like night itself
caught between her thighs.

He said, Your bones are shining wire.
My light will pierce through
to the filaments of your bones.
Your body will be as incandescent
as a lantern lit with flame.

But when he took the prints
out of solution, he saw only the woman
as she was.

He destroyed them all but the one:
she is biting her lip
and looking past the camera.

Between her fingers her nipples are hard
for the child who waits to nurse.
Her dark hair is as straight
at her temples as a scarf.

But a chance lens flare
surrounds her face
with a rim of fire.

Open Places   *Janet Beeler*

MORNING POEM

This is a morning of
white parakeets
      and red tea in rice porcelain.

It is tulips and hyacinths,
and ferns the boys cut one morning
before breakfast.

This is a morning of
      mahogany and pale orange
canaries
and the green voices of children.

It is
egg yellow and warm
as biscuits,
      a time of white plates
and embroidered curtains
      and little russian dolls
      conversing in wooden cabinets.

The Malahat Review   *Jennivien-Diana Beenen*

THE COLLECTOR

(for Jessica)

These children—with their careless hair,
with their fingers always stuck together,
with their loud, red mouths,
with their large, pale heads,

with their basement secrets,
and attic rituals,
with their convocations dry culverts,
porch stoops, abandoned houses, apple trees,

with their seeming smiles,
with their moonlight cries
like crows in cornfields in winter—
these children bear us a message:

Each human heart
is really a stone.

Inside each stone
is a clear, blue flame

that sings, is
always singing.
If asked,
the children claim

the song has no words.
Their eyes grow wide and dark
as polished obsidian mirrors,
and they say: It is simply

a song with no words.
But I think they know.
When the moon is full and high,
I crouch outside their doors,

and collect the strange runes
that fall from their dreaming mouths.

The Greenfield Review   *Richard Behm*

ELEGY FOR 41 WHALES
BEACHED IN FLORENCE, ORE., JUNE, 1979

(There was speculation that a parasite in
the whales' ears may have upset their bal-
ance and caused them to become disoriented.)

In the warm rods of your ears
forty-one parasites hummed
and you came rolling in
like tarred pilings after a hurricane.
What song were they piping for you?
What promises did you follow, past the coral
and mussels, and out from the frothy hem
of your world?

These are people.
They dance around you now like hooked marlin.
Some are weeping. Some are trying to pull you back.
Some crouch above your blow-holes
and drill their cigarettes into your skin.

All night your teeth are clicking.
All along the beach you are clicking like wind-chimes.
Is the song still piping for you?

This is sand. You cannot swim through it.
These are trees. Those houses on the cliff
are also trees. And the light that blinks
from them now is made from water.
We have a way of reworking the vital:

This is a pit. That was quicklime.
And here is fire.

New Letters   *Linda Bierds*

AT 21

Fashion me strangely in the human mold
And shape my manhood in a noble cast
Though I am not the first nor yet the last
Whom thou, long-practised, love, do cunningly hold
And with such painful artistry, yet bold,
Shape all my future being, as thine art
Has done before to many a human heart.
Still, what I am, it cannot yet be told.
But if of stone, the stone of which I'm made
Will whisper to the hand that guides the knife;
Or if of clay, from some dark pit first drawn,
Then I shall sinew up to be of aid;
Or if of bronze, wishful of sharp clear life,
Create me well, or I shall be self-born.

Harvest Magazine   *Eugene L. Belisle*

THE NEW FORMALISTS

These attempts to drink coffee
late at night
have got to stop. Besides
the free-floating fatty acids,
there's the usual effect:
you think you're smarter than
you are; you're just "up."
Two cups and you'll concoct
a school: Volcanic Verse,
Projective Paranoia or The New
Formalists, whose motto will be:
"Everyone talks about poetry
but no one does anything about it."
You'll try a French form again—
a Verandan, perhaps, wherein
every line must end
with a piece of porch furniture.
Could it be fun again?
Isn't part of a sestina's intention
to be boring? Do we need
a re-definition of achievement?
Do we need to neutralize
the line, in contradistinction to
a generation ago who gave us
a hundred ways to write free verse,
the subject of which
was lines and enjambments.
Is poetry in our time prose?
Was it always? Were you livid
to imagine Crane listening to *Bolero*
while he wrote? Or were you
a good drinking companion?

I see now the work of our generation:
to restore content by allowing
the old forms to fall apart naturally.
Prose-poems that were prose
are a part of this and, while it takes
years of bad work to make a thing
well, it is not a matter of how many.
Nor a matter of how long.
It gets late. But we make a mistake
in thinking it late for others.

Antaeus   *Marvin Bell*

GOOD WEATHER

What a morning! We haven't had a day
like this one since I don't remember when.
It opens your heart, like coming out of a cave.
You feel yourself starting to breathe again.

There's a touch of balsam on the breeze.
The wide sky is one delicious blue.
Get yourself together, is what it says.
Get out and get going, it says. There are things to do.

We've had some bad days, but this one looks
like spring if I ever saw it. Everywhere
all sorts of things are changing—even the rocks

are splitting open. As soon as I poked my face
outside the window this morning, I knew for sure—
What a perfect day! What crystal! What paradise!

Cutbank   *Giuseppe Gioachino Belli*
                                          —Translated from the Italian
                                              by Miller Williams

DEATH WITH A CODA

Either we're liberals or we truly do
Believe in the law of the Lord. We can't have both.
If we do believe, red-blooded or blue,
The heart freezes when it comes to death.

You go to taverns, run to a theatre, dash
From party to party, take somebody to bed,
Make your deals, pile up a little cash,
Grab everything you can—and then you're dead.

And then what? And then the soul swaps
The world we have a while for the world to come,
One that goes forever and never stops.

The word is *never* and it's so damned final.
Floating or sunk to the bottom, it's all the same.
The bitch eternity is going to be eternal.

Cutbank   *Giuseppe Gioachino Belli*
                                   — Translated from the Italian
                                        by Miller Williams

THE OLD BIOGRAPH GIRL

Not even the angels could bring a breath of air
to a white-hot day in Los Angeles.
A blue jay sits in the lemon tree, surrounded by bumpy
half-painted Easter eggs. He's
dead calm; a still life, you see.

In the photo, that's me,
my bound black hair and silk lashes bent beneath
the engorged gaze of—Walter Long?
One of the Beery's? Anyhow, "a human pig," rooting
    toward me
with sag belly and straining braces, bent on playing
his hot customary part. But the humid human hand
never touched this star. (Ramon Novarro
rescued me. I wept. He kissed my hand.) And at premieres
I was the orchid lady in the black sedan,
and Mother the earthy turnip
stumping at my side. As for money—
never mind: I noticed in time the dictionary truth
that *star turn* is next to *starvation,*
but just a little way from
stash. I'm sitting pretty on mounds of nest eggs.
The one thing I could use, like the blue jay,
like that girl

running along the beach in her sandy maillot,
is some relief
from the blood heat of the day. Otero died
between one bite of rabbit stew
and the next, under a sky of crockery blue. All of us,
the bird, each leaf of the jacaranda tree, my rouged lips,
exhale the same parched scrap of dialogue: Send rain.
I address at last
a browbeating golden hairy lover, and I remember
how coolly
my face once glowed in the dark.

Poetry   *Margaret Benbow*

AT SUMMER'S END

Months of waiting: then everyone
clamoring down the hill
to the orchard for its meats.

Winter long, rooted
snug in bed with books

up to our armpits, we plotted
summer's populations:
the musty peach, the sex
of pears; the sorbs and apples.
Amulets for our mouths to dream.

Differences are what count.
I can tell by the actual thump
whether it's an apple
or a sorb that's hit the path
or the soft or hard ground.

Apples recite: delicious, sweet.
Sorbs are blunt.
Some of us need ladders,
but others have only
to reach for what they need.

Lowest branches deliver up
their goods with least objection.
But even topmost fruits fall down
to mumble from our wooden crates.
Delicious bitter, delicious red.

Then falling light: the mind at war.
In search of what we might become,
we strip the summer down to seed,
and lug our thievings up the hill:
we steal what we already own.

The American Scholar   *Saul Hillel Benjamin*

POETRY IS . . .

"I am the sea"
murmurs a shell.

Gurgles a bucket,
"I am the well."

"I am the wind"
tinkles a bell . . .

Silent the sea
the wind and the well.

Midwest Chaparrel   *Bruce Bennett*

TO A YOUNG POET

(for P. L. A.)

Those who split wood know
that ax heads can lie buried
in the trunks of trees:

knife blades, old hooks, the tips
of rusted saws, lodged and left
by strangers years before,
can sit so deep within new growth
that on the bark no trace
or scar remains
warning they are there.
We are the same and grow
around our injuries,
until they seem no more
than somewhat bitter memories,
fragments, rusted and disused,
broken from experience,
and left by chance behind—
their power still to mar
known only from inside.

Focus   *Paula Bennett*

BOGEY

san quentin, sing sing, alcatraz.
if he busted out the slammer once
he did it a dozen times.
the smoke he pushed at you
no hazard to your health, mild even,
against narrowing eyes, flared nose,
lip curled so nasty.
robinson, cagney, raft were no match.
he'd whistle down bacall,
and hepburn was easy.

think of him—leeched tugging the QUEEN.
trenching the MADRE, crazy for gold.
grounds in his coffee, nails or glass.
but what about CASABLANCA?
the song sam played wasn't just any song,
ilsa just another dame
when rick grazed her eyes,
clinked her wine, said
"here's looking at you kid."

Seems   *Lee L. Berkson*

THE BLESSING

Cleanliness is godliness
Said the brindled cat
Rolling in sunlight on the rug
Caressing itself with cleansing spittle, nose to tail

Cleanliness is godliness
Said the marmalade cat
Sniffing the smell of soapsuds
Staring at a human in a tub

Cleanliness is godliness
Said the calico cat
And would not eat until the bowl
Was moved away from the catbox

Cleanliness is godliness
Said the tortoiseshell cat
Shouted away from the salmon
(When frustrated, wash)

Cleanliness is godliness
Sang the unneutered strays in the alley
Fur matted, tails ragged, scar-ridged, and limping
They littered their unwanted kittens
And taught them to bury their droppings

For the cat is hunter not hunted
And none shall follow the spoor
Of cats as they rove in the cities
Through forests to deserts
Back through the years
To the sandscoured sphinx

Cleanliness is godliness
Said the sphinx.

Poem   *Ruth Berman*

GLADIOLI FOR MY MOTHER

Too proud you are,
and impossible to deceive;
nature, before the winters' snuffing out,
displays her most passionate colours;
you, each moment so terribly aware
of the inevitable end, swollen-eyed,
pull the covers over your tormented head
and give up the battle.
I have seen you
rise anew as if watered by your own tears,
a rising wondrous as the hard green knobs
on the spring branches which you watch with me
through the quiet kitchen window as they
burst open and clothe the tree in our garden.

Now I rifle through drawers
in the cool basement, pulling out programmes
and black & white stills
of a stunning young gypsy
with dark wild eyes, gold hoop earrings,
and I secretly weep, though if you do the same
I still bully you out of it
as I did before I understood.

No matter how I try to say it, you'll never know
how much you are with me;

but each week, as I push my load
up and down the aisles, the shadow of my childhood
with one foot still on the cart,
I take for my own home
the brightest, strongest blooms,
carrying them out of the store like spears
into the battle for which
you have so well prepared me.

Poetry Canada Review   *Harriet Bernstein*

IF LOVE'S A YOKE

If love's a yoke
and lovers are mules,
　　blinded fools,

pray, may the yoke
be like a peal
　　of thunder, a wheel

without any spokes
hitting a hole
　　and no neck broke.

Pray lightning's flash
be both hope's reins
　　and hope's light lash.

Quarterly West   *D. C. Berry*

SECOND READING

Sunday morning restlessness
takes down
from a shelf we seldom browse
this reputable, yellowing periodical,
brushes off the dust of the years
since publication,
seeking something we said,
something we were,
something we meant.
Metering out our periodical span
each from a different perspective,
seeking something:
growing from sonnets to sestinas
to sonorous symphonies
in search of the meaning
of restless Sunday mornings.
We seek to remain
reputable,
grow yellow with years,
brush off the dust
less often,

are ultimately taken down
and finally go
out of print.

Pteranodon   *Richard Beyer*

BEAST ENOUGH

Now I am sure
I am beast enough to live
in this city.

Noon Saturday, walking
south from Yonge and Bloor,
I am caught up in a scurry
with or against a grain I am
powerless to establish or
even discern. Each bumped elbow,
upper arm or full shoulder
is a failure for *homo sapiens,*
an inability to cope with space.
I am adept. I give
and take with the best.
And I anger easily: only one
or two jolts and I am ready
to kill or turn up Isabella St.
to vent my best love for
thirty dollars in a narrow room.

But I persist. I linger
in Longhouse Books, finally
leave and take the gauntlet back
to the subway. I hold a book
as if it were a fresh kill. By
Summerhill, I have a lust
for words in my mouth.

Poetry Canada Review   *Robert Billings*

WOMAN IN AN ABANDONED HOUSE

When the clatter of reckless thought
no longer resounds or even echoes,
my mind will be as still
as this front room of our old house.
Come, rub your quiet, dirty hands
along the peeling trim and curling paper;
rummage through the corner-piles
and pick my love out from among
leaves and rubble and straw.
Sit in this dusty window ledge;
let your vision of the green wheat
blossom in these limestone eyes;
let the echo of your mourning dove

seep into these wooden eaves;
let your breath fill my crumbled walls.

Sou'wester   *Michael Bily-Hurd*

FAMILY HISTORY

My Jack Spratt parents, full of spite and bile,
Would measure out their words in stunning ways
And amplify each other's torn-tongue style
In hard-barred, door-locked rooms of disarray.
They'd defend each maneuver and slowly stockpile
An arsenal of faithless things to say;
As their days grew black (when their hopes grew thin),
They danced a vicious dance, alluring, grim.

My fairy-tale sisters (white slips for hair)
Would dress-up to kill and watch at the door.
They seemed to understand what was happening there.
If I knew a little, they always knew more;
They'd dress me in silk or knot-up my hair,
Convince me horses would move in next door,
And never divulge just what they divined;
But I was content to spy on their spying.

The Master is dead (and the Mistress breaks);
The children are married but few are festive.
If we dream of those days it's with distaste,
For the hours were hard and our hearts were restive
And we felt each night that familiar ache
As the spirit of our household wasted
And love-lost faces fed on spite and guile.
We continue their life, fearing their style.

Western Humanities Review   *Wendy Bishop*

THE REACH OF SILENCE

Silence beside the Pacific
Reaches a long way, to Norwegian waters
And into the mountains seen from these

On passage thrusting for the Pole;
There is a Spitzbergen
In every easeful summer swell.

Silence of the earth, silence
Is perennial cold, under the rustle
Of surf, winter here and there.

Spring reduplicates itself
Certainly, as such things go,
But winter lasts forever.

Arizona Quarterly   *Charles Black*

BARD

Who plays the hand that plays the instrument?
You see the hand; you hear the music sent,
The magic of the music in the strings.
Who plays the hand that plays the instrument?

Who is it sings the present voice that sings?
You hear the voice; you hear how passion flings
Words into rhythms, into flames of sun.
Who is it sings the present voice that sings?

Who thinks the thoughts and lets the feelings run?
Whose is the music when all's played and done?
My hand, my voice, my passion I have spent.
Who thinks the thoughts and lets the feelings run?
Who plays the hand that plays the instrument?

The Emissary   *Theodore Black*

BILLIARDS

The positions of the angles
are infinite. It is always
worth finding the good
in small things.
To leave the moves to chance
is like trying to leave
your breath in the wind.

The air carries a weight
of its own. Diagrams
are pasted in players' minds
like spider webs
in the hot summer breeze.
There is no game
like one that creates
its own good geometry.

The Greenfield Review   *Laurie Blauner*

THE CONVERTS

(for Jane and Stanley Moss)

On the holiest day we fast till sundown.
I watch the sun stand still
as the horizon edges towards it. Four hours to go.
The rabbi's mouth opens and closes and opens.
I think: fish
and little steaming potatoes,
parsley clinging to them like an ancient script.

Only the converts, six of them in the corner,
in their prayer shawls and feathery beards,

sing every syllable. What word
are they savoring now?
If they go on loving that way, we'll be here all night.

Why did they follow us here, did they think
we were happier?
Did someone tell them we knew the lost words
to open God's mouth?

The converts sway in white silk,
their necks bent forward in yearning
like swans, and I covet
what they think we've got.

California Quarterly   *Chana Bloch*

FROM THE ICE AGE

1.   The Woman with 3,500 Beads
All that remains now is her skeleton,
there is no name
to speak across the thousands of years,
no way to ask now
"What was your life?
Did you have children?
Were you loved?"
And yet her bones
are wrapped with hand-carved beads;
3,500 beads,
like tiny rough moons
that would circle her always,
bone against bone.

2.   Two Stags Crossing a Stream at Salmon Time
How the deer look out
from thirty thousand years,
as if it were no distance at all.
And the salmon leap up,
in a world full of animals we will never see.
I imagine the artist
bending over the bone,
carving the remembered scene,
and I want to tell him
how hard it is now,
knowing things the heart cannot hold—
the distances of space,
the lifespans of suns—
when what he has carved
is enough for a world,
and the woman wrapped in beads
shines in her familiar bones.

Sou'wester   *Barbara Bloom*

RETURN TO PRINSENGRACHT

(A Found Poem in an Article By Otto Frank)

I can no longer live in Amsterdam, he writes;
I often go there,
but I can't stand it more than three days.
I go to Prinsengracht
where we hid for two years.
Sometimes I look at our hiding place;
it has not changed
though the rooms are almost empty.
The map of the wall with the pins showing the Allied troops
is still there.
On a wall I still see the lines I drew
to show how the children grew,
the pictures of film stars
Anne hung up for decoration.
    I look around
and then leave.
I cannot bear the sight longer.

It is the anniversary of Liberation Day in Europe
when we visit the house on Prinsengracht,
near noon
when our footsteps echo
through the abandoned rooms, the wood
flooring creaking
and history and holocaust
overtake us.   We cringe
at the loud-voiced Americans
desecrating the quiet.
We are Canadian and sedate.
We want to understand.
    In the last room
overlooking the street
the air-raid siren tests the air
and we are seized by the cold terror
and sudden realization of discovery.

The Malahat Review   *Janice Blue-Swartz*

THE FLIRTATION

I am tired of looking at you through this glass.

Up close, I'm sure your eyes are a deeper green,
your hair the scent of lilacs, the texture
of Vermont in September. I am sure
we are in total agreement about the importance
of milkweed, the intrusiveness of money.

I see you cruising the ferns and coffee tables
of this building, eyes beating your forehead
for a glimpse of me, legs a chorus of violins.

You must know I am not really up here working,
that I am holding you like a key to the threatening sky.

I watch you washing other men's hair,
your fingers dancing like ribbons around
their temples. Your breath fills them with foolish
suggestions, makes me want to curl my own hairs
around you, discuss the justice of distances.

At night, two high-priced whores,
we go home to strangers, make love
in satin sheets, sipping imported brandy,
whispering each other's name to the impossible windows.

Poetry   *Michael C. Blumenthal*

STILL WRESTLING

My son leaps across my back
And we go down, his arms and legs
Locked around me, his flesh,
Femurs and finger-bones.

My daughter dives on;
Her shoulder in my stomach
Knocks the wind out of me.
My body tumbles in the blades,
Cold grass making me laugh.

I catch my breath, but they
Have not had enough. We roll,
Clavicle in my eye,
Scapula in my palm,
Hair on my tongue, the surround
Of the smell of skin.

They have me in a secret hold,
One that cannot be broken.
Baby teeth sink into the nape of my neck.
I am pinned by memory,
Slapped to my senses,
Still wrestling with the father.

Aspen Anthology   *Phil Boiarski*

SWALLOWING

I mastered the easy ones first.
I began with avocado pits
and lollipops, belt buckles and keys.
I learned that the trick was not to chew
but to swallow and savor the wholeness
of the thing itself. I nurtured
a taste for the outrageous.
Goldfish and swords had no allure,
nor would I swallow anything alive,

less from squeamishness than a fear
(absurd, I know) of being consumed
by the thing consumed. I have swallowed
lost love and my life-insurance plan.
I have swallowed the impeccable decor
of my brother's suburban house.
I have swallowed half the numbers
of the metropolitan telephone book.
I swallowed poignancy and inattention
when they were in vogue. I swallowed
a handlebar once, my most difficult
swallowing, not for the shape of it
but for the coldness of the chrome
moving down my throat. I have never
swallowed a lie, although (God knows)
I have tried, gagging and retching.
I have no pity for what I swallow.
I have paid with stomach pumpings
and a constantly sore throat.
I swallow for the headiness of it,
for the joy of feeling the thing inside.

Ploughshares   *Harold Bond*

NORMAL AS TWO SHIPS IN THE NIGHT

After a while, in the larger cities, we
do not talk or think of *normal.* The young
student, blond, clipped, whistling

the *allegro* of Sibelius' violin concerto,
is not normal; his lips
are too tight, his soul

is not in this frenetic tooting,
only his fear, flared-up; it is

his lighthouse & his horn as we pass self
to self in Harvard Yard. We pass quickly

in Harvard Yard. I am hiding in the dark
funk of a Laura Nyro tune; we know we're

incompatible, but grateful we will
probably not mug or harm or murder

but *unknowing, imagining,* we pass

quickly in Harvard Yard, in Harvard
Square, in Copley Plaza, in America.

We do not talk of *normal,* we whistle
odd snatches of song, violent passions
composed for solo instruments.

Dark Horse   *Walta Borawski*

GRANDFATHER YONEH

I never saw my father's father's face.
No one ever told me what he looked like.
No photograph of him ever graced
our home.
He is the grandfather *absconditus,*
the hidden grandfather who died
in Russia—of what, who knows?
To my repeated questions my father
said that grandfather Yoneh drove
the Russian nobility in his
horsedrawn wagon. He took them on
long trips. That was how he made
a living. But my cousin George
said he thought our grandfather
owned a tavern. Which was it?
Who knows? My mother said in a
hushed voice that false charges were
brought against him and that as a
result he was thrown into prison
where he suffered a long time.
He refused to eat because the food
wasn't kosher and so every day
my grandmother Fruma (the pious one)
visited him and brought him food
so he wouldn't starve to death.
When grandfather was finally let out
of prison he was a broken man.
He died soon after. He never made it
to America. He probably wouldn't
have left Uzda anyhow for he was
deeply religious, a *Hasid,* father said,
who made yearly pilgrimages to his
revered rabbi.
I never saw my father's father's face,
not even in an old photo. My father
repressed the memory of his death.
The only picture I have of him
is in my mind. He is standing tall and
thin, next to his horse, gazing
straight ahead into the uncertain future.

Jewish Currents   *Emily Borenstein*

ODE WRITTEN IN 1966

　　No one is the homeland. Not even the horseman
Who, tall in the dawn of a deserted square,
Rules a bronze charger for the time,
Nor the others who stare from the marble
Nor those who squandered their warlike ashes

On the countryside of America,
Or left a poem or a deed
Or the memory of one perfect life
In the just exercise of the days.
No one is the homeland. Not even the symbols.

No one is the homeland. Not even time
Charged with battles, with swords and with exodus
And with the slow population of regions
That border the rising of the sun and the setting of a star,
And with faces that grow old
In mirrors that tarnish themselves
And with the patient, anonymous agonies
That endure until dawn
And with the cobweb of the rain
Over the black gardens.

The homeland, friends, is a perpetual act
Like the perpetual world. (If the Eternal
Spectator were to cease dreaming us
For a single instant, he would hurl
Blunt, white lightning, His forgetfulness.)
No one is the homeland, but we all must
Be worthy of the ancient oath
Those noble gentlemen gave to us
Of being what they were ignorant of, Argentinians,
Of being what they could be because of their act
Of having sworn in that old house,
We are the future of those men,
The justification of those dead men;
Our duty is the glorious charge
Those shadows have bequeathed to our shadow
That we are obliged to save.

No one is the homeland, but all of us are.
Let this burn in my breast, and in yours, incessantly,
This fire, limpid and mysterious.

Willow Springs Magazine   *Jorge Luis Borges*
—Translated from the Spanish
by Lynn C. Jacox

NOW AND AGAIN

Night should be fuller than this.
Lying on our backs in scratchy twigs,
There aren't enough stars in this place;
the brightest lights are the distant buildings
in a circle around us, two people
without a thing to say to one another, or things
that can't be said, right beside us:
whole societies of frogs and insects,
as we in ours.
I don't want to be made of words and feelings.
I don't want to be a body that craves.

We get up and stumble through bushes,
back to civilization. Who are we
to be holding hands? The pond gives back
the reflection of two creatures a little startled
at being brought up to date
on their own existence.
How old can a person get?
Now and again it seems like it's time
to pass the baton and let somebody else
run their little way into the future.

The Malahat Review   *Roo Borson*

THE COPPERHEAD

A dwarfed limb
or a fist-thick vine, he lay stretched
across a dead oak fallen into the water.
I saw him when I cast my lure
toward a cluster of stumps near the half-buried trunk,
then pulled the boat to the edge of the limbs.
One ripple ran up his back like the tail
of a wake,
and he lay still again, dark and patterned,
large on years of frogs and rats.

I worked the lure around the brush,
oak and poplar stumps rising out of the water
like the ruins of an old pier,
and watched his spade head shift on the dry bark.
But no bass struck
so I laid the rod across the floor of the boat,
sat for a long time watching the shadows
make him a part of the tree,
and wanted more than once to drift into the shaded water,
pull myself down a fallen branch toward the trunk
where he lay quiet and dangerous and unafraid,
all spine and nerve.

The Atlantic Monthly   *David Bottoms*

COASTING TOWARD MIDNIGHT AT THE
SOUTHEASTERN FAIR

(for Jim Seay)

Stomach in my throat
I dive on rails and rise like an astronaut,
orbit this track like mercury sliding
around a crystal ball.
Below me a galaxy of green and blue neon
explodes from the midway to Industrial Boulevard,
and red taillights comet one after another
down the interstate toward Atlanta.

In the hotdog booth the Lions are sick of cotton candy.
Along the midway Hercules feels the weight of his profession,
Mother Dora sees no future
in her business,
the tattooed lady questions the reason
behind each symbol drawn indelibly beneath her flesh.

We all want to break our orbits,
float like a satellite gone wild in space,
run the risk of disintegration.
We all want to take our lives in our own hands
and hurl them out among the stars.

The Southern Review   *David Bottoms*

WHITE

Lying awake,
I watch the sky whiten,
the silence of the mountain
reaching into my room

like wild scents.
Familiar sounds melt away
until I am adrift
sitting beside a drawn woman,

watching with her
the silk spool unwind
to its last shimmer,
her face in the mirror

as she touches her hair,
blue eyes dark with fatigue.
I cannot tell her
how everything changes:

the walk between the trees
with freshly spread gravel,
a curve in the road
with an unfamiliar bench

on which two children play cards,
how a new world takes hold,
busy, absorbed,
knowing only the moment.

Southwest Review   *Marguerite Bouvard*

AT THE SPA

You have to be depraved to go at all
and suffer working out, endure the kitsch
decor (short plaster Greeks on pedestals
amid stainless steel), then the hell's kitchen
of steam room and sauna bath, hot whirlpool

where our heads like apples bob in thick fog.
(Yonder comes Dante in his cresting sloop,
dark and scowling. Virgil beside!) The dog
missed them. No. Not poets, not Cerberus,
just Rog, who works here, and a proselyte.
They pass on. Blank-eyed libation bearers
(two, from the same mold) are placed in our sight
but out of reach. What? Who is it comes here?
All sorts and conditions—ectomorphs, jocks
(a few), others old with slack dugs, some queer
(most aren't), some fat, I'm average, but tell jokes.
I climb out past furious Poseidon
aiming his fork, arrange for a massage
by a lithe tart in white boots, clothes hiding
tattooed hams. She is whistling a passage
from *Don Juan*. I'm in training, I explain,
for hell. She laughs, continues mixing pain
with pleasure, says, unharnessing a tit,
"Why this is hell, nor are you out of it."

Kansas Quarterly   *James H. Bowden*

ARCHETYPES

Even my dreams are hackneyed,
rising above my bed in comic-strip balloons:
corny one-liners,
stale TV plots,
eroded symbols stuck for generations
in the frightened mind.
Why not some new monster,
something unspeakable,
as shapeless as death but more terrible?
Anything but the chase,
the fall,
the soft seduction:
Lord, let me wake up dead, but not bored.

Southern Poetry Review   *Neal Bowers*

BEFORE THE STATUE OF A LAUGHING MAN

(Laugh more. It helps you forget yourself.—Overheard advice)

So advised, did you laugh and forget
yourself? And if so, is that self
the one we have standing here—
poised in laughter but vacant,
papier mache, waiting to be inhabited?
—What happened?—Where are you?
Not laughing, certainly. Standing,
like a question mark?—That's it:

I find you leaning over odd dials
filling up with the luminous facts
which are reading out as you—
O Discovery! You've found yourself,
in fact, and—*No! No!*—start
laughing again, forgetting another
self and how it is these selves,
recently, are coming more quickly.

Cimarron Review   *William C. Bowie*

HOMING

("Researchers have shown that a homing pigeon
flying over Chicago can hear the roar of both
oceans."—Heard on the news, 5-17-78)

It is nothing I understand any better
than flying: the drop of earth
and weightlessness, this lightening blue
around me. I am just there
and it happens.

                         My claws
above another city, each wing
tapping a rim of earth. And
I hear them again, whispering
in two voices

the same words: that I am
where I should be, balanced
between them again
in the place I am meant for
where air collapses.

Yankee   *P. C. Bowman*

THE CRANE'S ASCENT

Standing at the edge of the warped dock,
the thick scent of orange blossoms
sticking in his throat, my
grandfather sows corn on the water.
The small bass rise like birds
feeding from the open palm of a meadow.
It is not yet dawn.

He eases himself down
into the boat, breathing heavily in the heat;
he bends to the motor, pulls hard on the rope.
His heart pulses once and tightens.
Like a waking animal,
something stirs behind his eyes . . .

The outboard catches, chokes and dies.
Cradled in the slowly rocking boat,
my grandfather cannot see the clouds of moss
move in the trees, or from the shallows
the shadow of a crane
lift itself on impossible wings
above everything, and the sun

rising.

Carolina Quarterly   *Nick Bozanic*

CASUAL MEETING

We meet. And meeting repairs attention.
You're here, I'm here, and either may say
    what's pleasurably said.
Indeed, nature defers to nature,
    head bobs to head,
        "Good day!"—
the day is good by convention.

Enough. Or is there more to say—
shall we mention the weather?

Complete in ourselves and without much to tell,
two protagonist strangers: unwary together,
    we watch the young day
grow chronically older.
    Oh, I'm well, and agree:
        "Yes, a good day."

Your world passes. What I can apprehend
I take in stride, and drift again.
Not long will I look your way
though anxious for what is or has been
    lost to this thin-clouding
        sky of today.

Arizona Quarterly   *Sam Bradley*

THE STRINGER

Called from my room to a death,
It is your unknown face that frightens me.
I drive past the city limits
And park my car. I did not know suicide
Could look that simple: your caretakers in white,
The beer-joint's neon script
The only bright color in the damp light.

I walk to you at the field's edge,
To you lying more still
Than the ground beneath you.
The sheriff pulls back your smooth sheet.
I absorb your half-opened mouth and eyes,
Your blue lips.

Everything you could not finally abandon
Is evidence.
I am infatuated with your wound, wet
Empty socket with its eye stolen.
I want to put my finger there,
The shallow well
Where someone will split you,
Gather your limp machine into a plastic sack
And never answer what dam broke
That so many rivers at once
Washed over you.

Columbia   *James Brasfield*

POEM AFTER A SPEECH BY CHIEF SEATTLE, 1855

When the buffalo are all slaughtered,
When the wild horses are all tamed,
When the secret corners of the forest
Are heavy with the scent of many men,
And the view of the ripe hills is blotted
By talking wires, what will man be?

Where is the thicket? Gone.
Where is the eagle? Gone.
What is it to say goodbye to the swift?
What is it to say goodbye to the hunt?
It is the end of living;
It is the beginning of survival.

Denver Quarterly   *Charles Brashers*

SONG FOR A LOST ART

Weed and herb and foxy flower,
Each has a poison or curative power.
Wherever the poison is, they say,
The antidote grows not far away!

But they hanged the wizards in dead of night,
Burned the witches for fear of blight,
Hounded the gypsies who knew the lore,
Kept the poison and lost the cure.

Yankee   *Virginia Brasier*

CURTAIN SPEECH

I've been around a long time,
so long this life of mine can best be reckoned
not in years that make up calendars
but in events said to make up history . . .
World Wars, Number One and Two, with sideshows like holocausts—
the punishment meted out for sundry and assorted cruelty:

another flood, not of water but soldier blood
in Korea and Viet Nam, in Ethiopia and Sinai . . .
Yes, I've been around a long time:
revolutions against tsars in Russia, against shahs in Iran;
brown- and black-shirted counter-revolutions in Germany and Italy,
and, in South America, counter counter-revolutions,
too many even for a computer to count accurately.
In North America, thanks to a law and orderly succession of power,
a relay race of presidencies beginning with—
could it have been Taft or Woodrow Wilson?—
all the way down to the present incumbency
by a twice-born Southern Baptist
reigning over the uncertain destiny
of an East European non-believing Jew
who will die only once, hopefully never to be born again . . .
Jimmy Carter telling him in fireside chat after fireside chat
to conserve energy, pay taxes, observe speed limits.
I obey, as a rule, except for occasional lapses:
now and then I might take one too many at a bar
or, in a poker game, sneak a sidelong glance at an opponent's hand
and, ignoring whatever pangs of conscience, bet accordingly.
I am also apt to covet a neighbor's ass
or lust after his wife if she should have a pretty ankle—
a venal sin I will no doubt be punished for
now that I am a step or two removed from Judgment Day.
Still, fire, brimstone and flogging by devils do not frighten me:
nor am I elated by the prospect I will be forgiven
and spend every moment of the hereafter in heaven . . .
The carrot and stick props appropriate in juvenile theatre only
and the play not worthy of being taken on a tour,
certainly not that wide ranging as to include the other world.
Limbo is something else again—
appealing like a resort on the French Riviera
or, if that is asking too much, Palm Beach, perhaps,
with "Do not disturb" signs hanging from every door knob,
with strangers and only strangers moving about the vast lobby
and the morning newspapers strictly censored
except for the obituary page . . .
Limbo! Limbo! Now and forever!

Midstream   *Michael Braude*

SEEING IN THE DARK

Below my father's house lies a river valley
where the Minnesota rolls, lifting mist
in the morning till sunlight consumes it,
slowly, the way dogs dally round dishes
when watched. At night, barge-warnings
echo up the bluff and die at our doorstep.
Sometimes, if the moon strikes you right,
and the cold air smells clean, the night pulls
you inward before you can stop

and, as you're swallowed, turns
you inside out—there

                        in pitch darkness
blindness becomes sight, and you see
how the world looks to those dying,
before first dawn light, when the moon
is glowing like a darkroom lamp
and the landscape is a negative,
undeveloped, waiting for
immersion.

Kansas Quarterly   *Matthew Brennan*

PICKERS

Seeing them over and over each
season covering the landscape,
passing with the harvest
we see them emerge from their
apple baskets ready to pick,
ready weighing in dreams by
the ¼lb. And their kids, a
thousand arms hung out the
window, are quick to under-
stand everything, hoes under
arms

mushroom out of the back seat
nervously and, full of quick
eyes, stare at the beanfields,
hear of Xochqual, invent pictures:

they follow it down the sideroads
at thirty, lunging toward Romeo,
Michigan, on two bad tires, full of
the night in their faces.

Tendril   *Peter Brett*

PLAYING THE BONES

I found the black bones one day in a trunk,
almost the only possessions of my father
there are left. I remember he played them
when I was a child, told me
"They're black ivory, elephant tusks."
I touched them then and thought "Africa."

They belonged to him and him only,
like his shaving mug with pink roses,
the gold ring with his initials,
his favourite red neckties,
the long succession of his pipes.

My mother gave everything away
after he died,
moved to another house
so as not to be haunted
by his ghost;
but, by choice or chance,
she missed the bones.

So there they are,
after all these years,
solid as ever.
And they make me think, his own bones
must still be white and solid.

Flesh, hair,
his eyes' blue jelly—
these will be dissolved.
What's left is bone:

that, and the ghostly notes
of jigging music
tapped out long ago
for a child.

The Ontario Review   *Elizabeth Brewster*

SITTING IN BIB OVERALLS, WORKSHIRT, BOOTS
ON THE MONUMENT TO LIBERTY IN
THE CENTER OF THE SQUARE,
JACKSONVILLE, ILLINOIS

("The mystic chords of memory, stretching from
every battlefield to every patriot heart and hearth-
stone over all this broad land, will yet swell the
chorus of the Union when touched as they surely will
be by the better angels of our nature."—A. Lincoln)

The names of those who fought and died
In civil strife are inscribed around the pedestal
On which I slouch watching anonymous townsfolk
On foot, in vehicles, hurriedly enter the Square,
Then leave, return, retreat like blood
Coursing toward death. I imagine them in uniforms,
Cap and bayonet, marching for a common cause.
Only the vision shatters into pieces of ordinary citizens
Pursuing personal liberties and individual freedoms,

While the bodiless names raised on bronze plaques
Turn black-green from municipal neglect and weather.
Vigorous as Aladdin, I rub the lackluster letters
With my shirttail: a kind of magic brings images back
From shadow; voices beneath the granite base
Come unentombed from the ageless incarceration
Of having to outlast the memory of their deeds alone;

They form a chorus only I can hear this Easter:
A resurrection of a sort for a non-believer!

Hiram Poetry Review   *Louis Daniel Brodsky*

DEATH COMES TO THE SALESMAN

It happened so fast,
The sun slipping past the black gates
Into this hoary morning,
That I felt compelled to frisk the mist
Lifting from roadside hills and valleys
To allay my anxiety that sunlight,
Not the ochreous body of death,
Had thrown its shadows
Over my future with so little notice.

Yet when I sent out my eyes
To scrutinize its vapors, they were gone,
And in their place, everywhere,
Vision was a painfully blinding haze
Clawing across a tender sky.
In defense I drew the visor down,
Limiting sight to the pavement on fire,
A bubbling river Styx,
Until I was no longer the driver,

But a victim drowning
In mid stream in a nether world,
Ferried to the earth's furnace.
By the time I finally arrived for my meeting
I'd completely forgotten the reason
For leaving home so early, or even
In whose body I'd slept last evening
Before dying with such abruptness
On this perfectly normal Saturday morning.

Harper's Magazine   *Louis Daniel Brodsky*

ANCESTRY

I stand knee-deep in the ocean
Examining the tepid, eddying sand
Collecting about my feet like hungry minnows.
These particles are the oldest creatures
That still exist, older than Moses,
Younger only than the planet itself.
My own bones are composed of granules
That once came awash on desert shores.
Is it possible that I can recognize
My ancestry beneath these sunny shallows,
Associate blunted shadows with families
Buried 1000 generations ago?
I stoop to pick up a fluted rock
Alive with fossils. I can almost feel
Worms wriggling in my wet palm,

Almost hear its captured voices
Asking me for my body to inhabit again.

Four Quarters   *Louis Daniel Brodsky*

OEDIPUS, PENTHEUS

A sliding step unlocks a hero's cure.
Where three roads met he stayed for no reply.
Only in death we make ourselves secure.

The mind that in its own place caught the spoor
And laid it was of final causes shy.
A sliding step unlocks a hero's cure.

Would any cage the god's caprice endure?
A fatal trick though human to deny
Only in death we make ourselves secure.

By softer tricks untethered to procure
Sandal, thyrsus, and rope, and rending cry,
A sliding step unlocks a hero's cure.

We see the new-plucked limb and are not sure.
The green is altered when we know the dry.
Only in death we make ourselves secure.

The tropic senses decently abjure
All epigrams or read them half awry.
A sliding step unlocks a hero's cure
Only in death. We make ourselves secure.

Poetry   *David Bromwich*

ROUTE 29

i

It curved below the house,
like the last plow tracks
where a hill rises—
but always level with my mind.
Along with Amherst County farmers
going to Faulconer's General Store,
used cars being towed tandem
southwards, and Behemoth trucks,
I rode it every day,
and again a hundred times
from my windows at night, before
dreams, in the hollow hours worse
than sleep, watching the lights
round the bends of my mind.

ii

Dorothy Faulconer who lived
downstairs told me how one night
she had lost her headlights

driving down from Charlottesville,
and how a trucker, beams
on high, followed her all the way,
lighting her from behind.
Often I could feel
the dark room expand
about me and the fields beyond,
into a dizzy sea;
and then the beacon of a late car
below would cross my wall,
and the bed found its keel again.

iii

As the hills flushed red,
flowing into an idea of other
autumns, sometimes I thought back
toward the similarities of time,
and the child at the center.
Where the roads crossed,
I would remember the conjunctions
of love; but Valley winds
would drive the diverse
clouds down the Ridge and, climbing
the switchbacks through the gap,
I foresaw a thousand miles
of flight; my lives dispersed
like scattered birds.

iv

The mountains watch, flawless,
coeval with no one; we
are movement, marked like an edge
of road crumbling after winter's
bite. Half-knowing the dénouement,
I still drive those curves
in dreams; they are my wise serpent,
uncoiling in the past, part
of the arc of time—never joining
with tomorrow as I ride forwards—
since all revelation is revision,
figures in a rear-view mirror—
never the meaning coming,
never the connection, the return.

The Southern Review   Catharine Savage Brosman

THAW

In spite of mid-winter, the air is risen
from fires; we live in a babble of warm winds
flapping me this way and that,
and I tug against the fixed ends of my age.
All night I roll in the greenest grass

while you sit in a nearby tree
laughing at something, pointing away.
"Come down," I call, "the grass is fine,"
but you look beyond me.

I wake in a buffeted dark,
certain I hear your voice
outside my window. Someone's wooden chimes
speak for the wind. I do not doubt
my urge is the unacceptable yammer
of bones that will never be still,
but can not forget how it is to float
on the first touch of any bare clasp.

The slats of my cage are rattling,
so loose I could brush them aside.

Poets On: *T. Alan Broughton*

MIGRATION

Birds find their way
not by sight alone
or memory printed
into their genes,
but by the sounds,
so deep, so slow
that human ears
can never know them.

They fly, hearing
the surf from shores
a thousand miles away,
following the thrum
of winds against
the peaks of distant mountains—
Adirondacks, Smokies,
Sierras, Andes . . .

Their flight, it seems,
is a slow dance
done to a music
which never ends,
as if the seasons
were a bow
and the whole earth
a violin.

The Pikestaff Review   *Joseph Bruchac*

ORATION ON THE TOES

While the heel rears up in petty arrogance
at the upswing of every stride,
and the ball of the foot, with casual muscle,

controls the swing,
toes, the most sorely oppressed members
of our entire body politic,
languish in damp cells.

Without them, our high-stepping would unbalance,
yet we repay them with the worst
of civilization and its discontents. Would we forget
that age when, toes nimble as fingers,
we swung through the trees,
or even, fingers lending support to toes,
loped along the savannah?

If we would forget, surely they will not.
Twitching at unexpected moments,
furtively ripping holes in socks,
these pudgy brats are waiting—
to flick away the sandals of compromise,
to lunge up and make monkeys of us all.

Dark Horse   *Edward Brynes*

LIGHT RAIN

(for Steve & Barbara Schiefen)

Driving to Santa Barbara,
I am thinking of a light rain
in the last of summer,
and, as it clears, the partial clouds,
the sea light sharp to the foothills—
I find myself saying simply,
blue, blue, as if it were something
I was always forgetting . . .
The air is settled with sun,
with the gradual exhalation of flowers,
and I recall the white cymbidiums,
the parochial blouses,
the seraphim-like voices of the girls.

My friend's wife is in the back yard
pinning her freshly laundered sheets;
the mulberries are flushed and heavy,
the ropes of bougainvillaea
are crimson up the houseside.
I hear the Courthouse chime out the hour
and think of the heart
under my body's ineffable weight,
what is lost to us day by day.

Yet, here it all is, passing again
on the thin September light,
or so it seems as I take the old drive
along Alemeda Padre Serra—
the embroidery of iceplant,
the swan-necked agave, holding on just for us;

the pods of the pepper trees,
the rose scattered clouds,
deep as the memory,
this blue chapel of air.

It is like this after years,
after the longing gives way, we're still here;
and I am thinking—it is a light rain, just after . . .

The Chariton Review   *Christopher Buckley*

MY STYLE

I watch the jocks come out in the post parade
and one will win the race, the others will lose;
but each jock must win sometime at some race
on some day, and he must do it often enough
or he is no longer a jockey.

it's like each of us sitting over a typewriter
tonight or tomorrow or next week or next month.
it's like the girls on the street trying to score
for their pimp,
and they have to do it well enough
or they are no longer whores
and we have to do it well enough
or we're whores who can't score.

I would like a little less deliberateness
in the structure.

I became a writer but when I was a boy
I used to dream of becoming the village idiot;
I used to lie in bed and imagine myself that idiot,
planning ways to get food easily and sympathy easily,
a planned confusion of not too much love or effort.

some would claim that I have succeeded
in this.

Poetry Now   *Charles Bukowski*

REVELATION

The problem, surely, is to live with Here;
to spell *as if* so well we willingly suspend our disbelief
in the nothing that was here, is here, and will be:

till the overcast extensions of snow and ice,
black conifers on the stream's far ridge beside the highway,
whatever shakes us with its rusty splendor—till these

are not mere nature—no more than hell and heaven
when we knew them in the yearnings of our flesh
were mere—but compose instead the haven we must praise:

this gritty snow, our onyx; the walked-on moon, still there,
its televised rock our true calcedony; the wrong paths
we take, the concrete sorrows—these, our streets of gold.

The Hudson Review   *Jerald Bullis*

SABBATH

Rain seeps through the olives,
slicks the feathers of the morning bird.

Retreating to bed,
I unfurl the world:
bombs in Belfast, riots in Lebanon,
a plane lost over
Iceland, civil war in Spain.
The Sony at my touch
brings prophecies from pyramids,
and something less
than Bach.
(O give us this day
our Alfred Hay
Mallotte.)

The dove is snug against the rain.
The lily has turned inward.
It is time to polish silver,
read T. S. Eliot
to my cats.

Before the sun is down
I will gather roses and lemon blossoms,
play Mozart's *Requiem*
or the *Trout Quintet.*
I will watch leaves
shimmer in shadow on the wall.
Before I sleep
I will count the stars,
speak softly to the trees, baptized
by rain.
I will live six days in one,
naming the holy names.

Images   *Jean Burden*

WORDS

(for Mark Strand)

These are the words that leap
from the page: *gathered, field,
cold, nameless, sleep;*

all words for counting time:
*north, weather, silence,
dark, winter, keep;*

words to pierce the eye:
portent, dust, water,
nothing, window,
weep.

The Milkweed Chronicle   *Jean Burden*

CONCERTMASTER

(for my father)

Imagine your old bow father,
And a birth from violins.
That I might be among arpeggios
I discreetly scattered my sins.

When I was nine, you sixty-six,
That I might not dwell
Among dead violas
I began to dread your death—
You still seem one of God's tricks.

That we could ignore our mutual flesh
We played chess and talked of Mahler.
We pledged to avoid "exteriors,"
We scarcely remembered to dress.

These things I can now remember:
We were always composing lists.
Our society was usually sky.
We longed for invisible trysts.

He that he may need him.
He that he may rest from need.
He that he may follow him.
He that he may rest from sin.

Listen Father to what I know:
Fathers are Time and sons are loss.
Listen Father to what I remember:
Fathers are Time
And sons are rhyme.

New York Arts Journal   *Richard Burgin*

THE TEACHER TO HELOISE (AFTER WADDELL)

I have sometimes thought
this the difference
between loveliness and beauty:
the knowledge of what has passed,
the memory of the tree in Eden.
Loveliness is easy,
an appletree in blossom,
and for a shining while in youth
woman has it.

But beauty
is for the one or two:
Persephone come back
or Helen,
fierce kingdoms in her face.

And happiness?
A dog asleep in the sun.

And after beauty and great love?
Tragedy as great.

Commonweal   *Daniel Burke*

LONG-DISTANCE

I have these words you sent me—
strong, reassuring on the page—
but I want your voice,
the touch of your hand.
Days I find myself stopped
thinking of you—
what I would say,
how you would listen,
how together we would celebrate
each word,
each green blade.

Today I woke up thinking
maybe, if I open one eye slowly,
I'll find you beside me.
I look at the big towel by the shower,
the one you used
that would fit around us both,
and I see you standing there naked,
waiting.
I close my eyes to remember:
your voice,
soft as the shade of hemlocks
woven over head;
your touch,
little fingers of rain,
the steady gentle sound of it—
of breathing,
of leaves,
the long, deep shiver.

Soundings East   *Carol Burnes*

A HANDFUL OF SMALL SECRET STONES

When he had tired of playing big,
he took rocks—
the largest, crudest he could find: fool's gold, sandstone,
schist, granite—

gathered them like bodyguards, bruisers, ex-cons.
Mica: infiltrator, instigator;
flint: accomplice, arsonist. The other rocks: followers,
common thieves, two-time losers,
sandstone and pumice the first to crack.
Marble: the mastermind, the old pro.

The boy worked them loose from walls,
sprung them from cells
in a state pen. He conspired with rocks
against the handful
of polished stones he had saved, small as his fingernails:
Fatboy, Dark Thought, Freckles, Spinner,
Lucky, Little Digger,
The Twins, Old Blunt, Phantom, Riddlestone, Starnose,
Fiddlehead, Shadow, Gray Nun,
Kid Silver, Flood, Faithful.
The boy placed them in a circle, shut his eyes tight,
made them think hard:
if they were in a circle, they could not be touched;
whatever smoothed a place
and closed ranks around it, could not.
They did not give ground.

The boy overran them with rocks:
granite and sandstone shoved their way into the circle;
puddingstone ground them into the dirt;
Scarface and Wart
threw their weight around like gangsters;
marble and mica finished them off.
They were scattered, trapped under grass the boy tramped down,
buried in wet leaves, wilted petals, and loam.
All morning the boy flung his stones away
and found them again.
He dug them out from under the roses,
wiped each with his sleeve,
made a cave for them in his cupped palms.

He shut his eyes tight again,
held his mind to one thought
till he felt it press and flatten against his brow,
and he quivered, his head shook.
The names were breathed back into the stones
and he placed them in the same order
in the same circle they believed would save them.
He went to look for bigger rocks.

Box 749   *Chris Bursk*

SLEEPING AT THE BEACH

We are hypnotized by the flash of sun
on the hammered medallion of the sea.
Heavy-lidded, we surrender.

Noon sun turns the dozing world crimson.
The whine of one fly grows close,

becomes an engine whine
of a plane careening earthward
out of the nightmare sunfire.
Bomb-doors open; whistling shells
fall in slow motion, growing huge.
I hold my breath wondering how
they will separate our parts for burial.

I come awake like a whip crack
and watch the dream retreat,
focused on the thin membrane
at the base of your throat
where breathing is always visible.

Tendril   *Lucile Burt*

ON THE EDGE OF A SAFE SLEEP

In the silent ridges of a late
winter afternoon, when the city
settles into its stupor of ice

and I can feel the pulse of cars
on distant roads, streaming
toward certain destinations,

the slow disappearance of birds,
the crawl of raccoons and field mice
toward sleep,

I turn from my white pages
blurred with words, the walls
of my study lined with confessions

I had not planned to make,
and I meet the cold sidewalks,
the snow-washed evergreens

eye to eye. I run slowly
into the clear stretch of road
that wings away from the city,

leans toward trees and earth,
and emerges by a large pond.
I enter the woods furtively,

find a path by the water,
dip with the hills into darkness,
into the still breath of frozen ground,

the haunts of invisible animals
lying like fossils on the underside
of bushes. Rounding the pond,

purple with the last glimmer
of sun on winter cloud,
I run now with the path,

my feet on ice,
my legs exploding with a momentum
of muscle,

my mind clean of thought,
clear of any longing, except
the desire to live,

always like this, on the edge
of a safe sleep, lost in flight.

Tendril   *Teresa D. Cader*

REUNION

It is dangerous to visit you in your woods in May.
Not that I gash myself passing hawthorns
or get struck down by your electric fence.
Coasting hawks don't eye me.
It's this thick confusion we speak between us.
Coming on like a sudden fog when I arrive,
it settles in like a heavy blanket.
We beat our way through it with muffled words.
It stays put. We are muzzled dogs walking.

You tell the children to hurry. I've stopped them
to point out a may-apple.
You say our sons are good friends. I see cold looks
between them and scarcely two words. When you shout—
Watch it—we know and we don't know.
This fog may be cultivated: it seems perennial.

We talk about what you know all the answers to.
I duck, surface, cut you off in mid-stream,
lie, play dead, and you say
how nice to see me.

Your dogs leap and seethe. All the cats are in heat.
I see double, snap at the children, kick dog bones.
You yell from a barnful of horses.
Your voice cracks my watch.
It's time to leave.

The Fiddlehead   *Heather Cadsby*

MY SON, MY SON . . .

As the night ended,
And the long wake,
And the mother's hard labor,
You came forth
On that new day.
The first thing I saw
Was the back of your head
Crowned with red silken curls—
And you came forth crying

Into the world outside the womb.
You came forth glistening
Preternaturally lengthened
In my weary, sleepless eyes,
Held up there in the morning light
In the young intern's arms—
An awesome biblical-memoried
Strange and numinous moment—
A forever time when the real broke in.
And then after that apocalypse
Came the little helping tasks,
Feeding you tenderly the little spoonfuls of water.
Oh, all those newspapers and boiled water
On that day!—
Holding you carefully in my father arms,
Oh my son, my son!

And now estranged from the world and self,
Locked in the barbed-wire closure
Wrought by your lacerating mind,
All that is nulled for you
Nor never was.
And now I stand—
Your hated despised adversary,
First cause of your fallen state,
Architect of your irremediable doom.
And now that shapely little head,
Seat of your imagery and wit,
Becomes a terrible temple
Indwelt by all the furies.
And now here I stand helpless,
Unable to aid thee.
Oh my son, my son,
Mine enemy son!

I pray for you
To come forth once more
Into the light again,
Into the formed demanding world
Outside the womb.
Do not go back, my son,
Into that darkness again.
Breathe.
        Make.
            Be.

Midstream   *Seymour Cain*

NIGHT CHARACTER

Florence below was an abyss of lights of trembling sordidness:
On wings of fire the faraway rangling
Of the tram faded, the enormous dull river
Flashed its serpent's scales.

Above the indefinite spirals the disquiet smirking faces
Of thieves, and I between two equal rows of cypresses like
    sputtering torches.

More bitter than cypress hedges,
More bitter than trembling box-trees,
As from my heart this love,
As from my heart, the love a pimp breaks into song:
I love the old whores
Swollen with the fermentation of sperm
Who flop like toads on all fours on their red mattresses
And wait and pant and gasp,
Flaccid as bellows.

Cutbank

Dino Campana
—Translated from the Italian
by Frank Stewart

YOU CAN GET DESPONDENT

You can get despondent over not being a poet,
over your genius being just a bird in your head,

a bird that can only repeat endlessly
the same song causing the fir-trees to embrace,

when there might be so many things to say
about the clouds, the prairies, the smile,

like a fresh cherry, of very young girls,
about the horses round which the wasps are glittering,

about dawn which uses the weirs of wheat
to rescue its pearly fish from obscurity,

about the angels you see sometimes high overhead
in a triangle—and you think they're birds;

about God himself, God who is everything at once:
man, blade of grass, pebble, squirrel and great forest.

Poetry Now

Maurice Careme
—Translated from the French (Belgium)
by Norma Farber

NOVEMBER SNOW

The wind is enough to stack the snow
in odd, hard-packed shapes
one like the barrel I stole
for the oleander

which died all the same, the cats
clawing it down behind the curtain
for no apparent reason

And now the neighbours tell me
in that excited, too hungry tone

a child slipped out from the barrel
air-borne   snowbanks receding

from sight,
into the half-ton's wheel

We must have been in bed, your body
miraculously shaping my hands
And afterwards, taking the snow in
through the window I wondered
where the earth went in that moment

Out for a walk the spot is irresistable—
like love we love to look things over
try it on for size, discover its limits
too large
seeing only the spiked red blotch
like some mysterious snow blooming weed

Tonight my head swims aimlessly
searching in the room a way out
wondering without shame
what must have been

just then   not before
                   or after

The Canadian Forum   *E. J. Carson*

FOR JACK CHATHAM

For Jack Chatham, and his brother Tom,
Both without helmets, their red hair
Streaming behind them in the wind;
For all those who rode big Harleys
And Indians back in the fifties,
Who dropped out of school, of work,
Of everything, to drive again and
Again down the dark cylinders of air.
For Jack on that bright day hitting
The slick on the bridge and landing
Exactly in the center of Fall Creek,
So that coroners from adjoining counties
Argued over his body while the deputies
Took Tom down the road to a place
Where the Klan hung out and bought him
A few beers and patted him on the ass
Saying it's all right, kid—
Go on riding while you got the chance.

Pteranodon   *Jared Carter*

WINE FROM THE CAPE

There will greet you at the end, Vasco,
Blood, and as its recompense this vintage:

Light of skies that flint the glass with gold;
Spray, as of seas, to fill the stem with cold.

The measured seasons of the land and grape;
Their compressed forces that as foam escape.

For all your daring and for all your loss,
A little wine that snares the Southern Cross;

That as a sapphire keeps one star alive,
Inside the glass repeats its four, its five.

The Southern Review   *Turner Cassity*

CLASSICAL AUTUMN

They have left us, all the summerly mornings.
The simple season's mischief, the autumn, comes
varying tempers. And, therefore, days wake
watchful and urbane.
The warmth is civilized.
The nights delimit every wandering thing
and bring it home to flesh in simile
as if they brought an end to lonesomeness
in the small flavored winds now basketing
the folded air; yet saved this solitude
in the here and now, pointed and ardently.

Indian summer . . .

                    Sheerly derivative,
it takes from other seasons other weathers
—the doubt from spring, the innocence from it,
smearage of summer, and the winter's snap—
as an old precious scholar over his notes
takes all, gives little, yet is longly itself.
The hours are legendary even as we
saunter about them and they seem complete,
rather like poems for an exegesis
or like a song that sings its alphabet
. . . finely, slenderly made.

Wascana Review   *Robert Clayton Casto*

PATIENCE

We had to make catalogues—
divide things,
put them in the calipers,
weigh them.
It did not add up, things
often changed color,
consistency, taste, dimension.
Then we chose by sight, smell,
trusting instinct.
The results were not better.

In any case, suffering was needed:
the patience that wears out the flesh
in order for the bone to shine.

Poetry Now   *Bartola Cattafi*
                                    —Translated from the Italian
                                            by Rina Ferrarelli

IN THE TAXIDERMIST'S SHOP

In the taxidermist's shop
lids of eagles open up
to reveal each eye
of glass,

        and row on row
upon the counter
you can count the perfect eyes
for peacock, parrot, lion, bear,
one by one, pair by pair,
guaranteed not to fade,
guaranteed to stare.

Why would a pair of lovers go
to the taxidermist's shop
to speak politely to the man
behind the counter,
        to ask
how the feathered shrouds of birds
are kept intact
        or the hairy hide
of any hunter's pride?

Not knowing why, they do.
They touch each other and talk
of playing marbles with the eyes
of tigers—
cat eye, snake eye, eye of needle,
eyelet, they laugh, Immortal Eye;
while in some place they know
the eye of "I" has already seen
reflected in the other's eye,
twinned and focused,
in the stare,
that, like love,
mortality is there.

The Georgia Review   *Siv Cedering*

THE RUNNER

("A man too gentle gets left behind."—Nancy Schoenberger)

The roads go on, ending only
in reduced images.

> Running
is my way of returning
to a place,
> > to this room infused
with foliage, the street lights
merged in a single lamp.
> > > Already
you are awake. I lean to kiss
your waist, the muscles
like spreading water,
> > > > but skin
is anonymous. I am spared
my face. Only later
will we need words,
> > > > > the spaces
between them, a distance
we must try to cover.

The Sun   *Jerah Chadwick*

TO DRIFT DOWN

Perhaps when I am gaunt
and sorely tried by life
I will welcome death
as a brittle brown leaf
tired of clinging
in a harsh winter wind
finally must welcome
> freedom to let go
to drift down
to become one
with earth once more.

Quercus   *Janet Carncross Chandler*

THE EDGE

(Chugiak, Alaska)

Wedged into a hard huddle
by weight of ice and years,
clutches of stones
(the glacier's eggs)
lurk in the yard
where I would garden.

Pry with the shovel.
Brush away damp quartz crumbs
with the bent trowel.
The clunk of steel on stone
becomes a hymn
to unyielding wilderness.

I cannot loosen one boulder
without unearthing
adamantine siblings,
tangled in filmy roots.
One cold shoulder
cleaves to another.

Sometimes a pocket of ice crystals
winks in the unaccustomed light—
a reminder that here
we are always on the edge,
the edge
of winter.

A tongue of frost
curls upward;
an odor of cold sand.
Sweat drips from my chin
into the uncivilized
crevasse.

Permafrost   *Ann Chandonnet*

LOVE SONG

wherever your voice moves
        to touch me

wherever your hands will refuse
        to let go

wherever there are odors of your face
        remaining on me

wherever your muscles
        begin to breathe

wherever in the noise
        of cities

it is still
        possible for your dreams to begin

wherever your words
        burn the sky

wherever you are
        I will come to meet your hair

to touch your hands
        wherever you are

to be touched
        by you

Ararat   *Kosrof Chantikian*

YOUR EYES

your eyes are
      the other side of night's dreams

roses where silence
      becomes a sound of perfumed dawns

are mirrors
      through which death watches me asleep

your eyes are
      the sound of morning becoming the wind

Ararat   *Kosrof Chantikian*

EVERGLADE

Promising a river of grass, you guided me
south, through the red hills of my past,
the ridges of pine and oak, bitter shacks
and white, dreaming houses. The cities fell

behind us; no dwelling but the boat. The world
was low and endless, yellow sawgrass sharpened
in a hot wind. You grew into me, a white root,
but your hands were blue as water.

You taught me names for a land that was not land—
marl and slough. The eyes of marsh deer held us
transfixed. Over me, your ribs arched,
ferns imprinted in stone. And the days

slid into each other, sweet water into salt.
First I cried when I woke to find you gone.
I threw out the paddles and lifejackets,
I sunk the anchor, and I was adrift

in the estuaries. Herons watched me, pelicans
begged for fish though I had none. I listened
to the sad calls across the mangroves,
my hair a mess of roots, my legs beaten

and brown. And when the grasses caught my boat,
I tried to call them as you would: coinwort
and love-vine, but my voice rusted in my throat
and they slid their knots over my head.

Tendrils attached to my arms and I felt myself
growing pliant, dissolving, the sun over me scarring
my vision; and then I knew, suddenly I knew,
that it was as you had wished.

The Louisville Review   *Anne Cherner*

AN APOLOGY FOR A LOST CLASSICISM

I was writing a trenta-sei for the boat-people
when I ran out of chocolate mints and lost rhyme.

There is no conspiracy against creativity.
One yet notes art must be a precise encounter.
It is possible only in the fullest concurrence
of every circumstance of concept and creature.

When I ran out of chocolate mints and lost rhyme
I was alone in grieving for my failure.
The boat-people, adrift in their killing freedom,
could not care that the demands of art are total.
They were too busy bailing. And thirst lacks style.
I was alone in grieving for my failure.

There is no conspiracy against creativity.
It is the conceiving creature, not the concept,
falls belittled by its creature craving.
And also that one's subjects, caught in their agony,
refuse to see how they matter only as instance,
as dismissable witnesses to perdurable form.

One yet notes it must be a precise encounter.
I had been nagged from an epic sympathy
by nothing more than the teasing of my sweet tooth.
A stupid insistence. Yet concept cannot be riled,
can be shaped only by undistracted energy
freed of all need to provision its own survival.

It is possible only in the fullest confluence
of a reverent classicism, whose tradition
testifies to us that Ideal Greece herself,
our Gods' cradle, was raised to the noumenal
on the bones of slaves, whose otherwise pointless *soma*
subtended the *neuros* of the master encounter.

Within the circumstance of concept and creature
I tried to make do with Oreos. But there are
no substitutes for essence. Perhaps tomorrow
when I buy another paper—and infinite mints—
I shall fix their dying from *incidence* to *summa*,
and need not grieve alone for the boat-people.

West Hills Review   *John Ciardi*

MAP READING

You see, my darling,
where I place my finger's Cleveland,
standing sensitive and proud,
its radius swollen with culture and art,
gorged with the sculpture of sense;
matched on the other side by Toledo,
slightly smaller, less developed
because of neglect and location.

Watch carefully as I slide my hand
down route 71, fingertips savoring
the topography, the thrilling ache
of rushing past a world of landscape.

We've come at last to Columbus,
the very center of your state—
everything begun between your borders
seeks conclusion here—
and when something's whispered
in this very important place
your extremities shiver in response.

Try to concentrate; please lie still—
I'm about to show you a mighty river.

West Branch   *David Citino*

MYSTERIOUS BRITAIN

That gray morning I left you asleep
in the room overlooking Agincourt
Square, with the statue of King Harry
of Monmouth, and caught the bus to Trellech—
there being just one bus daily, and that one
so early there was no place to have breakfast
but a counter where regulars traded a patter
I couldn't make head or tail of—I was on the
scent of something a whole lot older
than Monmouth or the Battle of Agincourt:
the Wales of the Little People, a whiff
of huge unaccountable forces those
who are into the Craft believe they've
gotten in touch with.

                              The bus—I was
its only passenger—wound upward
through beechwoods dazzling with holly
over a foot-thick purple carpet of
bluebells. Trellech was at the top,
overhung by a towering wizard's hat
of a spire: too wet a place (even in
hospitable Wales) to be quite friendly.
The Standing Stones I'd come thinking
would leap at me were so hard to find
I began to think somebody'd moved them.
But in fact they were where they'd
always been—lichened, leaning every
which way, in what was now a cowpasture.
Supposedly anyone coming too close, or with
unseemly intent, will be thrown back by
powerful oracular forces. Whether it's
true or not I can't say, I couldn't
get close enough because of the cows:
big Herefords, mythic nostrils
the size of caves, totem faces and
enormous rimmy eyelashes a frightful,
milk-curdling white. I know cows
just enough to tell these weren't friendly.

There's a so-called Virtuous Well at
Trellech, clearly marked and such a cinch
to find, my guess is it's lost its virtue.
I'd intended to go back on foot,
get involved with holly and bluebells
if nothing else. But before I'd walked very far,
one of the hospitable Welsh came along in a
red sports car and offered me a lift.
There are some things, it seems,
you just can't get close to.

The American Scholar   *Amy Clampitt*

THE EDGE OF TOWN

Somewhere out past the high walls
of the garden, away from houses
standing one against another
and the garbage rotting right outside
combed over by chickens and dogs,
it is a morning, a Sunday
in Cholula. I am nearly recovered
from the long wringer of
hepatitis and this cursed season
of confusion and struggling.
Ernesto and I walk out
through the still damp
plowed fields, as his
big black retriever runs off
through furrows, irrigation
troughs and mud.

It is cleaner here, away
from the center of town, the husks
of fruit, pig carcasses hauled
from the trucks to *carnecerías*.
We move toward the huge
and calm volcanic cone.
The dog runs farther off.
We feel the fine lightness
of the air, and how we'd like
to hold this unearned peace
suspended right here; despite
an impenetrable city, foreign
to us both. Cholula, perhaps
the oldest city in the hemisphere,
unmoved like the glacial volcano.
I think how comforting
is just a fist of earth,
the quiet green brown plain.
A place we never quite belonged;
pained now to sense these are the last
mornings. The big black dog

comes running, wet and smelling of
the fields, the mud, the edge.

The Chariton Review   *William Clamurro*

BONNER'S FERRY BEGGAR

You are a beggar.
That is a door.
A door is a knife
that parts your world in two halves.

If you stand in front and knock on it
because you're a beggar,
then perhaps it will open to you
as the smell of roast meat
and fresh washed clothes streams out.

It is the smell of northern Idaho homes.

You who have a fine beggar's nose
can smell tears too.

But the Bonner's Ferry housewife says
        No, I can't help you today.
and
        No, there is nothing you can do for me.
and
        No,
says the closing door.

Kansas Quarterly   *Duane Clark*

DEATH COMES FOR THE OLD COWBOY

Night breathes in the window
like a steel guitar.
He asks her
could he have this dance,
and the Red Road Ranch Band
leans coolly into *Yellow Rose*
just the way his mother
would sing it to the wet moon
of the San Angelo sky
long after he'd been put to bed
and she was drinking her coffee
alone on the porch, her voice
taking him to the stars.
Blankly she says yes,
and they walk untouching
to the middle of the crowded
floor. He puts his arm
to the small of her back,

swipes his free hand
at his jeans, and carefully
takes her soft palm.
In the thick smoke
of the August night, he nods,
spins slowly left,
and *Lord!* how she follows—
like a dream, circling
on the endless curve
of that sweet pedal steel.

California Quarterly   *Kevin Clark*

SUMMER VISITORS

The poodles are in the basement again so my aunt
is angry. Uncle is in the living room feeling sleepy.
Living rooms always make him feel sleepy. Kitchens
make him feel hungry. You can imagine
what bedrooms make him feel. My two cousins
are outside in the tall grass in the back yard
playing "Doctor." I would love to join them
but my mother has a firm grip on my shoulder
as we sit together on the screened-in front porch
listening to my grandfather tell bad jokes.
He knows several terrible puns about nuns
and carrots and he tells them all.
I try to laugh but it comes out as
an insincere chuckle. Grandfather is very rich
and my mother is trying to make me appreciate him.
Meanwhile, I can hear ominous growls
coming up from the basement. The two poodles
hate each other and there is going to be trouble
soon. Auntie paces nervously and worries
about rabies. Uncle has at last gotten out of
the living room. He has made his way to the bedroom.
He wants to show his wife something there.
I have a vague understanding of what that is all about.
I keep thinking of my cousins. They are probably
naked and having a good time. My grandfather lights
a bad cigar. I cough, surreptitiously as possible.
My mother frowns. There are strange, muffled noises
coming from the bedroom, and barking from below.
Things are happening like an absurd play. I begin
day-dreaming about becoming a great writer, falling
in love with a great writer. The situation is
out of my control. I have to go to the bathroom
but grandfather is pointing at me with his cigar.
He begins telling a long, boring story about how
he first got rich, about how hard he had to work
to get rich, but it was worth it—he says.
Wouldn't you like to be rich? he asks.
As a young idealist, being rich is the last thing

in the world I would want to be. Money
is for helping the poor. But I nod and smile
and he chuckles and begins telling me about how
he is going to help me on my road to riches
(pointing the way to the proper and prosperous
schools and businesses), all the while ignoring
the rising crescendo of bedroom and basement
noises. He maps out my future for me. Mother
nods approval. (Father is dead. He will always
be dead. Mother is not exactly Mother. I am not
her child, I am her duty. She does her duty.)
Relatives infest my life: they visit and leave
scenarios I feel obliged to live.
There is more than cigar smoke clouding
my vision now. The summer outside fades as brightly
as adolescent pleasure. It is grandfather, not me,
who gets up to go to the bathroom. Mother and I
hold the scene steady for his re-entry. Her hands
are on me. *He's a good man,* she says. *He's rich,*
he'll help you. I hear laughter outside while
boisterous but muted animal sensuality stirs the house.
Running water—a toilet flushes. The future
is happening, it has already happened. Immediately,
I realize my life isn't going to turn out
the way I had planned.

Poetry   *Stephen Clark*

AFTER THE SEANCE

Cars disappearing from the driveway, carrying
their cargo of vague hope. She stands thin
behind the shades and watches three times a week.
When the last lights tail away, she pulls down
another night of rigging. The tambourine,
her father's once from show days. The fan,
whose low speed blows the right disturbance.
The tape recorder, humming dead silence in a drawer.
Her part is the practiced sweat, the eyes
sealed closed and dumb. This is the Next Life
that comes easy. Years of keeping the same secrets.
She knows working up the voice is hardest.
Each time learning how to beat the biggest drum,
a table full of ears, into believing.
The circle of hands has broken, scattered home
to dark houses. Her own hands pour coffee in a cup,
count money out of an envelope on the way upstairs.
Twenty dollars for Aunt Clara, fleeting,
taken by surprise in sleep. Another ten
for someone's Jacob, blown out at 80 mph.
Whatever was agreed on is all accounted for.
In her room, the door shut tight without thinking
twice. She's poured over the years before, maps

with holes where friends used to live. She knows
the minutes every night when she gives her gift,
her invention, time to slip away. Powers
of association fade. All money disappears or
grows too thin to handle. Tonight the radio
at her ear goes static. She can't get any station
clear. She's convinced again, no life beyond
this one. The familiar sweat beads a welcome back.
Half-formed voices ghost up her throat until
she finds the one she needs most.
Give me something to hold on to,
some jewelry, a shred of clothing. And who
will be the spirit guide tonight?

The Midwest Quarterly   David Clewell

TELEMACHUS AND THE BOW

He is the bow, firm,
smooth and aged, old
yet wonderfully pliant,
toughened with care.

I the string, taut
with untested youth, new
to these trials but fixed,
tempered for use.

And though the trial rewards
me, though I feel the stings'
strength in my own arms, power
to pierce the sharp arches and win

her, one look recalls me
and I decline, reminded
that this is not my contest
yet; I am another.

Occident   *Randall Colaizzi*

HOW THE SKY BEGINS TO FALL

When Skylab fell
into the wedding bed of gravity
it disintegrated in a reverie of many
colors—green, yellow, blue, red,
the spectrum of weightlessness
splintering east of Perth.
Come quick, mate, the wife of a station
manager said, if you want to see it
falling like bloody birds,
sonic wings drumming
until the horses run mad
in the wasteland.

Tonight, I dream I have
a sash made of many small brilliant
birds. It sang my life around
my body as I drove over the map
in an antique touring car. I wear
a dust veil like a beekeeper.
You slumber next to me
like an astronaut monitoring
vital signs. If this dark room
lacked gravity we'd never find ourselves.
Directions would mean nothing.

A bird
in the blackness above us sleeps
on a crooked branch,
stars burning along death row
like incandescent bulbs. Space:
the corridor of postulations. A door
the condemned enter breathing irregularly,
then not at all.

In my dream I give my sash
to a woman who is my friend.
Her eyes take flight; she may grow wings
where I failed. You groan in your sleep
changing orbit, beginning to fall
into my arms like a solar panel
melting with friction.

En Passant / Poetry   *Joan Colby*

A VEGETARIAN SINGS

(for Bruce)

We all must work with what we have.
So you're alone in Rome with words, a shave
away from dinner in an elegant trattoria,
and I compose with produce from the neighborhood emporia
carrot stick sunbursts, and rosettes of zucchini;
radishes, with finesse worth a Bellini,
balance on a focal eggplant; slivered green
cucumber peels marry with its violent sheen.
The urge toward form is bodiless, therefore requiring
media; our medium shared: bodies desiring
form and rhythm in one bed, one flesh
expressing mental thrust and mesh. It's fresh
each time, consumed with mutual relish.
I have made the tapanade. I roll it on my tongue,
imagine yours, and when tonight among
the guests your poems are quoted, I'll taste your body
transmuted, and they'll proclaim my funghi marinati.

Prism International   *Audrey Conard*

TONIGHT THE CITY

Tonight the city dreams uneasily,
For city dreams are restive, nightmare-ridden.
And, wandering through suburban streets, I see,
Unveiled then veiled as she's revealed and hidden
By skiffs and hulks of cloud, the placid moon.
And where she seems to float, the troubled sky
Is shot with phosphorescent blue and gray.
She silvers over roofs, beneath which lie
Trapped souls that stir, dreading the clattering day.
Now, while these skimming clouds escort the moon,
This cold, dark, hard-faced city almost seems
To assume a mask of loveliness; but I,
Having looked on purer beauty, through time's grace,
And lived, too briefly, where fantastic dreams
Acquire the sharpness of reality,
Never can take the mask to be a face.

The Arizona Quarterly   *R. L. Cook*

AN UNSEEN FIRE

i

We feel more than we see of the winter
Sun curving each day, petal by petal,
Toward some frank lush bloom. Now,
With the sap of laughter surging through our veins,
Who has the heartstrings to harp on
The next vicissitude, and darkness? The vessels
Of grief have no harbor amongst us, but ride
At bay, on springs of beatitude. No one tells
Of the flood that climbed the steeps last year;
Only the worst sufferers, perhaps, remember.

ii

And through it all the coal burns gloomily
Under the green hills all around Wilkes-Barre,
Under rosebush, gardenia, and pine.
Stunningly slow to form from humble
Origins, as slow to have chafed into flame,
This same coal will be seething aeons from
Where we stand, in its unsuspected cave
Of time, blind devotion and ashes.
It will get nothing more from the green
Things that fly under the decaying colors
Of the sun. It burns, unlike the inconstant
Geese, and, unlike us, aloof from the sun
And its incessant blind shuttle.

iii

We feel more than we know between the sun,
Unfolding petal by petal, and
The burning secret of this mountain, that coal.

The Yale Review   *Michael G. Cooke*

HOUSE POEM

Why do I see my house as a second body?
The disposition of the bed
like a hungry mouth? the dining room table
like the eye of Cyclops,
my third eye, the truth-teller,
perpetual Thanksgiving gathering all in?

Whoever knocks here, you enter a palpable skin.
All I ask is respect
for this skin of marble, walnut, leather, linen; this hair
of geranium leaves with its faint, dry breath;
even the vulgar conversation
of the air conditioner.
I am as vulnerable
to your least touch as a wandering clove of dust.

The Paris Review   *Jane Cooper*

HYPODERMIC RELEASE

Books, lips, hands,
ideas swirl, cram the brain
with insane pressures,
a balloon blown beyond its limits
straining to burst
in incoherent fury upon the world.

If I could only convert
this tiny pencil,
worn short from years
of scribbled tears,
into a hypodermic needle,
I'd insert
and suck each pounding poem out
and let it spill,
ooze through the paper
and seep like radiation
into the minds and hearts
and bones
of those I love.

Writer's Digest   *Del Corey*

THE BOSS MACHINE-TENDER AFTER LOSING A SON

When paper snaps in machines,
he pokes through greasy alleys, flashlight
beaming among clamoring wheels
and huge whirring belts.
He'll run himself ragged
getting sheets back on the reels,
shelving time for moments
when the clock ticks like a dream

of flawless paper. Then he smokes
his pipe in the office, and recalls
the smooth glide of his Old Town canoe.

He moves through waters
that sustained father and son
between slender, canvased ribs.
The two drift leisurely, machinery roaring
like distant white-water
inside his throbbing temples;
while somewhere back of his mind,
hidden like jagged river rock,
lies the night he shut down
machine number nine
to pull out his boy.

The Greenfield Review   *Paul Corrigan*

NOT THIS LEAF HAUNTS ME

No, not this leaf haunts me. Some year I might
Bring to your hand a leaf, but not this year.
This time I want to stand and watch the night
Come on. I want to see what has been clear
Come clouded, as some rare magic is turned
And made to look easy and everyday.
I want the leaves right to the limbtips burned
In rich ballooning flame, this air to play
A mass of pink into a shaded blue
And one last stream of sun and something blowing,
All the earthy huskiness so true
And so profound it makes me think of you
And this our stay on earth essential as our going.

The Antigonish Review   *Tony Cosier*

BRAILLE

The blind folding their dollar
bills in half. Giving the fives
a crease on each corner; leaving
the tens smooth as a knuckle.

There are ways, even in trust
among the rank and file
of the seeing,
not to be bilked.

The blind leading the blind
is not so bad—

how it is lost on us every day
that you can learn all
of the world you need to know

by tapping it gently
with a stick.

The Missouri Review   *Gerald Costanzo*

FALL AGAIN

("I say the gods are alive. And they are not consoling."
—May Sarton, "At Delphi")

Frost breaks across the dawn
    like crystal cracking.
All precious stones melt down,
        but build again
    in their secret chambers
    once day's short stay
        has erased itself
along the western slate.

The ministry of fear
    gave us long ago
our questions—when, where, who,
        what—but never
    why the diamond delves so
    far down into
            its chilly depth. That
    might ask too much of
human hearts in hiding,

cold, like the minerals
    that shape below the
dry wrinkles that the first
        flakes will wash to
    the blank brow of death, and
    long, long waiting
        for some dawn of gold,
mined out of total night.

This northern earth sinks to
    a dark stone turning,
turning from light around
        polarities of steel.
    The unseen why
    trails behind the geese,
        whose iron-bound,
    south-bound wedge shatters
down the emerald sky.

The Small Pond Magazine   *H. R. Coursen*

THE HINGE

(for Wendy)

Down on the beach we separate,
you to the sun and the morning *Times*,

I to the tidal pools and the casual
treasure last night's wind and rain washed in.
Beneath my toes the mud and the hard rounded shells.

We've been paired like the valves of these mollusks
for more than twenty years now, held
by the strong adductor muscles of children
and the old decencies. Mostly we've liked
the bond.
      Its toothed hinge clean
of detritus, the shell can stain food
through its siphons. We let it open
and close. Once a friend suggested
we'd been lucky. I flared—it wasn't luck,
it was hard work. It wasn't, not really,

not like digging clams or preparing a fine
bouillabaisse. Grit, weed, algae—all flow in
with the tide and out, even sewage
which, like crisis, urges growing.
Oh, things slip in and rankle,

a dear attractive friend wanting
too much solace, one dreary meal too many.
But it's when something rigid,
this guilt, a sliver wedged
in the hinge, fails to wash out in new tide,

then—then the breach—and the slow
relentless drying. To survive the daily
low tide becomes hard work.

Tar River Poetry   *Sheila Cowing*

PHONE CALL

Listen Sally
we must synchronize our watches
because at precisely eight o'clock
wherever you are
the phone will not ring
but if you pick up your hand
you will hear the words ringing over and over
in your ear
I love you

Footprint   *Tom Crawford*

AUGURIES FOR THREE WOMEN

Midnight, and three women
around a fire. We've done this
before. My cat worries
from lap to lap, and Claire
keeps crossing her legs,

corduroy asking which way,
which way?

The long bones of Gail's fingers
rest strong on her chair.
Tentative, Claire taps on the lip
of her wine glass. Grey
skims our hair the way
ice skims a pond
in the first fall frost.

The fire dies and I pile on driftwood.
The cat watches the salt blaze
blue and white, her long shadow
rousing itself across our legs.

I have dreamed us
big cats. By the full moon
we climb a prominence;
we don't need to look behind.
I have dreamed
how the jungle stops and the grassland
begins, golden
and perfidious.

We're three women solitary,
spelling the future,
looking for omens in words.

And then the time,
midnight, unexpected as mid-life,
that lioness knowing a path
through the savannah and seeing
just ahead the tall grasses
part.

Tendril   *Jacquelyne Crews*

GUNS

The blue-blooded Mauser's first cousin
this thirty-ought-six bolt-action Springfield
U. S. Army 1943 by Underwood Typewriter smells
of serious business gun oil metal and oily
hardwood fills your hands not at all
like a good woman lift

the bolt handle click pull
back click the brass jumps
halfway across the red carpet push
forward catching the top edge of
the new cartridge and out the
magazine smoothly into the chamber click
push down the bolt handle click locking
the three lugs that keep it from blowing
back half your head off that

last time when I made a fine pistol shot
at thirty yards the white fluff ran
only a few steps before falling over to lay
with a thin fading cry like a sick baby
heartbroken blood too red against white snow and
whiter fur I picked it up by
the hind legs kicking new snow over the red
like it never happened and holstered my
all-American Ruger single action revolver and walked
back to the cabin saying silently over and over by
god it was the last time and

this thirty-ought-six perfected in oh three is
the mousetrap of bolt-action rifles direct
descendant of the 1840 Prussian needle gun man has
always perfected his killing tools first and

even with my staunch resolution I stand here holding
it and all the pencils in the world cannot write
away this pull on my insides as
explicable as what pulls the goose south
in winter and that is the only reason believe
me all else is rationalization.

Permafrost   *Ronald Crowe*

IT MUST BE SUMMER

It must be summer.
Radios blare in the open windows
and the seamstress with the mane of a mare
leans on the windowsill;
her fashion magazines
sun themselves beside her.
A bitten-off basting thread dangles from her mouth
like the umbilical cord of an infant
who was born with wings.
My face flickers across hers—
had we once shared dreams?
Had I stood there, clutching a blackthorn branch
in the wide-open door?
A tousled fluff of a feather drifts by, numb,
in front of her eyes.
Then a piece of the sky, blue, uncreased,
The way it never is
inside a torture chamber!
It must be summer, truly summer—
the heart radar signals distant aluminum rain
and suspicious affairs.
With a throaty swan song.

Footprint   *Sandor Csoori*
                                        —Translated from the Hungarian
                                                  by Nicholas Kolumban

COUSINS

I am not cousin to thinking brain
Or upright stance.
I am pointed ears, cat-clawed feet,
A tusk-toothed fearsome thing
Living in shielded rock.

When it suits me, I am a child
Wet from the cavern, three breaths old,
My face screwed up in puzzlement
At a world turned hard and bright.

How did I come to such a crossing?
Was it space outgrown
Or ache to stretch straight my tiny bones
And hear unmuffled by her flesh
My howls of shock to taste the world?

I'd like to think my borning
Was such a consequence.
But to be true, I was moved by mountains
As are we all of small account
Moved by peaks of time and space.

By these we live our years,
But first the forces congregate
To push us from the womb
To greet a world
Gone mad with mountains.

Kansas Quarterly   *Paula B. Cullen*

ROSES, REVISITED, IN A PARADOXICAL AUTUMN

Poets have been writing about the death of flowers
at least since Ausonius, but these November roses
defy all images of autumn gardens. The Michaelmas daisies
left with the death of September, and the last late sunflowers
dropped and went dark three weeks ago. These silly roses
bloom like a hysterical couplet out of Rilke,
and new buds still blush like conventional metaphors.
Undisciplined endings like this offend us. We want cold in
                    November,
petals dropping like autumn leaves, earth slipping into seasonal
                    sleep
decently and in order, as in a late Latin epic
or a universe ordained by Thomas Aquinas.
Flowers and the bright day fail. What's left, we embody in elegies.
That's how we made sense of life, and the death of women.
These roses and hot sunlight in early November
decline responsibility for their scheduled mortality,
leaving us with old sonnets and our own uncertain wrists.

Poetry   *J. W. Cullum*

TO MY FATHER

Bellringing was another
of the things you didn't teach me.

How many crooked ladders did we climb?
How many belfries did we crouch in?
The musty smell of the years in the wood beams,
the giant domes balanced to move
against a man's pull.
Stories of jammed trapdoors and madness
in the deafening that draws blood.
Once you rang for the Queen
and I watched
all that pomp ooze into the cold stone of the cathedral.

I wanted to take the smooth grip of a rope
and lean my weight into it.
I wanted timing.
I wanted you to teach me
to teach my son's son.

Turning your back on that
brings our line down. What
have you left me? What sense
of the past? I could have lost myself in the mosaic
of Grandsires, Trebles and Bobs,
moved to that clipped calling of the changes.

I know now the churchbells coming over the folded
town's Sunday sleep carries me close to tears,
the noise of worship and weddings and death
rolling out,
filling the hollow of my throat.

The Malahat Review   *Tony Curtis*

MUSEUM WITH CHINESE LANDSCAPES

We walk past the Han stallion
captive in a glass box, its fierce
warrior long ago thrown,
on our way to the Chinese landscapes.
Together we wander
deep into painted mountains.
In thickening snowfall
elegant, green-robed pines
bend as in reverence.
Mist like milkweed,
winged shapes drifting off
until they are gone.
With each delicate brush stroke
we rise in blue sky that fades
imperceptibly into that whiteness,
our vanishing point concealed in time.

See how ice hardens to mantle,
the turquoise pond
where each thin reed sings
its own unvarying note.
That swirling of snow is the wind's work.
Who will remember this music
if the reeds forget when the wind stops?

America   *Walter Cybulski*

ANOTHER STONE POEM

Stones surpass the silence
Deep in space, where nothing is.
A stone in the hand is something,
Though it won't tell you what.
A stone in the hand can repair
The hole in your hand, be-
Come your hand, and give it
Stony silence, so that in touch,
Human tough, needy, ghosty flesh
To same, the words are slow
Slower, thankfully, to come,
And touch stays longer that way.
Lasts the better part of a day.

Cream City Review   *Philip Dacey*

LIKE AN IDEAL TENANT

Like an ideal tenant,
the bullet fits precisely in the wound,
closer than a friend,
a relative, a lover.
Removing it, what can we give
the body in exchange
to accommodate it
half so well?

Always the unexpected caller,
it only sleeps with strangers.
Never fails to find the perfect host,
and it in turn becomes the perfect guest,
bringing no gift but itself,
demanding nothing.

Lying cradled in the flesh,
never struggling to emerge,
cushioned in that hollow
as if it knew each curve,
it wraps itself in silence,
closing in on death

Southern Poetry Review   *Ruth Daigon*

NIGHT FLIGHT

The house lifts off. Down below
on the outspread map of night,
rivers branch like blood vessels,
new provinces emerge,
borders blur
until a sea of light
washes over the landscape.
Then phosphorescent dials
guide us back to the landing strip
and all our windows crack open
with the smell of lilacs.

The Smith   *Ruth Daigon*

CRABBING

(for Joan O'Connell 1935-1968)

See how easily our trap comes up
from the channel slime and seagrass,
where a little time and lures of flesh
have filled this iron press with crabs.

Thin as our lines from float to deep,
you wait, watching that snare rising.
Astern, the island beach lies clear,
the far shore shimmers out of reach,
wrapped fast in mist all morning.

Someone must sift keepers, saving males only.
Cast back to current, their mates drift down,
red shells fading as they sink.
You fade too, leaving us by fathoms
every day. When torn away, the magic claws
of crabs return. What grows back when you sleep?

Tonight at ebb with the catch consumed,
where the black beach glows with fire,
small crabs climb the waterline
to weep below the moon. No one tells how soon
the tide goes out, leaving us shells—
each to save from a wilderness of shell,
veiled by the eelgrass undersea.

The Seattle Review   *Marky Daniel*

GOING UP AND DOWN

You talk about the Soo Locks
and how you love to watch the water
go up and down, and the boats,
and I laugh,
"The water goes up and down—big deal,"

and grab the lunch you made me
and run out the door
and drive to the job
to stack steel
and I watch the press go up and down
and the more it goes up and down
the more steel I have to stack.
I understand this up and down of the factory—
it is simple and American—machines and steel—
and I eat the lunch you made me
and close my eyes
and try to picture
the water going up and down.

The Paris Review   *Jim Daniels*

NOCTURNE II

You who have listened to the heart of the night,
You who have heard—because of persistent sleeplessness—
Some door closing, some car resounding
In the distance, a vague echo, a slight sound . . .

In the moments of the mysterious silence,
When the forgotten surge from their prison
At the hour of the dead, at the hour of repose—
You would understand these verses steeped in sorrow.

As if into an empty vase I pour into them my grief
Over remote memories and dire disappointments,
And the sad nostalgia of my soul drunken on flowers
And the mourning of my heart saddened by festivities,

And the regret of not being what I might have been—
The loss of the kingdom which was meant for me,
The thought that for an instant I might not have been born
And the whole dream of my life from the moment of my birth—

All this comes in the midst of the deep silence
In which the night envelops the earthly illusion,
And I hear a kind of echo of the heart of the world
Which penetrates and stirs my own heart.

Poetry Now   *Ruben Dario*
—Translated from the Spanish (Nicaragua)
by Jan Pallister

ARMISTICE

On this day of longed-for peace
With the joy-peals bursting free,
What shall give our thoughts release?

Surge they with the city's glee
Press they like the charging crowd
Clamorous or strangely proud.

Wild-eyed women, mourners sad,
War-worn fighters, maimed & bowed,
Drunkards riotously mad,

Youths & girls who jest & sing,
Children frolicsome & loud,
Staring too & wondering,

Or above the town, on high
Airships, reconnoitreing,
All day, in the silent sky.

The Southern Review   *Elizabeth Daryush*

THE FOUR CARDINAL TIMES OF DAY

The black hen of the night
has laid another dawn.
Greetings, white; greetings, yolk;
Greetings, invisible seed.

Lord Noon, king of an instant,
strikes the gong at the height of day;
Greetings, eye; greetings, teeth;
Greetings forever to the greedy mask.

Upon the cushions of the horizon
the red fruit of the memory.
Greetings, sun, so wise in dying's art;
Greetings, you, our filth-distiller.

But in silence do I greet great Midnight,
She who watches while the others agitate.
Closing my eyes I see her without seeing anything beyond the
    shadows,
Closing my ears I hear her footstep as she does not walk away.

Poetry Now   *Rene Daumal*
                              —Translated from the French
                                        by Jan Pallister

HAVING NO EAR

Having no ear, I hear
And do not hear the piano-tuner ping,
Ping, ping one string beneath me here, where I
Ping-ping one string of Caroline English to
Tell if Edward Taylor tells
The truth, or no.

Dear God, such gratitude
As I owe thee, for giving, in default
Of a true ear or of true holiness,
This trained and special gift of knowing when
Religious poets speak themselves to God,
And when, to men.

The preternatural! I know it when
This perfect stranger—angel-artisan—
Knows how to edge our English Upright through
Approximation back to rectitude,
Wooing it back through quarter-tone
On quarter-tone, to true.

Mystical? I abjure the word, for if
Such faculty is known and recognized
As may tell sharp from flat, and both from true,
And I lack that capacity, can I say
That Edward Taylor's Paradise was seen
By other light than day?

The American Scholar   *Donald Davie*

ARMSTRONG SPRING CREEK

At mile marker 5 on Highway 89
north of Livingston, we turn left
through a field of bluebunch wheatgrass,
meadowlarks flying up in front of the car.
I hit the stream between the fence gate
and the bridge. The bottom is boulders
and gravel, except for patches of grass
waving in the cold clear current
that comes out of the ground.
At first I cast cream variants upstream,
but there is a wind (the sun sucking
the cool air up from the draws),
so I turn and fish down. Soon
a hatch is rising and trout are feeding.
It's a fine day.

Kansas Quarterly   *Lloyd Davis*

AFTERNOON AT CANNES

Just back of the beach at Cannes, the afternoon blue as angels swimming,
The old women hunch on benches, bent crows sunning themselves,
Their dark eyes squinted cunning as they lean to talk
Yards and years from the other women lobstered along the shore
who lie unspeaking, silent in the sun, stunning to those who breathless
See their nuded breathing out and in.
But back of women leaning into speech at Cannes
And women sprawling mute on view before them,
The mountains rise to shoulder trees seductive in their aging,
The weathered bark of trunks and limbs more winsome than skin
Squinting into words, more sensuous than broiling flesh spread dumb.

Kansas Quarterly   *Paul Davis*

TO MY SON, NOT YET BORN

I remember my father,
walking out in the deep fields at dusk,
his hands hung in his back pockets
whistling,
calling my name.
And how,
because I was not ready
for him then, I ran
in the other direction
and hid
when I heard him coming.

My son, not yet born,
I've waited
and planned for you,
remembering now,
how, before bed,
I'd stand at the bottom
of the stairs,
staring up into the darkness,
and reach out
and take my father's
roughened
outstretched
ready hand,
and how we'd climb the stairs together
without speaking.

Now,
waiting,
only these words between us,
I call to you
silently
and turn back from the edge
of a field where children are at play
and wait to hear,
between the barren trees,
so low and indistinct
I can hardly make it out,
the echo of an echo.

Wascana Review   *William Virgil Davis*

LIVES

On the far rock
the sea rushes in like a crowd.
You from the promenade window
watch an Atlantic dawn break
its first light on the bleak
high roads.
The rented house is up,

smells stale in the new day;
rose-papered walls swell,
their damp eyes blink like an owl's.
So this was what all the fuss
was over—when gulls
swung against a fierce wind,
you listened for a voice,
tender hands, a chance
to redeem yourself!
                    The house
stands—a great barracks of a place—
for others to live in
before moving somewhere else.

Prism International   *Gerald Dawe*

REJECT JELL-O

The man I married twice—
at fourteen in Reno, again in Oakland
the month before I turned eighteen—
had a night maintenance job at General Foods.
He mopped the tiled floors and scrubbed
the wheels and teeth of the Jell-O machines.
I see him bending in green light,
a rag in one hand,
a pail of foamy solution at his feet.
He would come home at 7:00 a.m.
with a box of damaged Jell-O packages,
including the day's first run,
routinely rejected, and go to sleep.
I made salad with that reject Jell-O—
lemon, lime, strawberry, orange, peach—
in a kitchen where I could almost touch
opposing walls at the same time,
and kept a pie pan under the leaking sink.
We ate hamburgers and Jell-O
almost every night;
and when the baby went to sleep
we loved, snug in the darkness pierced
by passing headlights and a streetlamp's gleam,
listening to the drifters and the Platters.
Their songs wrapped around me
like coats of fur, I hummed in the long shadows
while the man I married twice
dressed and left for work.

The Hudson Review   *Lucille Day*

THE WOMAN DRIVING THE COUNTRY SQUIRE

I'm tired of keeping my eyes
tethered to the same old roads,

seeing so much of so little of life
through a windshield.
Every day I have to strap myself in
for another go-round of errands:
to market, to market, and, broke,
to the bank, then there's the P.O.
for stamps, the laundry for shirts—
stores for every little thing.
Afternoons and weekends, in summer
all day long, my time's not my own.
I'm on call to chauffeur carpools.
Carpools! More than once
I've caught myself regarding
my children in the rearview's abyss
as though they were strangers on a bus.
Even with friends they act like that:
guardedly nonchalant, their eyes
as dull as when they watch TV.
What can I say? They mirror me.
The months spin by, boring landscape
on a long trip, seasons repeating
themselves like numbers on the odometer.
Yesterday the oldest, somber,
concerned, asked me what I'll do
once they're grown. I told him
I've driven the distance around the world
more times than I care to count—
there's no telling what I'll do.
The truth is I'm afraid of what I see:
a grim-faced woman catatonic
before a mirror she's just polished
for the second time that day.
Listening to the clock's pointless
tick-tock, she feels it echoed
by her heart.
                    —Oh,
you don't want to hear this!
Everyone's got complaints.
But when you find me in the car
next to yours at a stop, and I seem
sour, my eyes furious, my lips
twisted in a half-snarl, don't judge.
I'm really not like that. Really I'm not.

Southern Poetry Review   *David Dayton*

THESE TREES ARE

These trees are
black wicks of
flameless candles,
snuffed out. The

air is full of a
smell of old, cold
wax and my fingers
feel candle-dipped
and smooth.
It is the cold that
does this to the
mind. Plugs off
all the images
except the images
of frozen things.
The stars are too
far off and careless
to relight the
tapered trees.
Everything pools
in the dark and
hardens. Sets in
its own organic form,
like dipped, dark candy.

Cedar Rock   *Susan Strayer Deal*

SCHEDULES

Schedules come in different forms, all crushing.
They're like the helpful big brother, the teacher
Who showed you how and then never let you
Do it yourself. Schedules are devices

Of infinite exclusion. They'll keep out
What's most needed for your vision: fresh wind
Seeds, intoxication, eyes drowning down
In love, brain heat and the scream. They'll let in

Your salary, sleep, commuting, t.v. and
Acid baths of errands. Yet, at many desks
In hell, devils work daily scratching out

Blocks of wasted time on thin brain parchments,
Making out the menus of tasteless meals
You'll choose to devour, that'll devour you.

The Malahat Review   *John Dean*

SEEING AND DOING

Among other things, he smiles at lit lightbulbs,
Flowing water, porcelain figurines,
And the sound of the radio. I'll be
Damned if I can see the connection. But

He does: sees it and loves the interplay
As much as he does his riding high over
The house routine or lying back under
The palm plant and hallucinating once

Again about primordial forests
Alive with bananas in pajamas.
He sings too: an atonal acupuncture

That takes away all my pain, a song packed
With odd giggles, wriggling hips, and many
A satisfied sigh. Benjamin: six months old.

Dark Horse   *John Dean*

GOOD FRIDAY

Something is tearing, tearing a hole
Too wide for measuring
And something is grating, grating
As of a hinge, broken, and a door
Swinging in a deadly wind.
The lynchpin is pulled.
The ridgepole cracked.
Drawn through the needle's eye
We are crushed by a weight
With no name, and pray
The world will not lie splintered
By Sunday—
When all this will be explained.

The Christian Century   *Arlene De Bevoise*

BACK TO THE ANGELS

You who hunger and thirst
for amusement through an idle hour,
remember that in the Middle Ages
they debated how many angels
danced on the point of a needle.

(If you cannot laugh at this logic,
explain whether you have failed in
    algebra,
or keep hiding a secret sin.)

Since trouble rolls like thunder
over the plains of ennui
and the hill country of hope,
maybe it would be better
to go back to the angels.

Unitarian Universalist Christian   *William Walter De Bolt*

NIGHT OUT, TOM CAT

(for John)

Empty green wine bottles wink
wide-eyed at the moon and roll around

after each other on the bed
of the pickup going sixty miles an hour.
We laugh under our breaths, suck
the fury from new bottles,
pass them, toss them with the others.
It's a long white river road that slips
its hand under hot wool skirts of night
under bridges and out
past the honkytonks—
wildlife preserves for migratory passion
where barmaids peck and strut,
past houses where farmers' wives
toss in beds, dream us probing
their thighs, past the last bottle passed
and tossed aside.
Our instincts take us farther down,
further in. Our headlights sink in
the flesh of dark, the flesh of dark
          the flesh of dark.

Poetry Now   *Charles deGravelles*

THE ASTROLOGER ARGUES YOUR DEATH

There are more stars than people.
People and graves. Wombs too,
those soft coffins.
Perhaps yours shines tonight
—it's clear enough out—
a bubble rising in the dark wine
definable amid the sparkle
of other human miseries.
Lift your eyes. Search it out
and wait. How long is hard to say.
You slipped so suddenly into the world
from out of a starless night.
But be assured, the time was right.
Your death is moving towards you,
travelling at the speed of light.

Pontchartrain Review   *Charles deGravelles*

GOLF BALL

Pockmarked like a little moon, the golf ball
Is a veteran of trajectories
That sight on heaven in their earthward fall.
It makes its rounds within a universe
Of grass and sand. Beyond these boundaries,
Worlds could be better or they could be worse.

Players judge their shots and hit. Before them
Flash streaks of white light, each a falling star.

Wise, they already know where Bethlehem
Is—from experience or from their maps.
They know which ways are rough, which fair—that par
Is the true measure of their handicaps.

And so the placement of the pin intends
To challenge the mind's approach. We drive thought
Towards what we mean, trusting meaning transcends
The hazards of the words we utilize.
The shot we have is not the one we sought.
Perhaps. But golfers play it as it lies.

Sou'wester   *John Delaney*

THE CHOSEN

She lives by Cherry Hill where the dirt road
Drops down to the west across the valley.
Her husband has the egg route there.
After she walks the children to the bus
She weeds the garden, hangs out the laundry.
In the evening she reads by the warm stove
Or walks into town. She belongs to the choir.

If you see her nightlight from the road,
A star in the window, you imagine
That the door's unlocked, the table set.
Whatever you come to tell her
She'll find interesting;
Whatever remarks on the weather
She'll welcome them all
As metaphors, tokens of a plan
For self-amendment, a wish to be free.

If you say that your work has faltered this year,
She'll point to a few promising lines
And urge you to interpret your gloom
As the key to your true calling,
Your hunger for perfection. As you listen,
You'll gaze at her calendar on the wall,
A view of the sea, lovely Capri,
Where the old meets the new.
She's never been there, you're certain,
Never been anywhere,
And now she puts by the longing to go.

Both you and she, she'd affirm
If you ever asked her, can be traced back
To a noble ancestry, to heroes in the Bible tales.
For her it's the Hebrews pitching their tents at last
In Canaan, tired of their wandering,
Grateful as they water their camels at the well;
For you it's the Hebrews under Pharoah by the Nile
Whose calling is not to feel at home,

Not to tell themselves as they break stones
That it could be worse there after all.

The American Poetry Review   *Carl Dennis*

WORDS AT FAREWELL

Without tears
without sobs
though you mourn,
without pain,
let it pass,
let me go.

Leave my road
without light
mine alone.
Endless night.
Pull the sun down
and go.
Don't stand there
like a sister
to stare.

Don't remain.
Don't recall.
Don't evoke.
Leave the fog,
hopeless dark
and my work.

Don't stand there
with pity
to stare
like a sister.

Pluck the sun down
and go.

Ararat   *Vahan Derian*
                      – Translated from the Armenian
                      By Diana Der Hovanessian

TENNIS PRO

The air is one great dripping cloud.
The dark blue Atlantic rolls and yawns.
It *is* early; the gulls are up
And strolling scavengers,
Eking out their retirement,
Prod refuse.
Bus boys are slicking down their hair.
Waiters brushing their teeth.

He has had his sprinklers out for an hour.
Like thousands of small tennis balls,
Expensive water pocks the red clay's
Veils of grit.
Fallen, a gnarled palm frond
Spreads toward the base line;
Its yellow-freckled shoulder shines,
Shudders with each stab of the circling fusilade.

Eleven pair of smooth-soled tennis shoes,
Lace ends dappled with rust,
Canvas worn to translucence under raised nap.
Knees bent, back straight as pipe,
He lines them up where the sun,
If it come,
May dry them,
Freshen their musk of powder and lint.

He has three lessons this morning—
Two widows and a shy chiropodist.
At noon an insurance man
Will pay to win a few games,
Today, perhaps, a set.
The Pro will open overpriced cans of tennis balls—
Whoosh, sweetest of all God's breezes;
His shoes will return a usurer's rent.

The racquet feels good—
Good? Wonderful—in his hand.
(He beat Riggs, in '43, with this one.)
He dances back, *glissade, relevé,*
Sweeps round to his left,
Racquet head behind his ear,
Muscles stretching, deliciously coiling.
A hesitation, a glance across the parking lot:

The sky, the dark blue pool,
Three Cubans warming themselves around a coffee urn,
Patio tables, waiting.
Then into it,
Through it.
Down the line
A backhand explodes
Like a cloudburst.

Cornfield Review   *Lawrence Jay Dessner*

THE AGED WOMAN TO HER SONS

There is grey in your hair,
the poet said to the loved woman
before she was old
as now I say it to you, whose boyish head
shone bright and brown as your eyes,

and to you, the younger, who ran
sunnily in the sun,
you whose cheeks were "like apples that the sun hath rudded."
There is grey in your hair.
Nor will it be long before your cheeks are scored
by the hurrying years.
I shall not see you
in your old age, but seeing these grey hairs
I flinch from what further years will do
to two men loved more than in boyhood and early youth,
before the possible had shrunk to what will not change.
Little in life is strange as the gulf between
the actual and the imagined truth,
between the youthful dream
and the brute fact seen plain.
Oh, let it be long before
you turn to the young who are nearest your heart, and your heart
wrenched with pain.
There is grey in your hair.

Paintbrush   *Babette Deutsch*

JEALOUSY

How it sits, like a muddle
in your brain, like the taste
of someone else's anger. On
the icy road to work you imagine
her waking next to a warm
body that is not yours, you
remember the way her skin
feels in the middle of a night-
mare, when you need its warmth
and she yields it. But now
you are too far away from her to cry
your need so you imagine yourself
out of love, you swear you don't
need her voice over coffee, her
body claiming yours in bed. You
will not call to set things
right: your pride is galloping
like an unbroken horse.
You'll tame this one yourself,
you say, squinting your eyes
against the sun that glints
too brightly off the hard-packed
snow.

Cedar Rock   *Rachel deVries*

THE FRIENDSHIP GAME

Once every so often the risible makes me think of my friends
and how they arrange for their own disorders, like a drop

of blood, like a hope, like a long ride into a resort town; I
think of how they are always riffling up their passions to make
a go of the month's end. I think also of how they are greatly

disregarded by their own esteem. They try hard, lack patience,
and have all the brains of a tulip trying to make petals out
of just sitting there. So in spite of themselves, I must love
them. Someday I will tell it to their faces, look! be like me,
be a happy son-of-a-bitch with a mouth full of stars
and wag your tail in bed. I want to occur to them risibly, and so
I do,

and we will walk to heaven with a stop watch and a song

and somewhere along the way some one will kick us in the ass,
and we will take this as an illumination and kiss one another.

Waves   *Pier Giorgio Di Cicco*

HORN, MOUTH, PIT, FIRE

These are the kinds of injury that,
under the Civil Law,
may be done to you.
For which recompense can be made.

They are less clear than at first they seem.
If my dog bites you, if I have
told her to bite you, that is not
an injury of mouth, but of horn.
It is aggressive, it is a bull goring.

If my dog bites you casually,
almost as if she did not know
what it was she had intended,
if it is for her own satisfaction,
that is an injury of mouth.

It would be the same if my dog
leaned against your wall,
not meaning injury,
but the wall fell down.

This is what my correspondent, from Berkeley,
reading the Talmud in translation,
has so far told me. Pit, she says,
is a nuisance, as when someone
digs a pit in the road before my house
and forgetting about the pit, moved
by who knows what problems, what
metaphysics, questions of degree,
walks away, scratching his head, leaving the pit,
and I fall in.

Or perhaps he takes the pit away with him.
There are moveable pits:
as, motorcycles,

voices that when we hear them
are not music, that prevent music.

The Civil Law reaches me
only in installments, and so I do not know,
now, at this time, what I am to think of fire.
I can only wait.

I expect, though,
that the exactments fire makes of me
will be easily as large
and as ambiguous as the rest.

The Massachusetts Review   *William Dickey*

LOOKING DOWN ON WEST VIRGINIA

The shadow of the plane
on thin trails of the mountains
on fields of horses and ponds of ducks
on enchanted rivers of swans pulling barges
on deep pools of blind fish
and counties of poemless land.

The shadow of my hand
on tidy towns of steeples and schools
and singing taverns
and death arranged neatly on hidden hills
on farms of seclusion
on farms of escape
locked in their valleys with no roads out
on families of beds and meals and beer
on women left alone with their days
talking to the empty chairs
alone with the rustle of their clothes
each waiting for her lost prince
to whip his horse through a mountain pass
and sit at his meal of heavy evening
bleeding loneliness through his pores
a candle the sword between them.

But the Appalachian hills slip by
with their clanging steeples
and signalling dogs
and my shadow is lost in the thin smoke
of new steel and sulphur and coal
and grey trains
and home.

The Spoon River Quarterly   *John Dickson*

ART GALLERY

Nude Beneath the Willows, leaves hanging down.
Nude Descending Staircase, beige and brown.

Nude in an Armchair. Nude on a Train.
Nude Bathers bathing in the summer rain.

Nude in the Forest. Nude in the Street.
Nude on the Sofa, lonely and discreet.
Nude Under Pine Tree, bent out of shape,
breast for an elbow and head like a grape.

Nude without bikini, tan here and there.
Nude in the Meadow drifting through the air.
Nude in the coffee shop glaring at me,
wearing dress and raincoat that I can't see.

The American Scholar   *John Dickson*

PICCANTE

My mother was old
when she turned 29,
after her third child,
her third country,
after *Italia, Belgique,* Canada,
the new world
and sixty extra pounds.

She was old.
She no longer wrestled
with my father on the couch,
while I giggled in a corner
with a strange excitement,
knowing I was left out.

She was old,
but my father never aged,
as he played cards and drank wine
and made love to foreign women.
I never saw him kiss her.
I never saw them touch again.
I only watched the first arid lines
etch themselves around her mouth.

She was old
and she bent her back
to the grave art of cleaning and cooking,
to the art so like the taxidermist's
of stuffing and preening the children.

She was old
and only her meals
would she eat with gusto,
the hot chillies to spark
her appetite,
mi piace, piccante. *

**piccante is Italian for hot and spicy
mi piace, I like it*

I'm 29.
She tells me I'm old.
I have no husband, no children, no house.
I rent an apartment downtown,
unlike her suburban bungalow,
more like the tenement of my nativity.
I write poems,
daughter of a woman who only reads
the captions in the balloons
above the empty faces of the beautiful men and women
in the caricatures of life,
the photoromance of a *Grand Hotel* or *Intimita.*
I write poems about the appetites that strangle
my life, wrestling
with strangers on the couch.

The Canadian Forum   *Mary Di Michele*

ADVICE

You to whom the earth's
a hand-me-down, a ripped rug,
go look upon your children's eyes,
watch the moon skip
like a jumping bean
around your telescope,
see the blue halo on trees
and the circles of light
around your lover's head.

You to whom the earth's
a hand-me-down, a ripped rug,
wash the blur off your eyes,
see small streams
grow fat with rain,
slip into seas
and feel the moist cracks
in your body.

You to whom the earth's
a hand-me-down, a ripped rug,
shake your fingers down your throat
and gag yourself awake.

Poem   *E. di Pasquale*

ON CHRISTMAS EVE

On Christmas eve the river children torch
bonfires stuffed with bamboo and roseau weeds
that pop and fling idiot speech beyond
the river road to banks of gem-lit rooms.
I watch the wind lifting wild seeds
as when I was a boy, the air an animal thing,

all claw and muzzle, never friend or guest,
ten times itself but always plenty left.
The windstorm source, blue heart of the hour,
clear lightbreaking pitch of heat in motion,
tongue stuck skyward as if to chant
the river on its way, levee voices
hollering and spitting at barges
shipped deep with bauxhite and tin.

Great brown light-murdering Mississippi
too dark to give back pictures of children
hurling cherrybombs from bikes,
bodies halved by the stalk's blazing shadow,
belief only in fire and its devouring.
There's a pause somewhere at the core
where we are all a ring of children,
aspects of light, beginnings of firestorm
lashing the night past mudbank and river
toward next year. Trusting the picture
to give us back our own selves in the flickering
pieces of strangers. Perfect fire
when the dance outside is the dance inside
and we all emerge entirely where we are.

Carolina Quarterly   *W. S. Di Piero*

CHAMBER MUSIC

She pauses in the act of dressing
—having caught sight
of a stranger there in the full-
length mirror. From nearer

on, she finds a fascination
in a body's unfamiliarity,
stares at its bare entirety
closer still: a thrill,

a shock of non-recognition
shivers her frame; again
she presses forward. More.
At last, she's pressed undressed

full-length against
the glass, loving the self
that scares. Her makeup left
upon the second face, she smiles.

The Malahat Review   *John Ditsky*

MICHELANGELO: "THE CREATION OF ADAM"

How can this boyish and uplifted face
reveal a calmness so assured and clean,
and this arm, extended with a careless grace

toward the hurtling God, so repose upon
the upright knee, and the unflinching hand
relax before the vastness that approaches?

Our Adam, like a sleeping child, has found
perfection in his marbled pose, and knows
that love still rounds him in his solitude.

But should he look beyond the face of God
toward the unborn, wide-eyed Eve who stares
at his becoming in wonderment and fear,

would he begin to doubt his purpose here
before that light touch binds him to those eyes?

The Hollins Critic   *Gregory Djanikian*

THE ENGINE: A MANUAL

Whatever damn thing goes wrong,
Begin with a curse.
Then look at the engine and remember:
Everything here *always* works together.

The fan belt in its place
Has nothing to do with you.
Socketed tight
Into their mysterious holes,
Spark plugs are content
Without praise or blame.

Count on it: this whole enterprise
Is not meant for you,
Who are human.

If you must
Lie across it, place your arms
Entirely around the sides,
Your face touching some metal part.
Now you are grounded.
To get in tune,
Straddle something electric

And have someone start the engine.
Now listen: you are the part
That knows how everything works
Together. Painful at first,
This rhythm in time
Will contain all rhythms.

This will change you forever.
When they lift you out,
Sing: now you can tell
Exactly what's wrong.

Cimarron Review   *Michael Dobberstein*

OATMEAL DELUXE

This morning, because the snow swirled deep
around my house, I made oatmeal for breakfast.
At first it was runny so I added more oatmeal,
then it grew too thick so I added water.
Soon I had a lot of oatmeal. The radio
was playing Spanish music and I became
passionate: soon I had four pots of oatmeal.
I put them aside and started a new batch.
Soon I had eight pots. When the oatmeal cooled,
I began to roll it with my hands, making
small shapes: pigs and souvenir ashtrays. Then
I made a foot, then another, then a leg. Soon
I'd made a woman out of oatmeal, with freckles
and a cute nose and hair made from brown sugar—
and naked except for a necklace of raisins.
She was five feet long and when she grew harder
I could move her arms and legs without them
falling off. But I didn't touch her much—
she lay on the table—sometimes I'd touch her
with a spoon, sometimes I'd lick her in places
it wouldn't show. She looks like you, although
your hair is darker, but the smile is like yours,
and the eyes, although hers are closed. You say:
But what has this to do with me? And I should say:
I want to make more women from Cream of Wheat.
But enough of such fantasy. You ask me
why I don't love you, why you can't
live with me. What can I tell you? If I
can make a woman out of oatmeal, my friend,
what trouble would I make for you, a woman?

Poetry   *Stephen Dobyns*

THREE SUNRISES FROM AMTRAK

Mountains
Rails rise through dimness,
course along the stone,
and moonlight turns to snow.
The iron wheels breathe
slow rhythms upward.
Stone and snow and sky
spiral about us, and suddenly
snow flashes sunlight like a semaphore,
and startles us
with landscapes far below.

Desert
Star-lit, the desert dreams
the night away.
Ghost-shapes merge and pale

and vanish. Vista
fades into vista under stars
that swirl like fireflies
and fail. Dawn fumbles at the rim,
and sky and desert like a mammoth shell
open their distances in mother-of-pearl.

The River

My last night's sleep is real;
the night still dark when wheel-sounds blur
and seem to sing. I wake to see
wide water, moving smoothly with small waves
and water-sounds, running beside us.
We curve into it. A red edge
of light touches the farther side,
rises, and thins to orange,
grows round, and leaps
out from the water's burnished track.

How serendipitous
that as we cross the Mississippi
the sun should choose those minutes to rise!

Home Forum: The Christian Science Monitor   *Florence Dolgorukov*

HOTELS

Hotels are all alike—you lie on the bed at four o'clock
in the afternoon and watch the flies crawl up and down
the grey windowpane like tiny fighter planes about to plummet.
Everything you really need is spread out on the small desk
and the bureau: a typewriter, five folders and some pens.
The water glass on the bureau has an inch of whiskey in it
and three towels and a clean shirt laid out in the bathroom.
Heaven, Augustine might have said, is having enough space
in which to perform your thoughts without distraction.

Hotels are glamorous in the same way office buildings are dull.
Hotels are like a vertical diagram without a park.
After a while you begin thinking about the other rooms,
about the bar downstairs, the city stretching out like a hand,
some travelling salesmen eating a corned beef sandwich
over an argument about last night's hockey game.

There must be whores in this hotel, you think to yourself,
feeling your manhood pushing against your pants from side to side,
there must be young girls from the midwest in search of fame.
The cleaning woman knocks, she has been trying to get in all day.
"Ok," you tell her, "I'm going out for supper around five."

Two months ago in Vermont there was a young girl out of high school
who came and did the room each morning while you sat and wrote
or walked around the room naked except for a towel after your shower;
and when the towel fell she gave herself as easily as malt liquor
without even taking off her shoes or undoing her dress past the waist,

the confusion of her clothes somehow adding to the romantic spirit.
Great sex always goes with a rising up in the world. Biology.

You have forty-seven dollars and five new poems for the day
stacked on the bureau with some addresses and a bus schedule.
Hotels are all alike—you think about the other rooms,
about diplomats and men playing cards and women undressing
before their long bath, before they go out to eat homard aux provencal.
Provencal is expensive. One of the women bends over the tub and laughs.

You get up and put on your coat and take the elevator down to the street.
There will probably be someone attractive on the bus,
someone with great eyes and a funny sexy way of straightening her dress
travelling to Toronto to start a job as a personnel consultant
or something like that. You smile as you step around an argument
and think of the hotels in Toronto, the short days
and the great bars that go on forever.

Poetry Canada Review   *David Donnell*

THE WORKING MAN

I know I've got a job
waiting for me to arrive.
My truck threads the easy curves
of a rural Carolina two-lane;
the radio bangs some noise
and the tires slap time.
So I step on it, but I'm shocked
at a peacock in the road; he spreads
his magnificent defense, those rattling
bright feathers, and it works:
I'm off the road and in the ditch.
The peacock accepts his fate,
ducks his tail and hops away;
I'm after him up the roadbank.
Unknowing, I chase him back
to his pen. He clears the fence,
scrambles for his territory. What
did he want, standing in the road?
I sit down in the dark grass.
Overcast makes the colors deep,
the dandelions glow. A wind
lifts my hair and a bird
sings three notes in a bush nearby.
A car whines distant, close, gone,
and like that inmate of an asylum
in his red gown who, I've heard,
made his harmless escape
only to be lost in a wonder
of trees, only to sit looking
until they came to fetch him,
I sit waiting, giving thanks for this

until someone comes to take me
to the place where I belong.

Quarterly West   *Gregory Donovan*

INDIAN

This desert still remembers Eden,
says the Indian who lives next door.
He keeps a lizard in a Mason jar.
I swear they see which one of them
will blink an eye first every day.
But that's another tale, how the lizard
came to be content inside that jar.

The Indian, too, wants telling
but no one knows. Not even the lizard.
If he did, he'd tell me so, don't you suppose?

Beside the Indian's adobe house, cacti grow,
a solitary Joshua Tree and, huddled at its base,
a spread of purple yellow desert flowers
and a common scrub. That Indian—he knows
about how it was back beyond my grandfather's
remembering. He can track a legend down and say
if that was Old Man Jones who shot the one-eared
deer or if Jeb Hollins it was who caught
the white raccoon. I suppose, though, you would
think the Indian not quite fitting in with how
life should be today, what with garages built
for two, three cars, fast food stores all
over desert land. He doesn't need to fit,
my daddy says; the rest of us grow all around him
like land round some deserted Eden.

I can see my Indian from where I'm sitting.
From my porch to his is the same as from my room
three doors down to our kitchen.
That old Indian, he's sitting and rocking
on his porch, with the lizard jar between his hands,
the sun catching its rim, back and forth
as the Indian rocks and stares and waves one hand at me.

America   *Jeanne Doriot*

INSCRIPTION IN A BOOK

Who will find this when I am lost indeed,
lost to the spring wind and the summer cry
of thrush and river; who will idly read
"for Leo and Elaine" and wonder why
this tale of Tristram and Iseult the Fair
was given to these two by one called "John"
and if it was a gift picked out with care
or just a book to write some name upon.

With care, with caring, with compassion sweet
as wine enchanted and as love returned,
this gift of truth was given to complete
a tale of faith and three who, steadfast, learned
to live with love. Now, soon, death writes The End—
dear death, kind death! oh, read this idly, friend.

Poem   *Gilean Douglas*

NOVEMBER WALK

The color of the year spills down the street
and breaks its fragile edge against her feet.
The tender shoots in frost and, underfoot,
crisp fire, artillery of leaves, will root
her there, for all her rigid discipline.
They come, the gooseflesh and the sigh again,
as though some brazen girl had turned and tossed
her gaudy dress before her. Love of loss:
the brilliant momentary end, the Fall
shot through with blinding freeze and flame, holds all
the beauty that she wished she did not see,
or seeing, saw as deadly company

The Southern Review   *Susanne Doyle*

ON THE NIGHT EXPRESS TO MADRID

I stare into the dark of night to see,
Instead of moonlight from the passing train,
Myself reflected, staring back at me;

My eyes seek out familiar things—a tree,
A road, a house, a hill, a star—in vain;
I stare into the dark of night, and see

Nothing but myself, impenetrably
Curtained by the blackness, entertain
Myself reflected, staring back at me,

My obscure features, blurred, illegibly
Scrawled upon the glass. Dreaming of Spain,
I stare into the dark of night and see

No monuments or castles to accompany
The cadence of the wheels, view with disdain
Myself reflected, staring back at me.

What moonlit vista through a glass could be
Entrancing as the vista of the brain?
I stare into the dark of night and see
Myself reflected, staring back at me.

The Bluegrass Literary Review   *Lora Dunetz*

I COME HOME WANTING TO TOUCH EVERYONE

The dogs greet me, I descend
into their world of fur and tongues
and then my wife and I embrace
as if we'd just closed the door
in a motel; our two girls slip in
between us and we're all saying
each other's names and the dogs,
Buster and Sundown, are on their hind legs,
people-style, seeking more love.
I've come home wanting to touch
everyone, everything; usually I turn
the key and they're all lost
in food or homework, even the dogs
are preoccupied with themselves.
I desire only to ease
back in—the mail, a drink—
but tonight the body-hungers have sent out
their long range signals
or love itself has risen
from its squalor of neglect.
Every time the kids turn their backs
I touch my wife's breasts,
and when she checks the dinner
the unfriendly cat on the dishwasher
wants to rub heads, starts to speak
with his little motor and violin—
everything, everyone is intelligible
in the language of touch;
and we sit down to dinner inarticulate
as blood, all difficulties postponed
because the weather is so good.

New Letters   *Stephen Dunn*

NURSING THE HIDE

Charges I seek, dependent things,
the clawed cling of the small and artless,
the animals tremendous.   The tusked

ones and ones of horn, any
bird or brindled hound
all blunt of function and nippled bare,

a manger of my droning dears, a lowing herd.

To sit in the tent of their tepid breath,
muggy lovers all,
to treat for fever, to fatten, to quench, to

neglect my fretful brain awhile for
the feckless, simple scent

of feathers, of fleece, of wet fur
in winter rain.

Tendril   *Carol Dunne*

MORNING FOG

I can remember the fine image
of the woman, sheets drawn over her
to suggest the perfect rise and fall
of her body in my imagination. My hands
slowly trace the path of her eyes
moving under the lids, nervous
in so much darkness.
Shadows move in the room . . .
this is the way dreams begin.
You rise, dress, and leave.
Take the room, the stairway,
the whole house and leave it.
In the morning like this,
when it is dark and quiet,
you dream your body is cold,
and clothing won't keep the heat
from rising and going.
Smoke is the vision—it fills
the surface of the river, travels
on its own green highway.
The island in the middle is like flesh
exposed through her dark stockings.
You are back in bed, in love, filled
with wonder at this warm body next to you
that sleeps and sleeps and won't wake up
when you need it.

Colorado-North Review   *Quinton Duval*

ON THE EDGE

(for Frank O'Hara)

I hoped to see the sun today, but ice,
and darkness, and this powerful wind prevail.
It is the first day of death in the season
of indifference, a dark day, spinning
in a shower of ice, which the wind blows
sixty-five miles an hour, a cold ending
for people who live outside.

Little facts invigorate like coffee.
It is 7:03 A.M., December the second,
nineteen hundred and seventy-four: dark morning.
Outside, there is nothing indulgent, nothing kind.
Inside, on such a day, people touch more,
laugh more. They know this icy wind would kill them,

prising their calendars out of their hands, like taking
candy from a baby.

The Centennial Review   *Frank Dwyer*

THE CUBISTIC LOVERS

As long as they were standing, they were all that
        passion dares—
But once they fell uncomfortably in bed,
Something blockish happened to his head,
The virile stud in him a lumpish heap of squares.

To him her legs became abstract as cylinders:
Roll with the punches, yes—but with a tube?
Too much friction and too little lube?—
Standing, supple, subtle, they were surely keepers,
        finders.

How, in fact, did sacks of cubes undress,
Why did it begin, this awkward sense of burden?—
Also standing by, grace put its cryptic word in,
But rolled together, they went mechanically to press.

I do not mean to heap rectangular abuse—
Here a cube quivers with the letter L,
But H makes a move, suggests its counter cannot
        spell:
Their bodies scatter type as if block letters make
        the news.

The Canadian Forum   *Charles Edward Eaton*

STORM AND QUIET

(for Red Warren)

The difference between reacting to a storm,
Whose eye is malevolent, and whose violence
Kills hundreds of people, knocks properties apart,

And reacting to a poem, whose violence
Is of a different caliber and may disturb
A reader sitting in an armchair contemplating

Ancient mysteries of Chinese dynasties,
Infinite subtleties of Indian mythologies,
Is a question of thinking and of being.

If you are being yourself and a storm comes,
The violent force of nature, you have to move
To put your vessel up in a safe harbor,

To take steps not to be destroyed by nature.
But if it is not a question of survival,
Of the vessel or of yourself, and you are allowed

To think, that is a delectable proposition.
You are allowed to think while the storm passes,
Chance has opened your mind to possibilities

And you say, I have survived the hurricane nature
And I am allowed to think of the meaning of things.
You think of the meanings with gratitude,

But you do not tell your fellows what they are.
For what if you had told them everything.
You would have named the monster destroying the vessel

And you.

Kentucky Poetry Review   *Richard Eberhart*

FEAR DEATH BY WATER

I like to see the bay filled up with boats,
Which argues interest and continuity,
Argues that man controls the ocean,
Which he does not, but seems to do.

None of these vessels has been sunk or damaged
And short of a hurricane will not be this month;
The pleasure mankind takes in defying the seas
Grips him as he raises a sail, or increases a throttle.

He will defy the ocean waters, take a reef
If necessary, love life from a flying deck;
Yet yesterday a man drowned in Buck's Harbor,
Drunk, capsized, took salt water in his lungs.

Poems will not save him. I am afraid of the sea,
But he was not, was not, so he is nought.

Gryphon   *Richard Eberhart*

WAR POEM

There was little mignonette in life,
much blood, ashes and misfortune.
I do not complain about my lot.
I would only like to witness
such a day, an ordinary day,
when the dense sombre foliage of trees
would mean nothing else
but Summer, silence and sleep.

Harpoon   *Ilya Ehrenburg*
                    —Translated from the Russian
                    by Leonard Opalov

TURNING THIRTY

It isn't that I fear
Growing older—such things as fear,

reluctance or desire
play no part at all
except as light and shadow sweep a hillside
on a Sunday afternoon,
astonishing the eye but passing on
at sunset with the land
still unchanged: the same rocks,
the same trees, tall grass gently drifting—
merely that I do not understand
how my age has come to me,
or what it means.

It's almost like some small
forest creature one might find
outside the door some frosty autumn morning,
tired, lame, uncomprehending,
almost calm.
You want to stroke its fur,
pick it up, mend the leg and send it
scampering away—but something
in its eyes says, "no;
this is how I live, and how I die."
And so, a little sad, you let it be.
Later when you look,
the thing is gone.

And just like that these
thirty years have come and gone;
and I do not understand at all
why I see a man
inside the mirror when a small
boy still lives inside this body
wondering
what causes laughter, why
nations go to war, who paints the startling
colors of the rainbow on a gray vaulted sky,
and when I will be old enough
to know.

The Pub   *W. D. Ehrhart*

GRANDPA BEAR

He wasn't *my* grandpa but we
all called him Grandpa Bear
because he was so
old and as small as a child
and always sat in the cushioned chair
                    wearing his yarmulke,
                    reading the prayerbook.

When I was four
                    he was seventy-four,
looking up from the prayerbook

to squeeze my cheek and
smile, "hello, my dahlink."

*

Ninety-eight now—
he comes from the nursing home
to the graveyard
                    to bury his first-born.
At ninety-eight, who worries
for public niceties: his
anguished gruntings break
above the reassuring psalms.

When he raised his dwarfed body
beside the wheelchair
and waaaailed the *Kaddish,*
I swear death and life
              stood together
              and all my uncles wept.

Dark Horse   *Susan Eisenberg*

UNTER DER LINDE

In the diaphanous fall of your gown
your breasts firm into moonlight.
We trouble the night at arm's length.
Over glasses of wine we languish
between distance and passion, as far
from the turned up bed as walls allow.

Fragrance of lilac contains the room,
its heavy scent hangs like an amnesty,
an argument pressing against
us, thigh against thigh.

In the cool of the night
you curl in love against me—
like a morning flower
before the first light.

Canadian Author & Bookman   *George Ellenbogen*

HOW STARS AND HEARTS GROW IN APPLES

Grandfather showed me how stars grow in apples,
slicing a Gravenstein crosswise
as though he was topping a breakfast egg.
There, sure enough, stenciled in seeds:
an asterisk, stamped like a kitten's
single astonished footnote
on the year's first snowfall.
And he split a Winesap lengthwise,
twisting it open between the heels of hands
as gnarled as the tree's own knotholes;

then on his half he traced with a finger
twin curves of the pale green valentine
cupping its core. Even today,
come orchard harvest, I can walk rows
of young graftlings such as he never knew—
Golden Delicious, Ida Red—and spit out stars
by the mouthful, eating the heart out.

Yankee   *Virginia Elson*

THE UNDREAMED

*("Some species are necessary as prey and others as
predators . . . . One cannot rationally conceive
a state of things where there were flies without
swallows, and vice versa."—Cuvier)*

We have states of things you never
            dreamed of, Sir:
Flies without swallows dipping,
            scooping them with tiny
Bills open, ringed with sticky bristles;
            twilight without
Twitterings and grace to trap the heart.

We have fish without bald eagles, deer
            without wolves.
We soon may have Dutch-elm beetles
            without elms—
Only hopefully vice versa.

Nor was your vision long enough to see US,
            predators,
            with disappearing prey.

Kansas Quarterly   *Elaine V. Emans*

DOESN'T IT SEEM TO YOU

Haven't you wondered
When a shooting-star showers
The ground with shards,
Or when fragments of a meteorite
Fall to earth from distant stars—
Hasn't it seemed to you
That from far-away planets
It's the remnants of star-ships
Flying towards us,
      Burning in heaven
As they drift to our globe . . . ?

. . . And now, when our rockets burn
And scatter down on alien globes,
Do they know it out there?

That these flamed-out stars
Are fragments of smouldering ships?

Or do they call them falling shooting-stars
And write poems, or,
    Maybe . . . make a wish?

Poetry Now   *Gevorg Emin*
                            —Translated from the Armenian
                                    by Martin Robbins

WHY HAS THIS ACHE

Why has this ache returned,
the pain that's more
than one man's share?
There's no love left,
but still it hurts
as if it still were there.

What is this punishment
that banished love leaves
as unfair as revenge?

I wake up in the night
as the old soldier does,
with pain in that amputated arm
that is no longer his.

Ararat   *Gevorg Emin*
                            —Translated from the Armenian
                                by Diana Der Hovanessian

VANISHED

Connecticut summers recede and flow:
Thirty-two years ago
I first felt the breath of the pine-sweet air
Whisper a welcome there.

I walk through the bramble-thick paths and look
For a lost, laughing brook;
I find it at last, but still I can't see
Boyhood that used to be.

August Derleth Newsletter   *Steve Eng*

THE CROWS

When it was spring in Wisconsin, and the roosting crows
screamed every morning from the birches across the lake,
alarmed at the first, predatory light,

I used to push out from shore on the little, waterlogged raft,
awash to my ankles, and could believe myself standing
on the still water, over the dangerous place

where the sand bottom dropped away into the muds
of the springhole. When it was spring in Wisconsin,
and morning, the nights never far away,

and the stars always preparing to burn in the rising field
of the lake; when it was spring, and what I stood on
did not fully bear me up,

and if I could drown or fly or hurl myself
into the left and right of the powerful distances,
I had not sufficiently fathomed

how to believe in it, intent as I was on the instance
of morning when the voice of the crow became small
shivers of air in my bones.

I would stand on the lake in the jaws of the opening light,
a deepening beneath me, a greater overhead, the gesture
of my reaching out to either side

a movement of so little extension, I might, but do not remember,
have shouted in anger aloud, and heard in reply my own voice
fly at me, back from the trees

of the far shore, the words jumbled and raucous, prolonged
into something like warning, back like the joyous alarm
of the sun-greeting voice of the crow.

Salmagundi   *John Engels*

SONNET SONNET

The sonnet is a sleek iambic beast
that stalks its verbal prison endlessly,
its fourteen tongues all licking for a feast,
its seventy feet all struggling to be free.
Captured and cornered in a cage of rhyme,
pentametered in numbing nets of steel,
and tied to echoes of another time,
it still can win affections that are real.
Though music-lulled and even-beat-beguiled,
though fed on tripe of triteness, in its eyes
are all the freedoms known but to the wild;
for here the joy of endless jungle lies.
    And here the poet, paradox his fee,
    learns to cage his truth to keep it free.

Northwest Magazine   *John D. Engle, Jr.*

MIDWAY

Ever the green memory
of youth,
ever the ripe memory
of love.
The first,
a mountain stream

weaving its music
in my veins;
the other,
a slow, warm wind
passing velvet hands
over the flowering meadows
of meditation.
God leans lightly
against my mind
and smiles,
blessing all my dreams
before their birth.

Unity   *John D. Engle, Jr.*

DICHTERLIEBE

I doubt life is fulfilled, or love let go
by singing a Schumann song cycle
while your convenient wife plays piano.

There is, you know, a proper way to stand:
with your right hand on polished wood
and your back in the curve of the grand;

and there is a way to breathe the verse
for good German diction,
with one hand vested, for better or worse.

But in this new church, made to look old,
the music echoes without wonder
through the limestone columns, still and cold.

Long practice, discipline and denial
make such performance possible,
perfect technique and certainty of style,

for Heine's words could never live on lips
alive with the sweat of love,
kissing the flesh between a lover's hips.

We go home to practice, not to screw,
in sun-lit rooms with plants, holding
scores as a rose, pressed and saved from dew.

Asleep in separate rooms we sing our psalms;
in May we plan to do Schubert
and in September the course on Brahms.

And as the pure notes rise and fall,
the traffic of the world moves by.
Old women with furs, sitting near the wall,

dream of something they should have done.
Each recalls alone in ivory rooms
how stone and strange our days have gone.

Was there a time once like this song?
I remember now, the stones fired to lava,
the columns fused to one. What went wrong?

Kansas Quarterly   *Robert Klein Engler*

LUCK

("Why scold a child who knows nothing of zoology
and wants a bird with five wings?"–Rimbaud)

Dictionaries cannot
define luck
as accurately as an abacus
can count cards.

So, let the boy
dream of indecencies
or money. In time,
luck will turn toward him

its tortured face,
and he will recognize
a thousand risked moments
fused into the fact

that luck is not a lady,
spell, or sin. It resides
in the sheets of lovers,
the graves of parentage—

in the whiskey bottle,
the perfume, the milk.
It is always entering,
it is what we mistake for love.

The Virginia Quarterly Review   *Elaine Epstein*

THE ROCK

You can, of course,
undo the sentiment.
Somehow, its very indolence
requires perfection—
as if roses were
more pungent
than harmony
and burned brighter
than beeswax.

I have seen
the orchids
of Narcissus undermined
by black-eyed, diffident
logicians and believers.

These instances return
with powers inherent,
for no matter where
you look or stray
there *there* is,
pinned down,
obliquely known,
confessed and credible.

One can't achieve
infrangible solutions
outside the rock.

Occident   *Mary Fabilli*

LATE GAME

If this is soccer,
the moon's up for grabs.

It floats low over the goalie,
whose father waits downfield
measuring the distance—
several white lines
that flame then fade
like breaking waves.

The players pull night
behind them.
Luminous uniforms
move the white ball
quietly here, there.

Then out of these blurred
frail bodies
the ball looms—
a seagull rising.

His son's arms flash
against the moon,
catching it.

and one pale cry leaps
toward the stars.

The Texas Review   *B. H. Fairchild*

THE DAY DEATH COMES

What will it be like, the day death comes?
Perhaps like the gift at the beginning of night,
the first kiss on the lips given unasked,
the kiss that opens the way to worlds of marvels
while, in the distance, a Spring of unknown flowers
agitates the heart of the moon.

Perhaps in this way: when the morning,
green with shimmering buds, begins to sway

in the bedroom of the beloved,
and the tinkle of stars as they rush to depart
can be heard on the silent windows.

What will it be like, the day death comes?
Perhaps like a vein screaming
with the premonition of pain
under the edge of a knife, as a shadow;
the assassin, holding the knife,
spreads out with a wing span
     from one end of the world to the other.

Whichever way death comes, whenever it comes,
there will be the same word of farewell to the heart:
"Thank God it is finished, the night of the broken-hearted.
Praise be to the meeting of lips,
    the honeyed lips I have known."

Cutbank
          Faiz Ahmed Faiz
        —Translated from the Pakistani
          by Naomi Lazard

NOTHING GOLD CAN STAY

(Robert Frost)

Day's end. A Midas sack of cloud has spilled
this wealth of coinage down the chutes of air
into the river. Let me gather gold

surging as wide as though the treasure welled
up from water. Whom to thank for the rare
day's end a Midas sack of cloud has spilled?

The giver's gone. A sun's dropped from the world.
Let me surviving plunge my vision bare
into the river. Let me gather gold

to keep at heart. The night is forecast cold.
Hot rays of sun worked westward to prepare
day's end. A Midas sack of cloud has spilled

sheer gain. Here's an inheritance that's spelled
light. I claim it, searching deep as I dare
into the river. Let me gather gold

against a pauper dark. Here, stranger, hold
my hand. I'm rescuing—so so enriched I stare—
day's end a Midas sack of cloud has spilled
into the river. Let me gather gold.

Yankee
            Norma Farber

CAMPING AT THUNDER BAY

In the morning there is bacon.
Its smell fills up the poplared universe,

drowsy flies are driven to frenzy.
Sun vacuums the white September frost.
Someone's dog, far away, howls.
There is an echo, then silence.

This is strange country.
The Lake has conquered it,
the land has been beaten, the granite splayed
from Duluth on north,
the back portages stealing secrets from the old earth,
the wilderness surrendering.

There are ways to penetrate the past.
Thrust your fist into the Lake
at Pigeon River or Wawa
and feel the cold:
out of shivers come tendrils
of pain and love and greed
that led adventurers and brigands here.
The water betrayed the hills,
bore the logs,
carried the stone—
made and lost fortunes.

The land was emptied,
and into the emptying land came the people.
Others died
or sought escape where there were no roads.
It was the end,
though this lovely park,
perfectly civilized,
gleaming in morning light,
steadfastly maintains the illusion.

South Dakota Review   *David Fedo*

CUT

Filming a motion picture
about small town life in Minnesota
must be difficult; things happen
so slowly that when the director says
"action" the crew must be content
to watch a short farm boy pick up
his bicycle from a dusty road
and, imagining it to be a close friend,
walk beside it toward the creek,
kicking pebbles like dreams
into a ditch. They told him
he was being filmed but he
wouldn't believe them because
nothing interesting ever happens
here. After he reaches the creek,
the bicycle falls from his hands
and the boy picks up a few

flat stones to skip across
the water. In his mind he pretends
each skip betters his chances
of any dream coming true. He throws
another only to watch it sink.
Discouraged, he turns toward
home but finds a camera crew
surrounding his fallen bicycle,
filming that one wheel still spinning
in the motionless air.

Outerbridge   *David J. Feela*

SPRING

Meteorologists, like old lovers, know
That Spring is getting shorter year by year
Until, like neighborhoods and family trees,
It will, without a protest, disappear

And no one will show films of it, unless
Business demands a Spring nostalgia craze:
Robins lined up on branches like Rockettes,
Bing Crosby bluejays warbling Passion Plays.

Spring is for marriage, not indifferent sex,
For propagating history and art.
No, social intuition is precise:
A glacial age demands a glacial heart.

Southwest Review   *Frederick Feirstein*

NOCTURNE: HOMAGE TO WHISTLER

Night moves in fast. Across the Charles
a grid of bulbs above the soccer field
paints grass a green that never was, bathes
white-clad players in unnatural brightness.
The checkerboard lights cast silver-gilt trails
on water striped by reflections
of black trunks and branches.

A jogger's double outruns the current.
Lights come on in a fieldhouse, adding
long gold bars. Red tail-lights glimmer by
like lightning-bugs children capture
under tumblers, to watch them glow.

A black oarsman in a black scull
knifes across the reflections,
shattering their quiet. They shiver,
then settle back into place.

The sky makes good its threat: rain falls,
the floodlights fizzle out.
Under my window, roads

turn to running rivers. Snug and dry,
I sit in the friendly dark,
grateful to Whistler,
who flung a pot of paint in the public's eyes
and opened mine.

Green River Review   *Ruth Feldman*

THE "DUKE" AND THE "COUNT"

For Black folks,
loving the Lord and
loving ourselves
was always
one and the same thing.
Saturday nite boogie/blues is
Sunday mo'nin' praisin' dues
(if the Spirit moves you that way, and
you ain't jivin').
A joyful noise
can end with an "A-Men," or
a "Yeah, man!"
Music is our sweet Soul's meat.
They cut off our tongue and
stole our drums, so
we danced and sang
the things we couldn't say.
We swing into the world
to the beat of the conga, the chingle
of the tam-bo-reen, and
the mellowy moan
of moma's "C'mon, little baby,
come to me!"—and
when the midwife cuts the chord,
it's in B-flat, and
we *wail* right on key!

The Greenfield Review   *Richard Fewell*

TO SLEEP

My drooping eyelids veil waking
with half-sleep. In half-light
you step toward me, bubbles
rising upward from your lips,
vowels I can hardly make out.

Your eyes bulge with what
you've given up, held in, and you
step among the furniture as if
it were coral on an ocean floor.
I lie here some mermaid, fat fin

of a behind, alien, a sleeping
foot. You lift me, drape me

over your arms, and I remember,
suddenly, you can't swim, must be
drowning in my dream. Like most

sailors, you trust boatboard
and bottom, and I cry, my eyes
heavy as sleeping fish. You place
me on the bed, your body's patience
at end, while I drift through

white foam, drunken, waving,
thinking: *Dear, sweet sailor,*
go back, back to your life.
I am still too awake
to do what I do.

The Ohio Review   *Barbara Fialkowski*

THE END OF A MEANINGFUL RELATIONSHIP

Your face has almost disappeared—a leaf
pressed in an album shattered with a touch;
yet memory still keeps fresh the roots of grief
that send their shoots into my sleep. I clutch
at hands that I let go and hear the door
fall shut, the stairs go stumbling down the well;
silences stamp out your path across the floor
like waves that hide in sand the names we spell.
Lips that have tasted tears upon a face
turned to the wall taste bitter and grow cold,
no longer speak in whispers and in prayers—
then we unlearn the formulas that hold
self to a self and flesh to flesh; in place
of two is one who hurries down the stairs.

Blue Unicorn   *Kurt J. Fickert*

FARM WIFE

Beyond her window in October sun,
gilded maples rule in silent state.
Now days draw in, the harvesttime is done.

While she watches wondering, a lone
Canada goose trails south behind his mate,
beyond the window frame against the sun.

Cool shafts of late sunlight strike the pane
signalling there is not long to wait,
for day draws in. The twilight has begun

to fold her room in quiet. There within,
the kettle chirks and whistles in the grate.
Inside her window in the setting sun

she spreads her kitchen table once again—
blue willow cups and brown bread on its plate.
The day draws in, the evening has begun.

She sets her dreams in order, one by one,
welcoming the seasons as she does her fate.
Beyond her window in the dying sun
the days draw in, the winter has begun.

Ball State University Forum   *Matt Field*

NIGHT TRAIN

The only moment held
is held hours on a night train.
It is warm. You have stopped.
You wake alone among the six strangers
sealed with you in the dark; the breath
of each, slow, signalled. Look out
on the station platform: one light
casting no shadow, an empty bench;
no sign, no clock; clean lines of bare
concrete. The train is still.
The light outside the window hums.
Somewhere out of sight voices begin;
foreign men who watch the night train
walk along it and touch it; you
can hear them. You do not move
but lie eyes open at no name.

There is one click beneath you. Then another.
The station moves away. One man at its edge
waves, then slides past as the hills come in—
now a house, now a light in a field, now the land
passing until darkness closes your eyes
and you listen to the sounds of this journey
to nowhere you know.

Carolina Quarterly   *Mary C. Fineran*

TO ONE FAR AWAY, DANCING

Evening, here, and the gray garden
With frost on its lips says,
"Where are you, darling?"
And here the final light
Standing in its burly coat
Among cold clothes on the line.

But you, you are dancing
In a room of old boots,
Where something ageless
Moves along with you and lifts you.
Where your feet have never found a lover.
In that place the cold

Climbs into quiet boats
And goes downstream past bridges,
And sounds arc gently
Out of brown barrels
Into the wooden bowl.
Time forms rafters in the ceiling there,
And books in the hall send out
Their old clocks of praise,
But their words undress before you,
Content to touch you without speaking.

Yet, in this house, the earth is turning,
And the moon rising up:
One or two times its bell
Has knocked on the windows; I have
Knocked on the wood of my desk.
But it's autumn, autumn, anyway,
When tea darkens in the cup
As the light gets smoky,
And the last tomatoes sit
Against the panes, watching leaf-fall
And waiting for their turn
To ripen and be gone.

Tar River Poetry   *C. Stephen Finley*

THE DEAD OF THE WORLD

What would we do without them,
the dead of the world?
Leaves are the immigrants
in autumn, feathers flung loose
by blood, littered like coal
or old toys, out of mind
until the spring crop's flow.
Or the tinplate faces
tethered and lost in albums,
trunks, like patient animals
waiting to go home—the cheekbones
of one, eyes of another, the
composite photograph, the child,
the prodigal. And the newly dead—
how quiet they are beneath
their cries of stone, fitting in,
straddling flux, mapping their towns, assuming
their duties. And the river of dreams
late at night, a shutter poised,
the vivid, indelible lens that
clicks in the brain's dark backwash—
these are the gifts of the dead,
postcards from little junctions
on which they write
here I am, as you remember,
with no address or postmark.

And after waking,
having been signalled, the arc
nearly imperceptible, the image
filmed as a cataracted eye, we think no,
it is not so, they are stasis;

and they shrug, and go on
rising, and we mourn them
as the yeasty leaves in winter,
thinking they are gone.

The Centennial Review   *Jeanne Finley*

SPASSKY AT REYKJAVIK

("Wenn Sie so, dann ich so, und Pferd fliegt!"–Nabokov)

It was easy to see
that my opponent was mired
in his brilliance. I played
brutal, colorless chess, and allowed him
several brilliant moves,
each of which
cost him something.
My game was subtle and crushing.
It was on the forty-sixth move
(I was already practicing
the rueful smile, the
reassuring handshake)
when I made a terrible

                              mistake.
By the time I got my breath
I was one move short of the draw
and we sat there
king to king
with the single pawn.

Back Roads   *David Fisher*

AUGUST 12, 1952

(in memory of 30 Yiddish writers executed under Stalin)

One month after my 10th birthday
Markish/Kwitko/Bergelson were dead:
men I had no knowledge of. 27 others.
One month after I'd zoomed noisily
through the city   writing no poems
knowing only the little deaths
that could nuzzle in my hand,
Hoffstein/Fefer/Der Nister left
blood on stone. Even if I had known
even if their obituaries had reached me,

had—miraculously—appeared in electro-
luminescent air   even if I'd stumbled
out of my boyhood, become inevitably
human and not merely grown, nothing
could be done.   There was no time
to fabricate superman out of my prayers
no time to save the novels   poems
stashed incautiously in cupboards   no
time to stop their remarkable bones
from walking away from them: Markish/
Kwitko/Bergelson. I had to climb up
18 years to hear their names.

Ararat   *Charles Fishman*

A FAREWELL

My cat was a southerner and a lady.
She had two names, neither fitting,
Never conferred by me—
Peanuts, and Molasses.
I wish I had called her Jasmine
Or Magnolia, after two great flowers,
Perennials, performers of repute and style,
Of which she possessed none in abundance.
Yet her frequency of sweet greetings,
Her amiable approach and tagging
Of my footstep in the garden,
Her affectionate stroll between my ankles,
Always about to pitch me on my head—
How endearing!

She lies now, her sweet greetings stilled,
The white bloom of her paws,
The dark bloom of her head—
How still.

Oh, I wish I had given her a familiar
Name of a local flower, Pimpernel or Gilia;
Surely she would answer.
Come Kitty, come Madia, hurry, Cream Cup,
Whispering Bells or Filaree, come,
Come home!

Yankee   *Hildegarde Flanner*

MOON SONG

Naturally it was the naked moon
That lay in naked trees in quiet woods.
Only the naked moon gives half her light
And lets the rest seep downward to the roots
While I am waiting. But she did not rise.
Get up, you shining slut, I called at last.

And when, in spite of her eternal habit
She did not rise, I could not comprehend
The poor bright sagging shape, and felt
Bristles of animal fear stand on my scalp,
So close she lay, so close to me she lay.
Tonight, I think, some weary spiritual light
Wastes from the souls of men away,
My error to call it the moon, my grief.
Let me guess again and give it a holy name;
Whatever it is, it suffers for us,
So give it a holy, suffering name
As the light goes down, as it goes out
And the pale fire
                    relinquishes its flame.

Yankee   *Hildegarde Flanner*

LET GO: ONCE

Swimming is a gift
of hope. One bit
of ill ease & it's over,
you're the mountain jet
trailing its sound
behind.
Fish introduce themselves
with nuzzling snouts.
The years, in layers, lift,
plummet. 1954. Deeper,
colder, '32. Past that
is relaxation, like a swimmer
climbing onto shore.

Webster Review   *Gerald Fleming*

NANTUCKET'S WIDOWS

Always you begin the same.
On the balcony. Caught
in the moon's ragged tear.
Your footsteps tamping down
the powdery darkness
that will not let you sleep.

Pace. Clockbeat. Pulse.
I fill the silences you leave behind.

Somewhere beyond the balcony
you are wandering with Nantucket's widows.
I can see their ghosts against the wall,
their backs turned to empty bedrooms,
solid in their precise rectangles.

But oh how they can ease themselves into the air
and race with dolphins at the prow.

The Nantucket Review   *Richard Foerster*

LOVE IS LOATHING & WHY

You dreamed up a bottomless lake down South
& spied a species like your own in caves
Around it. Monkeys (more so than you, no doubt)
Were wondering wide-eyed in their dark amaze,
What is that strange unhairy thing out there?
& when your threatgrunt, or was it greetgrunt, came
(The danger was that love would seem like fear),
The sleekest of the she-apes called your name;
At least you took it for your name. Skirting
The rim of the bottomless pit, she bared bright teeth
As if declaring war while hotly flirting.
The more you loved, you loathed the threat or treat
Of life not ever being what it seems,
Not waking, not in deep primordial dreams.

Concerning Poetry   *Dan Ford*

SLEEPLESSNESS OF OUR TIME

This is a decade of insomnia
The nights white with fear
Every dawn is a sight every day
Seems to greet another year

If in the dark you lift your hand
Or move the counter-pane
I know you wait with choked breath
As I do for the rain

Or for a wind to stir the leaves
Or touch the window sill
And all the ghosts detach themselves
From the corners of the hall

And when we do sleep brokenly
With dusk in our eyes
We are afraid of suddenly speaking
The truth in any guise

Every day is a year gained
And two lost every night
The wonder is we do not fall
Faster out of sight

Maybe there is a pill to take
Against this century
But I think our conscience is too bad
For any remedy

Canada Poetry Review   *R. A. D. Ford*

POEM FOR A NEIGHBOR

All summer you have been
pulling out, pulling in,
your flat green car
burrowing in my dreams
like a slug.

You are tall and ordinary
unpacking groceries
from the trunk,
then producing the key
to your dark apartment
while I turn sixty
behind curtains.

All summer I have been
swallowing tea biscuits,
cupcakes, easy listening tunes
on the AM dial and
watching you, my nearest neighbor,
always driving away.

Did I ever tell you
about my husband,
I ask one morning
after you pull out with
a blond woman in your car.

Did I describe his death
in a high hospital room
looking out on the highway
where at night the cars
glow like moving stars?

Did I tell you how he
gave out watching them,
waiting for a crash,
an engine fire—something
to justify his burning?

All summer I have been
watching you, waiting for
the hottest night of the year
when you will open
all your doors and windows,
and I will catch
the strange rays of your TV
rising off the screen and
moving through the space between us
like cars, like meteors,
the mosaic of a common light.

Tendril   *Pat Therese Francis*

CHEKHOV COMES TO MIND AT HARVARD

Sheltered from the falling snow, inside the stable
the bent old man blows on his hands and unharnesses
his horse from the worn wooden wagon. Burning with
the day's events and no listener he stomps his feet
on the strewn hay, forcing life into his frozen feet
and pours words in the horse's ear. Far across snow-
covered time and the vast space of ocean somewhere
in Vermont, Solzhenitzen turns off the sound of his
closed circuit camera attached to the tree overlooking
the entrance to his farmhouse. He settles himself at
his typewriter and prepares a speech for Harvard. He
strokes his fur-like beard, fingering memories from
across the ocean.

Something in him rises and the ache in his bones,
intimate of ancient ice ages, remains attached to his
body. This is what it means to be spiritual, he hears
again, envisioning crypt-like moments experienced in
cold camps across the timeless ocean. A moment without
words filled with past moments of nothingness. And this
is what they do not know, can not know, this is what it
means to be spiritual. He will not tell them this; he will
tell them that they do not know what it is to be
spiritual, that they are afflicted with affluence, that
too much fat rides between the flesh and bone and
the words they speak are nothing more than spoken words.

The Greenfield Review   *William T. Freeman*

I CAN'T FIGURE YOU OUT

"I can't figure you out," she said.
"Can't get a handle on you."
"You're not in touch with your feelings."
Her eyes performed discos of possibilities
as if I should join a feeling franchise
so they would all come out the same way,
neatly wrapped and easily digested,
not to mention cheap.
No, not I. The chef runs amok
in my kitchen. I never know
how it will turn out—souffled, over easy, burnt.
I never want to know the sauce that pours,
nor when, upon what savory thick caloric thing.
My microwave is crazy—it won't shut off.
My Cuisinart cuts pirhouettes of poems
and my Perrier gurgles obscenities
in French. "Can't figure you out," she said.
O lady of the cosmic restaurant,
your boneware tingles even as I speak.

Your moving mouth, lips pyrex-cool,
sizzles like ice cubes in hot spray.

Electrum   *Elliot Fried*

REVOLUTIONARY

You cannot talk of violence
as you would
of putting the cat out at night
can you hear the skull cracking
flesh pouring over willing fingers
like blood
that is violence
revolution
beware of warriors
who plan their battles
in the sky
then go away
leave the earth
to die

how many bodies will be enough?
when will "justice" have drunk
full?

that man should live better
he must die

it puzzles me
it must be a new kind
of christianity
though Christ gave
his own life
now the air smells
of takers
too young
to ever have given

The Christian Century   *James P. Friel*

THE RECKONING

We meet tonight to pass the point of blame
dealt out like a marked deck
Sticky from past games and fingers.
We meet in the hole of last week's fire,
scorched grass, scrub. Two bloodhounds
sniffing at the blackened stones.

On a nearby twig, a mantis
mates and mangles in the same clutch.
It is an old confrontation, an ancient fire:
the horse-drawn gift of Greeks
wrapped in the ribboned knot of Helen's legs;
the wet slick that licks the scrotal sac

oils the flare and rages.
The pyre of Troy was struck
when the bed of Paris heaved with heat
running fire down the sweet sheets
scenting blood with lavender.

No wonder of it:
The angel's sword was struck in Eden.
It roots where it fell, blazing in orchards.
And we, promised by blossoms, run gathering
bushels of cinders, black and still as nuns.

The Georgia Review   *Alice Friman*

MEETING ANAIS NIN'S ELENA

Her flesh sticks to my hands, something held
long ago and released as one lets go
a starving beast. Not that she was lean,
skeletonic. Not that she lacked full bosom
and butt, nor that her belly wasn't full.
It was another hunger, womanly in a fate
which demands its ration of fury. My hands
are empty of her reason, though it flows
through my blood thick and sweet as maplesap.
The body's design, such a demonic maze,
thwarts the straight answer of my love.
Poet, dramatizer of the sensual will,
she "pined to be raped anew each day
without regard for her feelings." Elena,
tender as her labia, fled from me
to tear at love, devour its cold meat.

Beyond Baroque   *Gene Frumkin*

FICKLE IN THE ARMS OF SPRING

Sometimes the wind is all I need
to feel you on my lips
like violets waiting patiently
for stones to sing.
Even as I spin across your eyes
I feel them tremble,
moist and spilling stars
crocheting gold illusions from my hair.
And I remember how you moved across my fire-thighs
like Autumn:
russet
amber
and gone.

Colorado-North Review   *Susie Fry*

WHEN I HEAR YOUR NAME

When I hear your name
I feel a little robbed of it;
it seems unbelievable
that half a dozen letters could say so much.

My compulsion is to blast down every wall with your name.
I'd paint it on all the houses,
there wouldn't be a well
I hadn't leaned into
to shout your name there,
nor a stone mountain
where I hadn't uttered
those six separate letters
that are echoed back.

My compulsion is
to teach the birds to sing it,
to teach the fish to drink it,
to teach men that there is nothing
like the madness of repeating your name.

My compulsion is to forget altogether
the other 22 letters, all the numbers,
the books I've read, the poems I've written.
To say hello with your name.
To beg bread with your name.
"She always says the same thing," they'd say when they saw me,
and I'd be so proud, so happy, so self-contained.

And I'll go to the other world with your name on my tongue,
and all their questions I'll answer with your name
—the judges and saints will understand nothing—
God will sentence me to repeating it endlessly and forever.

The American Poetry Review   *Gloria Fuertes*
                                                   —Translated from the Spanish
                                                   by Ada Long and Philip Levine

I THINK TABLE AND I SAY CHAIR

I think table and I say chair,
I buy bread and I lose it,
whatever I learn I forget,
and what this means is I love you.
The harrow says it all
and the huddled beggar,
the fish that flies through the living room,
the bull bellowing in his last corner.
Between Santander and Asturias
a river runs, deer pass,
a herd of saints pass,
a great load passes.
Between my blood and my tears
there is a tiny bridge,

and nothing crosses. What
this means is I love you.

The Missouri Review   *Gloria Fuertes*
                                        — Translated from the Spanish
                                        by Ada Long and Philip Levine

OPEN YOUR HAND

Truth, like a mysterious, silken cat,
eludes one's anxious grasp, yet comes
silent and unbeckoned to the
motionless lap of a quiet mind.

Love, like a fragile bubble from a child's pipe,
is broken by the anxious grasp, yet settles its
delicate rainbows gently on an
outstretched, open hand.

Peace, the silent presence holding Truth,
the warm wind that carries love, cannot be grasped,
for it is in us, and around us, yet beyond us,
our beginning, our conveyance, and our journey's end.

Unity   *Dorothy R. Fulton*

HAMMER

The hand is not always extremity enough.
At times we must go farther,
and so the hammer comes to mind.
It leads the strength of shoulder
down through diverse fingers
to a solid head the way
horses are led into canyons,
or thunder.

In hammering, as in domestic matters,
balance determines all:
too little weight
wears the striker out,
too much may mar the stricken.

Repetition is the key, and aim.
Such is the magic of concentration:
every nail slides down
its passageway as if
that destination
had been chosen.

Dark Horse   *Erica Funkhouser*

HAND SAW

Through the soft pulp
of farmed pine, the saw moves
with the incessant logic of progress.

Why stand up when you can fall down?
Why be a tree when you can be a house?
Here there is nothing to hope for
but branches.

As the saw works, it whispers
of soft flanks weathering
in lumberyards. It never sees
the nightmares that come to the tree
in the form of windows and doors.

The saw knows only one fear—
the heat of steel
aging as it passes through
throbbing cells.

Ploughshares/Dark Horse   *Erica Funkhouser*

QUILLS

In the old photograph, my sister and I
are boxed in crepe de chine, socks
and slippers of white. Grandmother Reilly
stands between us, an hourglass of satin
and dark beads, blocking from full view
the child's tea table set with small porcelains.
Her bosom balloons. Her hair is piled high
and pierced with jeweled quills. If she stepped
from the sepia, she would waddle like a porcupine
to keep her thighs from rubbing in their corset-
confine. Hers would be the sow strut of an animal
straddling grass and foliage to eat
what bends in its path. This is the way she tried
to consume her son, my father: slow, cumbersome,
elegant, coiffed with a headful of poison.

Southern Poetry Review   *Charlotte Gafford*

WHATEVER IS, IS RIGHT

This night's calm water,
like a black museum floor,
relaxes me.
I pick up stones
reflecting the moon
and flip them in the lake.
They send circles
against the irregular shore:
pine cones, flowers,
dead grass.

The full moon on water,
the blue gills steady
around
their shallow nests:
the earth creates in spheres.

We build the corners
nature lacks. We measure,
slant, survey, and spin
our thoughts and gods
on perfect planes.
Sundials are inaccurate.
No one lives in round huts
any more, or caves, and as a child
I rolled a bread slice into a ball
only to eat it. Nothing
is perfect in the world.

Ball State University Forum   *Frank Gaik*

CREPES FLAMBEAU

We are three women eating out
in a place that could be California
or New Jersey but is Texas and our waiter
says his name is Jerry. He is pink
and young, dressed in soft denim
with an embroidered vest and my friend says,
a nice butt. It's hard not to be intimate
in America where your waiter wants
you to call him Jerry. So why
do you feel sorry for him
standing over the flames
of this dessert?

The little fans of the crepes are
folding into the juice. The brandy
is aflare in a low blue hush, and golden
now and red where he spills
the brown sugar saved
to make our faces wear the sudden burst. We
are all good-looking and older and he
has to please us or try
to. What could go wrong? Too much
brandy? Too little sugar? Fire
falling into our laps, fire
like laughter behind his back, even
when he has done it just right. "Jerry,"
we say, "that was wonderful," for now
he is blushing at us
like a russet young girl. Our lips
are red with fire and juice.
He knows we could go on
eating long into the night until the flames

run down our throats. "Thank you,"
he says, handing us our check, knowing,
among the ferns and napkins, that he has
pleased us, briefly, like all
good things, dying away
at the only moment, before
we are too happy, too
glad in the pioneer decor: rough boards,
spotted horses in the frame.

Open Places   *Tess Gallagher*

WALKING AROUND

What great relief to stand here in the street,
With maybe two-thirds of a life behind,
And have no destination in my mind
Nor anger that the same course may repeat
As yesterday and the day before, but go
In some direction, arbitrary as where
Sunlight falls, and let anxiety fare
Through talk's haze and traffic's undertow.
Thus to be self-sufficient, on the loose,
Should be enough: to walk until I tire,
Not needing to account for where I've gone,
What done, or what expect. Let me desire
Only the here and now, no longer torn.
Walking around should be its own excuse.

Midstream   *David Galler*

HERON'S BAY

There is a space for winter here
to grow its ice. There is a place
for a small boat with oars and sail.
There is a piece of water here
for a fish farmer and his old wife,
turned by the wind into the wind.
We say the night heron stands and waits
for breaking water. He knows that water yields,
that fishes break. His neck is a white slake,
fishing for the water's sake and his.
He takes only his place which is as small
as he needs. He leaves the rest to you
and me, a small boat, winter and a pair
of old crabbers leaning in the wind,
space for oceans to turn in, things that bend.

Commonweal   *Martin Galvin*

THE CARPENTER'S REAL ANGUISH

He calls: no answer from his folks.
Cutworms hit his plants.
He laughs: everyone knows his jokes.

The doors he carves won't shut.
His setter snaps. His cat
Won't kill. Nails bend with rust.

His lover leaves no address.
The kitchen marches with ants.
He hits his apprentice, who says

It's for the best. Both eyes
Go blind. Legs, lame. Skin,
Numb. The motion of his thighs

Jerks still. His level's off.
Yesterday he bought a hat
Too big today. The wood is rough

Where he has planed. The shelves he builds
Fall in thunder. And in the end
It is the universe he kills.

The Hollins Critic   *Stephen Gardner*

BAR HARBOR

We drove as far east as we could
that summer, distance more than space
on a map, more like silence
pulling us apart.
At the coast, I climbed alone where the rocks
give way to the sea—
intent on ripping itself open, closing
its ripped seams up.
In back of me, a cave. Empty,
but for clay nests lining the wall.
Like urns, each shaped
to a solitary swallow. As close
as hunger is to a child.
Free to come, or go, and they did,
fluttering nervously as if decision meant
changing their minds. Always
they returned. I felt their need
to be held again
in that stationary circle:
not unlike this human pattern
by which each of us moves
toward the other
in a series of subtractions.

West Branch   *Marita Garin*

PATHS THEY KEPT BARREN

Short grass and the hillside, a level road,
all sunlight and green feeling, like love;
someone singing in the sweep of the land—
these I remember from my shoeless summers.

A person grows on. The purgatory of adolescence
gives into hell's rage of age, all hectic;
the terrible sparrows peck at middle-aged eyes.
Then there comes the sweet dream of summer, all
the long days that held out against dying, all
the beautiful young bodies swaying in the dusk.

I do not care to remember, or I get the memories
wrong. Old fruit jars we canned the peas in, that
sweet corn with our own cows mooing in the fields,
telling us their happiness as we delighted. Those
paths they kept barren are lost now. This was not
meant to be sad!

A person can casually walk away from death, at least
when it's in the third person. But those nights
when we sleep alone in strange motel rooms
beside the raucous freeways—then we have nightmares
even the huge storms of the prairies cannot overcome.

Tailings   *John Garmon*

LETTER TO MY KINDER

Just past the clockhouse is a building of cinder
blocks. The sky is very dark and threatening to storm
this morning. I work in the cinder-block house.
On the street between here and the clockhouse
amber pebbles are embedded in the asphalt, sunk
where they were poured years before I came.
They seem to glow in the strange light
this morning as I cross them, passing
in my 21st gray February here. They are
like fossils on some old and crusted shore
of some early Cambrian sea. The rust on the
metal windows is emitting gold and blood
and starlight from some midnight escarpment. The sky
is a dead fish. It will change and be the same.
All timecards lie. There is little I can say.
I am old. I have the feeling all's been told.

Cedar Rock   *Bob Gaskin*

ON BEING PHOTOGRAPHED

The lens is not an eye. It will not leave you
where you are. The black case carries you a-
way. The eye makes no signifying flash. The

camera cries: I seize! And one understands why
some feel dispossessed, slightly less real, as
a result, and why the cameraman believes he
captures things on film. Black eye? no. Not
the lens. Its fixity is the fixity it will
give you; and you freeze in front of it, anti-
cipating what it will do, executing a gesture-
less gesture, the opposite of a flinch. What
are images anyway? Not footprints, or even
toilet wipings, not even ash in a tray which
might be used by a magician to do you in. Not
the impress of your body in the bed. They are
shadows which cannot even travel with the sun,
diminish or enlarge like shade. Beneath this
skin there is no second, but I suppose it is
appropriate that a writer should end as an es-
sense fading into paper. As a harmless cloud.

Webster Review   *William H. Gass*

THE VISIT

Sometimes my mind is like a house where no one lives.
When I close my eyes, I can picture the house.
Whoever lived there is gone now, I can picture that.
Sometimes I sit for hours with my eyes closed
Looking in through a window, waiting to see
What will happen, waiting to see.
Nothing happens. I can't help it if
Some things are hard to imagine, much less see, if
In order to picture a window the eyes must look
Like windows, if in dreaming a door the mind
Becomes doorlike. The dead pose
An obvious problem. I can't help it that

It's such a lovely and specific morning on the day
I visit the house. That weathervane, the roofline,
Those dark shutters reproduce
With painstaking clarity the picture that I have.
Ah! the sea and the cornfield are perfect and so
Nearly where they belong. Above the fields, clouds
Assume their positions. Look at that fence! So often
I picture myself standing just where I'm standing, out
In the world, beside the house, in a field of oh,

Uncanny signals: the flag on the mailbox, the numeral.
Everything that is is about to happen, I can picture that;
The world is clairvoyant, its large eyes are closed.
As clouds move, shadows pass
Over the cornfields. The sun comes out with all
That represents. Oh, and
The empty house in a field of sunlight, I carry

That image with me always, it's so
Untenable, but such a quiet place to rest.

Poetry   *Jim Gauer*

OLD ARGONAUT

Old man, old father, old argonaut,
Hero, adventurer, old guy,
Stop with the red light, go
With the green. On your eyelids
Will not be seen love's glinting dust,
Around your thin legs the Laocoön will not
Wrap its ropes, your swollen feet will not
Follow the Minotaur. Between these two
Crossings, between the green light
And the red, old man, old father,
Head bent against no wind of any weather,
Rest on the island for which your
Dues were paid amply, in full. It is
Now yours, the last land where the fleet
Flying charabancs of the young
May not assail you, everything else
Having failed, all weights on all shoulders
Having fallen from yours, empty, pitiable.
Yet pity like fear is contraband.
Here on this stinking asphalt spit
Now make your unwavering last stand.

Southwest Review   *Sara Saper Gauldin*

RELICS

I have packed away your clothes
folding your aroma
like a signature
someday
I will open the box
and know you again

the 20 pairs of shorts
acquired by you like treasures
nearly lost
the day you fainted at the laundry
and when I rushed to see you
in cardiac arrest
you said, sternly,
you've got to find my shorts
before someone steals them
and I looked, thinking
if I find them, he'll live
if I don't he'll die

we celebrated their recovery
and yours

now they wait safe and neat
asleep with your pajamas
that I smoothed like covers
over dreaming shirts
whose fabrics recall
the cut of your pattern
like the design in a bolt of memory

Poets On: *Suzanne Gegna*

A HOUSE ALL PICTURES

The windows vanish: we cannot afford to buy
a Vasarely. Our house is already weighted
with the evening light of framed squares of sky,
and the frame house itself is far too heavily matted.

The walls are literate with the grammar of prints,
the plaster is stalked by the lion of Jerome,
deep in the bricks you see Piranesi's intangible light,
enter the wall and you've entered the city of Rome.

Is home what we hang? It was Gertrude Stein's style
to have her pictures slightly crooked on her walls,
and you can't peel her Roman emperor smile
from the imperial plaster of a Paris atelier;
the Picassos, oh, her Braques breathed the air of those halls,
an era's gesture entombed in their crackling dismay.

The Hampden-Sydney Poetry Review   *Emery George*

HOMECOMING

My homeward barque is stocked with treasure;
White is the flag that tops the mast;
I'm steering west into the sunset;
Skiff after skiff I've raced and passed.

Old shores seem new, old bells, old buildings,
Each landmark's dusk renewed as dawn;
And with the pledge of new rejoicings
The soothing breezes ease me on.

What's bobbing up from blue-green breakers?
A voice, a face of briny flame:
"Why have you strayed so long with strangers?
Our love enfolds you all the same.

"You journeyed east into the sunrise,
The strand, the mermaids still at play,
And the first star of sunset greets you
As if you'd only gone a day."

Poetry Now   *Stefan George*
                                        —Translated from the German
                                        by Peter Viereck

SIX DIVINE CIRCLES

Cool to the wrist
are these six bangles—
no mixed metal, but ore
true as sun's tongue.

Displayed for me
on this velvet cloth,
six divine circles
whose mystic symmetry
delays my tongue.

How wise of you,
my devoted love,
to choose a perfect metal.

Perfect sun.
Perfect gold.

How do I wear you
on this imperfect arm?

The Malahat Review   *Gail Ghai*

CHILD BEARING

She always played Mother as a child,
talking to her dolls like children,
cradling her kittens like babies.
At eighteen, her playing ended.
She lay open and swollen on the table
straining to hear the first cry,
the white masks floating above her
while the scalpel did its work
to keep her from splitting in half,
the bare, white room spinning in silence,
spinning in silence.

Kudzu   *Charles Ghigna*

DANA POINT

I stood where real estate, measured in always smaller and more precious
portions, on the brink of height and vistas of the sea, ends
and will hardly be augmented more than a very little, westward
along the air or pillared and propped on dwindle of stone
over the bellow and driven bawling and battering that will not
be stalled in the long cave-head mining the cliff.

                                        I thought:
I would not lie down in consent to the earth we are trampling in passage,
not even here, where ash of ancient campfires sweetens
the gardens that supplant the bitter sage that made the wind
what it was.

No need, there may be no need: in a little while,
though we pray against it, and talk, and shout for another outcome,
the foretaste of ash that embitters the prospect of hope may come
into all our mouths, however we argue it away, however
we cry (however I whisper) against it (into the westwind).

The Blue Hotel   *Brewster Ghiselin*

MIDWESTERN MAN

I am the inland man,
he of capricious creeks,
deliberate rivers, a certain
shallow reading of the
testament of water.

I was a deepsea thing
when I was born and on
through youth, a treader
in moon-torn currents,
a dreamer of storms.

Nowadays the heart itself
seems to pump dust; but
at times the ground swells,
flashfloods startle the night,
the season drowns me.

Focus Midwest   *Paul Giandi*

MICHAEL'S ROOM

Your hand in your grandfather's—
as though the bone just beneath the skin
had cleared his thin flesh
and called out the skeletal glow
in your own fingers, too soon.
Bone against bone, surprising you,
bruises you both with dread.
Morphine, stitched incisions, nausea—
and your father sits in a chair,
his hands on his knees, still
brooding on the blood that made him faint.
While you wait now, holding yourself
together with the hurting that threads
its way through you, cold and hot.

A neighbor has brought her preacher.
"May we say a prayer over you, son?"
An unreasonable hope clarifies
their own cloudy pain, and his voice
climbs into a high monotone, as if
he were speaking to someone who's far off
or deaf or . . . . Your grandfather?
He's not really here.

He's been banished for good by your mother,
who blames him for the wreck.
Everything he's ever done . . . . Everything
you might have. But he hovers
in your dream of waking up healed
and you stare at his hand holding yours.

The Hudson Review   *Reginald Gibbons*

ALL THUMBS

We thumbwrestle and I
think of women I have
thumbwrestled; thin-boned, hysterical women, women with quick
tongues and hard knuckles, a hand I grasped at a peace rally
in 1968, ah, sister! How we wrestled over sociopolitical doctrines!
I think of how your thumb
is connected to your hand
and now to my hand, how such
connections compose the essence
of sensory experience and
how I am in love with you.
I grip tightly, thinking of games-playing women
I have known; my gambling partner who finessed my suit,
dealing me an uppercut, and the one who played Monopoly,
stole my railroads and hotels, then left me on Boardwalk
without carfare home—
and I think of how
you are twisting my arm, imagining what will happen
if I capture your thumb, your hand, or even perhaps
your arm and shoulder but
I cannot hope, feeling my thumb becoming depressed
beneath yours, knowing that no one will win
because your eyes have ruled this a mismatch already.

Back Roads   *David Giber*

LONG WALKS IN THE AFTERNOON

Last night the first light frost, and now sycamore
and sumac edge yellow and red in low sun
and indian afternoons. One after another

roads thicken with leaves, and the wind
sweeps them fresh as the start of a year.
A friend writes she is tired of being one

on whom nothing is lost, but what choice
is there, how can she close her eyes?
I walk for hours—either

with hands behind my back like a prisoner,
neck craning up to the sky where chain-gang
birds in tight nets

fly south—or with hands swinging free at my sides
to the brook, the water so cold it stings
going down. Either way, I whisper

to dogwood, fern, stone walls, and the last
mosquito honing in, *we're in this together.*
Here is the road. Such honest dirt

and stone. Some afternoon, heading home before dark,
if I walk by mistake, lost in thought, far beyond
the steep trees, the satellites and stars,

up over the rim to a pitfall, past any memory of words—
even then I can give my body its lead,
still find my way back.

The Michigan Quarterly Review   *Margaret Gibson*

PORTRAIT OF MY MOTHER ON HER WEDDING DAY

A young woman,
lilies gathered to her breast—
the moment of the wave
before it crests—
bride,
incandescent,
even in this sepia image
dazzling me, like a wedding guest.

Fifty years later, I uncover
in the movement of her swept-back veil
the life that was to come,
seeing revealed
the cunning of those hands
that clasp the flowers;
the will to shape a world
of her devising.

And once again I feel
how evil seems to fall away
before the power of her candid gaze
while everything in us that answers to good,
crowds round her lap
hearing itself spoken for.

Ploughshares   *Celia Gilbert*

RISSEM

I was sixteen, a freshman, a former Catholic Buddhist,
a sonnet-writer, no longer overweight but more than ever
ambitious for romance. At night in my lumpy dorm bed
I counted the number of would-be "lovers" I had,
sometimes adding the names of even my mildest fans
to fatten the list.

> You were a poet of twenty.
Your forehead was too high, your IQ (you said) one
    hundred eighty.
and I called my mother in Queens to tell her about you.
You'd already had mono and worried about potency!
You had loved many brilliant girls in Brooklyn!
But none like me.

We put our initials together—your R.I.S., my S.E.M.—
and signed all our poems *rissem.*
We collected Tagliavini records for the high C's.
We stole steaks from the IGA, gave your English bicycle
a name I've forgotten, kissed on campus in front of the
    statues.
People thought we were disgusting.

But when you came to my archery class
on the windy hillside beyond the dormitories,
you always made bullseyes,
even when the wind was strongest.
One night I cried all night in a narrow rooming-house
    bed,
wedged between you and the wall:

I saw the truth: the day would come
when I'd be twenty-eight, you'd be thirty-two,
we'd be married to other lovers, have other names.
And you were going to invent a solar battery!
You were going to discover the truth about aging
and perhaps prevent death!

When you died, fifteen years and three marriages
after we'd said goodbye on the Fifty-ninth Street
    station,
your best friend told me the driver of your hearse
    got lost
on the Brooklyn-Queens Expressway.
It was incredible, he said. *He would have loved it.*
He would have thought it was a great scene!

Sometimes I like to think we are still *rissem,*
a slender ageless androgyne from another planet.
With bow and arrow we hunt among strange craters.
Breathlessness doesn't bother us, or weightlessness.
The list of our lovers is long but we are indifferent
to all of them. On our planet

we bicycle faster than the speed of light.
In our extragalactic language
there are no words for "love" or "death."

Poetry   *Sandra M. Gilbert*

BEQUEST

Poppa left no will.
Apprenticed in Roumania at age eight,

Worked hard all his struggling life,
Had few personal possessions, fewer vacations,
Never went to a dentist,
Saved every string, used soap to last sliver,
Deeply devoted to duties, "musts," and "shoulds,"
Worn out, faded like a wave along the shore.

He bequeathed me no estate,
No monies, no bonds, no gems—
Just an old Tallith and a tattered "Seder Service,"
Some pages still stained with wine
Smelling of strivings, hopes, and bitter herbs;
A scratched snuff-box, a cracked shaving mug,
One pair of antique "specs"
Bought on a pushcart in Orchard Street.

But also a love for poetry, picnics, and pigeons,
Chopped eggplant, home-made plum brandy,
Horas, zither and accordion music.

A goodly inheritance!

The Jewish Spectator   S. Gale Gilburt

INITIALS

Most people think
I can't control my strangeness.

Well, I don't look for myself in closets
Or stare all day at mirrors

seeking hairs that need to be plucked.
My friends say I am losing touch,

that I need other people to keep me
from loving my loneliness too much;

they say I should stop looking
for dustballs under the bed,

explain that fatherhood
has been bad for my head

and mumble how my skull was bleached by winter
way back when wars were fought by youth.

I don't understand their talk.

Yesterday I went for a walk
and spent six hours watching

a caterpillar
cocoon its initials to a tree.

Right now, I'm looking for matched socks,
hushing my old grandfather clock

and drafting a memo to my son
to help him understand

that though I can no longer
hold his hand,

life is only a matter of degree
and when he learns to do

what his jailer tells him to,
he's just as good as free.

Poets On: *Michael S. Glaser*

STAYING AHEAD

(New South Wales/Tennessee, 1969)

Fire runs faster than emus, rams,
or 'roos across the outback scrub.
The bald landscape lies there
asking for it; and once the wind
and flame concur, a wall of hell
ten feet wide scrapes the pastures
and hills to cinder black.

"The worst thing you can do is run,"
Jack told us. "You'll end up trapped
or run down. You can drive back
through, if you have to. It's risky,
but if you're caught on the downwind
side of home, you have to chance it.
Turn up wind, floor it, heads down,
hold your breath, and pray. Chances
are you'll shoot right through."

"And if you're home and the fire
is moving your way, close up the house
and sit tight. The damn storm
of fire moves so fast it washes
right over the house. It's gone
before you realize it got to you.
The house will save you. It gets
a good blistering, but a good house
like this one—iron roof and stone—
will make it."

          Like an ark, I thought.
But it wasn't until I got back home,
safe among the familiar trees,
the labelled streets and nameless
hills, back in the heavy green cover
of this land I was born to travel
from, that I realized how many times
I had walked out the back door
onto scorched ground—safe again.

New Letters   *Malcolm Glass*

NIGHT SONG FOR AN OLD LOVER

I

Memory of you may be
attenuated by time
but your shadow still spans
my night.
      Beyond you,
the amble of patient constellations;
      Beyond you,
the winking of happier lights;
      Below you, below your mastering arch,
my body thuds and thuds against
the rim of the dark.

II

Dammed-up river; the metaphor
is old, but like all venerable things accrues
a patina of use. I feel
in this urgency of spring
fingers of curious water struggling through
the gaps. I feel the bridge
that anchored me to you, the bridge of you over me
collapse.

III

It's only the night
making distances invisible
that joins us under the same sky.
Continents snuggle closer together
in sleep.
      I still keep one side of the bed
for you, for whoever joins me
in the ceremony of dreams.

Dalhousie Review   *Susan Glickman*

NOTE FROM AN EXHIBITION

In a crosshatched 16th-century print, a
squadron of precisionists, each with his
compass, telescope, astrolabe, nets the
world. Their black tangents, black lines of vision,
mesh—till the gallerygoer's attention's
caught plunk like a ball in la crosse. It's

not that easy really: You don't whip a star
in on taut black fishline. You don't nail sun to the
cross in your lens. It will rise
without your faith. And behind the perpendicular
weave of nylon, the heat of you that's
calling me sexually defies measurement. On display,

small brownish spirals, fungal and breathy, eat
16th-century paper with no regard for the geometrics

neatly sectioning Renaissance air. The postal worker
will flick this note for you in its designated cubicle—zip
code 60625—but at night, under flap, under stamp, he'll
hear it: the thousand sorted tonguelicks

come alive in that grid: small ocean, small mercator.

Salmagundi   *Albert Goldbarth*

ON THE HAZARDS OF SMOKING

Rainy morning. Don't get up. Don't even smoke.
Don't read too much. Isn't it a queer spring!
Isn't it a queer spring. Darkness in the morning as though . . .
Don't read too much. Isn't it a cloudy spring!

Once you were a complainer. Did it help? did it bring back your
    dead?
What pain in the flesh, in the poem, in the papers, in the Song of
    Songs.
Limits to wisdom? Maybe. Just as well we learned meanwhile
Not to wake the neighbors, not to trouble friends.

Rainy morning. Don't get up. The night passed peacefully.
The night passed. And now—isn't it a cloudy spring.
Morning like night. All right. Only the stillness strangles.
Isn't it an oppressive spring! I told you: Don't smoke.

Poetry Now   *Leah Goldberg*
                                    —Translated from the Hebrew
                                    by Bernhard Frank

BECOMING REAL

We began this conversation in the spring
walking through a new meadow to the house
that shimmered in the late chill, white
and welcoming. There we sank into a long dream
of one another, of entering for shelter,
while our bodies, loyal, riotous,
wrestled in a hot satiric parallel.

Who we were then, whose thigh
and whose mouth was opening, and hands flowed,
we could not separate. You, opening your eyes,
slowly, taking hours, brown, with clear lines,
before I vanished into them, I seem
to remember, though I cannot tell you
whether early or late.

It is winter now. Waking in our deep bed,
small under heavy blankets, huddled
figures in a shrinking room, the wall
crowded with assembling ghosts, arriving
in sibilance and humming up the hall,

and we are hammered into one another's dreams
of comfort in the pure imagined past.

Salmagundi   *Barry Goldensohn*

AMBULANCE CALL

In the morning I went out with my bow:
slippery, after a little rain, but pretty:
the sky like a peeled bone,
and the trees so fresh, restful and straight.
I climbed the big apple by Bartlett's,
and sat up there a long time,
growing into it;
as if there were no spaces
between my flesh and the flesh of the tree,
the ground rising gladly with me,
and bringing in that sweet, slight sting
of apples rotting below;
and the wet black noses of the animals—
dogs, deer, coons—all feeling for life
with their heads cocked, and listening. I listened:
and there came such a black rose spreading,
and such a wave of sleep, a whole sea of sleep
that I could trust, could

lean down into:
I don't remember falling.
But there was a moment of no holding back,
Of a rushing so big and dark
before I slammed my body back into life,
my spine into its permanent sleep. It's

real bad, isn't it? Tell me.
I know it's bad.
What do I do without my legs?

The American Poetry Review   *Lorrie Goldensohn*

READING FAUST

Robin, I've been reading Faust
in the copy you left behind,
one side German and the other
English, to trot back and forth with.
I can't tell you how far you read in it,
though dog-eared pages hint
where you halted till the next bend;
but once you located a passage
I asked for, and copied it in your printscript
(the letters like midgets on parade:
how we laughed as we sillied together)
tidily on a loose leaf of memo pad
for my purpose (what was it, what purpose?)

I now use as bookmark and warning—
7/24 you wrote, not the year,
that was self-evident, as the present
always is to the unsuspecting—
denn eben wo Begriffe fehlen,
da stellt ein Wort zur rechten Zeit sich ein.
Whenever my memory of you fades
and I strain to remember your face,
the eyes abandoning hope,
the lips disdainful of coloring,
I recall these Mephistopheles lines.

The American Scholar   *Judah Goldin*

ON PHILOSOPHY

Philosophy, the love of wisdom,
    Is somewhat lost to me.
Perhaps it's because I haven't mastered
    Its epistemology.
The metaphysical ramifications
    Of the lamarckianism involved
Cannot be denied rationally
    Unless the dialectic is dissolved.
With due consideration, it's quite a rarity
    For the writing of philosophy
To exhibit clarity.

Ball State University Forum   *Jonas Goldstein*

SHATTERED SABBATH

I rose in joy at the pinking sheared sky—
a dawn of delight—
the dew-kissed lilacs scented the day
with their fresh fragrance.
God's covenant seemed alive
in the shimmering light!
Song sparrows and robins peeled away
the last grey shreds of night
with their melodic blessings.
The Sabbath morning blossom filled
with pink purple and white lilac May.

My feet turned aside from the House of Prayer,
where I might drink from the freshets of
Torah, and led me instead to the House of
Commerce where another day's work awaited.
The secular and the profane ensnare my soul.
Although the heavens should open up
by God's own volition,
for me there is no balm of Gilead.
Nowhere is there an ointment sweet

enough to heal the wounds
of my shattered Sabbath.

The Jewish Spectator   *Roberta B. Goldstein*

ARROWHEADS

For years we collected arrowheads,
the flints like dark tongues
mute under our plows and shovels.
Incomplete legends
clenched into centuries of silence,
they persist
in this forgetful land
    (homestead land:
    we are the owners,
    we are the settlers,
    we are the first).
They persist,
and us only inheritors
of a people
that buried its blood
under our thick crops.

    At the museum, at last,
    they kept only a few.
    "A dime a dozen," they said.
The memories so cheap, eventually,
and all of us harvesting still
that history.

Dalhousie Review   *Leona Gom*

WORDS

I want to give you words
    beautiful words
They're used but they last a lifetime
I want to tell you: forever
Don't talk about lack of perspective
Words mean whatever one wants

Denver Quarterly   *Ulálume González De Leon*
— Translated from the Spanish
by Sara Nelson

ORCHARD SNOW

Peaches in, and pears late
Brought down, the season ends.
Now under a different weight
The orchard bends.

April's fat bees done
And October's lean wasps lost,
Now in a pale sun
Ripens the frost.

Eden endures another year:
Snow on brown apple, brown leaf,
Pips holding Eve's promise here,
And Adam's grief.

The Nantucket Review   *J. B. Goodenough*

MARRIAGE

He told me, you'll end up
a fat wife, wiping your hands
on an apron, your children outside a screen door,
like geese flapping in the grain.
You'll have wrinkles
and veins on your legs, at night
little trumpets will sound in your ears,
bleating she-goats from a hillside
green with rain.

Your husband, he said,
will be strong as leather, always hungry,
the hairs on his face red
as clay. Mona,
he will call you, Mona my dear,
and you, pinching roses
into sallow cheeks, will wander
to his chair. Fights, oh yes,
worm holes in the plum tree,
lost animals, drought, death beneath a tractor . . .

It is true
there are children in the bald fields—
I forget their ages. Today
one of the boys undressed
my youngest girl, her skin a white slip
of fur. In time they kiss
and marry, grow old and stout out here, turning
the black soil again and again in a memory
of love.

Denver Quarterly   *Marea Gordett*

FREE FALL

I do not have faith in those
Who know who they are:
They have already done
What is never possible.

Like a ship in a doomed port,
They are low in the water
    and lifeless.

I take to those who are mistaken
    each day,
Whose nightmares occur in the light.
They have few facts but they fly
In the slipstream of undiscovered planets.

I prefer those who go in and out
    of the psyche.
They enlarge horizons, there are
Two blue lines in their distance.
The chosen are to speak for us all
In re: man's birthright and despair.

May we be delivered
From a nation of burghers
Who know where they are.
Meanwhile, I stand with
The free-falling ones
Who believe the parachutes
Will open some day.

The Greenfield Review   *Don Gordon*

OCTOBER

When the last child left
she wept, and her tears
grew cold in the empty
refrigerator, and sprinkled
the lone housedress
in the ironing basket.

There was an eerie silence,
an absence of telephone bells
and radios. Tired of the sound
of weeping, she began to hum,
and discovered a new voice,
softer and deeper than the practiced
tones that knew, "You didn't do . . . "
and "When will you learn . . . "

She noticed outer changes, too:
beds did not expose their rumpled
linen; newspapers stopped tumbling
around the floor; shoes no longer
danced from their closets at night.

She paced the tidy rooms of her house,
a tame lioness exploring her cage.
Her heart pounded and her mouth went dry
as her footsteps echoed, "What will I do,
what will I do?"   And when a gust
of October wind forced open her front door,

the lioness left her cage
to roar across the countryside,
to romp in the falling leaves.

The Centennial Review   *Judith Goren*

WHO OF THOSE COMING AFTER

We are all rushing nowhere
together—flocked constellations—
forming and unforming
around each other
to temper our presence here.

Centuries will pass.
Our vagabond earth drift
a remaindered planet
in a universe grown old.

What words, what code
will remain
on the string of existence,
of the signals we tried to send
as the dark grew flesh
behind our backs?

Who of those coming after
will ever know
that seeking the center of grandeur
we tried to make of love
a celebration?

Outerbridge   *Darcy Gottlieb*

ON WHY I WOULD BETRAY YOU

Because this is the way our world goes under: white lies,
        the now,
each flake a single instance of
nostalgia. Before you know it,
everything you've said
is true. The flakes

nest in the flaws, the hairline cracks, the stubs
        where branches
snapped—only unbroken lines, unwavering,
for building on. How easily our tracks
are filled. How easily
we are undone,

knowing the events
without the plot: caution and light and the odor of skin
        threading
the secret, a loom. What will happen?
What I do
in betrayal

is play at being small, the body a protectorate I can
    win back
at will; is alter the rules
in the pattern,
what happened.
It snows

like there is no tomorrow, the world growing younger
in her new attire. Who wouldn't love to render
her white lies to their flawlessness like this,
in brushstrokes
dagger-true

yet kind. For is it not true, this smooth new skin,
were we not also good? Each indiscretion
a caress of faithlessness,
a feather to touch
you by.

Anteaus   *Jorie Graham*

HOW I WAS HER KITCHEN-BOY

The saucepan of shining copper.
Her early morning voice. Here! I called. Here!
and ran into her, each time I tried
to run from her pots.

At Easter, I took lamb-tongues, protestant
and Catholic—and skinned them like my own sinful soul.
And when she plucked geese in November,
I blew fluff from the feathers,
so that the day would hang in balance.

She was built in the same proportions as the Church of Santa
    Maria,
but there were no mystic draughts,
it was never chilly, inside her.
Oh, her blanket pile,
where it smelled of goats' milk
into which flies had fallen.
Caught up in her odor of stables.
Her womb was cradle.
When was that?

Under her nun's-shirts—she was an abbess—
Time did not stand still.
History was made,
The dispute over flesh and blood
and bread and wine was resolved without words.
As long as I was her kitchen-boy,
I never had to freeze or suffer shame.

Fat Greta: half a pumpkin
laughs and spits out seeds.
Not often did I see her
stir beer into bread-soup;

but lots of pepper: her grief
left no after-taste.

Poetry Now   *Gunter Grass*
–Translated from the German
by Betty Falkenberg

THE GIRL/THE GIRLIE MAGAZINE

Who is that third always with you?–from Eliot
"The third rail . . . runs there beside him. He
regards it as a disease he has inherited the
susceptibility to."–Elizabeth Bishop

She is in full color,
her legs splayed
on a page glossy as any
displaying dolls
in Sears' Christmas book.
She's been creased at the crotch
and shoved under the front seat
of my father's Buick,
which it's my job to clean.

To look at her
is better than to be her—
she with her flume exposed,
her steamy regions
laid open.
Is my father a haruspex?
What does he augur?

I did not want to be her,
but to view her.
Viewer-controller
of pitted extremes,
of the animal slouching eastward,
"moving its slow thighs."

Now—
sometimes now—
in the silky moonlight
as your hand strokes my thigh,
if the bed seems cold or I distant,
it is this: I am the third
watching, coolly
touching finger to tongue,
turning the slick, creased page.

Calyx   *Pat Gray*

LINES FOR MY FATHER

Last Christmas, Father,
You were almost dead. You sat

In your concrete-block house
Above the Nowata and fought
The cancer; you lost weight,
Your clothes hung upon you
Like sacks. I heard you rustle
In your bed like dry cornsilks
After midnight. On Highway Fourteen,
The motorcycles spluttered like children
Tossed into a pool.
"They should muffle those things," you said,
"A man can't hear himself pray."

Father, now your eyes
Are closed; bluejays divebomb
Meadowlarks, and cats kill
Mice that squeak like the gates
Of hell; on the neighbor's farm,
His Saturday night son
Blasts with a shotgun everything
That moves on his lawn, just
For the hell of it, and I try
To pray amidst the noise.
The bluejays fall in triumph,
Their crests tousled by the fight,
Like your unruly hair.

Prism International   *Patrick Worth Gray*

JUDGE KROLL

Judge Kroll
is going deaf. He hears
rough language in his head. His voice
keeps coming back at him.
It says. It says.

He says he isn't
hard of hearing, it's
the arteries, the kind of hardening
his mother had who whacked her ears
to drive the echo out
and never could.
What's hard is getting old
before your time, he says,
and whacks his head
to silence it.
Fuck you, it says.

What what? he says
to something in his sleep
and calls it by a woman's name
and hears it say
such words she never said,

and hears the knuckle-cracking in his brain
turning his hairs white.

Northwest Review   *Barbara L. Greenberg*

COMPLINE

There is a litany
for the prone, the secular, the profane.
I don't mean in church but where,
behind the leading of leafless trees,
the sky's glass is stained by the sun's
departure. Or, rather, by the earth's
inclining toward the dark side. Leaving
an incense of leaf-mold and winterkill
in the hollows of your steps,
you head back toward indoors
and the horizontal, the stationary.
You should sleep like an animal,
dreamless or unable to recall its dreaming.

What did the mystic mean
when he termed prayer just holy
breathing? It takes on the slow
rhythm of chant, falling away
and away:

> *Small hours, gather us.*
> *Heavenly bodies, pin us*
> *to this ground.*
> *Nighthawk and owl, watch us*
> *as you watch a worm.*
> *Nurse, between rounds, drugged*
> *by fatigue, sleep for us.*
> *Night letter, leave us*
> *for daylight.*

The Georgia Review   *Debora Greger*

THE WORLD WAS NEVER REAL TO ME

The world was never real to me.
I played in corners of loneliness
with child's toys that could trap time
and hold it like a ball to be tossed.
I played games and never lost.
I hid and seeked and tagged with rag dolls and
        markers.

But the world is real.
The laughter of friends I could never somehow join
would reach into my room and grab my
        ball

and to hold back the tears I would jump
    on my bicycle
and ride far away.

The New Magazine   *George Randall Griffin*

LETTER FROM GERMANY

Though it is only February, turned
less than a week ago,
and though the latitude is upward here
of Newfoundland's north shore,
Mother, spring is out. It's almost hot,
simmering above and underground,
and in my veins! where your blood also runs.
The hazels dangle down
green flowery catkins, and the alders too,
those bushy, water-loving trees,
have a like ornament, in purple-red.
Spring is so forward here.
Snowbells swing in garden beds;
the pussy willows that you liked to bring
inside, to force their silver fur,
are open in the air;
witch hazel in the formal park,
still leafless, wears a ribbon-petalled bloom
of yellow and pale orange.
Once or twice I've walked through clouds
of insects by the river to the east
of town; the ducks are back on the canal
now that the ice is gone, loud and in love.
I wish that I could bring you here
to see this fast, unseasonable spring;
I wish that I could write a letter home.
But since a year you are not anywhere,
not even underground,
so that the words I might have written down
I say aloud into the atmosphere
of pollen and fresh clouds.
I say the litany of my desires,
and wonder, knowing better, if you hear
through some light-rooted organ of the air.

The Hudson Review   *Emily Grosholz*

AT PONT-AVEN, GAUGUIN'S LAST HOME IN FRANCE

If you come here and it is barely fall,
as it is now, and the sky is thick with leaves,
a few ducks squawking downstream, you will wonder
what made him leave. It must have been like this
even then: a few stores, mostly closed
with the season over, some old men

playing *aux baules* in the park or feeding
the pigeons, and the faint smell of salt
in the air, the first hint of the sea.

I do not know why he came, only
that he stayed awhile, then left. The stream
widens here to join the sea he must have dreamed.
First this ocean, then the next stretching
like a great plain to the place he had to go.

We drive through the town until it ends
and do not follow him past here. Above
the stream there is a path, first stone,
then a narrow trail of earth that takes us
the other way, back into ourselves. This forest
would have been here too—the deep moss floor, ivy
wrapping itself in the trees. And this stone house
long abandoned to a field dense with weeds.

Is there always this faint calling, curious
as the moon's effect on blood, that draws us
where we've never been until all our journeys
seem the same, our lives like baggage left
too long at the station—destinations
too faint to read. For now, we are happy
stopping in this wood. But still, I think of you
and wonder why we leave those places
we know will never change and could change us
if we let them, for distant islands
so remote we can never know their names.

Quarterly West   *Andrew Grossbardt*

THE ART OF LOVE

Technically they were all the same:
responding to the same pulsed, enflamed

in the same general ways.
And when they pulsed *together,*

it was the same pulse.
The shepherd said,

The art of love is the first art:
making somebody soar.

Coming together,
All beings devolve from pleasure.

Two spirits became one in heaven
without pain,

and the entire universe was created.
Now we strike out dumbly, wounded

by ignorance. Our hearts are dead
and no longer shimmer in their pools.

And when we combine, it is matter
doing and doing and doing and doing.

Cedar Rock   *Richard Grossman*

KNOWLEDGE

Things I do not understand
Are many; most of them lie with me,
Festering. I have dreamt
Of a great tree, sheltering
And informing. What I do not know

Grows greater while I become smaller
As I age. The tree must grow somewhere
Outside of good or bad dreams.
I lie. I do not wish more knowing.

Reverse: I would be the tree,
With the long sleep holding
Snow, contending with wind,
Able to wait, holding
Against the day the sun shines.

I would shade and give solace
Through being. I could even bear
A Kilmer making poems of me,
As I rested and gathered and waited
For another time, another chance.

Ball State University Forum   *Harold M. Grutzmacher*

BACK ROAD

Winter mornings
driving past,
I'd see these kids
huddled like grouse
in the plowed ruts
in front of their shack
waiting for the bus,
three small children
bunched against the drifts
rising behind them.

This morning
I slowed to wave
and the smallest,
a stick of a kid
draped in a coat,
grinned and raised
his red, raw hand,
the snowball
packed with rock
aimed at my face.

Poetry   *Bruce Guernsey*

PAINKILLERS

The King of rock 'n roll
grown pudgy, almost matronly,
Fatty in gold lame,
mad king encircled
by a court of guards, suffering
delusions about assassination,
obsessed by guns, fearing
rivalry and revolt

popping his skin
with massive hits of painkiller,

dying at 42.

What was the pain?
Pain had been the colors
of the bad boy with the sneer.

The story of pain, of separation,
was the divine comedy
he had translated
from black into white.

For white children too
the act of naming the pain
unsheathed
a keen joy at the heart of it.

Here they are still!
the disobedient
who keep a culture alive
by subverting it, turning
for example a subway
into a garden of graffiti.

But the puffy King
lived on, his painkillers
neutralising, neutralising,
until he became
ludicrous in performance.

The enthroned cannot revolt.
What was the pain
he needed to kill
if not the ultimate pain

—of feeling no pain?

The Michigan Quarterly Review   *Thom Gunn*

RAMBLE ON WHAT IN THE WORLD WHY

Making a meaning out of everything that has happened,
The there-it-is, plainsong, pitch and pinnacle:
All is blanket-plucking otherwise. My father
Lighted a pipe out in a rowboat on the lake
When he fished and brought up Leviathan on a wormy

Hook, Ahab's pegleg in the belly,
So the watching boy said. Brahms
Percolated coffee, something to fiddle with;
The cup, the pot, the burner, to duck having
To write down music. Meaning is wearying—hammers,
Level, hacking out hunks of marble to raise
Cathedrals. I travel to get out of it to walk in them—
And run slambang into gospels of course,
Pegasus loose and the barndoor slammed.
Berryman took poems and jumped off a bridge.
It all comes down to making oneself one
With sea-slime. Knowing what is OK,
It's the why we've got to, the prehensile toes
And all the rest of it, slops, jade and Jesus,
Venice, murder, virgins and music, that counts.

Canadian Literature   *Ralph Gustafson*

THE LIFE NOT GIVEN

Far from the sea and hard
in the pack ice of this
delta, I think
nonetheless of a boy who
rides his horse across
a sand bar and into
a sun-reflecting pool of the tide.
He stops for a second
but for only a bird
turning in the sky.
The water means nothing
at the hooves of his mare.
He's a boy squandering his days
like pennies. He thinks nothing
of tundra or the hungry.
But I am thinking
nonetheless and wonder which of my
light sons this is and which hour
of my life has so changed over
the years that a man who was
born in the hills of Alabama remembers
a boyhood at the sea
and knows how it feels in the shallows
to neglect life underfoot
and forlorn men far away
in exchange for the smell of salt
and the graceful arc in the sky
of a hawk he can hardly see.

The Black Warrior Review   *David Habercom*

EMILY DICKINSON

Rather slender. Rather tiny.
Always neatly dressed in white.
Well-bred steps about the household,
mainly staying out of sight.

Wipes the dust and waters flowers
in the parlor that she tends.
Bakes the bread and strolls the parkways,
writes to relatives and friends.

Loving sister. Loyal daughter.
This, at least, was how it seemed.
But the hidden flames were raging
and the silent screaming screamed.

Deep behind the lace and louvres
and the image that she gave,
lay a stranger no one knew of.
Much too lonely. Much too brave.

Lay a cool and careful surgeon
practising the surgeon's art.
While her pillow stilled her screaming,
she dissected her own heart.

Paintbrush   *Inger Hagerup*
                          —Translated from the Norwegian
                                  by Harold P. Hansen

ADOLPH HITLER MEDITATES ON THE JEWISH PROBLEM

Take this flyswatter and exterminate the angels,
then with big clawhooks force out their wings.
Now I see their stumps, now I see them crawling:
desperately they try to fly.
Take this insecticide. I hear them catching
and muffling their white coughs. A sunset
or a settling of angels is doubtless the same
because the night now lifts up its hump
and they slowly sink to the ground.
Raise your foot slowly. Likewise. Crush them.
Plunder their feathers with boiling water and stick
those stripped bodies into freezers.
Now the toy sudaria and corded coffins pass by me.
Now the tiny crosses pass by me,
so that the dead infants might amuse themselves.
Hand me the mountingboard and black pins.
Take this flyswatter and exterminate the angels.

Alembic   *Oscar Hahn*
                            —Translated from the Spanish
                                   by James Hoggard

A JULY STORM:
JOHNSON, NEMAHA COUNTY, NEBRASKA

There are two landscapes
in the Nebraska summer: one true,
one illusion. One floats
five thousand feet above
the other, a Front Range
displaced upon the Plains—

it will leave, rushing
through the flatlands like a tourist.
Below are the level fields, unbroken
save for windmills, a daub
of trees, the brick stores
of Main Street ambling

up the long slopes
like tired Herefords.
All else is plain and sky,
meeting where the eye can
see, the tongue taste,
the damp terror of space.

Kansas Quarterly   *Steve Hahn*

AT THE SMITHSONIAN

The trumpeter swan's neck was curved
like something drawn to reflection
in wavering water, while flying
squirrels, fixed in flight,
stopped mid-air between the branches.

Laboring for years, the taxidermist's
hands bloomed with the touch of feathers
or animal fur, and yet in the end
they gnarled from caresses, trying
to make them natural—poses of the dead.

And the hummingbirds are mourning,
wings spread like diadems, all blind:
Lazuline Sabrewing, Lucifer,
Magenta-throated Woodstar, hover
endlessly, never tasting columbines.

He forgot to give them eyes, too small
to bother with, or his hands had already
begun to stiffen. Black-eared Fairy
listens for nectar, its eyes
blank spheres of white, searching
in stillness for jewels of sight.

Poetry   *Vanessa Haley*

THE HOMELESS

At a Jewish wedding
the groom smashes a wine glass
under his heel,
not as I once thought to signify
the hymen shattered at a stroke,
but to recall
amid merrymaking
the destruction of the Temple
and centuries of the Diaspora
ending at barbed wire.

As I paint my house,
focused on the wood grain
under each horizontal
stroke I see refugees
lining documentary footage;
the camera pans quickly
but the faces are endless, alike,
dark; on the horizon
the glare of flames, famine.

This stroke of luck
I learned as a wartime child:
to be born here
and in a small slip of time
while children just like me
were gassed and burned
out of less lucky houses.
I called my left fist Hagar
and tortured it to cry.

I know my house both temporary
and well chosen: in the fireplace
only logs burn.
Once we were slaves in Egypt,
my grandfather said,
which meant suffering for others,
subdued rejoicing.

The Georgia Review   *Joan Joffe Hall*

THAT BRINGS US TO THE WOODSTOVE IN THE WILDS, AT NIGHT

It isn't freedom, that
old heron's call, or cowboys
singing in the other room
or things that scamper
sideways in the dusk.
Always you stand
in the first grade
cloakroom of Detroit,
the other children playing
in the open fields beyond

and the years healing
like broken fingers
until an early cold
catches you out. You drag
an animal that freezes
wild, unhung; the wood
stays wet for months.
Always, each night,
it speaks to you again:
Stay here; I'm warm; You're right.

Open Places   *Walter Hall*

LATE

(after Elizabeth Bowen)

It is late and the others have turned
off the lights to their rooms.
They are sleeping, or they are about to sleep,
or they are holding each other
in arms wrapped for sleep.
In the hotel only the lights in my room
call out to the solitary boats
staked to the warm bay.
What keeps me awake is indistinct.
You told me that without their indistinctness
things do not exist, you cannot desire them.
I think of you, what has not been said
and what remains unknown.
I lie awake to claim what is unclear,
as the guests of the hotel
finally release themselves to the night,
give the hotel over to its own settling in—
the natural progress of the night here
which I follow. It becomes what is clear
as I hold the two ends of dialogue,
asking my questions, answering for you.
If there were a truth in this hotel at night
it would bring me no sleep,
it would make nothing clear.
I say what comes to mind.
What comes to mind is the unsaid—
inflection your sweet device—your profile
at the window the day you turned to me to say
that those who never lie are never wholly alone.
It is late and the night air is fat with water.
I sit with you here, waiting for you to turn
again from that window and talk to me.

Poetry   *Daniel Halpern*

GNOSTOLOGY

Each return is a blessing,
a birthing. I come back
again in the last light
of evening and the blue cups
the camas raises to catch
the mist are dripping,
the blackberries turning
blue from green, and down
the narrow Strait of Juan
de Fuca, the fog horns
faintly call. I stand
a long time outside listening
to the dripping of leaves
and nighthawk cries. Behind
me the dark house drips
from the eaves. I slide
the wide door open
and breathe the scents of
stale beer and cigarettes
I smoked last week. The same
books clutter the table.
The same poem dies
in the crude last
unfinished line I couldn't
make to breathe. I ease
into my tattered chair in
trembling light as the sunset
slides into a shadow
ghosting the dark Pacific.
Somewhere, the tide is
staggering over stones at
the feet of incoming swells,
the gulls are scavenging, looping
a last time over the brine
searching for edibles
tangled in the wrack. The moon
slips between two cedars,
razor thin and curved into
a dazzling sliver of ice
shimmering through the fog.
The dark of night settles in
on strong steady feet.
The silence is not
profound—it's an old
friend, my beautiful dark
daughter I haven't seen
in years, a longing, a soft
exquisite ache. An hour
flies. Another. My life's
a summer reverie, a dream
that flashes past unnoticed

at the edge of sleep,
a simple gesture, a touch
or kiss of a friend.
                    Finally,
I rise and step out
of my clothes. I stand
on the porch in the mist,
suddenly naked, lightly
goose-fleshed, more alive
than I have been in days:
my whole body responds,
to mist and air, the moist
touch of evening bristling
hairs of belly and legs,
and I feel my nipples
harden, my scrotum
draw up against my groin,
my toes count every grain
so damp beneath my feet.
Out in the blank space
of night, the thousands
and thousands of systems
are at work lighting
galaxies, whirling the
billions of years into a ball.
Are the ants asleep
inside their catacombs
of fir? Are the chloroplasts
resting their eyes?
With no prayer on my breath,
without hope or fear,
without asking what it is
or what the seasons know,
I gather a long slow breath,
breathe it, and then
I kneel and bow.

Willow Springs Magazine   *Sam Hamill*

TESTING GROUND

(for Stanley Kunitz)

He said an old poet, meaning himself,
I imagine, ought never be caught
with his technique showing.
I see slips of words hanging
from the hems of tongues.
The baggy legs of poems bandied
back and forth. Some other poet's
flaw. Not his. He keeps his craft
well hidden, like the rugged inner
linings of a child's pocket.

What marvels for the unsuspecting:
a clever metaphor, a sly parable or two.
And once a witty oxymoron lay its snare
for me. He has the glint of genius
and places value on everything
he touches. Someday I'm going to ask
him why poets just get by and
what it means to be a pangolin.

Gryphon   *Karla M. Hammond*

BLUE BOTTLE

The blue-black flare at the bottom
of the red tulip. Inside,
the sticks of sex are alert and wet.
The eye of the penis
and its first glistening drop.
That's what happened
last night—not night
but the pink moment of dusk
when every eye, even the sky's,
sees clearly through the pastel motes
of daylight
into the navy steel of night.

Remember that cheap perfume
they used to sell in the dime store
next to the orange face powder?
Evening in Paris.
It came in a blue bottle
with a silver cap shaped like a star.
That's the blue I mean.
I twirled off the star
and smelled what was in there.
Sex was in there.
I drew that blue, bruised fragrance
deep into my nostrils.
I was at the cosmetic counter of T. G. Grant's,
and my cousin had just explained
that the man puts *his* on *hers*
and "they have to line their breasts up too."
I wasn't afraid, no matter
how odd it was.
I just pulled in that heavy blue smell.

Much later I was afraid,
for many years I was afraid with you.
But last night
I looked at the small, sleepy
eye in the intelligent stalk.
The blue light was caught there.
I recognized it.

You I recognized.
I said, blunt as that eye and as innocent,
Your penis smells like the rest of you.
The star opened, the flesh opened.
The night and the body
which are blue bottles
opened and opened.
It was the first day of Spring,
the tulips which had been aloof
bent out of themselves,
blue night was exposed.

The Iowa Review   *Patricia Hampl*

I LOOK AT MY HAND

I look
at my hand. The one I forget
so often,
leaving it among the most
vulgar objects.
Now it's like a bird
which has abruptly fallen
from my body to
this spot.
Another discovery: here is
my body. I live
in it without knowing
about it, almost without feeling it.
Sometimes it stumbles,
all of a sudden,
against another inevitable body.
And it is love. Surprised,
I then feel it isolated,
whole, different;
other times the sun
outlines its warm
profile, or the wind surrounds it
with a concrete and confining
boundary.
But now it is a cold
foreboding.
Tree, standing erect
in front of me, sudden body
of mine!
Blood runs through it. How
it descends! Listen to it:
this is the heart. Here sleeps
the pulse, like the water
of a quiet river.
There is the clean
white bone in its river-bed. The skin.
The long muscles, tough and concealed.

It is on the earth. On the earth:
tall spike of wheat,
young and green aspen, old
olive tree.
On the earth it is. It was.
I've seen it.
For only a moment.

          . . . it stands tall
between me and those yellow fields.

Cutbank   *Angel González*
— Translated from the Spanish
by Joel Hancock

AFTER VACATION

"Well," we say, "time to go." So then we pack
And sweep and straighten. This soft, sun-drenched
        week
Will warm the winter; now we journey back
Into our city. We forever seek
Small ways of holding this our gentle time,
Reminder during grayer days: we take
Stones home or bits of driftwood, scraps of rhyme
In keeping for that other place's sake.
So summer lingers in one perfect shell:
Our Eden-glances follow us as well.

The Christian Century   *Katherine Hanley*

THAT IS NOT INDIFFERENCE

I would exorcise you like some common demon
fallen, like Lucifer, from the upper firmament
to prey upon the shackled night,
did you not still bear, in that fitful gloom,
some remnant of former majesty
and that opposite of love that is not indifference.
Ours is a mutual bondage.

Those who must stretch their fate
must stay rooted deep in the creature heart
that can always hope.
Thus, oh my enemy, I drag you on my feet
from star to greater star,
extending your bleak shadow
into the bright web of song.

Arizona Quarterly   *Howard G. Hanson*

IN SEARCH OF A SHORT POEM FOR MY GRANDMOTHER

Last time I left, you pulled your chair
before the window glass to wait until

the bus had passed from view. All evening
I have moved from memory to photograph
searching the riddle of pain to find
an answer to the stringent indignities
you knew. I've tried to count your losses
as if a sheer sum could buy you time
for life to recompense all that it extracted.
I've tried to celebrate the calm with which
you slowed the late bad news that sped
across the waiting room. "How d'you spell that?"
you said. No word brave enough will come.
A snapshot of you at five, in soft batiste,
has come alive within my hand:
in the side yard, by the oleander bush,
you've been surprised at tears, your cheek is smudged,
a ribbon loosed; the amateur's flash has fixed
the shape to come of small outcries unheard,
scattered like a flush of birds from a bruised tree.
I cannot phrase an answer to the raveling
of your days. Here, from the ironwood chair,
I offer your name to the keep of anonymous air;
I dream you abroad in the night's vast maze,
pressed against the membrane of the world,
mouth open to these syllables of praise.

Southern Exposure   *Louise Hardeman*

FOOLS

"It's only a dream."—Champion Jack Dupre

They say one good shot deserves another.
They say the largest catfish wait.
They say in any kind of weather
good fish will run to good bait.

So with this chant dancing in our heads
we're off to the creek in the hills
like children looking for treasure,

looking for the aimed moment,
the arrow in the heart, still looking,
the years through, the time by, waiting.

For to still desire is to hurry death,
but with the silver white ghosts
of the hooked fish in the moonlight

we will dance along on the bank,
full of the music of pure movement,
more liquid than light or the luck

of the loved;
          we will dance all night
with the moon in our eyes,
like a true lover's dream come true.

They say in any kind of weather
good fish will run to good bait.
They say one good shot deserves another.
They say the largest catfish wait.

Pontchartrain Review   *Glenn Hardin*

THE VILLANELLE

Regard the motion of the villanelle:
Its ins and outs and comely dips and sways.
A couple must unite to do it well.

The two of them will make a carrousel,
For dancing circles which are roundelays,
Around the motion of the villanelle.

They never touch until they bid farewell
And then they meet in passionate embrace.
A couple must embrace to do it well.

Impassioned in the dance's magic spell,
No single movement of a foot betrays
The comely motion of the villanelle.

Each step by step their movements parallel
And compliment the partner's dancing ways.
This couple must conspire to do it well.

The moment's coming when the rules impel
The dancers now to fuse in final phase:
Regard this motion of the villanelle:
Our couple have embraced and done it well.

New Letters   *Donald Harington*

YOU ARE GROWING INTO MY LIFE . . .

You are growing into my life like ivy,
Slow-covering my walls with your dark tangle:
I can smell the dust settle on your leaves
As you crumble my mortar and stone,
As time etches you into me.

You are hanging from my thoughts, an endless
        vine
Growing deep shades of green under cool winter
        suns,
Then flashing shiny lime-colored leaves into
        warmer dreams;
Insinuate your tiny fingers into my every fissure,
Grow thick and close to me, blanket my harsh
        facade
With your ancient mask: I will carry you.

The Sun   *Louise Harris*

EVE'S VERSION

Another time I'll let him pick his own
apples. Since then all he's done is bitch
about how I was the one responsible. Which
I suppose I was. But before then it was moan
and groan that of course we mustn't but if on-
ly we could . . . . How else to maximize the rich
potential of . . . ? It wasn't the sales pitch
so much as the thought
                of hearing it morning, noon
and night that got to me. The serpent was quite
superfluous, really, and slunk off after the act
like your average phallic symbol.
                So now we know
how to tell good from evil. So what's new?
Except, of course, to Adam; God was right
about him—he wasn't ready to be imperfect.

The Canadian Forum   *James Harrison*

BLEMISHES

Tales of witches warned me
not to play with toads,
whose urine would
leave ugly warts.

So I gazed more closely
into the clots of white foam
dripping from the dog's jaw
to see the toad's blemish,
and mark it for my own.

Leaving the dog to snap at toads,
I might have stared deeply
into the mildewed eyes
forming in dark damp places
and seen its spreading truth,
like time foxing pages of books
with tracks of its passing.

Out of some such freckled books
I was taught to gauge my faith
in the red blemishes of spiked
hands and feet, a severed groin.
I learned in one book
that squid ejaculate ink
as writ against betrayal.

Heavy with remembered dreams
this night, I awake to find
pores oozing on my neck.
I feel my strength ebb,
like bat wings at dawn.

I distrust the shadows darkly
playing in the corners of my room
where the last days' dust covers cracks.

The Chariton Review   *James Hart*

TONIGHT WHEN YOU LEAVE . . .

I'll give you the weight of my hands, not knowing you want only
the hands, those two blue-veined mementos that scarcely
bleed. for months they lay between us like lovers, like
windows, opening and closing in this rough, dark season.
for months I've courted your silence, your own hands forever
circling like sea birds, poised to desert this city
of unpredictable tides.

it is evening. your absence leans in the doorway. I offer you
the weight of my hands and you refuse, wanting only the hands,
those two bitten faces singing softly to each other, like souvenirs,
years from now, wanting to be remembered.

The Spoon River Quarterly   *Gayle Elen Harvey*

IN RANDOM FIELDS OF IMPULSE AND REPOSE

A man moves toward himself as old,
as his own ancestor: hunting and hunted
though never feeling foreign, his boundaries
set by smell or height, cold or density,
water or none, as though earth herself
had said, Stop. You are too far from your
own home. And so he stepped back, read
the stars or birds, bargained with some
offering—brother, lamb, jug, weapon—
and stayed just there, at the edge
of the earth's command, preferring that
tremor caused by strategic defiance
to the simpler continuity of return.

A man moves toward himself as he will
always return to the man before, the man
inside himself who is for thousands of years
making the bread, lighting the cave, and
wearing well. He will call this man
something else, another sex or race or even
a place as in a dream. But he is just
himself returning, carrying his flute and
shovel across the breast of earth and her
ragged history, home.

The Georgia Review   *Jeanine Hathaway*

COLORING MARGARINE

On the top step with soft kitchen light
behind us and dank cellar glooming below,
we sat together kneading the yellow into
white margarine. Older and stronger, you
always got the longest turn, I remember.
Mother's radio was always playing "tunes"
by Percy Faith and his orchestra, I think.
That was the music we beat and squeezed to,
and it seemed the yellow product tasted better.

I lack patience with the college girl who cuddles
her new kitten in my class. She lets it crawl
underneath her sweater, between her terrific
breasts, and because I am weak I force a sickly
smile. This is not innocence, but its cynical
use. I would be labeled cynic if I leveled
a reproof, since the girls pretend to think
the cat is cute and the boys are dazzled by her tits.
Could I work this little vignette into the text-
book honesty of Cordelia and Kent? Instead,
I take a tangent with aimless anecdotes
of sibling rivalry. This kitten, class, and play
do not interest me as much as a memory of you
sliding back in focus—clutching our cat
in such sweet dishonesty when I came to punch
you back. O you knew my frail honor
would permit me to pound a girl, if she was
sister, but parental rules forbade
the striking of that cat. Other things come
back: the time you were spanked too for not
telling that I alone ruined Grandmother's fox
with gum. Later, shut together in the scary closet
with that dripping beast, its glass eyes
strangely lit with malice and reproach, we
were as close as we ever were. Your senseless
sacrifice made sense to you, I am sure. Though
I did not understand your female moods,
grown-up talk at table, or the love mush
on the radio. I still don't. Let me confess:
In *Lear,* the only character I full understand
is Edmund. Listen, do you remember what
I'm remembering now: *When-e-ver we kiss/*
I wor-ry and won-der/ you're close to me
now/ but whe-re is your he-art?

Columbia   *William Hathaway*

THE LONG SEASON

A man bows out the employment office,
leans into a blast of snow: you can see
where the horizon has lost definition.

And as you speak your voice
blows away, letter with no address.

In a diner the window clouds, as hunters
close their stained hands around mugs of coffee
and talk of bucks from past seasons.
All week they appear in town, permits
fastened to their checkered backs,
the oiled black rifles pointed toward the ground.

Cars pass quietly, deer tied to fenders.
Clouds move like hands and fold over us.
Each day we take home less,
there is one more word not said.
All evening a dog howls in the cold.
Let us talk, lean on each other's voices
in this long season of killing.

The Nantucket Review   *James Haug*

MUSIC BY THE WATERS

Out of the marbled underwaters,
artifacts of surf, comes the shining
of bubble and frog-green weed; the salivated
quartz egg; purple dye of greater storms
in minor shells; all things touched by tides;
patterns of water not of water;
castoffs, like speckled eyes from deeper sight,
tones on the mind. I pick them and they sing.

The Massachusetts Review   *John Hay*

THE STORM

The wind's overbearing voices
hit me laterally, beating up such seas,
waking such reminders of the drowned,
I ran off course, hiding in reeds,
covering myself as best I could with land,
to mute the storm within my living skull.
I ask of some Capacity,
what has us listen to what we may not hear?

The Massachusetts Review   *John Hay*

MAPS FOR A SON ARE DRAWN AS YOU GO

I say what Lindbergh's father
said to Lindbergh: "One boy's
a boy; two boys are half
a boy; three boys are no
boy at all."

> Which helps explain
why Lindbergh kept his boyishness
for life, which meant he stayed
himself, which means a lot.
What else is destiny?
>   After
you learn that governments lie
and happiness is undefinable
and death has no patience,
you'll understand me.
>   Meanwhile
the ignorant but well-informed
will try to keep you mute
as a shut book.
>   Forecasters of the best
and worst will hurry to retreat
infallibly into the future.
>   Ministers
who talk on cue with God
will weigh you down like serious
furniture.
>   Assume that what
you lose to such distractions
you will gain in strength.
>   By then
you'll learn that all you know
will help you less than how
you think.
>   The rest is memory,
and memory's the graveyard of the mind
as surely as tomorrow is its myth.
Nowhere but the time at hand
is when you'll see that God's
geometry is feast enough.
Within the world's closed circles,
everything's the sum of halves
that rhyme.
>   From coconuts to butterflies
to lovers knotted on the soft
battlefield of any bed, the halves
add up to one, and every one
remembers where it came from,
as a trumpet note recalls
the song it was a part of
and the listeners who heard it
and were changed.
>   What Lindbergh's
father meant and what I mean
are two roads to the same country.

Knowing how long it takes us
to be young, he left his son
some clues to get his bearings
by . . .
And so do I.

The American Scholar   *Samuel Hazo*

PAUSE BETWEEN CLOCK TICKS

Like a caught breath
the pendulum stays,
a dew drop hinges
to a leaf's edge,
an ant spies a crumb,
a ray of sun meets
its reflection, a bird's
wing arches to beat,
a glance begun, pulse
on tiptoe, a wave crest
hovers, a sigh breaks—
all held at zero motion
while "yes" trembles on lips,
"no" waits to be said.

Yankee   *James Hearst*

THE WRECK OF THE GREAT NORTHERN

Where the Great Northern plunged in
The river boiled with light, and we all stood
In the tall grass staring at a tangle
Of track, and four orange coaches
And one Pullman lying under the current,
Turning the current clear. We stood staring
As though it had been there all along
And was suddenly thrust up out of the weeds
That night as a blessing, as a long sleek hallway
Dropping off into fields we'd never seen,
Into the pastures of some great god
Who sent back our steers too heavy to move,
All bloated and with green seaweed strung down
Their horns. And we all looked down
Into the lit cars at businessmen
And wives, already back to breathing water,
And saw in the cold clear tanks of the Pullman
A small child the size of my son, a porter's
White jacket, a nylon floating gracefully
like an eel.
What the train and the river
Were saying, no one could understand.
We just stood there, breathing what was left
Of the night. How still the cars were,

How sleek, shimmering through the undertow.
And I saw the trees around us blossomed out,
The wind had come back and was blowing
Through the tall empty grass, through the high
Grain fields, the wind was rattling
The dry husks of corn.

The Greenfield Review   *Robert Hedin*

BEST FRIENDS

When you call, your cheerfulness thick as armadillo hide,
I'm supposed to help you keep it up.

You say I have no small talk. Well, you're right.
I don't care what color your new drapes are.

I want to know what you've done with her,
the girl who was you.

Remember that bad book you helped me write, our childhood?
The night your parents begged you to take sides?

The time our race to the toilet ended a dead heat
and we sat together laughing on the seat?

You scotch-taped your wedding pictures, but the rips still show,
ugly as a set of stretch marks.

Christ! If only you would barnstorm out of there.
Instead you call, circling like a wounded jet

through your spiral of topics—safe, banal—
your private holding pattern over hell.

The Hudson Review   *Judith Hemschemeyer*

THE MARTYR AND THE ARMY

The performer numbs toward the moribund,
Grabs with killer claws for the jugular
And strangles himself to death.
From his throat, tin soldiers strut into a
Battle circus. Puppet wraiths rush out
From the perverse gullet, of necessity,
Mortal but ready to die at arms.
One by one, they go to the maniacal attack.
See? Beneath the night shroud
An entire army arises from the trachea
Of one singular martyr, now divine,
With the rigor mortis of military design.

Commonweal   *Jock Henderson*

INTERNATIONAL MOTHERHOOD ASSOC.

Certain women, I think, are born
with a baby already in them. They

grow up feeling it push and claw below
their hearts, and know
the shape of its face while they are still virgins.
They then marry and it is proper
to let it out, and it squalls, and they love it forever.

I favor this. I was brought up
squished against the bosoms of various females
who were famous in 5 states for their skill
at cleaning up drool and stool
and a genuine and heroic Tolerance of me.

If I later married a girl more like my father
there was nothing Freudian about it. But
sometimes now when it rains I search the shopping centers
for a familiar silhouette; there's one—
a certain heavy grace gives them away—

their arms and hearts are always open
like an all-night superette, and I know
the angle of their shoulder fits my head
if I need it again.

The Literary Review   *M. L. Hester*

RYÓKAN

After an evening of drinking
amid peach blossoms by the river,
the seventy-year-old priest has lost his way.

Looking/not looking for home,
remembering the boy he once was,
he follows his own footsteps
in front of him:

"Before I was born,
I'd wear my favorite vest,
and ride a chestnut horse,
and go to play . . . . "

Now here he is again, laughing,
our friend, old poet, beloved fool,
next to the brothel, adjusting his robes,

after an evening of drinking
amid peach blossoms by the river.

The Ohio Review   *William Heyen*

THE ROAD ALONG THE THUMB AND FOREFINGER

The road all the way up along the coast
Is beautiful: the thumb reaching
Away from the mitten and into Huron,
Toward islands shown only on the better maps.
Never before timbered,

Secluded stands of virgin pine
Leap white against the paleness of the sky.
Violent storms visit them but afterwards
The water stretches away like a shimmering blue throat,
The stones laughing upward from depths of twenty feet,
More. And the towns, the towns:
Croswell, Harbor Beach, Sebawaing,
The land going from lakes to Polish
Dairy and back to the mitten,
Up to Sault Ste. Marie finally, and the ghosts of the Ojibwa
And names like Tawas, Au Sable, Oscada,
The snow high and late in leaving but
Warmer than no snow and low temperatures,
Up to Superior where the water is
Drinkable, if only the hand could hold it.

Many a car has died along the way,
Seen the water and the tiny port
Towns and given up the ghost
With a broken heart, almost in sight of the water.
The farmers grumble and wonder at the number
Of them and tow them away; but the road
Along the water goes on, the water
Glistening in its skin of blue and gold,
If only the eye could hold it.

The Cape Rock   *Mark Hickey*

THE TRUMPET SHALL SOUND

(to Garry R.)

A thin lip, it is said,
is most serviceable; able to counterpart
the quivering reed, the couch blade
taut between thumbs of children.
The sensuous contour is,
among equalities, certainly no asset.

Blow firmly, friend;
the trumpeters of this world
cut their way through gentler orchestrations
with a honed edge. There is seldom
an answer, but echoes from peak or forest
refresh the ear.

Blow when you will; consider
Gabriel at his cloud's core
hunched disconsolate, no summons
to press mouthpiece to lip, the dead
cumbent as ever in their graves.

Nothing ripens on the earth, there are few fruitions,
armageddons foregather unannounced.
Make your own music.

The Fiddlehead   *John V. Hicks*

LAST RITE

We will remember, surely, how we stood,
one with the silence in the grouse-grey wood,
and heard the wind pronouncing overhead
its benediction upon all things dead:
the ravished petal, the spent year's desire,
the upland's scattered and extinguished fire;
and how it lacked but winter's setting in
to still the memory of what had been:
the surge of light, the quickened pulse's heat,
the vernal thrust, the venturing wing's beat.
We will remember that we marked the sound
of the last leaf upon the littered ground,
and all about us, as we turned to go,
soft as a sigh, the sift of the first snow.

Poetry Canada Review   *John V. Hicks*

SOUP ON A COLD DAY

Visibility stretches for miles, bringing the sea
to the back lawn. It was worth waiting through the dark season
for the horizon to reappear like a fist
or a poem that scoops up facts of life.
We want familiarity in our lives, from room to room,
mirrors or brick walls or the opaque stones on the road
that shine alike in heat or cold: Break them.
The cook crushes eggs by the window while she daydreams,
looking at the table of green ocean. On the wall she has posted
a poem overgrown with braids of onion, garlic,
basil from the garden. Chew on the words
as if they were your intimate wishes—free, unceremonious.
Mix them. Boil them. Swallow.

The Centennial Review   *Nellie Hill*

IDIOT BOY

Though he's turned forty, they call him Idiot Boy
Here. But I wonder if some of us could take
Some tips from him, remembering the thefts
Of plants in hanging baskets from our porch
by teenagers who ripped the flashing off
Our neighbor's chimney base with long boat-hooks
And later stole a television set
From kindly Father John, retired priest.
Compared to them, Charlie, our Idiot Boy,
Seems like a saint. Once, to be sure, he took
A duck from out the pond; and when reproved,
Said, "It's the town's pond and I am of the town,
and hungry." Mostly, though, all bundled up
Even in summer, he cycles by serene,
With great-coat flapping in the brisk sea breeze,

Like a huge bat on wheels, cradling with care
In wicker-basket tied to handlebars
Some empty bottles he's cleared from the roadside
To exchange for a beer. He's been seen to plunge in the lake
Fully dressed, and lather himself and his clothes with soap.
He's kind to cats and small children and invalids,
And cheerily calls to me as he pedals by:
"You're looking good for your age today, old man."

Dark Horse   *Rowland M. Hill*

BALLET

After the class I taught my father French:
Lundi, mardi, mercredi and the slow months.
He learned the R the way I learned to move,
A little stiff and dramatized and breathless.
I held my arms round like the full moon
Wanting pointed shoes, the intractable
Lace of a real dancer. It makes me sad
To see them leap across the stage. Father
Mispronounced the French. But he had grace.

The Iowa Review   *Brenda Hillman*

WOOD BUTCHER

(for my father)

After the Navy and war,
You drafted big prints and started a summer house
In Bay Springs. I was your helper, and that first year
We worked weekends through most of the winter.
The wind, your cold immaculate tools, the hole
In the floor of the Ford we traveled in . . .
I hated it all. Especially my carpentry. I ruined doors,
My tape never returned,
I couldn't saw for shit. "Measure twice, cut once."
You said it a hundred times.
I tried everything to please you,
You my ex-flyboy, the perfectionist.
Even your smile was mitered. Your hands cool and silky
On the tools, brown as the lining
Of your flight jacket. Mine were white,
Mitts of a wood butcher.
You never said that,
But when you came across the scarred paneling,
The wrong nail, the split grain,
Doughnut grease on the new glass,
I'd watch your eyes, the drained bluebirds
That flew your face.
I fucked some screens up once,
Wrinkles, wavy frames;

You broke them out with a chair.
My best day I spent hauling dry wall,
Holding while you fitted and tacked.
For years I would devote myself
To carrying and fetching.
Strong, good with mortar, but squirrely.
A world class gofer.

I want you to know
That today I finished a boat, designed it,
22 feet, foredeck, wheel,
A transom you could hang a Pratt & Whitney on.
But none of this is challenge or revenge:
The boat is a way of speaking, a tongue
Saying I still want to please you,
That it's your disappointment that drives me.

Hawaii Review   *Norman Hindley*

NOT-KNOWING

(for Matisse's "Blue Nude")

I feel my stomach
like a blind physician:
with woman's intuition.

God needs no megaphone.
He talks with a soft tap
inside me;
little question mark
of worry.

This awful not-knowing
has made me relive
that one haphazard moment . . .
like stepping off the curb
or forgetting just-this-once
to lock the door:

It meant nothing.
It means everything.

Paintbrush   *Dawn Hinshaw*

FACTORIES

Everywhere in New York City there are factories
flinging their broken windows into the streets
raining sawdust and glass crying out with the
soft voices of women whispering Puerto Rican names
whispering my name and wearing their dark shadows
like petticoats and their graffiti like too much makeup
over their scarred bricks their used up bodies

yes they are always stained they have walls
broken off like the stumps of cripples
I'm sorry but this is how it is with me
everywhere I turn I find the ruined mouths
and damp animals of yes and when
I lie down to sleep at night I hear

dry pistons setting into motion like
galloping horses yes their hooves are echoing
on concrete their hearts are hammering
they are churning like diesels bursting out of
tunnels out of mountains out of factories
and shedding silence like an extra skin yes
pumping blood through the stillness of my arteries

Partisan Review   *Edward Hirsch*

LITTLE POLITICAL POEM

(after Nazim Hikmet)

Tonight I saw so many windows
lit up in so many different houses,
each little square of glass
lit up separately, like a flame,

so many flames together, the repetition
of so many lights in so many houses
all lit up separately, but

somehow all flaming together, too,
like a single fire, say, a housewarming,
an entire block blazing with the light
from a single window, so many windows

in so many houses on so many nearly
identical streets in so many different
neighborhoods in so many different cities . . .

Listen: tonight I saw so many windows
blazing alone, almost blazing together
under a single sky, under so many
different skies all weaving together

through so many different countries . . .

Skywriting   *Edward Hirsch*

A.M.–P.M.

At midnight the heart's
Valves close momentarily,
The planet draws its breath
As if listening for silence.
Coming from the stair of noon,
Tilted on the sun's edge,

The day has come crashing
Down to this: my hand
Smoothing the nervous sheets
In expiation for the day.
Life is the real dream,
Plato's curse, and we know
Ourselves best at midnight.
I watch you sleep, your
Breathing not your own.
What does the heart count?
Who keeps and measures
Each beat beside me?
Who counts and files
Away the spent dreams,
The constant diesel-throb
Of your heavy-duty heart?
We are perfect in sleep,
Not ourselves—forgiven.
It reminds in me some
Sadnesses beyond belief.

The Cape Rock   *Theodore H. Hirschfield*

BASE CHAPEL, LEJEUNE 4/79

the man before me stands, black muscles
gleaming, for the hymn. no planes are on the
runway; quiet heat reverberates from
pine walls and organ pipes. in channels on the bay
crepe myrtle bursts to purple; when he lifts
into the carolina air, the pilot sees
it marking out each inlet. now with his family
he is beside me as the music ends.
"peace be with you": turning to each other
we exchange the ritual wish. this day,
released from details, men come from soldiering
to hear themselves address their brothers
with these words. outside, we pause to catch a breeze,
relax, and wander off to pass the holy day.

Southern Exposure   *Archie Hobson*

TRUE CHILD

True Child of God, stand innocently awed
Before the furious stars of the night,
Before the dark passions of living beasts,
Before the processes of juice and blood,
The flight of birds, the deep sounding of whales,
Before all that is made, and the Maker.

True Child, greater is your Lord than the crude,
Violent, jealous God of the frightened,
Greater by far than bumbling, lusty Zeus—

He is Maker of worlds, Lover of life;
A million cultures marvel at His forms;
Fish dawdle in the moisture of His mouth;
Slugs decorate His forehead; standing in
His hands, horses copulate and drop foals;
His hairs are vegetables and fruit trees;
With His eyes, hawks hunt.

                    True Child, stand erect,
And love your self, not as a creator,
But as a creature who makes his own worlds
In sacred imitation. You are great;
The humble beggar scrapes, receives your alms;
The priest who dresses in tinkling symbols
Is your acolyte; you see and behold
While the blind stumble and grope for pleasure;
You speak, and though no one listens, he hears;
You prophesy, and the future unfolds.

Among the bones of the mighty and weak
You stand, True Child; the fleeing universe
You catch and hold aloft amid ruins;
Implacable, you stand among the wolves,
Your feet awash in the blood of all men
Who, before you, have worshiped at the sword;
Then go, jump and leap, turn a somersault;
Go, True Child, heart of song, sing out, sing out!

The Hollins Critic　　　　　　　　　　　*Marion Hodge*

BLUE RIDGE

In the mountains, there is more than slate
and red clay. There are more vivid images
than this: the sunset and twisted limbs
of pear trees against the sky. There is
tobacco. A stone chimney. Old clapboard
place. An ice house. Caverns of time
and space. Slowly, the narrow road winds
into the hills, the arbor of trees comforting
in their natural confines, and, then, with
just one turn, the ceiling disappears and
I am engulfed in a past that has no dimensions.
Figures bob between the rows in the field,
shadows against the wall. Once, there was
a cabin beside the chimney; already it is
buried with its persona. Hand tools
and bottles. Songs in the wind. As it
whistles through the broken windows of
the ice house, I listen from where I stand
rigid in the corner. I have reached the edge.
I am afraid of what the dark might hold
if I lose my footing. Sighs in the wood. *Fear*
is for the unknown. You have nowhere else

> *to go. There is no place you would rather be.*
> *You cannot rest unless you be here. Another*
> *shadow that will pass.*

The North American Review   *Elizabeth Hodges*

OUR ANNUAL RETURN TO THE LAKE

We never know what to expect:
Windows broken, the roof commandeered
By moss, the dock, perhaps, drifted away.
But this year there is no vandalism
Except the subtle hostility of nature.
A green battalion of grasses has
Held and occupied the entire back yard.
Mold has slowly advanced over my last year's
Paint, indoctrinating it with the concept of rot.
Ferns have thrown up road blocks
In what was once a well-worn path.
Even the trees have flown war missions
In a twelve-month bombardment of needles and leaves.
I will counterattack, of course, with broom
And brush and a rusty machete,
Clearing and cleaning and reclaiming my own.
But I wish that, just once, nature
Would greet me with "Welcome"
Instead of "Take me, if you can."

Blue Unicorn   *Robert D. Hoeft*

TO A LITTLE BOY LEARNING TO FISH

Yes,
You must crucify the worm
To catch the fish.
As much as your Sunday school training
Goes against the act,
Jab the barb through,
Thread it on,
Leave a portion dangling.
Lesser creatures
Don't feel pain
(But the dance
Is so convincing).
Men feed on worms
Through the intermediary fish:
That quite the reverse is true
Is too much too soon
As you stand in wet tennis shoes
On the gently bobbing dock
Casting your baited hook
Into the world of men.

Event   *Robert D. Hoeft*

THE SECRET IRISH

(for Karen McGullam)

Would you have me brand it, scars
healed green, across
my forehead? Sweat whiskey, flaunt
my sotten ways? I don't hide
it; if my name's not clue
enough, what of my nose,
something like a shrunk potato
sprouting from my face? I've tamed
my drinking, haven't picked
a fight in years and can't recall
when last I pitched a man
across a tavern by his face.

You try and tell me women
the world over nod, knowing
what you mean when you mention Irish
men. But only Irish women, warned
by their mothers as their mothers
cautioned them, possessing
total racial recall, know
that damning shred they're loath
to speak of, that you claim
stains my Celtic soul.

The Texas Review   *Allen Hoey*

ODE TO JOY

Your hand trailed over the hammock's side
And, like a netted mermaid, you hung in air
Lending the net the languorous shape of your
Lithe body, and the curved air
Swerved around you bearing scents
Of old shrub roses and of new-mown grass.
I sat on the steps beneath the sun that poured
On sun-filled lawn and sun-splashed holly bushes,
Sun-crested trees, magnolias afloat where sun
Like a summer shower thrust itself upon
A glimmering sea. Each new breath I drew
Was joy—I knew no name for this delight
That flowed through arteries to crest, recede,
And crest again, as endless as the tide.
The grass below was a metaphor of gladness,
The beetle underneath its blades, a trope;
The earth still damp with dew bespoke its kinship
With the linked constellations of the night.
The ivy on the wall had shone forever.
Each object of our sight, each breath
Crowded with speech this love outlasting death
That flowed through me as though it would not cease

Ever to flow, and knowing this I knew
Nothing else there was that we need know.

The Southern Review   *Daniel Hoffman*

WHAT'S LIVING?

("What's living-fission of mother and child?
    Snake with tail in fangs?"—Takahashi)

The amphibious bedlam of mothers
opens a door and locks it at the same time.
I have come to bring my daughter fruit.
The first bite is sweet
as a shape formed out of dust
as her dark hair I wash and comb.
The second is walking on fire
and the third,
that briney water cleaving apart
the way birds break off one way,
fish another.

Your sweet singing flesh
and myself, flaming ridge of back
edged sharp with anger and love,
this rare lizard who makes a wound
in the sleeping bird,
then waits until the soft neck weakens.
One hiss from my mouth
sets thin bones inside your ear
to violent motion, splinters the silent door.
We step so close to one another
we return to ourselves,
feathers and scales.

And the naked Medea
felt this love, wrapping her tail
about the beautiful ruins of children.
What's living?
The creature swallows herself,
swallows all the bodies
struggling to death and birth.

The Small Pond Magazine   *Linda Hogan*

WASHING MY SON

Zack's eyes can't
focus, but his skin
can. He squirms
as I hone him down,
tickle his feet, lather
up his neck, erase
these foamy four-lane

highways down his back
and wash around
his thimble-size wet
cock. He wants to be
touched all over,
rubbed behind his ears
like this, his neck
stroked, even
his navel's little map
explored. Scrubbing
him is polishing
this whittled spear
of wood until
that new wood shines
and he's firm,
sanded down all
over with my hands,
healed up
like a model airplane
you just made over
into silver. I kiss
him again. All
the decals go on
perfectly.

Kansas Quarterly   Jonathan Holden

TURNING POINT

Midnight in midwinter: the dead land laid
in a coffin of snow.
                              As I walk into my yard,
each step thumps through a drumskin
that drizzle has frozen. And I too,
when I stop, am quickly glazed:
                                             coatsleeves,
boots, eyeglasses glisten as for display
in winter's closed gallery: "Object
Frozen in Midthought, Medium:
Ice on Man. 1979."
                              Under snow I feel the earth's
stones and furnace; deeper still
the anticipated crust of life; beyond it
the sun, at this moment, passes underfoot
on its way to dawn and delicately
as a mother rocks a sleeping baby is tilted
toward spring.
                    And I thank God tonight
for those who first marked this moment. For
the moment has become the creator
of this world and king of jailbreakers.
I have met him here, at midnight
in midwinter, real and invisible

as a baby among refugees, and trust now
to find in every winter
a point on fire
with the friction of turning.

The Christian Century   *W. L. Holshouser*

OTHER LIVES

Some days a road streams back, a road you took
past someone's house: the porch propped up with boards,
the car dismantled in the yard, a door
where half-dressed children watch you with a look
you'd save for God. They're someone else's kids,
distant as someone else's needs and rent,
the life you never wanted if you tried.

Or it's a train you're riding: past a field
you catch a glimpse of someone hanging clothes,
long days you dreamed of, and she never looks.
Or it's a town where boys grow up to leave:
the two of them, still joking near a store,
stall like a sepia photograph, a scene
glimpsed in a 'forties movie that's run out.

Some nights you wake to this: in every house
on your own block, dark speaks with different names.
A door slams shut, dogs bark, your neighbor coughs,
a car drives up and leaves. The night's the same,
and yet its worlds are different, worlds apart.
You dream of rooms. You enter someone's life
some nights as though his heart beats in your heart.

The Centennial Review   *Patricia Hooper*

9:00

Waking up late this morning, in full sunlight,
I hear your voices already down in the kitchen,
trying to find the cereal, telling a joke
you've already told, and water faithfully running,
blessing the ceremony. Touching the cupboard,
touching the plate, or each other, we touch something
invisible, like a secret we almost remember,
which earth hints at. Quickly, I touch the blanket
as if in an ancient ritual, taking on texture
and strength from the threads that were once animal-fur.
If I woke in heaven, I'd say *wood, bread,* and your names.

The Centennial Review   *Patricia Hooper*

BARNABOOTH ENTERS RUSSIA

I sit with you at the window
of the lush but battered railway car,

observing the "worn billiard cloth" that is Russia.
We talk sometimes about cities.
Once I saw a city, a dark spot in the distance.
You said it was a cloud. It may have been a cloud.
We agree the trips are going nicely,
for it isn't a single trip but like Russia herself
something pieced from many occasions.
Now and then it occurs to us a trip has been concluded.
Yet we haven't slowed an instant. The throttle hand is steady.
We know these endings with certainty,
and I make a note in my book:
>   what was outside the window,
>   what I was doing at the time,
>   Where you were placed in the longish car.
You are happy with this arrangement.
There is no need for the final arrival
and anyway there is no Russia,
just the large blue "R" laid across a map.
I sit by the window holding your hand.
The sun comes up over blurred fields.
A porter wipes the mist from a glass,
and every few minutes, by common consent,
the trip ends, the trip begins.

Canto   *Paul Hoover*

THE HAIRDRESSER

Years, years she came to me to dress
that thick brown hair.
Short, it took ten years from her
and the brown eyes were a girl's.
Long and scalloped on her head:
a great lady rich in herself
without silk or diamond.
When she got up from the chair
her beauty was my beauty.
The work of my hands turned heads
at traffic lights, stopped men midway in their words.

It was sudden. When she died
they called me in
to make her lovely in the blue boat of her casket.
And I did.
They all said so.
Then they shut the lid of roses on her.
Then they put my beauty in the ground.

Kansas Quarterly   *David Hopes*

SUPPOSE . . .

Suppose the ruler used to mark our days
were magic. Suppose like magnets it could pull

a moving freightload of tomorrows close
enough not just to hear the train whistle
but near enough to check the contents of
each car against the cargo listing. Love,

we'd take off on our private detours then.
Foretell the weather: when the melted ice
would pool the road, when freeze across again,
a ring closing. Beaver and geese have ways.
Indians once, they say, could read the signs.
So, too, old prophets. But we're without the means

to scan the syllables of chugging time,
the links of aye and nay. At best, we can
just read the signals of the birds and arm
against the windmill of the seasons. Dawn
and dusk roll black and white, keys upon
which fingers recapitulate and learn.

Event   *Lewis Horne*

ON HEARING A BEAUTIFUL YOUNG WOMAN DESCRIBE HER CLASS IN PHYSICAL ANTHROPOLOGY

She handles bones, dull gray or ivory hued,
Complete, or chipped and shattered as the age,
The history, explains the true condition of Exhibit X.
She lifts a tibia, examines it with care,
Runs calculations of the height, the weight,
The age, the sex of the fleshed skeleton that strapped
This bone in place and helped articulate a leg
That carried someone somewhere at some time.

There is no grave, nor is this Yorick's skull.
The questions were not answered in that scene.
They are unanswered still and she who holds
This tibia in her hands must still respond
To ancient mysteries, must wonder if all life
Is nothing more than dreams and consciousness
And flesh and breath and love reduced to bones,
The lipless skull of Yorick final cause.

But bones reduce to dust. Then dust is final cause
And desert winds prove arbiter of all that was
Or is or ever will be through all time to come.
The image clears. She sees our vibrant tropics
Wilt and die, our oceans shrivel and distill
To arid wastes until our earth becomes as barren
As the moon, dust layering dust upon the empty plains.
She sighs, then tags a femur, pondering the remains.

Princeton Spectrum   *A. J. Hovde*

OF A MOUSE AND MEN

It came sniffing and nibbling about on the rock terrace
In quick starts and stops, like an animated cartoon image
That wandered off the screen and now, whiskers atwitch,
Scrambled madly about in search of food. Ludicrous mouse!
Ignoring us giant humans behind the window glass
(Who could squash it beneath a boot with a single step),
Ignoring the cat (that could have crunched it in its jaws),
Chittering like a squirrel in its eagerness to play
At life and death with that round body but one leap away.

Most ludicrous indeed! A tail much too long, too thin,
Too stringy pink to trail at ease behind that fur
(A shape too disproportionate to please the eye of man).
The mouse finds crumbs or seed, freezes in place
(Only the jaws and whiskers live until the eating's done),
Becomes so vulnerable we almost shout, "Beware!"
But do not shout. Instead, half fearfully, we look about,
Then turn to the glass again, relieved at last
To find our suicidal surrogate no longer there.

Poetry Newsletter   *A. J. Hovde*

NEWSPAPER HATS

They are no substitutes for gas masks
or lead helmets. But you can shape them
any way you want yourself. Here is one:

the Bishop's hat, and maybe if you make up
a prayer in your head, this one will funnel it up
and save something. Fold this here

and back over, tuck it in: the soldier's dress cap.
The headlines might rub off in your hair,
but that would be part of the job. Unfolding,

back to the original triangle hat—when the sun
blasts through what was an atmosphere, the brim
could provide a brief shade. I had a friend

who taught me these. He lives two states west now,
under the shadow of a mountain on giant shock absorbers,
a hollowed-out mountain no one climbs. Uniforms

with men in them go about their business there,
driving dark trucks over fluorescent streets
underground. Their families pass the food

and talk sometimes at dinner. The way they look
at each other is a story. I sit tonight,
give instructions to no one but the room,

and make newspaper hats for those people, for a friend
I had, for myself. And I try them on, hoping to see
how we wear the things that happen in the world.

New Letters   *Jim Howard*

MONOLOGUE THROUGH BARS

Take this stabbing or that rape—
I've got a record as long as a road.
In seven states I've looted citizens
and left them cooling in their blood.
Ardor's not my problem. Ask my wife.

She says I've got a temper, sure, and that
now and then I'm sulky and withdrawn.
I tend to pull at things—scabs, loose threads,
my love; I lean heavily on sex and friends,
and when they fail me, I'm off.

Chicago last week: on the South Side
I caught a queer looking sideways at me.
He never saw what hit him in the neck—
my fist—or felt the floor. His chin
chipped porcelain from the puking urinal.

Another time, out of cash,
in a whiskey-funk,
I stopped in Tennessee, pistol-whipped a grocer,
then leapt aside, pumping bullets at a noise.
I killed the stockboy, then left, too dazed

to check the register. So what? I wasn't born
this way: no fists, no gun, no rage,
only a dull composure, a settled fetal grin.
I think I shocked my mom—eyes wide,
I snickered at six months.

I've never swung in anger at a friend
or pumped myself for insult or revenge.
My crimes have been haphazard, coming in a tide
that sweeps my senses. Once a doctor
played a game—I went along—he asked me
how I saw myself, if I was like
an ocean or a train. I chose a rifle,
broken down and lightly oiled.
"Who put you together?" he asked,
and I was silent. He left an hour later.

One thing I should tell you: I love my wife.
No matter what, take care of her.
I know I've leaned on her, but even when
I came home blood-drunk, she kept me whole,
she fed me cartridges, she clicked my safety off.

Rhino   *Nelson Hubbell*

CATS AND EGYPT

I've left the thin autumnal air
to come inside for warmth. On the grate
logs dry to dust, then into fire.
The cold reminds me of my age,

and every fire I contemplate
returns my soul to Egypt and bondage.

Back there, the work is massive, crude
beyond the smallness I prefer.
All work is shared in servitude—
no task is small enough for one.
In the harsh demands of man's grandeur,
it's death on death and stone on stone.

The cat regards the ruthless fire,
and I the fire reflected in
his eyes, the mastery they acquire.
He could, if he wanted to,
walk through the fire and turn Egyptian;
it's something any cat can do.

He'd merge into the flames, and then
step out beside the opulent
brown Nile. Like a desert religion,
he blinks forbearance from his eyes.
Curled on my lap, he seems content
to warm himself on my cold thighs.

Southern Humanities Review   *Andrew Hudgins*

PROSPECTUS

I want to live in an old adobe house on the outskirts of Santa Fe
and grow red geraniums in great masses (scarlet against the
                              brown adobe earth)
and walk to the plaza and read my poetry to the multitudes,
standing with my head bare and my heart open in the clear bell-fragile light.
Summers, I'll live like a bird cadging crumbs in the streets
and, winters, I'll be a bear and hibernate till the last snow melts.
And year by year I'll grow browner till I am the color of aged adobe
and year by year my gaze will grow more distant and more clear
till nothing stands beyond my vision.
And then, on the first clear day of an early spring,
I'll walk off toward the mountains, singing a song I made for just
                              that occasion,
a song saying all that I've done and been and all the beauty I've seen,
in a voice like the river coming down in the night out of the mountains.
I will walk till the world is behind me and there is no one
and then I'll lie down still singing and close my eyes and the light
                              will enter me,
gentle as the first light of a New Mexico autumn morning
and clear as that first moment when you find yourself loving someone.
And I'll drift on that light out of my brown used shell toward the mountains,
not singing anymore, but sung.

Cedar Rock   *Albert Huffstickler*

BLACKBERRY WINTER

Though here it is already hot,
The red clover cut, the blackberries
Picked and eaten,
I imagine a place in Tennessee
Where winter tries to outlast
The first of May—

To no avail, like calling Arcady
Again, to say be as you were,
Not modified,
Not changed but as you were only:
The color of the past recurs constantly
In living minds—

And in living minds the past lives,
If only as the stain of blackberries
On a white shirt.
It is the taste that does not remain
The same, that mocks the memory
With sweet, not sour.

The Texas Review   *Peter Huggins*

STRAWBERRIES

PEAR TREE, the sun has reached the corner;
papercup tea and the minor sad singsong
of the Chinese radio station, the slow sun
spelling it: PEAR TREE FRUIT MARKET.

With the round toil, always the round forms of these
    Koreans—
do they think of their terraced farms in the mountains of
    Korea—
snapping the slatted crates, gently lifting the lettuce,
oh careful, the foggy grapes, strawberries.

On either side of the path to Setauket, if you looked
(the spiny leaves hid them), were strawberries,
tiny wild sweet, still warm from the sun,
enough to pierce the heart.
                        That was a lifetime away.

Now, in this piston street, the strawberry lifted
fragrant, freckled, by its green tuft, hangs
like hope
            With these Koreans, in their rumpled clothes,
unpacking parsley, and wet cress, on Second Avenue.

The Massachusetts Review   *Dorothy Hughes*

LETTER TO GARBER FROM SKYE

Dear Fred: I hope this finds you, Marge and children O.K.
We're living on Skye, in Uig, in a homey cottage
high over the bay. Below us two rivers, the Conon

and Rha, enter the sea. Both look trouty and aren't, a trick
peat plays staining the water dark brown and mysterious
where the rivers begin high on the moor. It's windy nearly
all the time, and when you look out the window you think
it's cold. You go out, and it isn't. The people too are like that.
Warmer than you think on first sight, with no throw-away charm
like in cities. The sky, water, vegetation and wind are Seattle.
The panoramic bare landscape's Montana. For me, two
homes in one. More than that, consider how many here live
silent inside like my surrogate father. Don't laugh, but
today I told my wife if I die here, here's where I want
to be buried. She said, me too. I wish I could explain.
Something young inside me says when they visit my grave
I want grass moving sadly and the prolix sea in sight.
On the other hand, dead I won't give a damn. The Scots
are good at that too if that's what you prefer. They are
most accommodating, the Scots, most given to accepting
fate. To be good as these people are, you must have cruelty
deep in your history, must have tested your capacity
for hate long ago and know how bad it can be and what
it can do. There are castles of the cruel in ruin
and megalithic forts. The blood of our mothers has dried.
An old saying: The fate of the Gael is to lose everything.
From my upstairs window where every morning I write hard,
I see Uig pier across the bay. It reminds me
of a small dock years ago on a lake that didn't look
trouty and was. Remember? And these passionate gales
that stunt trees and leave grass bent permanently east
are the same force that took your dock. They're still taking
and still worth it. So what if it all burns out? It burns.
It is the fate of the Gael. It is the fate of the headless
spectre to be forgotten by all. Once his howl was legend
on this island. Now I can't find a soul who knows him.
Not one. They stare at me when I ask. And only a few
old timers remember the water horse. And now what shall
become of us without monsters to pity and fear? The quest
for the autonomous man must have ended in this place
the day before the first tourist arrived. It was, as you
can't imagine, not the failure some scholars maintain,
you included. But you'd have to meet this wind head on
every day with no friend and no family and no
critical vocabulary before how alone we become
would hit home. The fate of the Gael is to lose. Everything
matters because everything dies and that includes storms.
It is calm. The sea does not stir. The hawk has no hard air
to hang on. Up on the moors, the autonomous man is lost
in this autonomous land. He does not answer our cry
to come home. When we light fires, he replies with the dark
silence of early warriors. Until he returns
he remains a threat to all of us who need others, who
need a good time on a dock catching trout, in a cottage
writing a poem for a friend far away. A new saying
I just made up: it is the fate of everyone to lose

the Gael. Five months to go and already I'm rehearsing
good bye, setting my weak mouth hard in the mirror, keeping
tears in check by thinking bad jokes. Did you hear the one
about the American who found so much quiet inside
he couldn't shut up, the way the lonely can't. I can. Dick.

The American Poetry Review   *Richard Hugo*

THE NAMING

i

In the boys' room at Macon Elementary,
Somebody had written something on the wall in black
Ink, a small neat word I thought
Was a name like other names
Scrawled there, a name like Huck or Buck,
Somebody I hadn't met yet, somebody older,
Maybe already walking the dark
Halls of the high school.

But something inside me knew better
Than to ask about it. Whoever
Belonged to a name like that
Could not be spoken of lightly.
Likely he drove fast, smoked,
Carried a quick bright knife.

ii

They brought the bull over in the back
Of a black truck. Lord, he was big. It was big.
The heifer in the pen smelled him and lowed
Loud enough to let him know
It was time. He came down quick
And ready. From the top
Rail of the corral, I saw him rear,
Saw the red flesh swollen bigger than my arm

Go in. They did their dance
In the hoof-marked mud of the pen,
And when they were done, my father
Turned and looked at me hard.
I didn't know what I had seen. But in the spring
They gave the calf my name.

Cimarron Review   *Terry Hummer*

ALL THINGS BEING EQUAL

Folks stopped by our place yestiddy 'bout dinner
  saying the government had sent them
to learn me how to spend my poverty
  brought out buckets of paint
to slop up our two seater
  what hangs over the creek
neat and clean like sunrise

wanted to put a decorative half-moon motif
in the door and move it wuz their very words.

Told 'em warn't nothing so good for purging the soul
  on a cracking cold morning
as to jist set on them seats with the breeze
  blowing upwards.

Funny highfalutin words like de-prived and de-praved
  they laid on me here in Appalachia.
Reckon they knowed now how
  my shotgun talks big too
When I blowed out their tars as they lit out
  a running with their government forms flying in the aire.

Me and a couple a sonsabitches we done got equal yestiddy.

The Mountain Review   *J. Lee Humphrey*

INDIAN SUMMER, 1927

We are watching our old aunts
who sit like eggplants on their cedar chairs
under the beech trees.

The cement steps cool the backs of our legs
and give our skin the fabric
of sand. It is better to color out here
where we can blacken

the margins of our pages and fill in the clouds
with words without being scolded.
The trees are dropping their apples, and if
we kick the overripe ones

which lie on the ground, yellow-jackets fly up
and fly up and the toes
of our shoes turn dark with juice.
How can we believe

thirst when we know the dry grasses
are hoarding moisture in
their secret tunnels and the gourds are swelling
with damp messages?

Der Altweibersommer, ja, ja,
they murmur, and crochet
daisy-patterned bureau scarves,
and sweat in their purple dresses.

Our mother is dying slowly in
the house. Our father has locked
himself in his study with his boat models
and accounts; and we

crayon princesses with hair the color
of loganberries and a river
that falls in love with a maiden but destroys
her image in its flow.

Our elbows hurt from leaning on them,
and our leathery collection
of leaf-money pulled from the rhododendron
is growing curled and brittle.

Inside, the house smells of old bandages,
and the porch cushions are stacked
like toast in one corner of the hall. Mat
is playing Schumann's "Träumerei" on the Victrola.

The air turns its thin music,
and we lie face-down on the blue slate in the hall,
softly tracing the mortar with our fingers.

The Southern Review   *Anne Hussey*

THIS YEAR

I've slept in five houses, but wakened
in one body over and over. My eyes
stung by headlights, sore-boned
at the struggling wheel, I've steered
our goods through each bad weather.
Now our blood's jazzed again
on thin air; the money's ample,
the Rockies huge. We feel
on our way somewhere.

And yet, I ache at how dreams
can swerve to a cliff-edge, wheels
holding barely . . . I think
how prodigal longings are (sparks
echoed in a house of mirrors), how far
from home our destinations: Han-shan
high on Cold Mountain; Lowell
struck down in his cab.

The Ohio Review   *Joseph Hutchison*

IN NO WAY

I am of the family of the universe, and with all of us together
I have no fear of being alone; I can reach out and touch a rock
or a hand or dip my feet in water. Always there is somebody
close by, and when I speak I am answered by a plane's roar or
the birds' whistle or the voices of others in conversation far
apart from me. When I lie down to sleep I am in the company of
the dark and the stars.

Breathe to me, sheep in the meadow, and sun and moon, my father
and my father's brother, kiss me on the brow with your light;
my sister, earth, holds me up to be kissed. I smile at you
both and spread my arms in affection; I lay myself down at full
length for the earth to know I love it too and am never to be
separated from it. In no way shall death part us.

The Ontario Review   *David Ignatow*

SUMMER STREET

The dry afternoon scraping the rooftops.
Two children skipping amidst a whirlpool of orange dust.
A shadow like an ancient woman that passes
leaving a wind of sadness.
The time that elapses.
The soul that turns the color of the earth.
The afternoon that bends over like an arch
through which the children pass
taken by their mothers' hands.
The rain that does not fall.
Only the ashen air that whitens the forehead's temples.
Only the fire that penetrates the blood and dyes
the eyes yellow.
Only the life like a dead animal
stretched out beneath the sky.
And in the air the sun drying the black-and-blue marrow of time.
And the dismal wind from the vast plain.
And the heavy steps.
And the children already aged returning beneath the arch of the
    afternoon.
And the stones.

Northwest Review   *Ana Ilce*
                         — Translated from the Spanish (Nicaragua)
                                          by Steven White

THE LETTERS OF A NAME

How many names for what bees see?
Leaves hear them humming in the blueprint
of eons to come in the summer.

How many names for what leaves see?
Figure the angle of the sun's descent.
Go draw a flower to the light.
Marigolds, Four O'Clocks.

Some are made to tally up the sums
of artifacts, spoor, fossil remains,
to count the letters of a name.
Not I with my back to the St. John's

Fire in a garden where you sketch me
in a few brief strokes starting
with the circle of my eyes. How many
names for what they see in waves

of the evening? Blue rising in the stem
of a flame, the fastening on of stars
to the sky, is not listed in the manual
of how love looks in a crouched position.

Tomorrow you will draw me out of the shadows.
Tomorrow I will let you take my name away.

Beyond Baroque   *Colette Inez*

MEMORY, A SMALL BROWN BIRD

From the balcony you watched her walking
among fallen masonry on the hillside,
golden dust-light of autumn sprawled at your feet,
a small brown bird cooing in the hazelbush.

The wooden floor of your room leaned
to the window where you first saw her
with two brown dogs,
asleep in the dry fountain.

Use your imagination. Take her
to England. Let her sit with gentlemen
in the parlor discussing birds,
sipping the soft red glow of the best years.

Walk with her on Sundays. Stand quietly watching
a small group of nuns talking softly by the dock,
a flight of teal wheeling out over the lake.
Help her imagine swans

gliding under a wooden bridge,
the moss-covered stones, the wood
and coconut smell of chestnuts
cracking under foot.

Don't tell her about your past.
It will mean nothing unless her own
grew choices. Memories select themselves.
Teach her to choose the future.

And from the rooms of the sad orphans, watch
as the quiet stranger who has finally reached you
turns to look back at his daughter.
There is no one to keep her from leaving.

The Virginia Quarterly Review   *Rich Ives*

GULL LAKE REUNION

Finally you will grow tired of it all.
Even when you settle your rustling self
on a beach with home and pines,
the lake people spill their vodka
in your sand and curse hilariously
on your precarious dock. In moonlight
they replace your door with an open invitation.

Tonight you urge the lake breeze to carry
no sounds but the muffled creaking of wood
and the small confusion of waves against the shore.

In this part of the world, summer has come
in its most shy and captive mood,
the sun having slipped away in a chill,
the pines folding their branches on one another
shadowing the darkest minute of light for miles.
The breeze that folds back strands of hair
against your head suggests a reason
for staying, and being, and settling yourself
alone in the cool sand. The lake can untangle
your spirit in the way it cannot untangle itself.

Down the beach, near midnight,
the mumbled phrases of neighbors,
and the drone of a boat across the darkness.
A buoy sops the water beyond the dock,
the land barely speaks.

Poetry   *Kelly Ivie*

OUT OF THE DEEPNESS

High in the mountains of Soviet Armenia
at Lake Sevan: the sun, clean, bright,
warming the cool thin air off the reaches
of the lake, the skin of our arms and faces.
Dark, hopeful eyes of children wanting gum,
candy, something American. They bring
bouquets of wild red flowers.
The bus driver, after the long engineheating
climb out of Yerevan, opens the gray hood,
shows me the leak in the radiator, shrugs,
and adds more water. I buy a bottle
of one ruble wine at the "gastronom" here
(for later, for the remainder of the run
over the cloudhung mountains to Georgia).

We stop for lunch, for trout freshly brought
out of the deepness of the lake.

A busload of Istanbul Armenians
fill up a long table beside us.
They have yet to know their first, cherished
glimpse of Ararat. Now they rise, singing
the saddest sounding song I've ever heard.
Their wineglasses catch the light of the sun.
The eaglefaced grandfather, surprising
with a voice of warm mercury, vibrant cadences,
leads them in a toast:
"To the Americans! To Peace!"
My skin buzzes. I turn,
and touch my glass to his.

The Spirit That Moves Us   *William (Haywood) Jackson*

SONG OF THE INTRUDER

So cool and so composed
butter won't melt
in the hollow of your chest
where I can see a heartbeat
just the same

So tranquil, so alone
your eyes so shuttered
lips so closed
as if they never spoke
though I have felt them whisper
just the same

So far, so inaccessible
that I despair of touching deeper
than your outer shell but
just the same

I have to try
bend over and bite hard
the inside of your thigh, and
roaring
with startled
pain and pleasure
you pull me down
for my just
punishment
which
just the same

for all its giddy laughter
holds a smarting edge

The Malahat Review   *Maria Jacobs*

THE FAMOUS OUTLAW STOPS IN FOR A DRINK

I ride into town.
The moon splatters above the buildings
like a bullet
hitting sand.
I hear
the piano clanking in the saloon,
a burst of laughter,
doors swinging and clapping together,
the buzzing of chairs moving in and out.
From every window, women stare,
their faces like dim candles.
With a glance, I blow
them out one by one.

When I push in the swinging doors,
everything stops.
I order eight whiskies

and two women.
Behind me, the hiss of voices.
In a few minutes, the music starts up again.
As I drink, pinching a woman's fat breast,
I see
the image of my gun
on every eye.

Poetry Now   *David James*

CASE

This is a tale of the body, its inert
material, sullen texture, which I do
not understand. Passive and massive it is
tedious, tedious, as it sits in a

fatherly armchair, refusing to get up
to look for its slippers and the day's paper.
While the mind is no doubt worrying about
how bloated and repulsive the body is

becoming and wondering why it doesn't
care to rise and jog several times around
the block in the rain. The mind thinks, without a
body, hair would not need to be blown dry, chins

squared, eyebrows lifted and so forth. All of us
could thus and in such a manner have more time.
This is a marriage between a drugged slug and
an aerial acrobat. The mind has more

than once applied for divorce, but the body
doesn't want to be bothered with procedures.
The body wants to be left alone to sit
in the sun's way and to spread, like some kind of

vegetable matter, into the loam of the
garden. The mind would like to strangle it, but
lacks that kind of strength. Oh no, this is not a
blissful coupling! Often the mind is as quick

as some sprightly animal traveling by
way of hanging vines with all the ancestral
energy the body lacks, in its torpor,
waiting for supper, the smell of food raking
through its middle like a red hot fingernail.

The New Yorker   *Phyllis Janowitz*

SKIN

We know that skin is the border of life,
the tight fit that describes our place,
and that we are remains of the dense matter
sculpted away by the cosmic knife.

We enjoy the mind's rush to extremities,
its thirsting at each windowed pore;
we avoid the freakish mirrors that put us *out there*
with the needless rocks and trees.

And we thrill to the laws of motion
by which we change the shape of things
with every stride and stretch,
bringing the wavering world to redefinition.

But in saying "we" we think "I"—
growing cold, we tell tales of transcendence,
union, spirit. We denounce the frailty of flesh.
And yet our skins hold the one and only life.

The Greenfield Review   *Philip K. Jason*

ENCIRCLEMENT

The day turns heavily on its axis.
Clearing the grimness behind the window,
My shadow follows at my heels,
While a hundred times around the table I revolve.
The sky sweeps me up. The earth pulls me downward.

I envy the immobility of objects.
Along the length and breadth and in the depths
They endure—do not touch them!
As a trunk springing from the earth
Penetrates the heart of a tree,
So has the force of gravity propped itself against them.
Dust has settled. A hundred years may wait
Peacefully. Time has taken a rest for them,
As the world has come to a standstill in four silences.

Yet I—Oh, how I suffer and agonize.
In vain to an unyielding corner I cling
With my paces. I cannot budge.

New Orleans Review   *Mieczyslaw Jastrun*
                                     —Translated from the Polish
                                          by Benjamin Sher

STARLINGS

Outside the window, at the top
of a chimney, two starlings are bathing
in soot. In a flock they grind away
at the grass, fly away like wagons
with sticking wheels. How they make
their presumptuous wishes,
what they practice in solitude
must be therapy, concord, and sleep.
They hang there in some indifferent
tree, dream their boring dreams
which they consider luminary.

They have always just-sprung from some horn
of plenty, they hop like rabbits,
like a gang of kids. As they pound
up to the trees they are like a veil
trailing, a veil you pray beneath.
They are like prayers for the lifting
of that veil. They are not beautiful.

It is cold. I lean at the radiator.
In one of my panes of glass, a man fills
his birdbath, the stream of water glitters
all this way to the other side of the street.
They might bathe, they might bathe forever
and be yet speckled, gritty, holy only
by name. They bear their stars
crudely, yet believe me, they are Earth's
creatures; suet and seed are cool and good.

The Iowa Review   *Laura Jensen*

PLEXUS AND NEXUS

I can prove who I am. I draw my wallet like
a six-gun. Look what all these numbers show:
core, corpse, corpuscle in many systems. Stopped,
I see in the mirror an upturned radio.

That tall young nun studies the mirror daily,
learning to show emotion on her face.
That black boy sits in the darkness staring at
the image in the mirror of his race.

But I with light and sticky step may travel
the web of the world, springing the tense strands,
sensing the signals at each intersection,
darting the way my heart (it seems) commands.

I am the fly in the network and the network.
I exist at many levels, if at all.
I am the thousand images receding
in every surface of the mirrored hall.
I diffuse at the speed of light.
                              Remember me!
the honest ghost, the wave, pulse, the fleet shape
imprinted on and by all I have met.

Experience runs through me like a tape.

Passages North   *Judson Jerome*

PSYCHOLOGY TODAY

My belly joined the Belly Potential Movement.
My brain took EST, my left eye last was seen
swimming with Swami Riva, my right was rolfed.

I'm actualized, if you know what I mean,
transcending, getting ready for the future,
fulfilled with helium, unstressed, piecemeal.

My organs drift asunder above the circus,
each bulbous with capacity to feel—
eastward the nose and south the probing tongue,

each toe afloat and powdered like a clown,
aurora borealis genitalia
higher than acupuncture can bring down.

Why then this aching? Surely not my soul—
for none was found when all was picked apart.
And, strings all cut, who would expect such
        throbbing

from one gland left on earth—my leaden heart?

The Sun   *Judson Jerome*

NIGHT FLIGHT

The others are tunneled in sleep
sprawled under blue airline blankets
like the late-comers to her last
family reunion.

She is the only one awake.

Trying to fix their place
by the vague constellations
of roads and mountain towns
rolling off in the dark
below them,
            she watches the inside
starboard engine die.

The prop slowly resolves itself
from the shined disc of its spinning,
stops,
            then slants like a broken limb
off the wing. She has already
tightened her belt. Leaning
to counter the lurch
that doesn't come, she swallows
the urge to scream,
lets even her grown daughter sleep
while she waits for the calm voice
to wind around her fear
like a tourniquet.

THERE IS NO NEED FOR ALARM

On the midnight flight
from Denver to Chicago
She is the only one who knows.

The others are deafened in sleep.
Her listening pierces the mask
of snores and air conditioning,
slips into the regular stroke
of the three sound engines.
Her quiet breathing fuses
each rivet, snugs the plane's
lapped skin around them.

As long as she breathes
like a surgeon, listens
like a mother with a sick child
sleeping in the next room,
her family is safe.

All night the truth
of the frozen engine
burns in her eyes.

Tendril   *Don Johnson*

NANCY, YOU DANCE

Nancy, you dance your days
with pizzicato steps
and speech precise as glass,

your small, powerful heart
hummingbird fast in flight,
body taut as a snake

gracing its way through grass.
Nancy, thinking of you,
I think of life on point,

slimly muscled and tuned
to respond and to move
delicately and quick,

with subtlety and strength;
I think of the ballet
of elegance you share,

the play of your sure lips
on mine; the skeleton
tiny, fragile beneath

your sleek skin; and your scent
in the still-spinning air
once we have done our dance.

The Texas Review   *Michael L. Johnson*

BECAUSE

she married him because
he was always bumping into walls
and when he saw the moon

he saw the coin of an ancient empire
and when he saw a tangle of woods
he saw a stained-glass window
and when she left him
he saw a joy in winged flight
and no walls could hold him

Focus Midwest   Paul Johnson

BECOMING IS PERFECTION

Something about your smile is more than you—
That curves in a long tangent to the light
Or lofting in a spiral on the air
Rides a current of silence out of sight:

Something about you seems to soar. And yet,
Though yours, it is becoming more than you
With every smile, with every arc of wing
Through empty air to sweep out only blue.

Nothing is simple; nothing that you know
Explains the easy arching of the light
Over the world that lies deep and unchanged
Below in certain turning toward night.

Becoming is perfection. If your heart
Takes flight like robins in the morning sky,
Catch at the wind and never wonder why:
The secret of flight is hidden from those who fly.

The Southern Review   Tom Johnson

JULY

You came with your sorrows drifting through your eyes
Like blossoms the great wind had seized and strewn
Over a field of sunlight. O my love,
My heart commends that hour, though it has cost
Enduring grief, enduring rage. You are
The silence and the trembling of my blood
Today as then. Near thirty years and still
My hand relives the tightness of your hand.
My mouth and eyes remember all their hunger,
My mind still feeds upon our weary calm,
Our silences, our quarrels and our joy.
I am fit to praise your beauty, I confess
This haunting purity, this brave dismay.
Whatever good I have is what you gave.

Occident   W. Ralph Johnson

THE HOT DAY AND HUMAN NATURE

Three little ones splash in the shallows along the beach
As the four young adults lounge, and shift positions,
Advantage, and slowly strip
(The offspring arrived in their bathing suits).
The older male reclines on his back and inflates
A large white plastic water toy which rests
On his knees and chest as he purposely breathes, and then,
Paternal, finds his kids safe places to play in the lake
(Who are now clambering in the Y's of tree trunks
And changing places, and squealing with anger or joy).
The younger male is chippier, more aggressive,
Simulates mounting the younger female, jokes
And sometimes sulks. His turn amusing the youngsters
Consists of taking away their toy for himself,
And then, repentant, letting them climb aboard him.
The females are siblings; the younger primps and shouts
At her niece and nephews; the older wears
A white polyester suit which stretches to show
The effects of giving birth. She calls her mate
From the water; he comes, and after a scolding
Submits, lies face down, while she sits astride
And the three friends closely examine the skin on his back
And make a fuss about whatever they find. He is forced
To turn over, and wonders why he thinks of deja vue.
When bluish clouds obscure the godlike sun
And doubting breezes rearrange the surface of the lake,
They thoughtfully dress, summon the children,
And head for the car
                    and head for home
And soft drinks from the fridge in thermal cups
Of plastic; on the outside, pretty summer scenes.
And up in the kitchen cupboard in the heat,
The chocolate coating on the biscuits softens
And readies to melt on their fingers
And their opposable thumbs.

The Canadian Forum   *Gordon Johnston*

THESE DAYS

These days the river
echoes softly under ice,
and grasses stiffen,
and love puts on a hardened face.

And I, the scholar,
can but quote
the words of others
and add a little note.

Winter is a bookshelf full
of choices I can own

when the grass is green again
and bending and half grown.

The Christian Century   *Robert Jones*

ANNE SEXTON

(a photograph)

Luminous almonds have
a straightforward
effect of serenity.

Yet, they shall
remain open only
on this print.

I would not
accept the fact
without that October
date in 1974.

For the hair
swirling about those
ivory cheek bones—
like Leonardo waves—
outlines élan vital.

But your lips
appear compressed as
if they closed
over The Death
Notebooks with an
absolute need to
redeem The Christ.

Did you believe
that he rescinded
the much vaunted
Auto-da-Fé
when the blood
vacated his brain?

We wanted you
to live!

However,
you had already
sniffed eternity and,

in spite of
us, were savoring
your last concealment . . .

Anne,
have you made
peace with peace?

Pteranodon   *Hans Juergensen*

CORNELIA'S WINDOW

She was newly betrothed, and
etched her name on the window
in the fashion of her time.
There it is—Cornelia Lee—
see how it glitters like a patch
of Jack Frostwork the sun missed,
a hundred years after her death?

The glass is so rippled that
each tree seems to bend like
a silver iced tea spoon
piercing a drink; and if you
squint, you see the blue Virginia
hills in the distance turn to
air-starved dolphins, and ascend.

If you could sleep in her bed,
you'd sense an ocean overhead
in the attic, where the rainbarrels—
dozens—were kept in case the house
was hit by lightning; and, rising,
you would see through rippled dreams
the world as witnessed by Miss Lee.

Ponchartrain Review   *Julie Kane*

LIFE STORY

(for Jeff Schwartz)

I know the story, how
the spider mates and dies
and then the old haymow
is thick with spiders,

how in generic terms
there is no death, and life
cleaves to starfish and worms
under the knife,

how the word just learned
appears in every paragraph
until it is burned
like a lover's epitaph

into the brain, how
even a stupid passion will
not be killed, but now
in a blizzard of fine silk

will fasten its filaments
and dormant seed
on any object for the chance
to breed.

The Massachusetts Review   *J. Kates*

IN THE YEAR OF TWO THOUSAND

Dovid,
my twenty-
three year old son,
good to see you in
the year of two thousand,
in mid-August of your life,
when I will be a near and far
memory to you. O I know how
I will yearn for you, biting my own dust.

You may
still dream of
me as a torn
leaf dreams in wind to
return to its father
tree. You may see my poems
burn, in late autumn, in the sad,
flickering gold of the tameracks,
before the needles fall in splendid death.

O see
my life cleansed
by the brisk light
of the first frost, at
dusk, when the scorched sun wheels
as a windfall apple, hear
me calling you as a brook locked
beneath ice: Dovid, my only one,
you are beyond my last night, my first dawn.

The Smith   *Menke Katz*

CUBA

In my dream, Joey, both of us were alive
& walking in Delaware Park, the dew
glistening on our shoes.
Neither of us spoke of your death.
We talked of other mornings, in winter,
when we'd drive up Hopkins
home from Bethlehem Steel—

two washed-out Marxists, sure suckers
for the good intention & the dialectic
under every rock. The blue snow
swirling the blue streets of South Buffalo,
& the streetlights hazed into swell-bellied
moons.   And to pass the time
you always had a story . . .
about the Navy, or a woman,
or the way the sea shimmered
at night off the Moroccan coast.
Next year, you'd say. Next year for sure
you were going to Cuba, leave the snow
& the mills, cut cane for a living.
Come on, Joey, I'd say, you'll be lucky
to make it out of the country; & anyway,
I've heard it before—you change your life
more often than your underwear.

Something was always trying to get out
when you'd talk. Friday nights
at *Locklin's,* you'd be pouring existentialism
down some 15 year-old's throat, & her
loving it: your hands flapping, your cigarette
leaving a smoky trail of enthusiasm
you could never bring yourself
to believe . . .
                            Who needs it.
Who needs it, you said
that time after Michael's funeral.
Our backs to the bar, we nodded
in unison. For once
we believed you, knew what you meant,
all of us stuck with what we knew
we were—sentimental & drunk
& fattening into our thirties.

All winter, brain reamed by booze,
you wanted to die. None of us knew,
though anyone could see it:
that grand gesture of denial
hovering just outside
your skin . . . that it was as close
as you'd ever get to Havana.
Sundays on the West Side,
weighing 260 & browsing for a coronary,
how you'd hit the bakeries for cannoli.
Or those mornings after work,
dreaming you were out in the cane
as we roared up Hopkins in your Olds 88
& you'd lean out the window shouting
eat dust you bourgeois creeps,
how it was one jazzy epiphany after another
right up to the moment

you shoved the gun in your mouth
& took off.

New Letters   *Lawrence Kearney*

THE TOURIST

I have not gone like a pilgrim.
I have walked on earth a tourist,
Annoyed, and thought myself solemn—
Neurotic to know the surest

Route of traveling without missing
An attraction. I've lived my life
A loud-mouthed, legend-dismissing
Intruder, rude to guides and wife,

A handler, a foolish spender
(Sucker for any swank hotel,
Big dealer with the fruit vendor),
A fallen angel loosed from hell

Shopping all the brimstone bazaars.
I have been frankly unabashed
At cultivated valleys, stars—
Confident my hours could be cashed.

But now, passport and injection
Void, the autumn changes find me
With a tetanus-like infection
In my heart. Rusty leaves wound me—

Saffron leaves—a glory like theirs
Gladdens, homesickens me, and I
Vacation from vacation's cares,
Aware I have begun to die.

Poem   *Garret Keizer*

BEFORE THE DIVE

If only I could love
as a whale, simply and directly
without fear of drowning or failing.
If only I could brush my arm
against your side
or caress your belly and open myself
in spite of harpoons and guns,
risking scares, wearing wounds like banners,
crying:
        "See! See! I have been brave
enough to love.
I have laid open my breasts
        to kisses and knives,
Trusting, completely trusting
another human, that species

most dangerous and untrustworthy of all."
If only I could swim beneath your body
    and reveal my colors
resplendent
in the morning light,
and move, slowly, lithely, full with joy
above the reef
and awaken to play, to plunge
to the abyss and sing,
    streamlining, surfacing, soaring,
        sounding
for miles,
a burst of breath, again and again and again
till once more I plunge,
we plunge, together,
      flukes flashing
  silver
before the dive.

The Hollins Critic   *Elizabeth Kempf*

OLD MEN PITCHING HORSESHOES

Back in a yard where play has grooved a ditch,
Old men in shirtsleeves congregate to pitch
Dirt-burnished iron. With appraising eye,
One sizes up a peg, hoists and lets fly—
A clang resounds as though a smith had struck
Sparks from a shoe, and his fling, out of luck,
Rattles in circles. Hitching up his face,
He swings again—fresh weight inhabits space
To drop as gently as a new-laid egg
And land with loving arms around its peg
Like one arrived to greet a distant brother.
Shouts from one outpost, mutters from the other.

Now changing sides, each pitcher sternly moves
As his long-ripened dignity behooves
Down the bare path of earth where August flies
And leaves of air in warm distortions rise,
To stand ground, fling, kick dust with all the force
Of shoes still hammered to a living horse.

The Hampden-Sydney Poetry Review   *X. J. Kennedy*

FISH STORY

*(for the Brown Hotel, Des Moines, Iowa,
and its aquarium-walled lobby)*

Once the family meeting place
  on shopping days
  to the capitol city,
  now it looks at me

with its fish eyes
across the years.

We kids, passing time,
stare back
eyeball to eyeball
with fish in the wall aquariums
on every side
of that fishy lobby.

Identifying everyone:
aunts, uncles, neighbors,
but especially teachers,
we see Miss Fugatt
frustrated to a frazzle
bumping her nose on the glass
and breathing bubbles of despair.

Never mind, never mind, Miss Fugatt,
that we didn't study our Latin
or our history as you wished.
Now we, your students,
are caught with you
in the swish of history's currents.

Like you, we swim hard and long
and on and on,
bulbous eyed
and bloody gilled,
straining upstream
against the current,
we swim the watery years.

Blue Unicorn   *B. Jo Kinnick*

CUBIST BLUES IN POLTERGEIST MAJOR

A Classical key:
        the harmonic interval

is limited.
        Appreciated by the
distance of at least
        half a century.

Taken apart,
        John Cage is still
        degenerate.
        You can still cube
Chopin.
        Apostasize him
into new music.

Yet somewhere
        resurrected nazis
are still burning Mendelssohn.

The Christian Century   *Allan F. Kipp*

LETTER TO FRANCES

Was that love or just a room on the outward stream
we wandered into and couldn't leave,
with its bed too short for sleeping
and the passion and the anger and the dreams
that mixed like blood along the walls
and burned the air each time we came in.

And I never wrote you. And after all those letters.
It wasn't you well know for lack of caring.
No, it was simply that so much was spoken,
so much written and felt and seen,
that only silence itself could both
give back and open. Was that Frances?

Was it separate? Did we ask?
Yes, and just as I remember curving
into a silence this very evening
as of the bone and blood wrap of your arms,
it wasn't just sex the flesh I kissed,
it wasn't only breast erect to my touch—

it was the all of the whole warp,
eye, mind, and spirit force stretching
out beyond each sense I could arouse.
And it's all always you altogether
waking out toward me and bringing
that sheer cloth of life and womanness,

that bent and turning, difficult, not
quite devious, up and down interior
constantly seeking and masking itself
in an endless, perpetual, perpetuating change
which, like a river branching and forking,
you alone have and keep and know.

And if there were any simplicities
I might have some proposal or ending,
this might be a letter or you might
walk on in, sit down, let fall those hands
and the alabaster grain of your face, and stay.

Harper's Magazine   *William Kistler*

THE DOLL HOUSE

I view the backless rooms
cluttered with miniature life
tiny beds and tables and chairs
tilting mirrors and porcelain tubs
and I slip into tunnels of time
child-tears ago and dream
of rag and wire mothers and fathers
and boards and nails
and know that sorrow dust

can slip beneath the best of puttied doors
and the safe ward is never certain
nor remorse long lost in that tiny
potbellied kitchen and with love
beside myself I haul the baggage up again
to breathe in a new moon and
swallow family with pain.

Cedar Rock   *Darlene Button Kitzman*

J'ACCUSE

                    I denounce those who are normal
for being so dull and so cruel, and
the authorities who encourage this. I denounce
those who believe with evangelical passion
for reminding us not of belief
but of passion.
                    I cite volume twelve,
The Need to Punish, for volume one, *The Duty
to Punish.*
                    I denounce the vacancy.
Mutton for jackal, bishop for bludgeon, logician
for wart;
                    I denounce footpads, de Lesseps,
Curnonsky-le-grand, I denounce Danzig, Warsaw, Prague.
Evenhandedly,
with malice aforethought, based on the evidence,
bearing no grudges, in spite of the odds, considering
the consequence, without premeditation,
in nobody's pocket,
I denounce Ras Tafari Makkonen for Finland.

                    Day for night I blame, I blame
the weary for the rested. Arse upright
the same way round, I blame those chronically
in limbo for those
eternally under sedation.
    Exquisite tincture: I drink from your etched crystal.
    Spiritual healer: here is your nameless tonic.
    Coat tree: where is your empty nest?
                    Let us blame
Bismarck for Napoleon, Mussolini for Julius Caesar.
Mended stocking, torn pyjama.
                    This sullen wine
I impugn, this sour waiter. I implicate
this baguette and that brioche.
I bring Hetty Green to the bar
and Martha Hanau to the bar, and I accuse them.
I bring Sigmund to the bar, I bring Karl and Carl
and Albert. I bring the fullness to the bar
and I accuse the fullness for this pod of earth
and for the vacancy,

for which I equally accuse the vacancy.
I cry out against the visible star
and recriminate the invisible ax.

                     Right hand
and left, I denounce them.
Second rib and first, I denounce them.
Pomegranate, serpent's skin,
microscope, paramecium,
busted bunion, broken shoe,
ironmonger,
toothache.

           Eye for eye, palm for palm,
cuspid for cuspid,
laughter for laughter for laughter
long forgotten comme tout le monde *je les en accuse.*

Antaeus   *Peter Klappert*

"CHEW MAIL POUCH"

when i was young
the old man would muster us together
every sunday for ritual rides
in the country to see america
while it was still here and beautiful
my sister and me in the back seat
playing the games
parents always instruct kids to play
to keep us behaved and occupied
she'd count the billboards on the right side
i'd count the ones on my side

she always won though
each time i noticed cows or horses
or farm girls feeding chickens
i'd lose count

but i got to see america
while it was still here and beautiful—
long ago rides on country roads
my sister taking
accurate billboard census
mom and the old man arguing
about whose fault it was
about something i did wrong again
and i never counted enough billboards

no matter how i tried
my sister won the prize
of naming the next game
which was always billboard counting
while i became lost
among trees and streams

and big gray barns leaning
slightly to the wind

The Georgia Review   D. L. Klauck

BRIGHT WINTER MORNING

I watch airplanes land
and fly from a hidden field.
They are silver birds that dive
and sweep bare silver trees.
Part of me flies there,
a bright dream in blue air.

But I find all dreams age silver.

South of here flies a dream
flag above a red land. Its blue
field, silver tree and crescent
moon deep under night sky
are a dream standard. In light
the land's a swamp of scrub and clay
that's no dream in Carolina.

Now I think of you . . .

At a great distance I dream you
silver. My thought, a bright star
or comet in a forest of dark trees,
smiles and brightens
before your eyes.

The Sun   *Chris Klein*

MY LOVE FOR ALL THINGS WARM AND BREATHING

I have seldom loved more than one thing at a time,
yet this morning I feel myself expanding, each
part of me soft and glandular, and under my skin
is room enough now for the loving of many things,
and all of them at once, these students especially,
not only the girl in the yellow sweater, whose
name, Laura Buxton, is somehow the girl herself—
Laura for the coy green mellowing eyes, Buxton
for all the rest, but also the simple girl in blue
on the back row, her mouth sad beyond all reasonable
inducements; and the boy with the weight problem,
his teeth at work even now on his lower lip, and
the grand profusion of hair and nails and hands and
legs and tongues and thighs and fingertips and
wrists and throats, yes, of throats especially,
throats through which passes the breath that joins
the air that enters through these ancient windows,
that exits, that takes with it my own breath, inside
this room just now my love for all things warm and
breathing, that lifts it high to scatter it fine and

enormous into the trees and the grass, into the heat
beneath the earth beneath the stone, into the
boundless lust of all things bound but gathering.

The Hiram Poetry Review   *William Kloefkorn*

TO MY SISTER, FROM THE TWENTY-SEVENTH FLOOR

They're beautiful, really, three
ebony flowers staining the screen
above the chief resident's chrome projector.
We meet daily in a sane yellow room
to chart their growth, low voices
more toxic than the disease. Earlier
I ran out into the corridor, wandered
its antiseptic space until the nurse
found my hand. Her own, silk like yours,
guiding me back to the shifting
of perfect flesh, thighs
vibrant under careful white skirts,
all starch and efficiency . . .

Nights, I'm awake
above the denseness of morphine and Seconal,
grateful for the small light
escaping the bathroom, the flood
of faces from our childhood
ridiculous against formal blue porcelain.

More surgery, they· say,
is out of the question. *Francine,*
you would not recognize me like this!
Balding, eyes drawn against the pallor
of cobalt. I would not tell them
where you live, can't
let you see any of this. Mornings
are more difficult: the hard
fluorescence, poached eggs and toast.
It's morning *now* and they violate my bed
with fresh linen. I pace the floor
avoiding windows, while the earth,
twenty-seven floors below, is absorbent
beneath its veil—black asphalt and cars,

weeds inching up as flowers, unopposed.

Willow Springs Magazine   *Michael Knoll*

PRIMARY NUMBERS

You look at yourself in the mirror, nothing;
you look at your neighbor, nothing;
you see people in the distance, nothing;
nothing when the sun shines,
nothing when it's dark,

nothing time and time again
and somewhat less composed.
You step over the threshold onto the street,
into the darkest brightness
and the brightest darkness,
and suddenly you're there
in the midst of clarity.
That's you, that's he
and that's me—
no other salvation,
no special doors to go through,
no skills needed—
Everything's simply as it is
and yet linked to
pure primary numbers.

The Malahat Review   *Edvard Kocbek*
—Translated from the Slovanian
by Herbert Kuhner and Peter Kersche

ISOLATION WARD

These germs are medusan: a touch,
A careless breath and pulsing men
Stiffen cold and rigid as stones.
All that comes near must be fed
Through chutes to the furnace jaws.

Parasites reign in these rooms:
Patients glow inside like steel boilers,
Stoking the feverish fires of infection
With food that once quickened their blood.

I must seem a vampire in their eyes:
Hovering in my sterile robes, searching
For the gaudy clues to their diseases.
Mummified from toxic touch, I reach
With plastic hands and breathe through gauze.

It must be morning now: I hear the whine
Of garbage trucks as their jaws clench down.
Shift's done; I shed my plastic skins
And feed the hungry furnace with these robes.

Outside, the stone chimney sucks the furnace
Of fevered flames, blowing flakes into the sky:
Ash swirls like snowflakes on the passers-by.

The Hiram Poetry Review   *Robert L. Koenig*

THE MAGIC WORDS

are not Abracadabra or anything slippery and remote.
The real magic words are these: I love myself
more than I love you.

Anyone's life can be transformed if he actually loves
his ass more than all the others, believes that those
blue veins in his legs are lovely as major waterways
and will own those thoughts that are always there
in the dark behind the eyes.

At one time or another we all exclaim, "Oh, how
wonderful. I'll say them first thing tomorrow."
But few really mean it because it is more fun
to be coached.

Can you remember? Or do you want me to whisper
in your beautiful ear.

Beyond Baroque   *Ronald Koertge*

PICTURE OF LITTLE LETTERS

I think I like this room.
The curtains and the furniture aren't the same,
Of course, but the light comes in the window as it used to
In the late morning, when the others had gone to work.
You can even shave in it. On the dresser with the mirror
Are a couple of the pictures we took one afternoon
Last May, walking down the alley in the late sunlight.
I remember now how we held hands for fifteen minutes

Afterwards. The words meander through the mirror
But I don't want them now, I don't want these
        abbreviations.
What I want in poetry is a kind of abstract photography
Of the nerves, but what I like in photography
Is the poetry of literal pictures of the neighborhood.

The late afternoon sunlight is slanting through the window
Again, sketching the room in vague gestures of discontent
That roll off the mind, and then only seem to disappear.
What am I going to do now? And how am I going to sleep
        tonight?

A peculiar name flickers in the mirror, and then disappears.

The Paris Review   *John Koethe*

PHIL

I remembered today
that you were afraid of birds.
Once, as we walked along,
you stepped out of your way
to avoid meeting a sparrow.
A sparrow, Phil.

You are dead of cancer
at forty-seven. The phone rings
at six in the morning,

and we press the cold news
to our cheek like a doll
with a horrible face.
Down a gray road at dawn,
from pole-top to pole-top,
the black bird of your death flaps,
calling our names.

Cottonwood Review   *Ted Kooser*

HOME

You arrive in Paradise feverish with anticipation, assuring
yourself that everything will be perfect: no migraine headaches,
no ambulance sirens, no goodbyes. & it's true—the view from
your sitting room is breathtaking, the service is impeccable, the
food enticingly garnished, & altho the water tastes slightly
metallic, there is always the coke machine in the lobby. & the
climate—the sort of weather you love—one glorious day on the
heels of another. You stroll down the beach under the mangroves
& seagrape trees in love, as you were on Earth, with the word
oceano, white seagulls, the bronzed & half-naked women. Women
who are everything you have always dreamed, & yours for the taking.
Truly a lecher's heaven. Yes, everything's perfect—perfect
by definition. Till one afternoon in an unguarded mood you confess
to yourself that the cuisine is without flavor & the wine flat,
that the celestial muzak piped into your suite, however mellifluous,
jangles your nerves. How you wish you could turn on the radio &
hear Monk or Dylan or even the 6:00 o'clock news. You long, if
the truth be known, for a cup of cold water. As for the women,
however lovely to look at, to the touch they are as lifeless as
the pages of the magazines from which they were drawn, & as weightless
& predictable as the figments of your own imagination. It is just
then—at that very instant—that the thread of a name & face catches
the light on what remains of the delicate film of your cortex—
the wraith of a memory—& escapes. You call to it desperately
over & over, but it will not return, tho its residue lingers on
your tongue. Such is the other side of God's marvelous amnesia.
From that day forward you are lost. You pace in distraction along
the Elysian beach obsessed with the need to recall who it was &
what it must have been like. How insufferable, at such moments,
is the glare of Paradise! & so it is that with only your foolish
heart for a witness you begin to long bitterly for home.

Cedar Rock   *Steve Kowit*

NOW, BEFORE SHAVING

The blanket loosens.
But if she comes in, I'll pretend to be sleeping.
I'd rather not make orange-juice,
slice fruit into cereal,
seek out the darkest suit

and argue which tie goes best with it.
I'd rather not promise to fetch home as trophies
a hospital's name,
its autopsy chart.
I'd rather not have the mortuary pinpointed on a street map,
my scene with the widow coached.
I'd rather not hear from a metal box it will be a sunny day.

To have fallen asleep without five minutes of mourning!
Now, before shaving, I want to see us
at college, the cafeteria group;
our Washington reunion, the Mellon Gallery concert;
home from war, still in uniform at that crazy party;
weddings, housewarmings;
New Year's Eves in that finished basement,
his improvised deadpan dance, lifting a partner in air;
The Merchant of Venice at Stratford
disputing Carnovsky in Shylock's dressing-room
over Shakespeare's intentions,
driving home the excitement, keeping it up till four,
spilling it over through brunch the next day;
our first quarrel: Israel, the Arabs;
a misfired phone-call, declined invitations,
rumors of a musician son, an architect daughter,
his name in the paper once,
an unmailed note.

Now, before shaving, is the time to feel.
Three friends buried in three months' time
and a feel not of heartache so much as cold feet.
The blanket comes loose, I lie at the edge of a sea,
the tide covers my toes, my ankles.
She comes in, fixes the blanket,
but there is no time.
A drowned face waits at the mirror.

Carleton Miscellany   *Aaron Kramer*

FOR AN OLD FRIEND

What a cruel way to learn
the news! The hometown newspaper,
arriving well after the fact,
tactfully placed your picture
and story on the second page.
I almost overlooked it that late
Friday afternoon when I settled
in, tired, for the weekend.
The same fine features I remember
from ten years ago, the look of
the hometown boy destined to go
far, very far. But, for whatever
reasons, you came back home
from New York. You came back

to the town you once loved
but could no longer accommodate
your needs, couldn't even give
you the simple urge to keep
breathing. You were drinking
heavily, I hear. Last time I
saw you, at the town library,
you appeared on the street with
a flushed face, said hello,
offered a nervous hand, hurried
back home through the alley.
I still cannot believe what
I read. I cannot accept
even the idea of you hanging
from a belt in the bedroom.
I want to sing you back out
of the darkness, onto your feet.
I want to release the tension
around your throat and sing
the breath of life back into
your lungs, hear that whiplash wit,
listen to deaf Beethoven's
ecstatic last symphony as we
sip from mugs of beer, argue
American literature, discuss
the merits of various cuisines.
But it's no use, Jeff. The poem
is always too much after the fact.

The American Scholar   *Norbert Krapf*

TELEPHONE LINEMAN

If fired upon, he cannot fire:
His gun-belt holster's full of tools.
His lariat's a loop of wire
Too stiff to lasso running bulls.
His spurs applied will not inspire
A burst of speed in wooden poles:
His mounts are rooted to the spot.
And yet we stare at him like fools
And see the figure he is not.

The Christian Century   *Ernest Kroll*

WHITE

White. A slashed tablecloth.
Someone waves it, white hand
of the east wind.
One says it snows.
Slowly
the slashed air
opens its eyes with cold.

Snow is beautiful for writing.
For the length of a white letter,
time gives in and smells
of frost and apples
until it melts.

Northwest Review   *Karl Krolow*
                    —Translated from the German
                    by Paul Morris

OUR GROUND TIME HERE WILL BE BRIEF

Blue landing lights make
nail holes in the dark.
A fine snow falls. We sit
on the tarmac taking on
the mail, quick freight,
trays of laboratory mice,
coffee and Danish for
the passengers.

Wherever we're going
is Monday morning.
Wherever we're coming from
is Mother's lap.
On the cloud-pack above, strewn
as loosely as parsnip
or celery seeds, lie
the souls of the unborn:

my children's children's
children and their father.
We gather speed for the last run
and lift off into the weather.

The American Poetry Review   *Maxine Kumin*

THE SNAKES OF SEPTEMBER

All summer I heard them
rustling in the shrubbery,
outracing me from tier
to tier in my garden,
a whisper among the viburnums,
a signal flashed from the hedgerow,
a shadow pulsing
in the barberry thicket.
Now that the nights are chill
and the annuals spent,
I should have thought them gone,
in a torpor of blood
slipped to the nether world
before the sickle frost.
Not so. In the deceptive balm

of noon, as if defiant of the curse
that spoiled another garden,
these two appear on show
through a narrow slit
in the dense green brocade
of a north-country spruce,
dangling head-down, entwined
in a brazen love-knot.
I put out my hand and stroke
the fine, dry grit of their skins.
After all,
we are partners in this land,
co-signers of a covenant.
At my touch the wild
braid of creation trembles.

Antaeus   *Stanley Kunitz*

THE PURPLE BLEMISH

I assume the grievous penitence
of not looking at you for days and days, because my eyes,
when they finally see you, are flooded with your essence,
as if shipwrecked in a purple gulf
of melody and vehemence.

Monday goes by; Tuesday; Wednesday . . . I suffer
your eclipse, oh solar creature!, but in my grief
the eagerness to see you opens wider
like a prophecy; it draws slowly together
like a curtain; it purifies itself like honey; it assays itself
like the precious metal in rich ore;
and it hones itself like the latchkey
to the cell of a ruined monastery, where lovers go.

You do not know the refinement of bliss
there is in fleeing you, in the furtive joy
of loving you secretly, of courting you
beyond the shadows, of lowering the scarf from my face
but once a week, and exposing my pupils,
for a fraudulent moment,
to the purple blemish of your resplendence.

In love's forest, I am the furtive hunter;
I watch you through the dense, dormant foliage
as one watches a dazzling bird; and from these walks
into the thick woods I bring back the most dazzling
of plumages to my isolation:
the purple plumage of your resplendence.

Poetry Now   *Par Lagerkvist*
— Translated from the Swedish
by Lennart Bruce

AN OLD FOLKS HOME

Blind, palsied, halting, speechless, mad,
Chair or bed-ridden, for decades now
These have been dying inward like old
Elms. Though rotten in trunk and bough,

They have a tree's longevity
Which neither mind nor body willed;
Outlasting sibling, spouse, and child,
They will survive our love and pity.

Here, the sculptor drops his spoon,
The dancer stumbles to her chair,
The scholar's stricken mind and tongue
Are baffled by the calendar.
Each hieroglyphic face or name
Eludes the mind's rosetta stone.
The angel of the lexicon
Won't bless, though every Jacob's lame.

Go further: in another ward,
Like newborn infants caged in beds,
Are studies which redefine the word
Human: hairless, fleshless heads
Lolling in some dream of life or death
In a darkness deeper than the womb's.
Like sparrows nodding at bread crumbs
They peck at life. Yet each pale wraith

Is tended as though it were a child
Nurtured in second infancy.
One can't help thinking how the world
Throughout this furied century
Has murdered the innocent and young,
Has laid whole generations waste,
Yet spared these cancer, gas, the blast
Of bombs, and things that stop the tongue.

Because it's longer-lived than life,
This pain, which at another time
Would stir my pity or my wrath,
Freezes the heart—and a cold, dumb
And numbing fury rises up
Till I want to shake the rotten limb,
Root up the rotten trunk, or climb
However high to reach the top:

What kind of tree is it won't let
The green fruit ripen, or the rotten drop?

Occident   *Paul Lake*

WAGON WHEELS

About those wagon wheels
we saw half stuck in mud

at the edge of that slough
     brown as dried blood:
     for weeks
I have dreamed of making a song
about huge wheels
thudding through prairie grass
and wilderness, and old heroic ways
we have lost.

I have tried to imagine masses of buffalo on a green sea of grass.
Have tried to see wagons on the skyline like small white ships.
Tried to stand alone away from town on the lonesome prairie under
     stars, under sun.
Feel the isolation.
Sense how the wind might have stung.
The bleached sky. The hunger.
Space. Flies. Dust. A brutal
treeless earth tumbling to eternity.
The savagery. The sweat.

But the song has not come.
And the wheels,
     two rusted steel bands
     on busted spokes and rotted axle
     like dulled rings
     hanging on a bony old finger
dumped in mud
that smells of cowshit
at the edge of a lake as blank as a mirror—
rusted cans   bald tires
     wind.
—a huge tractor wheels by
at the edge of the sky.

Blue Unicorn   *S. E. LaMoure*

THE ROAD TO SCHOOL

Did you make the bluebells ring,
Swing on ivy vines,
Spread your bread from buttercups,
Count the hydro lines?

Did you wake the morning sun,
Stir the wind from bed,
Pour the dew in acorn cups,
Spin a spider's thread?

Did you walk a crooked mile
On your way to school,
Stop to watch a dragonfly
Skim a roadside pool?

Did you chase a dandelion,
Ask the daisy's time?
Better hurry; Summer's out.
Dew has turned to rime.

Tower Poetry Magazine   *Joy M. Lane*

SOMEONE SITS AT THE HARP

Deep inside me, someone sits at the harp
and plays this light into being. What I can see
of him I see from a distance, the way that one
might see the world from the stars. Far-off, unearthly,
perfected, his expression from here seems empty
of all sentiment, his eyes endlessly indifferent,
what five years ago I might have called in my poems simply
"a death." Tonight, in silence, I die into this shining
of his music that grows more beautiful with every
precious breath I let go of. If I did not
already understand the sadness at the heart of human
expression, I would call this song of our joining the Perfect
One. But this is the earth. Deep inside me,
someone sits at the harp. And there are no words.

Studia Mystica   *Jon Lang*

UPON HEARING HIS HIGH SWEET TENOR AGAIN

John McCormack, you are riding again the air
in Italian arias and Irish chants
   like an old boyish want.

My father saved your records, played your songs
for twenty-one years from nineteen-eight and on
   clear in The Depression.

Then I cut the wooden needles when the steel
gave out on the Victrola. And I watched
   your voice in static etched

go faintly skipping and flying in our home,
delicate, robust, and pure. Throat and tongue
   caressed each note and sang

so that a boy, all ignorant of music,
voice or life itself, could steal from the air
   such intimations there

that though we labored round an endless wheel
and rolled with it, resounding day to day
   vibrating in an old groove,

still neither death nor poverty nor crime
can ever from his ear or eye remove
   such resonance, such love.

Epoch   *Joseph Langland*

EXPECTING

I could've spent my life banging young chicks,
sorting forms, guessing what I could do,
or choose to do, or pretend to do, or du-
plicate. I think I know all the tricks

by now of teacher-boy and teacher-man;
I can tell when the auburn hair is ready
for long walks, deep talks, the slow and steady
road to Williams or to Ford, and man-
ly forms, to all I ever cared about,
or sought to care about; to Ezra Pound,
to drunken boats, to burnished dismal light,
to all the angels who keep death in rout,
to stories I have made of breathing sound,
to dreams (I tell my dreams) of something right.

It's not that I'm against it: it may be fine
to use the love of books, the hungry trust,
the shallows burning in the steady eyes,
to add a woman to the song and wine;
if we were voting I would vote for Lust,
for heady groping and a dear surprise.
But I have liked the other way, the way
of holding back, of seeming not to mind,
of crumpling up my body till my mind
is all that tells, is all that I can say.
We are not the driver and the driven
and it feels good, better than a lot of things
and yes, just as in love, the sweet blood sings
the beating lushness of the freely given.

Kansas Quarterly   *Daniel J. Langton*

SERENADE OF ANGELS

It is not my voice, it is not my voice that is tearing.
It is the wind levelling the plain and bending the capsized wing.
        Close your eyes, close your eyes—
        The wind passes on but I . . . I remain.

It is not the night, it is not the night that holds you in strife.
It is the shadow of my distress or my hand over your life.
        Close your eyes, close your eyes—
        The shadow vanishes, but I . . . I remain.

It is not my tears, it is not my tears that shine.
It is stars under tranquil water, candles in wine.
        Close your eyes, close your eyes—
        A star can drown, but I . . . I remain.

It is not the angels, it is not the angels moving in retinue.
It is the first dawn, or the first snow falling upon the yew,
        Open your eyes, open your eyes—
        You go off with the angels, but I . . . I remain.

Sackbut Review   *Rina Lasnier*
—Translated from the French
by Jan Pallister

NO DIFFERENCE

Sooner or later I will forget
flags, trees, windows,
the glass and steel humming.

I will sit by a quiet fire,
loneliness spilling from my lap,
fingers spinning it out.

Faces will float up from the flames.
They will want me to tell them stories.
They will leap up listening.

They will be your faces wearing
my mouth. You will understand then
there is one voice between us.

New Letters   *Beverly Lawn*

TWO COMMUNIST POETS

Hey, Neruda! Hey, Ritsos!
what do you think of the Soviet Union
today
where an honest man can't speak his mind
but draws 14 years hard labour
and abuse
for being Jewish and wanting freedom?

How does Leninism strike you now,
how do you like its stink
as it moves its mountainous pile of shit
to cover the world
and to silence men of spirit and independence?
Louder! Louder! No one can hear you.

Pablo Neruda is dead.
He's gone underground
and isn't available for comment,
but you, Yanni,
might just as well be dead
for all the protest you're making
from your comfortable apartment
in Athens.

Maybe, Yanni,
if you pushed aside
some of the honours that are weighing
you down
you'd see what was happening
in the world
and find your voice again. Surely
not all the fire's gone out of you;
surely, mutinous poet,
there's still fire left in you

to grill and char
the fascist goons of Russia.

Louder, Yanni, louder!

Matrix   *Irving Layton*

THE COMEDIAN

What a malicious sense of humour
this comedian has who makes us see
holes or rods in walls and lace curtains,
or dreams of trains and black bulls charging
through tunnels that end as faucets dripping
over long lush meadows of blond hair

To mock your Presbyterian austerity
he's made you revamp a small bedchamber
into white chapel whose walls you cover
with handsome blow-ups of men all raging
to possess your ill ungiving self.
And what, poor dear, about the poem

He had you frame like a certificate
and place in a conspicuous spot
for marvelling visitors to take in?
It plainly tells us the bard enjoyed you
while imaging famed sawyers between your thighs.
O that conjuror has so many tricks

Up his false sleeves. Making you reveal
what most you're desperate to conceal,
using your own lies to unburden the truth
—to others! Not to yourself. Yourself
you must try the hardest to deceive with chapel
and shrine and open-collared lovers in hot pursuit

Yet since our comic's kind to fair ladies,
even as you re-arrange your collage of stills
in ignorant worship of his clever spoof,
he lets you mistake your sad obliquity
and seem to yourself pious and spiritual
each time men touch you and you freeze in hell

The Canadian Forum   *Irving Layton*

OXFORD COMMINATION

Rising from the pale valley, the rivers unseen from here,
Shwangun Range is all apple light and dappled
definition, with sky clear between final spring
and summer. Round that bend (where five townies in
    a dirty
coon-tailed Ford always seem to be doing eighty)
lies Lake Minnewaska—pretty and phoney as Switzerland—
one has to be both old and rich to hire a glimpse of it.

I look down now, over past ugly Kerhonkson
sunken into rolling depth by height and green distance
and say to you: this is the last poem of mine, curse
or tribute, you will walk through. This is my world,
    not yours.
Get out of my hair and my system, out of my head.
It was never your poems, bad or brilliant, that obsessed me
but your world, the childhood I lived through without
    knowing it
and, grown and knowing it through you, could not grow
    out of.
You were the shadow my father laughed at that
    frightened me,
the Faith and Freud to which my mother lit her lean
    candles.

My Oxford was not your Oxford, but you turned up,
flapping incredible mukluks down the Corn and
    St. Aldates,
your famous hair in famous disarray, your belt
hanging loose like a lariat. Owning a mutual religion
we shared a mass in Christ Church, and you said your
    Sanctus
with belief only the gross or cruel could impugn.

I poured your wine, a face among literary faces,
and you talked about nothing of interest or importance,
though still a past I was too shy to come to terms with.
But it was my Oxford, not yours. I dined that last
term with names and opinions and drank sparkling hock
in Wadham and suffered a delicious season of Roman fever
at St. Mary Mag's and wrote tough elegant bitchy poems.
The days turned occasionally towards this or that war
but there was no tension between style and belief,
no silly high resolutions about freedom—
only sensible window-glass sent to gunned Budapest.
What were you doing in my Oxford, dispersing ease
like conscience or a cop, reminding me in Hilary air
that betrayal lays in me and everyone, like a smart whore?
You belonged in a strictly legendary Oxford
with the legendary names and the cautionary verses.

Now get out of the Hudson Valley and my heart.
Your acts and reasons are hidden in poems I do not read.
And there is a black-haired girl who has been shot down
and a boy stricken with Keats, and a green promised road
winding down along the Wallkill to a winery
and a day now, all of whom must be attended to.

Poetry   *Paris Leary*

THE LIZARD

He sat on a boulder, his miniature
saurian length rigid except for

the wedge-shaped head turned toward me. Scales
like small beadings made diminishing rows
down his gray-brown back. He stood
on curved forelegs, pumping
up-down—up-down,
each push-up baring
a turquoise-colored breast.
Then, measuring distance, he jumped
at a flick in the air above him,
five delicate fingers outspread,
then closing, to bring down
a small white-winged moth.

I watched, but couldn't discover
the number of toes on his feet:
in the half-light, half-shadow,
they stickily bunched together.
I was afraid if I picked him up
he'd cast his tail . . . And,
in a world increasingly fragmented by
the losing of tails (or heads),
I needed him complete.

So I asked the neighbor's children,
"Can you catch me a lizard?"
—They bring me one, in a shoebox
Kleenex and a green-leaf lined.
He has his tail. Gary strokes him:
"He won't bite. His back is hard, see,
But he's soft underneath. Sometimes
he stands up on his fingers."
—"Did you count how many toes?"
"No," Jane says, "but I'll look."
She lifts one of his feet, gently
separates twig-thin digits.
"Two long ones in the middle, one shorter
on each side, and a very
short one back here." Their heads
bend closer, faces taking the gift
of lizard wholeness. "Five!"
Their eyes glow. "So now," Gary puts the lid on the shoebox
carefully back.
"So now we know."

Buffalo Spree   *Ruth Lechlitner*

ROGER AND ME

In the old days when we were kids
and summer evenings gathered us
all together to play hide-and-seek
until it was too dark to see,
we used to hide together, Roger and me,
in the high sweet grass along the ditch
or under the bushes at the edge of the woods,

his arm warm against mine,
hearts beating madly against the earth
as we watched for that chance
to run home free, Roger and me.

It seems so strange to think of childhood,
to look back across the years
and recognize that child, myself—
like looking back across a border
to a land I can never touch again
and did not recognize when I was there.

And Roger, he's gone.
He left me behind before he left his childhood,
and I sometimes wonder where he is,
who he has become, whether life has
treated him better than his childhood did,
who joined us bruised but laughing;
he was always laughing, does he still laugh?

I remember the sweet dry grass,
the earth-smell strong in my nostrils
as we huddled against it, waiting.
I remember the darkening evening
alive with our games,
the shouting and running and laughing,
and Roger's arm warm against mine
in those sweet gone evenings
when we used to hide together,
Roger and me,
waiting for the chance to run
home free.

Germination   *Anne Le Dressay*

METAL FATIGUE

An axle quits,
spilling a quartermile of nectarines
along the interstate.
She just went for no reason
insists the trucker to the trooper
who must word a report.

Another routine approach.
But passengers near the tail
see the landing gear topple,
falling to land on its own.
The stewardess croons the word *malfunction*
like a lullaby, with finesse.
But travellers prefer abuse to misfortune,
would rather she sing *sabotage;*
it would be easier to take.

A man wakes up suddenly
in the middle of the night

A mirror has fallen to the floor
and shattered to a thousand slivers.
Deep in his heart he suspects the supernatural.
It's safer to blame ghosts
than to believe a togglebolt made of U.S. steel
might have secret, human desires.

Don't you get tired sometimes?
Tired of mornings,
of washing your face, tending your bowels,
tired of pulling on your clothes,
of eating, of working, tired,
tired of this vertical life?
Don't you get tired? I do.

When the boiler explodes,
I'm suddenly aware of our kinship.
When my key breaks off in the lock,
how much better I understand it than before.
Who am I to pass judgement on the submarine
that gives in to the ocean
and refuses to rise, I
who am alloyed likewise,
mind and flesh constantly debasing one another?
Shall I demand more from cast iron and aluminum
than from my foundering heart?

The mirror has fallen from the wall. Of course it has.
Someday I'll let go too and fall,
and sleep like ore, invulnerable
under a mountain.

But this cold, particular morning,
the radiator shudders and clanks.
When I turn it on, the faucet
moans and spits
as if it were dreaming again of the forge.
And weren't we cast also
forcibly by a changing fire?
Don't we dream all night too,
and wake up exhausted?

The radiator shudders.
I know how it feels.

Blessings on the pen that breaks
in the middle of my name.
And bless the fillings that desert my teeth,
exposing nerve.

The American Poetry Review   *Adam Le Fevre*

ODE

People in the middle ages didn't think they were living
Between two more important and enlightened eras;
Nor did they see themselves as the players

In act three of a tragedy in five acts.
It was not always late winter in the middle ages.
People in the middle ages were not all middle-aged,
Though it is enjoyable on occasion to assume that they
    were.
The sun was as bright in the dark ages
As it is now—maybe a fraction brighter, in fact.

Think of the middle ages and what do you see:
Gloomy cathedrals, students dressed like monks in the
    rain,
Or a band of drunken pilgrims telling obscene jokes,
Or heroes embarking for the nearest wilderness come
    April?
Your answer will reveal yourself to yourself
But you may not know it—may choose to hide
In hazy visions of a serene and indescribable paradise.
And paradise, as we all know, may be paradise when
    we're dead,
But is boredom on earth, alas.

We never think of ennui in relation to the middle ages.
Should we? Did Thomas Aquinas never get bored
Cooking up elaborate refutations of diminutive heresies?
No, and you shouldn't either. Nor did the clerks
Of Oxford tire of the sin against the Holy Ghost,
Trying to figure out what it was.

On chill September mornings when
I smoked too much the night before
And I drank too much the night before
And a sinister cough rises up
From the depths of the belly of my being,
I like to imagine living in Provence,
Or even in Rheims during the middle ages.

Poetry   *David Lehman*

IN PRAISE OF ROBERT PENN WARREN

Beyond the primitive powers of pain, of love at last
Recognized behind the windows of a departing train,
    helpless
To give chase; beyond the power of the eye to detect
The proper balance between beauty and bunk, to direct
Our attention to the final unterrified meeting in the dark,

Beyond the power of streetlamps to illumine; to direct
Our attention to what you insist is important after all
And shall remain in the mind long after the daily grind
Of apologies and phone calls, unwanted, unreturned, the
    feigned
Enthusiasm, commercial breaks, news breaks, oaths,
    alarms:

You know it's wisest to retain your anonymity as,
    distrustful
Of doctors, you wander, as though for the first time, in
    barefoot
Happiness over the familiar ground, though you are now,
    what?
Seventy-three years old, and wonder, as though for the
    first time,
How brutal the light can be, though faint in the chill of
    dawn,

And you, insomnolent, and in need of assurance, yet
    braced
For the return of the dreams that can kill. Go ahead,
    ponder
The fate of innocence in a forest of fear. Gnarled
Are the roots, but you, staring, are immune to complaint,
And beyond the primitive powers of pain and lament.

Poetry   *David Lehman*

SHOPKEEPERS

Who can grasp the gray hearts of shopkeepers?
In the gray dawn, with keys in their hands
And sleep in their shoulders, quiet as lambs,
They are the first to round chilly corners.

Among the shelves and sacks and pails
They woo small change and take stock each hour.
Engrossed, like a man praying by the bimah,
They measure their merchandise on the scales.

The last in synagogue the eve of Yom Kippur,
They carry the odors of their stores.
Next day they peer through sighs of final prayers,
Measuring windows for signs the day is over.

By the time for breaking the fast—bless His stars—
The shopkeepers have long lit up their stores.

Midstream   *Mani Leib*
                            —Translated from the Yiddish
                                   by Richard J. Fein

SHAMAN

I gather clay and work it with my fingers,
Not for pots—mere womens' work—
But for fierce fresh colors;
Paint to decorate the warriors of my tribe.
Reds, yellows, sienas—
The hues of infusorial earths.

I powder charcoal;
Mix pitch and resin;

Extract the purple of ink berries
And tints from myriad roots
Which grow inaccessibly.
I know where to find
The magic bones of mammoths
And I prepare them.

Learning much in my journeying,
I've antidote for every poison.
When I draw the circles and symbols
That exalt
And wear the chaplet of power,
Children gape at my gold-vermilion splendor,
While women
Widen the corners of their mouths for me
When their men are not looking.

Pteranodon   *Esther M. Leiper*

WOLF DREAM

He hunches into his fur coat
and waits in the alley behind her house.
Her bedroom window still is lit:
she sleeps with her husband once a year,
and he is waiting up for her.
Wife and lover watch from the alley
as her husband's shadow crosses the window, comes back,
stands still in the light.
After midnight, the window dark, the lovers
crawl behind the garbage cans into an empty field,
fall tight together, roll over and over,
arms locked into crooks around each other's chests,
breath pressed out in whistling gasps.
Their tongues loll into each other's mouths,
their nails bite through fur and cloth
into skin. When they feel each other's blood, they change.
He is the stronger. Her face, human again,
stares up at the black shape crouched on her chest,
its fur heavy and stiffening with her blood.
He no longer sees her. He is sharing her husband's dream
of night skies, shadows crossing the moon
on four legs, two; crooked trees knock in the wind,
their shadows on the snow waver around the dark cleft
where the eyes wait, and the harsh breath;
then the snow bursts in a flurry of claws, cries, a shot
and a new shadow falls, rolls
over and over, hunches itself into human form
as it dies at the feet of the one man fated to hunt it down:
a man scarred to the bone
who had lain mauled, had felt death enter his flesh
as a lover, as a great wolf.

Cornfield Review   *Edward Lense*

TWO POEMS BASED ON FACT

1/ *Country scene remembered from a great distance*

I watched the rain amaze me again that water
could make such a noise simply falling.

A crow lost itself in the sky's thick muscle flexing.
In the voluptuous air, mushrooms preened and poked.

The smoke from a farmer's trash fire piled up against
leaden air. It had to meander sidewise to slip into the sky.

Mist came curling through the stand of trees
above the pasture, the cows walked by and drank

from the creek and I doubt they noticed
for an instant the way the fog rose and fell

so cool and firm over their tracks in the grass.

2/ *Night shift leaves in Owego, NY*

The sun rises over roof full of exhaust vents.
In the compound, they're loading nitrogen.

Around the pylons, and the big white tank,
and tank truck and coupling hose, we see

rising, then blowing across the parking lot,
dampening home-bound workers, a substance

not unlike the fog that beads the meadow
so we leave tracks behind us,

so our shoes are soaked through to the socks.
As the night and the night shift dissolve from

the plant below us, we thread our way along
up-meadow, rising toward our crest of dawn.

The Texas Review   *Frank J. Lepkowski*

EVERYTHING HAS ITS HISTORY

In the common day I find a common fact:
The chair in which I sit,
The small wood table,
The sienna vase
Lie mute in my room
As if they belonged here
Before I moved in.
But I know different
From a place inside that admits difference.
I moved them in.
This chair occupies the space
I once needed
To fill with a chair:
Chair-space I called it.
I hunted for it.
When I found it

I carried it home.
I sat and read and ate
In a new thing.
I was new,
I was made new.
Now I sit here remembering
There was a moment of love
Between myself and the place I inhabit.

Denver Quarterly   *Phillis Levin*

ONE MORNING

It feels so good,
this can only be a dream.
My legs apart and something
pushing from between them.
No pain and many faces smiling.

Whatever this flesh is
surfaced while my muscles slept.
I am slippery
and my hair shines like onyx.

When I wake up I am all me,
smelling of sleep.
My fingers warm
and my breath light,
I coincide with my skin.

The Slackwater Review   *Ellen Levine*

NEWS OF THE WORLD

When the first bad news came, my mother
began to cry those perfect crystal
tears that were the envy of friends
and strangers. She sat in the big chair
in her bright wool robe with toast
and tea at the ready and went on and on
until the carpets dampened and the dull
red drapes darkened. Somewhere a lark
had slipped his perch and tumbled down,
somewhere a phalanx of inchworms couldn't
find its way to war or peace, somewhere water
hung on the lip of a falls and froze. Yes,
what little sense there was had gone
out of the world and even dollars were
cast down and shamed. For this the answer
was the ageless wailing of the skilled
at shorthand and typing on an eight-hour day,
during which no book would be balanced,
no check signed or certified. I was a child
surrounded by great childish things with names
like Esther, Gertrude, Sophie, Honor,

Yetta, Mollie, Belle, so skilled at grief
and lamentation that even on sunlight days
the mists rose from our house and cleansed
the morning, and for miles around an awed
and cold silence fell on thousands of Polish
cheerleaders and bald Ukranian upholsterers
who tiptoed through the alleys on their way
to work or play. By nightfall the clocks
were on their marks, a bored stew wakened
in the kitchen, and on the avenue the buses
returned the hollowed husks of people. The day
was saved and tomorrow could begin on time.
I stood in the wings, my yo-yo rising
and falling like the ancient heads at prayer,
bright and learned in my five scrubbed years
having found my way to my first wisdom:
that in an exceptional world like yours
and mine exceptional measures are required.

Antaeus   *Philip Levine*

MY ANGEL

How many times must I tell
you that this world is not
the one I wanted? You yawn
and tell me I can find another
if need be. You must have
the last word, like a husband
or a stubborn child. I know!
I know! It's late, and I've
been drinking, and you refuse
to take anything I say seriously.
Do I want rain tomorrow? you
whisper. Snow? Hail? Do I
want to come home from work
and find the waters of Lethe
where my room was? No. I
want to sleep until ten and waken
with sunlight streaking the room
and the full odor of coffee
filling my head. I want to sit
listening to music or the music
of my silent mind and think
how this day will be like
no other, and each one that
follows will have its savor,
and years later I will recount
the long mornings that reached
almost to darkness. But you
aren't listening. Now you're
rereading the morning paper
and chuckling over the wrecks

and hijacks. You mumble
the names from the obituaries,
mixing in tidbits of advice:
I'd stay home tomorrow, I'd
get a good night's sleep, I'd
be sure the windows are locked.
You think you can scare me?
You know everything and nothing,
and when you fall from grace
you'll fall into my heart
and spend creation in an ocean
of ice . . . I can see the future.
I can see you in this perfect world
turning suddenly to calm a child
on the edge of panic. I can see
you bending to the long grass
of the foothills to find
that tiny blue flower we called
a gift. See, it is spring,
and the pure sunlight flares
in your hair. You've stopped
beside a cold rushing stream.
We bow in wonder, and you? You
are touched and bow back to us,
and then you fall into my heart.

Antaeus   *Philip Levine*

MY LIFE LIKE ANY OTHER

And the new sun broke on fields of grain
as I walked home, tired and full,
and touched with grace, smelling
her smell rising from my own body
pressed all night to hers. That dawn
I entered heaven and understood
it was a light falling on still fields,
it was the first barn swallow over
my head, it was within a white shirt
stretched across this back which bowed
for years to engine blocks, vats of acid,
pans of broken parts, and then received
its final shape from two hands that traced
their needs in darkness. It had seemed
such a long wait until that morning
when the cool air swelled in my lungs
pushing out my voice in the old joy-songs,
and at last I knew there was nothing I
wanted, nothing, except the life I'd entered.

The Missouri Review   *Philip Levine*

TO A WALL OF FLAME IN A STEEL MILL,
SYRACUSE, NEW YORK, 1969

Except under the cool shadows of pines,
The snow is already thawing
Along this road . . .
Such sun, and wind.
I think my father longed to disappear
While driving through this place once,
In 1957.
Beside him, my mother slept in a grey dress
While his thoughts moved like the shadow
Of a cloud over houses,
And he was seized, suddenly, by his own shyness,
By his desire to be grass,
And simplified.
Was it brought on
By the road, or the snow, or the sky
With nothing in it?
He kept sweating and wiping his face
Until it passed,
And I never knew.
But in the long journey away from my father,
I took only his silences, his indifference
To misfortune, rain, stones, music, and grief.
Now, I can sleep beside this road
If I have to,
Even while the stars pale and go out,
And it is day.
And if I can keep secrets for years,
It is because men like us
Own nothing, really.
I remember, once,
In the steel mill where I worked,
How a man opened the door of the furnace,
And I glanced in at the simple,
Quick and blank erasures the flames made of iron,
Of everything on earth.
It was reverence I felt then, and did not know why.
I do not know even now why my father
Lived out his one life
Farming two hundred acres of grey Málaga vines
And peach trees twisted
By winter. They lived, I think,
Because his hatred of them was entire,
And wordless.
I still think of him staring into this road
Twenty years ago,
While his hands gripped the wheel harder,
And his wish to be no one made his body tremble:
He said it was like the touch
Of a woman he could not see,
Her fingers drifting up his spine in silence

Until his loneliness was perfect,
And she let him go—
Her laughter turning into these sheets of black
And glassy ice that dislodge themselves,
And ride slowly out
Onto the thawing river.

Poetry   *Larry Levis*

GIVE US THIS DAY OUR DAILY DAY

Some things are blessedly alyrical.
A stone, immobile in its rut,
is not a poem. A weed does not sing
but for a random fingering of wind.
The tree just hunkers down, a green fact.

The failed poetry of our intentions
is like this. The rhythms lag to a walk.
The fine threads unravel from the yarn.
We find ourselves beautifully entangled
in the unwinding prose of our days.

Kayak   *Robert J. Levy*

INTERVIEW

(Lake Shinobazu, Ueno Park, Tokyo)

I.
Lady,
how long you been driving a bus?
No long.
The bus rides me.
Drive, lady, not ride.
And why prefer you the night shifts?
Night? Who rides nights?
It's morning!

II.
We glide the sleek abandoned streets
face-high into morning,
snatch the roving sun from secret poise each dawn,
and plaster the fleeting gold on the windshield glass
like a fine shiny paste.
But don't it get lonely, lady, all night? So quiet is alone.
And lovely the quiet.
Who lacks company, when drunk?
A bus is roomy and the air fresh as ponds.
Each bend round the lake-edge enlivens.
A storm, now and then, is good for surprises.
But the calm jaunts are cleaner. And when it's clear
the views are so brittle and crisp
I wince each time I stare.

So close to the panes,
nestled erect and propped in the plummetting flat half-face
(a prodigious forehead,
no jaw to absorb the sensuous punch of the weather),
I traffic in close-ups
and feast on the graphs of my eyes.

III.
But lady,
what do you do for noise?
Such voices, those cries.
I wade ear-deep in a sky-full of birds.

New England Review   *Laurence Lieberman*

GETTING UNDER

Grandfather, bring me down,
down inside the soil,
down in browns in greys;
I must get under.

I remember,
even with these years around me:
your body lying straight,
longer than it ever was,
a grounded fish
no longer flapping.
Your stillness promised.

Grandfather, it is now your turn.
I need to know on which side
the lines converge.

I want that plunge,
the sinking down through layers
that have breathed the breaths
of ancient men.
Grandfather, tell me of the feel
of earth in lungs, wet and cool,
the bottom.

Dark Horse   *Alan P. Lightman*

PERIPATETIC

I walk
between the cobblestones
on bricks and paving blocks

Incessantly
the steps take on the tempo
of a funeral march
through grounds deserted, wet

until
beneath the feet

papered on the footpath
I come across
the Eye of God

The God Eye
looks up my sole
and through its darkness
sees it leathery

I salivate
to tread on Death
with expert feet
having overwalked
the Eye of God
without a consequence

The Literary Review   *Robert Lima*

TWO BIRDS

A bird, most likely a sparrow,
although at first look I thought
pine siskin; anyway, a bird broke
his neck against my view.
He featherprinted the window
and dropped down flat out
on the gravel. Careless God closed
his eye and the bird flew
straight into death near the barrel
and downspout where bluejays fought
for drinks. Then silence, short as *oh,*
and the jays renewed their quarrel.

That was yesterday. This morning
another, whose star held steady,
crashed into the same glass, was flung
to ground and stood stock-still.
He bright-eyed me, not killed but stunned.
I put a basket
over him to keep off cats. Long
minutes passed, the lattice
edged sideways, there was a struggle
inside the wicker cage. Spread-
winged, ready to chance a wobbling
star, he rose upward like a stone.

Yankee   *Kathleen Linnell*

ENCOUNTER

You know my secrets
I can tell,
So if you move
suddenly behind me
I can feel

the way your hands would move
on my breasts
chafing the nipples gently
until they ceased to ache—
then soothe me down
softly into love
and sleep

You know me well
even though no touch
will pass again between us
even although minds flash
with the old spark
and laughter whips between us
into that sort of sanity
that lovers love—

my dear, my dear:
when we smile together
your eyes belie
your talking mouth.

The Canadian Forum   *Dorothy Livesay*

PAUSE

Is it a sudden thing:
the bud opening into flower
at the first blink of sun?

It has taken a year
of the seed's life
to erupt this way

And I also am new born
suddenly today!
yet slowly
through seventy years

The Canadian Forum   *Dorothy Livesay*

PROTECTIVE COLORS

As regions may be known by their moths,
Some voices have a distinctive habitation.
Yours has seemed temperate, a long valley

Where the leaves are not violent, preferring
To die quietly in the heat. Seen from the ridge,
Streams descend to a snaking river shallow

In this weather. Natives of this common shore,
The hawk and crow shelter threats against
Minor animals and the crops reaching harvest.

Piles of palm fronds, strange to this country,
Wait burning on the fields, their dried fans
Reduced to dusty ribs. On a morning soon evaporated

Into plain sky, no one but a single jogger pacing
Herself through an orchard is visible, her white shirt
Appearing and disappearing, sweaty against

Her thin back. Narrowed by parallel ranges
Of mountains, the dense valley lies flattened
Along the axis of sight, its speech camouflaged

And isolate. To reach the river, one must cross
The watershed and descend, trespassing through lines
Of trees that have added another ring of growth.

The Georgia Review   *William Logan*

DRIVING HOME

this is a stray donkey wearing
a saddle of stars

this is the star-studded belt
with the straight sword
in search of God knows what

this is the Word winging it
on the spur of the moment

this is a black page with the moon
burning a hole in it

the light obliterated
by the driving rain now

this is a shower of leaves caught
in the headlights of your car
spinning out of control
in the hands of God

this is the dotted center line
finally found again flashing under your eyes

this is the last curve
in the last curve home

Antenna   *Jonathan London*

CYCLE

Your ghost steps are already gone,
Sweet minnow, now your small foot falls
On the way to the bathroom at night
With a sound heavier than before . . .

And next year or so I could wake up
Again hearing, and then these steps now
Might be ghost steps for me too.
Through part-ignorance, or design, we parents

Could stymie your way, could place around you
Iron stayings from the past, causing you grief:
Asking—Your sweet future, where will it
Leave us? . . . Never calling it Lion's Share,

But blessing your dreams with your own . . . incense!
Daughter, walk free, be good, but please don't leave . . .
Near sleep again: my own parents gaze back at me
Through your ghost steps . . . to be forgiven.

America   *Frank Lonergan*

SAYING ONE THING

(for Daisy Jacobs)

Today, the angels are all writing postcards,
Or talking on the telephone.
Meanwhile, in Nowheresville,
A rabbit is running into a bush. This, I tell my friend,
Means good luck. The next day,
The sun is out, the fix is in

And we're ready to throw in the towel.
Anytime now, our number might come up,
And the telephone will finally stop ringing:
Don't call before three,
Knock four times,
Show me the way to go home,

Back and forth and back again,
Like some idiot boomerang.
"Kerpow" and "schlock" are our favorite words,
Lately, and are about what things are amounting to.
Still, the stories of airplane disasters
And overnight flings in faroff cities have a kind of
     allure,

Like metallic paint, or something expensive
You want and can't have.
O toothpaste commercials, common housefly,
Fall is in the air again. On this spaceship
The code word is "blonde," or "good dog."
Night begins to fall, the atmosphere is electric.

Poetry   *Robert Long*

MARES OF NIGHT

All night long they race above my bed,
necks arched to the wind, pale manes
streaming into milky mist, legs
stretched thin as sticks
in the umber fog.

The sound of their hooves
pounds into my dreams, a pulse
of terror beating prophetically
against a phantom of unease.
With instinct wiser than reason
they flee an unknown peril,

some dark danger, all the more
terrible because it bears no name.

In the morning
I drag myself up the dim stair
of waking, into the mad stampede
of another day, a day that
at any moment could blossom
in annihilating brilliance.
My mouth is dry, my throat clogged
by the taste of doom.

On the canvas above the bed
my four golden mares still race,
manes and tails flowing
like spilled cream
into a wild wind.

Cedar Rock   *Virginia Long*

FLIGHT 382

Above the clouds the sun is warm,
The sky dome cobalt blue.
Clouds below look
Like the backs of sheep—
Firm, resistant.
And they're in orderly rows
Mile after mile.

Now the sheep are gone
And it's an arctic vista.
Snow piled on snow
To the horizon,
With dangerous crevasses
And no guideposts.

Again, the clouds change—
Feathery soft
Blown spindrift
Gracing the skyways.
Chicago, in half an hour.

Great Lakes Review   *Doris Longman*

LIVING IN THE PRESENT

Sometimes your medulla
slips so low down
on your spine
that when somebody slips
his fingers underneath your hair
to stroke your nape,
your cat-brain,
you do not remember
whose they are.

So.
You curl your eyes up
in your fur and slip
into a room as warm
and warmly lit as this one,
slip through to another
and another,
and in each
there gently breathes
a tiny you.
No trick. No mirrors.

To descend a flight
of stairs—now
that would be a trick
all right: right foot
left foot right foot
left foot right foot
every moment hung in air
between a narrow
"there" and "here."
So.
You do not try to leave
this gently breathing room,
you do not try
the loud bare flight,
the plush flight,
least of all the marble
flight outside.
You fall
asleep, and when
you dream you dream
that you are sleeping

The Hampden-Sydney Poetry Review   *Clarinda Harriss Lott*

PEEK-A-BOO

Does Almighty God know about His sneaky competition?
A ferris wheel of alter ego satellites
eavesdrops the earth, branching out
to spin a telemetric web that bugs our steps.
It scans us to the bone and taps our optic nerve
to intercept "eyes only" messages.
They say now that a billion or two on R&D
will make it possible to monitor our shadow's EEG.

A thousand years can come and go in one blink
of God's unflappable eye and leave Him
unaware of changes at the hub,
but in that time we have gone from Domesday Book
to dossiers in a central data bank.

If we could manage to get word out to Him
He would surely ordain a Fourth Amendment for the sky.

The Small Pond Magazine   *Robert Lowenstein*

ON LIVING WITH CHILDREN FOR A PROLONGED TIME

Now I know
why God ordered Abe
to bump off Isaac;
not that God
was pulling rank
or had created
the ultimate Tide Test of Faith
(everything comes out in the wash)—
just that Isaac
was such an unruly
little bastard
and God, of course,
had to keep His nose clean.

Now I know
why the usually stoic Greeks
hurled their newborn
like dialogues
and theorems
from high cliff foreheads.

Now I know
the bloody brotherhood
of stooped Herod,
who parted the reeds
as I dipped my hands
in the bullrush slaughter.

Event   *Mark Lowey*

LLANBERIS SUMMER

You talk peaks and golden eagles,
I, foothills, sheepbells, slopes
Ranging foxglove and heather.
Mica peels from the cliffs.
I gather it. Intent
On your red coat I hum
With the slow rumbling
Pulse of the mountain.

You ascend slowly, past boulder
And scrub, past the sun,
A red bird winging
Toward rock face, toward aeries
Where eagles shadow the precipice.
The long grass sings
Of your night-camp, a single tent
Pitched on the summit.

Jewels in the morning.
Bring me something—
A wet quartz splinter, a kernel
Of moss agate. Tomorrow
I will whisper
Wyddfa's song for you,
Gather you foxglove.
Vapors shudder, tonight
Streams hush the foothills.
Breathe with me now,
Splitting the mountain,
A rockslide of agate.

Sou'wester   *Marianne Loyd*

BUT, STILL, HE

(for Jimmy Lohman, worker for the Florida Clearinghouse on Criminal Justice)

unhumans walk around
and jazzchant down.
                        jazzchant,
one down, in the name of God.
one down, in the name of morality.
one down, in the name of the law.
                        one down.

we killed one down, they say,
so people can have humandreams.
oh, one down!
but, still, he
screams the silent screams.

and after death, truculent rhythm
flows shoutingouts: T-shirts!
get your T-shirts
from the governor's mansion.
get your T-shirts
sanctified by the church.
get your T-shirts
dipped in J. S.'s blood. get your T-shirts.
with iceblooded winks, they whoop,
have electrical dreams.
but, still, he
screams the silent screams.

in a bebopping solo
that spiritpains against life,
they scat justice.
Florid-id-id-id-
                idian justice
burned God's soul in the chair
Florid-id-id-id-
                idian justice
wouldn't let a penniless drifter live.

Florid-id-id-id-
             idian justice.
got to have money
before you get any.
          Florid-id-id-id-
               idian justice.
you killed the good in America's dreams.
but still he screams.
but, still, he
he screams the silent screams.

Southern Exposure   *Henry N. Lucas*

MOTHERHOOD

Think of gentleness, as when
a head lifts and nods to a child,
easy permission. I remember
going back and forth to the kitchen
in winter, where the oven held us
like small lovely moths to the light.
Mother would hand us warm bread
with jelly, and we'd flit away
until we were cold again.

Now all my gestures are lost.
Too late for a bowl of cookies,
a hug, to make any difference.
He's younger in my dreams,
sometimes a brother. I walk out
to the barn to find the mare
I love, to give it to him.
But he can't understand,
and thinks she's dangerous.

I would begin again, have children
late, when I've learned
not to rely on words, but on
bread rising each Saturday
in a life that would stay
as firm as a boy's deliberate stride
onto the soccer field.
I'd know what can be forgiven,
what grace warms the air like steam.

The Georgia Review   *Susan Ludvigson*

BEYOND BELIEF

Water tower enclosures
are unimportant.
Everyone ignores
the baroque, triumphal arches
and Italianate pavilions
that adorn the rooftops of this city.

Nobody believes that water is the fundament,
the essence,
of all things.

Times have changed;
divinity has withdrawn from water.

And this week
we awoke to find that semblance
had spread itself over everything we own.
The finish on our antique mahogany table
is irreversibly opaque.
No amount of sanding will remove it;
denatured alcohol will not restore its clarity.

It seems
as if divinity has withdrawn
from every object in the visible world.

A month ago,
as we were driving from the city,
a convoy of huge, unmarked trucks
surrounded our small car.
We could not see the road signs, the exits,
the sumac trees that grow beside the highway;
for one hour we barely moved.

Only one said he felt lost
in an unknowable universality,
only one.

The Georgia Review   *Tom Luhrmann*

"TITUS, SON OF REMBRANDT: 1665"

Math. It's deliberately solutionless.
Even after you've closed the primer,
got up and stoked the fire,
the problem waits. But your father
doesn't expect an answer.
He's after the inexplicable gaze
that's you. You wonder why
he cuts strokes for hours
across a canvas you cannot see
and why, if he's so busy,
he keeps looking back at you
stretching your legs by the fire
and pulling the seat of your pants
from your behind. By the window

Your father arches his brow,
awaiting your face above the primer.
One of his students could easily paint
the lines along his eyes
and talk of the master, the painting
within the painting, the adult burden of art.
But you're still his favorite, thus the problem:

if there are eight rocking chairs before you,
which one, with the door three inches open
and the wind blowing hard,
will creak enough to cut the cat's tail?
What's all this seriousness.
You just want to sit in one,
scare the cat a little, watch its tail
flip over and under the rocker.

Salmagundi   *Richard J. Lyons*

LEAVING ONE OF THE STATE PARKS AFTER A FAMILY OUTING

The grass was the green of parades when we'd leave,
loading the trunk of the car in the summer evening.
The trees were all elms, shadows immense, and our thirst
was waiting to go somewhere for ice cream.

You would say *Do this, Elizabeth,* and I would do it
as if it were a game, on afternoons like that: I'd
spread wet towels on the back seat, go and fetch things,
put mama's purse in the corner, close the door "click,"

like two people kissing. Then I always said *Can we coast
today? Can we?* Mama would mention, Carl, it was
    illegal;
but you put the car in neutral, in the shade facing the
long hill—released all the brakes.

In the back I would make small pushing motions
against the front seat, as if a little girl like me
could move an automobile. The car would sit, edged
with the chance of falling, then, slowly, begin to roll.

How I loved you then, your hands on the wheel in the
strong almost twilight, as you did something just for me
at last. The park lilac bushes pass us in shadow
as though about to stop. We falter, come up to

a slight rise. Then we begin the wild controlled descent,
silent as bicycles but weighing tons. The elm-tree
shadows fly over the hood and down behind; you begin
to brake for the main road approaching. *Had enough?*

Then of course you turned the ignition over, eased us
down to stop in second gear. We went from there
for ice cream or for root beer, without having
heard the question answered: *No!* if I could've known

how to say it, *It's never enough.* I want to go down
with you forever, without anger, pulled by the weight
            of the car
in the steady descending silence, always just before sunset,
rolling through leaves, in some perpetually loving motion.

Poetry   *Elizabeth Macklin*

AN AUTUMN DAY

On that slope
on an autumn day,
the shells soughing about my ears
and six dead men at my shoulder,
dead and stiff—and frozen were it not for the
      heat—
as if they were waiting for a message.

When the screech came
out of the sun,
out of an invisible throbbing,
the flame leaped and the smoke climbed
and surged every way:
blinding of eyes, splitting of hearing.

And after it, the six men dead
the whole day:
among the shells snoring
in the morning,
and again at midday
and in the evening.

In the sun, which was so indifferent,
so white and painful;
on the sand which was so comfortable,
easy and kindly;
and under the stars of Africa,
jewelled and beautiful.

One Election took them
and did not take me,
without asking us
which was better or worse;
it seemed as devilishly indifferent
as the shells.

Six men dead at my shoulder
on an Autumn day.

The American Poetry Review   *Sorley MacLean*

SUN AND I

The land I plowed last fall
Is ready in the April sun to turn again
And gives a perfect loamy smell
To springtime in the Valley.

Framed in the April light,
My love sits by the open window.
Her face, touched completely by the sun,
Tilts up in dreamy beauty to the light.
Her face is rapt as lovers
In the ecstasy of touched and touching.

I will move and stand beside her,
Touch her chin and turn her face to me.
And with my fingertips
I will love the sun-warmed skin.
I will feel the sun along her lips,
The fields of sunlight on her cheeks.

Am I this woman's only love?
Or do sun and I, in turn, move on her skin?
Are we both ecstasy to her?
Did sunlight melt her soft for me to plow?
Or have I turned her up for sun to warm?

I'll believe she loves us both.
And sun and I will take unrivalled turns
To give her joy.
And sun and I will stand together on a summer day
To see what we have grown.

Cedar Rock   *Ken Mammone*

I'M LUCKY

I have lucky teeth,
perfectly even
as dice.

They win me compliments,
as does my head—
perfectly shaped,
according to my hairdresser.

I am growing vain.

When I was a child, I waited hours
in the hushed parlor
of my mother's dentist.

On the mantel, a magic picture
sifted sepia shadows of a human skull
into the portrait
of a lady in love
with her vanity mirror.

A serious lesson.

But the old Puritan moral
keeps a secret:

The waters of my flesh
will ripple, and webs in my skin
shake loose,
and spinning dots
reshuffle a blur of
molecules flying into
chemical dashes of existence

as I go on grinning,
showing off

the bone symmetry
of my lovely skull.

West Branch   *Charlotte Mandel*

CONCERT AT THE STATION

You can't breathe, the hard earth wriggles with worms,
and not one star says a word;
but God watches, there's music up above,
the station shakes with the singing of the Aonians,
and once more, after the screeching of the locomotive,
the torn violin-like air comes pouring together.

An enormous park. The glass ball of the station.
The ordinary world, somehow bewitched.
To a loud-voiced feast in a fogbound Elysium,
my festive rail car is being drawn.
The screech of the peacock and the bang of the pianoforte—
I'm behind time, I'm frightened. It's a dream.

As I enter the crystal forest of the waiting room,
the order of the violins is in confusion and tears.
The night choir begins wildly.
There's the smell of roses in a green-house
where under the sky of glass are sleeping
many beloved shadows crowding together in the dark.

And I imagine that everything is music and singing,
and the iron world so shakes like a beggar
that I rest against the entrance hall of glass;
Violent steam blots out the eyes of the bowstrings.
Where are you off to? The funeral feast of a shadow—
for the last time, we seem to be hearing the music.

Poetry Now   *Osip Mandelstam*
                            —Translated from the Russian
                                   by Andrew Glaze

ABSENCE

Take, for instance, a woman at a desk in a white room.
All day the blond light washes each wall in turn;
above the roof the sun makes its perfect arc. Knowing this,
she tells herself she is happy. When a bar of light
pierces the window, she watches dust spin inside the shaft,
for a while. She writes, *I am here and nothing is missing.*

She might go out to the garden, pull one savage rose
to blacken her room,
but she does not. Sitting in an angle of darkness,
she writes, *my day is defined by shadow.*

Panels of sunlight lengthen on the lawns.
The western window flares silver;
the white sun sets. Dusk brings on
its feminine shapes. *I am comforted,* she writes, *by the grainy night.*

Later, if stepping outside, she would see the sky crowded with stars,
but she will not.
The room is pearled.
Through the window
across the grey bed she watches a white disc float, but
it is only you, moon, the old cold stone of consolation.

The Georgia Review   *Kathy Mangan*

SPRING DEATH

The humanity of Europe
drained into the sore of Torremolinos
hungry for the healing sun.
And I had drained with them.

Spring broke me free.
I drifted north with my healing tan
through winding tips of almond blossoms
to flowering Alicante, Valencia, Barcelona.
And then into France.

Looking out
of the gemutlichkeit of a Swiss tavern
spring crocus' pushed through patches of snow.
I took a cab to Zurich,
caught a plane to New York City,
and flew south into Appalachia,
traces of green leading me home.

My father,
his twinkle gone,
greeted me with
damp softness and surprising warmth
more like late Indian summer.
For the first time
we shared two weeks of somber manhood.

I left for Chicago,
my sprightly tan
following the trace of spring green.
It was a warm day in April,
tulips spiraling out of the earth,
when I received the telegram.
        My father was dead.
        In the year of many springs
                my father was dead.

Appalachian Heritage   *Russell Marano*

SURVIVORS

"Since you refuse to communicate by telephone,"
my sister writes, "please excuse me
for dialing your number
and thrusting the phone

into the frail hands
of your ninety-year old mother
and forgive her struggle
to put me on."

"Don't handle her that way!"
my brother barked from another city
when I explained how I always try
to make simple refusals
with reasonable kindness.

When I told my mother my pain
over chances missed
for serious talk with Dad
about my discarding a religion
I couldn't believe
(and neither could he,
though he made it the hub
of his daily identity),
she told me he would have loved
to share with me his kindness
about freedom of belief,
and when I explained my heartsickness
over his bigotry,
she drifted into a puzzle.

Telephone lines
criss-cross these places
and letter-boxes gape,
but sister, mother, brother
just want from me
lies of kindness
or lies of cruelty,
and none of us hears
forgiveness for lies,
regret for fears,
or a clean good-bye
to what can't be helped.

Midstream   *Mordecai Marcus*

SISTER ROSE

The hospital floors give away
the sound of your crippled leg,
patients know it's time for a kiss
and another sacred heart medal.
For thirty years you've kissed foreheads
and said, "You'll get better, Honey,
trust in God."

At night your dreams are filled
with withered men, blood red women,
and infants that vanish through holes
in their hearts.

"Trust in God, Honey. Trust
in God."

The Bellingham Review   *Richard Martin*

COWS GRAZING AT SUNRISE

What the sun gives us,
the air it passes through aspires
to take back, and the day's long
bidding begins, itself a sort
of heat. Up goes the warm air
and down comes the cold.
In the cows' several bellies the bicker
of use is loud. Their dense heads
spill shadows thirty feet long,
heads that weigh as much as my grown
children, who can crack my heart:
the right tool makes any job
easy. And don't the cows know it,
and the dewy, fermenting grass?
And isn't the past inevitable,
now that we call the little
we remember of it "the past"?

Antaeus   *William Matthews*

EVENING SONG

Evening: and we
        wait for a train to pass
And my daughter
        says she sees the
Guard's van
        coming round the bend
A quarter of a mile
        or so away.

*You mean
        the caboose . . .*
I say & she looks happily
        and firmly
At the guard's van
        and pulls
At white cow parsley
        by the fence at the edge
Of the tracks
        that William Carlos
Williams
        in America called
Queen Anne's
        Lace. There's nothing
Royal at all
        about the stuff in Suffolk.

Evening. Laura pulls at
    cow parsley; we
Await the rolling guard's van.
    We live here.

Somewhere in Ohio
    the lantern on the back
Of the world's
    reddest last caboose
Vanishes
    down singing rails
Into the darkness
    of my
        childhood.

The Greenfield Review   *John Matthias*

TO SHERRIE

Things start to happen. This is not
to say that they continue happening,
there are things starting all the time.
This does not seem important to you.
You notice them for a moment and then
forget about them. Your dog
is stolen. You get another, then another.
Each one is smaller and puffier.
Perhaps your next will not be there
at all. Men and women enter
your life. The dance goes on, propped up
by the assumption that music still plays.
There are those things you have forgotten.
That is not to say they have not continued.
Changes creep in like weight. There
are no such things as decisions anymore.
Things surprise you. Suddenly, you have acquired
a child, who holds you heavy between its eyes.
Things keep starting. They take their toll.

Cedar Rock   *Joseph Matuzak*

WOMAN'S LIBERATION

After her twelfth birthday,
when the blood stained her pants, she ran—
wildly—to her bed, the bathroom. Then
the housemother, and the nurse.
           Both were kind
and tried to tell her clean facts
she had heard covered with dirt in an alley
when she was six.
        "We'll have a movie
that will help," the nurse said. "All
the girls will come to it, and then we'll talk."

In the dark classroom the child sat
with her hands over her face. Even with
her eyelids tightly shut, she saw,
on the purple screen of her eyes, the blackness
of the closet, and her fifteen year old
brother holding her to the floor.
She ate pain.
Now, open or closed, her eyes saw him—
coming and coming and coming. She screamed.

Southern Humanities Review   *Sister Maura*

WE STILL MUST FOLLOW

We still must follow through brush and through briar
The mystery of things but never say
Supernatural, a useless term
Omitted from our proper dictionary
Because it mocks all definition.
Everything, everything can be explained
Once *modus operandi* is laid bare
And pixies, kobolds, gnomes, and elves probably
Have nothing to do with the case. Admittedly,
We still have a long way to go to explain
Everything, but we've made a good start,
And damned be he who first cries "miracle."

New Letters   *E. L. Mayo*

FALL COLORS

Rioting the roadsides, the fall colors
obscure, along these miles between Hamburg
and Eden, nearby streams and steady hums
of rushing water with their turning leaves.
My eye, that practiced hunter, ferrets out
a brimming river and its flow and one
odd man fishing those capped, dark blue rapids,
his hipboots severed by the river's line.
Along the roadways, too, wait empty cars,
while owners with their rifles underarm
stalk carefully the wilds for would-be game,
their blackwatch colors blending into brush.
In town, two youngsters claim a lonely bench
beside the movie house, waiting for cars
with girls and trophies of a summer sort.
A car appears, landing them with its catch.
So much like my own boyhood these scenes are,
and yet the present's truer to their marks.
Next week, the pearl grey mist of early fall
will mute like Abishag the few leaves left.

The Hudson Review   *Jerome Mazzaro*

IF THERE IS A PERCHANCE

If there is a perchance
In the saffron-colored air
Of your workshop, where wood
Curlings adorn like young girl
Tresses the waxed floor—
And of course there is—then
Night and day, like checkers,
Will, and do, in a second
Change into day and night.

Immense control
Is a sharp knife,
Precise and exacting, drowned
In light beyond reason,
So luck a million to one
Calls, for you, the decision.

Chance, whether sun
Through the window is enough
Or rain with its drowning sound
Is too much, begets itself:
The raft on the thick brown river
Is guided—who knows?—as much
By earth as water and never
To know by the calloused hands steering.

The Ohio Review   *Thomas McAfee*

STARSHIP

in this exploded diagram of my heart, the large
chambers, home of my love for you, are seen to enclose
constellations, memories of loves long gone, vague
designs hovering above the immense expanse of now.

watch as I try to bring one of these loosely-tied
bundles of light closer: a scene may form, hands & lips,
& stroke us both freshly as at first—but no, in coming
closer the stars move apart, identities dissolve. how

massive the past is, & the unknown! everywhere faces gleam
in every shadow, but recede or reveal other faces below,
beyond, beneath them.
                    I am voyaging out, minute from many
perspectives, but where I am, a light, and drawn to light.

and here you are, vast as the sky, object of desire, source
of light, yet still surrounded & pierced through with night.

Virginia Quarterly Review   *David McAleavey*

CAN-OPENER

a mockingbird shrieks & dives again & again at the squirrel
running along the phone wire in back of our lot,

while the puzzled cat looks on: he's used to the bird
strafing *him.*

       the garden gleams after last night's rain;
the fungal odor from the compost isn't yet so bad
the neighbors will notice; a downspout stuffed probably
with maple seeds drips perpetually . . .

                I imagine a huge
chrome can-opener to lift the lid of these appearances &
reveal the significance of this moment, obscurely
satisfying; & then, twisting turn by turn its handles,

I watch these surfaces drift into the ether as contexts
stream by & meanings chase after themselves, connections
swarming into a fabric so dense everything is accounted for—
squirrel, rain, grass, tree—which now the cat runs up.

Ascent   *David McAleavey*

SPRING

Down Route 2, the farmers
are hauling hen-dressing
in flat, open wagons.
The stink is terrific.

The fields on either side
fan out in long arcs
of mud and shiny stubble;
even the crows, laboring
from tree to tree,
seem fresh, and everything
is ready to start over.

So a tractor heaves off
over the shallow bank,
and the farmer hums
or whistles, thinking
of his cows, his taxes,
or his woman, while today
paints a first wash of red
over his face and forearms.

Saddled to his big John Deere,
he throws the spreader switch,
flinging the stuff
in every direction, then rides on
through the stench and roar
like a free man, like a man
on top of something other
than a half-ton
of chicken shit: like how
you imagine a rich man, maybe,
with his money.

Poetry Now   *Linda McCarriston*

THE JUDGE

(for Bruce Wright)

The judge, as he is good, wants to listen, accept.
He sees in the eyes of this straggler
much: a premature darkening, a closing
of the room to wonder; all the evidence
of sorrow—the way breakfast came, was washed down.

The judge remembers
how doubt often seemed a saving, a birdcage
raised in poolhalls and supple
thighs; how the street
seemed to drone in the head.
The blues, the hot lonesomes, the lame
nights when nothing would promise.

The judge turns into this young face
and sees the heat
of capitalism; he knows his voice
is worthy
if only it might surge
through knives.

Now his reason
ambles, grows stony, deepens:
The judge (accountable only to life)
sees this boy, a bent sapling, a rich stem,
which need not break.

Freedomways   *Kenneth A. McClane*

PETITION

O Maker of the infinite starry spaces
That scared Pascal and now attract our bold
Spacemen and flying saucers, swiftly unfold
The rose of meaning in the bleaker places
Of earth's diurnal manifold disasters—
The stifling cities, the backcountry shacks,
The mortgaged homes of Wasps and angry blacks,
The factories and boardrooms of the masters.

And more especially, O Father of Jesus
And of the waters where the great whales go,
Teach us to know what we already know:
That your Creation was not uttered to please us,
But to incarnate Mystery, and to show
Love on the Cross and in our star-crossed faces.

The Christian Century   *Harold McCurdy*

FROST WARNING

After midnight the bright moon
teases me from bed like a rumor.
Full of innuendo and pale light,
the moon insinuates it is the lover
of my garden. Its cold rays
play among the tomatoes, seize
the last beans shriveling like green
penises on the dying vines, fondle
the riches of the crook-neck squash
I left to ripen one more day.

Strange cuckold, I stumble outside
guided by vague notions of honor,
reputation. Grass and weeds thrust
and twine among the neglected vegetables.
In the shadows I pull snaky
morning-glory from the strangled throats
of my squash. My icy fingers race
to save the tomatoes before they are
touched irrevocably. The second crop
of corn will not make. Already
the cukes grow bitter. In bed
my sweet wife dreams of an old lover
whose name she cannot remember.

Poem   *Ron McFarland*

BUSTER KEATON

Into the frenzy of falling bodies
and chaos of pastry, apollonian
and sober even as an infant,
he came, just as decades later
he would calmly step into a frame
and never leave. In the curious
oracle of his face, distant and mute
and abstracted perfect as statuary,
the lesson of his life could be seen:

Patience. Be humble. Believe in grace
and miracles of our own foolish making.
Words are mostly waste. Laughter,
like love, is a rigorous discipline.
Think slow. Act fast. Persevere.

After the sacred grove of Hollywood
has babbled, flushed, and scattered,
his image quietly endures, surviving
even when the small boat of his career
launches bottomward sudden as an anchor,
his body stubborn as a buoy or pile
fixed on the horizon, until he sinks
(soon to return, grave-faced) beneath
his flat hat floating on the water.

Or angled over some final tombstone:
the god of light, poetry, and movies
still laughs at that one, Buster.

The Hollins Critic   *Michael McFee*

INVITATION OF THE MIRRORS

I pack the mirrors again and again
until the destinations are confused
and look to each other with startled eyes,
knowing reflections cannot be trusted,
knowing that the last morning
is but the beginning of morning—
the looking out and looking in,
until the last moon jars the glass
and disappears.

The mirrors see everything: the spider
on the dresser, the woman dressing
and undressing a thousand times, the lovers
rising and falling until the night is dizzy
with their arms and voices, until the mirrors
themselves waken and darken, until they reflect
nothing but the brittle faces of despair,
a cold shining.

I go on packing the mirrors, knowing what
they hold is theirs or what they hold
is too great or too small to ever pack away;
and the mirrors, if their lives are long,
shall see me contained and carried, myself
becoming mirrors, seeing backwards
and forwards as light allows, as the invisible
world flourishes and diminishes, itself
grown wise in its own mirrors,
balancing on the horizon.

Kayak   *Tom McKeown*

THE BALD SPOT

It nods
behind me
as I speak
at the meeting.

All night
while I sleep
it stares
into the dark.

The bald spot
is bored.
Tired of waiting
in the office,

sick of following me
into sex.
It traces
and retraces

itself,
dreaming
the shape
of worlds

beyond its world.
Far away
it hears the laughter
of my colleagues,

the swift sure
sound of my voice.
The bald spot
says nothing.

It peers
out from hair
like the face
of a doomed man

going blanker
and blanker,
walking backwards
into my life.

Poetry   *Wesley McNair*

WATER

There is always a journey
to the sea, friend.
Put my bones in a good jar
for the salt is very hungry

and I want to rest
a while on the water.
Waves, like the cool white hands
of my dreams, lift me, carry me home.

Harper's Magazine   *Judith McPheron*

TREE MAN

Jacob can have his ladder,
angels, the whole business.
Give me any day the man
with gaffs on either boot

to jab his way straight up
a hundred-foot locust,
chain saw hanging behind
like a monkey's tail.

Give me the man
who hangs from a strap
in the middle of the sky,
lets go, stands on air

with the sun at his back,
saves the tree
and drops down to earth by
a single strand.

Yankee   *Rennie McQuilkin*

THE CHINESE GRAVES IN BEECHWORTH CEMETERY

What can I say? walking here, aware
to the rim of my eye of what earth is for,
and that this wedged century
keeps coming on like night,
stronger and darker all the time,
these graves in the slanting early sun
release speech somewhere, they seem right.

There would have been the old,
their mouths sagging imperceptibly
in the narcotic haze,
their long life-spans stretching out
in hope towards the small coins of sleep;
they would have been
dead Chinese anywhere.

For those who were quietly digested
when the mine-shaft's yellow mud stomach
caved in,
for those who died young, unjustly or sick,
the glittering blood-crimson characters
spattered across their stone plugs,
then so be it; you have gone back to earth
anthropos, where speech is nothing.

The dead forget life only because they have to,
the living try to fix the memory of it—
these with the spastic time of fireworks
and smouldering pig;
while their earth-fed and root-gripped
neighbours were ritualled with fuming censer
and the little moon of wafer—
no less totemic.

Now I hear them
in their right, private earth-houses.
Their silence is part of the historical one,
like that of the Somme, of Verdun.
As the sun says,
it is still early morning;
silence has passed to speech
and back again to silence.

New Letters   *Philip Mead*

THERE GOES A GIRL WALKING

There goes a girl walking,
Glinting, hurrying.
Everything bounces—
Little cap flopping, book bag alive, antic and tasseled
Jouncy jeans in motion
Up and down;
Loose thongs slapping,
Walking, walking, smooth-skinned, lower lip caught in
    perfect teeth
Totally young, clean,
Slim, smooth-legged, hurrying. It was in the Spring
They moved him
In the long black car from one white room to another,
One brick building to the next
After the long, pale months inside
Blinking in the sun, moving just his eyes,
Saying softly
Wait. Ah, can you wait a moment?
They could not. They did not. Anyway,
No girl was there. That was what he wanted, just to see
Just such a girl bounce by. She really—
Ah. She has no idea. Not at all. She is just a girl
Hurrying in the early sun, in March,
Through the first sweet thickness of Spring.

The Windless Orchard   *Dodie Meeks*

MARGINAL MUSIC

In the old photograph the two of us
stand in the center; people crowd around,
blurred toward the edges. The fiddler and I,
frozen, silent. I, tuning the banjo
with seven hummingbirds and twined flowers
painted on its head; the fiddler, clutching
the bow in his right hand, the fiddle held
under his right arm; there we stand, waiting.

With his cap pulled low, cigarette jutting
under his sharp nose, he has a profile
like a Yale key thrust toward a lock lying
beyond the margin. Hummingbirds hover
over their flowers, probing for music.
My eyes are hidden behind shades and hair,
head bent, listening for some key of my own.

I am waiting here in this empty house.
Sun falls on my paper. The music stops
in the next room. The family has left me
and I don't blame them. Empty room, quiet
house, where I sit, lonely, collecting all
the old images I can remember.

How fast they are all growing immortal,
splendid. We're becoming our own idols.

Another page, another photograph:
my grandfather looks like Charles Darwin.
The silvered glowing dead are all around
me, listening; I am becoming one
of them and all of us are listening,
staring out beyond the margins as though
we heard out there some vanishing music.

I sit here, leaning over my paper.
In the next room the instruments huddle—
banjo, mandolin, guitar, and fiddle—
all silent as me in this silent house.
Everything is as quiet as an old
picture that's fading into history
where the music is about to begin.

The Centennial Review   *R. K. Meiners*

AWAY FROM YOU

Away from you, it is you I shall love
from that tranquil distance
where love is detached desire
and passion fleshless persistence.

From that divine place
of joyous non-existence
love lies in eternity,
in pure, absolute absence.

Should I explain
the moment and the fragrance
of the Rose, which persuades
in being utterly without arrogance?

And, at the bottom of the sea,
the Star, without violence,
stares, shining, an ineffable truth,
oblivious of its transparent silence.

Poetry Now   *Cecilia Meireles*
— Translated from the Portuguese (Brazil)
by Harriet Zinnes

MOTIVE

Since the instant exists I sing
and existence is full to me.
I am not glad nor am I sorrowing:
I make poetry.

Brother of things that are runaway,
I taste neither torment nor cheer.
I range through the nights and each day
upon the air.

Whether I construct or overthrow,
whether I persist or melt away,
—I know not, I know not. I know not if I go
or if I stay.

I know that I sing. And the song is all.
Its wing is rhythmic and its blood abides.
And I know one day will still my call:
—nothing besides.

Sackbut Review   *Cecilia Meireles*
                                          —Translated from the Portuguese
                                                       by Don Wilson

THE SLAUGHTERHOUSE BOYS

Abandoned. My brother and I tiptoed
in. A cement floor
where pink stains
stuck flat fingers
into a drain.
Everywhere: hooks, rusted chains,
iron pinchers the color
of the liverwurst sky.
Our bare kneecaps felt the tips of butcher knives.

What did they once kill here?
Why did this black door keep
its mouth open for us?
We remembered cutting
our fingers on broken bottles,
part of our childhood dripping out.

In bed that night we both heard the moans
of ghost cows or pigs or
whatever died and died there
at midnight with no one looking.

Each night after that we were middle aged, fat,
wore white aprons with stained hearts showing.
Each night we slapped the silver cleavers
against our own wrists.
Each night, in that cement silence,
we were the only witnesses.

Poetry Now   *William Meissner*

OPEN POETRY READING

If body were not Art,
How many paintings, the incompleted master's piece,
The sculptor's hands would bend against clay,
The musician's ears would melt without sound?

That the writer's pen would stumble in slumber,
The dancers would lay dead in the dawn.

This shell,
        this tissue that we abuse—
It may not say all that is the truth of us,
It may all, in fact, be a lie.
But it is here.
It is what these eyes see.
So let it lure me to where you stand
That I may hold you in these human arms
Where dreams exile themselves to secrets.
In the midnight madness nights that break
Material dawns, let me confess my love
For you.
So many secrets that we would keep
From the open minds of children,
We would not dress a flower
Before their naked eyes.

The Greenfield Review   *Jesús Papoleto Meléndez*

MIDNIGHT, WALKING THE WAKEFUL DAUGHTER

(for Emily)

Late on a summer night maybe twenty years from now,
when these touches are lost as unnecessary covers,
you and a man nothing like me lie in bed,
through for the moment, though not asleep—lovers.

There is moonlight and the pulse of crickets.
His head, by your head. His arms, a weight
across your chest. All is shadow and the smell of sweat.
He breathes into your neck, "Baby, you are great."

Your fingers gauge the soft geometry where your belly ends.
The calm constriction in your throat is rising tears;
so much at peace, there is no reason to recall
the first man to hold you close, back all those years.

Father and lover, distinct. So it should be.
But, if there is comfort in the weight of his arm near your heart,
if you feel the crickets as fingers tapping lightly on your back,
then, remembered or not, these touchings were the start.

Kansas Quarterly   *Joseph Meredith*

MY MOTHER'S LIFE

A woman neither young or old, she moves
along the dark suburban street
swaddled against the night and cold
in a bright cloak. Only her face
and her small ankles are exposed
as she walks briskly towards some life she walks toward.
She is tired, and I think at this moment
she is expecting nothing. Not this. *Not this:*

A klieg light spots her from the sky
across the street. Out of the air it asks.
It asks something of the face she turns upward
to the supernatural light. I don't hear the question,
the illumination dazes the other senses.
And in the dream I watch the woman's face
as composure and surprise dispute its plainness.

I think she gives the right answer, before
the light dims, bluing, then purpling the retina.

Poetry   *William Meredith*

DEVELOPERS AT CRYSTAL RIVER

Elysian glade—
Roilings, upshudderings
Of tinsel, mirror-sycamores in wind . . .
No, we are underwater.
These are the Springs:
From deep below the bottom of white sand
Mercurial baubles effervesce
To aerate
A glassed-in bower of bliss
They keep at 74 degrees.

The mother manatees,
Brought here as babies, bring their babies here
To see the year-round decorations
And revel in each "tree's"
Renewing fruitlessness.
Muses of sheer
Indolence they are, and foes
To nothing in creation
—Least of all, those
Luscious undulating lawns downstream

Plowing through which, a sudden
Tenor scream,
The power launch veers—on guard!
Paths widen blue, then redden . . .
The huge, myopic cows go unheard. Poor
Finely-wrinkled humps
Over and over scarred
By the propellers, gaffs and garden tools
The boatmen use on them for fun,
Each year are fewer.

Sweet heaven, here comes one!—
No heavier than a sigh
Or small dirigible
Gone limp, or adipose
Naiad walking through murk, on knives. Unmarriageable
(Unless to the Prince of Whales)
In her backwater court
She'll have escaped our human hells—?

Look how the blades have cut
Even into her.

Intuiting the visitor,
She drifts closer;
Flippers held out, deprecative but lonely,
Makes to salute
Her long-lost cousin with *his*
Flippers, his camera and visor.
Time stops as, face to face,
She offers what he'll only
Back on Earth find words for—a rueful, chaste,
Unshaven kiss.

The Yale Review   *James Merrill*

ZEYDE

He had habits, my grandfather,
like tugging his beard,
pinching my cheek,
always pointing at everything
with a printer's inky finger
that made his nails shine
like mica.

He was a *tummler* whose affection
I couldn't shake no matter
how many dirty words I tested.
He knew the world, he said,
and stayed young
for a long time.

His black shoes flew like swallows
because he never walked, running
his *yarmulke* off his head.
Reading me stories on his knee,
he was too excited to follow
the words. But the ride was fast.

I didn't mind the fat white socks
he said gave his shoes a tighter fit,
or the way he used a currycomb
on his great white head.
I looked forward to the halvah
melting in his pocket
and my swoop into the air.

He called me his little heartbreaker
and taught me how to snap my thumbs
and stop bad dreams and evil eyes
with bibles and *"red bendles"*
beneath my pillow, sewed under
my dress.

When my canary died, he was
the only one whose comfort
stopped my weeping. He leaned
over and cupped his hands
over my ears, and then his own,
allowing that the Torah rejoiced
in *mitzvahs* more than miracles.

He wrapped the songbird, stiff
as a toy, tightly into a handkerchief,
eased him into the sliding matchbox,
burying everything under the blooming lilac
in the backyard, reciting prayers,
rocking slowly back and forth,
humming softly, something ancient.

---

tummler   — a joker, one who likes to celebrate

yarmulke — a skullcap often worn by Jewish men and
boys when at prayer or study, at meals, etc.

red bendles — lucky charms

mitzvahs — good deeds

Urthkin   *Roberta Metz*

THE CONTAGIOUSNESS OF DREAMS

You wake, shuddering, and as I kiss your back
I sip the dream that brought you up from sleep.
You tell me of the horror, and the dream
Has now two entrances: my mouth, my ear.
My body is the host now of your fear.
Tonight in dream I slowly press a door:
A startled woman waits upon a bed—
Enormous eyes—a hand upheld in shock—
Waking alone, I wonder who she is.

In like disturbance, poetry begins.

The Southern Review   *Diane Middlebrook*

FOR YOU, FALLING ASLEEP AFTER A QUARREL

May your sleep be calm as snow in the pleats of clouds
        we'd dream, if we had peace.
And may it smell like the aftermath of love
In the smallest crevices of flesh where we bury our heads,
Diving into the ambergris of earlier touch,
Opening it like the sky, our happiness.

The Southern Review   *Diane Middlebrook*

LIVES OF THE POET

To biographers, in rebuttal,
these facts. We whored little
and only for reputation's sake.
Alcohol and drugs were like
chocolates to the matron, merely
ensuring the inevitable, rarely
adding an ounce to the burden.

Politics? Aesthetics? Metals to harden
the mind, apologies for drought.
Sweethearts abandoned, friends we fought,
only the hazards of living enough.

What remains, to explain, to rebuff,
massive egos and sexual perversion?
More meek, more natural than a third-hand version.

Canadian Literature   *Ron Miles*

NOSTALGIA FOR 70

I think I could live at seventy miles an hour
traveling south like this forever, trees slipping
past on either side of the car while the farthest
green fields, keeping pace a little longer, fall
slowly behind as the grille eats miles of gray concrete
or forages for gnats like a whale in a shrimpbed.

It's easy calling a different room each evening home.
For when we are home, behind those mountains at our back,
trees and fields are always falling past our windows,
the house whines like an engine held at seventy, and evenings
we come to the same room a little further south.

And if, there at home, each morning before we pull
away, fields and fencerows back of the house
stand motionless, it's only because they are keeping pace:
house and field are holding steady like two cars
side by side at seventy on an endless interstate.

And though we seem to stand, we know we are traveling
steadily south, the weather is growing pleasanter,
and we are entering a season of orange groves.
Every day now for many days, perhaps for years,
ocean will lie on the horizon, a destination.

Green River Review   *Jim Wayne Miller*

MARCH LIGHT

Into gray March light,
and air
barely stirring,
these skinny, twigged branches
of an ash

tug up
resolute, unbroken
by winter storms.

You look out at the shapeless
pillowing clouds,
a rainslick street below
familiar
as this room where
you've turned around,
and again
round,
to arrive without ever leaving,
never to arrive.

But with dusk,
seeing grasses blacken
the years of wind have humbled,
you long
to wade among them,
plunging down suddenly,
wordlessly—
ankle, knee and elbow—

as into deep water
or beneath a covering wing.

New Letters   *Ralph J. Mills, Jr.*

ELEGY FOR FORMER STUDENTS

How dared you die before me? It was not
your turn. There should be order in these things:

Brilliant Gerald, elegant even in a jeep,
tossed from it, broke his neck, leaving the friend
with whom he was spending Easter
forever guilty.

Madcap Donny, on one New Year's Eve
wrapped his shining car around a tree.
Reckless Bill, flamboyant Mike,
and Ben, racing to get his auto home
in time for Mother's Day—
and Gene, warm-hearted only son
of a widow, went to death in steel.

But then those others? Gentle Jim,
tall and lovable, adored by his parents,
non-competitive (I kept for years
his letters back from college that first year,
his final one). He knew guns well,
but death came as he cleaned one.
Was it the gun? Or was it truly
the normal curve of distribution?

And Al, his father dead in skies of World War II—
Al, who came to take our pictures that last Christmas
and planned to visit us in Indiana
the coming summer: Newly engaged,
he stayed too long, kissed her goodby,
hit his head on a rail, and died.

Those were only eight out of nineteen,
and I am haunted by them and recall
how, reading "Julius Caesar"—not studying it,
twisting each word's semantic tail,
but *being* Caesar, Brutus, Cassius, Lucius—
when class was over, one of you would come
and ask, "May I be Cassius—or Mark Antony
tomorrow?"

And when the ghost scene came, each year I'd say,
"It is not likely any of you
will pre-decease me. If you should,
remember I should like to see a ghost.
Come visit. I shall welcome you."

Focus Midwest   *Virginia Scott Miner*

LETTERS TO MY DAUGHTERS

(11)

Lunching with you at a restaurant on Commonwealth Ave.
in this alien city of subways and accents,
I smile at your dark hair that wanted to escape the rain
and half-listen to two law students on my left. They are
closer to me than you, cutting your sandwich across the table;
I could touch the arm of the neck-tied young man
next to me, if I wanted. In this crowded place
all conversations blend. "In the case
of Jacobitz vs. Muller . . ." I ask if you need money;
you shake your head and fine wisps lift in the motion.
"Professor Hewitt said we should pay particular attention . . ."
I speak of the woods I just left, but your eyes wander.
She will marry one of these Boston men, I think, as I watch
my neighbor, holding his fork in mid-air, still talking the Bar.
Their hands, I want to tell you. Beware of hands
Too pale and soft. These hands have forgotten
the bark of trees. They have never sanded wood to its skin,
never felt rope slide across the palm. These fingers
have never reached into the earth, never touched
the heart of a deer. How can I tell you my fear for children
born of these men, children with vestigial arms,
two fingers to hold a fork, a pen, nothing more.

Paintbrush   *Judith Minty*

FIELD TRIP

(for Barbara Beauchamp and Susan Raymo)

Not one of them has seen it, but the fox
lives in the fields of these children's minds
as sure as real trees send roots their own size
into the balding earth. Say the word "fox"
and their eyes become dim windows that ancient
moths beat against from behind. Say "flower"
and they think "foxglove"; "song" and they sing:
"Oh the fox went out on a chilly night."

One of them, Leslie, a little older, says:
"We could get back to the school before it got us."
She's big on distances this year—the metric
system, her mother moving to another state.
It will do no good to tell her I was a child once
myself, or that foxes are the least of her worries.
All fear is equivocal. The only thing hers lacks
is accuracy, and when did content ever count?

"Maybe," I suggest, "we could get it to sit
for a portrait. You could all paint it."
"Foxes don't do that," Seth says—serious,
protective even, not telling me what they do do:
lurk behind bushes like gargoyles—lewd, toothy,
carnivorous—the strangers you don't take
candy from, their eyes terrible stars, burning,
their mouths foul with mucous . . . but why go on?

I think of those alphabet foxes—Disneyish-
cute and shy-eyed, not even sly. I think
of the leopards that pagan priests invited—
making them part of the ritual—into the temple.
The more I think, the more I like the fox
these kids concoct, that will strike like a match,
the blue-green of its eye adding an edge
to what we expect from fire, from foxes.

Soon enough their fox will become our fox.
But now, as they walk, the children tighten
their circle around me—an eye with its pupil,
frightened: Colin, the youngest, fingers
the tail of my jacket; Seth discusses weather;
Leslie looks up. Overhead, a jet trails
a thin line of vapor that widens and reddens.
The great eye of the sun burns in its socket.

The American Poetry Review   *Gary Miranda*

OPEN RANGE

Captivated by the strange, buzzing
movement of the fluorescent desk lamp,
the wallpaper gives back the familiar

blue-gray pattern, hounds-on-the-track-
of-a-hare, and I lose myself, momentarily,
gazing at the intricate maneuvers
of the horsemen, the horses, vaulting
various schoolboy fancies, fences,
rows of pale green shrubbery. There's
a breeze, perfectly flat like paper,
that doesn't rustle the motionless mane
of each horse, but sets the teaspoon
clicking on the surface of the desk,
draws my attention to the window,
the curtains shifting across the old moon
that climbs the clouds before I have time
to do something in life, to shove
my feet into a fire until the knee boots
are a brilliant red. The dogs, wagging
over a hill in the distance, are no more
than vague patches, their heads bobbing
in the moonlight. They know night
has blossomed into a living love,
and the walk home always seems longer.

The Chariton Review   *Thomas Mitchell*

CITY

Night hides outside
locked from well-lit rooms
where we reside.
Stars and moon would blind
so they too are kept
behind drawn draperies.
We must feel safe
and lock
all that we fear.

Arizona Quarterly   *Timothy P. Mocarski*

A GOOD START

Outside my window,
nothing but the patient
sound of windchimes
tempered from tropical shells.
When the wind dies
in the leaves of the ailanthus,
I can hear the garden
hose spray in the courtyard.
Always a child
playing *Heart and Soul*
with stone fingers
on a stone piano,
and the moans of Marie
under the weight of her lover.

All night I tossed
off dreams like a bargain hunter.
I begged and I grubbed
for a kind of sleep
that would keep me
strange when I woke.

But this morning I woke thinking
there is nothing in life
that I miss or would change
myself into. Not the tree
blessed in heaven,
nor the casual music of the chimes.
Not the child learning
the difficult mathematics
of the music, not the wind,
not the man on top of Marie.

How is that asking
so much from the life
of a dream I can wake
to accept so little?
There is so little of anything
that I know, and what that is
I've lived with long.
It is almost dull.
I know to greet the day
by listening carefully first.

The Black Warrior Review   *Larry Moffi*

JERUSALEM

On the verge of the infinite
Stands the city of Jerusalem.
Half divine,
Half earthbound—
In partnership with the heavenly realm.

Mountain rocks screen her,
White rocks recite psalms,
Fearsome desert rocks
Beards gray as mythic titans.

You journey there a thousand years
And arrive in the twinkling of an eye—
There stands a city
Like every city—
And she's Jerusalem.
And already you're standing in her midst—
Still yearning for Jerusalem.

You want to weep—and can't—
Such joy abounds there.
You want to laugh—it's not allowed.
Heaven offers up the afternoon prayer.

A man stands he can't say where
And every bone cries out:
Great God Merciful God
How hard to be your partner.

Jerusalem breathes a divine calm.
Burnt—she blazes into prayer;
Abandoned—she is bastioned by caves.
The hungry flock to her for bread
And the royal shepherd
Keeps watch over
The crowns of Jerusalem.

And when the city's under siege,
Jews rush there, column after column—
Vilna, New York, En Harod—
To pave the path of courage.
And seventy tongues are sanctified
And "Hear O Israel" echoes in every utterance,
And every word is a chapter of Psalms,
And every letter is a sign of prophecy.

Our eyes have seen visions—only yesterday it was.
In terror and anguish the wonder was seen.
Eye to eye,
On the verge of the infinite
In Jerusalem.

Midstream   *Kadia Molodovski*
                                  —Translated from the Yiddish
                                            by S. F. Chyet

REFLECTIONS

At the river's edge I study my form and face
that the water has taken and given back anew,
as if it were a wild lotus that grew
as if by grace
there in the tug and churn
of current and wind.
This chill and shifting shadow of my life
that smiles or frowns or frets the brow in thought
seems equally a toy of circumstance and change
as I who came to study and was caught
by that which is and never could be me.

Bitterroot   *Merle Molofsky*

LIFE'S EVIL

Often have I stumbled on life's evil:
it was the gurgling of the choked brook,
it was the crumbling of the parched
leaf, it was the felled horse.

I knew no good except the miracle
that discloses divine indifference:
it was the statue in the somnolence
of noon, the cloud, the soaring hawk.

Poetry Now   *Eugenio Montale*
— Translated from the Italian
by Jan Pallister

HETH

Purified, I struggle
to sin again:
reborn in solitary death
with no definitive being:
would that I had been born forever
or the instant of birth been denied me,
to remain pure, without the stigma of life.

Denver Quarterly   *Carlos Montemayor*
— Translated from the Spanish
by Nigel Grant Sylvester

JIMMY BRUDER ON QUINCEY STREET

I never would have remembered your name
if I hadn't driven through Allentown.
You drove your dad's car that summer
over the edge of Marsh's Dump
because I went out with a guy
in a White truck.
Jimmy Bruder afraid
of losing me,
blonde and suntan
in spaghetti shoes
and tight white shorts.
You knew, Jimmy Bruder,
I would tap my wrap-around foot
in a bigger truck,
but it was too soon
and the moon was full that night
and the dump was lush with
other left overs.
You got over me
even though your dad was mad
for a month.
Jimmy Bruder,
are you still driving
the dark green sedan?
Still grabbing girls,
rubbing your rough hands on their back blades
saying, "Don't you ever forget whose you are"
with your truck-driver mouth and tongue?

Jimmy Bruder, are your arms hard
and shiny and skinny?
Your hair still the color
of soot?
Jimmy Bruder,
I see you
in a truck's rear-view mirror
shifting and shifting,
your arm in a tee shirt
out the window.

Creative Pittsburgh   *Carol Artman Montgomery*

ROTHKO

He saw the gray on black, and that
was that. Two shapes of dark
came on him, parted, waited.
Shapes had been like chairs before.
He could always rest in a shape.
Before the gray came,
every oblong was a way to say the world,
a pitched tent of color in the wild
and arbitrary forest of all our longings.
He even found his own Matisse,
his homage, in oblongs, like a window
thrown open on yellow and orange, on patterns
that only the casual eye, lazy with joy, can find.
Sometimes he dreamt the world pastel,
dreamy curtains of color he hung
over bars of light, and left to be opened.
But he couldn't drench the black.
So, he painted what he owed it: square
after square. He gave the black
that final gray, a last oblong weight,
the simple and furious grave above the black,
the last place he had to go to paint. It was
hardly dry, but he went in to stay, inside
the shape he had made himself of himself.

The Paris Review   *James Moore*

OUT OF BODY

I search for familiar hair
of the child among swimmers,
eye-measure the distance
from diving board to concrete siding,
shudder at a story of toes
caught in an underwater drain.

As I drive my son from the pool,
he tells me he has seen himself
beside himself,
drifted out of his body certain times . . .

mothers do well to keep a foot
poised over the brake.

He remembers at three watching himself
smile at the beagle
peering through the back screen door.
Once he left his red wagon and
saw himself ride down a hill.

My fears walled in his body
must come to a certain stop.

Phantasm   *Janice Townley Moore*

LOIS IN CONCERT

Surely A-flat may be forgiven
If in a sudden flight of Bach,
Upward and intricately wrought,
The finger accidentally strikes
The black key.

The nerves' choice, though trivial,
Comes faster than the mind can master
Its consequences: whether to
Play on, to compromise the Logic
of Bach's line,

Or to restore the perfect curve,
To repeat the phrase and so disrupt
The settled audience upon
Whose casual ears the jarring flat
Rang true enough.

The nerves, the training, the character
Decide. The measure is redone,
Her peace and that of Bach restored.
"Doesn't it seem to you she's fumbling
About up there?"

The Texas Review   *Charles Moorman*

CASTLE ROCK

We climbed to the very top that August day
while the others waited below
and time reached back one hundred years.

The immense stone forming the capital of the cone
was bare of soil except in crevices,
overhanging by several feet on every side
the huge earth mound on which it rested;
it had the look of being gravely poised
on its own center—a trifle insecure.
Would our small added weight set it tilting?

No matter—we climbed. Insinuating ourselves
lithely into fissures and over projecting knobs
we worked our way, ascending, around the sides
to the upper surface, a breezy platform
smooth as a table-top and open to all four points.
Hawks wheeled and screamed from their colonies of nests
on one side of our pedestal
while down below us little hares were playing
in the ashen furze that thatched the earthy mound
and antelope grazed, far off, on the grey plains.

I dreamed I was my grandfather recalling
the landscape of a lost America—
and took your hand. Hours passed. When we descended,
the sun, declining, bathed the far brown mountains
in a rich amber glow, and deepening shadows
shrouded our patient friends . . . "It's the true end,"
you whispered musingly—and all was silent
as we resumed our memory of the present.

Harper's Magazine   *Frederick Morgan*

THE CHOICE

A clear sky may tell it wrong
when its warming light crosses
eyes and arms of a woman you have loved
and a blue pitcher standing on the window table.

All is bright, and must rejoice
in the sea-light gleaming across to the foothills
as wordless the barley sings outside,
"Think now of November."

Pinned by the exacting sun, the heart
grows its second skin,
but always fire has a last word
and speaks it out, no matter—

speaks it out to the troubled ghost
rising at night from a wakeful page
who moves in the shadows of the woman's room
like a man of ash and water.

The ocean girdles this sliding earth
as the hopeful lover chooses,
not knowing the face that will be revealed
to a new sun shining through . . .

The woman has a tranquil look,
but the room seems gathering in a tear
as he sits in his studious chair all night
reading the breathing book.

The New Republic   *Frederick Morgan*

ALEXANDER

Alexander cut the knot,
couldn't be bothered to untie it:
he wasn't good at solving riddles,
wouldn't even try it.

His adolescent blade addressed
the ancient hide and pierced clean through it.
Triumphantly he failed the test
and never even knew it.

The American Scholar   *Frederick Morgan*

THEN

        we lay, the air-conditioner on
low to cover our ardent unfolding,
as I wandered through blouse and bra
down to the pink shore of your delicate
small breasts, and your strong concentual hands
played through my hair like the green and
frothy lap of the tide, while sun
filled all the pencil-thin gaps
in the blinds with its yellow stain.

In the cool half-light and on the bed
which had so often seen me work my sex
alone, I rose on my knees over you,
grasped the flimsy slip that covered
your thighs, crotch, and "No,"
you cried, "John, no!"—more than ten years ago.

The fear in your voice brought me still
and I thought, Now
she's no good to me at all:
the late summer evenings when nothing
happened between us but a single
kiss that went on and on, weeks wasted,
and I saw life slipping back from this
high passionate hour to the randomness
of other bedrooms gummed with shallow sex,
while the body I wanted most would lie
through afteryears, a blade at my back.

I want to explain honestly what happened then,
because you were so young and there was
nothing but your youth
I wanted. Not marriage—I had never
wanted that, but you. And teasing
at the edges of my thought,
this thought: that I might marry
and screw you and then
walk away. Believe me,
nothing in that moment seemed final

but the youthful innocence of your body
beside me.

Beside me still.

Permafrost   *John Morgan*

AVIS

Four jays (I
have never seen them
flock before)
confuse the cool
air-space over
the lake with their
chasing. They
dogfight like
biplane pilots,
calling names, catching
the updraught up,
riding loose
thermals down.
They threaten each
limb, squalling,
unaware of tedium, the
predictable blue of
afternoon sky, the dim
light of a first star
trembling.
Their crests cut
the air to a puzzle.
They are among
the workers of the earth
as they
skirmish overhead,
threading day with
geometric freedom.
Yes, they
are blue and
now gone—
amazing.

Baltic Avenue Poetry   *Ted Morison*

THE SHIRT

No leaf moves. The weather
hangs in a daze.
                    Scarcely a bird-call.
By what am I pierced?
                    The sharp point of
what instrument drills through me?

There was a blue short-sleeved shirt
        I bought for you

one summer,
                    with beautiful long bone-buttons
made for frog-fastenings.
You loved & wore it till the threads showed
white from wear:
                    I can see nothing else but
this & the shape of your neck rising
out of the collar & your head—the oval
"of a second-century man" as Olson saw it,
                    & your hands
short-fingered with black hair on their backs.

                    Nothing
is clear to me except the smell of you
                    & the feel
of your skin.

Harper's Magazine   *Hilda Morley*

HIGH PLAINS HARVEST

Undulating golden waves of ripened
Rapeseed rush in lapping black loam
As gusts snap back heads
          then softly ebbing—
An intimation of north country chill.

Anxiety settles and resettles as
Sediment. Listening, whispers only,
"If it doesn't freeze before October
We have got it made."

          Reaper and winter
Traverse the field hand in hand, arm in arm,
Quarrelling lovers silently testing
Each other, walking the hard straw-strewn beach.

Kansas Quarterly   *Bruce Morton*

BIRTHDAY: TARA REGINA

memory parachutes in
like pure blue moon
and cages my thought in an old picture:
i cannot help
but to ease this too-tender image
out from my hidden wallet
among these walls
and men of stone:
it is my second daughter
whom i have not touched in four years
who's eight years old tonight
who riles my deepest rivers

the picture is a smiling one
which carefully captured her
as she dreamt in a basket
on my cousin pearl's kitchen table
it is the only one i have of her:
she fondles a teething ring
in her left hand
swinging from her neck are a pacifier
and a bib which holds a rearing zebra
her hair is walnut curly
her face round
and naturally tan
as a copper tinted sun
memory tells me that behind their covers
her eyes are pearly pecan

i am on my second pack of kool filters
my second quart of cold black coffee
into my eighth straight hour
and still i have not found the words
to say to this almost eight year old picture
that can justify all these years
that have escaped our togetherness:
like the puffs over the yellowstone springs
doubts hang
asking the question: "do such seeps of sound
in fact exist?"

regret is a word too much like *sorry*
it erases nothing that is already done

but a daughter shouldn't be a picture
on a prison bunk
on her birthday

Images   *George Mosby, Jr.*

FALL SONG

The headlights show that old
coloured leaves are milling

across the road. The atmosphere
tonight is rubbing all branches

clean, the lowest
last. Everything, rustling

included, must make
way for the sky. As the car rolls

past, a star comes
loose, slipping down like a sigh.

The Canadian Forum   *Daniel David Moses*

NIGHTMARES: PART THREE

There is some great sensitivity I want to rip
from within me. "Here, love it."
Some great flopping thing of a consciousness,
a morbid curiosity shaped like
an atavistic fish-monster:
half gills, half water-clogged lungs,
webbed, confused, half blind.

This of me is hidden:
Dark growlings. An urge to rape
many arrogant men. Secret
orgasmic sessions with myself: liquid release
of the slithery she-male.

I need some lightning, thunder, rain.
This rapt dreamer covets nature's storms and
sweats in frightened endurance of her own sudden emotions.

Intermedia   *Lynn Moskowitz*

SM

With spray-can paint,
I illuminate my name
on the subway cars and hand ball courts,
in the public school yards of New York:
S M
written in sky-above-the-ocean blue,
surrounded by a valentine splash
of red and white—not for Spiritus Mundi,
but for a life and death, part al fresco,
part catacomb,
against the city fathers
who have made a crime of signaling
with paint to passengers and pedestrians.
For the ghetto population of my city
I spray my name
with those who stand for a public art
that doesn't disillusion our sacred lives.
In secret if I must
and wearing sneakers, I sign with those
who have signed for me.

Graham House Review   *Stanley Moss*

MASADA

Masada rises like a rusted ax-
Head in the Dead
Sea plain.

We hack away at history, sift
The sands of man
To find bones

Molted for the moment
By those who chose
To survive survival.

The Jewish Spectator   Isaac Elchanan Mozeson

THE WEAVER

I would rather sleep
with the remembered map of his body
than learn a new one. It is that simple.
I wish I could tell them this,
instead of investing time,
the idea of a floating tomorrow.

But they won't believe it's ease,
not virtue, that keeps me faithful:
affection, the long habit
repeating itself like meals
and sunrise, a daily grace;

nor that my fingers have finally grown
to fit my wedding ring
and the knuckles swollen
into doors that will not open.

Chicago Review   Lisel Mueller

SATURDAY AFTERNOON, WHEN CHORES ARE DONE

I've cleaned house
and the kitchen smells like pine.
I can hear the kids yelling
through the back screen door.
While they play tug-of-war
with an old jumprope
and while these blackeyed peas
boil on the stove,
I'm gonna sit here at the table
and plait my hair.

I oil my hair and brush it soft.
Then, with the brush in my lap,
I gather the hair in my hands,
pull the strands smooth and tight,
and weave three sections into a fat shiny braid
that hangs straight down my back.

I remember mama teaching me to plait my hair
one Saturday afternoon when chores were done.
My fingers were stubby and short.
I could barely hold three strands at once,
and my braids would fray apart
no sooner than I'd finished them.
Mama said, "Just takes practice, is all."
Now my hands work swiftly, doing easy
what was once so hard to do.

Between time on the job,
keeping house, and raising two girls by myself,
there's never much time like this,
for thinking and being alone.
Time to gather life together
before it unravels like an old jumprope
and comes apart at the ends.

Suddenly I notice the silence.
The noisy tug-of-war has stopped.
I get up to check out back,
see what my girls are up to now.
I look out over the kitchen sink,
where the sweet potato plant
spreads green in the window.
They sit quietly on the back porch steps,
Melinda plaiting Carla's hair
into a crooked braid.

Older daughter,
you are learning what I am learning:
to gather the strands together
with strong fingers,
to keep what we do
from coming apart at the ends.

Open Places   *Harryette Mullen*

THE REAL MUSE

He hovers at the back door,
Biting his cigar, always buttoning,
Unbuttoning, his raincoat.

He is nondescript: no long scars,
No fierce recession of the hairline.
When you walk toward him, he acts

As if he owns the place: an impatience
With the lawn, that nailed-down look.
You've met his kind before.

They keep your thoughts awake for nights
Afterward, replaying the scene,
Slowing down at each detail or word.

They never mean you any good.
The phone calls that precede them
Are hysterical, cluttered with loud

Radios and voices gathering coherence.
Then the dial tone; then the quiet.
And now he waits for you again.

Shadows darken just above
His upper lip, as if the things he says
Were burning their way through.

This time the stories are all new
And smell of incense, at times of brandy.
As you fall into his tales' reach,

He frisks you for your valuables,
Leaves you penniless, in underwear,
Speeding through white water like a log.

The Hollins Critic   *Fred Muratori*

CONESTOGA

Creaking by pancake plateaus,
the water barrel sloshes
for a sailless prairie schooner
rolling on the horses' waving rumps,
slicing through this sunlight—
all snorts and flapping lips.
The sky's a whistling open door;
the road, a funny stumble down a hill
toward an echo of the clacking of my wheels.

The canvas, bleached and rippling,
smiles white up at the clouds, just daring them,
and stretches like a yawn above our days,
stitched with a wife's good patches,
bandana blues and calicos
to cover all the times we've left
like dust along the trail.

There are children in my groin
who dance like windchimes
on a fancy porch.
Home is out where my eye is leading,
waiting, looking like a field, but rich
and spitting water like a lady's laugh.

When you're looking for the beautiful truth
and sailing hard,
you sleep with your head upwind
of both your boots and your butt.

The Greenfield Review   *George E. Murphy, Jr.*

SOUTHERN EXPOSURES

Whenever you want to leave the clay, the deep
    furrows of your dignity, your seed
Fallen in place, you can smell cool mountain
    air in Asheville and sea bass
In Wilmington. Midnight: freight trains switch
    cars in rusting Hamlet, pass
Great silos, ponds, fields and farting sleepers
    all the way to Way Cross, Ga.
A sorority of birds knows the distance, angles
    southward, runaways of love

Flocking home. What is it ahead we see dodging
    in scrub pine, in cottonwood,
In the light we dream, the nearsighted light
    of our solemn dissipations?

Always the Piedmont will have its intimacies
    told in song; the stray sea-bird
Confused by long swells of inland foothills;
    kudzu reigning, rainfall or not.
Tobacco country: acres of white nets flutter
    in the face of Baptist restraint.
Under cattails and bladed elephant grasses,
    a marsh wind rises August hot,
Bearing the weight of morning, the gray turd
    of plover, heron, red-tailed
Hawk—cousins who never meet in this life,
    this beauty of rock and stubble
We love, blowing wild-eyed, random, laid open
    to the weather of hard words.

Chicago Review   *G. E. Murray*

TELLING THE COUSINS

Sydney? It's a building site now, says Kevin,
waiting to shovel. Ambition has gobbled the city
in towers for companies borrowing to build more towers.
Less than half the space is used. Lights burn up there to soothe
    America.

My father says it's farm boys proving their point again:
Look, Mum, we can fight! Look, Mum, we can build a city!
He and his friends keep preserving buildings and scrub
against each other. No one likes what they'd build now.

My grandfather reckoned when he knew Sydney first; it
was a lazy dangerous town five stories high
with razors up lanes, trams crushing stained corn, hawkers spitting,
straw hats on the ferry, shopgirls indignant about everything—

It was never a village. But now it would hold even more
people who never in their lives have to know the score.

New Letters   *Les A. Murray*

AMEN

That which brings death upon you
with all your dreams unbroken
returns in a childish rage
to eat the empty spots you never spoke of,
prancing over your death with a simple placard
as you open your eyes and their endless waters,
as you adjust to the daily breezes of the afterlife.

Death confuses you with its dreams,
and in them you recognize
symbols from life among the living—
like a hunter who in his return
recognizes his wasted shells in the woods.

Poetry Now   *Alvaro Mutis*
                        —Translated from the Spanish (Colombia)
                                  by James Normington

MOCKINGBIRD, COPY THIS

Mockingbird, I've been working hard
on a small routine,
a series of one-liners,
a word meant to keep me going;
please keep me going,
toward what I am.

I heard your woman sort of moan
behind your song.
But it's a job, isn't it,
the same old song
that God performed
when he made himself appear:
I Am Who Am.

Some God. Delusions of grandeur,
dissatisfactions, loneliness
that keeps us changing
a rivulet of whistles
into a river, a world,
the same old song.

Mockingbird, I don't know how you sleep.
I imagine you just hang on,
eyes wide open,
until the first star appears;
then you sleep in its billion
blinking echoes.

I won't ask if you're happy.
Don't ask me.
But there's such a thing
as courage.
It's in your gaiety.
That's what I listen to.
Then sing.

The Ohio Review   *Jack Myers*

THE FOURTH DIMENSION

Some part of us lives
always in the fourth dimension,
the invisible part

which can pass through walls,
falls hopelessly in love with light
and asks us in bad dreams
what touching is like.

This is not the soul
or anything God made,
only the imperfection or miracle
of being at last human.
It looks out of Einstein's eyes
as innocence or sorrow
for a time never to be lived in.

The Georgia Review   *Leonard Nathan*

MODERN ARCHITECTURE

to escape from internal dragons
shredding us as we shiver within ourselves
we avoid day and night;
for lack of light swallows
our distance from disaster;
the sun would bludgeon
our retinas with dark
after-image bandages,
and we can't run the treadmill-earth
at the speed of dawn or dusk;

safe in our thermal bag we savor
the logic of modern buildings
air-conditioned to a degree,
reverse-cycled against cold,
without glare or shadows
fluorescent into crevices;
no windows admit distortions of clouds
or odd views defacing constant heaven
as we breathe prescription air
in this eden of the drawing boards;

programmed from nine to five
we commute by elevator
to our homes on a higher floor,
then descend to a subcellar movie
or a mezzanine smorgasbord;
everywhere lumens are softened
for shapes we want to see;
climatized, we make love;
the electricity never relaxes
except perhaps when we sleep;

we're snug in receptive arms,
barbiturated against the sole trauma
    that   suddenly
the fuse or circuit breaker
or commissar or profit motive
or   simple   human   error

will crush us into uncirculating
freezing wet or hot humid black
in a dragon's belly.

San Jose Studies *Norman Nathan*

WINTER NIGHT, COLD SPELL

The stream has taken its shred of sound
under the ice and snow.
I trudge around the house
knocking icicles off the eaves with a stick—
they shatter and plunge into the snow.
The mercury sinks past zero.
The cold has sunk its teeth into the house
and means to hold it for days.
Inside this clear bitter night
there are many nights—
ice grinding stones,
chilled blood asleep in pond muck, the pulse thick,
and shining eyes staring among pines.
How many crouchings
near flaring fires
in houses of skin or stone,
faces shadowy
in the flickering circle—
huddlings
under robes taken from the animals,
and later under quilts in thin-walled farmhouses
with no electricity or telephones,
miles of drifted roads from town?
The woods click,
an owl rotates its head,
the stubble in the fields is buried,
a horse rustles its straw in the deep barn—
and in the house,
children asleep in their beds,
and a man and a woman lying close together
at the borders of sleep,
under heavy blankets,
within wooden walls,
circled by the pale fields cut into the forest
and the icy sprays of stars.

Carolina Quarterly *Howard Nelson*

ANABASIS

I left the valley, no longer heard
The nervous music of the farmland,
Rose into a lemon-colored reach
Of hills that led to hills more quiet.
I remembered spaciousness but not

This total sky nor the earth bending
Into itself again and again:
Lonesomeness, not the beauty of it.
My search was only for a gone time
In a place too far to matter:
Childhood and the high Missouri drift,
Nothing before and nowhere after.
I found in a ranch-woman the eyes
Of a girl who began to love me
And in her view I was kept unchanged
Along with the land she had married,
My past and future hummed by her voice,
A solo clarinet in western wind.

South Dakota Review   *Rodney Nelson*

IMMIGRANTS

My own family
Came out of the lumber forests
                of Hungary and Poland. Pregnant
Aunt Esther
                bit her tongue and kept quiet
Under a load of hay
                        when the border guard's
Pitchfork pierced her thigh.
                            Uncle Strool,
Who died an American millionaire,
                        worked by day
At a garment machine, at night
As a baker's helper,
                and slept when he could
                on a park bench. But no one
Had that soft romantic dream
Like my father.
    Half pitchman, half melamud, he deserted
The Russian Cavalry
("When they sent me to Minsk
I went to Pinsk") and embarked
Before they could hang him for treason.
                            I knew him
Mostly in his old age
                when he sang Yiddish songs
                about marguerite and raisins
And his voice rang
                        from the bathroom tiles.
            "Only in America," he would say,
"Can you buy tomorrow's paper today,"
                                forgetting
The apostatic neighbors
                        and the peddler's route,
                            blissful

in his Flatbush apartment overlooking the Brooklyn
College campus.
Immigrants!

Footprint   *Stanley Nelson*

THE THREE TOWNS

The road from Adonoi to I Don't Know
Runs on, our elders say, to I Deny.
Whatever won't let us stop won't let us go.

The erected spirit, with its will to know,
Leaves the home town in its own good time to try
The slope from Adonoi to I Don't Know.

The slope so steep, it takes us who knows how
Further from God and closer to the sky;
Whatever won't let us stop won't let us go.

The elders warn, but it is always so:
The beautiful and brash are they that try
The road from Adonoi to I Don't Know

And sometimes in their brilliance mount up so
They wind up further on in I Deny;
Whatever won't let us stop won't let us go.

The clear Satanic eminence of How
Runs further to the hermitage of Why.
Whatever won't let us stop won't let us go;
The road from Adonoi? I just don't know.

The Georgia Review   *Howard Nemerov*

TO SILVESTRE REVUELTAS OF MEXICO, IN HIS DEATH

When a man like Silvestre Revueltas
goes back into the ground at last,
there is a rumor, a wave's
voice and cry that makes ready and makes known his
     departure.
The tiny roots tell the grains, "Silvestre died,"
and the wheat carries his name in waves to the slopes
and then the bread knows it.
Soon every tree in America knows it,
and the frozen flowers of our arctic region.

Drops of water transmit it,
and the indomitable rivers of Araucania
                              take notice of it.
From glacier to lake, from lake to plant,
from plant to fire, and fire to smoke,
every thing that burns, sings, blooms, dances, and lives again,
every thing that lasts, high and deep in our America
                              welcomes it:
pianos and birds, dreams and disturbances, the quivering net

that unites in air all our weathers,
tremble and translate the funeral chorus.
Silvestre has died, Silvestre has entered his fullest music
in his sonorous silence.

Brother of the earth, son of the earth, from here you pass into
    Time.
From now on your name full of music will fly up as though
    from a field
                whenever it touches your country,
with a sound never heard, with the sound, brother, of you.

Your heart like a cathedral covers us in this instant, like the
    sky,
and your song, loud and magnificent, your volcanic
    tenderness,
fills to the roof like a burning statue.
Why has your life run out? Why
has it spilled
like blood into this cup? Why
have you searched
like a blind angel, groping against dark doors?
Oh, but out of your name there comes music,
and out of your music, as though out of a market,
there come wreaths of fragrant laurel,
and apples of perfume and symmetry.

On this solemn day of departure you are the departed,
but you no longer hear.
Your noble face is missing as if a man were missing
a great tree in the middle of his house.

Yet the light that we see from now on is another light,
the street that doubles back is a new street,
the hand that we touch from now on has your force;
everything takes its strength in your rest,
and your purity will climb out of the stones
to show us the clarity of your hope.

Lie still, brother, your day has ended,
with your sweet and powerful soul you filled it
with a light more luminous than the day's light,
and with a sound blue like the voice of heaven.
Your brothers and friends have asked me
to say your name again in the air of America
so that the bull of the pampa will know it, and the snow,
so that the sea will take it under, and the wind discuss it.
Now the stars of America are your country,
and from now on the Earth without doors is your home.

The Michigan Quarterly Review

                                   Pablo Neruda
                  —Translated from the Spanish
                        by Harry Thomas

MY BEST CLOTHES

I take my old clothes out of the cupboard and deck
my body with them. My old clothes are really my best.
They always bear the scent of time, the faded color of oblivion
and a single wrinkle of memory. Perhaps that's why I don't like
new clothes that have glamor and chic but not
the touch of your fingers and that one hair shed when
you leaned with your head on my shoulder. Oh, how many new
clothes have I worn in my life! None among them can equal
the shirt frazzled from age you wiped your tears with.
Or the battered shoes in which I once stood, on a rainy night,
under your window. I am wearing old clothes which
are really my best and I notice that a new button gleams
in the place of another once lost in your bed. And I weep.

Poetry Now

Eli Netser
— Translated from the Hebrew
by Bernhard Frank

AT MASADA

Where are they that barred the way,
Amalekites and Jebuzites,
the Hittites and the Perrizites?
Where are the taunting Phillistines,
the hordes of the Assyrians,
the might and pride of Syrians,
the grandeur of the Persians?
Where is the glory of the Greeks,
the conquering legions of great Rome,
the brutal blight of Ottomans?
All are perished from the land,
but little Israel shall stand,
as David stood,
again and again,
and even will, if need there be,
until the spirit that here abides,
shall overcome all Amalekites.

Midstream

Ernest Neufeld

MR. CHERRY

Two parts lye, and one part quicklime,
he beat his wife daily with words that bounced
and splattered like a rubber hose.
She faced him gushing through the nose.

He had a look of hot distaste,
of grim blood-pressure under black
eyebrows and black hair, a thick neck,
a fighter's look of quirky impulse,

razor quick. He played golf. One day he hooked
through eighteen holes and broke
every club across his knee, one by one.
He'd rather play baseball with his son,

he said. In the Thirties, a man he'd fired
tried to fire him with a Colt forty-five.
Mr. Cherry saw him coming and grabbed a chair.
"Batter up!" He pitched, it combed his hair.

He had a cataract. They said, "Cut it out!"
His wife who had the same, survived it.
But patience was never Mr. Cherry's forte.
He had a stroke. He sneezed and really blew it.

They carried him out. The little knife
that killed him, no bigger than a flake of rice,
went crawling into its case
of scalpels, thin as hungry lice.

The South Carolina Review　　　　　*Paul Baker Newman*

PASSOVER DACHAU

Now there are no walls
only pyramids
of brick

in the snow
we came to visit
you, Dachau

the visitors
who pass over me sign
their own obituary book

Speak to me
Dachau
Sprach

I put on my Joseph's coat
lined with many colors
round an Egyptian wound.

Midstream　　　　　*B. Z. Niditch*

RETURN TO DACHAU

Do explain to us
what has transpired
from these chimneys
in milestones of dust
embalmed in the sleep houses

Across a bare parchment
of wreathes and swathed trees
resembling a prayer shawl
once breathing of my children

the wind whispers only ashes
and I begin to be afraid.

Midstream   *B. Z. Niditch*

VILLANELLE

Like twilight bleeding on a winter day,
smiles clack and gossip to the eye
black with birds of carrion prey.

I am sick of those pinched lips that say
a love so violent as ours will die
like twilight bleeding on a winter day.

I am sick of those lean hearts that say
our flesh will burn and blow about a sky
black with birds of carrion prey.

I am sick of those thin souls that pray
a love so violent as ours will die
like twilight bleeding on a winter day.

I am sick sick of all the dead can say
of our damnation in an envious eye
black with birds of carrion prey.

Despite the certainty of all they say,
my God, beloved, how easily they lie!
—Like twilight bleeding on a winter day
black with birds of carrion prey.

New Letters   *John Nist*

HE FISHES WITH HIS FATHER'S GHOST

After his death we wade together
Chest-deep in a cold river. He smiles
And winds a silver thread
Into a silver reel and lands a fish.

Next I catch a fish and put it with the first.
They lie behind us in a wicker creel,
Dying. We cast out again and again and
Catch other fish. They also breathe the killing air.

Mother said he was not tender, she said
There never was so sexless a man.

I look back and see my fish have human faces,
Dwarfish arms and legs; his are sleek and bloodless,
Their flesh impersonal silver.
Grieving, I catch other demi-men.

When all are cooked and crisp,
He eats whichever are closest to his reach.
He ruined everything, my mother said,
He was not tender, I cannot love his memory.

I wade again into the same water
And again he casts beside me.
Again his fish are silver and mine
Dwarfish monsters. But now I know

They love their torture.
They love my grief.
All lie squeaking and beating their legs
And arms against the earth.

My first silver strikes the final cast.
It leaps at the end of my silver thread
At the end of my silver reel, and I look
At my father, who is proud of me and not tender.

The fish's sweet flesh dissolves
Upon our tongues. The last sweetness in the pan
We sop up with warm white bread.

Southern Humanities Review   *Lewis Nordan*

WE SEPARATE THE DAYS

We separate the days from each other
with nights,
the nights from each other
with days.
This way we remember our lives.

We separate the words from each other
with pauses,
the pauses from each other
with words.
This way we talk about life, about death.

We separate our lives from our lives
with our deaths,
our deaths from our deaths
with our lives.
This way we experience both

without knowing either of them.

International Poetry Review   *Henrik Nordbrandt*
                                        —Translated from the Danish
                                              by Nadia Christensen

YAHRZEIT CANDLE

The candle fit the glass
the way my body
fit the case it came in
but I'd heard of children
melted down
and of the fine
translucent leather.

Today they sell them
stacked like beans
in supermarkets.
Grandma bought her candle
from a Yiddish store
on Cherry Street
to mark the memory days

and set it on the stove
and lit it, wailing
while the wax
turned clear as water.
Milk to clear to flame
to smoke. It guttered
in a foreign tongue.

Her house was swimming
with the souls of animals.
It smelled of chicken
fat and grief, flesh
sagging on her arms and
body, water sloshing
in a bag of skin.

I was a *maedel* firm as wax.
I answered "No" to every hand,
but stuffed the word
back down my throat
before it sounded.
My mouth, a censor,
nothing passing in or out.

I'm eight years old.
I wear my leather
suit without a sigh
or wrinkle,
and I plan to sing,
to live on prayer alone,
to burn forever with a clear flame
and not be taken.

Kansas Quarterly   *Jean Nordhaus*

WHAT I HAVE

Suddenly in October the morning air
is sharp in my lungs. Each breath a blade.
The horses stamp and steam like dragons;
a gold dust of oats pours from the bucket,
filling the empty spaces. I am rich,
and each morning the mountains are closer.
Deer and lion still live in Box Canyon
and I have seen the fresh droppings of mustangs.
Summer floods took out the west fence,
but I expected that and in August the whole field

was covered with lupine and sunflowers high as my head.
You have been gone exactly one year.
The well still pulls sand by evening, two rattlers in July
and Tiger struck in the chest but lived. I am tired but strong,
all the does had twins; have you found something better?

Open Places   *Susan North*

SLEEPING IN A CAVE

Our toes touched stone.
Above our heads, the seamless face of granite.
You slept and I floated inside
the sound of your breath.

In the distance, the waterfall we had seen all day
roared down the mountain.
I thought of the steep trail, the miles behind us,
white cow grazing on the edge of a cliff.

Who would find us in those peaks and clouds?
There on that continent where no one knew our names
we had claimed a deep hole, shelter from rain.
You lit two candle-stubs while I stirred the thin soup.

Tomorrow we would climb farther, up to the second pass,
the burned-out slopes, the famous ruins.
We would lose ourselves again on that landscape
where any motion was swallowed by air.

I lay against you, thinking how fear moves in circles under the skin.
How loneliness folds up to fit in a pack.
I thought about everything which means life and closed my eyes,
knowing I was as far away and as near to it as I would ever come.

Alembic   *Naomi Shihab Nye*

TENNIS

In the hotel room, on tour,
before the match,
boy bringing bad coffee, burnt toast,

I answer the phone: my opponent.
"Peaches and champagne," I say,
winding up, serving breakfast.

If only I could jump the net, shake hands,
retire, design a line of sportswear,
redesign the sport: no judge

or score, no spin or slice or smash.
No cash. Green would be green
and white the light the players dance

within. "And croissants flown in
this morning," I add, as if winning
were flying, as if I loved games.

The Nantucket Review   *Nina Nyhart*

THE PRESENT TENSE

in which I live hurtles airless a razor's slash
so beautifully deep there is no blood for the first moment
no pain except to the eye the present tense is crammed
with fictitious memories yellowing snapshots in albums
the cheerful pretense of a history shared as we share stanzas
of embarrassing old love songs no one ever sings

the present tense in which I live is a morning of Canada geese
flying overhead in their supple formations crying to one
another in a language I can't decode and the single deer
bounding through the woods graceful as if it were the
Morning of Creation the present tense is a telephone ringing
and a stranger's voice *Who is that?* and I ask *Who is that?*
and a stubborn silence welds us together

the present tense might be called a rosary as the moments slip
by smooth as beads worn by the fingers one after another after
another as wordless prayers rise to the lips though just as
rightly it is a fallen nest in which tiny blue eggs rot or
yawning over a stained sink or the noise of air-brakes or
a child smudging a newspaper photograph with his forefinger
unable to comprehend what he sees

it is embraces and kisses and silly arguments lapping
around our ankles it is as warm with flying seeds gay and
prodigious as if even trees lived forever it might be a drawer
of snarled string and paperclips white creases suddenly ringing
a helpless eye it makes the charge *Now the day is gone, now
the day lies with the others, what did the day mean,
why did you see so little—*

the present tense in which I live hurtles so airless
a siren falling from the sky a Chopin cadenza too swift
to be grasped a bird's closing eye and slowing heart and
nothing to call it back when the eye-dropper and the egg white
have failed the present tense passes too swiftly to be
grammatical it is all one syllable shared as we share stanzas
of songs we never sing it is all we know it might be heaven,
or hell

The Atlantic Monthly   *Joyce Carol Oates*

MOVING OUT

There is much work to be done before we leave:
vacuuming, mopping, scrubbing, scouring:
the remorseless sorting of trash.

In the emptied house our footsteps clatter.
Our shadows veer across unfamiliar walls.
We have been toiling for days to detach ourselves,
To take leave, and to properly mourn.

What to make of these puzzles, old handmade gifts
quaint and dusty with love?
—How to cherish, how to honor
and discard, and feel no grief—
How to throw out outlived clothes.
How to clean house.

How to move out.
How to deal with dried cattails plucked from a jubilant
    Sunday afternoon,
and files of letters, a din of hurt voices,
debris of eighteen years.
Manila envelopes stuffed with snapshots.
Small bewildered smiles squinting against the sun.

There is much work to be done before we leave,
though the house sighs now with emptiness.
And somewhere water gushes hot and angry from a faucet.
The house is clean, but not clean enough.
It must be readied for the new tenants.
Steel wool, sponges, buckets, mops.
There are hours of work ahead, most of a night,
why did we think we were nearly finished?

For an instant I see everything clearly:
it has something to do with light reflected
in one window reflected in another.
It has something to do with quick footsteps overhead
as I have never heard them before.
The house will outlive us!
I will never be deceived again!

But the moment passes, like any other.
The faucets gush. We toil, we labor, loveless.
We will work through the night, the lights burning.
The house is a witness that must be effaced.

The Hudson Review   *Joyce Carol Oates*

PRISONER BETWEEN THE PANES OF GLASS

Prisoner between the panes of glass,
like insects which the naturalists examine,
were I able to approach myself, in front of
my astonishment, I would see me now.
Not the emerald of the scarab,
nor the flamingo's rose-white plumage,
nor the multiple eyes of the fly
would cause me such confusion.
Oh you who can see me from outside
tell me what is happening to the trees,
the corners and the flat roofs,
to Venus and the Moon, to men,
to the gardens, the alamedas,
to the diving suit with which I'm dressed,

to the resplendent river's margin,
the long paths of eucalyptus,
the unbreathable cane flowers,
to the anticipation of the future,
to the golden ring of David
the vain waitings, the hands
which taking their leave always return,
return without dialogue, in silence;
the intimate spikenards, the eyes
I seek without desire because they speak to me,
the stone lions, the docks,
the distant stream of dances,
to the marble Niobe, all in tears,
to Brahms' Requiem to which I did not listen
upon my failed deaths,
to the versatile course of
the divine and pathetic hours, burning,
to what I am, was not and perhaps will be,
to what I am and I will never be.

Jazz Magazine   Silvina Ocampo
                                   —Translated from the Spanish
                                          by Jason Weiss

ROBERT LOWELL

I read with him at Hopkins, substituting
For Theodore Roethke who was sick or drunk or dead;
No one could explain what I was doing there
With Wilbur and cracked Lowell on the stage
Reciting poems about our animals.
Dick Wilbur turned to me and said: "I like your
                              'Turtle'."
And I: "I like your 'Grasshopper', or was it your
                              'Groundhog',"
Confusing him with Richard Eberhart,
Another Dick. But it was Lowell held
My attention in the rostrum's glare
As almost incoherently he read
Poems of personal agony and the State
Engraved in furious speech—our anti-Horace
Of the nuclear American Imperium.

The Hampden-Sydney Poetry Review   *Richard O'Connell*

SLEEPING PILL

And then the drug takes hold
And goes down into your arms and your fingers,
Wipes the pain along in front of it, washes
Cells clear. The white moons come back in your fingernails,
The bed unfreezes and cradles you; it becomes

That nest you remember from childhood, coaxed from a
      mat of leaves,
Wedged up close to the oak tree.
You lie there with your friend with the pale green eyes,
      the one who was shot in Vallejo.

He smells of dust and soap, there are shadows of leaf on his
      face; he props
Himself up on one freckled elbow;
The hot California day wraps you in its dry tart smell.

And now the drug drowns the base of your spine, it floats
A pale warm ocean around the base of the tree, drowns
The lover in his khaki pants; pulls you
Empty as a new boat,
Home.

The Paris Review   *Diana Ó Hehir*

NUDE WITH GREEN CHAIR

Attending to some inexpressible wish
I assemble my paints and a nude woman,
A small thin towel draped around her shoulders.
She sits in my green and yellow chair before the window
And I shall paint her with her knee up
And one elbow crooked around her head.
It is a warm sunny Sunday with a blue sky,
And the birds are singing in a solid chorus outside
And the churchbells are tolling bass-voiced in the distance
And her eyes sparkle and move about the shadows of my room.

But she must be still. I will not look at her eyes,
I will not paint them till last
And then I will leave them blue horizontal ovals.

Curious, but I know already that the chair in my picture
Is alive and ready to discuss Plato with me,
I know the one curtain at the window is cold and shudders
                              in the wind,

That the red cushion I threw in a corner
Lies there in silent protest itching to be hurled
Out the window on the whim of the wind.
The red floor is awash with footfalls,
The prayer desk in the corner drowns with men kneeling,
The green foliage and birds in the wallpaper
Struggle to rise from their pigment and wave in the wind.

But the chalk and gray woman
Sprawls like an awkward statue
Pointy in a disapproving chair,
Frozen into the one still pose
Which is all I think I can manage.

The rocks and stones are more alive than my hands,
They are less afraid of the branches and vines

That wave about in the clouds and blue of her inner sky
And witness her whispery breezes and snow storms
And green spiders and surf and dog-barking fiestas
Where her eyes emerge from the dark lagoons
And dance with fire about the ships.

The Altadena Review   *Antony Oldknow*

THE END OF WORLD WAR ONE

Out of the scraped surface of the land
men began to emerge, like puppies
from the slit of their dam. Up from the trenches
they came out upon the pitted, raw earth
wobbling as if new-born.
They could not believe they would be allowed to live;
the orders had come down: no more killing.
They approached the enemy, holding out chocolate
and cigarettes. They shook hands, exchanged
souvenirs—mess-kits, neckerchiefs.
Some even embraced, while in London
total strangers copulated
in doorways and on the pavement, in the ecstasy
of being reprieved. Nine months later,
like men emerging from trenches, first the head,
then the body, there were lifted, newborn, from these mothers,
the soldiers of World War Two.

The Massachusetts Review   *Sharon Olds*

ADDRESSING HIS DEAF WIFE, KANSAS, 1916

The clear obsession that holds up the walls
and rafters of sunlight and pulls everything down
isn't what holds my talk together.
I touch and you touch. Just
who am I talking to? Explorers
made names on lies,
there used to be passenger pigeons in numbers
far beyond understanding,
but the stories outsized the flocks:
fur traders said the Mandan tribes kept
unthinkably huge pots of the pigeon oil
boiling grey at both sides of a village.
Remember how once in anger you dipped my hand
in a vat of boiling red dye?
When I screamed to have you hear my pain
I had committed a lie
of intention, and the lie, like love,
was larger than either you or me.

Sometimes I'll tell you stories
to have you watch me listen. For instance:

I should be walking outside
a while on the dirt road that leads to town.
Stand alone, with you at the window;
the clouds now dragging curtains of rain
across the Great Midwest,
that holds to very little.
Yes, the details matter: even in rain
the hills bursting from their seams.
I'm terrified both by what
I do and what I don't do, and terror,
like anything human and said,
survives just beyond understanding.
For you, the wind among the apple trees
is more dynamic for its unheard strengths,
unquestionable as my sitting up just now.

New Orleans Review   *William Olsen*

IN DESPAIR HE ORDERS A NEW TYPEWRITER

I want a typewriter
Without any letters
Just punctuation marks
Letters make words
Words make language
There's too much language
Too little punctuation
It all runs together
There's no content anyway
When every advertisement
Annuls another
Every politician's speech is
A try and see what you make of it
Rorschach inkblot

Cut down on the question marks
My mind nowadays
Is so full of question marks
They could make enough coat hooks
For the congressional cloakroom
But let's have some numbers
We can number all clichés
All platitudes all promises
I yearn for a future
When all advertisements
All political rhetoric
Will be nothing but numbers
And pornographic novels
Nothing but asterisks
And convulsive commas

Or for at least a return
To those simpler days
When it went without saying

That an enemy could be
Hazardous to your health
When enemies meeting
Used punctuation only
Could exclaim merely
By the definite emphasis
Of war club or battle-ax
And with dagger or spearpoint
Put an absolutely final
Unmisquotable
Unmistakable period.

The American Scholar   *Elder Olson*

FALSE PROPHET

My father was not inarticulate,
yet he could share so many ways
that did not call for speech:
his finger lifted from the wheel
could point a swarm of bees,
an earnest flock of migrant geese,
a pawpaw thicket rich with fruit.

Sometimes it wakened me to wings
before the flash of color
betrayed the bird.
Once it marked a possum
on a persimmon bough,
tail arched with young,
poised against an autumn moon.

Later, a waxen finger prophesied
Spring would never come again.
Yet when herons we had watched together
in November wheeled north in April,
the world was suddenly alive
with long-familiar promises of more
than trumpet vines and humming birds.

Kansas Quarterly   *Emanuela O'Malley, CSJ*

MY GRANDMOTHER AND THE VOICE OF TOLSTOY

Many years ago my mother and I skated
And walked and rode the train all
The way downriver to Odessa for the baths,
The over-sharp odor of mud that sank into
Me and into her like the voice of Tolstoy.
A handsome young man in Odessa told me
That Tolstoy was fatigued by a thousand
Years of history. But how terrible even
To remember those odors into which we sank,
That they mingled with the odors of spring
Off the Dnieper. Her death, too, must have been

A sudden awakening. I skated downriver
All night for the start of a long dream
Off a dirt floor to America, where everyone
Eats and drinks. As the lamps in the shtetles
Went out it seemed impossible to tell
If that world was real, though I could shift
From one leg to another with ease. Never did
Tolstoy quite understand what it is to be common,
To fall asleep having sung all the songs
You knew. Tolstoy didn't need to.
His desire to seek in the skeleton and muscles
And jaws and paws of the Russian Bear
Kept him from seeing that bear scattered
In the bricks of the new world over
The ocean. The thick ice near the middle
Of the river caused the sun to rise
Out of itself. This, too, was the voice of Tolstoy,
An army of imps striding on water, tugging
The eye of the world open and it saw me.

The Gramercy Review   *Steve Orlen*

SIGNATURE

The chinese written character
for tree
signifies height and grace.
Insignia of a hand's ingenuity.
This tree is tree
just as I am
my signature. I write and swear
its spelling
spells me magically
entranced into a net
of rune and rebus. Hieroglyph
for who I am, have been,
am willing to be. Emblem caught
in thread of ink,
name of my name. A slight ideogram
scripted picture, whose stitch predicts
a map cut in my skin
on forehead, elbow, palm.

The Greenfield Review   *Carol Orlock*

THE CHILD

A nameless presence on the paling green
Across from your windows: one who looked to be
The offspring of our complicated joy,
Who watched, like distant promises of birth,
Our kiss in the doorway.

                    Grown more distant now

Her inkling of embraces in a room,
As I no longer cross the patch between
The gaps in the hedge, the fence's shattered rung,
Nor you come to the windows as you did,
Expectantly.
           And so she must begin
Again her play, unparented, the grass
Tinged with the colours of a gone-off spring,
Your curtains drawn. Darkness is falling
And no voice calls, "Come in."

Prism International   *Frank Ormsby*

FOR YOUR INFERIORITY COMPLEX

an old man
on st catherine street
told me
impossible dreams
are the only ones worth believing in

these drunks
you can't take them too seriously

i thought
before i first saw her

met her
touched her warm body
(and was told to
get my hands off)

it was love at first sight

now i listen
to cab-drivers, television repairmen
and plumbers
hoping to learn her secrets

her weaknesses
and what she is like when tired
and alone

i am an idealist
whose love
knows no bounds

a product of the north american soap opera
the hemingway hero of the seventies

her tall boyfriend
with the fast car
and paul newman smile
is no competition

The Malahat Review   *David O'Rourke*

A SMALL ELEGY

My friends have left. Far away, my darling is asleep.
Outside, it's as dark as pitch.
I'm saying words to myself, words that are white in
      the lamplight,
and, when I'm half-asleep, I begin
to think about my mother. Autumnal recollection.
Really, under the cover of winter, it's as if I know
everything—even what my mother is doing now.
She's at home, in the kitchen. She has a child's stove
      toward which
the wooden rocking horse can trot.
She has a small child's stove, the sort nobody uses
      today, but
she basks in its heat. Mother. My diminutive mom.
She sits quietly, hands folded, and thinks about
my father, who died years ago,
and then she is skinning fruit for me. I am in
the room. Sitting right next to her. You've got to see us,
God, you bully, who took so much. How
dark it is outside! What was I going to say?
Oh, yes, now I remember. Because
of all those hours I slept soundly, through calm
nights, because of all the loved ones who are deep
in dreams—now, when everything's running short, I
      can't stand
being here by myself. The lamplight's too strong.
I am sowing grain on the headland.
I will not live long.

International Poetry Review

           Jiri Orten
      —Translated from the Czech
         by Lyn Coffin

OLD MEN

It seems to me the kindliness of old men
Is something incommunicably vast.
My grandfather, behind them all, plays chess
With learned Yiddish Socialists in Heaven,
Where he awaits me slipping onto his knee
To hear "The Story of the Man Who Travelled
From Place to Place." My other grandfather,
Who sat in a brown chair near the piano,
Not permitted by his wife to talk,
But smiling shyly, like a house aflame,
Waits also. And an Irishman named Frank,
Who trimmed the bushes in the Project gardens,
Called me "Margaret O'Brien" for my braids,
And let me use the shears. Lastly, my dad's friends,
Who lived like sheep in lonely East Side playgrounds,
Petted me, taught me checkers patiently

For many windy autumns.
It seems to me, then, God's a grandfather:
Infinite tenderness, infinite distance—
Not that I have any religion, but
It seems the way to talk about old men.

Poetry Now   *Alicia Ostriker*

THE OWL

It's his eyes
that you can't forget.
He is seeing through
darkness to the death
of a mouse.
He doesn't breathe, blink.

His claws have locked
him onto a branch.
He is wearing a coat
of feathers to hide
the turn of his thoughts.
All the trees
here become skeletons.
Only their shadows bow.

The gravity in his heart
is pulling the forest
closer so he can
focus on the smallness.
A toad inside
his stomach is, at last,
turning into an acid.

This is how the owl's
mind must turn.
This is how it is
to be so awake the mind
is too large for a skull,
eyes almost lidless.

The intensity of the will
burning down
to the hottest coal.
His eyes set the forest
on fire, the dark fire
that even the moonlight
cannot put out.

The Nation   *Sue Owen*

CUDWORTH'S UNDERGRADUATE ODE TO A BARE BEHIND

The female bottom is a sight
Unveiled, to ravish with delight.

Ripe plenitude's duality,
Fused thus in buxom symmetry,
Provides our best reflection here
Of Plato's primal, perfect sphere.
It's true the breast's expressive curve
Aesthetically excites the nerve;
But nothing else can quite inspire
Such rising to a pure desire
As your retreat, enticing me
With its fulfilled entelechy.
I know why Adam, self-deceived,
In all his blazing veins believed
That apple dangled by his wife
Was offered from the Tree of Life.
So, goddess, neither frown nor freeze
At love's impulsive liberties;
My pinch is tribute to the spell
Suffused from your symphonic swell.
Nor is my forward finger's thrust
To deeper mysteries, mere lust.
That boy, begotten in the stars
On Venus by triumphant Mars,
Is unabashedly direct
When his theophany's erect.
O feel his stiff divining rod,
The potent sceptre of a god,
To exercise unquestioned sway
When, cleft with ecstasy, you splay,
Your buttocks cupped in my firm hands,
Soft putty to their strong demands.

New England Review   *John Ower*

BABEL

Isaac Babel is riding with bloodthirsty Bolshevik soldiers.
The settings are poetic: sun, moon, stars
Shining like sabbath candles, frogs croaking
Like old peddlers, wheat flapping in the breeze.
But Babel records, too, the severed head of the old Jew
And the hurt, half-dead cry of his daughter:
"And where in the world is there a better father?"
"Come on, Babel, get your ass in the saddle
Or your head will roll on top of that old kike's head."
Babel is off and riding, telling funny stories
To his fellow revolutionary soldiers,
Stalin glaring from that rising sickle moon.

The American Poetry Review   *Gary Pacernick*

FIRE

In the wood that dissolves in spark and flame
then in silence and vanishing smoke

you watched your life come apart with a silent clamor
And you ask yourself if it has given heat
if it knew some of the forms of fire
if its flame ever burned and illuminated
Any other way it will all have been in vain
Smoke and ash will not be forgiven
since they were powerless against the darkness
—like firewood burning in a deserted room
or in a cave which only the dead inhabit

Denver Quarterly   *José Emilio Pacheco*
                                        —Translated from the Spanish
                                                by Frederick Luciani

THE KISS

A glaze of ice glistens in the manure
and rutted mud of the plowed-under garden,
as the brittle crack and squish of my greased boots
leads me plodding beside my vague reflection
this crisp April morning, as if my image
still were in the thawing earth I planted,
and last year's buried spring still stirred and shined
within the slick clay of the chunky soil.

With boot-grooves packed with mud, my cold cleft toes
imagine they can feel the rising moisture;
stopping by a three-year *red delicious* tree
to scrape a fresh bud with my fingernail,
I see that it is green inside—alive,
having survived the winter in my care.
Yes, it is soft and moist, it has come through
under my care, and I remove the wrapping—
aluminum foil and tape—around its trunk
that saved it from the gnawing mice and voles
who girdle fruit tree barks beneath the snow.
Now on the yellowed grass, the perfect turds
of starving deer, glimmering like planets,
circle the tree, and the faint waft of skunk
brushes me with a puff of wind; I like it,
it quickens my sense at the exquisite edge
where pleasure cloys, where one knows surely
what the human limits are. I kneel
beside another tree as if to dress
a child for school, snipping a dead branch,
as sharp sun strikes the creased foil by my knee,
catches my dazzled eyes and makes them tear.
A stranger here might think I truly wept.

Spring blood sings in my veins even as it did
some thirty years ago when I planted
my first apple tree. No lessening
of pleasure dulls the sun's feel on my arms,
a warming chill, or the female curves I see

along the hill that fruit trees make when my eyes
follow slowly, caressing every slope,
then moving on. I am gathering my life in
now with a breath, I know what thoughts I must
hold back to let my careful body thrive,
as bone by bone it was designed to do.

A gust of wind comes off the upper slope.
Having followed me, my youngest son,
crying "Watch me, Dad," runs along the ridge
much faster than I thought he could, launching
his huge, black birthday kite; catching the wind,
the kite leaps for the sky, steadies itself
as the string goes taut. It glides above me, swoops,
floating its shadow on my squinting eyes
that, pruning snippers still in hand, I shield
from shocking light. Designed like a great bat—
hooked wings and pointed ears and long white fangs
grinning like Dracula—it swoops again,
eclipsing the sun, hovers, dives at me;
I see the mock blood oozing at its mouth
and random dribbles brightening its belly
just as it crashes in the apple tree.

I take more shining foil from the tree
and roll it into two enormous teeth,
set them in my mouth like fangs, and chase
my son across the field, running faster
than I thought I could, until my ribs
smolder in my chest and my clay hooves ache.
He screams as if the demons of his sleep,
returning from the frozen underground,
were actually upon him—as I catch him,
grapple him down, sink my gleaming teeth
into his pulsing throat and suck, suck deeper
than I have ever sucked, tasting his life
sweeter than any apple I have known.

Poetry   *Robert Pack*

ON SITTING UP LATE, WATCHING KITTENS

The cats are home tonight. Unblinking eyes
Like gilded floating discs beneath the couch
Creep silently as kitten-tiger lies
Beside the fireplace. Her sisters crouch
And stalk their kill, but, pouncing, cuff her ear
And roll away, exposing bellies plump
With milk and egg to squeaking vengeance. (Here,
In this, the rage of jungle beasts—who jump
For fireflies, and dance with pipe-smoke shades.)
Their panther-mother smiles; her footstool-cave
Is too the surrogate of feral glades.
She stretches there, and knows that they behave

As she has taught them, living dual lives,
And even in the fat domestic, something purely *cat* survives.

Ball State University Forum   *Eric W. Paff*

ALL SONGS

The graveyard is wet
and white marble meets my hand
with careless kiss.
Angels, caught in forever flight,
guard the names carved in rock.
My shoes move through green
and rain slips down the faces of trees.
All songs can not be of love.
Some are written in green rain and stone.

Ball State University Forum   *B. Sanford Page*

COLORATURA

The groans of love
at 3 a.m.
A rickety hotel

spindled on
a spine of stairs
a block from Blvd. St. Michel.

Italian maybe,
she moans towards climax
and holds us fixed

next door,
involuntary voyeurs,
stick-figures
stuck by visions . . .

A fleshy prima donna
in her prime,
each breast a handful,

the lifted thighs,
her straight-man in between,
steel-eyed and silent,

bringing her to it
five or six times
before dawn.

Champagne and wireless
in occasional spaces—
her voice only.

A half hour
illusion of sleep—
and then again

the urgent
throaty cry
soaring to coloratura.

Stiffly we lie
in cold damp sheets
and listen.

So much, so little space
between two faces
of a wall.

New Letters   *Geoff Page*

PAINLESSLY OUT OF OURSELVES

Sometimes after the break of a bone
It mends harder in that place.
And properly stitched, skin can be grown
In a network of cells like lace.
The same nails we pare and throw away
Appear again out of ourselves without pain.
Hairs men slice in the mirror each day
Before another day grow back the same.

Flaps of flesh with which each eye
Is sealed at night in sleep
Open wide when the sun is high
And all the lashes leap
As the pupils recede from light
Like two black birds in flight.

Southwest Review   *William Page*

HIDE AND SEEK

In the backyard of the world
we played, he and I:
I covered my eyes, and he hid:
One-two-three,
not in front, not behind,
not inside me.

Since then I've been searching
so many years.
So what if I don't find you?
Come out already, out,
you can see that I've given up.

Poetry Now   *Dan Pagis*
                          —Translated from the Hebrew
                               by Bernhard Frank

THEODORE ROETHKE

1

Watcher of reedy places and cries,
he saw the pond teem like a thick broth,
and, parsing the moth wing's cuneiform,
observed the order of the mayflies' strict house.

2

Vision's trader, rich in the lore of mud,
he sent his poems out like argosies.
They returned from the next county
swollen with sheaves of light.

3

In August the marsh glowered like a solarium;
glassy flies skirred, but no one saw
a broad man wearing a slouch hat
muse through the brittle cattails and be gone.

California Quarterly   *Morton Paley*

RENAMING THE EVENING

After you have gone,
I turn out the light
in the front room.
From the porch I watch
the neighborhood children
play in an unmown corner of the yard,
and when their fathers call them in
from the darkness,
their laughter remains
like a splinter.
The moon begins to sleep
in the nest of branches above the house
and the night settles in the attic
beneath rags of cobweb.
I wish I were with you now,
driving south, past farms
and rusted machinery,
toward your home,
where the hills falling away
from the highway
are like two hands held out
revealing something hidden.

The Cape Rock   *Eric Pankey*

ALBUM

Having no past, I invent one
and pluck a once-upon-a-time from dappled glass:
ancestors picked fresh and prime
from someone's faded photographs
and fitted to my own creation.

Grandpa here, derbied, proud,
a genuine handrolled cigar slung from his lips.
How arrogant he looks, but for his twinkling eyes—
he was so good to me when I was young.

Farther now, creep on the rosied Aubusson and press your cheek
into a cloud of dimity and eyelet lace that billows up
in grandma's lap to hide a bashful face
from the chittering of whale-boned women
smiling high above brooched bosoms, figureheads
upon a bow, rippling out from yesteryear.

Gathered to me, every face consoles
and arms reach comfort out of history.
Kindly lips say, Come child,
beckoning across a century,
and when I choose to turn and leave these strangers where I live
they'll help me back to stand with them forever
in their ageless, safe oblivion.

Webster Review   *Carol Papenhausen*

SNAKE HILL

The dirt road rose abruptly through a wood
just west of Scranton, strewn by rusty wire,
abandoned chassis, bits of food.

We used to go there with our girls, those nights
in summer when the air like cellophane
stuck to your skin, scaling the frenzied heights

of teenage lust. The pebbles broke like sparks
beneath our tires; we raised an oily dust.
The headlights flickered, skunk eyes in the dark.

That way along the hill's illumined crown
was Jacob's ladder into heaven; cars
of lovers, angel-bright, drove up and down.

There was a quarry at the top, one strip
worked out, its cold jaws open, empty-mouthed.
A dozen cars could park there, hip to hip.

There I took Sally Jarvis, though we sat
for six hours talking politics. I was
Republican, and she was Democrat.

We talked our way through passion, holding hands;
the moon, gone egg-yolk yellow in the sky,
tugged firmly at our adolescent glands.

I kissed her once or twice, far too polite
to make a rude suggestion, while the stars
burned separately, hard as anthracite.

The city was a distant, pinkish yawn
behind our backs as we leant head to head.
The dead-end quarry held us there till dawn.

The Southern Review   *Jay Parini*

TUESDAY, 5 MARCH (MORNING) 1963

It was daybreak a little while ago,
an old, dying light, and now
the blueness of a Southern bay
in the icy blast of the north wind.
A day was upon us it was enough merely to uncover,
splendidly remote from all our sufferings.
A man soon to sit in the dock stares at that blue,
and yearns for a wonderful freedom—as when the thought
of a new day, born on the soft banks of northern streams,
seemed like the idea of a world held in the thrall
of the celestial rage of ancient wars, and the masses of wildflowers,
beyond the last streets of the Veneto countryside,
became, as the morning's frost began to melt, like people
naked under their armour, beneath the warm sun of Homer.
And you want to put a poet in this dock,
polished by the trousers of so many poor souls?
Well then, enjoy yourselves. But when Poetry downs tools,
Justice becomes like the blind calling of swallows.
Not because Poetry can claim the right to rave over
a bit of blue on a mere, sublime day that begins
with a mournful sadness. But because Poetry is Justice.
A Justice which grows in liberty, in the splendours
of the spirit, where the birth of days,
the beginnings and ends of religions, can be encompassed
in peace, where the acts of culture
are also barbarian
and he who judges is always innocent.

Alembic   *Pier Paolo Pasolini*
—Translated from the Italian
by Nigel Thompson

THERESA

In these, our first
few hours, deliciously
wet with each other,
I believe in everything

I've ever believed in
and loved best
and as well: your eyes,

hair, body in my hands,
beautiful mouth, murmurs
of pleasure. Theresa, you.

The Canadian Forum   *John Pass*

LISTENING

Wind and pines
strum
and speak
to each other,
sounding and echoing
like strings
lovingly plucked,
kissing the spring air.

They whisper
at the edge
of my house,
blowing my thoughts
in blurred rings
encircling tomorrow.
Wind-hugged,
I listen
for my name.

The Atlantic Advocate   *Nancy Passy*

ETHICS

In ethics class so many years ago
our teacher asked this question every fall:
if there were a fire in a museum
which would you save, a Rembrandt painting
or an old woman who hadn't many
years left anyhow? Restless on hard chairs,
caring little for pictures or old age
we'd opt one year for life, the next for art
and always half-heartedly. Sometimes
the woman borrowed my grandmother's face
leaving her usual kitchen to wander
some drafty, half-imagined museum.
One year, feeling clever, I replied,
why not let the woman decide herself?
Linda, the teacher would report, eschews
the burden of responsibility.
This fall in a real museum I stand
before a real Rembrandt—old woman,
or nearly so, myself. The colors
within this frame are darker than autumn,
darker even than winter—the browns of earth,
though earth's most radiant elements, burn
through the canvas. I know now that woman

and painting and season are almost one
and all beyond saving by children.

Poetry   *Linda Pastan*

ARMAMENTS RACE

and Mrs. Stephanopoulos said oh yes I am happy
I am very happy and why not for I have
a fine husband and beautiful children

and we have our health and enough to eat and we all
love each other exceedingly and if I had just one wish
this is what it would be

that when we die we should all go to heaven together
in the same instant so that none might feel
pain or despair at the losing of any other

and I said oh Mrs. Stephanopoulos oh my dear
you should be truly a happy woman for never
have so many been toiling with such a blinkered devotion
in the deep-down mines and the shiny laboratories
to make your one wish come true

Pequod   *Evangeline Paterson*

THE WATER TOWER

An engineer's dream, holding water
Over the town as if to dedicate it
To the heavens or keep it clean, the tower
Is painted blue that it may blend
Into the sky and disappear. It won't.

The sky's not so blue, and besides, only
Mirrors, giving us back ourselves, this
Town, would be invisible to us. Now
Its ladders and blue pipe-guts showing,
Its squat rotunda exalted like a parody

Cosmos, it is obvious and artful,
Realistic above the tangle of branches,
Mocking us and our fancy lives. We are
Just simple village folk. See—what thirst
We have we can quench from the sky.

Poetry   *James Paul*

EVENING HARBOUR

The bereaved years, they've settled to this
Bay-windowed guest house by the harbour wall.
Each of us loved a man who died,
Then learnt how to be old and seem cheerful.
I think of being young, in the coastguard station.
Those cement cottages with the washing

Swaying in the sea wind. What can she see,
The girl I talk to? Victorian childhoods
Where little stick figures go flickering
Along the roads? Such eagerness that used to be.
A butcher's shop, a boarding house, the dead
Are smiling from the windows there.
So many names, faces, and used things.
Dry calico, the smell of cedar wood . . .
I keep them in a drowsy kind of wisdom.
I have my drawer of rings and photographs.

The waves rustle on the beach like starched silk.
And girls come walking down a staircase
Into a wide room where lamps are burning.
Love was first danger and then children.
At sunset, when I saw the white beacon
On the quay, I felt a tear starting.
But I was happy, like a woman who opens a door
And hears music. It was your face I saw.
I heard your voice, its gentleness.
And I stared over the water at another coast,
An old woman in a sleep of voices.

Prism International   Tom Paulin

LINKS

Even at its edge the lake is no miracle,
flanked by copious reeds and the noise of birds
which from this wooden pier seem now to call
us to an instinct of images and words
born from shades of trees that frame the greys
of water knifed by a blinding solar path,
at times swelling on the backs of reptiles at day's
end, still ravenous and driven by the wrath
of ancestors, now bones, cutting water
and hyacinth roots with thick tails, lunging
at a slow snake or fish beneath the flutter
of dragonflies and the high shadow of a thing
they've never seen, wide-winged with the first feathers
sprouting through scales in the new coolness of the weather.

Epoch   *Ricardo Pau-Llosa*

REVISITING THE FIELD

I come back to cold lights
high above the field. We learned
how to lose every Friday night:
Jefferson, Madison, every goddamned team
in the league. Remember the last game,
when Henry ran that punt back in the mud?
Didn't we all block big as trees?
Later, the crowd outside, drunk, too cheap

to buy a ticket, threw insults
until Wallace swung his helmet
and ran them to their cars.
It was ourselves we hated:
the coach, the cheap shots in practice.
Knocking our friends down,
out of breath, out of confusion.
Isn't it all bull-in-the-ring now?
The terrible smack of our hearts
against our lives. Look, you sonsofbitches,
this is no sentimental crap-game.
I can still hear those cleats
echoing off the school walls.
I don't know how we got here.
I don't care.
I'm talking about this ugly ground,
a memory of forgotten dirt.
Go ahead, finish this beer,
Sing if you need to.
You'll get the same empty applause.
Look at this picture.
Can't you see the floodlights, blurring crowd?
Didn't we all block big as trees?

Tar River Poetry   *Walter Pavlich*

TWO FIGURES

What is bright or rare here, is called oriental.
This is the west, and it is home.
We are afraid of something here: the ornamental.
You know the pictures where the blue foam

Rises in vicious coils and stops above
Those two small figures, but it looks so calm?
Where home is, is plain, water only water, and the love
Those two must feel for one another under the bomb

And blast of their ocean is unspeaking—as the tiny
China figures in a closet in this house will not come alive
But are alive, even though they are cold to the tiny
Hands who wish them, will them, breathe them alive,

And almost see each mouth open in each head,
And if they be broken, be sure they are dead.

En Passant / Poetry   *Molly Peacock*

BEFORE THE WAR

We could not ignore the sky in those days,
Whether at cloudy dawn on a mountain road,
Half seen, half dreamed from the old car's back seat,
Through a web of sleep, chill air, and dusty cloth,
Or when it sang with the sun's triumphant vibration,

In August, over the apricot orchards.
We felt, without feeling, the weight of that presence,
Its absolute wholeness, clear and contained,
As everything then was supremely itself
And more than itself
In the light that enters new eyes undiminished.

And as birches spilled their seed down the wind
We were running, we shouted and leaped
In the span of that power;
We escaped from under our limiting roofs
To wander the mica-flecked sidewalks of infinite suns;
We shot blunt arrows up beyond our vision
And waited for their hissing return,
Shafts burying half their length in the ground.
Kites, gliders, skyrockets, balloons—we sent them all
To reach toward the brilliant separateness.
And so in the midst of our dazzle and sweat
We were tranced, silent watchers of airplanes
That came peaceful and solitary then,
Lulling the hot afternoons with the buzz of summer.

And while the red-tailed hawks drifted beneath the dome,
We drew our battle plans, conducted bloodless wars,
Rehearsing the truth for the oldest among us:
To die on their backs in the sand,
Staring up at the sky through the lightning of pain,
And a film coming over the cruel blue . . .

But those left to grow, young trees still standing
After the lumbermen passed through,
Would find our gaze drawn down at last
And held by the new geometries of girls,
Imagining in them the mystery come near.
Lying beside them in the grass,
We would see the sky grown pale and remote,
Fragile and impotent as a Chinese bowl.
It could not keep our eyes, we would turn from it
To shadow the glow beneath us,
Possessing sky and earth
In bodies met with ours,
Our arrows all come back,
All questions answered.

The New Magazine   *James Pendergast*

BEFORE THE BREAKING

When my father spoke in his natural voice
he made babies cry,
and that perhaps is the reason why
I stood my ground some distance from his dream
and never fully understood his hidden
gentleness, dark like distant rivers
climbing against the midnight sun.

Never knew, I say, until night
ripped it all away and rough
course hands held the wind at bay
before the breaking of the storm
above where my father lay.

Mountain Review   *Lee Pennington*

LAKE WALK AT NEW YEAR'S

All things are possible—

The life your hands, your soft mouth
breathe into me, is gentle, is real.
My first sounds: those of a woman
responding to woman. All night
we heal each other, make miracles.

Later, we leave Chicago
to go to a cabin at the edge of the year.
The party lulls: a few of us enter the woods, snow
and silence. Once you stop and hold me,
as your voice holds me when you tell me
I will be your lover. The night is a frozen expanse
of mist, sightlessness; all things are softened into gray.
Hand in hand we begin the walk across Wonder Lake,
walking on water.

The Beloit Poetry Journal   *Leigh Perez-Diotima*

THOSE TREES THAT LINE THE NORTHWAY

They called them shadblow or service bush
because when the long-boned, flat-bellied herring
choked the river, their white flowers pillowed.
Spikes of boys, their pant cuffs rolled,
their shrieks startling out cascades of frogs,
would spear and net the fish just climbing
into spawning streams, the moss stained blue-green
out of the Hudson. Their catch set by
for the communal feast, the boys knelt with their families
and the circuit preacher who came to help
them bury the long dead, marry the long loved
and christen babies and the mended living into spring.

The Greenfield Review   *Ellen Perreault*

PHOTOGRAPHS

You hold up your photograph;
I hold up my photograph
and in between
there's sand,
a swamp,

a plain,
an ocean teeming with life
until it's thickened like soup.
Also, there is
the survival of the fittest.

If we came out from behind
our loving faces
I'm afraid
we'd be at
each other's throats.
We've got hobbyhorses.
We each have
our own interests
to protect,
our ruthless genes
to push.

If the love were genuine
I suppose it wouldn't work.
We'd be laid wide open
to pirates
and gigolos,
cheats and hawkers
who could con us
and cuckold us.
They could charm their way
between our opportune sheets
and steal our fatherhood!

It's the way
we keep the tensions balanced
between the bodies
in the crowd.
An altruistic-looking skin,
a selfish programme
in the cell:
The photograph hides
the mechanism,
the love conceals
the care.

Prism International   *William Peskett*

STORY FROM ANOTHER WORLD

My father talked with ghosts—
would wake up in the pitch-dark night and see
them standing there, huddled at the end of the bed:
Grandfather in his scarlet regimentals
with the little stars for wounds,
Grandmother in her Irish shawl and bonnet—
and the other dead.
"Louie," they'd whisper, "Louie, can you hear us? Listen!
We've come to tell you something. Listen, Louie—"

And sitting bolt upright
he'd talk with them
of things from another world.

And over toast and smiles we'd listen, too—
to what they said and did,
to how they reached out flickering hands and touched
his cheek—just so—
and to prophecies
that did not come true.

But towards the end of his life,
when he was always looking over your shoulder
out of some far-off window—
banished by rum,
or by the cancer eating in his bowels—
they became
invisible—
and waking in the pitch-black night he'd sit
straight up—
                    listening
to his own veins beating in his ears,
the distant furnace hum, branches scraping the eaves,
but know
they were all there, standing
huddled at the end of the bed,
reaching out empty hands
and whispering—
"Louie, can you hear us? Listen! We've come to tell you
something. Can you hear us, Louie? Listen, Louie,
Listen!—"

No-one to answer them.
No-one to touch.

The Ontario Review   *Paul Petrie*

HOME AGAIN

Home again
with a bucket and spade.
And standing on an empty
Wind swept beach
I'll dig for China,
or build magnificent castles
on dreams
of golden sand.
And I'll watch them
crumble
into the froth-flecked edge
of the tide;
and the holes will
bubble full
of salt water;
and childhood will

fall away
like sand castles;
and life will fill slowly
to a brim,
like the holes dug
in the years ago
on a distant
empty beach.

The Atlantic Advocate   *Susan Petrykewycz*

OVID

The man could love the city he detested
Seeing its leafy columns, its columns
Of leaves on the seven hills in his mind,
Shelter for more than one man's good
Or bad luck, eternity stilted above
The sloppy Tiber. He hears fountains,
A childish patter of syllables, the plea
Behind his hexameters. His style lapses.
"Forgive me, Caesar, I want to come home."

Occident   *Richard Pevear*

LEAVING HERE

Up the river, where it thins out
And runs on pure north light
Like a white horse gone down the pasture's height,
Up the river, there would still be my mind meandering about.

Down the river, where even the water
Is filthy rich and the people talk black-eyed South
In a land red as beefsteak that brings water to the mouth,
Down river, there's still my poor north voice flat as the ugly
    daughter.

On the horny road, where it's all skin
From delta black to wool of Wyoming,
From big rigs and roaring oil to beer-blue light in the jukebox
    gloaming,
On the horny road, there's a part of me I can't get in.

Out from here, where it all gets wide
And only death could lie so far
And play as slow as that prairie guitar,
Out from here, I still couldn't die, not down deep, not inside.

But in my ear, there's still the story I'm so everlistening tired
    of.
When I want to feel her tongue or hear the evening fall without
    a shove,
It's there tick-telling me on the shelf.

To be alone, you only need yourself—
But to be lonesome, you have to love.

Poetry Now   *Stephen Philbrick*

UP AGAINST THE WALL

Up against the wall
hands high, feet wide
         apart
move an inch and I'll bust
your heart
spread 'em nigger—you know
how it go
move your ass, ain't gonna
tell you no more
you ain't got no rights boy
you going to jail
one funny move
                         and you going to
hell!

Southern Exposure   *Cleve Phillips*

A LETTER TO AUDEN

About suffering you were wrong, Wystan.
You who understood so much of this world
went askew on its human position:
how suffering occurs, how people react.
It is true that in Brueghel's "Icarus,"
for instance, everything *does* turn away
quite leisurely from the disaster. But:

Who has not seen countless real instances
where crowds, riveted to an accident,
try to save the bodies from the wreckage;
dive icy green waters for the drowning;
weep genuine tears at a stranger's fire?
All had somewhere to get to, but instead,
knowing that there but for the grace of God,
tarried to share the human condition.

Shenandoah   *Robert Phillips*

THE DIVER

Like a blind man, with eyes habituated to the darkness,
Until he sees only miracles,
My sight is constantly being seized
By fugitive sea shapes of a frightening animation,
Mutable identities
Like hallucinations; in this world

Of the dream and the unterminated
I find myself perfectly exposed.

I am a diver, if you should ask, who cut off
And vanished in the vast depths.
The sea controls my body, entangles
My footsteps; I am
An involuntary, deviated dancer
Who aborted his skeleton
That he may become at every moment
Terror of his terror, nightmare of his nightmare.

Poetry Now   *Nikos Phocas*
—Translated from the Greek
by Kimon Friar

H. S. BEENEY AUCTION SALES

A quarter century ago and
Lucky as MacArthur, they
Busted ashore at Inchon,
Blasted out of the Yellow Sea,
Across the mud flats of Blue Beach
To Seoul, to the Yesong, to
The hills of the forbidden north and
To ambush at the frozen Yalu.
They cursed the gooks and they cursed
The Joint Chiefs, and when luck turned
They cursed Truman and Acheson.
Three months they fought over the shoulder;
Then, tempered, fell in behind
Ridgeway and the U. N., grumbling their way
Home to a new luck.

Time teaches strange lessons.
Today their minds are elsewhere,
Puffing the crowd, coaxing the curious
From behind the tables,
Promoting next week's sale.
Now Charlie passes up a porcelain
Cup and saucer, and Joe adjusts his glasses
To read aloud, "J-pin.
Hand painted in occupied J-pin."
His finger circles the lip, and
He holds it to the light.
"I see nothing wrong with it,
And I want ten dollars to go."

A fat man offers two, snuffing his nose.
Children scamper among the furniture.
Behind me a young housewife whispers,
"Junk. There's a real auction
In Hanna City. Three generations,
Lots of history. Let's go."

The Spoon River Quarterly   *David R. Pichaske*

AN OLD POLISH LESSON

Imagine the shivers on the cold metal
table as you are waiting for the doctor
to conduct the backward count.

Imagine the last number.
Imagine the dove begging forgiveness outside the nest,
or the ground opening and closing over the face of a friend.

Wander through it.
Now let yourself be coached back
by the angelic voice of the white haired nurse.

Scrape the muck from your bare feet.
Remember those feelings, and tomorrow

the air will be thick with orange blossoms
and the willow limbs will dance the mazurka with the wind.

Cedar Rock   *Deanna Louise Pickard*

SNOW, SNOW

Like the sun on February ice dazzling;
like the sun licking the snow back
roughly so objects begin to poke through,
logs and steps, withered clumps of herb;
like the torch of the male cardinal
borne across the clearing from pine
to pine and then lighting among the bird
seed and bread scattered; like the sharp-
shinned hawk gliding over the rabbit-colored
marsh grass, three beats and a dip, crying
in talon-hooked cries to his larger mate;
like the little pale green seedlings sticking
up their fragile heavy heads on white stalks
into the wide yellow lap of the pregnant sun;
like the sky of stained glass the eye seeks
for respite of the glitter that makes the lips
part; similar to all of these pleasures
of the failing winter and the as yet unbroken
blue egg of spring is our joy as we twist
and twine about each other in the bed
facing the window where the sun plays
the tabla of the thin cold air
and the snow sings soprano
and the emerging earth drones bass.

Open Places   *Marge Piercy*

THE LABOR CAMP

Of her friends at the textile mill,
Anna, Hedwiga, Janina
Were shot, loaded into the oven.

Their crime was stealing scraps of cloth
To sew pillows.

My mother, her heavy flesh sunk
Into the sofa, recounts this incident
Without irony, without glancing from
The worn comforter she shreds
For the cotton filler. She's sewing pillows.

Germans trucked her from the farm in Jedynia
To a textile mill. It wasn't
That bad. As long as the massive spools
Kept spinning, their lifelines of threads
Stretched in spider webs overhead,
The bolts of cloth stacked,
She could eat and sleep.

There were never enough potatoes.
The barracks were cold, the women loud.
There were few lights. They slept on wood.
To this day she finds her bed too soft
And shoves planks beneath the mattress.

She raises her head to sniff the air,
Steps over the unsifted hair sprawled
At her feet, walks into the kitchen
To check if her loaf of rye
Is burning in the oven.

The Centennial Review   *John Pijewski*

WITH THE BAIT OF BREAD

Child, you were and
you learned to be.
For a while, Armenian was
a wish you could not fathom.
It is still a sea
and we fish in it for food
with the bait of forgotten bread.
The moon will be less specific
with the sun and the tides
if you wish it, Child.

You are yeast scattered upon the
ground and the rising dough
will grow into tomorrow.
You are the yeast of
your friends in one language
or another.
If not already, Armenian will
ring in one of your ears someday.

Ararat   *Helene Pilibosian*

RENOIR'S CONFIDENCES

She sits beside him
and leans slender hands and
arm against his arm.
Will confidences tell a deeper knowing
than she at first presumes?
The sun patches bright white on her dress,
the touch of red in shoes and hat
filter her fragile grace.

His pose: casual, too.
A hat, angled,
shades a black brown coat and dusted pants.

Her eyes drift down.

Will the landscape's dappled green hear
when their eyes meet?
Will they shatter the moment's quiet perfection?

Connecticut Quarterly   *J. Michael Pilz*

AN UNTITLED POEM, ABOUT AN UNCOMPLETED SONNET

Unpacking our summer house, I found
A sonnet that had wintered it out
Without the fourteenth line or final word.
It's always like that: just at the edge
Of pulling something off, a jealous lover
Appears, the phone rings, the door knocks.
Interruptions interrupted everything.
Even that poor, bedraggled poem,
With its half-couplet just sitting there
Like the ugly duckling at a high school dance.

The Spoon River Quarterly   *Sanford Pinsker*

DYING

Nothing to be said about it, and everything—
The change of changes, closer or further away:
The Golden Retriever next door, Gussie, is dead,

Like Sandy, the Cocker Spaniel from three doors down
Who died when I was small; and every day
Things that were in my memory fade and die.

Phrases die out: first, everyone forgets
What doornails are; then, after certain decades
As a dead metaphor, *"dead as a doornail"* flickers

And fades away. But someone I know is dying—
And though one might say glibly, "everyone is,"
The different pace makes the difference absolute.

The tiny invisible spores in the air we breathe,
That settle harmlessly on our drinking water
And on our skin, happen to come together

With certain conditions on the forest floor,
Or even a shady corner of the lawn—
And overnight the fleshy, pale stalks gather,

The colorless growth without a leaf or flower;
And around the stalks, the summer grass keeps growing
With steady pressure, like the insistent whiskers

That grow between shaves on a face, the nails
Growing and dying from the toes and fingers
At their own humble pace, oblivious

As the nerveless moths that live their night or two—
Though like a moth a bright soul keeps on beating,
Bored and impatient in the monster's mouth.

Poetry   *Robert Pinsky*

VIRGINIA BEACH

Those mornings in green mountains
when the air burned off blue,
        mornings of the fog coming up
    from all night in the ground,
mornings when the sky was down again—

    one blind morning I stood numb
as a child kneedeep in saltwater
        waiting for the cloud to lift.
    It lifted. It rose
by disappearing, rain back into sunlight.

    Water is one thing on water,
another, like smoke, on a mountain side.
        Mornings I can imagine the men
    still go out along the Blue Ridge
to handcut trees—summer and winter—

    hickory and oak, sycamore and maple.
Nineteen forty-something-or-other.
        I still see my father
    sawing on my sister with a whip.
Virginia green. Sometimes when you love someone
    you think of pain—how to forgive
what is almost past memory.
        All you can remember is the name,
    some place you have in mind
where all the blue smoke, all the ghost water collects,

    where the ground lets go. One year,
along the Shenandoah, the county flooded a farm.
        You could row out over the trees,
    the outbuildings, the barn, green.
You could almost see them down there drifting whole.

The first time people see the ocean
they say they are afraid because they feel anonymous.
What you need to name you save
by saying it out loud.
You stand in the visible, blue air, sure that your voice

will carry, clear that it will all come back in another form.

The American Poetry Review   *Stanley Plumly*

WRECK

Damn fool feeling her up
with both hands and one or more feet
pulled beside me at the light
—ice-blue Ford with a fire inside—
looked at me once and winked, then
left screaming, rubber smoking on a February street
behind him in a swath as wide
as jubilation. It was quick:
two can die
so fast; two blocks contain a life.
Outrageously they burned away from stop
and could not stop again except to meet
outrageous luck
in the face of a truck.

I saw the flame flare out,
I saw the chrome curled melting back
on flesh, and steel burnt crisply black,
burning hand on burning thigh
and panic frozen into burning eye;
                                        and

I have seen it since I have seen
meat on braziers grin and wink
and melt to ash. I have seen
fire freeze and ice burn
and bloody smoke blown upwind
into visions. I have seen
them die—
and waked,
cursing Ford and fire and two too dead
to cool the conflagration in my head.

The Southern Review   *Noel Polk*

RIVERSIDE DRIVE, NOVEMBER FIFTH

The sky a shock, the gingkos yellow fever,
I wear the day out walking. November! and still
light stuns the big bay windows on West End
Avenue; the park brims over with light like a bowl
and on the river
a sailboat quivers like a white leaf in the wind.

How like an eighteenth-century painting, this
year's decorous decline: the sun
still warms the ageing marble porticos
and scrolled pavilions past which an old man,
black-coated apparition of Voltaire,
flaps on his constitutional. "Clear air,
clear mind"—as if he could outpace
darkness drifting home like a flock of crows.

Poetry   *Katha Pollitt*

SONS

I take my son to visit in the distant
nursing home some months after
my last pilgrimage. The aged lady
here is almost cataleptic, I am warned,
and seldom leaves her ever-twilight room;
is mute unless approached.

I shout our introduction into deafened ears
and search her clouded eyes for light.
In some vague way she is aware that once I was
a part of her and mumbles questions to
the "little girl you've brought."

I catch the stain of dribbled vomit on her bib,
the acrid scent of urine in the room and wish
to run. Surely, I say, this isn't happening
—it's all a desperate dream. I sense being mocked
and want to shake her to her senses crying,
"Look at me, I am your son!"

The boy sits mutely, staring through the curtains,
as I dance my graceless dance with death.
But later, when we've left, the pangs of
my diminished self are softened as we smile
and seem to touch through moistened eyes.
He is my son.

Poetry Canada Review   *Don Polson*

THERE IS SOMETHING

There is something of every good-bye in this.
Somehow it is always winter,
there is snow at the curb,
the driveways are gray.
The soles of your shoes are turning dark and wet.
She stands there in her robe.
She has just come from packing sandwiches.
You are pushed by some schedule
and the weather,
compelled by her voice,
which is speaking.

She kisses your cheek
and hands you your life in the neat paper bag.
For this moment, in her face,
all your seams are mended,
your habits white.
You hug her and smile.
Your gift is your silence.
You leave.
Yet later, when you remember,
it will be that
always her eyes were sad,
her hand on your sleeve.

The Ohio Review   *Deborah Pope*

THERAPY

It wouldn't do to go crazy.
Impractical. One must still get in the crops.
The garden must be weeded. The dog
Wants for a bath. The fence
Has lost a board or two, and the gate
Squeaks. A madman about the place
Couldn't make a thing better. But evenings,
Lost before the fire, supper finished,
The paper read, weariness working at the tendons
Like high-priced city whores, it's okay.
I can stand full-up like a tree and let slip
Into the inward curve of an idiot's face
Hollering, *Here I am, beets! Here I am,*
Potatoes! Here, corn! Here, chicks! Here! Here!
Next morning, all is right,
And purged a bit;
I can take an old hand hoe out to the fields
And taunt them everyone just a tad more.

Cedar Rock   *Ken Poyner*

WATCHING MY DAUGHTER SEW

Her mouth is filled with silver pins.
Her hands move slippery through silk.
Together, in silence,
we listen to the whipporwill
out there behind the moon behind the house.
    All night she'll sing the heartbreak blues
    and plait her nest
    where we will never find it.
        Her nest is woven of shadow and smoke
        and her children hide
        in the leaves of her song.

Then we turn on the lamp and talk again.
"What are you making?"
Cautiously, she takes the pins from her lips.
"A dress for the dance."
>   Will you have a good time at the dance?
>   I think but do not say out loud.
>   The whipporwill is surer in the dark
>   than we are in the light.

Her needle goes in and out, in and out
of the shimmering cloth.
I also don't ask,
Why do you sew faster
when you're running out of thread?
>   And, watching you, why do I want to cry?
>   The whippoorwill is surer of her name
>   than we are sure of anything.

Carousel   *Katharine Privett*

THESE MAGICIANS

These magicians I mean,
they aren't the tired middle-aged men
in tatty capes, entertaining a room
full of sleepy after-dinner Lions
with a little sleight of hand
and pick a card;
nor the upstarts with big feet in sneakers
and buck teeth,
pulling the same old rabbit
out of a new hat.

These magicians I mean walk the streets,
with faces innocent as apples;
ordinary men who smoke pipes
and stop to pat a dog.

These are the dangerous kind.
Their eyes make you think
you are something other than yourself.
They speak in charms and portents
using ordinary words.
They tell you over and over again
their sleeves are empty, but still
you believe them full;
and when these magicians start changing shape,
one illusion after another,
the only mirror around
is yours.

Next thing you know,
they've disappeared,
leaving you wrapped with miles
of bright silk

and run through
with their painless swords.

These magicians I mean
have eyes that let you see
whatever you will,
and hearts of holy stone.

Yankee   *Sarah Provost*

REPETITION

I have seen the hardened innocence
Of a boy's large eyes locked on his mother
Dying, all questions set aside before that fact;
His father bending beyond their gaze
Into the fold of similar hands
Repeatedly clasping the same defeat.
No memory serves this brutal fact.

And I have seen the several patterns
Mourners take, as though the ritual
Put their blackening thoughts from them;
All, public in the ignorant eye
And anxious to the final touch,
Detailed habits keeping old questions down
Where memory folds like calloused hands.

Denver Quarterly   *Wyatt Prunty*

ELEGY

The way the hell-bent years consume my pleasure
Numbs me like a hangover—a vague pressure
My mind wakes with. Time is like wine, in fact:
The older it gets, the stronger its effect,
And age is like a sea I'm pledged to drinking—
Or I'm a damned swimmer, forever sinking.

Is this a toast to death? Oh no, my friends.
I need to live; my suffering depends
On it. Distilled from all the hours of wasting
Are bound to be some moments worth the tasting:
A few sweet songs, a story told to pass
The time, a tear or two shed in my glass—
And perhaps by the time I've drunk life dry,
Even love will drop around to smile goodbye.

Cutbank   *Aleksandr Pushkin*
                              —Translated from the Russian
                              by Robley Wilson, Jr.

GOING BACK

At night in Piazza Navona, I used to lie supine
on a bench in search of quiet
while my eyes with straight lines and spirals
joined the stars together—
the same ones I watched as a child
when stretched out on the pebbles of the Platani;
I stammered prayers in the dark.

Clasping my hands beneath my head
I remembered the times I went back home:
the scent of fruit drying on the wicker shelves,
of wallflower, ginger, lavender;
when I was about to read to you, but in a low voice
(you and I, mother, in a shadowy corner),
the parable of the prodigal son
that haunted my silences always
like a rhythm that breaks out
with every step
without meaning to.

But the dead don't come back,
and not even for one's own mother
is there time when the road beckons;
and again I'd go away, locked in the night,
like the one who fears to stay till dawn.

And the road gave me my songs
like grain full-to-bursting on the ear,
like the flower that whitens the olive groves
between the blue of the flax and the jonquils;
resonance in the eddies of dust,
the sing-song of men and the creaking of carts
with lanterns that sway dimly—
the light of a firefly.

Webster Review   *Salvatore Quasimodo*
                                 —Translated from the Italian
                                        by Rina Ferrarelli

AT TIMES I FEEL LIKE A QUINCE TREE

At times I feel like a quince tree, dated, old,
A tree no longer in fashion. I ask three girls:
"Do you know what quinces are?" They look at me
Strangely. Each autumn I go in search
Of quinces along unfrequented country roads.
Likely as not the best that I can do
Is to find a Kieffer pear tree as substitute,
A pear tree along some lane where nobody lives.
Such pears will do in a pinch, but how I long
For a few gold quinces, flannel to the touch.
There is nothing to match quince honey on a day
When snow is swirling, the past seems far away.

Kansas Quarterly   *John Robert Quinn*

VALEDICTION

Sometimes I can believe
it's almost a comfort,
that loss could be
like a blanket drawn above the shoulders,
snuggled into deeply. And how perfectly
it fits my body. So I'd remain

all night, sleeping as a child does,
surrounded and protected.
Waking at any hour I'd hear
the familiar slip and wash of water,
or a little wind high in the trees.

In this way your life
might be consigned to memory.
Though still I find myself asking:
Did you see me standing beside your bed?
Did you hear me speaking?

Yes, I saw you
beside my bed.
Yes, I heard you speaking.

When I turn to the window
the lake does not look so dark,
lit up with its stars,
the air does not feel so cold.
Could you hear what I was saying?

I wanted you to be happy.
That's all I ever really wanted.

So I might rise
quietly and walk downstairs,
across the porch and down
to the beach, to the lip of the water.
Standing there, I'd watch the shapes

of trees extend their darkness,
hear the water move a little toward me.
But it's only myself I'd find looking
back out of that stillness,
one shadow among others,
featureless and alone.

The American Scholar   *Lawrence Raab*

RAIN FALLS. IT DRIES . . .

Rain falls. It dries. Sun shines. A horse whinnies.
Look on at the world's minute flutters.

In the depth of a workshop a lamp burning, cat meowing,
girls with clouded fingernails sit there giggling, sewing.

They're eating cucumbers. It trumpets. Scissors snap.
They forget that Monday, Tuesday are so alike and drab.

Beyond the corner a cologne dealer is having his day,
I also know his wife, from her perfume's bouquet.

Her predecessor was old. She died. And like anyone else,
they plain forgot her. Like the square root of twelve.

They do know how to forget. Yesterday's dead
are nicely frozen in their hearts by today's bread.

A newssheet flies: now the wind is wearing a paper cap.
They also forgot a poet. I know him. He's still at it.

He still goes to a café. I see him, less on than off,
the shoulder of his dark suit is all dandruff.

What else, in this poem? Shall I maybe let it drift
as does an undressing plane tree its ancient leaf?

They'll forget as it is. Nothing really helps.
Listen on to the world's tiny flutters and yelps.

The Kenyon Review   *Miklos Radnoti*
                              —Translated from the Hungarian
                              by Emery George

ECOLOGICAL LECTURE

Consider fish: magnesium flows, slowly on the whole,
In their veins. They trap oxygen, gill it free,
And breathe comfortably under ice floes,
At the bottom of lakes, and in tanks behind glass.
Their spines bend double, their tails are mighty propellers,
Each eye turns a hundred and eighty degrees, independent of the other.
They track with their noses, their ears, talk sensibly back and forth,
Eat rapidly and often, sleep as if hung by invisible wires.
We eat them.
What a marvelous engine under God
Is the fish! Graceful, delicious,
Well employed cleaning our pools, lining our bellies,
Reliable, eternal, almost loyal
In dog-like fascination for our hooks, our lines, our baits, our flares, our nets
        and sieves and traps:
Consider if you will the glorious fish.
And next, the cow.

Waves: Two   *Burton Raffel*

DEMOLITION

The silence is first. Still water
not yet breached by fish or sin.
Then damnation as a wall explodes
like a heart attack in a man
relaxed in the sun.

The clock tower teeters. Old fears
that the first fall may be forever.
Then tumble as time and clay

collapse like ancient myths on
men's room walls.

The noise is cataclysmic. Suns on
dry lands pour in rains of fire.
Then hollowness, as broken things
hold to earth like sperm
to wet conception.

The dust is settling. Unshaped words
shift toward curse or prayer.
Then resolution, as warm debris
folds and forms like bones
on golden biers.

The silence is last. Wounds close
and heal in sacred wind.
Then festival, as dead bricks leap
to souvenirs like old women
remembering birth.

The Southern Review   *Philip Raisor*

FISHIN' BLUES

It was strange that morning
How the wind blew from an unusual direction,
Making the ocean clean, wide open and blue
Like sky, like a dream of my own.

Mom and Dad wished me luck,
Hoping I'd catch a big one.
Then they sat on the bay's edge and talked
About life; why the small, worn stones were mixed in
With boulders too large for this world of sky
And water meeting. I still remember how she turned,
Directing her argument toward the mountain
Across the water, saying how indiscreet it was
To expect more for an answer. For a while
Each thing there became glassy and quiet,
And they smiled, watching the rising chop
And tide cover each rock, as kelp drifted
Into a sky about to rain.

Pristine waterfalls, rockslides
Dismantling the mountain, and the summit
Crowned orange after each storm
Like a wing of epiphany, such was the source
And estuary of a time long out of my hands.
I'm waking up now, many hours after the incident,
After everyone has had their say and moved on,
Leaving their cups on the table, and me
Trying to sort out what I heard
Through the bedroom wall as sunlight
Streams into the window.

Hawaii Review   *Valentino Ramirez*

SPRING POEM

The loss of control, parquet, paraqueets
in a cage, the smell of sun
on the window pots, a hint of green
some morning and the surety
in the sound of water dripping in the kitchen:

all encroachments gather.
Morning light comes sooner every day,
for all it's worth, and free.

We walk quickly from the bedroom
tired as we may be. Enlightenment:
a phrase from history and the sound,
like a sigh, when her body gleams
between nightgown and morning robe,
a sight like lemons in a plate,
the certain taste and surer smell
of a dim-lit past when we slept well.

The Black Warrior Review   *Bin Ramke*

TENDING

It's no secret I've failed
with all our gardens. There were the tiger-lily bulbs
I never split that died of strangulation,
the roses with skeleton leaves,
the chrysanthemums with fungus,
and always the centipede grass with its root system
of runners.

So much you think you yank up
goes on with its underground tunnels
siphoning water and sun,
feeling for another nudgable crumb of dirt.

My children, I need to tend you more carefully
than gardens. When we moved here, deadnettle and thistle
had already taken over and it was almost a relief
to throw up my hands, say,
"All is lost," and turn inward.
And some things have happened to me
that have made me feel we have no more chance
than stems left to choke and rot,
that the only roots will be those tunnels
sucking us into the earth.

But I will never tell you.
Because maybe the yard is outside,
not connected to us, maybe weeds take over
everything but us. Maybe,
just because I fail in weeding out
my own duplicities, leaving them to run riot
all over my body, it doesn't mean

I can't learn some saving pull for you,
my arms towing you in over deep water.

The possibility alone keeps me reaching.

Quarterly West   *Paula Rankin*

AT THE BEGINNINGS OF THE ANDES

Above the clumps where feather trees
have quit their night creaking,
I sit on an outcrop. The sun
climbs the rise of the first felted mountain,
unrolls the valley into today's light.
Shadows shrink toward me.

It is so still—
the horses deep in their grazing,
a farmer hovering in his field,
one car touching the far road, moving
the dust tenderly—everything slows
in the time it takes to reach me.

And you in the house under the blue roof
are singing in your sleep, in your sleep
because these are the masked days,
the mute ones, carrying you
into a separate year.

Sadness wakes me like a new bird,
shy to touch this dawn of loss,
this strange arrival.
I will be happy for you,
later, when your music walks here
without shoes, when change takes us
beyond regret.

Now let the valley spread out,
let its green absorb my grieving,
let the cane fields bloom into white wands.

The Painted Bride Quarterly   *Barbara Ras*

EXTREME UNCTION IN PA.

No, not the last *Last Supper,* and yet
for the sake of the world I mumbled all
the holy poems I knew. They too
were dying. Outside the silver diner
rain fell and fell, and from the South
came wind that bore the glowing mask,
danced the silly saffron masque of hell.
And though I dreaded walking out,
inhaling tiny drifts from Satan's mills
that stood upon the earth like pots
of clay, turned on a loving wheel,
I'd try to tip my hat to the waitress

to keep her calm. *Go down gentle,*
I hoped to say, stay still upon your stools,
all you chubby drivers, innocent and hungry,
and feathered ladies on some worldly journey.
The sky went dark. Trees were trembling.
We had our share of cobalt blue,
but heavy lead had followed, and iodine
like that blind Homer kicked upon the shore, seaweed.

New Letters   *David Ray*

ROSE BAY WILLOW HERB

The willow herb, the
rose bay willow herb,
sweeps woods and commons
with pink sunset stripes.
It rises from black
aftermath of fire
that crackled through thick
undergrowth of trees.
Even after war
it flourishes in
empty lots, in bomb
craters, and like a
phoenix of flora
rises tall and wild,
true fireweed, indeed.
Should the air it spikes,
water it drinks, ash
it grows from become
radioactive,
the invisible
aftermath of a
great folly, perhaps
the willow herb, the
rose bay willow herb,
will still grow wild with
pink sunset stripes, and
bloom abundantly.
But who will there be
of our coughing, skin-
flaking, misshapen
kind to perceive a
symbol of hope? And
perhaps the only
phoenix to arise
from that blind folly
will be some tiny
flung molecule of
untainted earth with
no memory of

tall willow herb, wild
rose bay willow herb.

New Letters   *Judy Ray*

POEM FOR DOROTHY HOLT

(1905 - 1967)

Black walnuts litter the grass,
waiting for you
to tumble them into your skirt,
smiling, dropped to your knees,
holding up plump fingers,
stained and pungent. All the walnuts
are fallen now, the outer
shells dark and delicate; broken,
they mark whatever they touch.
And bittersweet is so wreathed
in the dead branches
that it cannot be removed
without the yellow petals dropping
off, leaving red centers,
lobed and naked.
A fragrance of earth and burning
sharpens the evening air.
I listen for your laughter,
high and rilled,
the last cry of a bird
before snow. Across the field
the final band of the sky flares,
the upper boughs of the trees
tinged red, even the tips
of the pines rouged, a burning hush
before the field drops into dark,
the grasses vanish.

The Pikestaff Review   *Susan Irene Rea*

LEAVETAKING

Is there anything left on the floor?
Only a shadow,
Only a gallery of shadows
Dancing close to the dust.
They will vanish when the neighbor's headlights
Scatter icy fires into the front yard
As he wheels, cleaving blank windows
On rainy black nights.
We stare at the floor:
Were things made different by us?
Is the wood more shiny
Smoothed like a tawny shell
That we cast off, now?

If we have abandoned anything,
Will it find its way to its proper place?
What we carried forward,
Pushed and pulled out of reluctant doors,
Sent by mail through the express
For us to find before we'd gone—
How recovered in this dark that stretches
Fathoms of miles further on?
We shall be gone now
To bend black apple boughs
And creak the rusty swing;
To stand at the top of the stairs
When you mount to the end of your nights.
You who come after us,
Tread lightly on
Our scarce effaced footsteps
Still placed in the path
That winds to the spring.

The Harvard Advocate   *Lisa Reape*

TO THE POSTMASTER GENERAL

He took the great bunch of letters and kissed it!
All those green stamps on the blue envelopes and on the white ones,
All those windowed debits and who knows a draft of credit,
All those missives sleeved in addresses and advertisements;
He grabbed the great bundle of envelopes off the mat and kissed it!
It proved the abundance of the world and his presence in it,
He blessed the postman and tossed them into the wardrobe,
Hung up his postman's uniform, and went out to fish.
Where silver creatures stamped with black and gold
Containing messages confined to issues of life and death
Swarmed, wrote and re-wrote themselves, fed, hatched and died
In the green-raftered halls of the water's sorting-office;
In the cool balsamic halls the watching flocks hung
Or turned swiftly to a new address: Blooded Worm, Esq.,
One A, Barbed Hook, The Line, Bankside: like letters with wings
Or a postman hurrying in his flowing pouch adventurous correspondence
    written
With energy and light on each leaf of the stacked flesh-pages.

The American Scholar   *Peter Redgrove*

THE INDIAN

I have found a way to capture color.
I take blue out of the sky,
condense it into a little bead,
and hang it on a string around my neck.
I take green from plants,
condense it into a little bead,

and hang it on a chain around my neck.
I take all the colors in the United States,
condense them into little beads,
and hang them on a string around my neck.
Then I build a cabin in the Rockies,
and stare through my beads
at the magnificent scenery.
After a few years, I leave my cabin
and go to New York with my string of beads.
Everyone is starved for color.
Everyone cries out in the middle of the night
for color.
I am magnanimous; I tell them I will share
my string of beads
if they give me Manhattan.

Outerbridge   *Thomas Reed*

SHADOW LIFE

Out of the corner of my eye
Something is always moving,
But stops
When I look up.

In the center of my ear
Something is always sounding,
But when I strain,
I can't make it out.

Against the back of my shoulder
Something is always pressing,
But when I turn,
Nothing is there.

In the hollow of my mouth
Taste is always yearning,
But when I eat,
It has been wrong.

In the caves of my lungs
Smell is always
Recalling—
I have forgotten what.

Tar River Poetry   *Robert F. Reid, III*

BROTHERS (I)

Eighteen years you beat me over the head
with the butt-end of our brotherhood.
So where are you now, Mr. Top
Dog on the Bunk Bed, Mr. Big
Back on the High School Football Team?

You hauled ass out of that town
with its flimsy goalposts.

Now you're down there with your Dead
Sea, your Jerusalem, busy
with the same old border disputes

that sparked our earliest fist fights.
Israel is just another locked toy
closet on your side of the bedroom, split
by electric train tracks. It's as if
you never left home at all: yesterday

in a bar in Washington Heights
I saw a man who could have been you.
The Jets were playing the Steelers with two
downs to go, and in the icy
lightshow of smoke

he lifted a pitcher of beer
and swilled it just as the screen
blazed red with an ad for Gillette.
And I thought, Here is my blood brother
whose only gifts to me were kicks

in the teeth, his castoff comic books,
and worst of all, wrapped, sharpened
for a lifetime,
the perfect razor of my rage.

The Ohio Review   *James Reiss*

"QUICK NOW, HERE, NOW, ALWAYS—"

Early morning quick coffee and bran,
                    his white Honda nosing
through fog. Anxious darting:
gradebook, texts, lesson plan,
a player on first (with a slow reflex),
the dull punishment of a dull "Raven,"
a long mellow note catching hold
                    of praise
and sacrament. To pause is to discover
                    an ancient florin.
"Come over, come over, beer and the team
                    on instant screen."
But even in slow motion the images flicker
                    too fast.
The game runs on ahead.
"What can I give? I can detail the blind man
                    seeing trees,
the Buddha, the Taos wail;
I can urge them to any spirit." The eyes
                    tell all.
"Give them wonder. Dissect your reluctance
                    to kneel
and chart for them the country of their heart."
The night is late for me,

but I am ready against the dark
to listen for more than love.

Kansas Quarterly   *William J. Rewak*

LOVE SONG FOR A TYRANT

No,
I never could talk with my father.

His ears were tuned to the thunder
of a fire and brimstone religion,
and that "Honor thy father" commandment
meant
you listened
but never sang.

So his sweet and obedient daughter,
his southern, well-bred lady
(never a moment's worry)
was quiet and meek,
and wild.

He had chiseled me stone commandments
and set all my limits in sin.

"Yes sir," I would say, politely,
and silently scream in my bed.

I honored,
but hated,
my father,

and loved him

but wrestled unblessed—
so I ran,
unforgiven,
through silence,

was free, at last, to sing
and I sing of my love for my father,

with songs that must shatter
on stone.

Pteranodon   *Marion Brimm Rewey*

GREEN FROGS

All night the surf bangs the coast.
The moon rises, a waxing, waxwork piece of itself,
but thunderheads slide shut over it.
I leave the trailer window and lie back
listening to the swamp frogs prattling
at the smell of rain, to the sea clearing
every hair-pin turn of my mind's darkening.
Troubled mind. The radio songs blaring
down from the pier were right about you.

In mercury vapor light the sailors hoist
the cargo—one more turn of the winch
and the whole world would budge. Do you hear?
Ghostly divers seed the oyster beds by night
while the glacial ferry steams overhead
to Connecticut. Surely they must be fearful
swimming rootless as snow in a paperweight.
Not one will rise who has not first felt
the hand moving away, and then nothing.

Here come the stars wriggling out of the sea.
O love, what night would you add to this night,
what darkness? Like a shell dropped in a chamber,
the time we count sits shadowless in our
stubborn barrel. We bolt it shut. The sea,
like a torch, gnaws the space between us.
Still, some things are simple:
when the rain comes down, the frogs break out
in a great green chorus of cause and effect.

Meanwhile the stars, vague as Greek, coast unseen
into formation. Their sob stories and seductions—
who remembers them? Tonight only clouds muscle
their way in from the Atlantic. How easy
to believe all they erase will not return.
At this distance the ocean shudders like a jet
plane turning toward the airfield. I think
I have slept too long in the fork of solitude:
sleep and truce have dovetailed to the heart.

As I come again to the window, the elemental
powers also come, and with them, the weird,
Gnostic unweaving of the sea, which only
holds our thin life according to its one value.
The moon reappears and the frogs hop out
over the sand, little fatigue-green frogs
like soldiers tossed into obscure battle.
But the surf drowns out what might have been
their battle song, a song beginning "O love . . . "

Carolina Quarterly   *David Rigsbee*

MACRAMÉ

We are the weavers
Of intricate knots that connect
Around the holes;

Of great hooting terminals
Switching massive trains of
        thought;
Of cloverleaves tied into vast
        bows
To wrap a world of souls;
Of trunklines that slither
        beneath concrete clothes

To form a net of news;
Above all, of synaptic flares,
More numerous than stars,
To surround dead space with
    clues.

Arizona Quarterly   Michael D. Riley

THE KNIGHT

Out rides the knight in dusky steel
Into the buzzing, blooming world.

And all is outside: the day and the dale
And the friend and the foe and the hall-served meal
And the May and the maid and the woods and the Grail,
And God himself on all streets without fail
Is placed to save his fold.

Yet in the knight's dark armor, under
And behind the grimly twining mail,
Crouches Death, who must ponder and ponder:
When will the sword leap flailing
Over this iron latticework,
The strange emancipating sword
Which draws me from my place of lurking
Where I spend so many bored, stoop-shouldered days—
That I might finally stretch my wings
And play
And sing.

Webster Review

Rainer Maria Rilke
—Translated from the German
by John N. Miller

THE GRIEF

Oh, how far away things are
and how long they have all been gone.
I feel that star,
in whose light I am bathing,
was dead thousands of years ago.
I feel in that boat,
that went sailing on by,
I heard something said full of worry and fear.
Inside the house an hour
has rung . . .
Inside what house? . . .
I would like to get out of my heart
and walk under the open sky.
I would like to pray.
And with all the stars there would have
to be one that is still real.
I feel I would know

which one alone
has lasted,
which one like a city of white
stands in the sky at the end of its light . . .

New Orleans Review   *Rainer Maria Rilke*
                                           —Translated from the German
                                                by Steven Lautermilch

TEAHOUSE

His villa in the mountains was made over
into the Berghof: vast rooms, oversized furniture,
an immense picture window with
a view of Untersberg. In his studio, a bust of Wagner and
a Titian nude. He slept late in the morning,
coming down at eleven.

After dinner, a stroll to the teahouse,
a round room with small-paned windows.
Waiters in white vests, SS men, served coffee and tea.
The Fuhrer unburdened himself of his long monologues,
droning on about Greek temples, the Catholic Church,
diet recipes, dogs. At teatime, he rarely talked about Jews.
Occasionally, his guests would fall asleep.
Now and then he too would doze off,
sometimes in mid-sentence.

Easy days and long, rambling nights.
Twilight over the Untersberg, where legend said
the body of Charlemagne lay sleeping,
waiting to rise again
and restore the Empire.

Flowers in a bowl at the center of the table.
Records on the phonograph. Simple white china.
His monogram on the silver.

Cape Rock   *Nicholas Rinaldi*

POEM FOR VLADIMIR

Time bagged you at last,
Pushed through your abdomen
That pin
Which holds you tight inside
A cabinet of earth.
Death classified you thus:
Genius, aesthete, athlete,
A type both rare and known,
Here local to the steppe.
When numbers moved and flexed
Against your sleep,
You mimicked life, made hours stop
With words, made worlds,

Holding the dream at bay and spreading wings
Above the plane and linden trees.

Perhaps you felt the night explode again
And multiply,
When time said you were dead.

Canadian Literature   *G. Ripley*

IN THE FALL

Even now, when the long white hair
frays on soft pillows,
my grandmother does not believe
in leaves falling, abandoning trees.
From her bed she watches
the slow inundation of browns.
Her sad arms turn into brooms. They sweep.

When letters from the children arrive
speaking of holidays to come,
she folds them neatly on her lap,
goes to the window and lets them flow
into the ochres of the afternoon.

River Styx   *Alina Rivero*

TONSILECTOMY

The doctor's aseptic popsicle stick
from his tongue depressor jar
is into your mouth and past your teeth
before you can yell shazam.
His evil beady yellow eyes
dance on a probing flashlight ray,
invade your mouth and inspect your throat
all the way down to the neck.
The boy's tonsils have to go
you overhear him say, and you're
Billy Batson with no lightning bolt,
Buck Rogers without his flying belt,
Red Ryder minus his horse.
Better off trapped on an asteroid
with no food or rocket fuel
or in a chapter of Jungle Tales
on an island of killer ants
than strapped like a dog
to a hospital table
with Doctor Ming at your throat.

You wake up silent in a ward
among the tongueless dead,
with your mouth cut out
and your throat slit through
all the way down to your neck.

You look around for the ether bomb
that blew you into space,
find only a slithering galactic squid
posing as a nurse:
it wants you to eat a plateful
of strawberry star saliva,
and you know by heart the secret rules
of the space ranger commando kit—
if you eat so much as a half a drop
you turn into a giant dwarf.
Before its slimy tentacle
gets the strawberry goo to your face,
you press a hidden nerve in your wrist
and completely disappear.

The Pikestaff Review   *James W. Rivers*

SPRING RITES

When the gray nets of winter skies hang
Mid-March as ragged as last chances
For the playoffs, the bedrooms of boys
Go still. No cheering crowds, announcers
Shouting goals or fouls, no north winds storm
Over covers quiet as June clouds.

What drifts in a baseball-lazy arc?
A boy's running, long strides getting him
Under a sure homer. Soaring with
The glove he's slept near all week, he leaps
high as a man. The cheers are now his,
But he shrugs to himself, hustling in

To bat. He limbers his stance with the two
Sticks that've rattled through raw nights,
Daring Florida to throw in spring.
After such snows, he's ready to make
The impossible catch again. Taller,
A little less shy, if he's not caught

His dream yet, waiting alone, his grip
On his vision and name is stronger;
And if he's not ready to stand up
To the curves they throw in the majors,
Leather and wood by his side smell like
A summer he'll knock clear out of the park.

The Greenfield Review   *Martin Robbins*

FOR MY GRANDFATHER

Autumn light, light of afternoon, the crows
you blessed last winter cross the yellow
corn rows homes have made of air. Inside,
a wall, here and there your furniture

in company with leaves. You'd expect your rug
to turn, domestic lawn, to red and gold
October. The trout you're cooking, kitchen
yellow as the flame, gives off all memory
of weed; the lake in summer, a hard green
light down thirty feet where fish swim and swim.

Coming into the world, fraternal, your twin
left all his air to you. Paired up
for those months, you swam the first dark waters
mindful of another heart, the way of touching
men are born with. You never found him
again. Stars turned over—
over London, Pocatello. Now, when you fish,
you troll for green light left behind you, gone
down lines the sun gives water in supreme
control of itself. It's the light where autumn comes from,

filling up your home, where the twin still
turns your colors, year after yellow year.

Carolina Quarterly   *Richard Robbins*

FARMERS

Gamblers they
who count on chance,
who trust the rain's
silver-falling touch,
the sun's bright hardness
to change the green
to gold.

Inlet   *Hortense Roberta Roberts*

AWAKENING

I bury my dreams well, under
Layers of night,
But sometimes I remember
That I am another person,
Living in a world
Where the calm light seems yellow
As it slants toward me
From a new direction.
At times I think this is the person
I imagined, as a child,
I would be as an adult;
Now it seems an earlier life
Swimming into momentary focus,
Or some life to come,
Impatiently casting glimpses of itself
Back toward time.

Concerning Poetry   *David Robinson*

KEYS

I hear their signal alert,
keys keeping time with my heart.
There grows the mechanical
breath of closed doors.

Chinks of passage are reflected
on the polished edges of a key:
he comes in the morning,
a little jingle and a tray.

One eats very slowly
in scrupulous white light,
fluorescence creeps into every corner:
it would be impossible
to lose a key here.

The Massachusetts Review   *Glen Rockwell*

FAT CAT

Six kilos of cat!
Quick as a house-
plant, she lumbers
up to the window,
and chooses a roost
for the afternoon.
Later, she nuzzles
the afghan, her body
seeping lower, lower
into the organized
holes—the prototype
and patron saint
of the leisure class . . .

 Mimic of wisdom, intercede for us!
 Tub of butter, hear our prayer!

Smug as sculpture,
cat does not care.
She's a species
of sphinx, wise
as silence gets.
She thinks: "I know
we're only on a planet;
let people pretend
it's the whole show."

Yankee   *John Ronan*

THE GERBIL WHO GOT AWAY

Jumped his cage
a whole week before I heard
scratching in the stove

& started for the oven drawers.
In the nested pans our eyes met,
& he took off on a dead run.
Under the cupboard he thumped
his hind legs—a gerbil sign for
Wild Animal Approaching.
With his interests at heart,
I found a tire-tool in the trunk
of my old 2-door Ford,
pried half an hour,
splintered a wall to flapping
sheetrock & sweating black pipes.
But he moved on.

       Swinging the tire-tool
like a club, I drew blood
when I kicked a cabinet door
tumbling
spilling flour, Arm & Hammer, honey,
Fruit Loops, wheat germ, Shake 'n Bake
till the linoleum was slick as a soaped ballroom
& I foxtrotted that stunted prairie dog
behind the refrigerator.

       Little fool,
Don't you know you'll never survive
on the outside?

Splitting fingernails on loose
drawer pulls, tripping the blender
to puree—
the kitchen fell;
         plaster in the Clabber
Girl, slivered wood, chipped & cracked crocks,
a spice rack sneezing clouds of cinammon,
cayenne, pale camomile,
         Constant Comment, MSG,
draughts of vanilla extract.

The Hollins Critic   *Judith C. Root*

A NATURAL HISTORY OF DRAGONS AND UNICORNS MY DAUGHTER AND I HAVE KNOWN

(Written on the Occasion of Her 12th Birthday)

Already we are both fans of the green and golden dragon
    who tumbles gloriously out of the terrible heavens
        not only in books and dreams

for us: He cascades also down the sides of the seagreen '61
    Valiant we painted once together by the ocean,
        trying to outrace the setting Mendocino sun

four years ago with mist rolling in, and he tumbles
    as well down the side of that van which resembles
        nothing so much as a forest dwarf's hutch on wheels

where he silently roars a great bouquet of flowers,
    while his green and scaley winding tail anchors
        round the side window.   Rose-white, a Unicorn

edged in icy blue rears opposite our flower-breathing
    fire-eater now, its jewelous horn shining
        by moonlight and headlight, glowing

with a proud shy promise of goodness pure as silver.
    We cannot always be together,
        you and I, and I would have you remember

our fabulous creatures always—the bold Dragon
    as terrible as the horned horse is wonderful, twins of a wisdom
        older by far than we are in our kingdom

of daily things.   Here, then, as a reminder, is the image
    of our Unicorn seen silver as he wades into waters ageless
        as the blue sky they reflect, hooves half tangled

in the world's common grasses.   Keep him with you
    where you go and try from time to time gazing through
        your eyes as he gazes through his: A sky beating slowly blue

as the heart of all the air, grass burning green as an
                     emerald's coolly imperial
    and incessant stare, the inner brilliance of all that is natural
    held in that eye of his, which is every bit as real
                as he is invisible.

Blue Unicorn   *William Pitt Root*

THAT WHICH YOU CALL "LOVE ME"

Look for a place in my skin that may not have been
written by your hand, and may not have
some trembling, some
light of your flesh in its blind memory;
look for a place in my eyes
that may not have been mirror and that will not see
that smile of yours crystallize
as it learns to walk on the earth:
that which you call "child"
now breaks into a lily in your hands;
that which you call "love me" is not blood
though it pulses, the same as the blood
and everything is yours!
                    and yet I feel
something that exists much closer
to me than hope, something that lives
from my own life and will make the same
life you surrender to me impossible.

Willow Springs Magazine   *Luis Rosales*
                                   —Translated from the Spanish
                                        by Lynn C. Jacox

CALLING HOME THE SCIENTISTS

The museum is gone from my bones now.
Labels and shelves gone,
scientists, equators, diagrammers gone,

leaving the sky and mountains to cover me
and the earth, nameless these days,
below.

The animals that quieted under their hands,
squawking and calling in the open,
spread my fingers to find their food.

All the names I could have had
stalk me through the desert
faster than antelopes, louder than bees.

How could I know pushing them away
in those white labcoats,
with those lined notebooks?

They were the angels of the new year
and the only names left, perhaps
all that is left, skeleton of humanity.

So here I am with my world now, soaring alone,
stripped naked to the bone,
free like lightning-struck trees

wanting it all back,
calling home the scientists,
calling home the museums.

River Styx   *Wendy Rose*

FOR LENINGRAD, AND MY JEWISH ANCESTORS

This is a city for old men.
All day they stand with crooked backs
along the Neva, fishing.
The water's gray face leaps with light
or blackens, further out.
Our window on the west has shut
its giant eye and slumbers heavily.
Only the bones gleam; domes.
I scan the streets for remnants:
an eye, a nose, an ear—
the darkened mirror of myself.
Citizens in threadbare clothing
shuffle, staring. I wave, they do not smile.

Soldiers in drab green stand and wait.
They file me through customs, silently.
Back in Finland again, I grieve,
remembering the lap of Russia, gray and dark.
The dark gray river, shifting always.
The water from faucets, urine-colored

that I dared not drink;
and the old men on the bridges,
waiting all day empty-handed
with newspapers spread,
hooking with their dark eyes
faint connections,
blood lines catching at my breath.

Midstream   *L. M. Rosenberg*

TO MY MOTHER

Mama, you turn from the sink, shaking water
from your hands, and I remember
how you coolly touched my head
to ease a fever. Strange,
I can't do as much for you in turn,
watching the years shed us like leaves.

When it comes time again for me to leave,
and I run from your house like water
down the hill of the front lawn, I turn
to watch you watching me. "Remember!"
you cry, "Call when you get there, don't let strange
men up the stairs!" I nod my head.

You stay behind, yet something of you runs ahead
of the carlights, your face under the wheels like leaves,
your voice that of some stranger,
your touch like lost water
in my cupped hand, like a thing remembered
in the stretch of dawn, forgotten in the turn

of morning. You turn to me now, only to turn
away, two-headed
goddess. It was always this way. I remember
how I'd beg you not to leave
the house, not even for errands; how I shook the water
from my eyes at each return of the beautiful stranger.

Midstream   *L. M. Rosenberg*

ARE YOU JUST BACK FOR A VISIT OR
ARE YOU GOING TO STAY?

How the place has grown. I hardly recognize it.
There is new construction everywhere. I had to look for
  the old landmarks.
A lot of the young people seem to be staying, at least for
  a while.
Everybody is building his own house, or is trying to,
The way he wants it or thinks he might be comfortable in.

The old zoning ordinances and building codes have all been
  allowed to lapse,
Which on the whole seems to be a good thing,

Although I suppose there is as much shoddy work in this
  new sprawl
As there ever was in all those old rows and boxes.

The rest of the state never did pay much attention to the
  town,
And still doesn't,
Which really never mattered:
To be well remembered in the town was all any sensible
  townsman ever wanted.

When I left
Everybody knew everybody else, or seemed to,
At least their names and where they lived.
Doc Williams and the lawyer in the insurance business
  had the best houses in town.

Most of the really old houses had been pulled down
  before I left.
I was surprised to see two or three have been refurbished
And seem highly regarded.
But no one seems to know anyone else now,
Although you can't really tell unless you live there.
Perhaps I should have stayed.

There is a lot of new building to the west.
On the south side there is a whole area of impressive new
  town houses,
Although as you drive by all the exteriors look pretty
  much alike.
There were always a visiting Britisher or two
And some townspeople who thought they were,
And I suppose there still are. You can't tell anymore
  from the architecture.

It was hard to make a living there
And I suppose it still is except maybe out by the college.
Win had a rich wife which helped and made it worse.
Miss Spencer who was black stayed mostly in her garden.
A lot of us tried it for a while and then moved away.
Among those who stayed the suicide rate was pretty high.

I recognize a lot of the old houses.
Somehow I thought I might hear a familiar voice say:
Hey, are you just back for a visit or are you going to
  stay?

Poetry   *Francis Coleman Rosenberger*

STACKING UP

A new professional group
calling themselves
      psychosexiatrists
explain one can tell
a great lover by the way
he treats his food—

lingering lovingly,
emotively gentle.

The more careless,
casual and quick the
appetite for food,
the same for sex;
both fundamental drives
divinely sensual experiences.

Gives me pause to wonder
about you, my love.
Very particular about
what you eat and how
it's prepared
and presented.

Then you wolf it down;
leave the table
yourself replete,
its surface in a shambles;
me dismally viewing the mess
as you glow thanks.

Neworld   *Rita Rosenfeld*

THE SECOND GENERATION

true, we are the children
of a nocturnal twilight,
the heirs of Auschwitz and Ponar;
but ours is also the rainbow:
in us the storm meets sunlight
to create new colors
as we add defiant sparks
to an eternal fire

Midstream   *Menachem Z. Rosensaft*

JUNE SONG

How blowsy the trees are today,
how full of flies the air!
And I am as listless as a ladle
stirring in thick soup.

My legs buckle under me;
June is this warm earth
on my kneecaps. And my fingers
are webbed with mud. And my mouth
is nearly stoppered
with a clump of grass.

Early graves of June!
Warm death! Who said dying
was a cold or spiritual matter?
In December I am not so seduced.

But this wind which makes
the grey leaves dance,
these funereal roses
clotted on their fence like blood,
like a slow, plump fire . . .

the presiding, infernal cardinal!

I was born in June, it's true,
but today I say, without bitterness,
I doubt I could do it again.

Kansas Quarterly   *Abby Rosenthal*

LOVE'S FOOL

If it's love, and if, as you say, it's ridiculous,
Then I suppose it must be love—since I have been love's fool
And still might be. It seems I have failed
To surprise myself once again; once again I am here
With this unfamiliar heart and these unfamiliar words.
I know what you mean, of course: some words are a waste of time.
They carry too much weight given our limitations
Which, thankfully, we have come to recognize. Love dies,
Love wanes, etc., and what of life's multiplicity! What of it?
A disguise word (what word isn't?), a mere symbol.
Such a word hands us over to the greeting cards.
Such a word is food for academics.
If one can be free, why should one be courtly?

Love's fool, my love, I speak but of my nature, saying,
"I'll settle for your heart, sweet, and nothing else."
Forgive me. This should not be said in a time of saturation,
When weighty dogs crow moonwards,
Not in hunger and longing, the old facts of passion,
But out of boredom and modest appraisal. I am guilty
Of bad taste, as if one, dining with friends,
Refused what was offered, what was available,
For the unserved possibilities of what was desired.
Even a fool with a foolish heart knows what's up:
Love is up, making way for something more organized,
Like flattery, perhaps, the queen's midnight drug
(Or even oil for the less cynical
Who dream gently among smooth hinges
And legs and deals of a seventh dull day).
Who needs fever, anyway, this neurotic malady
Of the senses, when it's ours to take mostly what we want,
And to leave, without confusion, what we don't end up getting?
Losing love, we may lose our best dreams,
But we are calmer, less lost, and of course, busier.

Even I who have ridden proudly with the prince
Cannot fool myself much longer. The wings are clipped,
Bow broken, and the arrow a rubber device
Made to amuse children. I say I love you
And hear the words echo among empty seats.

A political leader says, "Cut your losses," and I agree.
No sense in being a fool other than love's.
Eyes, ears, tears, moon-children moon-flowering—
I was a perfect fool a long time ago and sang
Wise songs to girls under the ridiculous moon.

The Sun   *John Rosenthal*

OLD WORLD, NEW WORLD

The engines thrum in their agile wilderness,
Oil, grease, gears—and the streets are not
What my mother thought she would find here—
Paved like a jewelry store with gold and diamonds.
But they are laced with tin cans left behind
On roadbeds, traffic arteries; the city's artistry
And banditry, in common moulds and fusion,
Flat, creased, shaped by thousands of ravaging wheels,
To new myths about our agile anthropology
Or objects of art, greased and suddenly run over.

I became a collector last night on Canal Street;
Enriched, said the wording on tin, with vitamins;
All natural, Hawaiian Punch; colored as if India
Under the Raj had created its shapes and colors,
Or whatever else is art in August 1979,
Or collected after an automobile expresses itself,
Rushing through the city's magical streets,
With curators on every corner and a red light.

New Letters   *Harry Roskolenko*

SOMEWHERE FARM

In winter, strangeness stained the fields,
The tongues of birds went stiff,
Water rotted in the stream.
And, till this, the farm was nothing.
Now to the spring even stones wake.
Martin-dazzled, the hay barn gapes.
And if at dawn the sun is cold as any star,
It climbs to show spring green
Greener than any evergreen.

Tonight, night will smell like clouds,
And, climbing the long east ridge,
I'll think about what's come, and coming:
Summer, meadows filled with light,
The hawking sun caresses like a beak.
Fall: that feeling: late day,
And weather coming in.
Winter, and want stands like an armed man.

Then the last light in the house winks out.
In my eye the whole farm shines—
Above the rooted stones, below the rooted stars,
Resisting, darkly, in the dark.

Tendril   *Guy Rotella*

THE PACT

Enclosed in a circle
I sit, toying with my empty pen;
Sucking on a minor finger wound,
I fumble through a family album
Where dried-up corners come unglued
And black flakes off the moulding leaves.
There people all are dead, and only I,
A phantom child, wander naked through
Their dreams. Time must turn around before
We meet, or lasers burn away the dark.
I had an understanding with her ghost,
But contracts aren't kept in Hell, or
Wherever mothers bless their stricken sons:
I would write the poems, and she—
She would haunt me just enough to guide
My hand. But now the leaves look blacker
Than before, and my pen is drier than
An empty bed. Sitting in the circle
Once again, I trace my signature in red.

Blue Unicorn   *Larry Rubin*

AMSTERDAM STREET SCENE, 1972

The cupid-faced hooligan standing on tip-
toe with his tin cup comes down

on the beat of the roar on the floor of glitter-
ing cement while turning the white wheel

of his music-truck, clapping coins in the cup
(a gull banks invisible to the eye to avoid a wall).

And with strange, charming deadness
puppets moved by wires drawn through their foreheads

move around a frail keyboard of bones, surrounded by
emblems and treasures, impaled on spikes (a great beast
     branded by

a Scarlet Woman, candlesticks, whips, wands, skulls, chalices,
a fox with a bird on a billhook, the lid of a tomb

flying off)—all done in fond, dreamy pastels.
(Light, drifting down like a bright brass puff,

lands on the rim of a cup like a halo) but no one gives.
People huddle by in ones and twos, smiling.

And as (no one hears it, now) the music runs down,
the wheel stops with a glad, eager grunt,

locking the puppets into the very dumbness
of each last gesture; he smiles once fast at them,

eyes as clear gray as the invisible eyes of glass
he gets behind, driving off—into the city's secret heart.

Open Places   *Raphael Rudnik*

WRITTEN

Nothing is pacified. It will be,
when it leaves, the one winter
still going on foot. The senseless
ongoing of our correspondence has been
driven to new heights by a storm
that has disintegrated into snow
in the time it takes to write this.

Edges in a still life
are lusting to be looked at,
alive against the grain
of tin plates, raw meat and new knives—
fruitskins curling on a block carpet
where light fallen from a leaded window
lands on an open letter because of certain
words I have no way of knowing
that are explaining the chemistry
of a moment.
Your postcard of the painted supper
is stuck by ice to the window ledge,
its message originating from an impulse
is forcing my heart into emptiness.

Friend, this is what I have planned:
Soon I will be walking out of myself
into the difficult welcome.
There will not be bells, so listen
carefully for the sound of anything
muffled, dense with light, falling
over the open land. In the time
it takes to read this
hands have opened doors
to let the dead wind in.

The Black Warrior Review   *Mary Ruelfe*

HOTEL FIRE: NEW ORLEANS

From first light we fear falling:
After the fever of birth, impetus
toward that natural window, we
reach, cling, our fingers and toes
curled to grip, after the fire ·
that tempers us for the sun.

There I saw them—I see them still—
thrust from windows, flailing

like children who know
that the earth has failed them.
They snatch at chinks, to ledges,
tumble to the wet street below—
the fire an old and certain death,
the leap the only faith that's left.

The Georgia Review   *Paul Ruffin*

LIMBO

*(I had come to Limbo because I had always wanted to
possess a country of my own. — Aubrey Menen)*

No one can come here for the first time.
It possessed us before the harsh startle of flesh,
will store our footprints forever. We travel our lives
inside its boundaries: This landscape we scour
for names to touch ourselves with; this prison
whose walls are fog piling up off an ocean decades wide.

Any escape is a thin disc of sun glimpsed
through closing shutters. Gratefully, we gather memories
like prayer beads, pass them and pass them through our fingers—
the gleam of one man's skin, another's voice.
The open lips of leaves. Summer's ochre moon.

And always the same blood lying to the arteries
and the same eyes denying their vision
of that place where we each received our enduring silver token,

that token we carry so carefully along all our invisible roads:
proof of fellowship, proof of passage, our coins
for the guardian of that last river which was the first.

Carolina Quarterly   *Marieve Rugo*

SUNDAYS

Church bells in gray air.
Across the city, lovers waking
into each others' flesh or waking
against bodies they no longer love.
Slowly the old pick up their lives.
Mailmen stay home.

Time for more coffee,
the fat *Boston Globe,* TV cartoons
for the kids. Lawns wait to be raked,
chickens to be roasted. Cat-like,
the hours stretch, then glide away,
unable to disguise the space between
what is and what should be.

Tendril   *Marieve Rugo*

THE PRICE OF PAPER

Her voice was cold as a bill collector's,
cold as a meat locker where the fresh,
stripped carcass steams.
She dragged up the times he'd worked days and nights.
Wrecks hauled up from a river of sludge. She said
he had no respect for himself.
Bitterly, he mutters, "Look how she cleaned

this place out — two lousy chairs and a couch."
But he can't stop worrying that something terrible
will happen to her. Her green car'll skid on ice
and crash in flames, like Christmas trees;
some man with a knife will force her down.
"What the hell does she want from me?"

Though the doors have clenched their teeth, he sees
he's got to get going. He carries
newspapers home from work, piles them
against the basement walls:
stacks of *Los Angeles Times'*, bi-weeklies from Winnetka,
"the same damn things"—the layoffs, terrorists,
rapes and wars. He tells himself he'll make some money,

if the price of paper ever goes up.
But meantime, these dirty stacks
just get higher and higher, one pile
after another, covering the walls, until
he has to sit and stare. And they start to look strange.
Like a fort made of snow in some kids' game,

or big waves, about to break over him.

The Greenfield Review   *Lawrence Russ*

STILL BIRTH

With my cousin
I practiced motherhood
on dolls, binding up
the expected wounds,
perfecting the magic kiss
that cures all bruises.
Now she has given birth
to a deformed child,
the salt-bag broken
on cataracted eyes and what
combination of limbs
and terror nothing heals.

On burial day in Montana
the house hides itself
in a veil of fog. Around
the small casket with its cruel
symmetry of lines, the family
converges into a pattern:

In the bitter kitchen women
cluck and whine, cooking up
reason for tragedy. I take
my place among them,
sifting the dark flour
for fortune, wondering
if it had a life-line,
wondering if it had a hand.
I want to break windows
with my fists. I punch
the dough down when it rises,
flour the board for kneading.

The Ohio Review   *Catherine Rutan*

THE FINAL CUT

Like my father I'm
an extra, like
him I disappear
from the final

cut, edited out,
coiled on the cutting
room floor,
my one walk-on

dark and swept
away with his
janitor's broom.
But we're together

at least, relaxing,
smoking, and talking
in the warm
gloom of the boiler—

room among shadows
and dust, among
spiders and push
brooms, the rags

of our profession.
Soon enough we'll
empty ourselves
with the trash

and whoop home
with a six-pack,
glad to be anonymous
and transient,

glad to have a room
and time and names
that are ours alone
and an address

forever unknown.

The New Yorker   *Vern Rutsala*

THE ALEXANDRITE RING

This is the ring my father gave me,
an alexandrite ring, a heart of stone
that changes in the light from sea
green to purple. I remember when he brought it home.

This alexandrite ring, this heart of stone
was his gift to me on my ninth birthday.
Green to purple. I remember he brought it home
in a velvet box. What did he say

when he gave me this heart on my ninth birthday?
I don't remember, probably nothing at all.
In a velvet box. What did he say?
He'd just had a fall.

I don't really remember. Probably nothing at all
was wrong with him then. I was thrilled with the ring.
He'd just had a fall,
a drunken collapse down stairs. He didn't live long.

Wrong with him then? I was thrilled with the ring.
Green to purple. I remember when he brought it home
and fell down the stairs. He didn't live long.
I have it still, the alexandrite ring, this heart of stone.

Cedar Rock   *Margaret Ryan*

WOMAN

When you were
a girl, you pricked
like a blackberry. Even your foot
was a weapon, O wild one.

You were hard to take.
                              Now
woman, still
you are beautiful. Tangles
of years of hurting tie up
our souls into one. Behind
the darkest hair that I wind
in my fingers, I'm no longer afraid
of the little white pointed demon ear.

International Poetry Review   *Umberto Saba*
                                      — Translated from the Italian
                                      by Christopher Millis

AMEN

They tell me I have to exercise to lose weight,
that around fifty, fatty foods and cigarettes can be fatal,
that one has to trim down one's figure
and battle time, fend off old age.

Well-meaning cardiologists and doctor friends
have recommended various diets and systems
in order that my life be prolonged by a decade,

and I'm grateful to them, grateful from the bottom of my heart;
only I have to laugh at all their vain prescriptions and wasted
  zeal.
(And death too laughs at all this silliness.)

The only recommendation that I take to heart
is finding a young woman for my bed,
for I have reached that stage of life when youth
can be contracted solely by contagion.

Poetry Now   *Jaime Sabines*
                              — Translated from the Spanish (Mexico)
                                          by Steve Kowit

CELEBRATION

My daughter has given me a grandchild.
She of the elegant stance, the faun-like grace,
the panic-filled dark eyes of a captured doe,
has all unwittingly bestowed
a kind of immortality.
The existence of this new wild creature
with long blonde curls and silver eyes,
a laugh that starts in his belly
and explodes like a ringing iron bell,
who teases, who is willful,
who must somehow survive,
has brought a deep inner peace
to some corner of my being
that didn't even know it was troubled.
The ancient rhythms of life
have been set right;
their circle is complete.

Paintbrush   *Elizabeth Newton Sachs*

MACHINE OUT OF THE GOD

In the twentieth century
who would dare imagine god?
A primitive invention:
god.
A novel concept
innovative as wheel,
as perfect as zero.
Concept of circles,
of all-things-at-once,
a spontaneous act
of creator creating creator,
the conceptual
creating
the concept

with craft,
contriving craft art,
ingenious innocence
savage as sin,
ingenuous act
naive as need
to survive.

Sophistication to doubt
evolved as small groups
pooled their civilized minds
and declared
that they dared
challenge stars.
That civilized mind
can envisage machines,
computers complex
as their makers.
Savage minds could see
god—
more complex than their minds—
an infinite complex
computed in fear,
compounded in pain,
constrained by the will
to believe.

South Dakota Review   *Thomas E. Sanders*

THE PART OF FORTUNE

I have been counselled
That my Part of Fortune
Lies in my eleventh house.
(The House of Friendship
And of Aspirations.)
So you see, that I am
Moved by you to act
Has been ordained
By the stars.

Should my pen rightly
Set down an image, or
Should my brush
Do likewise, or
Should my fingers
Strike the right chord,
It is only that
Your spirit, not mine,
Has led me to it.
Each act is an offering;
A quest for sanction.

Permit me, friend,
To use you thusly.

I would not have it so
But for the stars.

The American Poetry Review   *Ann Sanfedele*

CHILDHOOD

How it is I returned
to this one memory all
morning and through mid-
afternoon could not work,
confused still by what
had, or would not, come
back to me: a few small
drops of rain on my
Sunday shoes, the sun
plunged into the rose-gray
summit behind the woods,
and settling, overhead,
like waterbirds (you can't
tell how many, their wings
overlapping), the high yellow
clouds, and a voice, at
intervals, calling my name
across that farflung
sky—no, across the disced
back pasture where I
had wandered, not lost or
frightened, but as in a drift
of leaves—and so it was
I turned then and saw, not you,
but a winter moon rising
out of the suburbs like a pearl
earring lifted into place
by a hand, too long ago,
to be sure, to know what
it means, or the time
it takes, which was all
your life, Mother, and
all of mine.

Crazy Horse   *Sherod Santos*

AFTER ALL THESE YEARS

After all these years
When all I could caress
Was dog head and dog ears,
When all that came to bless
Was cat with her loud purrs,
With what joy and what quake
I kiss small naked ears
And stroke a marble cheek—

After all these years
Let sleeping beauty wake.

The New York Quarterly   *May Sarton*

RECONCILABLE DIFFERENCES

We wake to economical
late winter light.
Beyond the window
we can just make out
a few odd details:
Dark parts of pine trees
holding up ladders
of snow. A freeze-frame
of three puritanical
crows flapping off
the pasture's crust.
Nobody else out there.
How much of this
could we do without?
I put on my parka
and sweep snow
from the back porch.
You told me once
that on a certain day
in November the leaves
on gingko trees drop
all at once, the way,
in this clear air,
we'd like to be forgiven.
And when the pine boughs
let go their soft
snow pods, contradicting
our stillness, I
think again of turning
to you,
you brushing your hair,
you closing around me
like a cat.

The Sun   *Roger Sauls*

IN A NIGHT

The uneasiness of the night surrounds me,
everything is lost in longing.
I think of fields of snow in Montana,
the Greyhound stations during holidays,
the face of the blue miner in Butte
as he brings himself up into the light,
hitting his lunch pail against my back fence.

It is my father I think of tonight,
letting himself in the back door
and hesitating at the kitchen sink,

waiting for the slow hiss from the tap,
the slowness of the night to take hold.
Perhaps what he hates most about night
is the black grime he sees under his nails,
the bars closing too early and the edge
in his voice at the stiffness of his boots
as he pulls them off in the space left him,
behind the stove.

The uneasiness of the night surrounds me.
In it, the dark-grey eyes of my father
saying he will always be this way
and staring, sane as any man
into a whirlpool of dust, stirred up
one mile deep.

The Cape Rock   *Ann Marie Savage*

IN THE TIME OF THE ROSE

(for Sister Martin)

For this, Old Friend, we burn
Obedient as June;
We step and pause and turn,
Attending to the tune

The sun decrees. The wind
Plays poet, makes a line
To show us where we've been;
Plays scholar to define

The meaning of our play.
And what we loved in youth—
Unthinking, flushed with May—
Now settles to a truth:

Walking amid the late
Gold of garden and sun,
We pause to contemplate
The dancing we have done.

The Southern Review   *John Savant*

VIEWPOINT

From where I sit, I see
A trivium of roads,
A bivium of rivers,
An intersection of mountains:

In between, wild hedges map
The small farms into gatherings
Of young corn and grasses.
From a flower-starred meadow

Fringed with blue pines
Someone flies a blue kite
Against steamy white clouds
As clean as the church

On its sunlit knoll
In the middle distance.
Near to the church wall, half-
Hidden in shade,

One low, bent stone
Winks like a water-drop
Caught in green leaves
After sudden rain.

All morning I've read a book
In this upland pasture
Between a river and a mountain,
At the end of one road,

The beginning of another,
Liking the angle the land makes,
While close by a rose hoists itself
Up a staghorn sumac,

Contriving candelabra—
Which is only to say
That a poet needs to get under
His own light.

The Black Warrior Review   *George Scarbrough*

MIXED MEDIA

To meditate the marvel of mixed media
I turn on the television set, twist off the sound,
Tune in the radio, the stereophonic FM station,
Stare at baseball as Brahm's Fourth Symphony blazes.
Mix media, scramble eggs, bacon, beans and toast
To discover the romantic rhythms of American sport.
Baseball rhythm is pastoral, not pounding like Rock.
The pitcher's grace is confident-allegro,
Smoking the ball hard to exuberant strings.
The centerfielder dances floating to the wall
As strings climax in the green, soaring world.
Andante, the Boomer booms one over the leftfield fence,
Homerun as the high, circular rhythm of discovery.
An explosion of hits, hammering chords, records broken
To the Scherzo's jagged sensuous scattering.
Look! They're throwing everyone out at home plate,
Jolting music, spurts of plucked strings, bleating woodwinds.
On the edge of jaunty triumph, the players trot out
For the ninth as the brass begins its mysterious summons . . .
Wait! The finale fails, game shortened by thunder and rain.
Tomorrow I'll try again this crazy world of mixed media
To find the right mixture that cures my specialized life.

The Hampden-Sydney Poetry Review   *James Schevill*

WINTER TWILIGHT

These evenings,
out where the Lackawanna boxcars
curve into history,
I begin to understand nightfall.

Descending into the body
I notice the small flight of cardinals,
red birds of light
sweeping in prayers over the soul.

Yes, I know
that my bones are elsewhere, alone,
walking the orchard's road
rain-soaked in blossom.

Waiting on these tracks,
the world offers itself so easily, tonight.
May all that is flesh remain so.

Stilled sky.
Only the mind
allows its faint litany
to appear upon the tongue.
Forgive us that fear.

Distant world, allow us.
Redbirds cluster above each breastbone.
Let them speak.

The Ohio Review   *Jeff Schiff*

IN A MAPLE WOOD

Leaves were everywhere in air
and underfoot.
We chose carefully
those most crimson, those most green,
yet none around us in the air
or on the ground seemed half so bright
as those just out of hand-reach,
dancing.
And so you piled up logs,
climbed and balanced, reaching
farther than you comfortably could,
and touched the lowest branch
avalanching gold and red
in ancient cryptic blessing
on our heads.

The Small Pond Magazine   *Pat Schneider*

HUSH, HUSH, NEW HOUSE IN CHARLOTTE

Our new old house climbs a hill,
Backside sagging on stilts, porch chinning up

The short front lawn's long shaggy grass.
The hill drops down darkly behind the house.
Our eye-hooked back door isn't safe.
The basement is a wedge of black cheese
For a great, grinning rat. Trees,
With octopus roots and upward tentacles, tap the roof.
The floors slant, decks frozen in a pitch.
As to the furnace, it groans, goes on,
And heat hisses up from floor vents. Off,
Say a word in one room and you hear it in another,
Pad about and it sounds from somewhere else.
The former tenant was old and mad as bees.
He shot at shadows with a Magnum,
Out back, down there, in the tarpool.
He blew them out of the night, usually.
By day he walked out naked, hating neighbors.
He had the house boarded up, from inside,
And kept two sleek Dobermans. The kennel
Was in the black cheese-wedge down there,
Made out of all the inside doors in the house.
We broke it up, put the doors back on their hinges,
And now can smell them, doggy and dangerous.
That first was our initiation night.
Up the back steps: pumpf, pumpf, pumpf, pumpf!
My daughter woke my mother who woke my other daughter
And they listened by the basement door. Pumpf!
Six-footed, three-throated fear flew to us,
My wife and I, and banged on our bedroom door.
"What is it? What did you hear?" "Pumpf, pumpf, pumpf!"
I hoped it was the heat, or our own feet,
Padding about, leaping from the vents.
I went to the basement door, nevertheless,
And yelled down, "I've got a gun!" Pumpf!
I yelled down, "Get away while you can!"
Pumpf! I pushed open the basement door,
Snapped the switch, and darkness disappeared.
We're home now. We've had our first fear.

The Colorado Quarterly   *E. M. Schorb*

VOYAGE

I awaken to a flow of night
lush with drowsiness,
mirrored in your stroking hands.

Your fingers, light as a dragonfly
shrugging on a lupine stem, flush my skin.
I grow in the dark.

In the wide mouth of after-midnight
your silent words are inside out,
hung with seed and hunger.

The room trembles with transparency.

Rippled to the river bottom,
fluent, I turn over,
answering the shaped wind of your flesh.

In my half-sleep, not so deep
as the interdrowning of ourselves,
we race our protean bodies to the sea.

Beyond Baroque   *Donald G. H. Schramm*

WILLOWS

I sip the dregs, my tongue
Is drier than the wine.
You're disappointed, tired,

And I am not so young
That I will give a sign
To show that I have heard

Your slow retreat. The call
Of swans by the water's edge,
Metallic, strangely close,
Is where our thoughts must meet.

Or in the warmth, here still,
Of failing sunlight. Judge
My failure in your loss:
My silence not discrete,

But not unkind. I see,
But neither will I note,
How like this humid breeze

It was, that summer day
Alone I took the boat.
It stirs the willow trees.

Canto   *Laura Schreiber*

EDUCATIONAL MUSIC OR EROSION

In the innermost cavern of labyrinths
That constitute my being,
I hear the silence
Of a speck of music;
Sometimes it is strong,
Always it is fragile,
Connecting me
With the essence of all.
Can I make it grow?
Can I keep it from eroding?

Educational Studies   *William H. Schubert*

SOLAR SIGNALS

Wind has no language to be chipped
in stone, painted on parchment scrolls
or carved in bark.
Nor has it substance that will ever mold
to any shape round as a bowl, or
angular as wood.

Its voice is evident in slanted wheat
bent to a definition known as drought,
in all the tortured patterns of the oak
and epileptic dances of the dust.

Its words are heard at sunset when the clouds
stretch flat as flags, longer than north or south;
and at the center blows a crimson song,
bright as a bugle, redder than alarm—
the message unmistakable as fear,
warning that tomorrow may be blown
into the single eye of hurricane.

South Western Ontario Poetry   *L. Pearl Schuck*

MRS. APPLEBAUM'S SUNDAY DANCE CLASS

Her red pump tapping, her ankle-length gown slit at the knee,
Mrs. Applebaum lined us up while her husband tuned his piano,
his bald head shining under the Temple's big bay windows.
I can see it all again: the girls' shy smiles, the boys' faces
scrubbed bright as strawberries, 200 fingers crazy with anticipation,
the bowing & curtsying rehearsed to a nervous perfection
by Mrs. Applebaum's high German class. Oh it isn't hard to envision
Sarah Rosen, her bourbon curls tied in a ponytail, stepping forward
like an infant swan to choose that clod Charlie Krieger,
while smiling at me! Call it first intimation of splendor,
call it darker knowledge, but can't you see us, twenty dwarfs colliding,
Sunday after Sunday, until, miraculously, a flourish here, a pivot there,
suddenly Davie Stein dipping Suzie Fein to Mrs. Applebaum's shrill,
"Und vonce agunn, voys und gurdles!"

Oh Mrs. Applebaum, who could've guessed our wild shoving
would be the start of so much furor? You must've known
there was more to come when our lavish stretching left us spinning,
clumsy with desire. Weren't you, our first teacher, thinking of the day
when such passion would finally take our teeth & hair? I don't mean to
    pry,
Mrs. Applebaum, but what went on the night before to channel such light
into your eyes & sway your powerful bosom with such force?
What pushed Mr. Applebaum, never a prize winner, to such heights?
Ah, Mrs. Applebaum, did you notice how I sighed when Sarah
didn't change partners & stayed in my arms? I'm speaking
of that terrible excess, not the edging back, but the overflowing,
all that sudden color flowering in our cheeks! Please, Mrs. Applebaum,

remember Sarah in pink chiffon foxtrotting, her head back & braced
  teeth
pressed against all that which was to come, the world of such profound
  promise!
Yes, remember Sarah, her eyes, for so few moments, so blue
the room everywhere filled with light!

The Kenyon Review   *Philip Schultz*

BEDTIME

I had been watching the child appear
in years of poems, uninvited,
forcing my hand, a demanding
beggar, a king in rags.
At first it was play,
slatted wooden theatre, puppet drama
to earn my charity. Then the earnest,
the habit of catechism, words
to the figure riding my back.
Then the presence, the winking
stranger at the wedding feast.
And now the child is mine,
mythical only as children always
are, and parents. Now I walk home
to him, to her, with rhymes
about astonished animals, evil
lords and ladies, the bric-a-brac
of growing real. My hands seem so large
I must be giant. My child is right:
he has imagined me,
she has brought me home.
This is what it is like—
the confusion of skin,
the backwardness of memory—
to be born.

Descant (Canada)   *Hillel Schwartz*

THE STUMP IS NOT THE TOMBSTONE

The stump is not the tombstone for the tree.
It marks the birth and celebrates the living
Rather than points to where life used to be,
Providing now another kind of giving.
What once held root to timber, earth to sky,
Has now become the summer beetle's grotto,
The chipmunk's hide-and-seek. The butterfly
Brings signature to this old woodland's motto:
"There is no waste in nature, every cell
Recycles to produce another treasure."
May we, like this aged tree stump, do as well
When our diminished height the flowers measure.

Some one may live in deeds we leave behind,
However unrecorded and unsigned.

Quest | 80   *Ralph W. Seager*

SPRING MORNING: WAKING

("These are the days when birds come back."—Emily Dickinson)

Azaleas are funny plants:
they bloom abundantly in your back yard
but never so full in the front.
This I am told by gardeners
who labor to space plants by color and size
for that moment in late spring
when bushes bloom
and cars wind through suburbs
on Sunday afternoons.
That season is too brief—
two Sundays at best—
and the gardener finds her blossoms
litter the lawn,
soft and garish
as carpet in Grandmother's bathroom.

In the midst of new summer green
there is death:
blossoms gone to the ground
or browning on the bush
to drop late or be hidden by full growth.

"These are the days when birds come back"—
And they do come back
to eat berries from the tree outside the window,
to wake you with singing
as the heat of day begins.
Like old lovers, they filter into dreams
and I wake to find distance on regret.
Old loves gleam and rot in an instant.
Like the gardener,
I find myself cursing
the work too late realized,
too soon forgot,
the morning so early gone.

Feminary   *Emily Seelbinder*

TO ROBERT LOWELL AND OSIP MANDELSTAM

I look out the window: spring is coming.
I look out the window: spring is here.
The shuffle and click of the slide projector
Changing slides takes longer.

I like the dandelion—
How it sticks to the business of briefly being.
Shuffle and click, shuffle and click—
Life, more life, more life.

The train that carried the sparkling crystal saxophone
Osip Mandelstam into exile clicketyclicked
Through suds of spring flowers,
Cool furrowed-earth smells, sunshine like freshly baked bread.

The earth was so black it looked wet,
So rich it had produced Mandelstam.
He was last seen alive
In 1938 at a transit camp near Vladivostok

Eating from a garbage pile,
When I was two, and Robert Lowell was twenty-one,
Who much later would translate Mandelstam,
And now has been dead two years himself.

I sometimes feel I hurry to them both,
Stand staring at the careworn spines
Of their books in my bookshelf,
Only in order to walk away.

The wish to live is as unintentional as love.
Of course the future always is.
Like someone just back from England
Stepping off a curb, I'll look the wrong way and be nothing.

Heartbeat, heartbeat, the heart stops—
But shuffle and click, it's spring!
The arterial branches disappearing in the leaves,
Swallowed like a tailor's chalk marks in the finished suit.

We are born.
We grow old until we're all the same age.
They are as young as Homer whom they loved.
They are writing a letter, not in a language I know.

I read: "It is one of those spring days with a sky
That makes it worthwhile being here.
The mailbox in which we'll mail this
Is slightly lighter than the sky."

The American Poetry Review   *Frederick Seidel*

DANCE-SONG

It's been a long time since I wrote poems which dance—
And danced badly myself.
Still, sometimes even a stiff knee
Can beat good rhythm.

Now I go back shamefully
    To the first ones:
She had tangled bronze hair which hung
In one thick braid down to the waist,
And when she danced faster and faster,

It flew heavily after her
Like a tamed bird.

And I often return to Jindrishka
  (Although I don't feel like it).
She vanished in the deep grass of this world
And I haven't seen her since.
But then,
Just as my feet slide into my shoes,
  I remember her
And the shoes take me to that face circled with ash blonde hair.

The third one, the one who always believed
That love was just loud kisses
And gentle words,
Is now angry with me.

The one under whose window I used to whistle
When she refused to show herself to me
  Danced superbly.
She always lost her little combs,
Broke her bracelet,
Her madonna's medal spilled to the floor,
And who knows what else.

But there isn't enough of anything as long as we live.
The feet suddenly stop,
The dance breaks up in the middle;
No need for strong arms until winter comes
And the palms of hands save themselves
  For other work.

Finally, the last one appears.
She's confused, doesn't dance;
  That's why she's the most beautiful,
And is, until death, alone.

And now that one does not exist either.

The Hampden-Sydney Poetry Review   *Jaroslav Seifert*
                                      —Translated from the Czech
                                    by Paul Jagasich and Tom O'Grady

PATTERNS

When, on a yellowing hill, a tree
Opened its twiggy brown-ribbed fan,
In the interlacing of blue brocade
The stillness of one little bird
And the brightness of one gold leaf
Held autumn in its silk design.

Poet Lore   *Ruth Setterberg*

FALLING UPWARDS

A certain violinist had a beautiful violin,
But before he had had time to play her long and listen

To her tones as such, he was compelled to renounce music
And sell her, and go on a far journey, and leave his violin
  in the hands of the violin case.

What was there to do? It is said you cannot live life in
  quarter tones.
What was there to do? It is said you cannot live your life
  in silence.
What was there to do? It is said you cannot live your life
  playing scales.
What was there to do? It is said you cannot live your life listening to the
  Americans.

What was there to do? It is said you cannot live your
  life in your room and not go out.
What was there to do? It is said music disobeys
And reaches the prince's courtyard ever farther than smell
  and grits its notes like teeth and gives us food and drink,
And orders a fire to be lighted, famished silk to hang over it
  and repetitions to be sharpened.

What was there to do? It is said it is the violinists who
  do not sleep.
What was there to do? It is said we think and don't think;
  we are asleep.
What was there to do? It is said music sinks into the mire up
  to its neck, wants to crawl out, but cannot.
What was there to do? It is said the violin was a swan,
  seized by the boy, falling upwards to some height above the earth.

New York Arts Journal   *David Shapiro*

A JERUSALEM NOTEBOOK

1. A city of ascensions,
   nowhere to go but up.
   Forcing the spirit in New York
   is the commonplace; we live
   there as if we were in Jerusalem,
   Jesus and Mohammed touching down
   and going up, just another
   launching pad, as I get off
   the bus and head home.

2. *Postcard*
   It was not far from here
   that the parents stood
   and the child, placed into the priest's machine,
   heard the wail
   of Moloch. And the bronze god,
   arms outstretched, smiled at the smoke.
   Two of the kings of Judah
   burned their sons here—
   Hell, Gehenna, Gai Hinnom,
   the pleasant valley of Hinnom,

pink, scarred and silent
in the fading light.

3. If you begin housekeeping
   at the edge of Gehenna
   you have to expect a little trouble.
   She said to me: I like
   this place because there are no birds.
   No. She said to me: *Actually,*
   I like this place because there
   are no birds. The white lizard
   on the white wall seemed transfixed
   by the thought of hell. Looking east
   and south I see the Judean hills,
   a desert like a sea.
   Or dunes dropping off into a sea.
   Morning vapors rising off the land.
   Give me this place for my own,
   I cried, and I will live here forever.
   The prospect is as sweet
   as a Sabbath morning. Across
   the valley of Gehenna cypresses line
   the sloping hill. I can walk
   there any time I like, now
   I am old enough, and look back
   on this life I have begun.

4. *Tourists*

   She is crying over three olives
   that I threw out. Three olives
   but my food, she cries. She is
   not a child but a woman.
   Outside Zion Gate, Jaffa Gate,
   Dung Gate, she rubs my arm slowly.
   Gates excite her. Where I come in
   at night, the city is so beautiful.

5. It is the temple mount.
   It is a little like the temple mount,
   though I myself constitute
   the sightseers, worshippers,
   and sometimes the visiting god.

6. Whatever brought me here, to a new moon
   over Zion's hill, dark moon
   with the thin cusp silvered,
   help me believe in my happiness, for
   it was guilt that woke me. A voice
   on the telephone crying breakdown.
   Illusions of my own ego causing destruction,
   while outside the marvelous
   machinery of day has opened, light
   traffic on the road to the citadel.
   And as I look again, it is all
   swept clean, except for the small birds,

faint pink in the sky and on the old
stones of the city, and language in my head
that I brought with me, that I carry,
that I use to mark my way.

7. My way of being in the world:
not perfect freedom or the pitch
of madness, but that the particulars
of my life become manifest
to me walking these dark streets.

8. *For C. R.*

When I dropped permanence from my back
and saw what I had taken for
solid buildings and good roads
was desert all about me and within me;
how bright became the sunlight,
how sweet the evening air.

9. *The Old Jewish Poet Floats in the Dead Sea*

It is the lowest place on earth
but he has been lower.
For example, he has been on the heights
of Massada, watching the Roman soldiers
jack off in the baths below.
He knows his turn will be next.
Beneath him floats a crow.
Beneath the crow floats the crow's shadow.
Beneath the crow's shadow is another Jew.
These Judean junk hills
fill his head with sulphur.
Every hill is a hill of skulls.

10. I understand we are like smoke.
It streams from my cigar into the morning air,
silken, prism-like in sunlight
as I sit by the window.
Nothing I do with my life
could be as beautiful.

11. Lizard lines in his skin.
Striving to become one with the stones
like the lizard, even as the pen
darts into the shadow of the page.

12. I have dreams coming out of my ears,
she said. Why not? This city has seen
so many mad dreamers, their stale dreams
even now looking for new homes.
The stones dream in the sun,
the lizards. In the golden mosque,
riots of line and color, shapes dream
in the marble columns, pulsing in
and out of sleep. When the city wakes,
the action is brief and bloody.
Let it sleep. Let the gabardined Jews

dream of the Messiah. He approaches
the blocked-off gate of the walled city.
Taste the dream of the Jews.

13. Why did I want to sit out all the time—
was the air so special? Yes,
soft and today dust-blue. But the smell
of corpses had been everywhere, and more to come.
Red buses and blue buses raced the roads
to the small towns, carrying infant Jesuses,
dynamite. Blondes from Scandinavia,
silver-toed, tried on Arab dresses
while the man in the stall scratched his crotch.
It was all happening inside the city.
And at the edge was desert.

14. Middle east music on the radio: Hebrew love songs,
Arab wails. Carmel Dry Gin
taking me up Zion's hill.
Lights on the stones of the ancient city.

15. Who needs more happiness? People living
on the edge (of pain, of death,
of revelation) need time in the sun.
A lengthening interval between
the sonic boom and the rattled glass.

16. I cannot dissever my happiness from language
or from your body. Light a candle for me
at the false tomb of David—I am of that line.
Let the young scarecrow who might be from 47th Street
say a blessing for me. Sway over the candle's flame
like the old Arab riding toward me on his donkey.
If I forget my happiness, let me be dust.
Jerusalem, here I am going up again.
It is your moon, your labyrinths, your desert
crowding east where the sun waits.

Poetry   *Harvey Shapiro*

PARTIAL DRAFT

My ear, still keyed to summer, failed to label
a murmur stirred by the mild October day;
so, lured at last mid-sentence from my table
(What was the word I wanted?—It slipped away).

I turned to see how, eased of my attention,
trees turning fast had scattered half their load.
What I was hearing, mind in meek suspension,
was former foliage hurrying down the road,

a fibrous faint grating, skip and bustle
made when the wind dispatches lemony shoals
over the asphalt. That doom-eager hustle
whispers a dry subversion to the souls

of those still undisposed to follow after,
intent to stay awaiting a later word.
A second wind: cicada-like but softer,
the sound is known this time when it is heard:

a noise more near to silence than most noises,
bordering silent moments when the pen
upon some puzzling brink or line-break poises
before pursuing its scratchy path again.

Poetry   *Robert B. Shaw*

TELEPHONE

This instrument
unravels your voice
and feeds it, wire thin,
from particle to particle of air,
bouncing inside a wreath of insulation.
Miles away, it is knit up again,
and lies like your blue sweater
against my ear.
You have little to say.
The pauses crackle.
Another conversation
fades in and out,
a woman's voice says
"I don't care." I say, "I do."
The cause of her indifference
filters off into another line
somewhere in the Arizona desert.
Small blue sparks, our words
rub against each other,
tumble their slow dreams
across the scrub-brush,
over the heads of Indians
spinning yarn, gathering grasses
in the middle morning.

Yankee   *Robin Shectman*

LETTING GO

you walk down the road
my young and only son
as if everything
were there for your pleasure
and you are right

you pause to touch a tree
and say *alligator juniper*
and again you are right

why should I be surprised
that you have learned

what I have forgotten
and more than I ever knew

my tall bright son
nothing I can do now
will alter the length
of your shadow
as you leave the desert
which has been your home

when you look back
the moon will set
over your shoulder
and the sun will rise
each morning to meet you

turn then
turn away and walk on
nothing I can give you
will forestall
the moment of your death
nor determine how long
how much you will suffer
between this point of light
and that point of light

you have learned
to accept your life
as if it were music
played with great skill
and would last forever
and you are right again
my son my only son
it will last long enough

The Gramercy Review   *Richard Shelton*

IN PASSING

Used years,
when we are done with them,
are gathered into decades,
given titles—gay nineties,
roaring twenties, turbulent sixties,
or the me-decade—then bundled,
tied and stored in that vast attic
of the aeons where they slowly sift
and settle into centuries.
While, in the meantime,
time itself (which, by the way,
is never mean), spins out
its fine, unbroken thread
along the weary labyrinths
to the moment with the minotaur

when all our yearly tributes
are delivered and set free.

The Christian Century   *J. Barrie Shepherd*

THE ENLIGHTENMENT

The woods have a way of slanting light
so one can see into its solitude,
into the deep green of fully developed spring,
to the deepest shade of green that is not black.

A mote of dust becomes irradiated,
drifting down the light beam
and through its edge,
musical,

the way it slips into harmony
with the light, like a note
heard inside the composer's mind,
without the flourish being sounded.

Trace the dance of dust back
to every degree of green.
There is this life.
Make of it what you will.

The Hudson Review   *Patricia Sheppard*

PILGRIMAGE TO HENNESSEY'S

It would be snowing back there,
grinding out the cold
till skin cracks, the rasp
in the wind snaps trees.

The old woman rocks
at the window, smiling with her
warmth like homemade pie,
a homespun plaid bandana
tieing up her thinning hair.

The river's frozen current
surges forward, snags
at the eye. She's knitting a
biography, laying out her years
end to end, stretched some.

Original flirting tools, her
wink and smile still secure
the past, never dug up by
its roots. Each sigh takes her
deeper into that secret.

Her eyes, already packed,
leave tracks in the new snow.
Shadow spreads over the distance

     where memory stays lit,
     embers of a dying winter fire.

Slackwater Review   *Steven Sher*

FIRST HOLES ARE FRESH

All his friends had gotten a hole—
their mark of maturity.
Eric needed to lose his first tooth.
From the swing he came running
to tell me he was ready.
I pushed back, then pulled,
breaking a bit of skin—
only a drop of blood really.
Young, proud, initiated,
he cradled that misshapen pearl.

My teeth were pulled at the dentist's,
then thrown away in a white pail.
I wish I had kept the molars
to string around my neck.
Eric will lose one tooth at a time,
keep my heart running back and forth
while I try to stop him
from knowing how early good men die
if they do not save their teeth.

We put the tooth under his pillow
as I had done at six for the tooth fairy.
Ropes of teeth wrapped her arms,
sequined her clothes,
flaking her hair like snow newly struck.
Even her mouth was full.

I tried to barter with her
for that first tooth of my first born.
But she took it and left silver,
teaching him to trade himself.
There are many things
I wish he would never learn.

The Greenfield Review   *Vivian Shipley*

FIRST ICE OF WINTER

I have hunted the first ice
Of winter eagerly, making
Rounds of each pond and creek
In my childhood land, rising
Before dawn to walk beneath
Wood's branches where the last
Red and black leaves sang
The coming touch of snow-whorled wind.

And like a hunter visiting his traps
I stood, watching for hairs
Of ice bloomed forth on those rippled faces.

I have hunted the first ice of winter
Skillfully, testing the thin
Shells of freezing planets
With heel and toe, urging them
Form solid mirrors to bear me,
Gliding in blue winter,
A manna of snow draped on trees,
Skies, the aimless circles of joy.

Buffalo Spree   *Michael Shorb*

TRACKS

So I've come south this time
and found a beach longer than anyone can run,
a sheath of fine white sand
stitched with tire tracks,
beaded with beer cans and glistening bodies.
Tailored to my life: I understand
when the tide reaches up, scoops out sand
beneath my feet: keep moving.
I move, I move.
Not a scene I can share with you.
I can't think of you here.
Lying on my back in the late afternoon,
sun coaxing all the sweat I have to give,
wrapped in salt-glaze,
                          lost in a heat daze,
I connect you with a northern heartland
undisturbed since you left.
Pine trees tremble in a frozen field,
the sun is calm and heatless,
the air too overwhelmed
by your passing to speak.
Frozen, fragile,
your tracks are still there,
beautiful bruises on the crusted
glittering snow.

Buffalo Spree   *Brad Lee Shurmantine*

THE CENTER OF AMERICA

The center of America is a whale
green, spreading quietly over the waters.
His mouth, hidden under the earth,
strains food for millions
as a fluke beats patiently near one eye.

He is not a whale to turn
upon the shadow that hunts him,

nor treacherously sink
marooning the children who take him for an island.

Instead, he will stretch to the summer sky,
his dreams shuddering upward like the heat
that dances before the combines
revolving across Kansas.

Cream City Review   *Robert Siegel*

GRAND HOTEL, CALCUTTA

One hot Bengali night returning home
Through yellow-lighted corridors, I found
our turbaned Indian bearer sitting down
With folded feet at ease outside our room;
Against his knee he wrote, in a script unknown
To me, a letter to his country town.
He mused and wrote, he dipped his pen, wrote on,
Ignoring me. One always writes alone.

How strange to hear the sounds of my father's pen
On paper, in his bottle of ink, at night,
To see his way of musing, writing again.
He also hummed in his solitary delight.
Remembering how my father used to write,
I was all drunk with India that night.

The Helen Review   *Layle Silbert*

CARTOON

Our lives are sketched in the simplest lines.
Four fingers suffice as a hand. Our eyes are
sets of round dice, rolling up one's time
and again. Two arcs and a line mean a bird
on the horizon. The color blue means sky.

It is like hell: nothing is impossible. Our
skulls might be split by grappling hooks,
and we would still report for work in the
morning. We might be blown to cinders by
uncertain design; there would be nothing to
do but assemble the ashes and begin again.

A childish anthem describes our lives. When
we move, we pass the same tree or building
over and over. We pretend not to notice.
When we speak, our words do not match our lips.

Carolina Quarterly   *Jim Simmerman*

THE FIRST GOODBYE LETTER

"Dear wife, I don't suppose you understand
my cheerfulness these days with passion cooling,

my love-songs of a bachelor,
my boyish fooling,

"the way I lie so easy on my own side
or rise to screw newspaper for the fire?
Crooning over breakfast pans
is all that I desire.

"Safely alive in the quiet light of morning,
indulging my fancy alone, acting the clown
is plenty, plenty. I'm reconciled
to letting us all down.

"Old girl, don't worry over it, don't argue.
The famous challenge of marriage, when all is said,
is not my scene, the legal arena,
the permanent double bed.

"Me? Famous for nothing but giggling, tiptoe,
avoiding parents and other dinosaurs
through fern and aspidistra jungles,
down dangerous corridors?

"I'm nowhere, home again, goodbye my honey,
escaping the duns of conscience with ad-lib ruses,
incapable drunk, but always deft
with wry smiles and excuses."

Ploughshares   *James Simmons*

WHY DO YOU WRITE ABOUT RUSSIA?

When I was a child
my mother told stories about the country
she came from. Wolves were howling,
snow fell, the drunken Cossack
shouted in the snow.

Rats prowled the floor of the cellar
where the children slept.
Once, after an illness, she was sent
to Odessa, on the sea. There were battleships
painted white, and ladies and gentlemen
walking the esplanade . . . white naval uniforms
and parasols.

These stories were told
against a background of tropical night . . .
a sea breeze stirring the flowers
that open at dusk, smelling like perfume.
The voice that spoke of freezing cold
itself was warm and infinitely comforting.

So it is with poetry: whatever numbing horrors
it may speak of, the voice itself
tells of love and infinite wonder.

Later, when I came to New York,
I used to go to my grandmother's

in Brooklyn. The names of stations
return in their order like a charm:
Franklin, Nostrand, Kingston.

And members of the family gather:
the three sisters, the one brother,
one of the cousins from Washington,
and myself . . . a "student at Columbia."
But what am I really?

For when my grandmother says, "Eat!
People who work with their heads have to eat more" . . .
Work? Does it deserve a name
so full of seriousness and high purpose?
Gazing across Amsterdam Avenue
at the windows opposite, letting my mind
wander where it will, from the page
to Malaya, or some street in Paris . . .
Drifting smoke. The end will be as fatal
as an opium-eater's dream.

*

The view has changed—to evergreens,
a hedge, and my neighbor's roof.
This too is like a dream, the way we live
with our cars and power-mowers . . .
a life that shuns emotion
and the violence that goes with it,
the object being to live quietly
and bring up children to be happy.

Yes, but what are you going to tell them
of what lies ahead?
That the better life seems
the more it goes sour? The child no longer
a child, his happiness all of a sudden
behind him. And he in turn
expected to bring up his children
to be happy . . .

What then do I want?

A life in which there are depths
beyond happiness. As one of my friends,
Grigoryev, says, "Two things
constantly cry out in creation:
the sea and man's soul."

Reaching from where we are
to where we came from . . . *Thalassa!*
a view of the sea.

*

I sit listening to the rasp
of a power-saw, the puttering of a motor-boat.
The whole meaningless life around me
affirming a positive attitude . . .

When a hat appears, a black felt hat,
gliding along the hedge . . .
then a long, black overcoat
that falls beneath the knee.

He produces a big, purple handkerchief,
brushes off a chair, and sits.
"It's hot," he says, "but I like to walk;
that way you get to see the world.
And so, what are you reading now?"

Chekhov, I tell him.

"Of course. But have you read Leskov?
There are sentences that will stay in your mind
a whole lifetime.
For instance, in the 'Lady MacBeth,'
when the woman says to her lover,
'You couldn't be nearly as desirous
as you say you are, for I heard you singing' . . .
he answers, 'What about gnats?
They sing all their lives, but it's not for joy.' "

So my imaginary friend tells stories
of the same far place the soul comes from.

When I think about Russia,
it's not that area of the earth's surface
with Leningrad to the West and Siberia
to the East—I don't know anything
about the continental mass.

It's a sound, such as you hear
in a sea breaking along a shore.

My people came from Russia,
bringing with them nothing
but that sound.

The Ohio Review   *Louis Simpson*

BACK IN THE STATES

It was cold, and all they gave him to wear
was a shirt. And he had malaria.

There was continual singing of hymns—
"Nearer My God to Thee" was a favorite.
And a sound like running water . . .
it took him a while to figure it.

Weeping, coming from the cells
of the men who had been condemned.

Now here he was, back in the States,
idly picking up a magazine,
glancing through the table of contents.

Already becoming like the rest of us.

The Georgia Review   *Louis Simpson*

ON CERTAIN DAYS OF THE YEAR

Sun and moon at the same time,
my boy looks up saying Carolina sky
is different from sky in Vietnam.
Nguyen Quoc Phong, Nguyen Quoc Phong,
he writes on the fogged windshield.

Anniversary of adoption, sun and moon—
he asks too many questions.
I try to explain day and night.
We are somewhere between
home and his dad's new house,
coconut cake on the back seat
and presents tied with white ribbon.
That is not enough.
He wants to know how separate worlds revolve,
the crossing of paths on certain days of the year.
I apologize for divorce,
driving us south to Atlanta, remembering
the day I reached half-way around the world,
$1600 in my fist, believing I could give him
the sun and the moon.

The Wayah Review   *Nancy Simpson*

FAMILY PLOT

Quite apropos that we should visit here
Who loved them in their flesh, and say their names
Aloud lest stones and graveyard atmosphere

Possess them utterly; recall lost whims
And graces that endeared or vexed, unique
Humanity no monument redeems

With chiseled text or ivy trimmed each week
To make death neat. Yet quick of eye and nerve,
We gather, never certain what we seek
Or counter. Is it kin or self we serve?

Bitterroot   *Sarah Singer*

OUTSIDE EVERY WINDOW IS A FLOWERING THING

This February in Berkeley
we slope down the pebbled sidewalk
in the morning fog, speak reverently
of the Victorian houses, wind through
students, small strands of vigorous
trees and formal buildings to the Women's
Faculty Club, appropriately, we discover
later, designed by a woman. By the steps,
a tulip tree works white and pink
slivers into the bright grass, explodes

against the sky, and as we move
inside, dark heavy beams
beg for the rhythm of hands, fingers
to trace the pulse of the wood,
contrast with the reticent
eggshell of the walls,
and the tall windows with dozens
of small squares
ask in the light.

Outside every window is a flowering thing,
a woman blooming in every yard
of this American landscape (behind the white
picket fences in Mississippi, the black iron
gates of Brooklyn, the rock walls
of the hill country), flourishing
in the costume of her territory, sharing
the secret language of women,
an Aunt Jemima, a Georgia O'Keefe.
We narrate the shapes, the places,
the routes of their stories;
we become the portraits
of many regions: the north, the south,
the self, the frontiers
of our intimacies, the definitions
of our lifestyles. We are not ornament,
intended to adorn, to freshen
the room, to add glory
to the age. We think
with our bodies as well as
our minds. Our words
are our photographs: learn what
is important, search for
what is left out.

Come sit with me on the floral
cushions of the big chair, wicker
or rocker. Look out over the lights
around the bay, the seeds of the great
city. Since we may never
meet again, let us say
how our lives have changed.

Cottonwood Review   *Anita Skeen*

HIS SIDE / HER SIDE

His Side

There can be no explanation
elaborate enough to satisfy your curiosity.
Don't you see that yet? When the hurt
has nowhere to go it becomes a kind of hunger,
a sad relish for lewd detail. And the questions
lead to nothing, like a series of doors

in a dream. Behind the next door
you keep hoping to find an explanation

but all you find is another door, a question
that opens and closes on curiosity,
so blank and wooden it hurts.
They say the best way to stop hunger

is abstention: for two days you are hungry,
then it disappears. Refrigerator doors
lose their pull, all the body's tiny hurts
heal themselves. I could explain
how the cells, freed from digestion . . . but you are not
    curious
in the least; you want to get back to the question.

She was nothing to me. You question
this, over and over, as if you hungered
for a different answer. I'm curious—
if I said it was love, wouldn't you open the door
and toss me out, screaming *Bastard?* Explanation
would be unnecessary. You would still hurt.

I'm not making fun of your hurt.
Nothing goes rancid like a promise. The question
is how many times must I explain
that what flared in me was momentary hunger,
an unexpected knock on some ancient door
I answered out of curiosity.

Like the cat, I gave in. And curious
as it sounds, though I wasn't killed, I was hurt.
Yes, me! You point to the door,
you cry, you will not stop your questions—
I'm trying to tell you it was hunger
for love that brought me back. To explain
further is to mock explanation: Curious,
I indulged a brief hunger. You were hurt.
Our love is not in question. Now, shut the door.

Her Side

It's like you to fall back on words
when what I need is the touch
of something real. Oh, how calmly you say the damage
is done, that I should forget her,
forget my sad, my pointless questions
so that we can go on living—

what a fairy tale you must live
in! To think I'd swallow smooth words
and idiotic, cliche reasons without question—
the height of arrogance! Touch
down from your cloud, friend. Describe her
face, her body; let the damages

take on flesh. Was she ever damaged
like me? Or did she have a life
you read about in *Cosmopolitan,* her
clothes sleek and shiny, good with words,

up-to-date on every kind of touch
to bring a man off? Does that question
offend you? Ha! What a question!
Tell me, did you satisfy her? Or would it damage
your pride to answer? It's touching,
your concern about our life
together, how it hurt to break your word,
how you wavered in agony. But what about her,

we have to consider her
feelings too, don't we? Now you question
my sincerity, call me sarcastic. Words
cannot express how sorry I am. It's damaging
evidence, I know, my disregard for her life . . .
You see, the thing is, I've lost my touch

for empathy. All I see is your hand, touching
her there, and there, lifting her
out of some hell, and into my life.
Why? why—that's the only question
I want answered. Why did you damage
a promise I thought went beyond words,

and now is just words? You can't touch
me now without damage: I think of her.
Answer the question, bastard. Don't waste my life.

Poetry   *Jeffrey Skinner*

IN BED

Jewish extremities—cold
hands and cold feet,
all that long history
stretching back before Christ
and the Magi
or going forth into who knows what
calamity.

Why do you have such cold hands?
he wants to know.

It's the history, I say to him,
while he blows on my fingers,
while he prevents me from wrapping cold
around his body.
The history blowing through these rooms,
I tell him. The Old story of exile
and assassination.

Why are your toes so cold? he says,
cradling my feet in his own.

The history, I reiterate, warming
to this dialectic. The way the history
goes from one desert to another. Or stalls,
I think to myself, in some cozy doctrine

certain as the yellow-backed antelope
bedded down in straw, the afternoon sun
encircling her.

Carolina Quarterly   *Myra Sklarew*

YOUR BIRDS BUILD SUN-CASTLES WITH SONG

Your birds build sun-castles with song; insects give shape
to the river; and the brilliant winds come with green intent.
Earth, all this one morning from my window; all this
irradiated on the eye, made part of my ever-atoms. I built,
I flowed, I was air upon memory.
And I loved. I dismantled dream-wings that would not fly;
I breathed in the deep moon and found her bitter; but sweet
the paths to the tree-tops to reach her,
overlooking what was to be.
Earth, all this one morning from my window,
As the rain was falling.

Descant (Canada)   *Daniel Sloate*

NEXT DOOR TO MONICA'S DANCE STUDIO

Over the hiss of the coffee urns,
The cash register registering coins,
The dancers speak low, their leotards curved,
Partially covered with denim-patched blue.
Orange slices swallowed for Vitamin C,
They talk, ballerinas, of enzyme in flow,
Muscle stretch, tendon strain, cartilage tone—
Sudden discoveries of arching back strength,
Of posture and space and of arm-filling air—
Rhythming bodies now turning
Art. I envy and hold
Wonder of painters, their bronzes and chisels and molds;
And sharply this moment, these torsos, these legs,
Breathing to music heard inside the sounds
Of me and the dishroom and business-tuned tongues—
Wonder of whether my soul can move
This pen into magic, this paper to dance.

Hill and Valley   *Barbara Smith*

TIDE POOLS

At dusk and long-distance they are the mouths
to another world, caves of silence that speak
only in light and, tonight, family packed
for home travel, we take a last, slow route
over sand the sea has been all day cleaning.
At driftwood the children stop, first veering
off wordlessly, and kneel to know some texture
of wood, or stand merely to dream themselves

freely into the gathering shadows of the land.
As we go ahead of them, we imagine their hands
collecting what seems to have waited for each:
shells, starfish, agates like a lover's eyes.
Then we also drift apart, each following deep
runnels the tide has left, and after a while
I see you hunched on a rock, almost part of it.

The light is almost gone and the wind chills me
so I think of my father's whistle, how it called
the sundered shadows of a family into the house.
But do not whistle now, through the lips he made,
for somehow we have come where we may be apart
and whole. Instead, I walk farther to the north,
until you are all taken into shapes of this place.

Then I find it, the deepest pool, rock-vaulted,
light bending and alive in water faintly moving.
I see the lacey deceptions, creatures disguised
as rock whose breath flutes in quick freshets.
A killdeer cries from the dark suck of the surf
and, though sweet, that darkness is not wanted.
This hole is filled with the last golden light
and by it I learn to see what I always suspected,
the small, quiet, incessant outcroppings of life.
For a while I stare into the spooling depth, for
here are hard black eyes and iron-shells, glitter
of hulls laid forever side by side like the dead
caught at last unwarily, perfect and untouchable.

When finally I whistle there is almost no light,
but there's enough. You come, then, invisible,
a sound made by the sand, a mingling of laughter,
and I duck under just in time, holding my breath.
How I love your squeal of delight when I burst up
like a king from underground! Soon we are all in,
all naked, splashing and crying like white birds.
The road home will be long and dark, the stars cold;
but collected like this, we will be buoyed beyond
the dark snags and splinters of what we once were.

Poetry   *Dave Smith*

FIRST STAR

Someone is smoking in the darkness
on the porch of the land.
Somewhere is falling the last
light-edged word, and wind
walks in from the west.

Hurry, you can feel the absence.
Hurry, call like a storm:
"It's me!" Use present tense,
for time is now the form
the surf takes, and it's urgent.

That star is not smoke. It deceives.
You are no child to declare
again, "But I'm not ready."
What, then, of surf and step-flare
always the same? "It's me—"

Why does that smoker on stairs not answer?
Is it wind? Is it distance? Is it anger?

Quest / 80   *Dave Smith*

THE BALCONY POEMS

i.

If I reach out
over the guardrail
I can touch
the elm's highest spears of chlorophyll
that will yellow and fall
from twigs thin as fishbones
all five storeys
without design or fear
of design

ii.

Above the TV aerials and chimneys
anchored in the glittering shingles
of the rained-on neighbourhood
the church spire
rises like a nose-cone
fueled with sin
Its sudden *gong*
scatters saintly-gray pigeons
They land nearby on a flat roof
like breadcrumbs
fallen from the mouth
of some greedy god

iii.

The sun falling on the river
a disaster of streaks

Across the water
the windshields and chrome of cars
flicker
like stars
through the thinning trees of the park

I stand on my balcony
and watch
these axioms of light
repeat their lessons to a failing world

Prism International   *Douglas Smith*

SOMETHING

Something massively large has slept
the last days in the valley reaching outside from my window;
something of unimaginable weight
along the far banks of the river outside my study;
and yet silent in the ease with which its resting limbs
uprooted trees and boulders, cascading earth and rubble
down to the water's edge, leaving an expanding pattern
of metal frames and abandoned summer houses
pressed flat into the depression of its presence.

Some thing which I do not have a name for
which has passed the night these recent days
quietly waiting while I slept,
so that when I rose in the gray of morning
the land outside was changed each day,
and the vegetation I remembered further crushed.
So that is why tonight I wait
long after my wife has departed for the bedroom,
and I smoke cigarettes or sip my drink
as I stare into darkness listening to the wind
as it builds along these valley corridors
and the air inside this room grows heavy with discarded time.

And I listen to the rain in its falling,
as it has fallen each of these past days,
rattling along the shingles and sliding off to silence.
And there suddenly I begin to hear
the distant splintering of wood and a heavy settling
as if the smoke which fills this room were taking solid form
and rolling to a final resting place;
and yet the room is filled with smoke and it is rolling
    without ceasing in the darkness,
moving in or out with the coolness of the partly opened window.

Even as I write this,
I am staring as intently as I can
out over the valley beneath the distance of the stars,
until almost I think there is a less substantial shape
transforming in the valley, or a gathering of gray within the night.
But it is too hard to tell about, and the shape
or shapes, if they are shapes, too hidden in their form.
The brighter focal points perhaps the flashlight
of some landowner puzzling over forgotten land,
his eyes every now and then reaching out to touch a stone
and glittering there. I do not know,
but only that something there is hidden from the light.
And I know that everything is fading as the morning comes,
and that the earth will slide down farther down its swollen river.

Poet Lore   *Jared Smith*

RURAL ROUTE

I have loved coming by the back roads,
knowing deer cross my path
and disappear into slash pine stands.
I have loved scouting wide fields
of slain corn and soy stubble,
passing the quiet silo against sunsets
or discovering roots revealed snakish
by floods eroding the soil.
Who has missed the lone creek's twist
through red slate and under the road?
Who has failed to taste woodsmoke
when first chill whets the hogblade?
I have loved the startle of switchback,
sweat of incline, the signs
of each season dissolving with time.
Have you seen wind awaken the dust
to dance its shapes in your path?
Have you seen dew spark on the combine,
heard cows low by barbed wire on a night
when each star promised a dawn?
I have loved watching each footprint
shape the damp weeds, then vanish,
each leaf trembling silent where
a surprised creature has eased
into the home maze of nettle and vine.
I have enjoyed the abbreviated steeples
of country churches, weather-wounded,
and reveled in the stir of April rain.
Have you touched the still warm
cleft heart of a fresh deer print
in sand that does not believe in form?
Have you heard the gunnery of limbs
under the ice left by storm?
A chainsaw snarls against the distance,
patchwork quilts flagging from the line
snap in wind, and neighbors wave.
I have loved coming by the back roads
whose curved amble will always lead
to a reservoir of heart safe from harm.

Buffalo Spree   *R. T. Smith*

POEM FOR DAVID JANSSEN

I am no worshiper, but a member
of your constituency. As a kid
I could never remember if your
legal name were Janssen or Kimball.
Your plight was universal,
a flight from law, pursuit
of the secret, the guilty maimed.

Now, late nights I know you
as wry private eye Harry O.,
wearing that carapace of scorn
to cover the widower's heart
you have borne from show to show.
Each week I watch you debate cops,
interrogate, and always pursue,
your hairline receding, middle-aged
breath resisting the chase. It's hard
to believe you're dead. The papers
said you had a heart attack at home,
but I have known what would happen
since your Kafkaesque career began:
you have found the one-armed man
and found him certain kin.

Ball State University Forum   *R. T. Smith*

THE DEATH OF CARMEN MIRANDA

Carmen Miranda died on my seventh birthday,
August 5, 1955.
I was climbing among mimosa blossoms
when the music stopped,
and her death floated like a scarf
from the kitchen window.
"The South American Bombshell is dead,"
the radio said.

Uncle Tully was home from Korea,
and I wondered if the death
of Carmen Miranda meant he'd go off
to another war.
He laughed
and answered in that careless fashion
adults use when answering children.
He said,
"Well, maybe it's like Pearl Harbor,
but with fruit in its hair."

Ten years later,
when word came that Uncle Tully's body
was suddenly somewhere legless in Asia,
I sat watching an old movie
on TV—
and there was Carmen Miranda,
fruitful headdress and all,
dancing a Samba in our living room.
"My God, Uncle Tully's dead!"
someone said.

Across this distance I wake from a
dream of August and mimosa blossoms.
Strange,
after so many years to fear

this scream sleeping inside me.
Sometimes I think Uncle Tully was right,
the pieces never come together.
Maybe the death of Carmen Miranda
was like Pearl Harbor—
but with fruit in its hair.

Southern Poetry Review   *Stephen E. Smith*

DAYSLEEP

Mid-afternoons
your consciousness,
its inner dial
left jangling,
becomes a canoe.
It rides through twigs,
logs its way toward
rest.
Low sounds, cicadas,
creaking wheels,
whir past.
The boat beaches up
laced by hollow grass.

Your canoe
is lulled by minnows
swarming,
and painted eels,
day's bad dreams,
slithering in the
quiet water's wake.

Electrum   *Virginia E. Smith*

STILL LIFE

This still life is still life after all.
These massed hydrangeas standing near the wall
as big as cushions puffed up on a chair
loll their heads like pink clowns in the air
who just perform and do not need to know.
They bloom with blue like heaped up mountain snow.

These flowers bring such fullness to the room,
They stand like resurrections from the tomb.
Now at season's end with tarnished golds
the year rots like a mirror which still holds
blue and silver merging with the frame.
These are colors with a flower's name.

We sit and watch their clouds of pink, their sheen,
the way they look both savage and serene
drawing the light and holding it at bay:

a storm inside a storm that has been stilled
with something finished, something unfulfilled.

New Letters   *Vivian Smith*

ANSWERS TO THE SNAILS

Yes, I said, go out there
And find that flawless shell you believe
You never wore before.
It is my answer to the snail: no matter
How deep down you may dig, you won't hide
The moist quivering soul you carry so quietly,
Even in this summer lawn hotter than
The devil's kitchen.

Your sluggish personality gives you away,
The starcharts on your backside; what galaxies
Drift beneath your perfect leg?

I said you were perhaps a disciple of dirt,
That without your shell life would always be
A stinging process, like quick deliberate hands
Made from air, holding the absences; they numb
The undoing of your nomadic ways. Nowhere is
Your home to be found inside an ocean's muscle;
Dried up in weight, you take on its shapeless body
The burden of the sea.

Chelsea   *Arthur Solway*

THE POWERS OF THE PAWN

("The pawns are the soul of chess."–Philidor)

The king can move a single square
without restrictions made;
but once he topples from his place,
no ransom to be paid.

The queen, as you might well expect's
a complicated dame;
she does most anything she wants
and quite controls the game.

The bishop is a sly old fox,
strategically oblique;
if there is trouble on the board
he is not far to seek.

And some are fascinated by
that most eccentric knight
who gallops rather awkwardly
but loves a bloody fight.

The stately rook's a mighty piece
and mainstay of the force;
he'll beat the bishop anytime
and overwhelm the horse.

But never underestimate
the powers of the pawn
who can promote into a queen
and put a kingdom on,

or moving humbly up the board,
killing on the side,
outpriest the priest, and leave the knight
without a horse to ride,

and trip the elevated rook
to bring it crashing down,
and nudge the psychopathic queen
into oblivion,

and stop before great Caesar's throne,
a tiny regicide,
and watch a cornered monarch fall
and ponder how he died.

Canadian Literature   *David Solway*

RESOUNDING

The sleep of late afternoon
in an undertow, pulling
my breath to struggle
with twilight as a child . . .

This is a glass dream.
Mirrors full of me rise
and fall, lit
by a single candle flame;
child eyes flicker
in the speckled age of looking-glass,
staring to a music box dying
midway through a nursery rhyme.

Glass-child, child with my eyes,
you're the splinter in me still,
breathing again the threat of evening
in the heavy smell of Four-O'Clocks.
I'm caught face down, held
to the solitary
lengths of afternoon and the long-term
reach of flowers: dried thoughts
rearrange themselves, unfold
on the wet cheeks of a child,
left alone to grow with dusk
as a scattering of wild flowers.

The Smith   *Katherine Soniat*

A VIET CONG SAPPER DIES

Those Chu Lai priests who raised me as a boy,
Those earnest soldiers calling me a man,
All spoke of sacrifice as the great joy
And shamed my acquiescence in their plan.
Alone here, far from family, with no wife,
I crouch before my comrades' saving fire
And purchase others' deaths with this one life,
As with my bleeding palms I part the wire.
Compelled by love of others, quelling dread,
I fall upon the concertina wire,
And hang here hearing bullets at my head,
The screaming of an awesome, furied choir.
To those who led me softly to this wild,
Let linger this reproach: behold the child.

The Centennial Review   *Stephen Sossaman*

NO SUCH THING

In another world, there may be utterances
that remind you of slow carriages
vanishing into the distance of the approaching night.
In this one, no such thing happens.
The sky is always what it is.
Yet it is also what broods above you as though sorry
for the interference of clouds and rain.
You have always taken the weather for granted
and have never questioned the blatant, aggressive wind.
There is a curious emptiness about the moon tonight.
It is difficult to decode its private language,
just as it is difficult to be sure that beyond one wheatfield
lies another, so that your thoughts can never flow easily
as from wheatfield to wheatfield to wheatfield.
You accept yourself as contradictory.
Though your thoughts are erratic
you are always constant,
in the way that one wave follows another.
In other words, what you are
is never quite as permanent as silence
or the granite sky. What you are is never as still
as the woods after rain.
You accept a part of yourself
in which your name is a foreign word,
in which the syllables you utter are the ticks of a clock.
It doesn't matter that spiritual progress
isn't always like dressing in the half-light
in anticipation of going forward into a new day.
And you *are* destined to be concealed in a body
that doesn't stroll casually down the street, laughing with others,
admiring the sunset.
You surrender to yourself

as to a protective shadow.
You forget that your life will eventually change direction,
like the needle of a compass toward true north.
You proceed with caution, as though you were an endless night
scarcely touching the earth.

Antaeus   *Marcia Southwick*

THE FISH WILL SWIM AS BEFORE

Over logs jammed between rocks
The river lunges, pouring
In a white arc to a pool
Where water never stills, where fish
Know a constant thunder. As the stream
Every moment smooths the cliff edge,
Mist rises as though it were fog
Moving up the falls. It darkens
The face of the cliff, clinging
To stone like the moss it moistens.

Spray forming drops on its needles
Like dew; a red spruce, its roots long
And twisted as snakes, leans too far out
Above the pool. Among its branches wrapped
In their silk, the budworms will be sleeping
When the tree falls into its distorted reflection.
After that one startling explosion
The fish will swim as before,
The submerged wood growing soggy
As logs jammed between rocks.

Poetry Seattle   *Michael Spence*

SHINING

A blue iris
marks an opening through daisies,
morning glories and wild
peas.
I am walking toward the sea.
The grass is shining with just-rain.
I want to say
so much and yet say nothing,
covert as a small animal
crouching in hay;
ahead of me
the water sparkles, a celebration;
the grasses wet my thighs.
I am trampling
wild strawberries, the scarlet hidden ones,
in my haste, in my haste.

Shadowgraph   *Kathleen Spivack*

HELP FROM HISTORY

Please help me know it happened,
    that life I thought we had—

  Our friends holding out their hands
      to us—
  Our enemies mistaken, infected by
      unaccountable prejudice—
  Our country benevolent, a model
      for all governments, goodwilled—
  Those mad rulers at times elsewhere,
      inhuman and yet mob-worshipped,
      leaders of monstrous doctrine, unspeakable
      beyond belief, yet strangely attractive to
      the uninstructed.

And please let me believe these incredible
    legends that have dignified our lives—

  The wife or husband helplessly loving us,
      the children full of awe and affection,
      the dog insanely faithful—
  Our growing up hard—hard times, being
      industrious and reliable—
  The places we lived arched full of
      serene golden light—

Now, menaced by judgments, overheard revisions,
    let me retain what ignorance it takes
    to preserve what we need—
    a past that redeems any future.

The American Scholar   *William Stafford*

OUR KIND

    Our mother knew our worth—
    not much. To her, success
    was not being noticed at all.
    "If we can stay out of jail,"
    she said, "God will be proud of us."

    "Not worth a row of pins,"
    she said, when we looked at the album:
    "Grandpa?—ridiculous."
    Her hearing was bad, and that
    was good: "None of us ever says much."

    She sent us forth equipped
    for our kind of world, a world of
    our betters, in a nation so strong
    its greatest claim is no boast,
    its leaders telling us all, "Be proud"—

    But over their shoulders, God and
    our mother, signaling: "Ridiculous."

The Hampden-Sydney Poetry Review   *William Stafford*

DEAD NECK

Salt flakes fleck my skin
after a circumambulation of the island.
The rough beach grass is turning gold.
I borrowed a boat to get here—
this sand spit not more than a mile long
and an eighth-mile wide—close to shore,
but with currents too swift to swim.

Among the terns and sandpipers,
skate cases—sea purses—
scatter like seedpods. The medusae
are white grapes or moonwort,
the barnacles like lichen.

Only a few days are as whole as this,
where a cove becomes the world, trading
down to smaller and smaller forms of life:
every few steps a horseshoe crab gives way
to one more shrunken, more transparent,
until the last can't be told
from the mermaid's fingernails.

The American Scholar   *Sue Standing*

THE DESERTED GARDEN

This garden needs you. Between its walls
a central path, iris and asters, pear trees in rows
and the blue of wisteria over the gateway.
But beyond the gate, matted grass and weeds
overrun the paths, splash against walls,
and ivy thickens over the fallen columns.
Once there were laurels here, now only traces
of ruined walkways. The deserted terrace
overlooks the sea gate and the broken hedges,
where the white, deep-rooted morning glory sprawls over
   broken rubble.

You long to pull at the weeds, clear out the paths,
cut the thicket of myrtle, set up the columns,
plant foxgloves and asters, rosemary, marigolds,
put lemon against the walls, trim the broken hedges
and sit at evening
looking over the garden and the wall
where the warm blooms mingle with the wind from the sea.

But it doesn't belong to you. Not for you to untangle
the smother of green, you with your hillside
waiting, deserted, unfinished, as you mourn for this lost
   garden.

The Southern Review   *Ann Stanford*

NOT BLINDLY IN THE DARK

This morning trimming ivy in
The yard, I found two strands had grown
Beneath the porch—long, white, and thin;
Somehow they had pushed through stone
And crept on blindly in the dark,
Cool dusty air, their dwarfish leaves
Wide-spaced, transparent, skeletal, stark.
This same vine in the sunlight weaves
Dense patterns all across the wall:
A mass of leaves, lustrous, green.
How strange that some stems turn and crawl
Away from light, and, in the growing,
Lose all color, purpose, which
Give plant life worth. Now I fling
The blanched ends by the backyard ditch.
Lord, turn me if I too should try
To grow my way instead of yours—
To shun Your light and Your bright sky
For a dimness worse than under floors.

The Pentecostal Evangel   *Robert M. Stanley*

MURDER MYSTERY

Unmasked, our friend confesses. Drained of hope,
He is more recognizable than ever.
I never meant . . . I loved her . . . Given rope,
We'd all contrive to hang ourselves. Too clever

Or else too thoughtless (the two being the same),
Our friend's led off. The hawkeyed sleuth, meanwhile,
Explains how he *saw through the poor chap's game.*
His is a lucid and discursive style

In which all things fit neatly: the paint smear
On the door handle of the summer house,
The faked call, the scarf tangled in the weir,
The button missing from the victim's blouse.

And yet such neatness sheds scant consolation
Among the vindicated. Even though
We're stunned by the detective's revelation,
We learn only what we already know—

That all our moods and humors are erratic,
That, in due course, dead bodies will confer
Distinction on drab stairwell and dull attic.
Adieu, Detective! Adieu, Murderer!

Your interests, as they should, end with the damned,
While we, the acquitted, are left to atone
For innocence which never would withstand
A law more true and thorough than our own.

The Southern Review   *Timothy Steele*

JOGGING

You drag by the knees before
learning the secret of toes, and running
comes last in the slow lessons
the leg unwinds. In time the pain
stops and the body becomes your own
idea; breath becomes sky and the soul
floats out from all dull pumping.

At a great distance you hear feet
ticking, just as the earth must. You
think nothing can stop the machinery
but even little deaths end. The soul
climbs down to its tree and legs
thicken into summer.

In this white season you stick
to the sheets and want to leave
your body again. You practice breathing,
set your shoes ready and twist
the clocksprings tight by the pillow.
Every hour the curtain flutters but
you remain inside drowning in knots
jealous of fish.

We want a summer to explode, good
death, space that is still. Why when
you run out of a body for miles
is there any more?

Washington Review   *Gary Stein*

MASON JAR

For lunch this noon, a mason jar full
Of yellow peaches, resting in the glass
Like lovers asleep in the autumn sun.

I nap for just ten minutes, and dream
Of lying in the field at home
Under the tall oak that stands bronzed
This month like a sweating smithy, dream
Of lying with you, your hand stroking
Only the inside of my thigh, over and over . . .

Waking, I amble outdoors, full of peaches,
To afternoon light like applesauce spiced
With cinnamon, to rake the gold leaves
The maple tree wept down.

Calliope   *David Steinberg*

OLD MAN

Tell us, old man—
And you tell us,
Sometimes leaving out important thoughts,

Sometimes repeating trivial ones.
And we nod, and perhaps
We speak a little bit louder into your left ear.
And much food is lost in the long, tremorous journey
Twixt dinner plate and dentures.
We speak slowly, that you,
You who were once a great man,
Can understand our simple words.
And we see old pictures—
Is that you, old man,
In the army uniform?
You of the cane and unsteady step?
And you must be awakened in the morning,
Or else you would sleep through the day.
But we understand.
Old men get tired,
Very tired.
Sometimes tired of life,
But never tired of living.
And that is why we love you,
Old man.
Because you were once a young man.
And that life of years past
Has sustained you to the present.
We love you,
Old man.
Please keep living that life,
Even when the cogs of memory creak and thump
Like the beating of that ominous distant drum.
Stay with us,
Old man.

Midstream   *David E. Stern*

YOUR ANIMAL

The final end of all but purified souls
is to be swallowed up by Leviathan,
or to be bound with fiery chains and flogged
with 70 stripes of fire.
I walk along the mule path dreaming of my weaknesses
and praying to the ducks for forgiveness.
Oh there is so much shit in the universe
and my walks, like yours,
are more and more slippery and dangerous.
I love a duck for being almost like a vegetable.
I love him because his whole body can be consumed,
because there is no distance between him and his watery offal.
Your animal is almost human,
distant from his waste,
struggling to overcome the hated matter,
looking up with horrified white eyes,
eternally hunting for space in the little islands of Riverside Drive
and the fenced-in parks of the Village.

I love duck and potatoes, duck and red beets,
duck and orange juice.
I love the head of duck dipped in sugar,
I love chocolate duck with chipolata sausages,
fragrant crisp duck mixed with shrimp and pork.
I love the webs and the heart; I love the eggs
preserved in lime and potash; completely boned duck
filled with ham and chestnuts, fried duck with pineapple
and canned red cherries or sections of tangerine.

This is a poem against gnosticism;
it is a poem against the hatred of the flesh
and all the vicious twists and turns we take
to calm our frightened souls.
It is a poem celebrating the eating of duck
and all that goes with it.
It is a poem I am able to write after walking every day
through the flocks, and loving the babies, and watching them slip
down the mud sides and float into the current.
It is a poem about shooting galleries and cardboard heads,
about hunters and their checkered hats and frozen fingers,
about snow-white cloths and steaming laced-up birds
and waiters standing in little regiments
getting ready to run in among the tables and start carving.
—It is my poem against the starving heart.
It is my victory over meanness.

The American Poetry Review   *Gerald Stern*

DAYS OF 1978

This is the only thing that clarifies my life,
this beautiful old living room
with the pink walls and the mohair sofa.
I walk out every night singing
a little song from Gus Williams or W. C. Handy.
I throw my yellow scarf around my neck
and pull my cap down over my eyes.
Even here I am dressed up,
walking through the light flakes and the ice puddles.
—Tonight I will think about Cavafy
and the way he wept on his satin pillow,
remembering the days of 1903.
I will compare my life to his:
the sorrows of Alexandria,
the lights on the river;
the dead kings returning to Syria,
the soap in my bath.
—Later I will lie on my own pillow
with the window open and the blinds up,
weeping a little—myself—at the thick blankets
and the smoking candles
and the stack of books,
a new sweetness and clarity beginning
to monopolize my own memory.

The Missouri Review   *Gerald Stern*

IN SCORCHING TIME

Note how the desert takes form, easily as wax. It moves
with light, and also with whatever on or above the surface
has scale or wing or claw. There are shadows and impressions, then,
from vulture, lizard, and toad. And those big cactuses that seem
firm as thoughts do in the head's acre (and just as thorny):
if you draw closer you will find that, far from solid,
this one is riddled with sockets, with eyes
of small birds that roost in a castle
defended by spikes, complete with turrets and spires.

And of the sand—let me tell you how it swings
in tides so slow they defeat the mind,
great hinges of gravity for a door you expect to be pulled open
to reveal within. And how one seed, hard and round,
caught in the undulation here, may wait
one hundred brown-edged years for rain.
                                        Yes, but
I wanted to say more about seeds, how the seeds of all things,
if they stay anywhere, rest here. For often when I slept
in the desert, I would dream of a sky like this,
but of a different substance, and of a sand whose image
always shimmered in the moon, beyond this sand;
and then, on waking, I still partly held
those other visions, like shadows of the day's true marrow,
before fire spread in the brass sky
and burned up the residue like cobwebs.
                                        Seeds,
that was what I wanted to tell you of, how
the one wet trigger during as many years
as would make three of my lives to date,
reduces that encapsuled patience
to nothing (which was nothing all along, anyway, lost
even to the hawk's superb eye), except, perhaps,
as an image of some past state which stubbornly clings
between the roots and branches of the growing network,
something that struggles to hold life in the spaces of ours,
and that some day, when the sands turn over, will resume sway.

The Georgia Review   *Alex Stevens*

ANOTHER COLOR

The dog gazes back at me. The pair of rats
he's brought up from behind the wood stack
to the lawn beside the house still
tremble. They're both as brown as dirt, organs
ripped open to the air, and one is broken
around the skull, one eye smeared and distorted.
They both tremble, and the dog
looks down. It's their disordered noises
at night I've hated most. But to kill them
I've poisoned the woodchuck, the best
breeder of its kind, you said, a flock of juncos,

the quail, the two pheasants. The cat is dying
and an amber stain's begun to grow
from the wood across the grass toward our
window. The dog's begun to limp, and I look
carefully at you and the child each day. I'm better
with poison than with growing, I confess. Hard
as my doubt of the soil, of the progress
of marriage and sons. And even the poison's
gone amiss. The dog looks up at me, smiling.
It's tongue is discolored. The brown rats
are dead and the dog, having forgotten them, turns
and walks away into the field. At night I look
for him, think of him in the mirror, but I can't
find him. The night, your face, the man's flesh
in this mirror, the world itself is another color.

Tendril   *Frank Stewart*

THE PLUMBER ARRIVES AT THREE MILE ISLAND

A plumber's price is high because he uses
equipment that can channel what diffuses—
since heavy duty's standard on some jobs,
and augers, threaders, clamps and come-alongs
can bring our flooded dreams another turn.
Unless a plumber has somewhere to stand
he'll wade right in among the toilet fish
and fumble with the break below the wastes,
among those places we will not admit,
where all our bright ideas turn to shit.
But now the whole trade's dirty—used to be
just septic tanks and sewers; it used to be
a plumber always had a place to wash
when he was through to tally up the costs.

New Letters   *Robert Stewart*

BREATHE ON THE GLASS

Along the river edge
     the stalled train
     waits

On the water
     faces float
     in drowned windows

Freight cars narrate
     backwards on the
     traveling water

MOHAWK
     FRIEND OF THE EAST
     SANTA FE

Beside the bank
     flowing gardens
     bloom again

> Over faces
> carried in the
> darkened stream.

Yankee   *Raymond Stineford*

EASTER FLOOD

> Even in the worst of times,
> God never really turned His back
> on the Jews.
> There must have been occasions, though,
> when they thought
> that He was out to lunch
> or on vacation
> and had not notified
> His answering service.
>
> Think of Jonah,
> his voice reverberating
> in the whale's dark belly;
> or Noah
> on that cramped and stinking ship,
> the nights and days
> running together like blood and water,
> the animals restless and on edge,
> their fur steaming
> in the damp malodorous hold,
> and his sons
> eternally bickering and complaining.
>
> Under such circumstances,
> a week would have been long enough;
> so when your voice came streaming
> through that thin taut wire
> like sunlight shooting through a cloud,
> I knew how Noah felt
> to see the dove returning,
> bearing in its beak the olive branch—
> or Mary Magdalen
> the morning that she stood before the tomb,
> astonished
> at the implications of the stone.

Southern Poetry Review   *Brenda S. Stockwell*

CHANCES

> For the most part,
> I have lived
> a safe, quiet life,
> regretting little,
> daring less—
> never, in other words,
> giving the heart

more than loose change
to gamble with.
I never once desired
to call Time back
or live my life
a different way—
until today.

Seeing your son
bareheaded
in the warm spring air,
suddenly I knew
that I would risk it all—
twenty years of careful thrift,
always hedging my bets
against heartache—
for the chance
to be his lover
or his mother.

The Texas Review   *Brenda S. Stockwell*

HOW I'D HAVE IT

I'd have no flowers
other than Mozart

A suit—blue—
not new, but worn

the knees
still in the trousers

for as long
as polyester is

And a fire
and someone there

to throw on
the oak especially

for the last movement
of the Mozart

As for the mourners
let's have them enter

STAGE LEFT
and pause and peer

over the side
and say mournful

things such as What
A Pity A Pity

And So Old, Too.
And then exit all

STAGE RIGHT

The American Scholar   *John Stone*

EVEN THOUGH

A = pi r squared

even if a body
continues to fall
32 feet per second per second

which I hope

it will continue to do
nevertheless
after careful calculation

and by the grace of algebra

I am persuaded that
if truth is a number
not only is it never

in the back of the book

but it never comes out even
ends in a fraction
cannot be rounded off.

Approximation
was the first art.
It is the only science.

The American Scholar   *John Stone*

FUNERAL NOTICES

At the side of the little black crosses*
As anchors cast in grim finality
Horizontally lie the names of those
Who died this day,
As the very corpses themselves.
Enormous now, menacingly, on the cold sheet
Close to the crosses, my own name dances about.

*Black crosses precede the funeral notices in Latin American Newspapers.

Poetry Now   *Alfonsina Storni*
                    —Translated from the Spanish (Argentina)
                              by Dorothy Scott Loos

WAITING

I believe in the fitness of surprises,
the feisty arrogance of hope against all odds,
the reckless spirit, testing
my blood like an unleashed dog.
Today I'm sure of miracles.
I knew it as I waited for the mail;
I knew it as I swung around the railing,
knee-bend, push-up;
I knew it as the weather tamed,
easing into fall, and I was seeing

you come, a stranger years ago,
like a gift
that explained the waiting.

Poetry Now   *Liz Stout*

SHABBAT MORNING

From high windows
light angles down
through dancing dust.
The chant drones up
and down the scale
of memory.

The scattered worshipers
drink in the sabbath
somnolence.
Wrapped in their thoughts,
like talisim,
they rock back and forth
on an ancient wave
of dreams.

The Jewish Spectator   *Bradley R. Strahan*

BEGGING ON NORTH MAIN

Should I worry about choosing
The right word if I can get what I want
By pointing at it?
                    What do I want?
                                    Is it this ghost
With the unslakeable past, this rusty child
Who keeps asking me to give him his eyes back?

Is it this stone man who disappears
Beneath my toes every step I take,
Telling me he's nobody's thoroughfare?
                                    If I were dreaming
Would I call them both *Father*
And follow them blind into the center of the earth?
Would I come out bright-eyed and raw on the other side
In a country whose people speak in pictures
Where someone could say *Look,* and point, and I would see my self?

It's hard to ask the right questions,
                                    yet the fire I have
Kindled with my vocabulary and its hungry years
Gives off a growing heat,
                            and the day I saw
My reflection in its bottom I gave my tin cup
To the mute on North Main Street.
When he sees me coming he smiles

And points the cup at me, slowly turning it
Until it flashes the sun into my face.

The Southern Review   *Dabney Stuart*

DEDICATION

In my dreams we are always together
In my dreams no tragic flames fall about us
In my dreams the paths we wander are enchanted
In my dreams the forms are of another world

I watch you by the darkening woods
Turn to speak as wind begins its murmuring
I see us gazing into shreds of mist
As though the message were ours

But there is no comfort even in love
Or the intelligence of time whose response
Is always to leave these words for you
And come between us a spell upon my night

In my dreams the forms are of another world
The way their shadows comfort
By transmuting pain to tenable themes
The violence of our fortunes into words

Whose veil binds us with perception
Whose image a garden of dissolving stars
Shudders to hide you in my arms
There to seek a further omen of the mask

Where beneath a month's beginning
The anonymous daylight over golden grass
As though every gesture were a metaphor
We awake and are renamed

New York Arts Journal   *Richard Stull*

FIRST COLD NIGHT OF AUTUMN

In the mountains
trees practice for winter,
dropping their leaves.
Birds, like thin farmhands,
sweep down on the rutted back roads,
begging for food.
I'm driving north to Montana
in a '68 Buick
with a heater that doesn't work,
past fields that slip away in the mist,
crusted over with the heapage of summer.
Soon the sun will burn
clear frost smoke pure as ice.
Snow will come as a white cloth
bandaging the hills with silence;
the fields will be smooth again.

Tonight I move through villages
huddling along the road for warmth.
Their half-open gates,
rusted cold until next year,
cry out in the night wind.
Then they give up and sleep.
Only the smoke from a cog-railroad
makes petals in the air over the Rockies,
a flower garden to open somewhere,
after a deepening Christmas.

The Seattle Review   *John Stupp*

AS SUN, AS SEA

It is easy to disturb
The current in another's soul, hard
To give more than you take away.
  What one must do
Is build his own nonentity
Into a thing worth referring to,
A standard of being. Then he can run
Without curbing the running in some other realm.
  Then he can be
As the sun is to the earth,
To the river as the sea.

Commonweal   *James Sullivan*

PROPHECY

(for Jean Cassou)

One day the Earth will be
Only a blind whirling space
Where night is merged with day.
Beneath the great sky of the Andes
It will no longer have any high hills,
And not even a small ravine.

Of all the houses in the world
There will remain only one balcony,
And of the human map of the world
A sadness without ceiling.
Of the late Atlantic Ocean
A slight salty taste in the air, and
One flying magical fish
Who knows nothing of water.

Out of the window of a 1905 coupé
(Four wheels and not a single road),
Three girls of the period will peer
Thinking that Paris isn't far away,
And will smell only the odor
Of the throat-catching sky.

Where the forest once was
A birdsong will rise
Which no one can identify,
Or even prefer or even hear—
Except for God, who will listen carefully
And say, "Why, it's a goldfinch."

Poetry Now   *Jules Supervielle*
—Translated from the French
by Jan Pallister

RETURN

When I said farewell
To land and cove, to cardinal and swan,
To mourning doves inhabiting the sun,
To slender egret, yellow-shod, immaculate
And white, where mallards congregate;
To gull and puffin, maple tree and yew,
Muskrat afloat and hornet dipping dew—
Disaster was the mad inheritance,
Till sanity, my singular concern,
Prevailed upon the long forsaken peace
To verify my ultimate return.

New England Sampler   *M. L. Sussman*

STATIC

Well, Old Flame, the fire's out.
I miss you most at the laundromat.
Folding sheets is awkward work
Without your help. My nip and tuck
Can't quite replace your hands,
And I miss that odd square dance
We did. Still, I'm glad to do without
Those gaudy arguments that wore us out.
I've gone over them so often
They've turned grey. You fade and soften
Like the hackles of my favorite winter shirt.
You've been a hard habit to break, Old Heart.
When I feel for you beside me in the dark,
The blankets crackle with bright blue sparks.

Poetry   *Barton Sutter*

LINES

There can be no power in a square.
Nor a straight line. Nor *lines* of
any sort. Lines take off directly
& find what it is they're chasing
isn't for catching. After a while,
they stop & lie still. More lost lines
cross them & lie heaped. As they cross,

angles for dust form, and angles
for darkness. Try as hard as they can
with whatever life is left, they cannot
turn and twist. They were meant to go
the shortest way
to the longest objects.
They cannot become the circle of the horizon
or the bowl of the sky.
They cannot enclose anything.
If they are made into a house,
whoever lives in that house
will continually be banging off edges
& looking at the waste space in corners
where no one can get at it.
So they'll make things with edges
to fit in those corners. They'll
fit & fit & fit till they grow
tired and scared and start praising
round things, things rubbed with hands—
tents, pitchers, the bellies of women.
They praise the power of round things.
Then they try making everything round.
They fit & fit & fit . . .

San Jose Studies   *Brian Swann*

MASKS

Smoke, shadowy deep smoke,
shadowing deep snow.
Tracks make the invisible
present. The air goes
warmer slightly. Trees
wear a mountain. The mountain
wears sky. The sky
wears clouds. Thus we see
how it moves. The wind
is plumed. It is the shape
of three deer coming
into the light to browse
lichen from oaks. They
drink. Their flanks
are cobalt silk from
the stream slipping through
collapsed ice arches.
                          At
evening the smallest of
owls, small as sparrows,
fly about with the sky
turning. They sometimes sit
on mens' heads. Their owl
masks are the souls of
certain men, as the souls
of hunters go toward

wolves, fishermens' to the salmon, twins'
to the Salmon Maker.
                              The
smallest of the small
owls is full of light. I'd
sleep if I could, outlast
him by the weight
of my bones. But I
walk out. Into a night
that is not dark
but masked.

The Yale Review   *Brian Swann*

FOR WE ARE ALL MADWOMEN

For we are all madwomen
in torn voile dresses
carrying groceries,
screaming at butchers—
impatient, decisive
on fire with love—
springing from beds in the morning,
jumping from windows in the afternoon,
tossing from side to side
those menacing glances of ours.

For we are all madwomen
laughing at parties,
showing our underwear to the men
and laughing some more.
We own silver forks engraved
with the names of dead aunts;
all codes, passwords and signals
belong to us.
We are the sails, and of course,
the wind behind the sails.

For we are all madwomen
stooping, hunting, faceless,
like nuns in a convent garden
proud of our children, dangerous, cast aside,
tired of the same old stuff—
waiting for the chance to change the world
back into a melon
where the cities would be seeds
held together by
something sweet in the dark.

The Malahat Review   *Barbara Sweeney*

THE PRO

She glows against
the glazed bricks of the motel
in canary hot pants and buxom blouse

as though oozed into them with a pastry tube—
her face made-up to the stylized rind of sex.

Across the mechanized order of traffic
that matches her only on the caution light,
she is a french horn signaling
the hunting call of humanity.

I, also, was once called to her profession.
As little boys yearn to be pirates or astronauts,
girls dream of Manon and Barbarella—
fantasies of individual power
in which death curls nascent as a cutworm.

Although presently cornered on 48th and 8th,
she has stalked Les Halles,
held her own downhill from the Parthenon,
sold oranges to profit in Covent Garden
and found the majesty of Persepolis convenient.

I watch her with an amateur's fascination,
recognizing in her phantom rebellion
the defiance of Carmen's last aria.
She is our first attempt at victory, our final
painted desert of defeat.

The Slackwater Review   *Karen Swenson*

NOTHING BUT IMAGE

*(And you ought to have heard him pronounce the
word "I." The whole man was concentrated in this
personal affirmation.—Miguel de Unamuno)*

If I am amazed by anybody
it's the bum on 34th Street,
who bears the abuse
of executives and salesmen,
and smiles at secretaries
rushing past his ragged presence.

My father once told me:
don't trust these men with no purpose.
They seem harmless, he said,
but look hard and you might see
your own fallen image
fading across their faces.

So I turned my head and walked away.
But one night, in a winter rain,
an old man mumbled,
spare change, for coffee . . .
and I stared into his bloodshot eyes.

Water dripped down his face
like sweat, and his busted nose
broke the dark,
perhaps the proud wound

of a forgotten middleweight fight.
As I handed him some coins
didn't he lower his head,
bless me, call me brother?

Now I love to look for those
whose faces and clothes deceive us,
this bum standing up
to the insults of the crowd,
who leaves us shaking our heads,
talking to ourselves,
like men lost in the heart
of New York, in an almost memorable past.

The Missouri Review   *Jody Swilky*

LETTER FROM DES MOINES

And I had forgotten about the stars—
I had been so busy moving again.
From eastern Iowa to central Iowa,
No relief in sight. But stars!
Hundreds—no—thousands of them
On a smokey August night.
And just over the blond chimneys
Of the low-rent housing project—
A constellation. Or I thought so:
Never having had a mind for science,
I'm not sure of the proper shapes,
Those illustrative man-made names.
So far away like that,
They seem often unimportant.

            At 12, I loved photography
And had a favorite book: an oversized paperback
Called *Trick Shots*. At a gathering of relatives
(They were frequent then),
I recruited my brother and our cousin, Ann.
Pretty Ann, the "baby" and best-looking
Among us. In an album of heavy,
Large-boned German faces,
Hers is a pale, foreign pole-star.
But *that* day my brother stood nearest the camera:
With his hand held away from him,
He stared where I directed him—
Into his shallow palm. And behind,
Down the narrow driveway,
Impatient and confused, now waving,
Now squinting into the afternoon sun,
Was Ann. I took the picture. Later,
when the film came back,
There was my brother with Ann,
An elf in his outright hand.

            And so photography
Is magic, because the eye is.

And tonight I closed one eye and held
A hand up to the stars: none of them
Was larger than a knuckle,
A cluster could have gathered on my nail.
I confess I had forgotten the stars—
But I can remember whole days,
Any number of details when I need to.
Between us—you and me,
Myself and those others
Who live in tall structures—
Between all of us and the stars,
Distance is pure metaphor.
And the cool night is a clear jewel.

The Literary Review   *Thomas Swiss*

COUPLE

If she had someplace to run to, she would run,
her heavy body laboring for breath,
arms reaching, hair outstreaming in the wind—
unkempt, unseemly, down some stony path.

Her scowling husband shuts the bathroom door
to sit alone, wrestling with his bowels,
his sense of having failed confirmed once more
in the day's headlines, his monogrammed towels;

while she, his once-beloved Valkyrie,
caught, mired in the sucking river mud
of their closed life together, picks up her key
to walk the dog around the neighborhood.

Dark Horse   *Mary Swope*

HOMECOMING

Birds have come back again early in the morning, in the spring.
Rejoice, dear intellect, instinct too may blunder,
Straying, yawning—and into the snow they tumble,
Perishing indifferently: a death incommensurate
With the structure of its own larynx, with its miniscule talons,
With its solid cartilage and thorough, compact membranes,
With the drainage-basin of the heart, with its labyrinthine intestines,
With the aisle of ribs and vertebrae in stunning array,
With feathers worthy of a pavilion in a museum of universal crafts,
And with the beak of a monk's sore forebearance.

This is not a lament—only an outrage
That an angel of authentic whiteness,
A kite fashioned of glands from the Song of Songs,
Single in the air, innumerable in our hands,
Bound, tissue upon tissue, to the community
Of place and time like classical art
In the colors of its wings—
Should fall and nestle by the stone,

Who in his own archaic and coarse manner
Looks upon life as upon cast-off trials.

New Orleans Review
Wislawa Szymborska
—Translated from the Polish
by Benjamin Sher

IN PRAISE OF A GUILTY CONSCIENCE

A buzzard finds no fault with itself.
A panther has no qualms.
Piranhas do not doubt the rightness of their actions.
A rattlesnake accepts itself without reservation.

A self-critical jackal does not exist.
Locust, alligator, trichina and gadfly
live as they live, and are pleased with it.

The heart of a whale weighs a hundred kilos,
but otherwise it is light.

Nothing is more bestial
than a clear conscience
on the third planet of the Sun.

Footprint
Wislawa Szymborska
—Translated from the Polish
by Grazyna Drabik and Austin Flint

THE MOON IS A DIAMOND

flavio gonzales, 72, made jackhammer
heads during the war & tells me
about digging ditches in the depression
for $1 a day. we are busy plastering
the portal, & stop for a moment
in the april sun. his wife, sick for
years, died last january & left a
legacy—a $5000 hospital bill.
i see the house he built at 15,
the ristras of red chili hanging
in the october sun. he sings "paloma
blanca" as he works, then stops,
turns: "i saw the tv photos of the
landing on the moon. but it's all
lies. the government just went out
in the desert & found a crater.
believe me, i know, i know the moon
is a diamond."

The Greenfield Review
Arthur Sze

IN THE PALMS OF ANCIENT BODHISATTVAS

In due time bridges collapse, handsome people get
  very old looking, call it deterioration, old age,
  erosion.

But look at the Ponte Vecchio, look at Rembrandt's
    self-portraits in old age: cliffs
can be ancient testaments, old Hebrew prophets can
    be mind-boggling in their power, beauty,
the signs of age on a magnificent enormous tree or
    elephant or elaborate Hindu temple
can make a new fluorescent bank look bland, blank.
    There is that rugged Ghirlandaio grandfather
with the bumpy nose; the admiring young Florentine
    grandson knows experience and kindness when he
    sees it;
listen to the old WINTER'S TALE; arrive at the
    breezy condition of taoist old wanderers.
We progress from one mystery to another like ageless
    grasshoppers summoned precisely.

Poets On: *John Tagliabue*

THE DEEPEST BOW

I want to dance.
I want to dance for you
in the gleam of a night-lamp.
You will undo my gown,
and my hair will fall free.

I want to dance a young dance
to a song within me
and to the notes from my taut strings.

You will be near.
You will fall to your knees
at my feet.
You will stay on your knees
in the half-light
a long time.

A man on his knees
before a dancing woman:
The deepest bow of all—
and the most painful.

Paintbrush   *Marie Takvan*
                                    —Translated from the Norwegian
                                    by Harold P. Hansen

SHAPES, VANISHINGS

1

Down a street in the town where I went
to high school twenty-odd years ago, by doorways
and shadows that change with the times, I walked
past a woman at whose glance I almost stopped cold,
almost to speak, to remind her of who I had been—
but walked on, not being certain it was she,
not knowing what I might find to say.

It wasn't quite the face I remembered, the years
being what they are, and I could have been wrong.

2

But that feeling of being stopped cold, stopped dead,
will not leave me, and I hark back
to the thing I remember her for, though God knows
how I could remind her of it now.
Well, one afternoon when I was fifteen,
I sat in her class. She leaned on her desk,
facing us, the blackboard behind her arrayed
with geometrical figures—triangle, square,
pentagon, hexagon, *et cetera.* She pointed
and named them. "The five-sided figure," she said,
"is a polygon." So far so good, but then when she said,
"The six-headed one is a hexagon," I wanted things clear.
Three or more sides is *poly,* I knew, but five only
is *penta,* and said so; she denied it,
and I pressed the issue, I, with no grades
to speak of, a miserable average to stand on
with an Archimedean pole—no world to move,
either, just a fact to get straight; but she
would have none of it, saying at last, "Are you
contradicting me?"

3

A small thing to remember a teacher for. Since then,
I have thought about justice often enough
to have earned my uncertainty about what it is,
but one hard fact from that day has stayed with me:
If you're going to be a smartass, you have to be right,
and not just some of the time. "Are you
contradicting me?" she had said, and I stopped
breathing a moment, the burden of her words
pressing down through me hard and quick, the huge
weight of knowing I was right, and beaten. She
had me. "No, ma'am," I managed to say, wishing
I had the whole thing down on tape to play back
to the principal, wishing I were ten feet tall
and never mistaken, ever, about anything in this world,
wishing I were older, and long gone from there.

4

Now I am older, and long gone from there.
What sense in a grudge over something so small?
What use to forgive her for something
she wouldn't remember? Now students
face me as I stand at my desk, and the shoe
may yet find its way to the other foot,
if it hasn't already. I couldn't charge
thirty-five cents for all that I know
of geometry; what little I learned is gone now,
like a face looming up for a second out of years
that dissolve in the mind like a single summer.
Therefore,

if ever she almost stops me again,
I will walk on as I have done once already,
remembering how we failed each other,
knowing better than to blame anyone.

Western Humanities Review   *Henry Taylor*

THE EGG OF NOTHING

Whether or not I watch
I know that night comes on,
And every nesting night must hatch
Somebody gone.

What do you want me to say?
The egg of being's bare?
That's news? I call it every day.
Nobody's there,

Nobody's there at all.
Somebody was there last night.
But then came somebody's own nightfall,
A fall, no flight.

West Branch   *John Taylor*

LAKE HARRIET: WIND

The coots are awash,
heads to the wind
like the tarp-covered boats
at their moorings.
Water sucks at the beach.
Dead leaves scuttle
over the footpath.

Along that path I come
in my hooded sweatshirt.
North and South desert the sky.
East and West lie numb.
The wind usurps all direction;
my lungs must wrestle
for each bit of air
torn from my mouth
in a long grey plume.

The lake flexes on its thick root.
Birds and boats ride anchor.
Bushes, trees, weeds
bend and bend in the same places still.
This wind scorns my bones
running like leaves before it,
cares nothing
for the flicker of my warmth.

Calliope   *Laurie Taylor*

THE FUTURE

The future smiles again
Like a beaten, sobbing boy
Who sees a monkey and its master
Coming down the street.

The future smiles at me,
That silent, black-veiled widow.
It smiles, and opens
Gold-filigree doors before my eyes.

Although the future is more bounded now
Than it had been—boundless hopes,
Loves, passions—when it shone on me

Beneath the sun of immortality,
It still speaks. It still smiles—
See: with the voice of my past and the face of my soul.

Ararat   *Vahan Tekeyan*
                                    —Translated from the Armenian
                                              by James Russell

THE NETS ON THE ANDREA DORIA

I have a feeling
the world occasionally settles in my net
swimming near the Andrea Doria.

These are sea anemones that
cling to the sides like
plastic flowers on a shower cap.

Divers setting dead fish free
Disturb the harmless sleep this sinking world takes
in the yards of net I've set around the anchor.

Italians once made good glass;
here you see it all intact,
the green floors well-preserved
without the disturbing effects of feet,
while ceilings puncture, peel, fall away.

Even the wily octopus could not avoid
the treacherous and arbitrary pull of these lost nets.

On the filigreed staircase leading from the ballroom,
ghosts without watches wait for the orchestra to resume.

Divers,
do not lose consciousness before
you reach the bell.

Anima   *Karen G. Tepfer*

FROM

Twelve years ago I was twelve.
I watched the angles of blue swallows, perfect as water.
Ferns and low shrubs scratched green on my arms and face.

My father's pocket compass lay comfortably
in his hand at my chin.

Today I climbed from a meadow to cool redwoods.
At noon a river, and the ocean was a backdrop always.
I never remember much I see:
a shriek at evening is maybe a blackbird,
quails drum to safety.
I imagine this the middle of my life
to someday remember more than actually was
—in wildflowers, gathering wood.
I imagine the center goes on from here,
mistakes me for where I've been.

The North American Review   *Richard Terrill*

LINEAGE

This is how forever is.

In Brigham's valley, secularized,
rising high into silence
securing me with my Mother,
is the mountain.

I can know my history here.

From a place other than Oklahoma;
from a place conceived of stone,
this mountain climbed out of earth
and called me;
called me back to Genesis
set down in the consequence,
the mutiny of time.

Stones   monuments
outlasting me or even God as some know him;
outlasting ashes   dust   historic loves
civilizations   marriages
or my caresses I bestow upon it.

Because it was here   misty with mortality
I was born.   Because my Father was bred
from these stones   where some giant oak
awoke one year in the beginning.

Pregnant with my first-born,
I rise up past the last mound of my Mother's womb
to walk in clouds;
wade through whiteness higher than seas;
climb toward the dawn higher than the plains
of Oklahoma.

I shall give birth to my daughter here,
holding up the sky.

Pteranodon   *Reba Terry*

SUMMIT LAKE

When snow melts, green mountains slope
to the cabin's door. I reach for my pole,
its lures like sparkling ornaments—
and mosquitoes, droning a distant highway,
hike down to shore.

Dragonflies, small black kites, hover
above the boat. I drift
wherever
slow currents
take me. Firs part
at the bow, slide together under stern.
I drop hook and worm, settle back,
wait for the pull.

Rocky Mountain Review   *Mark Thalman*

SMILE

The smile is already there
in the first snap, let's say 17,
under the mop of black
fuzzy ringlets, sitting on the back
steps of a granite cottage
in a Cornish village

the smile is still there,
decorative as a film star
at the wheel of a Model-T
(my father in drainpipe trousers
proudly draped against them both)
in front of a Spanish-white
bungalow in California

and is there, in the same white
place and in the same sunny
era, my sister in her arms,
and is there
under her early-gray hair
sitting on a donkey
on a Cornish beach

and is there
on a bright January day
having tea outside
with her sisters-in-law
and my grandmother,
while I stare solemnly
at my first-birthday candle

and the smile is there
under tight white curls
in a Melbourne park,
a plump floral woman
by my plump floral sister—
and I a fat youth poking his tongue

and is there, in the last snap
of my father, color Kodak,
on a Cornish quay, and is there
behind her glasses, hiding pain,
under thinning white hair
on her last holiday with us

and now that she is dead and gone,
having smiled in the undertaker's hut
so I shouldn't feel guilty,
and now that her death has faded
like the snaps,
the smile is still there,
some poems have no beginning and no end.

The American Scholar   *D. M. Thomas*

SPRING HAWKS

Excited, they sport high over our valley,
careless for once of all beneath them,
curvetting and dancing in the morning air.
They dare each other with loops and dives
peeling off at the last split second
to softly touch, rolling, falling away
to flare up again in triumphant flight.
We watch them out of sight behind far trees,
then splash through the mud to our cars, the drive
over rutted roads to school and work, some part
of us forever gone on loan to hawks.

The Spoon River Quarterly   *Jim Thomas*

FUNERAL

Wind comes like the chief mourner,
masking its face with sliding
taffetas and iron needles,
its voice a curling drone.

Mercy is not in it. It slaps
over the mouths of graves
and pushes our dark, reverent
clusters away. Edges of it
pretend to drag themselves

like children into our arms,
but the clasp it seeks
is bloodless, an unlined skull
to chafe.

We are
only impediments to the business
of death, as trees to the wind.
It does not break against
the mountains, but gullies

up a snake's track on slimed
grass. Trees open their mouths,
torn lips of leaves swallowed
and spat out like our oyster
screams in blue metal depths.

We crack. We roll away
in waxed limousines, leaving
it all, all, all to the wind.

The American Scholar   *Joanna Thompson*

THE GATHERING

Always I have been a cottonwood
in May, when the swollen pod
bursts and everywhere the air goes white,
all lawns returning
winterward under that burden of yearning;
seeds that long for lodging anywhere
and by the million die in flight
into the river, pavement, alleys, air.

Now I must learn to be the island instead,
which grew itself by grains from the bed
of the farewell river, lasting by staying put
and gathering whatever stuck—
collecting things the world thought were no good,
squeezing filth and death and junk so tight
they fused into a single stone that struck
sparks, the leaping green of cottonwood.

The Michigan Quarterly Review   *Dwayne Thorpe*

WHAT SHE WISHED

She only said she wished there was a place
where I could iceskate. That was what she said,
and that was thirty years ago. Today
the words return as I watch skaters glide
and turn beneath this canted roof upon
the sleek perfection of machine formed ice,
and I am certain she did not mean this.
What she wished for me were snowbanked days
along a frozen river, rough along
the edge and smooth above the quicker current.
What she wished was wind to skate against
chilly teething on my cheeks, and then
at dusk when I had skated far enough
to think perhaps it was too far, wind
to blow me down the river like a clipper,
effortless and eager sailing home.
And there would be a bonfire on the bank,
a beacon through the dusk to melt an arc
of snow into a shining mirror and draw

the tingling blood into my cheeks and toes.
And there would be new snow between dark pines
under brand new stars toward home.

Outerbridge   *Marilyn Throne*

MARCH SOUND

Purple-blotched and red-haired,
one eye closed by the instruments
attending a difficult birth,
I came one month too early
(an arm and a leg first)
And would not suck at my mother's breasts—

Here I am with these big things, she cried,
and he won't even look at them.

Forgive me: perhaps it was the wind
which howled three days on my arrival,
as if consciousness were a pricked
pocket of air.
Before my eyes opened or skin dried,
March sound was the first sign
of a new world.

Twenty-eight years in this atmosphere:
To celebrate, the wind has blown
three days.
I watch as it lifts the horizon,
sets it down elsewhere at will,
snuffs the sun's candle out.

Outside it grafts skin to ice,
blows at your back, then your face,
until you understand why men
curl up like babies in the snow.
Twenty-eight years in this atmosphere:
I know enough now to suckle comfort,
frost-bitten cheek blooming again
in the kitchen heat.

Prism International   *Harry Thurston*

NUCLEAR LAND

Salvador Dali almost foresaw it.
In his pictures, ghostly part-buildings stand
the way alleys made the backdrop
for the stage of Diocletian's palace.
Now, even these are ruled completely flat.

The condition is global.
Nearly half a world away
a bent blind man with twigs on his back,
hoping to arrive in time for trumpets announcing
twilight of his Himalayan village,
finds his mountain gone.

For all of us the hill, the mountain to
which we could turn, is gone.
Even the mind's inner landscape
is sealed off. There is no quay
no caique with taut sail,
not even an underworld ferry.

We see it. It is not a dream or sci fi.
Numbness or guilt keeps us from acting, voting
against nuclear power. The global
nightmare compounds as once in Germany.

Can't we change directions, walk back
to the original mother-father sun? For God's
sake and our own, can't we?
Or *is* the above to be our planet?

New Letters   *Ellen Tifft*

WOMEN HOPING FOR RAIN

Come Saturday morning, we bring ourselves,
Loyal as fall rain, to this cropped
Field to see our sons play out
Their skills. We gather in kind, familiar

As sisters, beneath these shallow
Skies where our sons run, switch
Inside, swing leisurely wide and cut
Their confident patterns into the dust

Of this playing field of boys.
Week on week, we come to surround
This field with mothers who think we can
Bear the hazard of full morning shifting,

Settling within itself. In the shadows
That float from the first leaves feathered
From these elms, we gather   as women hoping
For rain   and submit to the grace
Of morning the adolescence of our sons.

The Southern Review   *David Tillinghast*

THE ORIGINS OF ESCAPE

Sitting in the shelter of this porch, I struggle
For sunshine, a peephole in the cloudbank
Laying over us for weeks. The newspaper
You hold in your hands this morning,
And yesterday morning, will be the same one
Tomorrow that wilts on its foldings.
How do you survive the rainy season?
How do you survive the silence
Of your fingers?

Here mildew has invaded the woodwork,
Finding in its grooves the chlorophyll

Of darkness. I rub my palm against walnut,
Damp friction straining against familiars.
I hear the knock of the shaker,
Trying to free the salt, slow squeak
Of flesh on wood, the evolution of life
Grown from a thick comfort of union.
These are sounds of an amphibian who has learned
To drink his oxygen from water.

I breathe in humidity. Would Darwin have noticed it,
These origins of escape? My eyes acquiesce
To the garden. It has been a Noah's Flood
For the insect world. Ants have built mudhuts
In the podjoints of the peas. Figs are as big
As peaches. Under a leaf sit six daddy longlegs,
Sheltered from the rain.

New Mexico Humanities Review   *Charles P. R. Tisdale*

WITH DUE DEFERENCE TO THOMAS WOLFE

Fifteen years ago
I left this seacoast town
on a gritty train for New York.
Now I stake out old haunts,
find on the site of the railroad station
a modern shopping mall
where the cherry cokes of the Whistle Stop Cafe
have drizzled into concrete ribbon.
The cottage I lived in is gone—
that whole row of cottages
has been shorn; sprung in their place
are boxlike condominiums,
no green lawns or chaises,
no clothesline (where we beat out sand
from the braided rug).
Only a weekend traffic jam
where Shady Lane intersects Main:
small tugs of memory
become deafened by one thousand
revs of radial tires.

Yet Sunday dawns with New England precision.
Beyond the swish of beach grasses
a lone dory rides the billows,
and below Pegleg's corner
the old man still combs the sand
with his metal detector,
finding more pop tops than coins.
Herring gulls blast all quiet
with their raucous "kuk-kuk-yucca-kuk"
as, swooping low,
they dash clams against rock,
pry out breakfast,

then soar away—heedless of Sabbath
and immune to echoes.

Harpoon   *Joanne Townsend*

FEELING FOR FISH

Even in daylight, in murky waters,
As the ooze slides between your toes,
You can sense them around you, cautious,
Curious, nosing up close.

And often, swimming at night, you feel
Small ones nip at your flesh,
Then flick away with a little swirl.
But to make your catch,

Lie in the dark on a weedy ledge
Where the bank drops off sharply,
And troll your arm over the edge
Into the blind water.

You'll feel them nudging, cruising about;
Then one will strike your hand—quick,
Cock your thumb in the gills, hook
Your fingers through the mouth

And wrestle the slippery, thrashing thing
Out of its element into your own.
Later you'll find raw streaks the teeth have torn
And aching little holes from fins,

But you'll never use hook or net again;
You'll keep feeling back into black water,
And one night sooner or later
You'll wade out deep for the big one.

Poetry   *Leonard Trawick*

WAKING IN NICE

All the way from Florence in the train
the distances were gaining. You moved
from car to car restlessly, you smoked; I took
notes in my black book like a gumshoe
gathering evidence. In Nice, things have begun
to come apart: like a Las Vegas Mary & Joseph,
we trudged away the first night in search
of a room. We slept in the only place we found:
on a slanted floor in twin beds, our feet higher
than our heads, our faces cold above red blankets.

In the morning I discovered the boast
on the wall outside: Matisse and Chekhov
slept here, in different years of course:
much the way the two of us are sleeping. I made a note.

At night along the *rue Jean Medecin,*
shopping bag women sleep curled in the doorways

of fancy shops. They are bundles of rags
the tourists must look past
to see the window fashions. There are no simple
things here. And for us
language has become food. In Italy
neither of us spoke the tongue, but here
you are alone; you watch me like a spy.
The two oranges I bought in the open
marketplace have become community property.

Early mornings along the *Cote d'Azur*
the hobos gather
their blankets from the rocks, making room
for golden bodies on rented mattresses. You and I
lie directly on the rocks to prove our toughness
to each other. We stare. It seems as if we
have forgotten our own language. We settle
on silence. I draw faces on the rocks, leave them
when we go: bread crumbs. And if we should get home
again, language will no longer be the blanket
it once was; things will be uncovered
when we speak: the words
will be of an old language, untranslatable
into the present tense.

The Malahat Review   *Patricia Traxler*

CROW VOICES

On the Plains, crows speak in raucous caws,
circling corn fields, waiting for the weeding
woman to turn her back. In those open
spaces, their voices seem brazen
as they fly along highways looking
for the dead to pick clean to the bone—
devouring the remains, maggots and all.
Fat on road meat and grain, crows seem
always ready to play tricks, to outwit
themselves quicker than coyote,
to gossip with magpie, to gather light
and shine black against the sky.

In western Washington, crows speak
in steady, conversational tones, voices
muted as they convene meetings
among cedars. Speaking of spells,
they fly through mist—dark shadows
drawing dark to themselves like shamans
preparing some incredible magic
to frighten evil. Inside the rain forest,
crows act serious, whispering about enemies,
about food supplies, about how Raven
stole their wit when he proved
he was so clever he could take the sun.

Denver Quarterly   *Gail Tremblay*

THE SKULL IN THE DESERT

So dry and clean,
It lies amid
The harsh and brittle sage.
Pure, scoured of all but age,
All warmth has died
Except the sun.

In life, two ghosts
Of misty breath
Defied the morning cold,
And cloven hooves so laid
This desert path
That yet it lasts.

The skull now rests.
The sockets, blind,
Are stuffed with straw. The nose
And horns small mice traverse
And climb, to find,
Within, their nests.

The Southern Review   *Alison A. Trimpi*

FAILED FATHERS

(On a theme by, and with apologies to, Greg Pape)

Where do all the failed fathers
go? To Albuquerque? Cleveland?
After the slow slide down the drain,
where do they go? After the last
lay-off, the class reunion where they're shown

kissing the matronly Queen
of the Prom, where do they go? Where
do they go, these old young men, these
paunchy guys with the eyes that squint
into the lens at the family picnic,

the fishing expedition
near the falls, the baseball game where
they played second? After the fights,
the money fights, the brief affair,
after the spree and the morning after,

where do the failed fathers go?
Is there a bar where they gather?
Is there a bus they all take?
Is there a line at the Bureau
where they talk over their sons and daughters,

their Old Ladies turning cold,
the milkmen they caught spending time
drinking coffee in their kitchens?
Is there a motel in Cleveland
full of fathers playing poker,

smoking cigarettes, squinting
at their hands, drinking beer? Is there,
down in Albuquerque, some street
full of walk-up rooms full of dreams
of mowing lawns, of paneling basements,

propping children on their bikes,
walking down the aisles of markets
pushing shopping carts? Of course, we
know what happens to our mothers,
but where, oh where, do the failed fathers go?

La Fusta   *Lewis Turco*

THE SPIRIT

Again, Christmas, bright colored lights
dress the town and children
just can't wait for Christmas morning
so they can attack the presents
underneath the tree
and on the tv the tribes have united
and are stalking
towards Rhodesia bringing
presents of bullets
of rockets
of land mines
enough for everyone
and in Ireland
the bombs still explode, but a 3-day truce
has been promised
a time to build up
a time for some good cheer
and in Lebanon
the dead are being buried and the ceasefire
is marred by machine gun bursts
and exploding rockets in the not so silent night
and in Uganda Big Daddy plays Santa
for his crocodiles
feeding them extra good fat spies
in festive season merriment ho ho ho ho ho
belly jiggling like any good Santa
in a season to be merry
& I just can't help not really feeling
merry and festive, not with all the killing
and torture and suffering going on in the world
all in the name of freedom and peace and right
I'm not indignant, I'm used to it, kind of
the odd picture still makes me want to puke
just a little anyhow
a child with its legs blown off
a pregnant woman with a machine gun abortion
oh, jingle bells   jingle bells   bells
tolling for the dead
signalling an attack

and merry christmas happy new years
as robot armies prepare for victory
but I can't really condemn them
the soldiers   the warriors   the guerillas
like me they love and hate
and sometimes I see myself
in a uniform, an automatic rifle
determined in my hands
walking stealthily to the ambush
pockets bulging with grenades
scalping knife dangling from my belt
a perfect trooper, the perfect cause
blazing bright in my mad eyes
and just last night I drove my fist
into a wall in a murderous rage
wishing instead it was someone's face
a nose instead of plywood smashing
under my knuckles
the silent night holy night
broken by my loud cursing
filled with the electricity of the madness
that unites us all
the brotherhood of man
the sisterhood of woman
crazy creatures
convulsing
like a prehistoric monster
filled with stone age spears
screaming defiance
all the way to the end

The Malahat Review   *Doug Turner*

GEOLOGICAL FAULTS

And other wonders
Invade my fossil dreams.
He and I stand
On the Columbia Ice Cap—
Canadian tourist trap—
Testing the queer blue ice,
The kind they say "runs deep"
Miles and miles.

Solid, it held us up
Above the hot dog concession
And tramway, supporting
Hundreds of visitors daily,
And Sonja Henie
For years.

Nobody could guess
The adjoining crevasses would swallow
The whole Indian Trading Post.
The children and I

Wear our Saskatchewan mittens,
Hold our palms up bravely
As we slip through
Caverns of ice,
Our costume skirts
Tilted upward
Like broken umbrellas.

Now on the sunless side of the canyon
I fly alone on my home-made mechanism,
A downy giant bat,
Frightening lizards
Who scuttle under cold rock
Afraid of the woman
Who fell from the sky.

I soar, dive, touch bottom,
Then rise again into cobalt blue.
Around my webbed wings
Whirls a lasso of buzzards,
Moving soundlessly,
Waiting for
The thawed wax,
The faulty bolt,
The broken wing.

The Nation   *Barbara Unger*

TASTE

I have, alas, no taste—
taste, that Talleyrand, that ally of the minimal,
that foreign-accented intuiter
of what sly harmonies exist
betwixt the draped, the draper, and the drape:
that advocate of the *right* as it teeters
on its tightrope above the abyss of excess,
beneath the airy tent-top of not quite enough.

My first wife had taste.
White walls were her answer, and, Take that
to the attic. Nothing pleased her, quite,
but Cezanne and emptiness
and a shabby Oriental rug so full
of dust and virtue it made me sneeze,
descended as it was from her ancestors,
exemplary in piety and in the China trade.
Yet she was *right,* right in all things,
and draped herself in cocktail dresses
of utter black, her arms no less perfect than bones.

I know a man with taste.
He lives alone on a floor of a warehouse
and designs machines that make nothing
but vivid impressions of whirling,
of ellipticity, dazzle, and flow.
He cooks on a single burner

Supremes de Volaille aux Champignons,
has hung his brick walls with pencilled originals
by Impressionist masters,
and lives in smiling harmony with all that is there
and is not there,
minding only the traffic noise from the street.
He and my first wife would make a pair,
but they will never meet.

My second wife, that flatterer, says
I have taste.
All decisions as to pattern are deferred to me.
A chair, a car I chose is cheered
when it arrives, like a bugle note, on pitch
with all the still-humming chords
of our clamorous, congratulatory mingling.
It makes one blush, to be credited with taste.
Chipmunk fur, wave-patterns on sand, white asters—
but for these, and some few other exceptions,
Nature has no taste, just productivity.
I want to be, like Nature, tasteless,
abundant, reckless, cheerful. Go screw, taste—
itself a tasteless suggestion.

The American Poetry Review   *John Updike*

HIS SLEEP

In sleep he hunches away from me,
Thrusting a sharp shoulder
Into the dimness
(which here is never quite dark)
Like a mountain ridge across my horizon.

His legs are positioned for flight,
Knees bent like a runner's,
One higher than the other,
Muscles relaxed now, slack
On the long bones, femur and tibia;

Elbows bend to the shape of his dream.
One arm embraces the pillow,
The other grasps at nothing, until
His fist strikes the mattress,
Setting off a bed of earthquakes.

His night-breathing is louder than speech;
It rattles in his throat
Like the ghost of croup-kettles,
Heaving him over, exposing the vulnerable parts:
Tufted ribs, soft belly, idle sex.

Born new and naked every morning,
Soon he'll wake with a groan,
Every limb flying out in startled protest,

And squint wryly into the light
Of our common life.

Paintbrush   *Constance Urdang*

EXERCISE FOR THE LEFT HAND

Have I ever been other?
A wild girl, racing the clouds across the sky
Where like riderless horses they toss white manes and tails?
Was I that one?

Was I a sullen girl, glum
As the cloud that hangs, heavy with rain,
On the hill's narrow shoulder?
Have I been a soft girl, Daddy's darling?
Was I a vixen, snarling?
An Amazon, bestriding
Her conquered country? Or a wanton
In dark streets, casting sideways glances
At impossible romances?

Surveying the landscape of myself, molded
"By the trivia of circumstance"
Into woman-shape,
I see it all might have been foretold
By my mother's great-grandmother
On the other side of the world.

Paintbrush   *Constance Urdang*

VIEW

Pure spite, wanting
to escape the unexplained
even while I crave it.

In the shadows of my room I see
the leaves through my window,
and through the leaves the feather
of light from the wind off the sea.

Ring of trees, bending row of elms,
courtyard of memories, statue of sky,
of breath.   Nothing more.

Poetry Now   *Christian J. Van Geel*
                              – Translated from the Dutch
                        by Emilie Peech and W. S. Di Piero

LUMIERE

The cathedral window was a cliché
she hardly noticed,
and what she saw
of the stairs for years
was the carpet wearing thin.

Light now
is the only visitor.
The nurse leaves the door ajar,
and the pillows propped up high
from morning till afternoon.

She watches first the leaded glass
begin to glow,
and then the whole
body of light
leans toward the right.

It seems to grip the balustrade—
as a waiter might, carrying a tray;
and so carefully and slowly climbs
the stairs, he takes all afternoon
bearing up the light.

Harper's Magazine   *H. L. Van Brunt*

ENCOUNTER WITH HUNGER

The starving of Bangladesh
are visited.
They come from the sky,
the children tell me,
carry their eyes in
their hands,
stay at a distance
and stare.

I have been there,
I tell them—
T.V. land;
I grew up there,
overfed and fat.
They question old rumours
of whole rooms full
of food, of Big Mac's
and bread that is tossed
to the street
and stays there.

Their eyes bulge.

This is not the world,
they tell me.

I listen,
begin to feel
like a renegade with
a camera—
move in, shoot
what you can,
leave the rest for
the scavengers—
these children,

eating
themselves.

The Fiddlehead   *Brian Vanderlip*

WHEN YOU ARE GONE

One day a week I stay home
to make bread, to mop floors,
to try on your clothes.
Beside your dresser
I pull your jockey shorts up
over my thighs like a dancer,
stuff your huge billowing shirt tails
into the round belly of wool trousers,
slowly slip small feet into your shoes.
Finally, I shove myself into the suit coat,
going out on the porch
where I flap my arms like a scarecrow,
the wind blowing me out. Even
my toes stretch to caress wing tips;
and this is my day.
Anxious over bread dough,
I move alone in the house
airing the closet and
drawers of love.

Kansas Quarterly   *Nance Van Winckel*

CONCORDANCE

(from Keats)

Tall chestnuts keep away the sun and moon.
Some shape of beauty moves away the pall
that scared away the meek ethereal hours,
filled out its voice and died away again.
The breath of winter comes from far away,
charms us at once away from all our troubles.
Fresh morning gusts have blown away all fear
—will blow one half of your sad doubts away,
fanning away the dandelion's down,
chasing away all worldliness and folly
to a loud hymn that sounds far, far away.
     What can I do to drive away
all chaff of custom, wipe away all slime,
fade far away, dissolve and quite forget
I threw my shell away upon the sand?
Yet would I give my unworn crown away,
my life away like a vast sponge of fate,
and die away in ardent mutterings.
At this the shadow wept, melting away.

Sun and Moon   *Paul Violi*

EXPERIENCE

The vale of twilight filled with silver-gray
Exhalings of sweet mist, as when the moon
Seeps down through clouds . . . But still it was not night.
With silver-gray mist of the darkening vale,
My twilit thoughts merged into a liquid haze
And calmly I sank through the wavering sea
And its translucence, leaving life behind.
What fascinating flowers blossomed there
With darkly glowing calyxes!—a mass
Of vegetation through which topaz-light
Streamed yellow-red and glimmered warmly. All
Was filled to overflow with a deep swell
Of melancholy music. And this I knew;
Although I do not grasp it, still I knew:
That this is Death. And Death turned into music,
Big with yearning, sweet and darkly glowing,
Akin to deepest sorrow.
                                    Yet how strange!
A nameless homesickness wept soundlessly
Within my life-committed spirit—wept
As one might weep when, standing on a ship
With giant yellow sails as evening nears
On dark blue water, he moves past a town,
His town of birth and childhood. There he sees
The old streets, hears the gushing fountains, smells
The fragrant lilac shrubs, and sees himself,
A child, upon the shore, and with this child's
Own stricken eyes, which want to cry, sees light
Shine through an open window in his room.
But the great vessel carries him away
On dark blue water, gliding soundlessly
With strangely fashioned giant yellow sails.

Webster Review   *Hugo von Hofmannsthal*
                          —Translated from the German
                          by John N. Miller

UNDER THE SIGN OF MOTH

Having read and written myself almost to sleep, I stretch
For the light and see it
There on the otherwise bare ceiling:
A rust-and-black-winged moth
Motionless over our heads, waiting for something—
The scent of a distant, screened-off mate? Some hint
Of a flower to feed on? Another chrysalis?

My wife is already sleeping, not knowing
We will spread our dreams under the Sign of Moth,
A constellation presiding over us
(More plausibly than the thread-spinning of stars
That housed our births) by clinging

Somehow to the plaster heaven we trusted
To see us safely and vacantly through the night.

I turn out the lamp that might have tempted it
To flutter down and play its familiar role
As a fool for brightness, a hopeful dabbler
Aspiring long enough to expire, battered
And singed by what it thought it wanted,
To suffer a last demeaning transformation
Into a moral lesson.

In the near-darkness, its eyes catch at the streetlight
And gleam deep red, lidlessly staring
Downward at the beginning of our sleep.
What can I offer it but peace and quiet?
With heavy eyelids, I return its gaze
More and more heavily, now blinking, my body
Unable to rise to this occasion,

Either to hunt for love or food or light
Or to fashion a moth-net from some gauzy remnant
Or to manage anything but a spinning fall
Into a dream of becoming
A shape that wants to leave old forms behind,
Now hidden, now crawling upwards, now flying,
Endlessly new, endlessly unfolding.

The ceiling is blank in the morning.
I yawn and slip out from under, obeying the obscure
Scheme of the day, drifting from room to room.
The moth is somewhere in a dusty crevice,
Its long tongue coiled more certainly than a spring
Made to keep time, still waiting
For what it came to find and will die for.

Poetry   *David Wagoner*

FALLING ASLEEP IN A GARDEN

All day the bees have come to the garden.
They hover, swivel in arcs and, whirling, light
On stamens heavy with pollen, probe and revel
Inside the yellow and red starbursts of dahlias
Or cling to lobelia's blue-white mouths
Or climb the speckled trumpets of foxgloves.

My restless eyes follow their restlessness
As they plunge bodily headfirst into treasure,
Gold-fevered among these horns of plenty.
They circle me, a flowerless patch
With nothing to offer them in the way of sweetness
Or light against the first omens of evening.

Some, even now, are dying at the end
Of their few weeks, some being born in the dark,
Some simply waiting for life; but some are dancing
Deep in their hives, telling the hungry

The sun will be that way, the garden this far:
This is the way to the garden. They hum at my ear.

And I wake up, startled, seeing the early
Stars beginning to bud in constellations.
The bees have gathered somewhere like petals closing
For the coming of the cold. The silhouette
Of a sphinx moth swerves to drink at a flowerhead.
The night-blooming moon opens its pale corolla.

The Iowa Review   *David Wagoner*

LOVE IN BROOKLYN

"I love you, Horowitz," he said, and blew his nose.
She splashed her drink. "The hell you say," she said.
Then, thinking hard, she lit a cigarette:
"Not *love*. You don't *love* me. You like my legs,
and how I make your letters nice and all.
You drunk your drink too fast. You don't love *me*."

"You wanna bet?" he asked. "You wanna bet?
I loved you from the day they moved you up
from Payroll, last July. I watched you, right?
You sat there on that typing chair you have
and swung round like a kid. It made me shake.
Like once, in World War II, I saw a tank
slide through some trees at dawn like it was god.
That's how you make me feel. I don't know why."

She turned towards him, then sat back and grinned,
and on the bar stool swung full circle round.
"You think I'm like a tank, you mean?" she asked.
"Some fellers tell me nicer things than that."
But then she saw his face and touched his arm
and softly said, "I'm only kidding you."

He ordered drinks, the same again, and paid.
A fat man, wordless, staring at the floor.
She took his hand in hers and pressed it hard.
And his plump fingers trembled in her lap.

Poetry   *John Wakeman*

AGING

It is the light
in January, thin as a beautiful woman's stocking,
which I love.
It comes through my yellow curtains
in the morning
like clean underwear
and I,
warm and lazy under the down comforter,
can only wonder
why there is such a general rejection of winter.

I'm not talking now
about freezing, starving soldiers
in the snow at Valley Forge;
but the simplicity of suburban snow
that is experienced by an ordinary
man or woman
in East Lansing, Michigan.

This winter
is so beautiful to me.

Hawaii Review   *Diane Wakoski*

SIGNALS

My love is the red sky before a rain;
She lavishes portents and I know each one.
My love is the index of approaching pain
And I'd run for shelter if I knew which way to run.

My love is the calm space of a battlefield;
She announces confusion and mystery.
My love's in my brain, where the light has congealed,
And she has ruined forever my sense of history.

My love is the void of expectation,
The empty hub radiant with spokes,
The moment of wisdom before creation,
The spasm of laughter for untold dirty jokes.

True prophecies are never understood
And I see some things only when I'm delirious.
I've tried knocking twice on the same piece of wood—
My love makes death and death makes everything serious.

Open Places   *Keith Waldrop*

INSTRUCTIONS FOR A PARK

These apartment acres, good only
for living in, must go. Plant charges
at regular intervals, wherever
ceiling meets floor or flat ridge of floor
meets ceiling.
                Stand back the recommended
distance, hold traffic still as a photo-
graph, the city holding its moment, eased
upon a plunger, a lever, anything
on which to stand and pry the earth.

Allow a lifetime for the air to clear.
Allow twenty years for paint to be done
with cracking, another thirty for lumber
to burrow into the ground and emerge
as tree, twenty-five for brick to crumble
to stone, stone to pebble, pebble to dust.

Then hire dozens of dozers to push
the dust into mounds, the mounds into hills,

hills into mountain. Label the mountain
Erosion, and leave it for another
century.
      Mold your children, your children's
children, the children of the children
great grandchildren bear; convince them
that they are the reason for the past.

If their faces turn red, know that it is
only the wind in the park, the beginnings
of rain or snow. If they grow thirsty,
know that all rivers flow into one, and
that even that one, like a shadow
passing over a park, flows into air.

Shenandoah   *Brad Walker*

TRACKING THE SLED, CHRISTMAS 1951

It is the route you took through winter light.
The shadow of the sled I asked for then
falls across the pane again tonight.

From Bloomquist's Hardware, where the kegs of bright
nails dozed in the banter of afternoon,
you took the route through final winter light,

across the railroad tracks and to the right.
In the IGA the radio whined a tune
that falls across the pane again tonight.

It's more than memory, for I cannot quite
recall the shanties' tilt as dark drifts in.
It is the route you took through winter light.

You scarred the snow. Above, geese break in flight.
Now steady tracks of runners fail. They fan
and fall across the pane again tonight.

The sled leans by my doorjamb. Frail, bright.
There is no way to get where you have gone.
It is the route you took through winter light
that falls across the pane again tonight.

The Chariton Review   *Jeanne Murray Walker*

PROFILE

The living swim through their photographs
like fish
even the ones taken yesterday
cannot contain them
and it does not matter
which we choose
for the family album where
through the flicker of a page

the scrawny six year old can twist
and turn herself to bride or mother

But the dead move differently
though they seem fixed forever
on uncomfortable chairs
or grimly posed beside aging husbands
and though we search nervously
through overflowing boxes desperate
for happier expressions more
august occasions   the dead
retreat behind their frozen attitudes
and the yellowing surfaces cloud
with their wishes
their unfinished business
till we become like the man
who sorts through photographs
of someone he once loved
and is held   not by the ones
that catch her full faced to the camera
but the tentative profile
where the pattern
of shadows on her face and the way
her hair falls through them
imply a movement so hesitant
he cannot remember
which way she turned
when the shutter
reopened

Event   *Bronwen Wallace*

THE LINEBACKER AT FORTY

slouches over four-bit beers
at Hoagy's, dreams wide-eyed
about the bluster of scrimmage, the sweet
crunch of a blindside, randy schoolgirls
putting out in borrowed cars. Now

even love is work. His wife
wears muu-muus, tenses beside him in bed
like a guest. His daughter dates
sullen pansies in platform shoes, talks
to him as if he were a cop. Once, while
she stared into his shirt, he
explained why no one played him
one on one, how at 19
he was a lawnmower,
and a halfback's ass was grass.

                    While
the jukebox whines about love
gone sour, he feels his waist
thicken, his belt pinch. Life, he
discovers, is what makes him tired, like

another scrimmage. Only now the weariness
goes clear to the bone. Staring
deep into his glass, he imagines himself
       far away
   rising within a circle of light
      like a star.

Kansas Quarterly   *Jon Wallace*

THE REAL THING

The sea was as blue as the sky
and your eyes were as blue as the sea.
Could I help it?
I was happy. We were in love.

And the jellyfish floating in on the tide?
And the gulls in their lovely remoteness?
Who could see through
the blue angle of their descent,
the accuracy of stinger and beak,
the sea in its cool movement,
swelling? Who could care?

Oh the sky was our limitless future,
and the rhythmic sea laving the beach
was our love going on, and forever.
Could I help it?

And the bright starfish trapped in the shallows?
And the sea urchins reft of their spines?
And the shells with their ears full of memories?
Who could care? We were young;
how could summer and language betray us,
leave us stranded in this blue season,
our tongues blunt as husks in our cheeks?

The Midwest Quarterly   *Ronald Wallace*

FATHER AND SON

He sat at the foot of my bed
with authority, I thought, not love,
counting me down to sleep,
his stiff crutches propped in the doorway,
their shadow flat on my back, until
there was nothing I could do
but let go and float out of myself
toward that unattainable
galaxy of pretence—love and sleep.

But when he was finally satisfied
that I'd gone off, sometimes he'd weep.
I never knew why. And so, years later,
as I sat by his high bed,
watching him drift off beyond me,
I let him go, as he let me,

my silence flat at his feet.
I didn't try to call him back
from that calm, untroubled sleep.

The Midwest Quarterly   *Ronald Wallace*

TABLEROCK

Looking eastward from Tablerock
I realize how the darkness
that follows the sun from the east
is but the shadow
of a mountain reaching out from the west.
How interesting that our perceptions
change with position—
like those moments we fly backwards
into the source,
and see darkness falling
away from the self.

The Sun   *Darryl Wally*

HERBS IN THE ATTIC

(for Amanda Jordan)

A car by the fireside, purring.
But I don't stop there; I go
through the living room and up the stairs.
My little brother stirs in his crib,
My sister and I sleep in our tumbled rooms,
and our parents sleep together,
fingers intertwined.

The second stairway's narrow.
It darkens when I close the door
behind me. And I climb up to the attic,
to the bustles and pantaloons
hidden in trunks, the diaries and love letters,
the photographs, the rings,
the envelopes full of hair.

Here's the old silverware
Great Aunt Irene and Uncle Eric used.
Her fork is curved
from her life-long habit
of scraping the plate.
His knife is broader,
the better for buttering bread.

Here are the bookcases of discarded books:
Tarzan, Zane Grey, a textbook Shakespeare,
piles of *National Geographic, Look,* and *Life:*
enough to last me a while.

I sit on the dusty floor
and open a book.

Dream music fills the air
like the scent of dried herbs.

The Georgia Review   *Marilyn Nelson Waniek*

TENANT FARMER

This is the only way it can be. Twilight
finds the snow falling like balls of fur torn
from the sky. He watches it fill up the dead
eye of the deer, as softly as it knows how.
The willow branches have ceased to eddy
around the strung carcass. His wife
counts steaks from the window.
He has little to do now but to think
of what to tell the children at night,
sitting in the kitchen around the stove.
Tell them how he slept as they do, four
in a bed; and in the morning the frost
was so thick on the wallpaper you could eat
it with your fingers. Or when he was in the Army,
on maneuvers in Alabama, he saw the snakes.
Racing across the fields, their heads high
above the rye. Or how the fields have hardened
against him, his own water pushing him back.
That what they've earned is another year.
This morning he rose early for deer. Cross-lots
he found that nothing remained but light.
As always. But less congested. Clear and
empty. Then in a slough near his landlord's
barn, a doe. Tenant to the same land, he thought
momentarily, it is stupidity that brings them
both here. Then he felt the trigger's imagination.
Next spring the earth will open again. The wind
will be like a beggar once more. He will work
under the sun till he will think of nothing.
He has some rabbits left, and jars of black-
berry jam. Carrots and potatoes till March.
And now the deer. The moonlight reaches into
the drifts. He reaches for his wife. Living
on another man's land, he has learned
what can be owned, what can be borrowed.
He sleeps late, days before Christmas.

Kansas Quarterly   *Robert Ward*

ODE TO A HOMEMADE COFFEE CUP

These bright colors of red
and blue and brown
will never fade,
nor will you ever shatter,
cup my wife made pushing fingers deep,
deep into soft clay
to make a vessel out of a lump,

both male and female at once;
vessel I pour my morning cup
of black Brazilian fluid
into, fill you brimful

and take you upstairs, steaming,
away from the clatter of dishwasher,
sit you by my battered typewriter,
so that you may share with me
a moment of morning silence.

The Spoon River Quarterly   *Marine Robert Warden*

SEIZURE

Photograph: *an empty house, the windows intact,*
grass halfway to the sills, and rusty tracks
too near across the weeds. But once
upon this sparrowed porch the children sat . . .

I felt myself tense,
delighted, sensing a poem in it.

I stalked into my study's gloom,
fumbled for notebook and pen—

then,

suddenly,

knew something at my heart
or brain
or both:
the wanting-to-burst of death.

(They patched my seventy-year heart last week.)

I sat, my head upon my arms
a long and holy moment.

There
I felt the cold dizziness leak
out, drain;
gathered myself together carefully in the dark;
walked slowly back into the light
where
though arteries rotten,
though pulses grow sullen,
though hearts become silent,
the bright, clean, strong words still remain.

Daimon   *James E. Warren, Jr.*

COMMUTER'S ENTRY IN A CONNECTICUT DIARY

I finish the *Times.* Shut eyes. My head,
Inside, flickers like TV in a dark hospital room.

This is the world. Or is it? I
Hear the morning curdle of traffic on our pleasant
oak-shaded street.

Grab briefcase, kiss wife, discard umbrella,
Hum "Annie Laurie" as I back down the drive in sunshine,

And make ready the plastic smile to greet
The smiles that greet me on the platform of the 8:20.

What is the day but a dream, or the dream but a day?
And what is life but the day and the dream? I sit

In the evening bar car to nurse only one, as I catch
The last gleam on estuary, river, or sail,

And think of a body, white, in the open sea,
With stroke steady sunsetward, and water prismatic in eyes.

Yes, love is reality. Without it, what? I clasp
The hand, hear the breath now even and slow, and staring

In darkness, trust I'll not again dream the dream
Of fume and glow, like the city dump, at night

Outside Norwalk, Conn.

The Southern Review   *Robert Penn Warren*

VIRGIN PICTURED IN PROFILE

(This poem is derived from an Egyptian Middle Kingdom tomb painting.)

A white-gowned woman making offering
rests on one knee, the other raised.
Hands outstretched, palms down,
fingers slightly curved at the tips.
Spins a straight stem. The visible ear
left bare by the black, geometric coiffure.

Where does she gaze with that slant, blank eye?
The amphora before her is empty.
So are the bowl and narrow vase.
She kneels, rigid in ceremony.
No one stands near her,
and the world beyond is milk mist only.

They have gone: maidens, parents, the robed priest,
the people of her town, even the gods.
So rapt she was
in the rite, she did not hear
when they called and trundled away.
Beams crumbled on sand and shards, and wind
curled in from the desert.

She did not hear, nor will she ever.
"Child, child, wake up," they had cried,
but could not break her trance, and so
departed, with all their belongings
wrapped in bright woven cloth, their dogs at their heels.

They died. Somewhere, the river rises still,
fish feed, and fields are tilled,
the newly dead are laid in the living earth.
Of this she will never know.

It is the perfection of emptiness
she offers now, as she offered eras ago.

No river rises to her wall,
mud-roiled, flooding with spring.
Her landscape is pure dust.
Nor will it be granted
to her who never soiled her loins with life
to enter, lotus in hand, and dressed as bride,
the full-thronged kingdom of the truly dead.

The Atlantic Monthly   *Rosanna Warren*

ADAM, EVE AND THE BIG APPLE

Don't you love farce? All those bedroom doors—
Feydeau, Astaire, those sketches at the Palace,
All have revolved around them: erotic wars,
A Dionysiac tribute to the phallus!
More lighthearted romps these than skin flicks
With leather and chains to titillate the senses—
Lubitsch himself provides more cheerful kicks
Than X-rated peep shows for the jocks and wenches.

Send in the clowns, as Sondheim aptly puts it—
A delightful round, those smiles of a summer night:
Even a Bergman lover lightly foots it
When the Stockholm sun's still up and the music's right.
  For sex, the commodity of the Times Square man,
  Once was champagne and laughter, Lunt and Fontanne!

Song   *Edward Watkins*

MUSEUM PIECE NO. 16228

You lie there, with your line of stiff red griffins
dissolving into linen colorless with age:
a scrap of history pressed beneath some glass.
The museum card says "circa 1550."

Whose body-warmth enhanced your gaudy threads
and made those griffins prance
and dance with sixteenth-century flesh
now long dispersed and lost

but for this little linen scrap that says
"Remember me"?

Ball State University Forum   *Elaine Watson*

A GOOD LIFE

Memories of a good life are not enough;
The fade-out begins. I run to beat the dark,
I swim to light my eyes. I give up drink,
I diet on yogurt, squash seeds, herbal tea.

I take the lotus position, meditate.
Arising, I fly straight at the new day
(What's done, was done): make the new day
Fresh as home-baked bread, blueberries bog ripe,
Clams dug, steamed the same hour. My mind receptive
As a child's. Yes, I could wish for hail storms,
A city in flames, a hovering harem,
A visit from an angel. No, I train
For a different kind of tomorrow today.
I run to beat the dark, I swim to light my eyes,
To see the usual I have passed by.

I need a vision: Let me see an apple
That is tart, firm from a tree, an orchard
In Vermont, an orchard in winter snowfall,
The orchard blank as a white sheet of paper.
I walk in this snow. It squeaks in sub-zero.

I will not look over my shoulder, behind
At my footsteps, at the disrupted snow.
I am not ready yet to be the past in the past.

The Georgia Review   *Robert Watson*

MEMORY MOVIE

Kaleidoscopic memories fall in and out
Until the right picture is framed.
Father is watching television,
Mother whirs the sewing machine—
And I am ten years old again.
Father tucks me into bed,
Mother kisses my cheek,
And I dream of chocolate sundaes
And all-year summers;
But time tugs my sleeve.
Fast forward blurs the film,
And today takes charge.

Touchstone   *Diane Webster*

CALVIN IN THE ATTIC CLEANS

The trunk won't budge; I open it
and begin taking things out.
I find in an old purse
letters filled with love not mine.
The dates go back seven years;
wife and I ten.
I know some of the restaurants,
even took her to the same plays.
And here, isn't this when I went east?
But does it make a difference?
What I believe is what is.
The blocks of time love's built on

still hold if I let them.
I put the letters back, pull out
sweaters, yearbooks, the old uniform.
The trunk drags easily now;
dust climbs to the rafters.
And I stand, straight as I can.

Sands   *Craig Weeden*

THE LIMITS OF DEPARTURE

We edge the boat in tight among stumps
Stretching the long cane poles like arms,
But in that odd passing of time that is fishing
We do no more good than the conversation
Of strangers in a small boat
Out on a rough-hewn lake
Trying to right a bad day in a new town.

For a moment we watch ducks
Hover above a green open patch of water
Reeling and lifting at last in suspicion,
And I am afraid of nothing tonight:
Not the lull in our small talk when the wind stops
And the dark catches us too far out,
Not the thousands of desires that brought me here
For reasons I was too stupid to speak or know;

Not my love for that unnamable longing
To speak something that matters, that touch
Of words at the heart until pain
Thin as mist lifts
Until even the rotting jaws of catfish, catching last light,
Stuck on short stumps like totems,
Turn warnings we see more clearly
On the way back home.

Cimarron Review   *Bruce Weigl*

THE ARMLESS

The ends of dreams are acts of completion.
Well, usually. I know this, everyone does.
But tell me why I had this crazy dream for years,
this dream of waiting for the sun to go down,
cool, crystallize itself into an arm.
After that I grew up considering
the stories of amputees—
how they could walk toward stores
swinging their spectral flesh beside them,
how part of them went out futilely,
but still went out toward the doors.
Even this failed to materialize.
So I contented myself by telling stories
to the socialites of Graywood, Nebraska:
of catching soccer balls in grade school

with my left hand and my knees,
of offering my right side to my friends
as a plumb line for their home improvements.
But occasionally, while dreaming of a woman,
there was something in me
which had never heard it was deprived,
and how, in lying down,
I too came to know the right side
of the world.

Poets On: *Don Welch*

CAROLERS

Clustering up on my Christmas steps,
They crunch the snow, and whisper
Their positions: one with a pitch pipe
Brushing himself more forcefully over the door,
Which jars, as if some heavy shoulder
Of an animal put against it.
Book aside, I wait for their chorus
And the four-part broidery of hymns
To break the crust of silence: what
Have they come to sing except goodwill
Towards men, Hosanna to the King
Of Kings? and still, the silence.
Mocked by its emptiness and by
The unsteady snow, I throw the lock
And scan: four motley masks, misplaced
All-Hallows, each one soberly lifting
His book, bent open to the beginning
Of the Word and carols: carolers,
Evangelists of what their Christmases began:
The heavy-shouldered ox, and eagle, lion, man.

The Christian Century   *Nancy G. Westerfield*

THE COLLECTOR

It is not the words we work with, words we examine
like old coins under a convex magnifying glass,
feeling with sensitive fingers for a sharp edge or smooth surface.
Nor is it the slats we slip them in or the album's
completion or the return to relics so shiningly restored.
Not all the paper and ink in the world,
nor the window we stare through, postponing a poem,
watching the day decline into night, nor the shade
we draw over the darkness, nor the lamp
we turn on to light our labor, nor the love
we finally write about. No, it is not these,
but the writing in our love, the light in our labor,
the night in our day and the darkness between,
all the unspent silver and gold of our pride's collection,

the world's unshaded window lit by a single lamp,
feeling's magnification and the work in our words.

The Mississippi Valley Review   *Robert F. Whisler*

RETURN TO ASTOLAT

Dying for love is out of fashion.
There are other ways for women
to forget their troubles.
I could take up gardening,
could weed the lilies from the beds
on wholesomely dirty hands and knees,
could do crewelwork embroidery
and strain my eyes on minute stitches,
could take in retarded children
by the day or week,
could research titles to graveyards,
work for my Congressman
or give museum tours.
It's absurd to be fascinated
with the image of myself in death:
pale hands folded on a cold breast,
lovely chiseled features,
ivory face framed in long black hair,
floating on my swanboat down the river
to disturb the feasters with my apparition.
It is an image to be kept apart,
like old photographs in the attic,
for days when it rains too hard
to be trowelling in the garden.

Aspect   *Gail White*

LINDEMAN

Your last name's the one I remember. Director
of our all-American chorus, you led me alone

into the sandhills, told me how you were named
for the lindens that grow like smaller oaks
or elms in Europe's parks, and which, translated

into English, are "lime trees" usually.
You were smaller, too. Your head and profile
ought have crowned a height of six or seven feet.

Lindeman is spicy, now I've smelled a linden blooming
and been reminded a time or two of you
kissing me, first of anyone. A *lime* has always been

a green lemon to my mind, but I thought you yellower then,
with age. Now so many have kissed me, too.
Still, of them all, you were my good instructor,

the single, high-placed person I hoped to hold
as you would open your arms in preparation for a note
to break from, as I would guess, two hundred girls.

I was your girl, that one day only, at the beach,
where you noticed me out of six or seven. We'd worked

to bury you, helpless, to the neck. Dark glasses.
That left your voice and even teeth. Deep breath.
Sand broke off your chest. Alarming. Now I would rhyme

with my early thinking, call it *charming.*
Then we walked, not far, and sat without a towel.

No waves, no stars, no air to gasp to start with.
Your hand ran under my suit-strap and let it snap.
I thought probably I would hate you, but I have not.

Crazy Horse   *Mary Jane White*

MOOSE

My canoe slowly drifting downriver,
I close in for a detailed look, despite the dusk.
Trophy-sized, palmated antlers.

Rather bizarre predicament:
feeding on pondweed, head submerged up to huge ears
that swivel in the breezy world.

At last he lugs up his long face,
preposterous mouth soppy with aquatic greens,
gawking with incredulity,

water streaming down a solemn snout
and pouring from a dewlap ponderous as a cowbell,
cartoon of a spoony satyr.

He spooks towards the riverbank.
Not the rugged ease of elk, nor the fluency of deer.
Graceful as a contortionist,

he lurches, lunges through the water,
clambers over fallen trees, trundles through reeds.
Lost remnant of some remoter time,

he stops, smallish sappy eyes probing back.
Massive front, stilt-like legs, he rifles through spruce trees.
Called twig eater by the Algonquians.

And I catch a passing glimpse of myself
backpaddling to keep my spot against the current,
straight man in a masterly gag.

Poetry   *Robert Wiljer*

BUBBA ESTHER, 1888

She was still upset—
she wanted to tell me,
she kept remembering
his terrible hands:

how she came, a young girl
of seventeen, a freckled

fairskinned Jew from Kovno
to Hamburg with her uncle,
and stayed in an old house
and waited while he bought
the steamship tickets
so they could sail to America . . .

and how he came into her room,
sat down on the bed, touched
her waist, took her by the
breast, said for a kiss
she could have her ticket;
her skirts were rumpled, her
petticoat torn, his teeth were
broken, his breath full of
onions; she was ashamed,

still ashamed, lying
eighty years later
in the hospital bed,
trying to tell me,
trembling, weeping with anger

Radcliffe Quarterly   *Ruth Whitman*

LEARNING TO SPEAK

In college when a second language was required,
I learned to repeat *Hans und Fritz reden mit einander*
quite as if the same speech had not been used
to burn Yiddish out of the mouth of Europe.

The problem of children solved one million times,
the never-to-be-born bulldozed into ashes very fine.
Under the wand of a word
heaped hanks of hair
turned into pillows to dream on.
German magic.

Rain falls tonight like light on my skin.
My bare arms whisper, awakening ancestral agreements.
I must begin the study of the language of my flesh.
Like William Bradford, the Pilgrim Father, I too will read
"the ancient oracles of God in their native beauty."

And yet, before I die, I'd like to live between the pages of a book.
An American book.
But who would keep the book alive?
Am I in the wrong place, with the wrong people, using the wrong words?
Exiled in my native language,
I fear I am a problem for whom
some new sorcery may be in store.

Midstream   *Melvin Wilk*

LONG LONELY LOVER OF THE HIGHWAY

He turns his truck on its side,
strokes it in a burst of affection.

Side by side they fall fast asleep.
They pass once again
              through the little towns.
They dream of each other.
Neither has life without the other.
In the sharp dewy morning the trucker
mounts onto his truck
              and takes it in passion.
He pours out a decade of lonely silence.
He empties his power
              into the flank of his lover.
They shudder softly.
They draw even closer,
locked and dreamy
              until the first rays of morning.

The Canadian Forum   *Frederic Will*

WORDS

Strip to the waist and have a seat. The doctor
will be in soon. He smiles and the nurse smiles.
He sits on the table, bumping his knees together,
scratching around his navel, counting the tiles.

We never talk, she says, and so you talk
and everything you speak of falls apart.
This is how we come to understand
what they mean by chambers of the heart.

Some words are said to start a conversation.
Some, after which there's nothing more to say.
"Amen," for instance. "I said I was sorry."
"Tower, we're going down. This is PSA."

The Southern Review   *Miller Williams*

ASSIGNMENT: DESCRIPTIVE ESSAY

As I mark a set of essays,
each describing someone
the student has met,
the mechanical errors I see
are mere pebbles beneath the flow
of images sparkling with wit
and warmed by affection.
There is, I feel at this moment,
a bond of common feeling
behind all the grand old faiths
and the grand new anti-faiths:
a boredom with boredom, a joy in joy,
a hatred of hatred, a love of love.
To sculpt and polish phrases
may or may not be important:
what is important

is to revere
the irresolvable mystery
of the human heart.

The Canadian Forum   *Gary Willis*

SEAWAY

Sound not the depths for anchorage, but ways
To launch a foundered craft still set to sail
Beyond the sunny shores of quiet bays,
Its mended canvas bellied on a gale;
Its keel a plow whose furrows curl and steam
In seas where trough is matrix to the crest.
Chart a course along the North Star's beam
Or south by moon; by sun, plot east or west.
Taste the salt . . . inhale the searing cold . . .
Dream, dream of what you can't in memory name
That fills the darkened corners of the hold
And lives like moths around a candle's flame.
With land aport and starboard calling free,
Haul the wind! Put out again to sea!

The Lookout   *Grace Wilson*

YANKEE POET

A cup is bound to spill, a saucer to break,
Some blunder to bring on a clumsy lull
In civilized talk. I know. We're that full
Of Nature; a fair number of mistakes

Occur to us by instinct. But we are
Worth all the crockery. We make a show
For the sophisticated folks; we do
A homely trick or two with stones and stars;

We own, ruefully, to some trafficking
With Satan, and a middling taste for hate
Into the bargain. Virtue and sin debate
At the town meetings of our souls. I think

New England makes more poems because it lies
So far from Heaven and so near to Hell.
We know them both, and the old glaciers tell
Us truths in granite. Yet we are not wise.

Only this morning I raked up some leaves
The frost knocked down, but what they might have meant—
Portents of mortality, gravely sent—
I missed to praise the colors autumn gives.

I know it's foolish for a man to read
The splendid side of death. I ought instead
To think how grim it is to curl up dead
Across a gold and green October bed—

That's the new way. I hope my ignorance
Turns out to be real wisdom at the last.
You can't know anything except the past;
Tradition sets the straightest line to sense.

The Hudson Review   *Robley Wilson, Jr.*

PORCUPINES

Sometimes in winter you see one
by the roadside, drawn to the salt
men seed their highways with, or
in the top of a tree, where it holds
hard to the bare branches and looks
like fruit too ripe to fall; or at dark,
as you climb the graveled driveway
into the farmyard, you are startled
to see its small eyes shining red.

But oftener than not you discover
only the evidence of porcupine:
One morning you open the back door
and here is the family dog, whining,
bristling black and white quills
like an old beard. You fetch pliers,
you shoulder the dog hard against
the wall of the shed, and for hours
one by one you yank the bloody spines.

Next day, making much of yourself,
you brag your humaneness to a neighbor.
He says: I hope you clipped the quills
first—when they deflate, those barbs
let go and slide out smooth as butter.
Late learning. How else to understand
the subtlety of life's simpler machines
but by trial, or error, or second-hand?
O neighbors. O dogs. O porcupines!

Poetry   *Robley Wilson, Jr.*

THE LIMITS OF EQUITATION

You've already learned *heels down*
    elbows in
and how to keep dollar bills
against the saddle with your knees.
        Your hands
float above his mane
    quiet as if you were in a chair.
But now
    heading into the fence you
learn the thing that can't be learned:
the point of take-off is *his* choice.
        You feel

him gather himself between your legs,
then tilt to rise with his wide arc
    that flies him
independent of
    your knees, or hands, or voice.

Kansas Quarterly   *Barbara Winder*

FINISTERRA

Bracelets of cold spume wreath my city ankles
as I sink into the sand of Cabo San Lucas
for one quick and dangerous moment.
Two stray mongrels run alongside me;
I fear their frolic will turn to tearing flesh.
Instead, the black beast licks my salty leg
with his pink, raspy tongue; relieved, I sear in shame.
The Sea of Cortez speaks in an unbroken dialect,
its crestline ripples like carved aventurine—
viscous shimmer of undulating power.
Gargantuan cache for bird and flower,
these monstrous pockmarked cliffs plummet upwards,
redesign the placid sky with ciphers . . .
chipped Aztecan gods left to weather.
November hours hang like pearls, lustrous and singular,
gathering their own patina as thin violet shadows
box a marmalade sun to sleep.
Beyond my grasp, the constellations of Cancer
screen in the velveteen night, close and patterned
like heavy steel medallions.
When these stone towers were fragmented grains,
I slithered on the crosscut current
idle with indecision until I stepped from this tropical
spawn, glistening and different.
The caves of Cabo housed my primal Self—
that part of me attuned to rumble and roar;
it remembers something that no longer has a name . . .
When I must concede a new beginning,
let it be later when all joy and zest have run down to
empty. Then, I will be ready to jog
with the old dogs at Finisterra . . . lick the salty leg of the
sea with my own grateful tongue.

Clues To The Second Coming   *Bayla Winters*

DELAYING TACTICS

I think about where I'd really like to be.
Europe, perhaps—Holland sweet with flowers
and witty with lace; sipping brandy
at Zermatt in a high Alpine cafe;
sailing past the Drachenfels.
Or somewhere more exotic, more remote,
Like Patagonia, finding small scaly creatures

in the rocks; Galapagos with its turtles and birds;
diving some deep green lagoon for shells;
drinking coconut milk and eating
suckling pig tenderly wrapped in leaves.
Or would it be the East, the heat,
exploring fetid rivers in a leaky junk;
discovering old temples buried deep
in jungle, shining with snakes and jewels.
Antarctica—the white, the pure long white . . .

It's no good. She knows what I'm doing.
I give in, let it happen, opening
my astonished eyes to the same old
shell-shocked bed, the familiar walls,
the slow suburban cars outside.

Poetry Canada Review   *Christopher Wiseman*

MRS. ASQUITH TRIES TO SAVE THE JACARANDAS

I tried to save those glorious jacarandas—
African trees that made a purple cathedral
out of Bush St. when they bloomed each May—
went to the city council, got up a petition
to stop mad progress from rooting out that beauty.

Wasn't it enough to destroy the orchards,
couldn't they leave a single leaf in place,
widen some other street or not widen any?
Why do they think improvement means to erase
everything that's old and not spend a penny

to preserve and conserve what loveliness we have?
I lost, of course, crouched there behind my window
hearing those buzzsaws until I thought I'd scream—
it was my body they seemed to be ripping into.
Some spirit dies with the murdering of trees.

The Wormwood Review   *Harold Witt*

SURPRISE

Surprise, surprise, they're flying in today—
Grandma, 84, who's never flown,
and Grace and Bob, to make a fleeting stay,
out of the blue instead of on a phone.
The steps are swept, some of the windows shine,
oh, but we will never be quite ready
with odes and roses and with vintage wine—
we hardly even have the proper bedding.
However, here they'll be, right at our door—
and they will smile and lie we don't look older,
and we, too, won't be able to ignore
the deeper line and the more stooping shoulder.

But come on in, sit down—the proffered cup,
and then the awful, truthful catching up.

Wind   *Harold Witt*

COLD GLOW: ICEHOUSES

Because the light this morning is recondite
like figures behind curtains a long way off,
because the morning is cold and this room is heatless,
I've gone without sleep, I brood.
The protocol of memory: the faucet dripping
into a sponge, then thinking of the way
I watched White Bear Lake freeze over
twenty years ago in Minnesota, the carp oblivious below.
I still can't understand.

I thought last night of Soloman Petrov,
a Ukrainian rabbi in my college science books
afflicted with total recall, a pathological memory
that made perspective impossible.
Once for doctors he remembered running for a train
in Petersburg in winter. They recorded
his quickened pulse, body temperature plunging.
The death by fever of his first wife Tania
was not remembered, but continually relived.

And memory is not accomplishment.
Last night again you described for me
our child pulled dead from your womb. In sleep you talked
to yourself and the child, who passed unnamed
wholly into memory. Now you wanted peace,
some distance. And every memory, said Soloman Petrov,
must proceed unchanged in the mind, going on
like smoke to designate itself again.
Like a second floor window where I stood as a boy
to watch the fishermen park their cars
on the lake, icehouse lights in the evening below.

Or our child, whose name is only ash,
is only thought too hurtful to free.
Mornings like these, he floats at the window, waiting
and mouthing his name, there through a tangent of ice,
his face and hands ashimmer.

The North American Review   *David Wojahn*

SPARROWS IN COLLEGE IVY

Not now the sun yellows the vine
and brightens the stone. No shadow
reaches and the all-shadow grows.
Above the arch and up the tower
to eaves, in and out, yelping,
with strike of wings on wings, on leaves,
on air; bursts, breaks, hurtles, dives,

possessed, insatiable, this rout
of featured frantics, berry-grabbing
at bed-time, vying and playing
and gossiping, trying hard to be heard.

Kansas Quarterly   *Edgar Wolfe*

MORNING FROM MY OFFICE WINDOW

The cock-crow clouds wave like nebulous fingers,
fingers that say, "Good morning; goodbye,"
and night-rained-mornings' green-damp descends
curtaining the lumpy mountains, the lumpy town,
and surrounds this office building and me,
a floor from the top, looking off
through green curtains like a child
behind parlor portieres,
watching wordlessly a grandmother
and her all-gone ladies waving goodby
with their teacups and egg-nut sandwiches.
I would sometimes step from behind those portieres
and be called in for petting
and compliments and the last sandwich.
And later I'd drink the sweet juice
left in the bowl of carrot salad.
But I am grown now. The ladies have floated by.
My grandmother grows smaller,
and the clouds float by.
The morning lightens, the green lifts,
and I rise to my students,
float down the halls, enter my rooms,
and they watch me and think of me,
think I am waving "Good morning; goodbye."

The Southern Review   *John A. Wood*

LEARNING TO LIVE WITHOUT YOU

If desire is absence—the wind
whipping the bare branches, torturing
the sunlight so that it trembles
at four o'clock on a winter afternoon—
then absence brought us
together, and more than loneliness
divides us. The way our lives take on
the color of a Country & Western song, that blue
haze that smothers the interminable valley
like a scarf. Or a pillow on which
you dream each night of bodies
as rivers, your lungs filling
with flesh, of breasts parting

like water. I'd like to be the woman
whose lover wanted to reach
behind her ribs and cup her heart

in his two hands. But it's just you
trying to remember the origin
of your fear, what it meant to you.
You study your wife's palm lying open
on the quilt, the bones in your daughter's face.
You think of a trip to a museum, how I found
a postcard of Leonardo's "Last Supper"
hidden in Rauschenberg's "Odalisk," or this
description of Matisse's cut-outs: "As if
the hands that shaped those birds

were wings." Our letters cross:
words close over our heads like dark
pools. You take your wife's arm
and stand with her on the porch staring
into the hard shell of night, the snow
blowing across the road, rising up
the white body of the birch, into a sky
of blank and similar stars. None of it's true.
The night sky isn't a mirror absorbing
our light, only the space for stars
to die in. We both know there are two kinds
of betrayal. Even now, I dream
of choosing.

New England Review   *Susan Wood*

GREEN GRASS AND SEA

The grass is so green that
geese should be pecking there,
and the sun shines level and
honey-gold on the riders
strolling their horses
back to the stables. It
is the suspended moment,
time singing in a bright
still rush from day
to evening. I
stand empty and
receiving, already
joyful, when the car
surges beside me
like a boat backing water.
My heart jolts at the
hit of a girl's face,
apricot in that
brightness, gold
cowling hair and great
eyes green as the sea.
The car sails on,
the instant
ends, process continues
and colours ebb from

the darkening meadows,
from my eyes.

Next day in Safeways
sheepishly I stand, a
stale loaf in my hand.
I offer my quarter.
The girl looks at me. I
drown in that
green sea.

Poetry Canada Review   *George Woodcock*

TERRITORY

In the chapel
the floor was linoleum
and the air gorgeous with beeswax.
The sisters' stalls faced the altar
and one afternoon through the window
I had seen them chant and bow in unison
toward the aisle.
The stalls,
with slab drop seats, were old wood
dull with a century of breviaries
resting lightly,
the floor dull with heavy shoes
moving softly by.

Here the nuns in secret
who never mentioned religion
came to say what else they believed,
who else, besides the sick, they loved;
to try to make sense out of the flat days
in Galveston when the salt wind didn't lift starched veils,
when God did not make himself known,
when nothing was like growing up in Ireland
in the countryside, holding piglets,
housing and hiding gypsies.

Here I came in secret,
barefooted for quiet,
to smell the beeswax,
to catch the sanctuary fire flickering unseen,
to watch the moon whiten the curves of the stalls.
Silent as the pulse pounding,
I listened for soft steps and the words:
"You do not belong here."

My fingers swiftly handled the breviaries.
I peered at the sisters' holy cards, tried each stall
expecting the trap door to hell
to drop open under my knees
for coming in moonlight,
believing in fire
for not knowing
my place.

Feminary   *Susan Wood-Thompson*

MARK VAN DOREN

(1946)

You know, he didn't *teach* me any *thing;*
the Chaucer, Edmund Spenser, Dante—wait!
I'm often etched by what he said of trimmers—
(or by what he said that Dante said of them)
that they weren't wanted, even down in hell—
but otherwise (and that's the wise he was)
he taught me not a thing that I've remembered.

Why, then, is he the uppermost in mind
when I am asked—most often by myself—
"Who was the finest teacher you have known?"
The style, the style's the trick that keeps him
    kept—
no, not a trick; it must unfold as grace,
inevitably, necessarily,
as tomcats stretch, as sparrows scrounge for lice:
in such a way he lolled upon his desk
and fell in love before our very eyes
again, again—how many times again!—
with Dante, Chaucer, Shakespeare, Milton's Satan,
as if his shameless, glad, compelling love
were all he really wanted us to learn;
no, that's not right; we were occasionals
who lucked or stumbled or were pushed on him—
he fell in love because he fell in love;
we were but windfall parties to those falls.

The Christian Century   *James Worley*

EARLY FALL: THE ADIRONDACKS

Our private foliage has unscrolled
all summer, drifted imperceptibly
as oak leaves into fall, the burnt
red edges of a need. Around
the thickest trunks, the hopeful
start their raking. They overturn
the broken stems of older,
failed seasons.
          Now, aster
and wild carrot flourish
in the deep space of the meadows
like widening clouds of stars,
and slashes of early foliage
leap at the eye from shadows
grinding out longer and longer
across the afternoon.
            How many times
have we known this, outfitted ourselves
for departure, turned within our well-
oiled parts on the slanting axis

of the season? Now I would ask,
in the chill these higher altitudes
bring out, how is it that we've come
this far? What makes us stumble
over our own hope as if over a root
split off suddenly at a switchback?
What will we do with the truth
when it finally arrives: a season,
a sculpture marching clean and finished
from the stone, a light coming steadily
through an interstellar mist?

The Malahat Review   *Carolyne Wright*

SHAVING

When his match, when his match kept missing
his pipe, I knew from my father's face,
sharp grey stubs in a cornfield reaped and dry,
he hadn't begun a beard out of an old man's right
or November whimsy, but that his hands were going.
Watching him there fumbling the light again,
I went back to another Sunday with him
when on small boy's legs I fell behind him
in the snow going to church. He came back for me
laughing, and boosted me to his chest. My cheeks
touched then two smoothnesses at once:
the velvet collar of his Lord Chesterfield
and the warm plains of his best Sunday face.

I lit his pipe and said, "Smoke that while I shave you
for Sunday." He sat on the toilet seat like
a good boy taking medicine. My fingers
touched through the lather the cleft of his chin
and the blade made pink and blue swaths
in the snowy foam, and we were done.
Pretending to test, I bent down my cheek to his
a moment, and then we went to church.

The Spoon River Quarterly   *Charles David Wright*

VIEW FROM AN INSTITUTION

(for B)

Thirty miles or so south of L. A.
stand two hangars, like two tombs
on the plain between
the freeway and the mountains,
remote dark swarms of army helicopters every hour
departing and arriving: I still
feel too sick even to think
we lived in their presence,
their shadows,
for nearly a year. Oh yes, I remember

it. And when I can't sleep
I think of huge observatories parting soundlessly,
or those two domelike structures
we passed once on the coast highway,
the nuclear reactor eerily lit and crane-manipulated all night
                              long . . .

And when I'm by myself,
this is my demented song:
welcome to the University—
it seems you're the only one registered this fall.
You'll notice our nocturnal sprinkling-system.
You'll notice the library's books are all blank on the inside.

The Virginia Quarterly Review   *Franz Wright*

VENICE

Crumbling into this world,
Into this world's sea, the green
Sea city decays.
The cats of the early evening,
Scrawny and sly,
Gloat among lengthening shadows of lions,
As the great palladian wings lean toward the water and
     slowly
Fall and fall.
The city of shifting slime ought not to be
In this world.

It ought to drift only
In the mind of someone so desperately
Sick of this world
That he dreams of himself walking
Under crystal trees,
Feeding the glass
Swans there, swans born
Not in the fragile calcium spun among feathers
But out of the horrifying fire that
A sullen laborer spins
In his frigid hands, just barely, just just barely not wringing
The swan's neck.

Poetry   *James Wright*

THE VESTAL IN THE FORUM

This morning I do not despair
For the impersonal hatred that the cold
Wind seems to feel
When it slips fingers into the flaws
Of lovely things men made,
The shoulders of a stone girl
Pitted by winter.
Not a Spring passes but the roses

Grow stronger in their support of the wind,
And now they are conquerors,
Not garlands any more,
Of this one face:
Dimming,
Clearer to me than most living faces.
The slow wind and the slow roses
Are ruining an eyebrow here, a mole there.
But in this little while
Before she is gone, her very haggardness
Amazes me. A dissolving
Stone, she seems to change from stone to something
Frail, to someone I can know, someone
I can almost name.

The Hudson Review   *James Wright*

PAIN

The dog comes home with a mouth full
of quills and lies
near her dish. Slowly,
we unravel each shaft and point, push
and pull them through
as though we were darning her mouth with pain,
that everyone might see the thread of it
there like a decoration for battle,
or that she might wear its heavy scars
as a helmet, taste it like a jaw
full of pebbles, until she learns,
until she craves its absence
the way she already craves softness, the soft
raw hamburger for dinner,
a new bed of straw tonight,
and another creature's belly forever.

The Seattle Review   *Robert Wrigley*

THE OBSERVER

He observes. He has a great black notebook
and he checks what he observes. He sees life.
He watched Sherman march through Georgia, saw
plantations burn, saw women raped. He saw
Hitler comb his hair, brush his moustache,
watched Jews huddle at Auschwitz. He saw
the slaughter at the Alamo, saw Custer shrug
"What the hell!" at Little Big Horn, watched
the bombs fall on Vietnam. He's the observer.
He does not interfere. He watches. He saw me
kiss you last night under the stars, saw us
go to mass this morning and receive communion.
He saw the Astros edge the Reds, 2-1, in twelve
innings, saw a cigaret butt start a forest fire

in California, watched the wind whip the fire's
fury over 100,000 acres of pine, and the rabbits
and the spiders and the ticks and the mosquitoes
all burned. He never tires. His great eyes
never close. He's the observer. He sees stars
collide, galaxies form from milky gas. He sees
black holes suck up light, even time itself.
He sees our own earth spinning, sees where
it came from and where it's going. He checks
his notebook: duststorms on Mars, methane
disturbances on Saturn, moons exploding near
Alpha Centauri, me eating Post's Grape-Nut Flakes
at 6 a.m. Monday morning. He has big eyes.
They never tire. He sees everything. He saw
Buddha meditate, saw Christ cry out, "My God,
my God, why hast thou forsaken me?" He sees me
searching for a path, studying the maps. He sees
you combing your long dark hair in front
of the mirror, watching yourself, feeling and
worrying about your wrinkles. Everything we do
he sees. Everything we think. We can't hide. He is
the observer. He watches. He does not interfere.

Cedar Rock   *David C. Yates*

THE DISORDERING

She only lit the closet and the bathroom—
the dark concealed what lay about the room:
the shoes, worn and cast aside, the towels
damp from drying, the clothes both clean and dirty,
tumbled in together. Even if she stumbled over

some stray item, if the pile of books beside the
bed should topple in her path, she could upright
herself and still continue. Once she had dressed,
the disorder threatened her no more. She could
fix her eyes on the paper's narrow columns for the time

it took to have her toast and juice. But then,
although she locked the door behind her, she
could not shut it in. It reappeared, its form changed,
like a man with a bag of tricks. Outside was merely
replication. Her weeds deranged the sidewalk,

and by the wall where she parked her car, trash
from passersby mounted amid the rotting leaves.
An extension of her life—like her arm held out.
Wherever she went, it went too, defiled the streets
she drove down in the morning, filled her ashtrays,

shuffled endless pink and yellow forms. Each
evening when she returned, the same disorder
greeted her. It grew more adamant and she, unable
to subdue it, became entwined with what she had
created. To lift one item, to once disturb

the chaos, would ravel both of them. Much easier to
blend into it and, gradually, to be assumed.
No longer would she seek some way to solace her.
She would lie down among the clothes, mingle
with the refuse, wait for the weeds to rise to her.

The Southern Review   *Lynda Yates*

ON A FRIEND'S SUICIDE

The day you shot yourself
a spring snowstorm surprised
the tulips in the front yard
and the robin in the maple tree
brooded.
        We sat around the table
saying it wasn't like you to do that:
you always attacked life, clawing
at it like an insatiable lover—
how could we explain the oil-soft barrel
against your temple
and your purposeful finger
squeezing?
        Like detectives
reopening a closed case,
we reconstructed your collapse,
weighed the clues, and nodded knowingly
to one another.
            In the end,
we agreed it was elementary
and went away satisfied
there were no loose ends
to dangle in our dreams.

Tar River Poetry   *Michael Yots*

UNDER THE CATALPA TREES

At first I could remove the bandages
and look at myself the way I have looked
at photographs, curious but detached.
Later, I was filled with a kind of repulsion
and guilt, the same I felt
when passing cripples on the street
and I could not look away.
They tell me I'll get used to this
strange face that I cannot recognize as me,
but that is a lie. Even in my dreams
when I stand back and watch myself
chased, caught and dismembered,
it is my old face that grimaces and screams.
But it is true about the world, how it goes
on without us, or in spite of us, and even
the pain I feared would be the end of me

brings a kind of solace to these gray,
spring mornings. It does not disappoint.
I once craved latitude, the ability to become
someone different, someone strange. Now
I must learn to accept that my prayers
were answered and fulfilled. There is no good
reason for what becomes of us, but I have discovered
no malice. We move and are moved.
Standing under the catalpa trees, watching
the heart-shaped leaves open larger
than I ever thought possible, I feel comfortable
with my new face. I am even ready
for the children, for their mimicry. Let them
have my stooped walk, my grin and sullen gestures.
Then let them change.

The New England Journal of Medicine   *Gary Young*

TO AN ESTRANGED WIFE

August, another year and the same
sour air rises from the fallen fruit.
The days are too hot without the morning
fog to cool and subdue us; we agonize
with the birds and, like them, keep moving.
I cannot trust myself in this weather.
The air suffocates and the fruit trees
bend from their trunks and seem
to melt in the heat.
I listen to the birds and can make
no sense of it. It is another burden,
something I cannot keep or hold.
I think of the cold, of December,
when the little we believe we possess seems
lost to us. Indoors, I break the seal
on the mason jars and there comes to me
everything retrievable of summer:
the tender meat of the fruit, spices and
the succulent air like steam on the window,
your body, still here, leaning gently
against the cupboard doors.

Poetry   *Gary Young*

TAUGHT TO BE POLITE

His cry was always sad.
Even as a baby, anything
could set it off: screech
of an owl, siren of
ambulance, a cloud passing
over his face. He studied
art but hoped to be
a diplomat.
He was taught to be polite.

Honest in his letters. He talked
back to his sergeant, preferred
the buxom girls. On rifle range
he hit the bull's eye
nine times out of ten.
His carbine never cooled.
He was taught to be polite.

This soldier was a patriot. Almost
as good as religion when you're
dying. All he had was twenty years
and ti-ti from the Saigon girls.
He was taught to be polite.

The guns at Dong Ha boomed
when he died. A farmer cursed
the mess his body made.

The Pikestaff Review   *Virginia Brady Young*

LATE AGAIN

It's so hard to coordinate:
one hand over your head
like a halo
the other
perpendicular
to your navel.

Nevertheless it's a universal law:
people begin soaping
at their bellies
while other worlds
turn around in their heads.

Think with your stomach,
said the happy Buddha.
But we
ruminate with our heads.

Denver Quarterly   *Gabriel Zaid*
—Translated from the Spanish
by Eliot Weinberger

AS LONG AS THE HEART BEATS

Every hand is open to another's;
every face, even an ugly one,
yearns for kisses and fire.
On every street I see
all the young men approaching.
One of them must love me.
One of them must answer.

You belong to the dream
but I belong to no one,
cutting up hearts as a surgeon does,

squeezing the breath out of myself
and closing my mind like a lock.
Someone must belong to me.
Someone must care.

There's something imbedded under everyone's skin,
and as long as the heart beats
we'll keep on answering.
We'll give ourselves over
and make way for the fire.
Someone must dream of me.
Someone must cry.

There are warm meetings in the night
when you'll tell me who you are.
There are men that will pass by
with not even a murmur.
Fireflies gathering near the window.
Someone will be waiting.
Someone knows that time can't fly.

The Moonshine Review   *Christine Zawadiwsky*

POEM ENDING WITH AN OLD CLICHÉ

("Dr. Caldwell wants to trace the other participants in the exercise, the purpose of
which was to test soldiers' reactions to a nuclear blast . . . There have been some
erroneous accounts as to the amount of radiation those men were exposed to."
                                                 —PARADE, June 19, 1977.)

Last week my old cat fell to the worms;
I watched the clouds come down into his eyes,
The final twitch and turn of his muscles
Like the pinnae of a clipped fern,
Constricting in sadness, clutching in to ease
The final cravings, then the fearful resignation.
Seeing this, I can say the old cliché now,
Knowing at long last what it means:
Life is precious. It is all we have.

How was I to know, through all my long
And short years, that two decades beyond
The flash and ram of those explosions,
The vaporized towers and mangled animals,
Caved-in trenches and awesome dawn clouds,
I might finally bear secrets?

In whatever dimness and despair,
In the midst of terrible exchanges
From down on my knees in fear
Of early death, senility or loss;
Even in happiness it cannot be forgotten—
I will say it again. It has become the truth:
Life is precious.

Porch   *Paul Zimmer*

DRIVING NORTH FROM SAVANNAH ON MY BIRTHDAY

Surely most signs pass me by unnoticed;
Not the squares and octagons of the road,
But twirls of scud, magic rings of fungi,
Marks that tree limbs scribble
On the sky, subtle dances of insects,
Veerings of flocks of birds,
Things that form and point to me—
Signs that might have shown me
How to live the rest of my life.

Forty-four years old today.
I think, too, of the minutes I have lived.
Twenty-two million yellow butterflies
Migrating south, sailing and turning,
Tying intricate knots over the road.
I wipe them out by the thousands,
Driving my car hard north
Against their fragile yearnings.

Porch   *Paul Zimmer*

LILLY'S SONG

I hold my daughter up to the fire-
light: tiny blossom, perfect snail
whose heart blooms
in her like springtime, opening
and opening. The morsels of her cry
bend us in, saying *I, I,*
I'm arrived! and we curl around her
like fingers, weaving lullabies.
All the world's
hers now, her nest warm as desire
while her father croons over her:
My lover, he sings,
My lover, childbride.

Poetry   *Evan Zimroth*

WALLACE STEVENS GIVES A READING

("The unconscionable treachery of fate."—Le Monocle de Mon Oncle)

I saw his back
walk down the aisle
toward the platform
at the Y, the 92nd Street Y.
His back—broad, wide, enormous,
even monstrous: a monstrous back.

I do not remember his voice.
I do not remember his words—
Just his back:

a back that was large enough,
bulky enough, huge enough to carry
a supreme fiction,

a fiction that did not need the back;
a fiction that lasted longer than the back—
such tink and tank and tunk-a-tunk-tunk.

The Centennial Review   *Harriet Zinnes*

LOVE SONG

For love one must risk
everything (it has been said
before)—one must risk everything:
one's faith, one's hope, one's
sanity, one's pride, one's very
life, one's fate—as the
poet must sometimes (you will
not buy this comparison) get
out of bed and begin
to write the poem down,
or it is lost forever.
Everything for love! And if
one loses in that desperate
country, there is always the
shocking slime of life, the
grave earth beneath one's feet!
Or one can take the
fact of one's feet, and
continue to search for love,
unless one is so old
one cannot walk. Either way,
one must die for love.

Partisan Review   *Bob Zmuda*

BEACHHEAD PREACHMENT

from this beach i want to make a poem
into a stage presence
with some sex in it,
with some oo-wee-baby and trembling thighs,
with some tongue dancing in & out,
with some oo-la-la in it.

from this beach
a nightful of orgasms my audience
gives back to me,
a nightful of putting our hands and hearts together,
a nightful of surf giving me some head,
as my short leg strokes the gypsy waves
and i move thru a forest of desire.

i want to leave my sperm-seed radioactive
as i work some music thru a people

like uranium,
as my calypso testifies
and my zydeco shouts rock and roll bump
to the rhythm of the sea.

i would be preacherman hallelujah lover
challenging the seaweed wig that life wears
between her bowed legs;
i would be a hot sunday afternoon healer
jazzing sho nuf gospel blues
from this beachhead
(i want to praise the lawd
with this nude muse).

from this beach
let my voice be an echo lubricating the horizon,
let seagulls know my poem
that they might carry the word
in the sails of their wings.

Open Places   *Ahmos Zu-Bolton*

POND

In such a place
my father taught
me how to fish,
though to this day
I have never
touched a worm.

I'd look deep into the can,
poke it with a stick,
and watch in horror
how like fingers
worms can be.

I'd try to think of fishes' toes
sleeping beneath the waves,
or the gnarled grunts
of bullfrogs pouting
up more air in their chins.

Something in me
always grew lumps,
and the mind would divide
in the senses until each
was silent as a potato.

Nothing helped.
Those who have no eyes
molested every dream
the soul tried to close up,
and the tallest thing about me

would get up on all fours,
hear the willow weeds

whistle what the wind knows
when the bones
speak for themselves.

The Black Warrior Review   *Fredrick Zydek*

PA

When we got home, there was our Old Man
hanging just by his hands from the windmill vane,
forty feet off the ground, his pants down,
inside out, caught on his shoes—he never wore
underwear in summer—shirt tail flapping,
hair flying.

My brother grabbed a board.
We lugged it up the windmill and ran it out
like a diving board under The Old Man's feet
and wedged our end below a crossbar. The Old Man
kept explaining, "I climbed up to oil a squeak,
reached out to push the vane around, slipped, damn
puff of wind, I swung right out."

We felt strange helping him down.
In our whole lives, we never really held him before,
and now with his pants tangled around his feet
and him talking faster, getting hoarser all the way
down, explaining, explaining.

On solid ground, he quivered, pulling up his pants.
I said, "Good thing we came when we did." His eyes
burned from way back. His hands
were like little black claws. He spit Copenhagen
and words almost together: "Could have hung on
a long time yet. Anyway, you should have been home
half an hour ago."

Plainsong   *Leo Dangel*

CANCER PATIENT

Fire and sword cavort in her aging body,
and storm is having a lark in her wearied mind.
She is less, she is loss.
How could her own keep watch? She is entrusted
to other care.
The nurses find a grief in her wasting flesh,
but charts reveal a small surprise of comfort:
peace can invest calamities of pain.

Power is not said to peer above these ruins;
suffering with One who suffered hides its worth.
No one ascribes to her
an influence or faintest likelihood
of the apt plea or the transforming word,
and yet

I saw a river stopped by her lifted hand,
a tide turned back, a stubborn mountain moved.
I saw a history altered, wrenched to the light
by pain, pain.
After her war, I visualize her spoils
in a new springtime gathered, meadows of grace
miraculously given
to her loved, her lost, to all who come to her feast
in this faithless time.

Commonweal   *Jessica Powers*

VIGNETTE: 1922

On the cool porch of "Wannamasset"
Grandpa turned with the tides, black
As a beetle in his threadbare habit,
More than our darkness at his back,

And like a *girasol en deuil,* glared down
On the shove, the shout, the sheer of ocean
Or toward the empty moors, the white town,
The steeple—and death, an alien notion.

Then, with his major's cane pacing our dance,
"Hop, *fröschen!*" he urged as each stood mute.
He left but a few sullen tokens to chance:
A sword, a tin watch, a rumpled black suit—

Left with his gold eyes tarnished by sun
And his bearded marine chaps uptilted west;
As the tide ran out the long mackerel run,
He tucked a shrewd hand in his miser's vest.

Yankee   *Lawrence P. Spingarn*

Index of Titles

Index of First Lines

Books of Poetry by Contributors

This bibliography is included as an aid for those who wish to locate additional poetry by authors whose work appears in the Anthology. Most of the information was supplied directly by the authors.

A

Aal, Katharyn Machan: *Bird On A Wire.* Privately printed, 1970.
   —*The Wind In The Pear Tree.* Privately printed, 1972.
   —*The Book Of The Raccoon.* Gehry Press, 1977.
   —*Looking For The Witches.* The Fine-Arts Bluesband & Poetry Press, 1980.
   —*Where The Foxes Say Good-Night.* Scarlet Ibis Press, 1981.
AI: *Cruelty.* Houghton Mifflin Co., 1973.
   —*Killing Floor.* Houghton Mifflin Co., 1979.
Aliesan, Jody: *Soul Claiming.* Mulch Press, 1975.
   —*as if it will matter.* Seal Press, 1978.
Applewhite, James: *Statues In The Grass.* University of Georgia Press, 1975.
   —*Following Gravity.* University Press of Virginia, 1981.
Armand, Octavio: *Horizonte No Es Siempre Lejania.* Las Americas Pub. Co. (New York), 1970.
   —*Entre Testigos.* Graficas Urex (Spain), 1974.
   —*Piel Menos Mia.* Escolios (Los Angeles), 1976.
   —*Cosas Pasan.* Monte Avila Editores (Venezuela), 1977.
   —*Como Escribir Con Erizo.* Asociacion de escritores (Mexico), 1979.
   —*Biografia Para Feacios.* Editorial Pre-Textos (Spain), 1980.
Astor, Susan: *Dame.* University of Georgia Press, 1980.
Atwood, Margaret: *The Circle Game.* Contact Press, 1966; Anansi, 1967.
   —*The Animals In That Country.* Oxford, 1968.
   —*The Journals Of Susanna Moodie.* Oxford, 1970.
   —*Procedures For Underground.* Oxford, 1970.
   —*Power Politics.* Anansi, 1971.
   —*You Are Happy.* Oxford, 1974.
   —*Selected Poems.* Oxford, 1976.
   —*Two-Headed Poems.* Oxford, 1978.
Awad, Joseph: *The Neon Distances.* Golden Quill Press, 1980.

B

Baker, David: *Looking Ahead.* Mid-America Press, 1975.
   —*Rivers In The Sea.* Mid-America Press, 1977.
   —*Virga.* Owl Creek Press, 1981.

Balakian, Peter: *Father Fisheye.* Sheep Meadow Press, 1980.
Balazs, Mary: *The Voice Of Thy Brother's Blood.* Dawn Valley Press, 1976.
   —*The Stones Refuse Their Peace.* Seven Woods Press, 1979.
Barnes, Jim: *The Fish On Poteau Mountain.* Cedar Creek Press, 1980.
   —*This Crazy Land.* Inland Boat Series/Porch Publications, 1980.
   —*The American Book Of The Dead.* University of Illinois Press, 1982.
Bartlett, Elizabeth: *Poems Of Yes And No.* Editorial Jus (Mexico), 1952.
   —*Behold This Dreamer.* Editorial Jus (Mexico), 1959.
   —*Poetry Concerto.* Sparrow Poetry Series, 1961.
   —*It Takes Practice Not To Die.* Van Riper & Thompson, 1964.
   —*Threads.* Unicorn Press, 1968.
   —*Twelve-Tone Poems.* Sun Press, 1968.
   —*Selected Poems.* Carrefour Books, 1970.
   —*The House Of Sleep.* Autograph Editions, 1975.
   —*Dialogue Of Dust.* Autograph Editions, 1977.
   —*In Search Of Identity.* Autograph Editions, 1977.
   —*A Zodiac Of Poems.* Autograph Editions, 1979.
   —*Address In Time.* Dufour Editions, 1979.
   —*Memory Is No Stranger.* Ohio University Press, 1981.
Barton, David: *Notes From The Exile.* Elysian Press, 1980.
   —*Surviving The Cold.* Quarterly Review of Literature, 1981.
Beeler, Janet N.: *How To Walk On Water.* Cleveland State University Poetry Center, 1973.
   —*Dowry.* University of Missouri Press, 1978.
Bell, Marvin: *Things We Dreamt We Died For.* Stone Wall Press, 1966.
   —*A Probable Volume Of Dreams.* Atheneum Publishers, 1969.
   —*The Escape Into You.* Atheneum Publishers, 1971.
   —*Residue Of Song.* Atheneum Publishers, 1974.
   —*Stars Which See, Stars Which Do Not See.* Atheneum Publishers, 1977.
   —*These Green-Going-To-Yellow.* Atheneum Publishers, 1981.

Bennett, Bruce: *Coyote Pays A Call.* Bits Press, 1980.
Berkson, Lee: *Away From Home.* Spoon River Poetry Press, 1980.
Berry, D. C.: *Saigon Cemetery.* University of Georgia Press, 1972.
　—Jawbone. Thunder City Press, 1978.
Beyer, Richard G.: *The Homely Muse.* Pinpoint Press, 1973.
Billings, Robert: *blue negatives.* Fiddlehead Poetry Books, 1977.
　—The Elizabeth Trinities. Penumbra Press, 1980.
Black, Charles: *Telescopes And Islands.* Alan Swallow Press, 1963 (no2 in reprint by A.M.S. Press).
　—Owls Bay In Babylon. Dustbooks, 1980.
Bloch, Chana: *The Secrets Of The Tribe.* Sheep Meadow Press, 1980.
Bloom, Barbara: *The Myths Do Not Tell Us.* Blackwells Press, 1978.
Blumenthal, Michael: *Sympathetic Magic.* Water Mark Press, 1980.
Borenstein, Emily: *Woman Chopping.* Timberline Press, 1978.
　—Cancer Queen. Barlenmir House Publishers, 1979.
　—Finding My Face. Thunder City Press, 1979.
　—Night Of The Broken Glass. Timberline Press, 1981.
Borson, Roo: *Landfall.* Fiddlehead Poetry Books, 1977.
　—In The Smoky Light Of The Fields. Three Trees Press, 1980.
　—Rain. Penumbra Press, 1980.
Bottoms, David: *Jamming With The Band At The VFW.* Burnt Hickory Press, 1978.
　—Shooting Rats At The Bibb County Dump. William Morrow & Co., 1980.
Bouvard, Marguerite Guzman: *Journeys Over Water.* Quarterly Review of Literature, forthcoming.
Bowie, William C.: *Before The Statue Of A Laughing Man.* Veiled Horn Press, 1981.
Bradley, Sam: *Men In Good Measure,* Golden Quill Press, 1966.
　—Alexander And One World. South and West, Inc., 1967.
　—manspell/godspell. Routledge, 1975.
Brashers, Charles: *Whattaya Mean, "Get Out O' That Dirty Hole"; I LIVE Here!* Helix House, 1974.
Brasier, Virginia: *The Reflective Rib.* Pasadena Press, 1955.
　—The Survival Of The Unicorn. Creative Press, 1961.
　—The Sand Watcher. Golden Quill Press, 1974.
Braude, Michael: *Who's Zoo (A Bestiary).* Andre Deutsch (London), 1967.
　—Question Of Identity. Lieber-Atherton, 1975.
　—The Fishtiary. East Hampton Historical Society, 1979.
　—Village Vignettes. Street Press, 1980.
Brett, Peter: *Ghost Rhythms.* Blue Cloud Press, 1977.
　—Gallery. University of Virginia Press, 1977.
　—Borrowing The Sky. Kastle Press, 1978.
Brewster, Elizabeth: *East Coast.* Ryerson Press, 1951.
　—Lillooet. Ryerson Press, 1954.
　—Roads. Ryerson Press, 1957.
　—Passage Of Summer. Ryerson Press, 1969.

　—Sunrise North. Clarke, Irwin, 1972.
　—In Search Of Eros. Clarke, Irwin, 1974.
　—Sometimes I Think Of Moving. Oberon Press, 1977.
Brodsky, Louis Daniel: *Trilogy: A Birth Cycle.* Farmington Press, 1974.
　—Monday's Child. Farmington Press, 1975.
　—The Kingdom Of Gewgaw, Farmington Press, 1976.
　—Point Of Americas II. Farmington Press, 1976.
　—Preparing For Incarnations. Farmington Press, 1976.
　—La Preciosa. Farmington Press, 1977.
　—Stranded In The Land Of Transients. Farmington Press, 1978.
　—The Uncelebrated Ceremony Of Pants Factory Fatso. Farmington Press, 1978.
　—Resume Of A Scrapegoat. Farmington Press, 1980.
　—Birds In Passage. Farmington Press, 1980.
Brosman, Catharine Savage: *Watering.* University of Georgia Press, 1972.
Broughton, T. Alan: *Adam's Dream.* Northeast/Juniper Press, 1975.
　—In The Face Of Descent. Carnegie-Mellon University Press, 1975.
　—The Others We Are. Northeast/Juniper Press, 1979.
　—The Man On The Man. Barlenmir House, Publishers, 1979.
　—Far From Home. Carnegie-Mellon University Press, 1979.
Bruchac, Joseph: *Entering Onondaga.* Cold Mountain Press, 1978.
　—There Are No Trees Inside The Prison. Blackberry Press, 1978.
　—The Good Message Of Handsome Lake. Unicorn Press, 1978.
　—Ancestry & Other Poems. Great Raven Press, 1980.
Bukowski, Charles: *Flower, Fist And Bestial Wail.* Hearse Press, 1960.
　—Poems And Drawings. Epos Press, 1962.
　—Longshot Poems For Broke Players. 7 Poets Press, 1962.
　—Run With The Hunted. Midwest Poetry Chapbooks, 1962.
　—It Catches My Heart In Its Hands. Loujon Press, 1963.
　—Crucifix In A Deathland. Loujon Press, 1965.
　—Cold Dogs In The Courtyard. Literary Times, 1965.
　—The Genius Of The Crowd. 7 Flowers Press, 1966.
　—All The Assholes In The World And Mine. Open Skull Press, 1966.
　—At Terror Street And Agony Way. Black Sparrow Press, 1968.
　—Poems Written Before Jumping Out Of An 8 Story Window. Litmus, 1968.
　—The Days Run Away Like Wild Horses Over The Hills. Black Sparrow Press, 1969.
　—Fire Station. Capra Press, 1970.

—*Mockingbird Wish Me Luck.* Black Sparrow Press, 1972.

—*Me And Your Sometimes Love Poems.* King Press, 1972.

—*Burning In Water, Drowning In Flame.* 1974.

—*Scarlet.* Black Sparrow Press, 1976.

—*Love Is A Dog From Hell.* Black Sparrow Press, 1977.

—*Play The Piano Drunk Like A Percussion Instrument Until The Fingers Begin To bleed A Bit.* Black Sparrow Press, 1979.

Bullis, Jerald: *Taking Up The Serpent.* Ithaca House, 1973.

—*Adorning The Buckhorn Helmet.* Ithaca House, 1976.

—*Orion: A Poem.* Jackpine Press, 1976.

—*Inland.* Editions Generation (France), 1978.

Burke, Daniel: *Diptych.* Half Penny Press, 1978.

Bursk, Christopher: *Standing Watch.* Houghton Mifflin Co., 1978.

C

Carson, E. J.: *Scenes.* Porcupine's Quill, 1978.

Carter, Jared: *Early Warning.* Barnwood Press, 1979.

—*Work, For The Night Is Coming.* Macmillan Co., 1981.

Cassity, Turner: *Watchboy, What Of The Night?* Wesleyan University Press, 1966.

—*Steeplejacks In Babel.* David R. Godine Press, 1973.

—*Yellow For Peril, Black For Beautiful.* George Braziller, Inc., 1975.

—*The Defense Of The Sugar Islands.* Symposium Press, 1979.

Casto, Robert Clayton: *A Strange And Fitful Land.* Six Marks Press, 1959.

—*The Arrivals.* Studio Press, 1980.

Cedering, Siv (the following books were published under the name of Siv Cedering Fox): *Letters From The Island.* Fiddlehead Poetry Books, 1973.

—*Cup Of Cold Water.* New Rivers Press, 1973.

—*Letters From Helge.* New Rivers Press, 1974.

—*Mother Is.* Stein & Day, 1975.

—*How To Eat A Fortune Cookie.* New Rivers Press, 1976.

—*The Juggler.* Sagarin Press, 1977.

—*Color Poems.* Calliopea Press, 1978.

—*The Blue Horse.* Houghton Mifflin/Clarion Books, 1979.

Chadwick, Jerah: *The Country Of Water.* Seal Press, 1980.

Chandonnet, Ann: *Incunabula.* Quixote Press, 1968.

—*The Wife & Other Poems.* Adams Press, 1977.

—*The Wife: Part 2.* Adams Press, 1979.

—*At The Fruit-Tree's Mossy Root.* Wings Press, 1980.

—*Ptarmigan Valley (Poems Of Alaska).* The Lightning Tree, 1980.

Citino, David: *Last Rites And Other Poems.* Ohio State University Press, 1980.

Clark, Duane: *To Catch The Sun.* Scopecraeft Press, 1977.

Clewell, David: *Room To Breathe.* Pentagram Press,

1977.

—*The Blood Knows To Keep Moving.* Chowder Review, 1979.

Colby, Joan: *XI Poems.* Interim Books, 1972.

—*Beheading The Children.* Ommatiou Press, 1977.

—*Blue Woman Dancing In The Nerve.* Alembic Press, 1979.

—*Dream Tree.* Jump River Press, 1980.

Coleman, Wanda: *Art In The Court Of The Blue Fag.* Black Sparrow Press, 1977.

—*Mad Dog Black Lady.* Black Sparrow Press, 1979.

—*Alcatraz, An Assemblage.* Alcatraz Press, 1979.

Cook, R. L.: *Hebrides Overture And Other Poems.* Plewlands Press (Great Britain), 1948.

—*Within The Tavern Caught.* Hands and Flower Press (Great Britain), 1952.

—*Sometimes A Word.* Plewlands Press (Great Britain), 1963.

—*Time With A Drooping Hand.* Lomond Press (Great Britain), 1978.

Cooper, Allan: *Blood-Lines.* Fiddlehead Poetry Books, 1979.

Cooper, Jane: *The Weather Of Six Mornings.* Macmillan Co., 1969.

—*Maps & Windows.* Macmillan/Collier Books, 1974.

—*Threads: Rosa Luxemburg From Prison.* Flamingo Press, 1979.

Cosier, Tony: *With The Sun And The Moon.* Privately printed, 1979.

Coursen, H. R.: *Storm In April.* Arco Pub. Co., 1970.

—*Lookout Point.* Samisdat Press, 1972.

—*Survivor.* Ktaaon Poetry Press, 1972.

—*Inside The Piano Bench.* Samisdat Press, 1975.

—*Fears Of The Night.* Samisdat Press, 1976.

—*Walking Away.* Samisdat Press, 1978.

—*Hope Farm: New And Selected Poems.* Cider Mill Press, 1980.

Crawford, Tom: *I Want To Say Listen.* Ironwood Press, 1980.

Curtis, Tony: *Album.* Christopher Davies Ltd. (Wales), 1974.

—*The Deerslayers.* Cwm Nedd Press (Wales), 1978.

—*Preparations.* Gomer Press (Wales), 1980.

D

Dacey, Philip: *Four Nudes.* Morgan Press, 1971.

—*How I Escaped From The Labyrinth And Other Poems.* Carnegie-Mellon University Press, 1977.

—*The Condom Poems.* Ox Head Press, 1979.

—*Men At Table.* Chowder Chapbooks, 1979.

—*The Boy Under The Bed.* Johns Hopkins University Press, 1981.

—*Gerard Manley Hopkins Meets Walt Whitman In Heaven And Other Poems.* Penmaen Press, 1981.

Daigon, Ruth: *Learning Not To Kill You.* Selkirk Press, 1975.

—*On My Side Of The Bed.* Omnation Press, 1979.

Daniels, Jim: *Factory Poems.* Jack-in-the-Box Press, 1979.

Davis, Lloyd: *Fishing The Lower Jackson.* Best Cellar Press, 1974.

Davis, William Virgil: *One Way To Reconstruct The Scene.* Yale University Press, 1980.

Dawe, Gerald: *Sheltering Places.* Blackstaff Press (N. Ireland), 1978.

Dayton, David: *The Lost Body Of Childhood.* Copper Beech Press, 1979.

Deal, Susan Strayer: *No Moving Parts.* Ahsahta Press, 1980.

Dean, John: *Restless Wanderers.* University of Salzburg Press (Austria), 1979.
—*Foreign: Poems & Short Stories.* Handshake Press, 1980.

De Bolt, William Walter: *Mist From The Earth.* Candor Press, 1969.
—*Bricks Without Straw.* Candor Press, 1971.
—*Second Spring.* Candor Press, 1976.
—*Forty Sonnets.* Candor Press, 1979.
—*Buds And Blossoms.* Candor Press, 1980.

deVries, Rachel: *An Arc Of Light.* Wild Goose Press, 1978.

Di Cicco, Pier Giorgio: *We Are The Light Turning.* Thunder City Press, 1976.
—*The Sad Facts.* Fiddlehead Poetry Books, 1977.
—*The Circular Dark.* Borealis Press, 1977.
—*Dancing In The House Of Cards.* Three Trees Press, 1977.
—*A Burning Patience.* Borealis Press, 1978.
—*Dolce-Amaro.* Papavero Press, 1978.
—*The Tough Romance.* McClelland and Stewart, 1979.
—*A Straw Hat For Everything.* Angelstone Press, 1980.
—*Reason For Humaneness.* Intermedia Press, 1980.

Dickson, John: *Victoria Hotel.* Chicago Review Press, 1979.

di Michele, Mary: *Tree Of August.* Three Trees Press, 1978.
—*Bread And Chocolate.* Oberon Press, 1980.
—*Vicarious Lives.* Mosaic Press, 1981.

Doriot, Jeanne: *Diving After Flame.* Indiana University, 1978.

Douglas, Gilean: *Now The Green Word.* Wings Press, 1952.
—*Poetic Plush.* Story Book Press, 1953.
—*River For My Sidewalk,* J. M. Dent & Sons, 1953.
—*The Pattern Set.* Quality Press, 1954.
—*Seascape With Figures.* Prairie Press, 1967.
—*Now In This Night.* Harlo Press, 1973.
—*The Protected Place.* Gray's Publishing, 1979.
—*Silence Is My Homeland.* Stackpole Books, 1979.

Driscoll, Jack: *The Language Of Bone.* Spring Valley Press, 1980.

Dunn, Stephen: *Looking For Holes In The Ceiling.* University of Massachusetts Press, 1974.
—*Full Of Lust And Good Usage.* Carnegie-Mellon University Press, 1976.
—*A Circus Of Needs.* Carnegie-Mellon University Press, 1978.

E

Eaton, Charles Edward: *The Bright Plain.* University of North Carolina Press, 1942.
—*The Shadow Of The Swimmer.* Fine Editions Press, 1951.
—*The Greenhouse In The Garden.* Twayne Publishers, 1955.
—*Countermoves.* Abelard-Schuman, 1962.
—*On The Edge Of The Knife.* Abelard-Schuman, 1970.
—*The Man In The Green Chair.* A. S. Barnes & Co., 1977.
—*Colophon Of The Rover.* A. S. Barnes & Co., 1980.

Ehrhart, W. D.: *The Awkward Silence.* Northwoods Press, 1980.
—*The Samisdat Poems.* Samisdat Press, 1980.

Ellenbogen, George: *Winds Of Unreason.* Contact Press, 1957.
—*The Night Unstones.* Identity Press, 1971.

Eng, Steve: *Yellow Rider And Other Fancies.* Eidolon Press, 1981.

Engels, John: *The Homer Mitchell Place.* University of Pittsburgh Press, 1968.
—*Signals From The Safety Coffin.* University of Pittsburgh Press, 1975.
—*Blood Mountain.* University of Pittsburgh Press, 1977.
—*Vivaldi In Early Fall.* University of Georgia Press, 1981.

Engle, John D., Jr.: *Modern Odyssey.* Golden Quill Press, 1971.
—*Laugh Lightly.* Golden Quill Press, 1974.
—*Sea Songs.* Branden Press, 1977.
—*Spiritually Speaking.* Engle's Angle, 1979.
—*Cycle Of Beauty.* Engle's Angle, 1980.

F

Farber, Norma: *The Hatch.* Charles Scribner's Sons, 1955.
—*Look To the Rose.* Fandel, 1958.
—*A Desperate Thing.* Plowshare Press, 1973.
—*Household Poems.* Hellric Publications, 1975.
—*Something Further.* Kylix Press, 1979.
—*Never Say Ugh! To A Bug.* Greenwillow Books, 1979.
—*How The Hibernators Came To Bethlehem.* Walker & Co., 1980.

Farrar, Winifred Hamrick: *Another Fountain.* Privately printed, 1940.
—*Thru Our Guns.* Privately printed, 1945.
—*Rumshinsky's Hat.* Thomas Yoseloff, Inc., 1964.
—*Cry Life.* South & West, Inc., 1968.
—*The Seeking Spirit.* South & West, Inc., 1974.

Feirstein, Frederick: *Survivors.* Ultramarine Press, 1977.
—*Manhattan Carnival.* Countryman Press, 1981.

Feldman, Ruth: *The Ambition Of Ghosts.* Green River Press, 1979.

Fialkowski, Barbara: *Framing.* Croissant & Co., 1978.

Fishman, Charles: *Aurora.* Tree Books, 1974.
—*Warm-Blooded Animals.* Juniper Press, 1977.
—*Mortal Companions.* Pleasure Dome Press, 1977.
—*The Werewolf's Polonaise.* Northwoods Press (forthcoming).

Flanner, Hildegarde: *The Hearkening Eye.* Ahsahta Press, 1979.

Ford, R. A. D.: *A Window On The North.* Ryerson Press, 1956.

—*The Solitary City.* McClelland and Stewart, Ltd., 1969.
—*Holes In Space.* Hounslow Press, 1979.
Friman, Alice: *A Question Of Innocence.* Raintree Press, 1978.
—*Song To My Sister.* Writers' Center Press, 1979.
Funkhouser, Erica: *Natural Affinities.* Dark Horse Press, 1980.

G

Gallagher, Tess: *Instructions To The Double.* Graywolf Press, 1976.
—*Under Stars.* Graywolf Press, 1978.
Galler, David: *Walls And Distances.* Macmillan Co., 1959.
—*Leopards In The Temple.* Macmillan Co., 1968.
—*Third Poems: 1965-1978.* Quarterly Review of Literature Books, 1979.
Gegna, Suzanne: *A Phoenix Story.* Privately printed, 1980.
George, Emery: *Mountainwild.* Kylix Press, 1974.
—*Black Jesus.* Kylix Press, 1974.
—*A Gift Of Nerve: Poems 1966-1977.* Kylix Press, 1978.
—*Kate's Death: A Book Of Odes.* Ardis Publishers, 1980.
Ghigna, Charles: *Plastic Tears.* Dorrance & Co., 1973.
—*Stables.* Creekwood Press, 1975.
—*Divers And Other Poems.* Creekwood Press, 1978.
Ghiselin, Brewster: *Against The Circle.* E. P. Dutton & Co., 1946.
—*The Nets.* E. P. Dutton & Co., 1955.
—*Country Of The Minotaur.* University of Utah Press, 1970.
—*Light.* Abattoir Editions/Fine Arts Press, 1978.
—*Windrose: Poems 1929-1980.* University of Utah Press, 1980.
Gibbons, Reginald: *Roofs Voices Roads.* Quarterly Review of Literature, 1979.
Gilbert, Celia: *Queen Of Darkness.* Viking Press, 1977.
Gilbert, Sandra M.: *In The Fourth World.* Alabama University Press, 1979.
Glaser, Michael S.: *Marmalade.* Seasonings Press, 1976.
Glass, Malcolm: *Bone Love.* University Presses of Florida, 1978.
Goldensohn, Barry: *Saint Versus Eve.* Cummington Press, 1971.
—*Uncarving The Block.* Vermont Crossroads Press, 1978.
Goldensohn, Lorrie: *Dreamwork.* Porch Publications, 1980.
—*The Tether.* L'Epervier Press, 1981.
Goldstein, Roberta B.: *The Searching Season.* Queen City Press, 1961.
—*Fling Jeweled Pebbles.* Golden Quill Press, 1963.
—*Selections From The Searching Season.* Centro Studi e Scambi Internazionali (Rome), 1964.
—*The Wood Burns Red.* Golden Quill Press, 1966.
—*Cry Before Dawn.* Golden Quill Press, 1974.
Gom, Leona: *Kindling.* Fiddlehead Poetry Books, 1972.
—*The Singletree.* Sono Nis Press, 1975.
—*North.* League of Canadian Poets, 1980.

—*Land Of The Peace.* Thistledown Press, 1980.
Gordon, Don: *Statement.* Bruce Humphries, Inc., 1943.
—*Civilian Poems.* Beechhurst Press, 1946.
—*Displaced Persons.* Alan Swallow, 1958.
—*On The Ward.* West Coast Poetry Review, 1977.
—*Excavations.* West Coast Poetry Review, 1980.
Goren, Judith: *Coming Alive.* Stone Press, 1975.
Gottlieb, Darcy: *No Witness But Ourselves.* University of Missouri Press, 1973.
—*Matters Of Contention.* Aesopus Press, 1979.
Greenberg, Barbara L.: *The Spoils Of August.* Wesleyan University Press, 1974.
Greger, Debora: *Movable Islands.* Princeton University Press, 1980.
Grossman, Richard: *Tycoon Boy.* Kayak Press, 1977.
Grutzmacher, Harold M.: *A Giant Of My World.* Golden Quill Press, 1960.
Gunn, Thom: *Fighting Terms.* Fantasy Press, 1954.
—*The Sense Of Movement.* Faber & Faber, 1957.
—*My Sad Captains.* Farrar, Straus & Giroux, Inc., 1961.
—*Touch.* Faber & Faber, 1967.
—*Moly.* Farrar, Straus & Giroux, Inc., 1971.
—*Jack Straw's Castle.* Farrar, Straus & Giroux, Inc., 1976.
—*Selected Poems.* Farrar, Straus & Giroux, Inc., 1979.
Gustafson, Ralph: *Selected Poems.* McClelland and Stewart, Ltd., 1972.
—*Fire On Stone.* McClelland and Stewart, Ltd., 1974.
—*Corners In The Glass.* McClelland and Stewart, Ltd., 1977.
—*Soviet Poems.* Turnstone Press, 1978.
—*Gradations Of Grandeur.* Sono Nis Press, 1979.
—*Sequences.* Black Moss Press, 1979.
—*Landscape With Rain.* McClelland and Stewart, Ltd., 1980.

H

Haley, Vanessa: *Horse Latitudes.* Coraddi Publications, 1980.
Hall, Joan Joffe: *The Rift Zone.* Curbstone Press, 1978.
—*The Aerialist's Fall.* Ziesing Bros., 1980.
Hall, Walter: *The Spider Poems.* Perishable Press, 1967.
—*The Music Threat.* Trask House Books, 1971.
—*Glowing In The Dark.* Burning Deck Press, 1972.
—*Performance.* Beethoven Press, 1974.
—*Vestiges.* Diana's Bimonthly Chapbook Series, 1975.
—*Miners Getting Off The Graveyard.* Burning Deck Press, 1978.
Halpern, Daniel: *Traveling On Credit.* Viking Press, 1972.
—*Street Fire.* Viking Press, 1975.
—*Life Among Others.* Viking/Penguin, 1978.
Hamill, Sam: *Petroglyphs.* Three Rivers Press, 1975.
—*The Calling Across Forever.* Copper Canyon Press, 1976.
—*The Book Of Elegiac Geography.* Bookstore Press, 1978.

I

Editions, 1979.
—*Conversations.* Survivors' Manual Books, 1980.
Inez, Colette: *The Woman Who Loved Worms.* Doubleday & Co., 1972.
—*Alive And Taking Names.* Ohio University Press, 1977.

J

Jackson, William (Haywood): *An Act Of God.* Samisdat Press, 1979.
—*Fellow Travelers.* Samisdat Press, 1981.
Janowitz, Phyllis: *Rites Of Strangers.* University Press Of Virginia, 1978.
Jason, Philip K.: *Thawing Out.* Dryad Press, 1979.
Jensen, Laura: *After I Have Voted.* Gemini Press, 1972.
—*Anxiety And Ashes.* Penumbra Press, 1976.
—*Bad Boats.* Ecco Press, 1977.
—*Tapwater.* Graywolf Press, 1978.
Jerome, Judson: *Light In The West.* Golden Quill Press, 1962.
—*The Ocean's Warning To The Skin Diver And Other Love Poems.* Crown Point Press, 1964.
—*Serenade.* Crown Point Press, 1968.
—*Plays For An Imaginary Theater* (verse drama). University of Illinois Press, 1970.
—*The Village And Other Poems.* Trunk Press, 1976.
—*Public Domain.* Trunk Press, 1977.
—*Thirty Years Of Poetry, 1949-1979.* Cedar Rock Press, 1979.
Johnson, Michael L.: *Dry Season.* Cottonwood Review Press, 1977.
—*The Unicorn Captured.* Cottonwood Review Press, 1980.
Johnston, Gordon: *Inscription Rock.* Penumbra Press, 1980.
Jones, Robert: *Before The Last Goodnight.* Pocket Canyon Press, 1981.
Juergensen, Hans: *I Feed You From My Cup.* Quinnipiac College Press, 1958.
—*In Need For Names.* Linden Press, 1960.
—*Existential Canon.* South And West, Inc., 1965.
—*Florida Montage.* South and West, Inc., 1966.
—*Sermons From The Ammunition Hatch Of The Ship Of Fools.* Vagabond Press, 1968.
—*from the divide.* Olivant Press, 1970.
—*Hebraic Modes.* Olivant Press, 1972.
—*Journey Toward The Roots.* Valkyrie Press, 1976.
—*The Autobiography Of A Pretender.* Olivant Press, 1977.
—*California Frescoes.* American Studies Press, 1980.

K

Katz, Menke: *Land Of Manna.* Windfall Press, 1965.
—*Rockrose.* Smith Horizon Press, 1970.
—*Burning Village.* Smith Horizon Press, 1972.
—*Two Friends* (with Harry Smith). Smith Horizon Press, 1981.
Kearney, Lawrence: *Kingdom Come.* Wesleyan University Press, 1980.

Kennedy, X. J.: *Nude Descending A Staircase.* Doubleday & Co., 1961.
—*Growing Into Love.* Doubleday & Co., 1969.
—*Bulsh.* Burning Deck, 1970.
—*Breaking And Entering.* Oxford University Press, 1971.
—*Emily Dickinson In Southern California.* David R. Godine Press, 1974.
—*Celebrations After The Death Of John Brennan.* Penmaen Press, 1974.
—*Three Tenors, One Vehicle: A Book Of Songs* (with James E. Camp and Keith Waldrop). Open Places, 1975.
—*One Winter Night In August And Other Nonsense Jingles.* Atheneum Publishers, 1975.
—*The Phantom Ice Cream Man: More Nonsense Verse.* Atheneum Publishers, 1979.
—*Did Adam Name The Vinegarroon?* David R. Godine Press, 1981.
Kenyon, Jane—*From Room To Room.* Alice James Books, 1978.
Kinnick, B. Joe: *Time Is The Stream.* Golden Quill Press, 1961.
—*Miss Honky, The Black Flamingo And The Blue Guitar.* Wuerth Letter Shop, 1973.
—*Crying For Guyana.* Graphics Design, 1980.
Klappert, Peter: *Lugging Vegetables To Nantucket.* Yale University Press, 1971.
—*Circular Stairs, Distress In The Mirrors.* Griffin Press, 1975.
—*Non Sequitur O'Connor.* Bits Press, 1977.
—*The Idiot Princess Of The Last Dynasty: The Apocryphal Monologues Of The Doctor Matthew O'Connor.* Alfred A. Knopf, Inc., 1981.
Klauck, D. L.: *Everything Else . . .* King Publications, 1976.
—*Blood And Ashes.* Thunder's Mouth Press, 1981.
Knoll, Michael A.: *The Woman At The End Of The Mattress.* Broken Wisker Studio, 1981.
Koertge, Ronald: *The Father Poems.* Sumac Press, 1973.
—*12 Photographs Of Yellowstone.* Red Hills Press, 1976.
—*Sex Object.* Little Caesar Press, 1979.
—*Diary Cows.* Little Caesar Press, 1981.
Koethe, John: *Blue Vents.* Audit/Poetry, 1969.
—*Domes.* Columbia University Press, 1973.
—*A Long Lesson.* Bouwerie Editions, 1974.
Kooser, Ted: *Official Entry Blank.* University of Nebraska Press, 1969.
—*Grass County.* Windflower Press, 1971.
—*Twenty Poems.* Best Cellar Press, 1973.
—*A Local Habitation & A Name.* Solo Press, 1974.
—*Not Coming To Be Barked At.* Pentagram Press, 1976.
—*Old Marriage And New.* Cold Mountain Press, 1978.
—*Cottonwood County* (with William Kloefkorn). Windflower Press, 1979.
—*Sure Signs: New And Selected Poems.* University of Pittsburgh Press, 1980.
Kowit, Steve: *Climbing The Walls.* Proexistence Press, 1977.

—Last Will. Farpotshket Press, 1979.
Kroll, Ernest: *Cape Horn And Other Poems.* E. P. Dutton & Co., 1952.
  —The Pauses Of The Eye. E. P. Dutton & Co., 1955.
  —Fifty "Fraxioms." Cummington Press, 1973.
  —Fifteen "Fraxioms." Putah Creek Press, 1978.
Kumin, Maxine: *Halfway.* Holt, Rinehart & Winston, Inc., 1961.
  —The Privilege. Harper & Row, Publishers, 1965.
  —The Nightmare Factory. Harper & Row, Publishers, 1970.
  —Up Country. Harper & Row, Publishers, 1972.
  —House, Bridge, Fountain, Gate. Viking Press, 1975.
  —The Retrieval System. Viking Press, 1978.
Kunitz, Stanley: *Intellectual Things.* 1930.
  —Passport To The War. 1944.
  —Selected Poems, 1928-1958. 1958.
  —The Testing-Tree. 1971.
  —The Poems Of Stanley Kunitz, 1928-1978. Atlantic Monthly Press, 1979.

L

Lake, Paul: *Bull Dancing.* New Poets Series, 1977.
Langland, Joseph: *The Green Town.* Charles Scribner's Sons, 1956.
  —The Wheel Of Summer. Dial Press, 1963; ppk., Blue Triangle Press, 1973, 1979.
  —An Interview And Fourteen Poems. Gob Books (Clark Univ.), 1973.
  —The Sacrifice Poems. North American Review Press, 1975.
  —In The Shell Of The Ear. M. R. "Signature," 1977.
  —Any Body's Song. Doubleday & Co., 1980.
Langton, Daniel J.: *Querencia.* University of Missouri Press, 1976.
Lawn, Beverly: *Throat Of Feathers.* Pleasure Dome Press, 1979.
Leary, Paris: *Views Of The Oxford Colleges.* Charles Scribner's Sons, 1960.
  —The Snake At Safron Walden. Carcanet Press (England), 1973.
Lechlitner, Ruth: *Tomorrow's Phoenix.* Ronald Lane Latimer, 1937.
  —Only The Years. The Press of James A. Decker, 1944.
  —The Shadow On The Hour. Prairie Press, 1956.
  —A Changing Season: Selected And New Poems, 1962-1972. Branden Press, 1973.
Le Dressay, Anne: *This Body That I Live In.* Turnstone Press, 1979.
LeFevre, Adam: *Everything All At Once.* Wesleyan University Press, 1978.
Lehman, David: *Some Nerve.* Columbia Review Press, 1973.
  —Day One. Nobodaddy Press, 1979.
Leiper, Esther M.: *Christmas Colt & Other Poems.* Cookeville Press, 1974.
Levine, Ellen: *Notes On The Pumpkin.* Lynx House Press, 1979.
Lieberman, Laurence: *The Unblinding.* Macmillan Co., 1968.

—The Osprey Suicides. Macmillan Co., 1973.
—God's Measurements. Macmillan Co., 1980.
Livesay, Dorothy: *Green Pitcher,* 1928.
  —Signpost, 1932.
  —Day & Night, 1944.
  —Selected Poems, 1957.
  —The Unquiet Bed, 1967.
  —The Documentaries, 1968.
  —The Two Seasons, 1972.
  —Ice Age, 1975.
  —The Woman I Am, 1978.
Logan, William: *Dream Of Dying.* Graywolf Press, 1980.
  —Sad-Faced Men. David R. Godine Press, 1981.
Long, Robert: *Getting Out Of Town.* Street Press, 1979.
  —What It Is. Street Press, 1981.
Loyd, Marianne: *Across The Water.* Tamarack Press, 1981.
Lucas, Henry N.: *My Rhythm Flows From Ah Diff'rent Beat.* King Publications, 1975.
  —Silent Screams. Printing Express (pending).
Ludvigson (Bartels), Susan: *Step Carefully In Night Grass.* John F. Blair, Publisher, 1974.
  —The Wisconsin Women. Porch Publications, 1980.
  —Northern Lights. Louisiana State University Press, 1981.

M

Mandel, Charlotte: *A Disc Of Clear Water.* Saturday Press, 1981.
Mangan, Kathy: *Ragged Alphabet.* Rook Press, 1978.
Matthews, William: *Ruining The New Road.* Random House, Inc., 1970.
  —Sleek For The Long Flight. Random House, Inc., 1972.
  —Sticks & Stones. Pentagram Press, 1975.
  —Rising And Falling. Atlantic/Little, Brown & Co., 1979.
Matthias, John: *Bucyrus.* Swallow Press, 1970.
  —Turns. Swallow Press, 1975.
  —Crossing. Swallow Press, 1979.
  —Bathory & Lermontov. Kalejdoskop (Sweden), 1980.
Maura, Sister: *Initiate The Heart.* Macmillan Co., 1946.
  —The Word Is Love. Macmillan Co., 1958.
  —Bell Sound And Vintage. Contemporary Poetry, 1966.
  —Walking On Water. Paulist, 1972.
  —What We Women Know. Sparrow Press, 1980.
  —A Word, A Tree: Christmas Poems. Franciscan Graphics, 1980.
Mayo, E. L.: *The Diver.* University of Minnesota Press, 1947.
  —The Center Is Everywhere. Twayne Publishers, 1954.
  —Summer Unbound. University of Minnesota Press, 1958.
  —Selected Poems. Prairie Press, 1973.
McAfee, Thomas: *Poems And Stories.* University of Missouri Press, 1960.
  —I'll Be Home Late Tonight. University of Missouri Press, 1967.

—The Body And The Body's Guest: New And Selected Poems. BkMk Press, 1975.
—Time Now. Raindust Press, 1977.
—The Tempo Changes. The Lights Go Up. The Partners Change. Singing Wind Press, 1978.
McAleavey, David: *Sterling 403.* Ithaca House, 1971.
—The Forty Days. Ithaca House, 1975.
—Shrine, Shelter, Cave. Ithaca House, 1980.
McClane, Kenneth A.: *Out Beyond The Bay,* Ithaca House, 1975.
—Moons And Low Times. Ithaca House, 1978.
—At Winter's End. Emerson Hall, 1981.
McCurdy, Harold Grier: *A Straw Flute.* Meredith College, 1946.
—The Chastening Of Narcissus. John F. Blair, Publisher, 1970.
—And Then The Sky Turned Blue. Briarpatch Press, 1980.
McFarland, Ron: *Certain Women.* Confluence Press, 1977.
—Eight Idaho Poets. University Press of Idaho, 1979.
McKeown, Tom: *Alewife Summer.* Road .Runner Press, 1967.
—Last Thoughts. Abraxas Press, 1969.
—The Winds Of The Calendar. Road Runner Press, 1969.
—Drunk All Afternoon. Abraxas Press, 1969.
—The Milk Of The Wolf. Asari Press, 1970.
—The Cloud Keeper. Seafront Press (Dublin, Ireland), 1972.
—The Luminous Revolver. Sumac Press, 1973.
—Driving To New Mexico. Sunstone Press, 1974.
—The House Of Water. Basilisk Press, 1974.
—Maya Dreams. Wisconsin Review Press, 1977.
—Certain Minutes. Scopecraeft Press, 1978.
Meiners, R. K.: *Journeying Back To The World.* University of Missouri Press, 1975.
Meissner, William: *Learning To Breathe Underwater.* Ohio University Press, 1979.
Merrill, James: *Water Street.* Atheneum Publishers, 1962.
—Nights & Days. Atheneum Publishers, 1966.
—Fire Screen. Atheneum Publishers, 1969.
—Country Of A Thousand Years Of Peace. Atheneum Publishers, 1970.
—Braving The Elements. Atheneum Publishers, 1972.
—The Yellow Pages. Templebar, 1974.
—The Diblos Notebook. Atheneum Publishers, 1975.
—Divine Comedies. Atheneum Publishers, 1976.
—Mirabell: Books Of Number. Atheneum Publishers, 1979.
—Scripts For The Pageant. Atheneum Publishers, 1980.
Metz, Roberta: *Private Parts.* Omnation Press, 1978.
—Women the Children the Men. Laughing Bear Press, 1979.
Miller, Jim W.: *Copperhead Cane.* Robert Moore Allen, Publisher, 1964.
—The More Things Change The More They Stay The Same. Whippoorwill Press, 1971.
—Dialogue With A Dead Man. Georgia University

Press, 1974; Green River Press, 1978.
—The Mountains Have Come Closer. Appalachian Consortium Press, 1980.
Mills, Ralph J., Jr.: *Door To The Sun.* Baleen Press, 1974.
—Night Road/Poems. Rook Press, 1978.
—Living With Distance. Boa Editions, 1979.
—With No Answer. Juniper Books, 1980.
Minty, Judith: *Lake Songs And Other Fears.* University of Pittsburgh Press, 1974.
—Yellow Dog Journal. Center Publications Sumac Poetry Series, 1979.
—Letters To My Daughters. Mayapple Press, 1980.
Miranda, Gary: *The Seed That Dies.* Kedros Press (Greece), 1973.
—Listeners At The Breathing Place. Princeton University Press, 1979.
Moffi, Larry: *10 Poems 10.* Stanboy Press, 1976.
—Homing In. Ridge Road Press, 1977.
Moore, James: *The New Body.* University of Pittsburgh Press, 1975.
—What The Bird Sees. Momentum Press, 1978.
Moorman, Charles: *Epiphanies At Lux.* Texas Review Press, 1980.
Morgan, Frederick: *A Book Of Change.* Hudson Review Publications, 1972.
—Poems Of The Two Worlds. University of Illinois Press, 1977.
—The Tarot Of Cornelius Agrippa. Sagarin Press, 1978.
—Death Mother And Other Poems. University of Illinois Press, 1979.
Mozeson, Isaac: *The Watcher.* Downtown Poets, 1980.
Murphy, George E., Jr.: *Bicycle & Other Gifts.* Wampeter Press, 1976.
—Encounters. Wampeter Press, 1977.
—Teddy: A Christmas Story. Bear Essential Books, 1977.
Murray, Les: *The Ilex Tree.* Australian National University Press, 1965.
—The Weatherboard Cathedral. Angus & Robertson (Australia), 1969.
—Poems Against Economics. Angus & Robertson (Australia), 1972.
—Lunch And Counter Lunch. Angus & Robertson (Australia), 1974.
—Selected Poems: The Vernacular Republic. Angus & Robertson (Australia), 1976.
—Ethnic Radio. Angus & Robertson (Australia), 1977.
—The Boys Who Stole The Funeral. Angus & Robertson (Australia), 1980.
Myers, Jack: *Black Sun Abraxas.* Halcyone Press, 1970.
—Will It Burn. Falcon Publishing Co., 1974.
—The Family War. L'Epervier Press, 1977.
—I'm Amazed That You're Still Singing. L'Epervier Press, 1981.

N

Nathan, Leonard: *Western Reaches.* Talisman Press, 1958.
—Glad And Sorry Seasons. Random House, Inc., 1963.

—The Matchmaker's Lament And Other Astonishments. Gehenna Press, 1967.
—The Day The Perfect Speakers Left. Wesleyan University Press, 1969.
—Flight Plan. Cedar Hill Press, 1971.
—Without Wishing. Thorp Springs Press, 1973.
—Returning Your Call. Princeton University Press, 1975.
—Coup And Other Poems. Windflower Press, 1975.
—The Likeness: Poems Out Of India. Thorp Springs Press, 1975
—The Teachings Of Grandfather Fox. Ithaca House, 1976.
—Lost Distance. Chowder Chapbooks, 1978.
—Dear Blood. University of Pittsburgh Press, 1980.
Newman, P. B.: *The Cheetah And The Fountain.* South and West, Inc., 1968.
—Dust Of The Sun. South and West, Inc., 1969.
—The Ladder Of Love. Smith-Horizon Press, 1971.
—Paula. Dragon's Teeth Press, 1975.
—The House On The Saco. William L. Baughan Publishers, 1978.
North, Susan: *All That Is Left.* Desert First Works, 1976.
Nye, Naomi Shihab: *Tattooed Feet* (under name of Shihab). Texas Portfolio Press, 1977.
—Eye-To-Eye (under name of Shihab). Texas Portfolio Press, 1978.
—Different Ways To Pray. Breitenbush Books, 1980.
Nelson, Stanley: *Idlewild.* The Smith, 1970.
—The Brooklyn Book Of The Dead. The Smith, 1971.
—Chirico Eyes. Midnight Sun, 1976.
—The Travels Of Ben Sira. The Smith, 1978.
—101 Fragments Of A Prayer. Midnight Sun, 1979.

O

Oates, Joyce Carol: *Anonymous Sins & Other Poems.* Louisiana State University Press, 1969.
—Love And Its Derangements. Louisiana State University Press, 1970.
—Angel Fire. Louisiana State University Press, 1973.
—Dreaming America And Other Poems. Aloe Editions, 1973.
—The Fabulous Beasts. Louisiana State University Press, 1975.
—Season Of Peril. Black Sparrow Press, 1977.
—Women Whose Lives Are Food, Men Whose Lives Are Money. Louisiana State University Press, 1978.
Oldknow, Antony: *Lost Allegory.* North Dakota State University Press, 1966.
—In The Neon-Center Of The Street. Scopecraeft Press, 1967.
—Positive Poems For Twentieth-Century Anglo-Saxons. Scopecraeft Press, 1968.
—Tomcats And Tigertails. Poetry North Publications, 1968.
—Verses For The Beast. Scopecraeft Press, 1971.
—Sonnets By Oldknow. Scopecraeft Press, 1972.
—Anthem For Rusty Saw And Blue Sky. Territorial Press, 1975.

—Consolation For Beggars. Song Press, 1978.
—More Sonnets By Oldknow. Scopecraeft Press, 1979.
Olds, Sharon: *Satan Says.* University of Pittsburgh Press, 1980.
Olson, Elder: *Thing Of Sorrow.* Macmillan Co., 1934.
—The Cock Of Heaven. Macmillan Co., 1940.
—The Scarecrow Christ. Noonday, 1954.
—Plays & Poems. University of Chicago Press, 1958.
—Collected Poems. University of Chicago Press, 1963.
—Olson's Penny Arcade. University of Chicago Press, 1975.
Orlen, Steve: *Sleeping On Doors.* Penumbra Press, 1976.
—Separate Creatures. Ironwood Press, 1977.
—Permission To Speak. Wesleyan University Press, 1978.
Owen, Sue: *Nursery Rhymes For The Dead.* Ithaca House, 1980.
Ower, John: *Legendary Acts.* University of Georgia Press, 1977.

P

Pacernick, Gary: *Credence.* Professor H. Quinn Press, 1975.
Page, Geoff: *Two Poets.* University of Queensland Press (Australia), 1971.
—Smalltown Memorials. University of Queensland Press, 1975.
—Collecting The Weather. Makar Press, 1978.
—Cassandra Paddocks. Angus and Robertson, 1980.
Page, William: *Clutch Plates.* Branden Press, 1976.
Pass, John: *Taking Place.* Talonbooks, 1971.
—The Kenojuak Prints. Caledonia Writing Series, 1973.
—Air 18. Airbooks, 1973.
—Port Of Entry. Repository Press, 1975.
—Love's Confidence. Caledonia Writing Series, 1976.
—Blossom: An Accompaniment. Cobblestone Press, 1978.
—There Go The Cars. Sesame Press, 1979.
Pastan, Linda: *A Perfect Circle Of Sun.* Swallow Press, 1971.
—Aspects Of Eve. Liveright, 1975.
—The Five Stages Of Grief. W. W. Norton & Co., 1978.
—Setting The Table. Dryad Press, 1980.
—Even As We Sleep. Croissant Press, 1980.
—Waiting For My Life. W. W. Norton & Co., 1981.
Paterson, Evangeline: *The Sky Is Deep Enough.* Starglow Press (Scotland), 1972.
—Eighteen Poems. Outposts Unlimited (England), 1974.
—Whitelight. Mid-Day Publications (England), 1978.
Paulin, Tom: *A State Of Justice.* Faber & Faber, Inc., 1977.
—The Strange Museum. Faber & Faber, Inc., 1980.
Peacock, Molly: *And Live Apart.* University of Missouri Press, 1980.

Pennington, Lee: *Scenes From A Southern Road.* JRD Pub. Co., 1969.
  —*Wildflower: Poems For Joy.* Poetry Prevue Publications, 1970.
  —*April Poems.* Poetry Prevue Publications, 1971.
  —*Songs Of Bloody Harlan.* Westburg Associates, 1975.
  —*Spring Of Violets.* Love Street Books, 1976.
  —*I Knew A Woman.* Love Street Books, 1977.
Peskett, William: *The Nightowl's Dissection.* Secker & Warburg (England), 1975.
  —*Survivors.* Secker & Warburg (England), 1980.
Petrie, Paul: *Confessions Of A Non-Conformist.* Hillside Press, 1963.
  —*The Race With Time And The Devil.* Golden Quill Press, 1965.
  —*From Under The Hill Of Night.* Vanderbilt University Press, 1969.
  —*The Academy Of Goodbye.* University Press of New England, 1974.
  —*Light From The Furnace Rising.* Copper Beech Press, 1978.
  —*Time Songs.* Biscuit City Press, 1979.
Phillips, Robert: *Inner Weather.* Golden Quill Press, 1966.
  —*The Pregnant Man.* Doubleday & Co., 1978.
  —*Running On Empty.* Doubleday & Co., 1981.
Piercy, Marge: *Breaking Camp.* Wesleyan University Press, 1968.
  —*Hard Loving.* Wesleyan University Press, 1969.
  —*To Be Of Use.* Doubleday & Co., 1973.
  —*Living In The Open.* Alfred A. Knopf, Inc., 1976.
  —*The Twelve-Spoked Wheel Flashing.* Alfred A. Knopf, Inc., 1978.
  —*The Moon Is Always Female.* Alfred A. Knopf, Inc., 1980.
Pinsky, Robert: *Sadness And Happiness.* Princeton University Press, 1975.
  —*An Explanation Of America.* Princeton University Press, 1980.
Plumly, Stanley: *In The Outer Dark.* Louisiana State University Press, 1970.
  —*Giraffe.* Louisiana State University Press, 1973.
  —*How The Plains Indians Got Horses.* Best Cellar Press, 1973.
  —*Out-Of-The-Body Travel.* Ecco Press, 1977.
Pollitt, Katha: first book of poems will be published in Fall of 1981 by Alfred A. Knopf, Inc.
Polson, Don: *Wakening.* Fiddlehead Poetry Books, 1971.
  —*Brief Evening In A Catholic Hospital.* Fiddlehead Poetry Books, 1972.
  —*In Praise Of Young Thieves.* Alive Press, 1975.
  —*Lone Travellers.* Fiddlehead Poetry Books, 1979.
Powers, Jessica: *The Lantern Burns.* Monastine Press, 1939.
  —*The Place of Splendor.* Cosmopolitan Science & Art Service, 1946.
  —*The Little Alphabet.* Bruce Publishing Co., 1955.
  —*Mountain Sparrow.* Carmel of Reno, 1972.
Privett, Katharine: *The Poet People.* San Marcos Press, 1976.

R

Raffel, Burton: *Mia Poems.* October House, 1968.
  —*Four Humours.* Writers Workshop, 1979.
Ray, David: *X-Rays, A Book Of Poems.* Cornell University Press, 1965.
  —*Dragging The Main And Other Poems.* Cornell University Press, 1968.
  —*A Hill In Oklahoma.* BkMk Press, 1972.
  —*Gathering Firewood: New And Selected Poems.* Wesleyan University Press, 1974.
  —*Enough Of Flying: Poems Inspired By The Ghazals Of Ghalib.* Writers Workshop (India), 1977.
  —*The Tramp's Cup.* Chariton Review Press, 1978.
Ray, Judy: *Pebble Rings.* Greenfield Review Press, 1980.
Redgrove, Peter: *The Collector & Other Poems.* RKP, 1960.
  —*The Nature Of Cold Weather & Other Poems.* RKP, 1961.
  —*At The White Monument & Other Poems.* RKP, 1963.
  —*The Force & Other Poems.* RKP, 1966.
  —*Dr. Faust's Sea-Spiral Spirit And Other Poems.* RKP, 1972.
  —*Sons Of My Skin: Selected Poems 1954-74.* RKP, 1975.
  —*From Every Chink Of The Ark And Ditto.* RKP, 1977.
  —*The Weddings At Nether Powers And Other New Poems.* RKP, 1979.
  —*The Apple Broadcast And Other New Poems.* RKP, 1981.
Reid, Robert F., III: *Angels In The Mirror.* Kenmore Press, 1981.
Reiss, James: *The Breathers.* Ecco Press, 1974.
Rigsbee, David: *Stamping Ground.* Ardis Publishers, 1976.
  —*To Be Here.* Coraddi, 1980.
Rinaldi, Nicholas: *The Resurrection Of The Snails.* John F. Blair, Publisher, 1977.
  —*We Have Lost Our Fathers.* University Presses of Florida, 1981.
Rivers, J. W.: *From The Chicago Notebook.* Spoon River Poetry Press, 1979.
Robbins, Martin: *A Refrain Of Roses.* Alan Swallow, 1965.
  —*A Reply To The Headlines.* Swallow Press, 1970.
  —*A Week Like Summer And Other Poems Of Love And Family.* X Press, 1979.
Robbins, Richard: *Toward New Weather.* University of Montana, 1979.
Root, Judith: *Little Mysteries.* Stone Press, 1974.
Root, William Pitt: *The Storm And Other Poems.* Atheneum Publishers, 1969.
  —*Striking The Dark Air For Music.* Atheneum Publishers, 1973.
  —*A Journey South.* Graywolf Press, 1977.
  —*Coot And Other Characters.* Confluence Press, 1977.
  —*7 Mendocino Songs.* Mississippi Mud Press, 1977.
  —*Reasons For Going It On Foot.* Atheneum Publishers, 1981.
  —*Fireclock.* Four Zoas Press, 1981.

—In The World's Common Grasses. Moving Parts Press, 1981.

Rose, Wendy: *Hopi Roadrunner Dancing.* Greenfield Review Press, 1973.

—Long Division: A Tribal History. Strawberry Press, 1976.

—Academic Squaw: Reports To The World From The Ivory Tower. Blue Cloud Press, 1977.

—Poetry Of The American Indian, Part 2: Wendy Rose. American Visual Communications Bank, 1978.

—Builder Kachina: A Home-going Cycle. Blue Cloud Press, 1979.

—Lost Copper. Malki Museum Press, 1980.

—What Happened When The Hope Hit New York. Contact II Press, 1981.

Rubin, Larry: *The World's Old Way.* University of Nebraska Press, 1963.

—Lanced In Light. Harcourt, Brace & World, 1967.

—All My Mirrors Lie. David R. Godine Press, 1975.

Ruffin, Paul: *Lighting The Furnace Pilot.* Spoon River Poetry Press, 1980

S

Sarton, May: *Collected Poems: 1972.* W. W. Norton & Co.

—Selected Poems. W. W. Norton & Co., 1978.

—Halfway To Silence. W. W. Norton & Co., 1980.

Scarbrough, George: *Tellico Blue.* E. P. Dutton & Co., 1949.

—The Course Is Upward. E. P. Dutton & Co., 1951.

—Summer So-Called. E. P. Dutton & Co., 1956.

—George Scarbrough: New And Selected Poems. Iris Press, 1978.

Schevill, James: *Tensions.* Bern Porter, 1947.

—The Stalingrad Elegies. Alan Swallow, 1964.

—Release. Hellcoal Press, 1968.

—Violence & Glory: Poems 1962-1968. Swallow Press, 1969.

—The Buddhist Car & Other Characters. Swallow Press, 1973.

—Pursuing Elegy: A Poem About Haiti. Copper Beech Press, 1974.

—The Mayan Poems. Copper Beech Press, 1978.

—Fire Of Eyes: A Guatamalan Sequence. Copper Beech Press, 1979.

—The American Fantasies: Collected Poems 1945-1980. Swallow Press, 1981.

Schiff, Jeff: *Anywhere In This Country.* Mammoth Press, 1980.

Schorb, E. M.: *The Poor Boy And Other Poems.* Dragon's Teeth Press, 1975.

Schramm, D. G. H.: *Silences, Bones And Angled Rain.* Tipografia Hispana (Colombia), 1974.

Schultz, Philip: *Like Wings.* Viking/Penguin, 1978.

Seager, Ralph W.: *Songs From A Willow Whistle.* Wake-Brook House, 1956.

—Beyond The Green Gate. Wake-Brook House, 1958.

—Christmas Chimes In Rhyme. Judson Press, 1962.

—Cup, Flagon And Fountain. Wake-Brook House, 1965.

—A Choice Of Dreams. Partridge Press, 1970.

—Wheatfields & Vineyards. Christian Herald House, 1975.

—The Manger House And Other Christmas Poems (reprint of *Christmas Chimes In Rhyme).* Judson Press, 1977.

Shelton, Richard: *Journal Of Return.* Kayak Press, 1969.

—The Tattooed Desert. University of Pittsburgh Press, 1971.

—Calendar. Baleen Press, 1972.

—The Heroes Of Our Time. Best Cellar Press, 1972.

—Of All The Dirty Words. University of Pittsburgh Press, 1972.

—Among The Stones. Monument Press, 1973.

—You Can't Have Everything. University of Pittsburgh Press, 1975.

—Chosen Place. Best Cellar Press, 1975.

—The Bus To Veracruz. University of Pittsburgh Press, 1978.

Sher, Steven: *Nickelodeon.* Seagull Publications, 1978.

—Persnickety. Seven Woods Press, 1980.

—Caught In The Revolving Door. Love Street Books, 1980.

Siegel, Robert: *The Beasts & The Elders.* University Press of New England, 1973.

—In A Pig's Eye. University Presses of Florida, 1980.

Simmons, James: *Late But In Earnest.* Bodley Head (England), 1967.

—In The Wilderness. Bodley Head (England), 1969.

—Energy To Burn. Bodley Head (England), 1971.

—The Long Summer Still To Come. Blackstaff Press (N. Ireland), 1973.

—West Strand Visions. Blackstaff Press (N. Ireland), 1974.

—Judy Garland And The Cold War. Blackstaff Press (N. Ireland), 1976.

—The Selected James Simmons. Blackstaff Press (N. Ireland), 1978.

—Constantly Singing. Blackstaff Press (N. Ireland), 1980.

Simpson, Louis: *The Arrivistes: Poems 1940-49.* Fine Editions Press, 1949.

—Good News Of Death And Other Poems. Charles Scribner's Sons, 1955.

—A Dream Of Governors. Wesleyan University Press, 1959.

—At The End Of The Open Road. Wesleyan University Press, 1963.

—Selected Poems. Harcourt, Brace & World, 1965.

—Adventures Of The Letter I. Harper & Row, Publishers, 1971.

—Searching For The Ox. William Morrow & Co., 1976.

—Caviare At The Funeral. Franklin Watts, Inc., 1980.

Skinner, Douglas Reid: *Dreams From A World Place.* Tideline Press, 1979.

—Reassembling World. David Philip (Cape Town; London), 1980.

Sloan, Bill: *Ghost Images.* Hard Cider Press, 1980.

—Portraits Drawn From Memory. Hard Cider Press, 1980.

Sloate, Daniel: *Words In Miniature & Other Words.* Les Editions Maisonneuve, 1972.

Smith, Douglas: *Thaw*. Four Humours Press, 1977.
—*Scarecrow*. Turnstone Press, 1980.
—*The Light Of Our Bones: A Sequence For Lawrence*. Turnstone Press, 1980.
Smith, R. T.: *Waking Under Snow*. Cold Mountain Review Press, 1975.
—*Good Water*. Banjo Press, 1979.
—*Rural Route*. Tamarack Press, 1981.
Smith, Stephen E.: *The Bushnell Hamp Poems*. Green River Press, 1980.
Stafford, William: *Braided Apart*. Confluence Press, 1976.
—*Stories That Could Be True: New And Collected Poems*. Harper & Row, Publishers, 1977.
—*Smoke's Way*. Graywolf Press, 1978.
—*Things That Happen Where There Aren't Any People*. BOA Editions, 1980.
Standing, Sue: *Amphibious Weather*. Zephyr Press, 1981.
Stanford, Ann: *In Narrow Bound*. Alan Swallow, 1943.
—*The White Bird*. Alan Swallow, 1949.
—*Magellan: A Poem To Be Read By Several Voices*. Talisman Press, 1958.
—*The Weathercock*. Viking Press, 1966.
—*The Descent: Poems*. Viking Press, 1970.
—*Climbing Up To Light: Eleven Poems*. Magpie Press, 1973.
—*In Mediterranean Air*. Viking Press, 1977.
Steele, Timothy: *Uncertainties And Rest*. Louisiana State University Press, 1979.
Stern, Gerald: *Rejoicings*. Fiddlehead Poetry Books, 1973.
—*Lucky Life*. Houghton Mifflin Co., 1977.
—*The Red Coal*. Houghton Mifflin Co., 1981.
Stewart, Robert: *Taking Leave*. Raindust Press, 1977.
Stineford, Raymond: *Pattern And Voice*. American Weave Press, 1968.
Stone, John: *The Smell Of Matches*. Rutgers University Press, 1972.
—*In All This Rain*. Louisiana State University Press, 1980.
Strahan, Bradley R.: *Love Songs For An Age Of Anxiety*. Black Buzzard Press, 1981.
Stuart, Dabney: *The Diving Bell*. Alfred A. Knopf, Inc., 1966.
—*A Particular Place*. Alfred A. Knopf, Inc., 1969.
—*The Other Hand*. Louisiana State University Press, 1974.
—*Round And Round*. Louisiana State University Press, 1977.
Sussman, M. L.: *Light And Shady: A Collection Of Limericks*. Wings Press, 1980.
Sutter, Barton: *Cedarhome*. Boa Editions, 1977.
Swann, Brian: *The Whale's Scars*. New Rivers Press, 1974.
—*Roots*. New Rivers Press, 1976.
—*Living Time*. Quarterly Review of Literature Books, 1978.
Swenson, Karen: *An Attic Of Ideas*. Doubleday & Co., 1974.
—*East-West*. Confluence Press, 1980.
Sze, Arthur: *The Willow Wind*. Rainbow Zenith Press, 1972.

T

Tagliabue, John: *Poems*. Harper and Brothers, 1950.
—*A Japanese Journal*. Kayak Press, 1966.
—*The Buddha Uproar*. Kayak Press, 1970.
—*The Doorless Door*. Mushinsha/Grossman, 1970.
Thomas, D. M.: *Two Voices*. Viking Press, 1968.
—*Logan Stone*. Viking Press, 1971.
—*Love And Other Deaths*. Elek (England), 1975.
—*The Honeymoon Voyage*. Secker (England), 1978.
Thurston, Harry: *Barefaced Stone*. Fiddlehead Poetry Books, 1980.
Tifft, Ellen: *A Door In The Wall*. Hors Commerce Press, 1966, 1968.
—*The Kissed Cold Kite*. Hors Commerce Press, 1968.
—*The Live-Long Day*. Charas Press, 1972.
Tomkiw, Lydia: *Obsessions*. MOD Press, 1979.
—*Popgun Sonatas*. MOD Press, 1980.
Traxler, Patricia: *Blood Calendar*. William Morrow & Co., 1975.
Tremblay, Gail: *Night Gives Woman The Word*. F Limited Gallery, 1978.
Turco, Lewis: *First Poems*. Golden Quill Press, 1960.
—*The Sketches*. American Weave Press, 1962.
—*Awaken, Bells Falling: Poems 1959-1967*. University of Missouri Press, 1968.
—*The Inhabitant*. Despa Press, 1970.
—*Pocoaneglini: A Fantography & Other Poems*. Despa Press, 1971.
—*The Weed Garden*. Peaceweed Press, 1973.
—*A Cage Of Creatures*. Banjo Press, 1978.
—*The Compleat Melancholik*. Bieler Press, 1981.

U

Unger, Barbara: *Basement: Poems 1959-1961*. Isthmus Press, 1975.
—*The Man Who Burned Money*. Bellevue Press, 1980.
Urdang, Constance: *Charades And Celebrations*. October House, 1965.
—*The Picnic In The Cemetery*. George Braziller, Inc., 1975.
—*The Lone Woman And Others*. University of Pittsburgh Press, 1980.

V

Van Brunt, H. L.: *Uncertainties*. The Smith Publishers, 1968.
—*Indian Territory And Other Poems*. The Smith Publishers, 1974.
—*Feral: Crow-Breath & Caw*. Conspiracy Press, 1976.
—*For Luck: Poems 1962-1977*. Carnegie-Mellon University Press, 1978.
—*And The Man Who Was Traveling Never Got Home*. Carnegie-Mellon University Press, 1980.
Viereck, Peter: *The Persimmon Tree: New Lyrics & Pastorals*. Xerox University Microfilms, 1965 (reprint).
—*Terror & Decorum*. Greenwood Press, 1972 (reprint).

—Strike Through The Mask: New Lyrical Poems. Greenwood Press (reprint).
—The First Morning. Greenwood Press, 1972 (reprint).
—The Tree Witch: A Verseplay. Greenwood Press, 1973 (reprint).
—New & Selected Poems. Xerox University Microfilms, 1979 (reprint).
Violi, Paul: *Waterworks.* Toothpaste Press, 1972.
—In Baltic Circles. Kulchur Press, 1973.
—Harmatan. The Sun Press, 1977.
—The Reckless Sleeper. The Sun Press, 1980.

W

Wakeman, John: *Hopeless Loves And Happy Endings.* Midsummer Press, 1980.
Wakoski, Diane: *Coins & Coffins.* Hawk's Well Press, 1962.
—Discrepancies & Apparitions. Doubleday & Co., 1966.
—The George Washington Poems. Riverrun Press, 1967.
—Inside The Blood Factory. Doubleday & Co., 1968.
—The Magellanic Clouds. Black Sparrow Press, 1970.
—The Motorcycle Betrayal Poems. Simon & Schuster, Inc., 1971.
—Smudging. Black Sparrow Press, 1972.
—Dancing On The Grave Of A Son Of A Bitch. Black Sparrow Press, 1973.
—Trilogy (reprint of first three collections). Doubleday & Co., 1974.
—Virtuoso Literature For Two And Four Hands. Doubleday & Co., 1975.
—Waiting For The King Of Spain. Black Sparrow Press, 1976.
—The Man Who Shook Hands. Doubleday & Co., 1978.
—Cap Of Darkness. Black Sparrow Press, 1980.
Walker, Jeanne Murray: *Nailing Up The Home Sweet Home.* Cleveland State University Press, 1980.
Wallace, Jon: *Looking For Home.* Darian Ltd., 1981.
Wallace, Ronald: *Cucumbers.* Pendle Hill Press, 1977.
—Installing The Bees. Chowder Chapbooks, 1977.
—The Facts Of Life. Mary Phillips, 1979.
—Plums, Stones, Kisses & Hooks. University of Missouri Press, 1981.
Waniek, Marilyn Nelson: *For The Body.* Louisiana State University Press, 1978.
Warden, Marine Robert: *Beyond The Straits.* Momentum Press, 1980
Warren, James E., Jr.: *This Side Of Babylon.* Banner Press, 1938.
—Against The Furious Men. Banner Press, 1946.
—Selected Poems. Branden Press, 1967.
—Walking With Candles. The Print Shop, 1973.
—A Kind Of Fighting. The Print Shop, 1974.
—Bequest/Request. The Print Shop, 1976.
—Prie-Dieu And Jubilee. The Print Shop, 1978.
—Collected Poems. Harvey Dan Abrams, Publishers, 1979.
—The Elegance Of God. The Print Shop, 1980.

Warren, Robert Penn: *Eleven Poems On The Same Theme.* New Directions Pub. Corp., 1942.
—Promises: Poems 1954-1956. Random House, 1957.
—You, Emperors, And Others: Poems 1957-1960. Random House, 1960.
—Selected Poems, New And Old 1923-1966. Random House, 1966.
—Incarnations: Poems 1966-1968. Random House, 1968.
—Audubon, A Vision. Random House, 1969.
—Or Else: Poems 1968-1974. Random House, 1974.
—Selected Poems 1923-1975. Random House, 1976.
—Now And Then: Poems 1976-1978. Random House, 1978.
—Brother To Dragons. Random House, 1979
—Life Is A Fable: Poetry 1978-1980. Random House, 1980.
Watson, Elaine: *We, The Women: Limericks Liberated.* Reno Press, 1980.
Weigl, Bruce: *Executioner.* Ironwood Press, 1976.
—Like A Sack Full Of Old Quarrels. Cleveland State University Poetry Center, 1977.
—A Romance. University of Pittsburgh Press, 1979.
Welch, Don: *Dead Horse Table.* Windflower Press, 1975.
—Handwork. Kearney State College Press, 1978.
—The Rarer Game. Kearney State College Press, 1980.
White, Gail: *Pandora's Box.* Samisdat Press, 1977.
—Irreverent Parables. Border-Mountain Press, 1978.
Whitman, Ruth: *Blood & Milk Poems.* October House, 1963.
—The Marriage Wig And Other Poems. Harcourt Brace Jovanovich, 1968.
—The Passion Of Lizzie Borden: New And Selected Poems. October House, 1973.
—Tamsen Donner: A Woman's Journey. Alice James Books, 1977.
—Permanent Address: New Poems 1973-1980. Alice James Books, 1980.
Will, Frederic: *Our Thousand Year Old Bodies: Selected Poems, 1956-76.* University of Massachusetts Press, 1980.
Williams, Miller: *A Circle Of Stone.* Louisiana State University Press, 1964.
—Recital. Oceano De Chile, 1965.
—So Long At The Fair. E. P. Dutton & Co., 1968.
—The Only World There Is. E. P. Dutton & Co., 1971.
—Halfway From Hoxie. E. P. Dutton & Co., 1973; Louisiana State University Press, 1976.
—Why God Permits Evil. Louisiana State University Press, 1977.
—Distractions. Louisiana State University Press, 1981.
Wiseman, Christopher: *Waiting For The Barbarians.* Fiddlehead Poetry Books, 1971.
—The Barbarian File. Sesame Press, 1974.
—The Upper Hand. Enitharmon Press (England), forthcoming.

Wood, John A.: *Orbs.* Apollyon Press, 1968.

Wood, Susan: *Bazaar.* Holt, Rinehart & Winston, Inc., 1981.

Wood-Thompson, Susan: *Crazy Quilt.* Crone Books, 1980.

Woodcock, George: *Six Poems.* E. Lahr (England), 1938.
 —*Ballad Of An Orphan Hand.* E. Lahr (England), 1939.
 —*The White Island.* Fortune Press (England), 1940.
 —*The Centre Cannot Hold.* Routledge & Kegan Paul (England), 1943.
 —*Image The South.* Untide Press, 1947.
 —*Selected Poems.* Clarke Irwin, 1967.
 —*Notes On Visitations: Poems, 1936-1975.* Black Moss Press, 1977.
 —*Anima, Or, Swann Grown Old: A Cycle Of Poems.* Black Moss Press, 1977.
 —*The Kestrel And Other Poems.* Coalfrith Press, 1978.
 —*The Mountain Road.* Fiddlehead Poetry Books, 1980.

Wright, Carolyne: *Stealing The Children.* Ahsahta Press, 1978.
 —*Returning What We Owed.* Owl Creek Press, 1980.

Wright, Franz: *Tapping The White Cane Of Solitude.* Triskelion Press, 1976.

 —*The Earth Without You.* Cleveland State University Poetry Center, 1980.

Y

Yates, David C.: *Making Bread.* Cedar Rock Press, 1976.
 —*Riding For The Dome.* Cedar Rock Press, 1979.

Young, Gary: *Hands.* Illuminati Press, 1979.

Young, Virginia Brady: *Double Windows.* Folder Editions, 1970.
 —*The Clooney Beads.* Folder Editions, 1970.
 —*Circle Of Thaw.* Barlenmir House, 1972.
 —*Cold Wind From Aachen.* Catalyst Press, 1978.
 —*Shedding The River.* Catalyst Press, 1978.

Z

Zimroth, Evan: *Giselle Considers Her Future.* Ohio State University Press, 1978.

Zinnes, Harriet: *Waiting And Other Poems.* Goosetree Press, 1964.
 —*An Eye For An I.* Folder Editions, 1966.
 —*I Wanted To See Something Flying.* Folder Editions, 1976.
 —*Entropisms.* Gallimaufry, 1978.
 —*Book Of Ten.* Bellevue Press, 1980

Zu-Bolton, Ahmos: *A Niggered Amen.* Solo Press, 1975.
 —*Ain't No Spring Chicken.* 1980.

PART TWO

Yearbook
of American Poetry

The Yearly Record

The following bibliography lists books of and about poetry that were published, copyrighted, officially announced, distributed or that otherwise appeared in the United States and Canada in the year ending October 31, 1980.

(1) COLLECTIONS OF POETRY BY INDIVIDUAL AUTHORS

A

Aal, Katharyn Machan–*Looking For The Witches.* The Fine-Arts Bluesband & Poetry Press

Abercrombie, Lascelles–*Interludes And Poems.* Core Collection Books (reprint)

Adam, Helen–*Gone Sailing.* Toothpaste Press

Adcock, Fleur–*The Inner Harbour.* Oxford University Press

Akhmatova, Anna–*Way Of All The Earth* (translated by D. M. Thomas). Ohio University Press

Aldridge, Alan–*The Peacock Party.* Viking Press

Allardt, Linda–*The Names Of The Survivors.* Ithaca House

Allen, Mark–*Seeds To The Wind.* Whatever Publishing

Allingham, William–*Robin Readbreast, And Other Verses.* Core Collection Books (reprint)

Allman, John–*Walking Four Ways In The Wind.* Princeton University Press

Almon, Bert–*Poems For the Nuclear Family.* San Marcos Press

Aloff, Mindy–*Night Lights.* Prescott Street Press

Amis, Kingsley–*Collected Poems, 1944-1979.* Viking Press

Ammons, A. R.–*Selected Longer Poems.* W. W. Norton & Co.

Anderson, Emily F.–*A Question Of Hardiness.* Privately printed

Anderson, Maggie–*Years That Answer.* Harper & Row

Anderson, Wendell B.–*Season Of The Crow.* Namaste Press

–*Rocky Mountain Vigil.* Privately printed

Andre, Evelyn M.–*Places I Like To Be.* Abingdon

Andrews, Lyman–*Kaleidoscope.* Calder & Boyars (distributed in the U.S. by Merrimack Book Service)

Annensky, Innokenty–*The Cypress Chest.* Ardis Publishers

Apollinaire, Guillaume–*Calligrammes* (translated by Anne Hyde Greet). University of California Press

Archibald, Donald–*Chanty Chanson.* Privately printed

Aristophanes–*Clouds; Women In Power; Knights* (translated by Kenneth McLeish). Cambridge University Press

–*"The Acharnians" Of Aristophanes* (translation and notes by W. J. M. Starkie). Arno Press (reprint)

Armstrong, John–*The Art Of Preserving Health: A Poem.* Arno Press (reprint)

Armstrong, Patricia Mees–*The Rain Bids Me Listen.* Windy Row Press

Armstrong, Tom–*Love In Being: Poetry And Photography.* Jemta Press

Arnett, Gogisgi/Carroll–*South Line.* Elizabeth Press

Arnold, Matthew–*The Portable Matthew Arnold* (edited by Lionel Trilling). Penguin Books (reprint) –*Selected Poems And Prose* (edited by Miriam Allott). E. P. Dutton & Co.

Ashbery, John–*As We Know.* Viking Press

Ashman, Russell Smith–*High Pollards.* Privately printed

Astor, Susan–*Dame.* University of Georgia Press

Atkins, Russell–*Elegy, February Twenty-First, Nineteen Sixty Five.* Free Lance Press –*Whichever.* Free Lance Press

Auden, W. H.–*The Double Man.* Greenwood Press (reprint)

Awad, Joseph–*The Neon Distances.* Golden Quill Press

Axley, Jim–*Oranges And Sweet Red Wines.* Lightning Tree

Ayyildiz, Judy–*Smuggled Seeds.* Gusto Press

B

Bacharach, Burt; David, Hal –*What The World Needs Now Is Love: Poetic Selections From The Songs Of Burt Bacharach And Hal David* (edited by Susan Polis Schutz). Blue Mountain Press

Bad Al–*Punk Novel.* Macmillan Pub. Co.

Balakian, Peter–*Father Fisheye.* Sheep Meadow Press

Baloian, James C.–*The Ararat Papers.* Ararat Press

Banbury, Lance–*Michael Sin: A Lyrical Narrative.* Privately printed –*Poems 1975-1978.* Privately printed

Banks, C. Tillery–*Hello To Me With Love: Poems Of Self-Discovery.* William Morrow & Co.

Bargen, Walter–*Fields Of Thenar.* K. M. Gentile Publishing

Barnard, Mary–*Collected Poems.* Breitenbush Publications

Barnes, Jim–*The Fish On Poteau Mountain.* Cedar Creek Press –*This Crazy Land.* Inland Boat Series/Porch Publications

Barnstone, William–*A Snow Salmon Reached The Andes Lake.* Curbstone Press

Baron, Mary—*Wheat Among Bones.* Sheep Meadow Press

Barrax, Gerald W.—*An Audience Of One.* University of Georgia Press

Barrett, Eaton Stannard—*Woman; Henry Schultze.* Garland Pub. Co. (reprint)

Barrett, Susan E.—*Ms. Noah Touches Earth.* Artichoke Press

Bartels, Susan—*Step Carefully In Night Grass.* John F. Blair, Publisher

Bartlett, Elizabeth—*Address In Time.* Dufour Editions

Bartman, Joeffrey—*Habit Blue.* Apple-wood Press

Barton, David—*Notes From The Exile.* Elysian Press

Baxter, Carolyn—*Prison Solitary, And Other Free Government Services.* Greenfield Review Press

Bayes, Ronald H.—*The Casketmaker.* John F. Blair, Publisher
—*Fram.* Pynyon Press

Baylor, Byrd; Parnell, Peter—*Your Own Secret Place.* Charles Scribner's Sons

Bayly, Thomas Haynes—*Rough Sketches Of Bath.* Garland Pub Co. (reprint)

Bear, Ray Young—*Winter Of The Salamander.* Harper & Row

Beck, Thomas—*The Cause Of The Dumb Pleaded; The Passions Taught By Truth; Elegy On The Death Of The Rev. Henry Hunter; The Age Of Frivolity; An Elegiac Tribute; Poetic Amusement; Modern Persecution; An Elegy On The Death Of The Princess Charlotte.* Garland (reprint)

Beecher, John—*Report To The Stockholders & Other Poems.* Vanguard Books

Bemrose, John—*Going Under.* Fiddlehead Poetry Books

Bennett, Bruce—*Coyote Pays A Call.* Bits Press

Berkson, Lee—*Away From Home.* Spoon River Poetry Press

Bernheimer, Alan—*Cafe Isotope.* The Figures

Berrigan, Ted—*So Going Around Cities: New And Selected Poems, 1958-1979.* Blue Wind Press

Berry, Wendell—*A Part.* North Point Press

Bertolino, James—*Are You Tough Enough For The Eighties?* New Rivers Press

Betham, Matilda—*Poems And Elegies.* Garland Pub. Co. (reprint)

Betts, Donni (see listing for Betts, George)

Betts, George; Betts, Donni—*Seasons Of Love.* Celestial Arts Pub. Co.

Billings, Robert—*The Elizabethan Trinities.* Penumbra Press

Bita, Lili—*Fleshfire: New And Selected Love Poems* (translated by Robert Zaller). Lyra Press

Blackburn, Paul—*Against The Silences.* Permanent Press (London)

Bland, Robert—*The Four Slaves Of Cythera.* Garland Pub. Co. (reprint)

Bliss, S. W.—*Pyramids And Prisms.* Vega

Bloch, Chana—*The Secrets Of The Tribe.* Sheep Meadow Press

Blossom, Laurel—*Any Minute.* Greenhouse Review Press

Blotnick, Elihu—*Never Distrust An Asparagus.* California Street Books

Blumenthal, Michael—*Sympathetic Magic.* Water Mark Press

Bode, Carl—*Practical Magic.* Swallow Press

Bond, Harold—*The Way It Happens To You.* Ararat Press

Borson, Roo—*In The Smoky Light Of The Fields.* Three Trees Press
—*Rain.* Penumbra Press

Bosley, James—*Gargoyles.* Privately printed

Bosquet, Alain—*Instead Of Music* (translated by William Frawley). Louisiana State University Press

Bottoms, David—*Shooting Rats At The Bibb County Dump.* William Morrow & Co.

Bowie, John—*Screen Gems.* W. D. Hoffstadt & Sons Press

Boyd, Melba Joyce—*Cat Eyes And Dead Wood.* Fallen Angel Press

Boyle, David—*Seven Poems.* Obscure Press

Bradley, Buff—*The Honey Philosophies.* Center Publications

Brand, Millen—*Peace March: Nagasaki To Hiroshima.* Countryman Press

Braude, Michael—*Village Vignettes.* Street Press

Braverman, Kate—*Lullaby For Sinners: Poems 1970-1979.* Harper & Row

Brecht, Bertolt—*Poems, 1913-1956* (edited by John Willett and Ralph Manheim). Methuen

Bristol, David—*Paradise & Cash.* Washington Writers' Pub. House

Brook, Van K.—*The Hard Essential Landscape.* University Presses of Florida

Brodine, Karen—*Illegal Assembly.* Hanging Loose Press

Brodsky, Joseph—*A Part Of Speech.* Farrar, Straus & Giroux, Inc.

Brodsky, Louis Daniel—*Birds In Passage.* Farmington Press

Brooke, Rupert—*The Collected Poems of Rupert Brooke.* Dodd, Mead & Co.

Broumas, Olga—*Soie Sauvage.* Copper Canyon Press

Brown, Dorothy Hanson—*God And The Tree And Me.* Upper Room

Brown, Spencer—*Child's Game, On A Journey.* Elizabeth Press

Brown, Sterling A.—*The Collected Poems Of Sterling A. Brown.* Harper & Row

Bruchac, Joseph—*Ancestry & Other Poems.* Great Raven Press

Brydges, Samuel Egerton—*Poems; Odo, Count Of Lingen.* Garland Pub. Co. (reprint)

Buckley, Christopher—*Last Rites.* Ithaca House

Bukowski, Charles—*Play The Piano Drunk Like A Percussion Instrument Until The Fingers Begin To Bleed A Bit.* Black Sparrow Press

Bullen, Donald G.—*Rambles Of A Sedentary Anthropoid.* Celestial Otter Press

Bunting, Basil—*Collected Poems.* Oxford University Press

Burleigh, Robert—*The Triumph Of Mittens.* Boardwell-Kloner Press

Burns, Gerald—*A Book Of Spells.* Salt Lick Press

Burritt, Mary—*The Solera Poems.* L'Epervier Press

Burrows, Cecille Miller—*Clowns Of The World: A Collection Of Clowns And Verses.* Northwood Institute

Burrows, E. G.—*On The Road To Bailey's.* Fallen Angel Press

Burton, Wilma—*Sidewalk Psalms . . . And Some From Country Lanes.* Good News Publishers

Butcher, Grace—*Before I Go Out On The Road.* Cleveland State University Poetry Center

Butscher, Edward—*Amagansett Cycle.* Cross-Cultural Communications

Byrd, Emmett—*Byrd Thou Never Wert* (edited by John Crowe Byrd and Winslow Farquar; compiled by Michael Hinden). Ted Speed Press

C

Cardenal, Ernesto—*Zero Hour And Other Documentary Poems* (edited by Donald D. Walsh; translated by Paul W. Borgeson, Jr.). New Directions Pub. Corp.

Carothers, Robert—*John Calvin's Favorite Son.* Barnwood Press Cooperative

Cassity, Turner—*The Defense Of The Sugar Islands,* Symposium Press

Castleman, David Lee—*I Stammer It To Angels.* Privately printed

Casto, Robert Clayton—*The Arrivals.* Studio Press

Catullus—*The Poems Of Catullus* (translated by Charles Martin). Abattoir Editions

Cavalieri, Grace—*Swan Research.* Word Works

Chadwick, jerah—*The Country Of Water.* Seal Press

Chambers, Lela—*Reminiscence In Poetry.* Allegany Mountain Press

Chandonnet, Ann—*At The Fruit-Tree's Mossy Root.* Wings Press

　　—*Ptarmigan Valley (Poems of Alaska).* Lightning Tree

Chapman, George—*George Chapman: Selected Poems* (edited by Eirian Wain). Carcanet (England) (distributed in the U.S. by Dufour Editions)

Charlip, Remy—*Arm In Arm* (partly poetry). Four Winds Press (reprint)

Chaucer, Geoffrey—*The Isle Of Ladies; Or, The Isle Of Pleasaunce* (edited by Anthony Jenkins). Garland Pub. Co.

Cheatwood, Kiarri T-H.—*Valley Of The Anointers.* Lotus Press

Chernoff, Maxine—*Utopia TV Store: Prose Poems.* Yellow Press

Cherry, Kelly—*Songs For A Soviet Composer.* K. M. Gentile Publishing

Cherwinski, Joseph—*Relics Of The Spring.* Harlo

Chesterton, G. K.—*The Collected Poems Of G. K. Chesterton.* Dodd, Mead & Co.

Chichetto, James W.—*Stones, A Litany.* Four Zoas Night House

Citino, David—*Last Rites, And Other Poems.* Ohio State University Press

Clark, J. Wesley—*Daughter Of The South Country.* Free State Press

Clark, Marden J.—*Moods, Of Late.* Brigham Young University Press

Clifton, Lucille—*Two-Headed Woman.* University of Massachusetts Press

Coffin, Lyn—*Human Trappings.* Abattoir Editions

Cohen, Marion—*The Weirdest Is The Sphere.* Seven Woods Press

Cohen, Marty—*A Traveller's Alphabet.* Prescott Street Books

Colby, Joan—*Dream Tree.* Jump River Press

Cole, E. R.—*Acts And Potency.* Apeiron Press

　　—*Falling Up: Haiku And Senryu.* Kamazu Press

Coleridge, Samuel Taylor—*The Rime Of The Ancient Mariner.* Avon/Bard Books

Collins, Billy—*Video Poems.* Applezaba Press

Collins, Floyd—*Scarecrow.* St. Luke's Press

Colombo, John Robert—*The Great Cities Of Antiquity.* Hounslow Press

Comfort, Alex—*Poems For Jane.* Crown Publishers

Contoski, Victor—*Names.* New Rivers Press

Cook, Albert—*Adapt The Living.* Swallow Press

Coon, Betty—*Seaward.* Berkeley Poets Workshop and Press

Cooper, Allan—*Blood Lines.* Fiddlehead Poetry Books

Corn, Alfred—*The Various Light.* Viking Press

Cottle, Joseph—*Messiah.* Garland Pub. Co. (reprint)

Coulson, Charles Walter—*Visions: Selected Poems Written In Port Elizabeth In The Late 1940's.* E. M. Underwood

Coursen, H. R.—*Hope Farm: New And Selected Poems.* Cider Mill Press

Cowan, Alice M. H.—*The Roundness Of Things.* Pulmac Enterprises

Cowper, William—*The Poetical Works Of William Cowper* (edited by H. S. Milford). AMS Press (reprint)

Crawford, Tom—*I Want To Say Listen.* Ironwood Press

Creeley, Robert—*Later.* New Directions Pub. Corp.

Crenner, James—*My Hat Flies On Again.* L'Epervier Press

cummings, e. e.—*Complete Poems, 1913-1962.* Harcourt Brace Jovanovich, Inc.

　　—*Xaipe* (edited by George James Firmage). Liveright Pub. Corp.

　　—*Viva* (edited by George James Firmage). Liveright Pub. Corp.

Cummings, Michael—*Red Haw.* New Wave Press

Cummings, Peter—*Bicycle Consciousness: Poems And Prose.* Greenfield Review Press

Curnow, Allen—*An Incorrigible Music: A Sequence Of Poems.* Oxford University Press

Currey, Richard—*Crossing Over: A Vietnam Journal.* Apple-wood Press

Cutler, Bruce—*The Doctrine Of Selective Depravity.* Juniper Press

D

Damon, S. Foster—*Heaven & Hell.* Copper Beech Press

Dana, Robert—*In A Fugitive Season: A Sequence Of Poems.* Swallow Press

Dankleff, Richard—*Popcorn Girl.* Oregon State University Press

Dante Alighieri—*The Divine Comedy* (translated by Charles S. Singleton). Princeton University Press

　　—*The Divine Comedy Of Dante Alighieri: Inferno, Volume I* (translated and annotated by Allen Mandelbaum). University of California Press

　　—*The Divine Comedy* (a new verse translation) (translated by C. H. Sisson). Carcanet New Press (England) (dist. in U.S. by Persea Books, New York)

Firer, Susan—*My Life With The Tsar And Other Poems.* Three Rivers Press

Fisher, Aileen—*Out In The Dark And Daylight.* Harper & Row Publishers

Fisher, Anya—*At The Edge Of A Void, Waiting.* Remo Publishers

Fisher, David—*The Book Of Madness.* Apple-wood Press

Fisher, Harrison—*Blank Like Me.* Paycock Press

Flory, Sheldon—*A Winter's Journey.* Copper Beech Press

Floyd, Bryan Alec—*The Long War Dead: An Epiphany.* Avon Books

Forbes, Calvin—*From The Book Of Shine.* Burning Deck

Ford, Phyllis (see listing for Kachmar, Jessie)

Forster, Paul Q.—*Side Dishes.* Privately printed

Forsythe, Kathleen—*Phoenix Rising.* Fiddlehead Poetry Books

Francis, Luis; Friedman, David—*Her Beauty Likes Me Well.* Petrarch Press

Franklin, Jessie Merle—*Grandparents Are Special.* Broadman Press

Friedman, Barton R.—*You Can't Tell The Players.* Cleveland State University Poetry Center

Friedman, David (see listing for Francia, Luis)

Friedman, Richard—*Physical Culture.* Yellow Press

Friend, Robert—*Somewhere Lower Down.* Menard Press

Frosch, Thomas—*Plum Gut.* New Rivers Press

Frost, Robert—*Robert Frost 1981 Engagement Calendar.* Holt, Rinehart & Winston

Fulford, R. W.—*Powerland Minds.* Fiddlehead Poetry Books

Funkhouser, Erica—*Natural Affinities.* Dark Horse Press

G

Galloway, Terry—*Buncha Crocs In Surch Of Snac.* Curbstone Press

Galt, Tom—*The Wind And The Rain.* Shearwater Press

Galvin, Brendan—*Atlantic Flyway.* University of Georgia Press

Gandy, Doreen—*Poems For Twelve Moods.* Dragon's Teeth Press

Garcia Lorca, Federico—*From First Songs* (translated by Bill Herron). Chango Press
—*The Cricket Sings: Poems And Songs For Children* (translated by Will Kirkland). New Directions Pub. Corp.

Gardner, Isabella—*That Was Then: New And Selected Poems.* Boa Editions

Gegna, Suzanne— *Phoenix Story.* Privately printed

Gent, Thomas—*Poetic Sketches; Poems (1828).* Garland Pub. Co. (reprint)

George, Emery—*Kate's Death: A Book Of Odes.* Ardis Publishers

Ghiradella, Robert—*Fragments.* Apple-wood Press

Ghiselin, Brewster—*Windrose: Poems 1929-1980.* University of Utah Press

Gilboa, Amir—*The Light Of Lost Suns: Selected Poems Of Amir Gilboa* (translated by Shirley Kaufman). Persea Books

Gill, M. Lakshmi—*Novena To St. Jude Thaddeus.* Fiddlehead Poetry Books

Ginsberg, Allen; Orlovsky, Peter—*Straight Hearts' Delight: Love Poems And Selected Letters* (edited by Winston Leyland). Gay Sunshine Press
—*Composed On The Tongue* (edited by Donald Allen). Grey Fox Press

Giovanni, Nikki—*Vacation Time: Poems For Children.* William Morrow & Co.

Gizzi, Michael—*Avis Or The Replete Birdman.* Burning Deck

Glaser, Elton—*Peripheral Vision.* Bits Press

Gluck, Louise—*Descending Figure.* Ecco Press

Goedicke, Patricia—*Crossing The Same River.* University of Massachusetts Press
—*The Dog That Was Barking Yesterday.* Lynx House Press

Goepfert, Paul—*Chiasma.* Panjandrum

Goethe, Johann Wolfgang von—*The Eternal Feminine: Selected Poems Of Goethe* (selected by Frederick Ungar). Frederick Ungar Pub. Co.

—*Goethe, The Lyrist: 100 Poems In New Translations Facing The Originals.* AMS Press (reprint)

Gold, Harry—*The Dolphin's Path: A Bookman's Sequel To the "Odyssey" Of Homer.* Aberdeen Book Co.

Goldbarth, Albert—*Different Fleshes: A Novel/Poem.* Hobart & William Smith Colleges Press

Goldberg, Natalie—*Chicken & In Love.* Holy Cow! Press

Goldensohn, Lorrie—*Dreamwork.* Porch Publications

Gom, Leona—*North.* League of Canadian Poets
—*Land Of The Peace.* Thistledown Press

Gonzalez, Lorenzo J.—*As Shadows Fall.* Privately printed

Goodman, Linda—*Linda Goodman's Love Poems: Levels Of Love Awareness.* Harper & Row Publishers

Gordon, Don—*Excavations.* West Coast Poetry Review

Gould, Henry—*Stone.* Copper Beech Press

Grabman, Richard—*The Writing Lesson.* Writers' Center Press

Graham, Jorie—*Hybrids Of Plants And Of Ghosts.* Princeton University Press

Graham, W. S.—*Selected Poems.* Ecco Press

Graziano, Frank—*From Sheepshead, From Paumanok.* Porch Publications

Greene-Pepper, Dorothy—*Hate Poems For Ex-Lovers.* Citadel Press

Greger, Debora—*Movable Islands.* Princeton University Press

Gregory, Michael—*Hunger Weather.* Mother Duck Press

Grenier, Robert—*Oakland.* Tuumba Press

Griffin, Jonathan—*The Fact Of Music.* Menard Press

Griffin, Susan—*Woman And Nature: The Roaring Inside Her.* Harper & Row, Publishers

Gross, Betty J.—*Visions From Within: Collected Poems 1971-79.* Gainesville Letter Shop

Guenther, John—*Cihuateteo: New And Selected Poems.* Celli Press

Guiney, Louise Imogen—*Happy Ending: The Collected*

Lyrics Of Louise Imogen Guiney. Greenwood Press (reprint)

Gurian, Jay—*American Studies Singing*. American Studies Press

Gustafson, Jim—*Shameless*. Tombouctou Books

Gustafson, Ralph—*Gradations Of Grandeur*. Sono Nis Press
—*Landscape With Rain*. McClelland and Stewart, Ltd.

H

Hacker, Marilyn—*Taking Notice*. Alfred A. Knopf, Inc.

Hackleman, Wauneta—*A Lump Of Sugar And A Dash Of Spice*. Northwoods Press

Hakim, Seymour—*Iris Elegy*. Poetry Gallery Press

Haley, Vanessa—*Horse Latitudes*. Conraddi Publications

Hall, C. Margaret—*Giving Birth*. Antietam Press

Hall, Joan Joffe—*The Aerialist's Fall*. Ziesing Bros.

Hall, Kirk—*Angel Of The Cities*. Privately printed

Hamill, Sam—*Animae*. Copper Canyon Press

Handlin, Jim—*Where The Picture Book Ends*. Gusto Press

Hankla, Susan—*I Am Running Home*. Burning Deck

Hannan, Greg—*Instincts For The Jugular*. Washington Writers' Pub. House

Hansel, Alfarata—*Ribbons Of Melody*. Alpha Pub. Co.

Harasym, Sally—*Circles In The Sand*. Fiddlehead Poetry Books

Haring, Cynthia—*Songs For Solitude*. Hibiscus Press

Harper, Elizabeth—*Games Like Passacaglia*. Fiddlehead Poetry Books

Harris, Jana—*The Clackamas*. The Smith Publishers

Harris, Marie—*Interstate*. Slow Loris Press

Harrison, Jim—*"Letters To Yesenin" And "Returning To Earth"*. Center Publications

Harrison, Sarah—*In Granny's Garden*. Holt, Rinehart & Winston, Inc.

Harryman, Carla—*Percentage*. Tuumba Press

Harvey, Alexander—*Months And Seasons*. Hollow Spring Press

Hastings, Thomas—*Political Love Poems*. Writers' Center Press

Hausman, Gerald—*Night Herding Song*. Copper Canyon Press

Hayley, William—*Ode To Mr. Wright Of Derby: Occasional Stanzas; An Elegy On The Death Of Sir William Jones; Little Tom, The Sailor; The Triumph Of Music; The Stanzas Of An English Friend To The Patriots Of Spain; Ode On Leaving South Carolina*. Garland Pub. Co. (reprint)

Haynes, Diana—*Moving Inland*. Fiddlehead Poetry Books

Hazel, Robert—*Who Touches This*. Countryman Press

Hearne, Vicki—*Nervous Horses*. University of Texas Press

Heber, Reginald—*Palestine: A Prize Poem; Europe: Lines On The Present War*. Garland Pub. Co. (reprint)

Hecht, Anthony—*The Venetian Vespers*. Atheneum Publishers

Hecht, Roger—*Burnt Offerings*. Lightning Tree

Heffernan, Thomas— *Narrative Of Jeremy Bentham*. New House Publishers

Heller, Michael—*Knowledge*. Sun

Hellman, Dorothy Gurkin—*Let Go, My Love*. Bloch Pub. Co.

Hemans, Felicia Dorothea—*The Domestic Affections; The Restoration Of The Works Of Art Of Italy; Wallace's Invocation To Bruce; The Sceptic*. Garland Pub. Co. (reprint)

Hemingway, Ernest—*Three Stories & Ten Poems*. Bruccoli Clark Publishers

Henisch, Peter—*Hamlet Fables* (translated by Herman Salinger). Charioteer Press

Hennessy, Madeleine—*Pavor Nocturnus And Other Poems*. Washout Pub. Co.

Henry, Steve—*A Part Of Me Apart From Me*. $ Publishing

Heraud, Javier—*Season Of Disenchantment: Selected Poems Of Javier Heraud* (translated by Pilar Zalamea). Illuminati Press

Herron, Bill—*Rituals Of Our Time*. Carolina Wren Press

Hershon, Robert—*The Public Hug: New And Selected Poems*. Louisiana State University Press

Hesiodus—*Works And Days* (edited by T. A. Sinclair). Arno Press (reprint)

Hetenyi, Lazlo J.—*On Being Human*. American Studies Press

Heyen, William—*My Holocaust Songs*. William B. Ewert
—*The City Parables*. Croissant Press

Heywood, John—*John Heywood's Works And Miscellaneous Short Poems* (edited by Burton A. Milligan). Greenwood Press (reprint)

Hicks, John V.—*Winter Your Sleep*. Thistledown Press

Higgins, Dick—*Some Recent Snowflakes (And Other Things)*. Printed Editions

Hiller, Tobey—*Crossings*. Oyez

Hillman, Brenda—*The Train To Paris*. Penumbra Press

Hillman, Priscilla—*A Merry-Mouse Book Of Months*. Doubleday & Co.

Hindus, Milton—*The Broken Music Box*. Menard Press

Hitchcock, George—*The Piano Beneath The Skin*. Copper Canyon Press

Hobbie, Holly—*A Treasury Of Holly Hobbie*. Rand McNally & Co.

Hodgkinson, Edie—*Season's Edge*. Hanging Loose Press

Hodgson, Francis—*Saeculomastix And Sacred Leisure*. Garland Pub. Co. (reprint)

Hogrogian, Nonny—*The Pearl: Hymn Of The Robe Of Glory, A New Retelling*. Two Rivers Press

Hollo, Anselm—*Finite Continued*. Blue Wind Press

Holub, Miroslav—*Sagittal Section: Poems New And Selected* (translated by Stuart Friebert and Dana Habova). Field

Homer—*Selections From Homer's "Iliad"* (notes by Allen Rogers Benner). Irvington Publishers (reprint)

Honig, Edwin—*The Foibles And Fables Of An Abstract Man*. Copper Beech Press

Hoover, Paul—*Letter To Einstein Beginning Dear Albert*. Yellow Press

Hornsey, Richard—*Where Roads And Rivers Lead*. Fiddlehead Poetry Books

Hotchkiss, Bill—*Middle Fork Canyon And Other Poems.* Blue Oak

Hotham, Gary—*Against The Linoleum.* Yiqralo Press

Housman, A. E.—*A Shropshire Lad.* Greenwood Press (reprint)

Howe, Susan—*Secret History Of The Dividing Line.* Telephone Books

Hoyt, Helen—*Fire Poems.* Blue Oak Press

Huffstickler, Albert—*The Remembered Light.* Slough Press

Hughes, Daniel—*Falling.* Copper Beech Press

Hughes, Ted—*Cave Birds: An Alchemical Cave Drama.* Faber & Faber, Inc.
—*Moortown.* Harper & Row

Hugo, Richard—*White Center.* W. W. Norton & Co.
—*The Right Madness On Skye.* W. W. Norton & Co.

Humble, Christopher—*Subject To Turbulence.* Tamal Land Press

Hunt, William—*Oceans And Corridors Of Orpheus.* Elpenor Books

Hunter, Eileen—*Tales Of Waybeyond.* A. Deutsch (dist. in U.S. by E. P. Dutton & Co. New York, NY)

I

Ibsen, Henrik—*Peer Gynt: A Dramatic Poem.* University of Minnesota Press

Ignatow, David—*Conversations.* Survivors' Manual Books

Ivimey, John W.—*Complete Version Of Ye Three Blind Mice.* F. Warne

Iwaniuk, Waclaw—*Dark Times* (translated by Jagna Boraks and others; edited by John Robert Columbo). Hounslow Press

J

Jabes, Edmond—*A Share Of Ink* (translated by Anthony Rudolf). Menard Press

Jacob, Max—*The Dice Cup: Selected Prose Poems* (edited by Michael Brownstein). Sun

Jacobik, Gary—*Sandpainting.* Washington Writers' Pub. House

Jaffin, David—*Space Of.* Elizabeth Press
—*Perceptions.* Elizabeth Press

Jalal, al-Din Rumi—*Mystical Poems Of Rumi* (translated by A. J. Arberry). Westview Press

James, Candice—*A Split In The Water.* Fiddlehead Poetry Books

James, David—*Driving To Here.* Applezaba Press

Jeffrey, Susu—*Songs Of The Gypsy Women.* New Rivers Press

Jellema, Rod—*The Lost Faces.* Dryad Press

Jennings, Elizabeth—*Selected Poems Of Elizabeth Jennings,* Carcanet New Press (England) (dist. in U.S. by Persea Books, New York)

Jerome, Judson—*Thirty Years Of Poetry: Collected Poems, 1949-1979.* Cedar Rock Press

Johnson, Michael L.—*The Unicorn Captured.* Cottonwood Review Press

Johnson, Robert W.—*He Sends You Knowledge: Mystical Thoughts For Meditation.* Alpha Centauri Publishers

Johnston, Caryl—*Instead Of Eyes.* Anthroposophic Press

Johnston, Gary—*Making Eyes Thru Morning.* Blind Beggar Press

Johnston, Gordon—*Inscription Rock.* Penumbra Press

Johnston-Hale, Ellen Turlington—*What If There's A Rainbow?* Moore Pub. Co.

Jones, David—*Introducing David Jones: A Selection Of His Writings* (edited by John Matthias). Faber & Faber, Inc.

Jones, Rodney—*The Story They Told Us Of Light.* University of Alabama Press

Jordan, June—*Passion: New Poems, 1977-1980.* Beacon Press

Juan de la Cruz, Saint—*The Poems Of St. John Of The Cross* (translated by John Frederick Nims). University of Chicago Press

Juergensen, Hans—*California Frescoes.* American Studies Press

Justice, Donald—*Selected Poems.* Atheneum Publishers

Juvenalis, Decimus Junius; Persius Flaccus, Aulus—*The Satyrs Of Decimus Junius Juvenalis And Of Aulus Persius Flaccus* (translated into English verse by John Dryden and others). AMS Press (reprint)

K

Kachmar, Jessie; Ford, Phyllis; Winter, Helen—*Apertures To Anywhere.* Harper Square Press

Kamenetz, Rodger—*The Missing Jew.* Dryad Press

Kaschnitz, Marie Luise—*Selected Later Poems Of Marie Luise Kaschnitz* (translated by Lisel Mueller). Princeton University Press

Kavanaugh, James—*Walk Easy On The Earth.* E. P. Dutton & Co.

Kearney, Lawrence—*Kingdom Come.* Wesleyan University Press

Kelly, Dennis—*Chicken.* Gay Sunshine Press

Kelly, Robert—*The Cruise Of The Pnyx.* Station Hill Press
—*Kill The Messenger.* Black Sparrow Press

Kemp, Penny—*Changing Place.* Fiddlehead Poetry Books

Kendig, Diane—*A Tunnel Of Flute Song.* Cleveland State University Poetry Center

Kennedy, Mary—*New Green Over Old Green.* Gotham Book Mart

Kessler, Leonard—*The Mother Goose Game.* Garrard Pub. Co.
—*The Silly Mother Hubbard.* Garrard Pub. Co.
—*Hickory Dickory Dock.* Garrard Pub. Co.

Kim Chi Ha—*The Middle Hour: Selected Poems Of Kim Chi Ha* (translated by David R. McCann). Human Rights Publishing Corp.

Kimmel, Judith—*Animal Crackers.* Friends United Press

King, Karen Rice—*I'm Dead Now, But In Fifty Years I'll Be Reincarnated As a Potatoe [sic] And You'll Know Me By My Eyes.* Ruffled Feathers Pub. Co.

Kinnell, Galway—*Mortal Acts, Mortal Words.* Houghton Mifflin Co.

Kinnick, B. Jo—*Crying For Guyana.* Graphics Design

Kinsella, Thomas—*Poems 1956-1973.* Wake Forest University Press
—*Peppercanister Poems 1972-1978.* Wake Forest University Press

Kirstein, Lincoln–*Rhymes Of A Pfc* (revised edition). David R. Godine Press

Klein, Ernst–*My Dialogue With Death*. Judson Press

Kleinzahler, August–*A Calendar Of Airs*. Coach House Press

Klinge, Gunther–*Day Into Night: A Haiku Journey*. Charles E. Tuttle Co.

Kloefkorn, William; Kooser, Ted–*Cottonwood County*. Windflower Press

Kloss, Phillips–*The Great Kiva: A Poetic Critique Of Religion*. Sunstone Press

Knight, Etheridge–*Born Of A Woman: New And Selected Poems*. Houghton Mifflin Co.

Koehn, Lala–*Sandpoems*. Fiddlehead Poetry Books

Kooser, Ted–*Sure Signs: New And Selected Poems*. University of Pittsburgh Press

Kornblum, Allan–*Awkward Song*. Toothpaste Press

Krieger, Ted–*Bearing It Alone*. Ansuda Publications

Kudaka, Geraldine–*Numerous Avalanches At The Point Of Intersection*. Greenfield Review Press

Kuskin, Karla–*Dogs And Dragons, Trees And Dreams*. Harper & Row

Kuzma, Greg–*A Horse Of A Different Color*. Illuminati Press

Kuzmin, Mikhail–*Selected Prose & Poetry* (edited and translated by Michael Green). Ardis Publishers

Kyger, Joanne–*The Wonderful Focus Of You*. Z Press

L

Laing, R. D.–*Sonnets*. Pantheon Books

Lamport, Felicia–*Light Metres*. Everest House

Lane, Patrick–*Poems: New & Selected*. Oxford University Press

Langland, Joseph–*Any Body's Song*. Doubleday & Co.

Larsen, Jeanne–*James Cook In Search Of Terra Incognita: A Book Of Poems*. University Press of Virginia

Laviera, Tato–*La Carreta Made A U-Turn*. Arte Publico Press

Lea, Sydney–*Searching The Drowned Man*. University of Illinois Press

Lear, Edward–*A Book Of Nonsense*. Metropolitan Museum of Art/Viking Press (reprint)

Leckner, Carol H.–*Seasons In Transition*. Fiddlehead Poetry Books

Ledinko, Zora–*Wind Bound*. New Merrymount Press

Lee, Robert Edson–*The Dialogues Of Lewis And Clark: A Narrative Poem*. Colorado Associated University Press

Leon, Luis de–*The Unknown Light: The Poems Of Fray Luis De Leon* (translated by Willis Barnstone). State University of New York Press

Lepson, Ruth–*Dreaming In Color*. Alice James Books

Lesniak, Rose–*Young Anger*. Toothpaste Press

Levenberg, Diane–*Out Of The Desert*. Doubleday & Co.

Levine, Philip–*Pili's Wall*. Unicorn Press

Lewis, Claudia–*Up And Down The River*. Harper Junior Books

Li Ch'ing-chao–*Li Ch'ing-chao: Complete Poems* (edited and translated by Kenneth Rexroth and Ling Chung). New Directions Pub. Corp.

Lieberman, Laurence–*God's Measurements*. Macmillan Pub. Co.

Lifshin, Lyn–*Naked Charm*. Illuminati Press
–*Matinee*. Omnation Press
–*Madonna Who Shifts For Herself*. Applezaba Press

Lillie, Mary Prentice–*A Decade Of Dreams*. Dragon's Teeth Press

Lippe, Jane–*Silent Partner*. New Rivers Press

Little, Geraldine Clinton–*Separation: Seasons In Space*. Sparrow Press

Little, Janet–*Hecate The Bandicoot*. Dodd, Mead & Co.

Livingston, Myra Cohn–*No Way Of Knowing: Dallas Poems*. Atheneum Publishers

Locklin, Gerald–*Two Summer Sequences*. Maelstrom Press

Logan, William–*Dream Of Dying*. Graywolf Press

Longfellow, Henry Wadsworth–*Hiawatha's Childhood: From "The Song Of Hiawatha."* Dandelion Press

Lonidier, Lynn–*Woman Explorer*. Painted Bride Quarterly Press

Louis, Adrian C.–*Sweets For The Dancing Bears*. Blue Cloud Quarterly

Louthan, Robert–*Shrunken Planets*. Alice James Books

Lucretius–*On The Nature Of The Universe* (translated by James H. Mantinband). Frederick Ungar Pub. Co.

Ludvigson, Susan–*The Wisconsin Women*. Porch Publications

Lundkvist, Artur–*Agadir* (translated by William Jay Smith and Leif Sjoberg). Ohio University Press

M

MacBeth, George–*Poems Of Love And Death*. Atheneum Publishers

MacDonald, Bernell–*The Theories Of Fish*. Fiddlehead Poetry Books

Macdonald, Cynthia–*(W)holes*. Alfred A. Knopf

MacLeish, Archibald–*Six Plays*. Houghton Mifflin Co.

MacLow, Jackson–*The Pronouns: A Collection Of Forty Dances For The Dancers*. Station Hill Press

MacNeice, Louis–*Collected Poems*. Faber & Faber, Inc.

Magill, Arthur–*The Society Of Mutual Backscratchers: A Collection Of Poems*. Charles E. Tuttle Co.

Magorian, James–*Phases Of The Moon*. Black Oak Press

Mahon, Derek–*Poems 1962-1978*. Oxford University Press

Mahone, Ollie–*Vignettes For Harvesting*. Privately printed

Malloy, Merrit–*Beware Of Older Men*. Doubleday & Co.

Malone, Ted–*The Tapestry Maker*. John F. Blair, Publisher

Mandelstam, Osip–*Stone* (translated by Robert Tracy). Princeton University Press

Mansour, Joyce–*Birds Of Prey (Rapaces)* (translated by Albert Herzing). Perivale Press

Mariani, Paul—*Timing Devices*. David R. Godine Press

Marion, Paul—*Focus On A Locus*. Yellow Umbrella Press

Martin, Herbert Woodward—*The Forms Of Silence*. Lotus Press

Mason, Herbert—*The Death Of Al-Hallaj: A Dramatic Narrative*. University of Notre Dame Press

Mason, Scott—*No Dogs In Heaven*. Cleveland State University Poetry Center

Mathis, Cleopatra—*Aerial View Of Louisiana*. Sheep Meadow Press

Matthews, Patricia—*Love's Many Faces*. Pinnacle Books

Mattison, Alice—*Animals*. Alice James Books

Mattison, Judith N.—*Facing Up*. Fortress Press

Maura, Sister—*A Word, A Tree: Christmas Poems*. Franciscan Graphics

Mazzocco, Robert—*Trader*. Alfred A. Knopf, Inc.

McAleavey, David—*Shrine, Shelter, Cave*. Ithaca House

McBride, Mekeel—*A Change In The Weather*. Chowder Chapbooks

McCaffery, Steve—*Intimate Distortions: A Displacement Of Sappho*. Porcupine's Quill

McCombs, Judith—*Against Nature: Wilderness Poems*. Dustbooks

McCord, David—*Speak Up: More Rhymes Of The Never Was And Always Is*. Little, Brown & Co.

McCord, Howard—*The Great Toad Hunt And Other Expeditions*. The Crossing Press

McCue, Lilly—*Well, Butter My Bread!* DeVorss

McCurdy, Harold Grier—*And Then The Sky Turned Blue*. Briarpatch Press

McDaniel, Audrey—*Love's Promise*. Doubleday & Co.

McDonald, Walter—*Anything, Anything*. L'Epervier Press
—*Working Against Time*. Calliope Press

McGee, Shelagh—*What Witches Do And Other Poems*. Prentice-Hall, Inc.

McGrath, Thomas—*Movie At The End Of The World*. Swallow Press

McKuen, Rod—*Love's Been Good To Me*. Pocket Books

McMullen, Richard E.—*Rural Route 2*. Street Fiction Press

McNaughton, Duncan—*Shit On My Shoes*. Tombouctou Books

Meek, Jay—*Drawing On The Walls*. Carnegie-Mellon University Press

Megnon, Phillipe—*Ruby: The Food Poems Of Phillipe Megnon* (translated by Darrell Gray). Sombre Reptiles

Melhem, D. H.—*Notes On 94th Street*. Dovetail Press
—*Children Of The House Afire: More Notes On 94th Street*. Dovetail Press
—*Rest In Love*. Dovetail Press

Meredith, George—*Selected Poems Of George Meredith* (edited by Graham Hough). Greenwood Press (reprint)

Meredith, William—*The Cheer*. Alfred A. Knopf, Inc.

Merivale, John Herman—*Orlando In Roncesvalles*. Garland Pub. Co. (reprint)

Merrill, James—*Scripts For The Pageant*. Atheneum Publishers

Metzger, Diane Hamill—*Coralline Ornaments*. Weed Patch Press

Mihalyi, Martha—*Bloodflowers*. Red Weather Press

Miles, Josephine—*Coming To Terms*. University of Illinois Press

Millay, Edna St. Vincent—*Edna St. Vincent Millay's Poems Selected For Young People*. Harper & Row

Miller, David—*Primavera*. Burning Deck

Miller, Jane—*Many Junipers, Heartbeats*. Copper Beech Press

Miller, Leon—*White Bear*. Beatitude Press

Miller, Rob Hollis—*Shanghai Creek Fire*. St. Andrews Press

Mills, Ralph J., Jr.—*With No Answer*. Juniper Press

Mills, Robert—*Brown Bag*. Spoon River Poetry Press

Minshull, Evelyn—*You Teach Me Gentle*. D. C. Cook Pub. Co.

Minty, Judith—*Letters To My Daughter*. Mayapple Press

Mitcham, Allison—*Inuit Summer*. Porcupine's Quill

Monette, Paul—*Musical Comedy: A Poem*. Illuminati Press

Montague, John—*The Leap*. Deerfield Press/Gallery Press
—*The Rough Field*. Wake Forest University Press

Moon, Lawrence David—*Olympian Souls*. Clinton Press

Moore, Clement C.—*The Night Before Christmas*. Holiday House

Moore, Marianne—*The Complete Poems Of Marianne Moore*. Viking Press (reprint)

Moore, Roger—*Last Year In Paradise*. Fiddlehead Poetry Books

Moorman, Charles—*Epiphanies At Lux*. Texas Review Press

Morgan, John—*The Bone-Duster*. Quarterly Review of Literature

Morgan, Robert—*Groundwork*. Gnomen Press

Morice, Dave—*Quicksand Through The Hourglass*. Toothpaste Press

Morris, Herbert—*Intimate Letters: A Poem*. Illuminati Press

Morris, John N.—*The Glass Houses*. Atheneum Publishers

Morse, Rory—*Verisimilitude*. Prairie Poet Books

Mosby, George, Jr.—*Waves That Circle Him In Stone*. Greenfield Review Press

Moss, Howard—*Notes From The Castle*. Atheneum Publishers

Mozeson, Isaac—*The Watcher*. Downtown Poets

Mueller, Lisel—*The Need To Hold Still*. Louisiana State University Press

Mulligan, John—*Clutch A Dozen*. Beautiful Snow

Murphy, Richard—*Niches*. Deerfield Press/Gallery Press

Murray, Catherine—*The Transatlantic Flight Of The Angel Death*. New Rivers Press

Murray, G. E.—*Repairs*. University of Missouri Press

Mycue, Edward—*The Singing Man My Father Gave Me*. Menard Press

Myers, Neil—*All That, So Simple*. Purdue University Press

N

Nagy, Agnes Nemes—*Selected Poems* (translated by Bruce Berlind). Iowa Translations

Napora, Joe—*Portable Shelter.* Wolfsong

Nash, Ogden—*Custard And Company* (selected by Quentin Blake). Little, Brown & Co.

Nash, Valery—*The Narrows.* Cleveland State University Poetry Center

Nathan, Leonard—*Dear Blood.* University of Pittsburgh Press

Nelson, Bill—*Implementing Standards Of Good Behavior.* L'Epervier Press

Nelson, Harry W.—*Command Performance, And Other Poems.* Blue Leaf Editions

Nelson, Stanley—*101 Fragments Of A Prayer.* Midnight Sun

Newton, Norman—*On The Broken Mountain.* Fiddlehead Poetry Books

Nicholas, Paul—*I Want To Love: A Poetic Narrative Depicting Man's Struggles To Maturity.* Jade Publishing Co.

Nicolai, Adeodata Piazza—*Two Faces Of Janus: Translations And Poems.* Privately printed

Nikolic, Djordje—*Key To Dreams According To Djordje* (translated by Charles Simic). Elpenor Books

Nocerino Kathryn—*Wax Lips.* New Rivers Press

Nolan, James—*What Moves Is Not The Wind.* Wesleyan University Press

Norris, Leslie—*Walking The White Fields.* Little, Brown & Co.

North, Charles—*Leap Year.* Kulchur Foundation

Novalis—*Henry Von Ofterdingen* (translated by Palmer Hilty). Frederick Ungar Pub. Co.

Nye, Naomi Shihab—*Different Ways To Pray.* Breitenbush Publications

O

Oberg, Arthur—*Anna's Song.* University of Washington Press

O'Brien, Michael—*Conversations At The West End 1966-1974.* Sun

Oca, Marco Antonio Montes de—*The Heart Of The Flute* (translated by Laura Villasenor). Ohio University Press

Oldham, John—*The Works Of John Oldham, Together With His Remains.* Scholars' Facsimiles & Reprints (reprint)

Olds, Sharon—*Satan Says.* University of Pittsburgh Press

Oliver, Michael Brian—*To A Sister Loneliness.* Fiddlehead Poetry Books

Olson, Charles J.—*Ghost In The Trenches: Adventures In Verse.* Adams Press

Omar Khayyam—*The Rubaiyat Of Omar Khayyam/ Persian Miniatures* (translated by Edward Fitzgerald; notes by B. W. Robinson). Crescent Books

Ondaatje, Michael—*The Collected Works Of Billy The Kid.* Wingbow

O'Neill, Eugene—*Poems 1912-1944* (edited by Donald Gallup). Ticknor & Fields

Oosterhuis, Huub—*Times Of Life: Prayers And Poems* (translated by N. D. Smith). Paulist Press

Opie, Amelia Alderson; Tighe, Mary—*Elegy To The Memory Of The Late Duke Of Bedford; Psyche, With Other Poems.* Garland Pub. Co. (reprint)

Oppen, Mary—*Poems & Transpositions.* Montemora Foundation

Orlovsky, Peter (see listing for Ginsberg, Allen)

Overton, Ron—*Dead Reckoning.* Street Press

Owen, Guy—*The White Stallion And Other Poems.* John F. Blair, Publisher

Owen, Sue—*Nursery Rhymes For The Dead.* Ithaca House

P

Pack, Robert—*Waking To My Name: New And Selected Poems.* Johns Hopkins University Press

Padgett, Ron—*Tulsa Kid.* Z Press
—*Triangles In The Afternoon.* Sun

Paransky, Leah—*Ticker Tapes.* Lintel
—*Paper Napkin Poems.* Lintel

Parnell, Peter (see listing for Baylor, Byrd)

Parsons, David Mercier—*Life, Love, The Pursuit Of Happiness.* Arrow Pub. Co.

Parton, Dolly—*Just The Way I Am: Poetic Selections On "Reasons To Live, Reasons To Love And Reasons To Smile" From The Songs Of Dolly Parton.* Blue Mountain Press

Pastan, Linda—*Setting The Table.* Dryad Press
—*Even As We Sleep.* Croissant Press

Paulin, Tom—*The Strange Museum.* Faber & Faber Inc.

Pavese, Cesare—*Hard Labor* (translated by William Arrowsmith). Johns Hopkins University Press (reprint)

Peacock, Molly—*And Live Apart.* University of Missouri Press

Pease, Roland—*Held Up For Answers.* Imaginery Press

Pennant, Edmund—*Dreams Navel.* Lintel

Perchik, Simon—*The Club Fits Either Hand.* Elizabeth Press

Perry, Ronald—*Denizens.* Random House, Inc.

Persius Flaccus, Aulus (see listing for Juvenalis, Decimus Junius)

Peterson, Liz—*Weathering.* Spoon River Poetry Press

Petrarch—*Love Rimes Of Petrarch* (translated by Morris Bishop). Greenwood Press (reprint)

Pfingston, Roger—*Hazards Of Photography.* Writers' Center Press

Phillips, L. C.—*Twelve Muscle Tones.* Pulse-Finger

Phillips, Michael Joseph—*31 Erotic Concrete Sonnets For Samantha.* Privately printed

Piercy, Marge—*The Moon Is Always Female.* Alfred A. Knopf, Inc.

Pindar—*Pindar's Victory Songs* (translated by Frank J. Nisetich). Johns Hopkins University Press

Pittman, Edward M., Jr.—*The Graph Poems (Book I).* Privately printed

Pizarro, Agueda—*Sombraventadora/Shadowinnower* (translated by Barbara Stoler Miller and the poet). Columbia University Press

Poe, Edgar Allen—*The Poetical Works Of Edgar Allen Poe.* Weathervane Books

Polite, Frank—*Letters Of Transit.* City Miner Books

Polson, Don—*Long Travellers: Selected Verses*. Fiddle-head Poetry Books

Pomerantz, Charlotte—*The Tamarindo Puppy And Other Poems*. Greenwillow Books

Popa, Vasko—*Homage To The Lame Wolf: Selected Poems 1956-1975* (translated by Charles Simic). Field

Pope, Alexander—*The Selected Poetry Of Pope* (edited by Martin Price). New American Library

Portuges, Paul—*Aztec Birth: The Turquoise Mockingbird Of Light*. Mudborn Press

Posner, David—*Geographies*. Bellevue Press

Prelutsky, Jack—*Rolling Harvey Down The Hill*. Greenwillow Books

Press, Clayton M.—*Crepuscule*. Privately printed

Q

Quagliariello, Thomas A.—*Crumbs In My Crotch And Other Morsels*. Pageant-Poseidon Press

Quasha, George—*Giving The Lily Back Her Hands*. Station Hill Press

Quillen, Ruthellen—*The Bell Witch*. Sibyl-Child Press

R

Rabb, Antonia Phillips—*Encounters With Love*. William L. Bauhan Publishers

Radhuber, Stanley—*Flying Over Greenland*. Prescott Street Press

Radnoti, Miklos—*Forced March: Selected Poems* (translated by Clive Wilmer and George Gomori). Carcanet New Press (England); distributed in the U.S. by Persea Books

Raine, Craig—*A Martian Sends A Postcard Home*. Oxford University Press

Raine, Kathleen—*The Oracle In The Heart*. Dolmen Press/Allen & Unwin (London)

Raley, Tom—*Rodeo Fever: A Collection Of Poems Capturing The Spirit Of Rodeo*. Latigo Press

Ramage, Rosalyn Rikel—*A Book About People*. Broadman Press

Ramsey, Julian—*My Brother's Keeper*. Windy Row Press

Ray, Judy—*Pebble Rings*. Greenfield Review Press

Redgrove, Peter—*The Weddings At Nether Powers And Other New Poems*. Routledge & Kegan Paul, Ltd.

Reed, James—*Morning Notes To A Nighttime Diary*. Bits Press

Reid, Christopher—*Arcadia*. Oxford University Press

Reid, Monty—*In By One, Out By Four*. Instant Poetry Press

Reith, Alma Carmichael—*Smiles Ahead: A Book Of Light Verse*. Acre Press

Renner, Bruce—*Blue*. Sackbut Press

Rexroth, Kenneth—*The Morning Star*. New Directions Pub. Corp.

Reznikoff, Charles—*Testimony: Volume II, The United States (1885-1915)*. Black Sparrow Press

Ricard, Rene—*Rene Ricard 1979-1980*. Dia Books

Rice, Helen Steiner—*Mothers Are A Gift Of Love*. Fleming H. Revell Co.

Richardson, Dorothy Lee—*The Half-Seen Face*. William L. Bauhan Publishers

Richkin, Robert J.—*The Blind Receptionist And Other Poems*. Blue Mornings Press

Rigsbee, David—*To Be Here*. Coraddi Publications

Riley, James Whitcomb—*Afterwhiles*. Core Collection Books (reprint)

Rilke, Rainer Maria—*Sonnets To Orpheus* (translated by Charles Hazeloff). Privately printed

Rimbaud, Arthur; Verlaine, Paul—*A Lover's Cock And Other Gay Poems* (translated by J. Murat and W. Gunn). Gay Sunshine Press

Rinaldi, Nicholas—*The Resurrection Of The Snails*. John F. Blair, Publisher

Rinder, Walter—*A Promise Of Change*. Celestial Arts Pub. Co.

Rizzo, Peter Joseph—*Dream On, America*. Huntington Press

Roberts, Ellis W.—*The Mystik Mark*. Byron Books

Robinson, Kit—*Tribute To Nervous*. Tuumba Press

Rogers, Jill—*Alternate Endings*. Sono Nis Press

Rogow, Zack—*Glimmerings*. More Than Coincidence Press

Ronan, Richard—*Flowers*. Calamus Books

Ronan, Richard—*Buddha's Kisses And Other Poems*. Gay Sunshine Press

Ronsard, Pierre de—*Poems Of Pierre De Ronsard* (translated and edited by Nicholas Kilmer). University of California Press

Root, William Pitt—*A Journey South*. Graywolf Press
—*Coot*. Pipedream Press
—*The Storm*. Pipedream Press

Rose, Wendy—*Lost Copper*. Malki Museum Press

Roseliep, Raymond—*The Still Point*. Uzzano

Rosten, Norman—*Selected Poems*. George Braziller, Inc.

Rothenberg, Jerome—*Vienna Blood & Other Poems*. New Directions Pub. Corp.

Rothfork, John—*Indians*. Northwoods Press

Rozewicz, Tadeusz—*Unease* (translated by Victor Contoski). New Rivers Press

Rudder, Virginia L.—*The Gallows Lord*. John F. Blair, Publisher

Ruebsaat, Norbert—*Cordillera*. Pulp Press

Ruffin, Paul—*Lighting The Furnace Pilot*. Spoon River Poetry Press

Rukeyser, Muriel—*The Outer Banks*. Unicorn Press

Ruth, Barbara—*The Politics Of Relationships*. Seven Woods Press

Ryan, R. M.—*Goldilocks In Later Life*. Louisiana State University Press

S

Saaz, Johannes Von—*The Plowman From Bohemia* (translated by Alexander and Elizabeth Henderson). Frederick Ungar Pub. Co.

Salinger, Wendy—*Folly River*. E. P. Dutton & Co.

Saltman, Benjamin—*Deck*. Ithaca House

Sanders, Lewis—*Night Blossoms*. Prairie Poet Books

Sarton, May—*Halfway To Silence: New, Lyric, Love Poems*. W. W. Norton & Co.

Scalapino, Leslie—*This Eating And Walking At The Same Time Is Associated All Right*. Tombouctou Books

Schaeffer, Susan Fromberg–*The Bible Of The Beasts Of The Little Field*. E. P. Dutton & Co.

Schaffer, Ulrich–*Love Reaches Out: Meditations For People In Love*. Harper & Row, Publishers
–*A Growing Love: Meditations On Marriage And Commitment*. Harper & Row
–*For The Love Of Children: Meditations On Growing Up With Children*. Harper & Row

Schedler, Gilbert–*Waking Before Dawn*. Wampeter Press

Schevill, James–*Fire Of Eyes*. Copper Beech Press

Schiff, Jeff–*Anywhere In This Country*. Mammoth Press

Schiller, Friedrich–*Friedrich Schiller: An Anthology For Our Time* (edited by Frederick Ungar) (part poetry). Frederick Ungar Pub. Co.

Schmitz, Dennis–*String*. Ecco Press

Schneberg, Willa; Warren, Larkin–*Box Poems And Old Sheets*. Alice James Books

Schultz, Robert–*Vein Along The Fault*. Laueroc Press

Schuyler, James–*The Morning Of The Poem*. Farrar, Straus & Giroux, Inc.
–*Freely Espousing*. Sun

Schwartz, Delmore–*Last And Lost Poems of Delmore Schwartz* (edited by Robert Phillips). Vanguard Press

Schwartz, Howard–*Gathering The Sparks*. K. M. Gentile Publishing

Scotellaro, Rocco–*The Dawn Is Always New: Selected Poetry Of Rocco Scotellaro* (translated by Ruth Feldman and Brian Swann). Princeton University Press

Scott, Ann–*Inside*. Fiddlehead Poetry Books

Soully, James–*May Day*. Minnesota Review Press

Searle, Chris–*Mainland*. Calder & Boyars (distributed in the U.S. by Merrimack Book Service)

Seferis, George–*Poems*. Nonpareil Books

Seidel, Frederick–*Sunrise*. Viking Press

Seiler, Barry–*Retaining Wall*. L'Epervier Press

Service, Robert–*The Shooting Of Dan McGrew And Other Favorite Poems*. Dodd, Mead & Co.

Sewell, George–*A Gnome, A Candle, And Me: Reflections In A Candle On A Winter's Night– Poetry, Philosophy And Mischief*. Deluxe Co.

Shakespeare, William–*The Sonnets Of William Shakespeare*. Avenel Books (reprint)
–*The Sonnets Of William Shakespeare* (edited by Edward Dowden). Folcroft Library Editions (reprint)

Shapiro, David–*Lateness: A Book Of Poems*. Overlook Press

Sharett, Deirdre–*Language Of A Small Space*. Hartmus Press

Shaw, Sharon–*Auctions*. John F. Blair, Publisher

Sheppard, Susan–*Book Of Shadows . . . Book Of Dreams*. Merging Media

Sher, Steven–*Caught In The Revolving Door*. Love Street Books

Sherry, Pearl Anderson (see listing for Vidaver, Doris)

Siegel, Robert–*In A Pig's Eye*. University Presses of Florida

Sikelianos, Angelos–*Selected Poems* (translated by Edmund Keeley and Philip Sherrard). Princeton University Press

Silberg, Richard–*The Reckoning*. Oyez

Silk, Dennis–*The Punished Land*. Viking Press

Silkin, Jon–*The Psalms With Their Spoils*. Routledge & Kegan Paul Ltd.

Simic, Charles--*Classic Ballroom Dances: Poems*. George Braziller, Inc.

Simpson, Louis–*Out Of Season*. Deerfield Press/Gallery Press.
–*Caviare At The Funeral*. Franklin Watts, Inc.

Sitwell, Sacheverell–*Selected Poems*. AMS Press (reprint)

Skelton, Robin–*Landmarks*. Sono Nis Press

Skloot, Floyd–*Rough Edges*. Chowder Chapbooks

Slauson, Tom–*Natural Causes*. Red Weather Press

Sloan, Bill–*Ghost Images*. Hard Cider Press
–*Portraits Drawn From Memory*. Hard Cider Press

Smith, Douglas–*Scarecrow*. Turnstone Press
–*The Light Of Our Bones: A Sequence For Lawrence*. Turnstone Press

Smith, Robert L.–*Refractions*. Dragon's Teeth Press

Smith, Stephen E.–*The Bushnell Hamp Poems*. Green River Press

Smith, William Jay–*Journey To The Dead Sea: A Poem In Four Parts*. Abattoir Editions

Snow, Karen–*Wonders*. Viking Press

Solt, Mary Ellen–*The Peoplemover: A Demonstration Poem*. West Coast Poetry Review

Solway, David–*Mephistopheles And The Astronaut*. Mosaic Press/Valley Editions

Sophocles–*Ajax* (edited by W. B. Stanford). Arno Press (reprint)

Sotheby, William–*A Poetical Epistle To Sir George Beaumont; Oberon, Or, Huon De Bourdeaux*. Garland Pub. Co. (reprint)

Souster, Raymond–*Collected Poems Of Raymond Souster, Volume I, 1940-55*. Oberon Press

Spear, Roberta–*Silks*. Holt, Rinehart & Winston, Inc.

Speece, Merry–*Detail From An American Landscape*. Bits Press

Spenser, Edmund–*The Faerie Queene: A Modern Prose Adaptation* (by Douglas Hill). Newsweek Books
–*The Faerie Queen* (edited by A. C. Hamilton). Longman, Inc.

Sponde, Jean de–*Sonnets On Love And Death* (translated by Robert Nugent). Greenwood Press (reprint)

Stafford, William–*Tuned In Late One Night*. Deerfield Press/Gallery Press
–*Things That Happen Where There Aren't Any People*. Boa Editions

Stefanile, Selma–*I Know A Wise Bird*. Sparrow Press

Stephenson, Shelby–*Middle Creek Poems*. Blue Coot Press

Stewart, Pamela–*Cascades*. L'Epervier Press

Stone, John–*In All This Rain*. Louisiana State University Press

Stoutenburg, Adrien–*Greenwich Mean Time*. University of Utah Press

Strongin, Lynn–*Countrywoman/Surgeon*. L'Epervier Press

Sullivan, Francis–*Spy Wednesday's Kind*. The Smith

Sussman, M. L.–*Light And Shady: A Collection Of Limericks*. Wings Press

Sutherland, Elizabeth—*Mouth Of The Whale*. Prairie Poet Books

Suttles, Ella Mae—*Great Reunion In The Sky*. Prairie Poet Books
—*When The Lights Are Turned On*. Prairie Poet Books

Swados, Elizabeth—*Lullaby*. Harper & Row

Swanson, Karen—*East-West*. Confluence Press

Swetman, Glenn Robert—*Concerning Carpenters And Childhood Saints & Other Poems*. Pterodactyl Press

Swift, Robert—*Green Meadows*. Swift Systems

T

Tahara, Mildred M. (translator)—*Tales Of Yamato: A Tenth Century Poem-tale*. University Press of Hawaii

Takamura, Kotaro—*Chieko And Other Poems Of Takamura Kotaro* (translated by Kiroaki Sato). University Press of Hawaii

Tanikawa, Shuntaro—*At Midnight In The Kitchen I Just Wanted To Talk To You* (translated by William I. Elliott and Kazuo Kawamura). Prescott Street Press
—*With Silence My Companion* (translated by William I. Elliott and Kazuo Kawamura). Prescott Street Press

Tarwood, James A.—*Constant Change*. Privately printed

Taylor, Bruce Edward—*Idle Trade: Early Poems*. Wolfsong

Taylor, Richard—*Earth Bones*. Gnomon Press

Tedlock, Ernest—*You See I Don't Forget: Selected Poems & Stories*. Holmgangers Press

Thayne, Emma Lou—*Once In Israel*. Brigham Young University Press

Theriault, Frank—*I Am Justice: An Epic Poem Of Moral Determination In The Space Age*. Blain Press

Thomas, F. Richard—*Frog Praises Night: Poems With Commentary*. Southern Illinois University Press

Thomas, Lorenzo—*Chances Are Few*. Blue Wind Press

Thomas, Richard—*Poems By Richard Thomas*. Avon Books

Thurston, Harry—*Barefaced Stone*. Fiddlehead Poetry Books

Tighe, Mary (see listing for Opie, Amelia Alderson)

Toigo, Sister M. Angela—*Caves And Canyons: A Refreshing Journey Of The Spirit To Inner Realities*. Benedictine Sisters

Tolson, Melvin B.—*A Gallery Of Harlem Portraits* (edited by Robert M. Farnsworth). University of Missouri Press

Tomkiw, Lydia—*Popgun Sonatas*. MOD Press

Toomer, Jean—*The Wayward And The Seeking: A Collection Of Writings By Jean Toomer* (partly poetry) (edited by Darwin T. Turner). Howard University Press

Trammell, Robert—*George Washington Trammell*. Salt Lick Press

Transtromer, Tomas—*Truth Barriers*. Sierra Club Books
—*Selected Poems* (translated by Robin Fulton). Ardis Publishers

Treanor, Richard G.—*Parallax Poems*. Privately printed

Turner, James Houston—*The Earth Of Your Soul*. Seven Search Publications

Turner, Myron—*Rag Doll's Shadow*. Porcupine's Quill
—*Things That Fly*. Swallow Press

Tyler, Kathy—*Apple, Worm, And All*. Fiddlehead Poetry Books

Tyse, George—*Tea*. Burning Deck

U

Unger, Barbara—*The Man Who Burned Money*. Bellevue Press

Urdang, Constance—*The Lone Woman And Others*. University of Pittsburgh Press

V

Van Brunt, H. L.—*And The Man Who Was Traveling Never Got Home*. Carnegie-Mellon University Press

Venn, George—*Off The Main Road*. Prescott Street Press

Verlaine, Paul (see listing for Rimbaud, Arthur)

Vidaver, Doris; Sherry, Pearl Anderson—*Arch Of A Circle*. Swallow Press

Villa, Jose Garcia—*Appassionata: Poems In Praise Of Love*. King and Cowen

Villon, Francois—*Ten Poems* (translated by Arpad Barna). Westport Press

Violi, Paul—*The Reckless Sleeper*. The Sun Press

Virgil—*Aeneas In Libya* (a translation into verse of the first four books of Virgil's "Aeneid") (by Charles Cassil Reynard). Vantage Press

Vliet, R. G.—*Water And Stone*. Random House, Inc.

Volk, Stephen—*Exordium*. Harvest Press

Vonnegut, Kurt—*Sun, Moon, Star*. Harper & Row

W

Wakeman, John—*Hopeless Loves And Happy Endings*. Midsummer Press

Wakoski, Diane—*Cap Of Darkness*. Black Sparrow Press

Waldman, Anne—*Countries*. Toothpaste Press

Waldrop, Rosemarie—*The Road Is Everywhere Or Stop This Body*. Open Places
—*The Ambition Of Ghosts*. Seven Woods Press

Walker, Jeanne Murray—*Nailing Up The Home Sweet Home*. Cleveland State University Press

Warden, Marine Robert—*Beyond The Straits*. Momentum Press

Warren, James E., Jr.—*The Elegance Of God*. The Print Shop

Warren, Larkin (see listing for Schneberg, Willa)

Waterman, Cary—*The Salamander Migration*. University of Pittsburgh Press

Waters, Michael—*Not Just Any Death*. Boa Editions

Watson, Elaine—*We, The Women: Limericks Liberated*. Reno Press

Webb, Cornelius; Wells, Charles Jeremiah—*Sonnets; Summer; Joseph And His Brethren*. Garland Pub. Co. (reprint)

Weismiller, Edward—*The Branch Of Fire*. Word Works

Welch, Liliane—*Syntax Of Ferment*. Fiddlehead Poetry Books

Welish, Marjorie—*Handwritten*. Sun

Wells, Charles Jeremiah (see listing for Webb, Cornelius)

Welt, Bernard—*Serenade.* Z Press

Wendell, B. Leilah—*Threshold.* Privately printed

Wendt, Viola—*The Wind Is Rising.* Carroll College Press

West, John Foster—*Wry Wine.* John F. Blair, Publisher

Westcott, Nadine Bernard—*I Know An Old Lady Who Swallowed A Fly.* Little, Brown & Co.

Westlake, Diane—*Gentle Freedom, Gentle Courage: Poems On Friendship, Love And Life.* Blue Mountain Press

Whitehead, Fred—*Steel Destiny.* West End Press

Whitehead, James—*Local Men.* University of Illinois Press

Whiteman, Bruce—*Inventions.* Three Trees Press

Whitman, Ruth—*Permanent Address: New Poems 1973-1980.* Alice James Books

Whitten, Les—*Washington Cycle.* The Smith

Wicklund, Millie Mae—*Outlaw.* Mudborn Press

Wilcox, Hilda Mader—*Proving The Pudding.* Privately printed

Wild, Peter—*Jeanne D'Arc: A Collection Of New Poems.* St. Luke's Press
—*Wilderness.* New Rivers Press

Will, Frederic—*Our Thousand Year Old Bodies: Selected Poems, 1956-1976.* University of Massachusetts Press

Williams, Paul—*You And Me Against The World: Poetic Selections From The Songs Of Paul Williams* (edited by Susan Polis Schutz). Blue Mountain Press

Winter, Helen (see listing for Kachmar, Jessie)

Winters, Yvor—*The Collected Poems Of Yvor Winters.* Swallow Press

Woessner, Warren—*No Hiding Place.* Spoon River Poetry Press

Wolfert, Helen—*Landlady And Tenant.* Sheep Meadow Press

Wood-Thompson, Susan—*Crazy Quilt.* Crone Books

Woodcock, George—*The Mountain Road.* Fiddlehead Poetry Books

Wordsworth, William—*Benjamin The Waggoner* (edited by Paul F. Betz). Cornell University Press

Worth, Douglas—*Triptych.* Apple-Wood Press

Wreford, James—*Countryside Canada.* Fiddlehead Poetry Books

Wright, Carolyne—*Stealing The Children.* Ahsahta Press
—*Returning What We Owed.* Owl Creek Press

Wright, Franz—*The Earth Without You.* Cleveland State University Poetry Center

Wright, Jay—*The Double Invention Of Komo.* University of Texas Press

Wynand, Derk—*Pointwise.* Fiddlehead Poetry Books

Wyness, Jean M.—*I Am Part Of Every Poem: Poems For Everyone Over Seven.* Branden Press

X

Xerox, Anna May—*Dyke Tracy And Others.* Karmic Revenge Laundry Shop Press

Y

Yates, David C.—*Riding For The Dome.* Cedar Rock Press

Yau, John—*Sometimes.* Sheep Meadow Press

Yevtushenko, Yevgeny—*Ivan The Terrible And Ivan The Fool* (translated by Daniel Weissbort). Richard Marek Publishers

Yolen, Jane—*How Beastly!* Collins

Young, David—*The Names Of the Hare In English.* University of Pittsburgh Press

Young Bear, Ray—*Winter Of The Salamander: The Keeper Of Importance.* Harper & Row

Z

Zander, William—*Distances.* Solo Press

Zienek, Marilee—*Splinters In My Pride.* Word Books

Zinnes, Harriet—*Book Of Ten.* Bellevue Press

Zu-Bolton, Ahmos—*Ain't No Spring Chicken.*

(2) ANTHOLOGIES
(listed alphabetically by title)

Always Begin Where You Are: Themes In Poetry And Song (edited by Walter Lamb). McGraw-Hill Book Co.

The American Poetry Anthology (edited by David Halpern). Avon Books

Anthology Of German Poetry Through The 19th Century (edited by Alexander Gode and Frederick Ungar). Frederick Ungar Pub. Co.

An Anthology Of Modern Persian Poetry (selected and translated by Ahmad Karimi-Hakkak). Westview Press

An Anthology Of Spanish Poetry: From The Beginnings To The Present Day Including Both

Spain And Spanish America (edited by John A. Crow). Louisiana State University Press

Anthology Of Swedish Lyrics From 1750 To 1925 (compiled and translated by Charles Wharton Stork). Granger Book Co. (reprint)

The Batsford Book Of Country Verse (edited by Samuel Carr). Batsford (London) (dist. in U.S. by David & Charles, North Pomfret, VT)

The Batsford Book Of Light Verse For Children (edited by Gavin Ewart). Batsford (London) (dist. in U.S. by David & Charles, North Pomfret, VT)

Before Their Time: Six Women Writers Of The

Eighteenth Century (edited by Katharine Rogers) (part poetry). Frederick Ungar Pub. Co.

Best Loved Poems Of The American West (edited by John J. and Barbara T. Gregg). Doubleday & Co.

Best Of The Poetry, Year 6 (edited by Dannie Abse). Robson Books

The Birthright With Love (selected by Lecta Kate Falls). Moore Pub. Co.

Blood Of Their Blood: An Anthology Of Polish-American Poetry (edited by Victor Contoski). New Rivers Press

The Book Of Ballads (selected by John R. Crossland). Granger Book Co. (reprint)

Bring Me All Of Your Dreams (selected by Nancy Larrick). M. Evans & Co.

The Burning Tree: Poems From The First Thousand Years Of Welsh Verse (selected and translated by Gwyn Williams). Greenwood Press (reprint)

Ca Dao Viet Nam: A Bilingual Anthology Of Vietnamese Folk Poetry (edited and translated by John Balaban). Unicorn Press

The Capra Chapbook Anthology (edited by Noel Young). Capra Press

Christmas In Texas (edited by V. T. Abercrombie and Helen Williams). Brown Rabbit Press

The Colour Of The Weather: An Anthology Of Walloon Poetry (edited and translated by Yann Lovelook). Menard Press

Contemporary Irish Poetry: An Anthology (edited by Anthony Bradley). University of California Press

Contemporary Northwest Writing: A Collection Of Poetry & Fiction (edited by Roy Carlson). Oregon State University Press

Contemporary Poetry Of North Carolina (edited by Guy Owen and Mary C. Williams). John F. Blair, Publisher

Contemporary Poets Of America, 1979. Dorrance & Co.

Contemporary Southern Poetry: An Anthology (edited by Guy Owen and Mary C. Williams). Louisiana State University Press

Contemporary Swedish Poetry (translated by John Matthias and Goran Printz-Pahlson). Swallow Press

Dante And His Circle With The Italian Poets Preceding Him (1100-1200-1300): A Collection Of Lyrics (translated by Dante Gabriel Rossetti). Folcroft Library Editions (reprint)

Dear Dark Faces: Portraits Of A People (selected by Helen Earle Simcox). Lotus Press

Dinosaurs And Beasts Of Yore (selected by William Cole). Collins World Publishers

The Earthquake On Ada Street: An Anthology Of Poetry Of Members Of Paul Carroll's Poetry Workshop (edited by Paull Carroll). Jupiter Press

Easter Buds Are Springing: Poems For Easter (selected by Lee Bennett Hopkins). Harcourt Brace Jovanovich

Eight Idaho Poets: An Anthology (edited by Ronald E. McFarland). University Press of Idaho

The Faber Book Of Nonsense Verse: With A

Sprinkling Of Nonsense Prose (chosen by Geoffrey Grigson). Faber & Faber, Inc.

The Faber Popular Reciter (edited by Kingsley Amis). Faber & Faber, Inc.

The Face Of Creation: Contemporary Hungarian Poetry (translated by Jascha Kessler). Illuminati Press

Fairy Poems (edited by Daisy Wallace). Holiday House

Field & Dreams: Ohio's Wild Life: Poetry & Fiction (edited by Nikki Giovanni and Clarence Major). Arts Consortium

A First Poetry Book (compiled by John Foster). Oxford University Press

Five American Poets: Robert Hass, John Matthias, James McMichael, John Peck, Robert Pinsky. Carcanet New Press (England) (dist. in U.S. by Persea Books, New York)

Five Centuries Of Polish Poetry (compiled by Jerzy Pietrkiewicz and Bruns Singer; translated by the compilers and Jon Stallworthy). Greenwood Press (reprint)

Five Contemporary Dutch Poets (compiled by Hans van de Waarsenburg; translated by Peter Nijmeijer and Scott Hollins). Cross-Cultural Communications

Five Contemporary Flemish Poets (compiled by Hans van de Waarsenburg; translated by James S. Holmes, Peter Nijmeijer and Scott Rollins). Cross-Cultural Communications

Five Missouri Poets (edited by Jim Barnes). Chariton Review Press

4 Major Visual Poets: Ruth Jacoby, Richard Kostelanetz, Tom Ockerse, Michael Joseph Phillips (edited by Michael Joseph Phillips). Free University Press

Golden Harvest: A Collection Of Inspirational Poetry And Prose (by Gilbert Hay). Doubleday & Co.

Golden Songs Of The Golden Gate (selected by Marguerite Wilkinson). Granger Book Co. (reprint)

The Golden Treasury Of Longer Poems (edited by Ernest Rhys). Granger Book Co. (reprint)

Here We Come A'Piping (edited by Rose Fyleman). Granger Book Co. (reprint)

Homespun: An Anthology Of Poetry (compiled by Anita Browne for General Federation of Women's Clubs). Granger Book Co. (reprint)

Inventing A Word: An Anthology Of Twentieth-Century Puerto Rican Poetry (edited by Julio Marzan). Columbia University Press

It's All In The Wrist (edited by C. Michael Archer). Volume II Poets

Ko-Uta: "Little Songs" Of The Geisha World (edited by Liza Crihfield). C. E. Tuttle Co.

Last Translations—Russian Poems (translated by Eugene M. Kayden). Colorado Quarterly

Late Augustan Poetry (edited by Patricia Meyer Spacks). Irvington Publishers (reprint)

Likenesses (translated by Francis Golffing). Typographeum

The Listening Child: A Selection From The Stories Of

English Verse, Made For The Youngest Readers And Hearers (compiled by Lucy W. Thacher). Granger Book Co. (reprint)

Lithuanian Writers In The West: An Anthology (partly poetry) (edited by Alina Skrupkelis). Lithuanian Library Press/Loyola University Press

Living Space: Poems Of The Dutch "Fiftiers" (edited by Peter Glassgold). New Directions Pub. Corp.

London Poets And The American Revolution (compiled by James C. Gaston). Whitston Pub. Co.

Lyra Historica: Poems Of British History (compiled by M. E. Windsor and J. Turral). Granger Book Co. (reprint)

The Man In The Moon As He Sails The Sky And Other Moon Verse (collected by Ann Schweninger). Dodd, Mead & Co.

Men Who March Away: Poems Of The First World War (edited by I. M. Parsons). Chatto & Windus

Modern Australian Poetry (selected by H. M. Green). Granger Book Co.

Modern British Lyrics: An Anthology (compiled by Stanton A. Coblentz). Granger Book Co. (reprint)

The Modern Japanese Prose Poem: An Anthology Of Six Poets (translated by Dennis Keene). Princeton University Press

Modern Poetry For Children (edited by James J. Reynolds). Granger Book Co. (reprint)

Modern Poets Four: Philip Larkin, Ted Hughes, Thom Gunn, Seamus Heaney, Charles Tomlinson, Sylvia Plath (edited by Jim Hunter). Faber & Faber, Inc.

Modern Welsh Poetry (edited by Keidrych Rhys). Granger Book Co. (reprint)

Moments: Poems About The Seasons (selected by Lee Bennett Hopkins). Harcourt Brace Jovanovich

Morning, Noon And Nighttime, Too: Poems (selected by Lee Bennett Hopkins). Harper & Row Publishers

The Nature Lover's Knapsack: An Anthology Of Poems For Lovers Of The Open Road (edited by Edwin Osgood Grover). Granger Book Co. (reprint)

Nature In Verse: A Poetry Reader For Children (compiled by Mary I. Lovejoy). Granger Book Co. (reprint)

Nematodes In My Garden Of Verse: A Little Book Of Tar Heel Poems (compiled by Richard Walser). John F. Blair, Publisher

New England Poetry Engagement Book 1980 (edited by Eric C. Linder and Paul F. Marion). Yellow Umbrella Press

The New Limerick: 2750 Unpublished Examples, American And British (edited by G. Legman). Bell Pub. Co.

News Of The Universe: Poems Of Twofold Consciousness (chosen by Robert Bly). Sierra Club Books

Old Friend From Far Away: 150 Chinese Poems From The Great Dynasties (translated by C. H. Kwock and Vincent McHugh). North Point Press

Out Of This World: An Encyclopedia Of Contemporary Poetics (edited by Anne Waldman). Stonehill Pub. Co.

An Oxford Anthology Of English Poetry (edited by

Howard Foster Lowry and Willard Thorp). Granger Book Co. (reprint)

The Oxford Book Of English Verse, 1250-1900 (chosen and edited by Arthur Quiller Couch). Granger Book Co. (reprint)

The Oxford Book Of Victorian Verse (chosen by Arthur Quiller Couch). Granger Book Co. (reprint)

Pictures That Storm Inside My Head: Poems For The Inner You (edited by Richard Peck). Avon Books

Pipe And Drum (edited by Rose Fyleman). Core Collection Books (reprint)

Poems On The Abolition Of The Slave Trade (compiled by R. Bowyer). Garland Pub. Co. (reprint)

Poems Of Christmas (edited by Myra Cohn Livingston). Atheneum Publishers

Poems That Stir The Heart (compiled by Mary Sanford Laurence). A & W Publishers

Poemscapes (edited by Sheila R. Jensen). M. O. Pub. Co.

The Poetry Of Railways (edited by Samuel Carr). Batsford (London) (distributed in U.S. by David & Charles, Inc., North Pomfret, VT)

The Poetry Of Scotland (edited by Douglas Dunn). Batsford (dist. in U.S. by David and Charles, North Pomfret, VT)

Poetry Of To-day: An Anthology (edited by Rosa M. R. Mikels and Grace Shoup). Granger Book Co. (reprint)

Postcard Poems: An Anthology Of Poetry For Sharing (edited by Paul B. Janeczko). Bradbury Press

The Pushcart Prize, IV: Best Of The Small Presses (edited by Bill Henderson). Pushcart Press

Rapunzel, Rapunzel: Poetry, Prose And Photographs By Women On The Subject Of Hair (edited by Katharyn Machan Aal). McBooks Press

Restoration: Our Philosophy Through Inspired Poems (edited by Sister Sooty-Face). Sooty-Face

Ribaldry Of Ancient Greece (edited and translated by Jack Lindsay) (part poetry). Frederick Ungar Pub. Co.

Ribaldry Of Ancient Rome (edited and translated by Jack Lindsay) (part poetry). Frederick Ungar Pub. Co.

A Roman Collection: Stories, Poems And Other Good Pieces (by writing residents of the American Academy in Rome; edited by Miller Williams). University of Missouri Press

Roman Poetry, From The Republic To The Silver Age (translated by Dorothea Wender). Southern Illinois University Press

Sappho To Valery: Poems In Translation (edited by John Frederick Nims). Princeton University Press

Second Rising (edited by Stacy Tuthill). SCOP Publications

Serving Blood: New Poems By French Women (translated by Gloria Still). Wampeter Press

Seven Lake Superior Poets (edited by Rick Penn and David Kubach). Bear Cult Press

Seven Russian Poets: Imitations (edited by Rosemary Dobson and David Campbell). University of

Queensland Press (dist. in U.S. by TIC, Lawrence, MA)

Sextette: Translations From The French Symbolists (compiled by Dorothy Martin). AMS Press (reprint)

Silly Verse (And Even Worse) (edited by Joseph Rosenbloom). Sterling Pub. Co.

Six Voices: Contemporary Australian Poets (edited by Chris Wallace-Crabbe). Greenwood Press (reprint)

Social Writings Of The 1930s: A Selection (edited by Jack Salzman and Leo Zanderer). Burt Franklin & Co.

Soldiers' Verse (chosen by Patric Dickinson). Granger Book Co. (reprint)

Sun Through Small Leaves: Poems Of Spring. Collins

This Powerful Rhyme: A Book Of Sonnets (selected by Helen Plotz). Greenwillow Books

Three Russian Poets: Margarita Aliger, Yunna Moritz,

Bella Akhmadulina (compiled and translated by Elaine Feinstein). Carcanet New Press (dist. in U.S. by Persea Books, New York, NY)

Threshold (edited by Sheila R. Jensen). M. O. Pub. Co.

A Time For Poetry: An Anthology Of The North Carolina Poetry Society. John F. Blair, Publisher

Too Small For Stovewood, Too Big For Kindling: Collected (Irish) Verse And Translations (edited by John V. Kelleher). Dolman Press (dist. in U.S. by Humanities Press, Atlantic Highlands, NJ)

Twenty Contemporary Greek Poets (edited by Dinos Siotis and John Chioles). Wire Press

Two Decades Of Indian Poetry, 1960-1980 (edited by Keki N. Daruwalla). Vikas Pub. House (dist. in U.S. by Advent Books, New York, NY)

Visions Of The Enchanted Spirit (compiled and edited by Sal St. John Buttaci and Susan Linda Gerstle). New Worlds Unlimited

(3) BIOGRAPHY AND COMMENT ON SPECIFIC POETS
(listed alphabetically by subject)

Alberti, Rafael– *The Lost Grove: Autobiography Of A Poet In Exile* (by Rafael Alberti; translated and edited by Gabriel Berns). University of California Press

Aristophanes–*Socrates And Aristophanes* (by Leo Strauss). University of Chicago Press (reprint)
  –*Self And Society In Aristophanes* (by Dana Ferrin Sutton). University Press of America
  –*Aristophanes: Essays In Interpretation* (edited by Jeffrey Henderson). Cambridge University Press

Arnold, Matthew– *Matthew Arnold, Prose Writings: The Critical Heritage* (edited by Carl Dawson and John Pfordresher). Routledge & Kegan Paul

Ashbery, John–*Beyond Amazement: New Essays On John Ashbery* (edited by David Lehman). Cornell University Press

Auden, W. H.–*Conversations With W. H. Auden* (by Howard Griffin). Grey Fox Press
  –*W. H. Auden: The Life Of A Poet* (by Charles Osborn). Harcourt Brace Jovanovich

Awoonor, Kofi–*Four Modern West African Poets* (by Romanus Egudu). NOK Publishers

Baudelaire, Charles–*Baudelaire, A Fire To Conquer Darkness.* St. Martin's Press
  –*Baudelaire: Man Of His Time* (by Lois Boe Hyslop). Yale University Press

Beaver, Bruce–*As It Was* (by Bruce Beaver). University of Queensland Press (dist. by TIC, Lawrence, MA)

Behn, Aphra–*The Passionate Shepherdess* (by Maureen Duffy). Avon/Discus Books

Berryman, John–*John Berryman: A Critical Commentary* (by John Haffenden). New York University Press

Bishop, John Peale–*John Peale Bishop: A Biography* (by Elizabeth Carroll Spindler). West Virginia University Library

Blake, William–*From Blake To "A Vision"* (by Kathleen Raine). Dolmen Press (Dublin) (dist. in U.S. by Humanities Press, Atlantic Highlands, NJ)
  –*Blake And Freud* (by Diana Hume George). Cornell University Press
  –*Such Holy Song: Music As Idea, Form And Image In The Poetry Of William Blake* (by B. H. Fairchild, Jr.). Kent State University Press
  –*The Line In The Margin: Juan Ramon Jimenez And His Readings In Blake, Shelley And Yeats* (by Howard T. Young). University of Wisconsin Press
  –*Blake And The New Age* (by Kathleen Raine). G. Allen & Unwin
  –*Symbol And Truth In Blake's Myth* (by Leopold Damrosch, Jr.). Princeton University Press

Bontemps, Arna–*Arna Bontemps-Langston Hughes Letters (1925-1967)* (edited by Charles H. Nichols). Dodd, Mead & Co.

Bronte, Anne–*The Poems Of Anne Bronte: A New Text And Criticism* (by Edward Chitham). Rowman and Littlefield, Inc.

Bronte, Emily–*Women Writers And Poetic Identity: Wordsworth, Bronte And Dickinson* (by Margaret Homans). Princeton University Press

Browning, Robert–*Browning's Trumpeter: The Correspondence Of Robert Browning And Frederick J. Furnivall, 1872-1889* (edited by William S. Peterson). Decatur House Press
  –*The Browning Cyclopaedia: A Guide To The Study Of The Works Of Robert Browning* (by Edward Berdoe). Longwood Press

—Robert Browning's Poetry: Authoritative Texts, Criticism (edited by James F. Loucks). W. W. Norton & Co., Inc.

—Quest For Eros: Browning And "Fifine" (by Samuel B. Southwell). University Press of Kentucky.

—Robert Browning: A Collection Of Critical Essays (edited by Harold Bloom and Adrieene Munich). Prentice-Hall, Inc.

Bunting, Basil—*Basil Bunting: Man And Poet* (edited by Carroll F. Terrell). National Poetry Foundation

Byron, Lord—*Byron, A Portrait* (by Leslie A. Marchand). University of Chicago Press (reprint)

—A Heart For Every Fate (edited by Leslie A. Marchand). Belknap Press

Campbell, Roy—*Broken Record: Reminiscences* (by Roy Campbell). Scholarly Press (reprint)

Catullus—*A Commentary On Catullus* (by Robinson Ellis). Garland Pub. Co. (reprint)

Chateaubriand, Francois R.—*Chateaubriand: Composition, Imagination And Poetry* (by Charles A. Porter). Anma Libri

Chaucer, Geoffrey—*Chapters On Chaucer* (by Kemp Malone). Greenwood Press (reprint)

—Chaucer, Langland, And The Creative Imagination (by David Aers). Routledge & Kegan Paul, Ltd.

—Chaucer's Boccaccio (edited and translated by N. R. Havely). Rowman and Littlefield, Inc.

—Chaucer's "Troilus And Criseyde" And The Critics (by Alice R. Kaminsky). Ohio University Press

—Chaucer's Language And The Philosophers' Tradition (by J. D. Burnley). Rowman & Littlefield, Inc.

—Chaucer's "Troilus": Essays In Criticism (edited by Stephen A. Barney). Archon Books

Clare, John—*Homage To John Clare: A Poetical And Critical Correspondence* (by Peter Neumeyer). Peregrine Smith

Clark, John Pepper—*Four Modern West African Poets* (by Romanus Egudu). NOK Publishers

Coleridge, Samuel Taylor—*Coleridge's Secret Ministry: The Context Of The Conversation Poems, 1795-1798* (by Kelvin Everest). Barnes & Noble Books

—Coleridge And The Literature Of Sensibility (by George Dekker). Barnes & Noble Books

—Coleridge On Imagination And Fancy (by Basil Willey). Folcroft Library Editions (reprint)

—Romanticism And The Forms Of Ruin: Wordsworth, Coleridge, And Modalities Of Fragmentation (by Thomas McFarland). Princeton University Press

Collins, William—*Gray, Collins, And Their Circle* (by W. T. Williams and G. H. Vallins). Folcroft Library Editions (reprint)

Crane, Hart— *Hart Crane's Divided Vision: An Analysis Of "The Bridge"* (by Helge Norman Nilsen). Universitetsforlaget (dist. in U.S. by Columbia University Press)

Creeley, Robert—*Charles Olson & Robert Creeley: The Complete Correspondence* (edited by George Butterick). Black Sparrow Press

Croce, Benedetto—*The Romantic Theory Of Poetry: An Examination In The Light Of Croce's Aesthetic* (by A. E. Powell). AMS Press (reprint)

cummings, e. e.—*e. e. cummings: The Growth Of A Writer* (by Norman Friedman). Southern Illinois University Press

Dante Alighieri—*Dante* (by George Holmes). Hill & Wang, Inc.

—Further Papers On Dante (by Dorothy L. Sayers). Greenwood Press (reprint)

—Dante, Michelangelo And Milton (by John Arthos). Greenwood Press (reprint)

—Dante The Maker (by William Anderson). Routledge & Kegan Paul, Ltd.

—The Poetics Of Disguise: The Autobiography Of The Work In Homer, Dante And Shakespeare (by Franco Ferrucci; translated by Ann Dunnigan). Cornell University Press

Desbordes-Valmore, Marceline—*Memoirs Of Madame Desbordes-Valmore* (by C. A. Sainte-Beuve (translated by Harriet W. Preston). AMS Press (reprint)

Dickinson, Emily—*Emily Dickinson's Imagery* (by Rebecca Patterson; edited by Margaret H. Freeman). University of Massachusetts Press

—The Poems Of Emily Dickinson: An Annotated Guide To Commentary Published In English, 1890-1977 (by Joseph Duchac). G. K. Hall & Co., Inc.

—Women Writers And Poetic Identity: Wordsworth, Bronte And Dickinson (by Margaret Homans). Princeton University Press

—The Life Of Emily Dickinson (by Richard B. Sewall). Farrar, Straus & Giroux, Inc.

Dimmette, Celia Puhr—*Take Me Home: Life On The Family Farm* (by Celia Puhr Dimmette). Marshall Jones Co.

Donne, John—*John Donne's Lyrics: The Eloquence Of Action* (by Arnold Stein). Octagon Books

Dunbar, Paul Laurence—*Paul Laurence Dunbar* (by Peter Revell). Twayne Publishers

Duncan, Robert—*Robert Duncan, Scales Of The Marvelous* (edited by Robert J. Bertholf and Ian W. Reid). New Directions Pub. Corp.

Eliot, T. S.—*The Progress Of T. S. Eliot As Poet And Critic* (by Jyoti Prakash Sen). Norwood Editions (reprint)

—Jungian Psychology In Literary Analysis: A Demonstration Using T. S. Eliot's Poetry (by Joyce Meeks Jones). University Press of America

—Time And Poetry In Eliot's "Four Quartets" (by Rajendra Verma). Humanities Press

—Vortex: Pound, Eliot And Lewis (by Timothy Materer). Cornell University Press

—T. S. Eliot: A Bibliography (by Donald Gallup). Faber & Faber, Inc.

—T. S. Eliot: The Critic As Philosopher (by Lewis Freed). Purdue University Press

—Theory And Personality: The Significance Of T. S. Eliot's Criticism (by Brian Lee). Athlone Press (dist. in U.S. by Humanities Press, Atlantic Highland, NJ)

Elytis, Odysseus—*Odysseus Elytis: Analogies Of Light* (edited by Ivar Ivask). University of Oklahoma Press

Emerson, Ralph Waldo—*Light Of Emerson: A Complete Digest With Key-Word Concordance: The Cream Of All He Wrote* by H. S. Emmons). Folcroft Library Editions (reprint)
—*The Centenary Of The Birth Of Ralph Waldo Emerson* Folcroft Library Editions (reprint)
—*A Day With Ralph Waldo Emerson* (by Maurice Clair). Folcroft Library Editions (reprint)
—*Emerson, His Muse And Message* (by V. Ramakrishna Rao). Folcroft Library Editions (reprint)
—*Ralph Waldo Emerson: An Interpretive Essay* (by Lewis Leary). Twayne Publishers

Euripides—*The Phoenissae Of Euripides* (edited and notes by John U. Powell). Arno Press (reprint)
—*The Iphigeneia At Aulis Of Euripides* (edited and notes by E. B. England). Arno Press (reprint)
—*Euripides And His Age* (by Gilbert Murray. Greenwood Press (reprint)
—*The Violence Of Pity In Euripides' "Medea"* (by Pietro Pucci). Cornell University Press

Everson, William—*Earth Poetry: Selected Essays And Interviews Of William Everson, 1950-1977* (edited by Lee Bartlett). Oyez

Feng Chih—*Feng Chih* (by Dominio Cheung). Twayne Publishers

Foscolo, Ugo—*Ugo Foscolo: Poet Of Exile* (by Glauco Cambon). Princeton University Press

Frost, Robert—*Robert Frost: Studies Of The Poetry* (edited by Kathryn Gibbs Harris). G. K. Hall

Garcia Lorca, Federico—*Lorca's New York Poetry: Social Injustice, Dark Love, Lost Faith* (by Richard L. Predmore). Duke University Press

Glatstein, Jacob—*Yankev Glatshteyn* (by Janet Hadda). Twayne Publishers

Graves, Robert—*A Wild Civility: Interactions In The Poetry And Thought Of Robert Graves* (by Patrick J. Keane). University of Missouri Press

Gray, Thomas—*Gray, Poetry And Prose* (with essays by Samuel Johnson, Oliver Goldsmith and others). AMS Press (reprint)
—*Gray, Collins, And Their Circle* (by W. T. Williams and G. H. Vallins). Folcroft Library Editions (reprint)

Gumilev, Nikolay—*Nikolay Gumilev* (by Earl D. Sampson). Twayne Publishers

Hall, Donald—*String Too Short To Be Saved* (by Donald Hall). G. K. Hall & Co.

Hardy, Thomas—*Some Recollections, By Emma Hardy, Thomas Hardy's First Wife, Together With Some Relevant Poems By Thomas Hardy*. Oxford University Press
—*Hardy's Poetry, 1860-1928* (by Dennis Taylor). Columbia University Press

Heidegger, Martin—*Destructive Poetics: Heidegger And Modern Poetry* (by Paul A. Bove). Columbia University Press

Heine, Heinrich—*Heinrich Heine* (by Jeffrey L. Sammons). Princeton University Press

Homer—*A Guide To "The Iliad"* (by James C. Hogan). Anchor Books
—*Homer's Readers: A Historical Introduction To The "Iliad" And The "Odyssey"* (by Howard Clarke). University of Delaware Press
—*An Introduction To Homer* (by W. A. Camps). Oxford University Press
—*The Poetics Of Disguise: The Autobiography Of The Work In Homer, Dante And Shakespeare* (by Franco Ferrucci; translated by Ann Dunnigan). Cornell University Press

Hopkins, Gerard Manley—*Gerard Manley Hopkins: Priest And Poet* (by John Pick). Greenwood Press (reprint)
—*A Counterpoint Of Dissonance: The Aesthetics And Poetry Of Gerard Manley Hopkins* (by Michael Sprinker). Johns Hopkins University Press

Housman, A. E.—*A. E. Housman: The Scholar-Poet* (by Richard Perceval Graves). Charles Scribner's Sons

Hughes, Langston—*Arna Bontemps-Langston Hughes Letters, 1925-1967* (edited by Charles H. Nichols). Dodd, Mead & Co.

Hughes, Ted—*Ted Hughes: The Unaccommodated Universe* (by Ekbert Faas). Black Sparrow Press

Hugo, Victor—*Victor Hugo: Philosophy And Poetry* (by Henri Peyre; translated by Roda P. Roberts). University of Alabama Press

Jimenez, Juan Ramon—*The Line In The Margin: Juan Ramon Jimenez And His Readings In Blake, Shelley And Yeats* (by Howard T. Young). University of Wisconsin Press

Jonson, Ben—*Ben Jonson* (by Claude J. Summers Ted-Larry Pebworth). Twayne Publishers

Keats, John—*Metamorphosis In Keats* (by Barry Gradman). New York University Press
—*John Keats: The Living Year, 21 September 1818 To 21 September 1819* (by Robert Gittings). Greenwood Press (reprint)

Kunitz, Stanley—*Stanley Kunitz* (by Marie Henault). Twayne Publishers

Labe, Louise—*Love Elegies Of The Renaissance: Marot, Louise Labe and Ronsard* (by Gertrude S. Hanisch). Anima Libri

Laforgue, Jules—*Looking For Laforgue: An Informal Biography* (by David Arkell). Persea Books

Langland, William—*Piers Plowman: The Field And The Tower* (by Priscilla Martin). Barnes & Noble Books
—*Chaucer, Langland, And The Creative Imagination* (by David Aers). Routledge & Kegan Paul, Ltd.

Larkin, Philip—*Philip Larkin: A Bibliography, 1933-1976* (by B. C. Bloomfield). Faber & Faber, Inc.

Lazarus, Emma—*Emma Lazarus* (by Dan Vogel). Twayne Publishers

LePan, Douglas—*Bright Glass Of Memory: A Set Of Four Memoirs* (by Douglas LePan). McGraw-Hill Ryerson

Linderman, Frank Bird—*The Long Friendship* (by H. G. Merriam). Mountain Press Pub. Co.

Lindsay, Vachel—*Letters Of Vachel Lindsay* (edited by Marc Chenetier). Burt Franklin

Lowell, James Russell, Amy and Robert—*American Aristocracy: The Lives And Times Of James Russell, Amy And Robert Lowell* (by C. David Heymann). Dodd, Mead & Co.

Lowell, Robert—*Robert Lowell* (by Richard J. Fein). Twayne Publishers

Loy, Mina—*Mina Loy, American Modernist Poet* (by Virginia M. Kouidis). Louisiana State University Press

MacDonagh, Thomas—*Thomas MacDonagh: A Critical Biography* (by Johann A. Norstedt). University Press of Virginia

Mallarme, Stephane—*The Early Mallarme* (by Austin Gill). Clarendon Press (dist. in U.S. by Oxford University Press, New York, NY)

Marie de France—*A Metrical Study Of The Five Lais Of Marie De France* (by Katharine W. le Mee). Mouton

Marshall, Lenore—*Invented A Person: The Personal Record Of A Life* (edited by Janice Thaddeus). Horizon Press

Marvell, Andrew—*The Life And Lyrics Of Andrew Marvell* (by Michael Craze). Barnes & Noble Books
—*Andrew Marvell* (by Augustine Birrell). Folcroft Library Editions (reprint)

McClung, Nellie—*Tea With The Queen* (by Nellie McClung). Intermedia Press

Meredith, George—*Precarious Enchantment: A Reading Of Meredith's Poetry* (by Carol L. Bernstein). Catholic University of America Press

Michelangelo (Buonarroti)—*Dante, Michelangelo And Milton* (by John Arthos). Greenwood (reprint)

Milton, John—*Milton And The Baroque* (by Murray Roston). University of Pittsburgh Press
—*The Metaphoric Structure Of "Paradise Lost"* (by Jackson I. Cope). Octagon Books (reprint)
—*Milton And The Christian Tradition* (by C. A. Patrides). Archon Books
—*Milton In Early America* (by George F. Sensabaugh). Gordian Press (reprint)
—*Dante, Michelangelo And Milton* (by John Arthos). Greenwood (reprint)
—*The War In Heaven: "Paradise Lost" And The Tradition Of Satan's Rebellion* (by Stella Purce Revard). Cornell University Press
—*Poet Of Exile: A Study Of Milton's Poetry* (by Louis Martz). Yale University Press
—*Milton And The Martial Muse: "Paradise Lost" And European Traditions Of War* (by James A. Freeman). Princeton University Press
—*Milton And The Theatrical Epic* (by John G. Demaray). Harvard University Press

Morris, William—*William Morris* (by Frederick Kirchhoff). Twayne Publishers

Nemerov, Howard—*Howard Nemerov* (by Ross Labrie). Twayne Publishers

Nicander—*The Poems And Poetical Fragments* (edited by A. S. F. Gow and A. F. Scholfield). Arno Press (reprint)

O'Hara, Frank—*Frank O'Hara: Poet Among Painters* (by Marjorie Perloff). University of Texas Press
—*Frank O'Hara* (by Alan Feldman). Twayne Publishers

Okigbo, Christopher—*Four Modern West African Poets* (by Romanus Egudu). NOK Publishers

Olson, Charles—*Destructive Poetics: Heidegger And Modern American Poetry* (by Paul A. Bove). Columbia University Press
—*Charles Olson & Robert Creeley: The Complete Correspondence* (edited by George Butterick). Black Sparrow Press
—*Charles Olson's Maximus* (by Don Byrd). University of Illinois Press

Ovid—*The Metamorphoses Of Ovid* (by A. E. Watts). North Point Press

Owen, Wilfrid—*A Concordance To The Poems And Fragments Of Wilfrid Owen* (by Donald A. Heneghan). G. K. Hall & Co.

Peters, Lenrie—*Four Modern West African Poets* (by Romanus Egudu). NOK Publishers

Petrarch—*Petrarch's Poetics And Literary History* (by Marguerite R. Waller). University of Massachusetts Press
—*The Poet As Philosopher: Petrarch And The Formation Of Renaissance Consciousness* (by Charles Trinkaus). Yale University Press

Plath, Sylvia—*Protean Poetic: The Poetry Of Sylvia Plath* (by Mary Lynn Broe). University of Missouri Press

Poe, Edgar Allan—*Poe, Poe, Poe, Poe, Poe, Poe, Poe* (by Daniel Hoffman). Avon/Discus Books
—*Edgar Allan Poe, An American Imagination: Three Essays* (by Elizabeth Phillips). Kennikat Press
—*Selections From The Critical Writings Of Edgar Allan Poe* (edited by F. C. Prescott). Gordian Press (reprint)
—*Edgar Allan Poe: The Unknown Poe* (edited by Raymond Foye). City Lights Books

Ponge, Francis—*Francis Ponge* (by Ian Higgins). Athlone Press (dist. in U.S. by Humanities Press, Atlantic Highlands, NJ)

Pope, Alexander—*Pope: Recent Essays By Several Hands* (edited by Maynard Mack and James A. Winn). Archon Books
—*Acts Of Knowledge: Pope's Later Poems* (by Fredric V. Bogel). Bucknell University Press

Pound, Ezra—*Vortex: Pound, Eliot And Lewis* (by Timothy Materer). Cornell University Press
—*Ezra Pound* (by James F. Knapp). Twayne Publishers
—*The Poetic Achievement Of Ezra Pound* (by Michael Alexander. University of California Press
—*A Companion To The Cantos Of Ezra Pound, Volume I (Cantos 1-71)* (by Carroll F. Terrell). University of California Press
—*A Light From Eleusis: A Study Of Ezra Pound's Cantos* (by Leon Surette). Oxford University Press
—*The Formed Trace: The Latter Poetry Of Ezra Pound* (by Massimo Bacigalupo). Columbia University Press

–A Student's Guide To The Selected Poems Of Ezra Pound (by Peter Brooker). Faber & Faber, Inc.

–Ezra Pound And The Cantos: A Record Of Struggle (by Wendy Stallard Flory). Yale University Press

–Ezra Pound And The Pisan Cantos (by Anthony Woodward). Routledge & Kegan Paul, Ltd.

–Guide To Ezra Pound's Selected Cantos (by George Kearns). Rutgers University Press

–The Tale Of The Tribe: Ezra Pound And The Modern Verse Lyric (by Michael Andre Bernstein). Princeton University Press

–Ezra Pound (by Jeannette Lander). Frederick Ungar Pub. Co.

Rilke, Rainer Maria–*Rilke: The Alchemy Of Alienation* (edited by Frank Barron, Ernst S. Dick and Warren R. Maurer). Regents Press of Kansas

Rimbaud, Arthur–*A Season In Hell: The Life Of Arthur Rimbaud* (by Jean-Marie Carre; translated by Hannah and Matthew Josephson). AMS Press (reprint)

Robinson, Edwin Arlington–*Selected Letters Of Edwin Arlington Robinson* (compiled by Frederic Torrence). Greenwood Press (reprint)

Roethke, Theodore–*From The Notebooks Of Theodore Roethke 1943-63* (selected by David Wagoner). University of Washington Press

–Theodore Roethke: An American Romantic (by Jay Parini). University of Massachusetts Press

Ronsard, Pierre de–*Love Elegies Of The Renaissance: Marot, Louise Labe And Ronsard* (by Gertrude S. Hanisch). Anma Libri

Roumain, Jacques–*A Knot In The Thread: The Life And Work Of Jacques Roumain* (by Carolyn Fowler). Howard University Press

Rukeyser, Muriel–*The Poetic Vision Of Muriel Rukeyser* (by Louise Kertesz). Louisiana State University Press

Russell, Charles Marion–*The Long Friendship* (by H. G. Merriam). Mountain Press Pub. Co.

Salel, Hugues–*Hugues Salel, His Life And Works* (by Howard H. Kalwies). Applied Literature Press

Sandburg, Carl–*"Moonlight Dries No Mittens": Carl Sandburg Reconsidered* (by Daniel Hoffman). Library of Congress

Sarton, May–*Journal Of A Solitude* (by May Sarton). G. K. Hall & Co. (large type edition)

Savala, Refugio–*Autobiography Of A Yaqui Poet* (by Refugio Savala). University of Arizona Press

Schwartz, Delmore–*Delmore Schwartz: The Life Of An American Poet* (by James Atlas). Avon/Discus Books

Secundus, Janus–*Janus Secundus* (by George Schoolfield). Twayne Publishers

Sexton, Anne–*Anne Sexton: A Self-Portrait In Letters* (edited by Linda Gray Sexton and Lois Ames). Houghton Mifflin Co.

Shakespeare, William–*Shakespeare's Sonnets* (by Kenneth Muir). G. Allen & Unwin

Shapiro, Karl–*Karl Shapiro: A Descriptive Bibliography 1933-1977* (by Lee Bartlett). Garland Pub. Co.

Shelley, Percy Bysshe–*Sexuality And Feminism In Shelley* (by Nathaniel Brown). Harvard University Press

–The Line In The Margin: Juan Ramon Jimenez And His Readings In Blake, Shelley And Yeats (by Howard T. Young). University of Wisconsin Press

–Destroyer And Preserver: Shelley's Poetic Skepticism (by Lloyd Abbey). University of Nebraska Press

–Rousseau In England: The Context For Shelley's Critique Of The Enlightenment (by Edward Duffy). University of California Press

–Shelley In England: New Facts And Letters From The Shelley-Whitton Papers (by Roger Ingpen). Folcroft Library Editions (reprint)

Spenser, Edmund–*Spenser Studies: A Renaissance Poetry Annual, Volume I* (edited by Patrick Cullen and Thomas P. Roche, Jr.). University of Pittsburgh Press

Sterling, George–*George Sterling* (by Thomas E. Benediktsonn). Twayne Publishers

Stevens, Wallace–*Destructive Poetics: Heidegger And Modern American Poetry* (by Paul A. Bove). Columbia University Press

–Wallace Stevens (by Frank Kermode). Chip's Bookshop (reprint)

–Wallace Stevens: A Celebration (edited by Frank Doggett and Robert Buttel). Princeton University Press

–Wallace Stevens: The Poems Of Our Climate (by Harold Bloom). Cornell University Press

–Wallace Stevens: The Making Of The Poem (by Frank Doggett). Johns Hopkins University Press

Stuart, Jesse–*Jesse Stuart: Kentucky's Chronicler-Poet* (by J. R. LeMaster). Memphis State University Press

Swift, Jonathan–*Energy And Order In The Poetry Of Swift* (by A. B. England). Bucknell University Press

Teasdale, Sara–*Sara Teasdale: Woman & Poet* (by William Drake). Harper & Row, Publishers

Tennyson, Alfred–*Tennyson: A Collection Of Critical Essays* (edited by Elizabeth A. Francis). Spectrum Books

–Tennyson And Tradition (by Robert Pattison). Harvard University Press

–Tennyson's Debt To Environment: A Study Of Tennyson's England As An Introduction To His Poems (by William G. Ward). Folcroft Library Editions (reprint)

–Tennyson And His Publishers (by June Steffensen Hagen). Pennsylvania State University Press

–Tennyson: The Unquiet Heart (by Robert Bernard Martin). Oxford University Press

Thomson, James–*James Thomson* (by Hilbert H. Campbell). G. K. Hall & Co.

Tibullus, Albius–*Tibullus: A Hellenistic Poet At Rome* (by Francis Cairns). Cambridge University Press

Tompson, Benjamin–*Benjamin Tompson, Colonial Bard: A Critical Edition* (by Peter White). Pennsylvania State University Press

Viereck, George Sylvester–*Odyssey Of A Barbarian: The Biography Of George Sylvester Viereck* (by Elmer Gertz). Prometheus Books

Virgil–*Virgil's "Georgics." A New Interpretation* (by Gary B. Miles). University of California Press

Warren, Robert Penn–*Robert Penn Warren: A Vision Earned* (by Marshall Walker). Barnes & Noble Books
  –*Robert Penn Warren Talking: Interviews, 1950-1978* (edited by Floyd C. Atkins and John T. Hiers). Random House, Inc.
  –*Robert Penn Warren: A Collection Of Critical Essays* (edited by John Lewis Longley, Jr.). Greenwood Press (reprint)

Welch, Lew–*I Remain: The Letters Of Lou Welch & The Correspondence Of His Friends* (edited by Donald Allen). Grey Fox Press

Whitman, Walt–*Destructive Poetics: Heidegger And Modern American Poetry* (by Paul A. Bove). Columbia University Press
  –*Walt Whitman Among The French: Poet And Myth* (by Betsy Erkkila). Princeton University Press

Williams, William Carlos–*William Carlos Williams: The Critical Heritage* (edited by Charles Doyle). Routledge & Kegan Paul

Winters, Yvor–*An Introduction To The Poetry Of Yvor Winters* (by Elizabeth Isaacs). Swallow Press
  –*Language As Being In The Poetry Of Yvor Winters* (by Grosvenor Powell). Louisiana State University Press

Wordsworth, Dorothy–*Women Writers And Poetic Identity: Wordsworth, Bronte And Dickinson* (by Margaret Homans). Princeton University Press

Wordsworth, William–*The Making Of A Tory Humanist: William Wordsworth And The Idea Of Community* (by Michael H. Friedman). Columbia University Press
  –*The Egotistical Sublime: A History Of Wordsworth's Imagination* (by John Jones). Greenwood Press (reprint)

–*The Mind Of A Poet* (by Raymond Dexter Havens). AMS Press (reprint)
–*Wordsworth In Time* (by John Beer). Faber & Faber, Inc.
–*Wordsworth And The Poetry Of Human Suffering* (by James H. Averill). Cornell University Press
–*The Poet Wordsworth* (by Helen Darbishire). Greenwood Press (reprint)
–*Romanticism And The Forms Of Ruin: Wordsworth, Coleridge, And Modalities Of Fragmentation* (by Thomas McFarland). Princeton University Press

Wright, James–*James Wright: An Introduction* (by William S. Saunders). State Library of Ohio

Yeats, William Butler–*The Rhizome And The Flower: The Perennial Philosophy–Yeats And Jung* (by James Olney). University of California Press
  –*The Poetry Of W. B. Yeats* (by Louis MacNeice). Oxford University Press (reprint)
  –*The Line In The Margin: Juan Ramon Jimenez And His Readings In Blake, Shelley And Yeats* (by Howard T. Young). University of Wisconsin Press
  –*The Olympian And The Leprechaun: W. B. Yeats And James Stephens* (by Richard J. Finneran). Dolmen Press (Dublin) (dist. in U.S. by Humanities Press, Atlantic Highlands, NJ)
  –*Yeats, Ireland And Fascism* (by Elizabeth Cullingford). New York University Press
  –*W. B. Yeats: Images Of A Poet* (by D. J. Gordon). Greenwood Press (reprint)
  –*The Letters Of W. B. Yeats* (edited by Allen Wade). Octagon Books (reprint)

Zukovsky, Louis–*Louis Zukovsky: Man And Poet* (edited by Carroll F. Terrell). National Poetry Foundation

(4) COMMENT AND CRITICISM
(listed alphabetically by author)

Allen, Don Cameron (editor)–*The Moment Of Poetry.* Greenwood Press (reprint)

Allen, Roy F.–*German Expressionist Poetry.* Twayne Publishers

Andre, Michael; Rothenberg, Erika–*The Poet's Encyclopedia.* Unmuzzled Ox

Aristotle–*Aristotle On The Art Of Poetry* (edited and translated by Ingram Bywater). Garland Pub. Co. (reprint)

Barnes, Walter–*The Children's Poets: Analyses And Appraisals Of The Greatest English And American Poets For Children.* Folcroft Library Editions (reprint)

Bloom, Harold–*Poetry And Repression: Revisionism From Blake To Stevens.* Yale University Press

Bold, Alan–*The Ballad.* Methuen

Bove, Paul A.–*Destructive Poetics: Heidegger And Modern American Poetry.* Columbia University Press

Calder, Daniel G. (editor)—*Old English Poetry: Essays On Style.* University of California Press

Carruth, William Herbert—*Verse Writing: A Practical Handbook For College Classes And Private Guidance.* Folcroft Library Editions (reprint)

Cazelles, Brigitte (see listing for Johnson, Phyllis)

Chang, Kang-i Sun—*The Evolution Of Chinese Tz'u Poetry.* Princeton University Press

Clark, LaVerne Harrell—*Focus 101.* Heidelberg Graphics

Clark, Tom—*The Great Naropa Poetry Wars: With A Copious Collection Of Germane Documents Assembled By The Author.* Cadmus Editions

Cooper, Barbara Eck (see listing for Somer, John)

Cowley, Malcolm—*The Dream Of The Golden Mountains: Remembering The 1930s.* Viking Press

Dang, Shu-leung (see listing for Wong, Kai-chee)

Davie, Donald—*Trying To Explain: Poets On Poetry.* University of Michigan Press

Del Plaine, Frances Kelley (and Adah Georgina Grandy)—*College Readings In Poetry.* Granger Book Co. (reprint)

Francis, Robert—*Pot Shots At Poetry.* University of Michigan Press

Friebert, Stuart; Young, David (editors)—*A "Field" Guide To Contemporary Poetry And Poetics.* Longman, Inc.

Fry, Paul H.—*The Poet's Calling In The English Ode.* Yale University Press

Gibson, Robert (arranger)—*Modern French Poets On Poetry.* Cambridge University Press

Glassgold, Peter (see listing for Laughlin, J.)

Gould, Jean—*American Women Poets: Pioneers Of Modern Poetry.* (Dodd, Mead & Co.)

Graff, Gerald—*Poetic Statement And Critical Dogma.* University of Chicago Press

Grandy, Adah Georgina (see listing for Del Plaine, Frances Kelley)

Grant, Patrick—*Images And Ideas In Literature Of The English Renaissance.* University of Massachusetts Press

Greiner, Donald J. (editor)—*American Poets Since World War II.* Gale Research Co.

Grundlehner, Philip—*The Lyrical Bridge: Essays From Holderlin To Benn.* Associated University Presses

Halporn, James; Ostwald, Martin; Rosenmeyer, Thomas G.—*The Meters Of Greek And Latin Poetry* (revised edition). University of Oklahoma Press

Harrison, John Smith—*Platonism In English Poetry Of The Sixteenth And Seventeenth Centuries.* Greenwood Press (reprint)

Hartman, Charles O.—*Free Verse: An Essay On Prosody.* Princeton University Press

Hatto, A. T.—*Essays On Medieval German And Other Poetry.* Cambridge University Press

Heinzelman, Kurt—*The Economics Of The Imagination*—University of Massachusetts Press

Henderson, Stephen—*Understanding The New Black Poetry.* Morrow Quill Paperbacks.

Ho, Pung (see listing for Wong, Kai-chee)

Hogg, James—*On Poets & Poetry, Second Series.* Salzburg Studies in English Literature (dist. in U.S. by Humanities Press, Atlantic Highlands, NJ)

Hope, A. D.—*The New Cratylus: Notes On The Craft Of Poetry.* Oxford University Press

Houston, John Porter—*French Symbolism And The Modernist Movement: A Study Of Poetic Structures.* Louisiana State University Press

Howard, Richard—*Alone With America: Essays On The Art Of Poetry In The United States Since 1950.* Atheneum Publishers

Ignatow, David—*Open Between Us* (edited by Ralph J. Mills, Jr.). University of Michigan Press

Jackson, J. B. de J.—*Poetry Of The Romantic Period.* Routledge and Kegan Paul

Jackson, W. T. H. (editor)—*The Interpretation Of Medieval Lyric Poetry.* Columbia University Press

Jarrell, Randall—*Poetry And The Age.* Ecco Press

Johnson, Phyllis; Cazelles, Brigitte—*Le Vain Siecle Guerpir: A Literary Approach To Sainthood Through Old French Hagiography Of The Twelfth Century.* University of North Carolina Dept. of Romance Languages

Kohn, Murray J.—*The Voice Of My Blood Cries Out: The Holocaust As Reflected In Hebrew Poetry.* Shengold Publishers

Kostelanetz, Richard—*Visual Literature Criticism: A New Collection* (partly poetry). Southern Illinois University Press

Kratzmann, Gregory—*Anglo-Scottish Literary Relations, 1430-1550.* Cambridge University Press

Krieger, Murray—*Poetic Presence And Illusion: Essays In Critical History And Theory.* Johns Hopkins University Press

Kumin, Maxine—*To Make A Prairie: Essays On Poets, Poetry And Country Living.* University of Michigan Press

Kuzma, Greg (editor)—*A Book Of Rereadings In Recent American Poetry—30 Essays.* Best Cellar Press

Landy, Alice S.—*To Read A Poem.* D. C. Heath

Laughlin, J.; Glassgold, Peter; Martin, Frederick R. (editors)—*New Directions In Prose And Poetry 40.* New Directions Pub. Corp.

Lorenzatos, Zissimos—*"The Lost Center" And Other Essays In Greek Poetry* (translated by Kay Cicellis). Princeton University Press

Lyall, Charles James—*Translations Of Ancient Arabian Poetry.* Hyperion Press (reprint)

Mahoney, John L. (editor)—*The Enlightenment And English Literature: Prose And Poetry Of The Eighteenth Century, With Selected Modern Critical Essays.* D. C. Heath

Martin, Frederick R. (see listing for Laughlin, J.)

Martin, Robert K.—*The Homosexual Tradition In American Poetry.* University of Texas Press

Matthew of Vendome—*The Art Of Versification* (translated by Aubrey E. Gaylon). Iowa State University Press

Mazzaro, Jerome—*Postmodern American Poetry*. University of Illinois Press

McGhee, Richard D.—*Marriage, Duty & Desire In Victorian Poetry And Drama*, Regents Press of Kansas

Middlebrook, Diane Wood—*Worlds Into Words: Understanding Modern Poems*. W. W. Norton & Co.

Montale, Eugenio—*It Depends=Quaderno Di Quattro Anni: A Poet's Notebook* (translated by G. Singh). New Directions Pub. Corp.

Morrison, Blake—*The Movement: English Poetry And Fiction Of The 1950s*. Oxford University Press

Murray, Margaret A.—*Egyptian Religious Poetry*. Greenwood Press (reprint)

Murrin, Michael—*The Allegorical Epic: Essays In Its Rise And Decline*. University of Chicago Press

Opland, Jeff—*Anglo-Saxon Oral Poetry: A Study Of The Traditions*. Yale University Press

Ostwald, Martin (see listing for Halporn, James)

Pater, Walter—*The Renaissance: Studies In Art And Poetry* (edited by Donald L. Hill). University of California Press

Peyre, Henri—*What Is Symbolism?* (translated by Emmett Parker). University of Alabama Press

Powell, A. E.—*The Romantic Theory Of Poetry: An Examination In The Light Of Croce's Aesthetic*. AMS Press (reprint)

Powell, Neil—*Carpenters Of Light: Some Contemporary English Poets*. Barnes & Noble Books

Pritchard, William H.—*Lives Of The Modern Poets*. Oxford University Press

Reiman, Donald H.—*English Romantic Poetry, 1800-1835*. Gale Research Co.

Renwick, Roger deV.—*English Folk Poetry: Structure And Meaning*. University of Pennsylvania Press

Riccio, Ottone M.—*The Intimate Art Of Writing Poetry*. Prentice-Hall, Inc.

Rinaker, Clarissa (see listing for Zeitlin, Jacob)

Rivers, Isabel—*Classical And Christian Ideas In English Renaissance Poetry: A Students' Guide*. G. Allen & Unwin

Rosenmeyer, Thomas G. (see listing for Halporn, James)

Salinas, Pedro—*Reality And The Poet In Spanish Poetry* (translated by Edith Fishtine Helman). Greenwood Press (reprint)

Schmidt, Michael—*A Reader's Guide To Fifty Modern British Poets*. Barnes & Noble Books

Sewell, Elizabeth—*To Be A True Poem: Essays*. Hunter Pub. Co.

Snyder, Gary—*The Real Work: Interviews And Talks*. New Directions Pub. Corp.

Somer, John; Cooper, Barbara Eck (editors)—*American & British Literature, 1945-1975: An Annotated Bibliography Of Contemporary Scholarship* (includes listings for poetry). Regents Press of Kansas

Stanford, W. B.—*Enemies Of Poetry*. Routledge & Kegan Paul

Tennyson, G. B.—*Victorian Devotional Poetry: The Tractarian Mode*. Harvard University Press

Thomas, F. Richard—*Frog Praises Night: Poems With Commentary*. Southern Illinois University Press

Turner, Alberta (ed.)—*Poets Teaching: The Creative Process*. Longman

Van D'Elden, Karl H.—*West German Poets On Society And Politics*. Wayne State University Press

Vendler, Helen—*Part Of Nature, Part Of Us: Modern American Poets*. Harvard University Press

Viswanathan, S.—*The Shakespeare Play As Poem: A Critical Tradition In Perspective*. Cambridge University Press

Wagner, Linda W.—*American Modern: Essays In Fiction And Poetry*. Kennikat Press

Wakoski, Diane—*Toward A New Poetry*. University of Michigan Press

Wesling, Donald—*The Chances Of Rhyme: Device And Modernity*. University of California Press

Williams, Gordon—*Figures Of Thought In Roman Poetry*. Yale University Press

Wong, Kai-chee; Ho, Pung; Dang, Shu-leung—*A Research Guide To English Translation Of Chinese Verse*. Chinese University Press of Hong Kong (dist. in U.S. by University of Washington Press)

Young, David (see listing for Friebert, Stuart)

Zeitlin, Jacob; Rinaker, Clarissa—*Types Of Poetry*. Granger Book Co. (reprint)

Ziolkowski, Theodore—*The Classical German Elegy, 1795-1950*. Princeton University Press

Book Publishers Publishing Poetry

Following is a directory of publishers in the United States and Canada who issued at least one book of poetry during the year ending October 31, 1980; it is based upon publishers represented in Section 1 of The Yearly Record *in this volume. Not included are those specializing in reprints.*

A

Abattoir Editions, University of Nebraska, Cleary House, P.O. Box 688, Omaha, NE 68101
Aberdeen Book Co., Chapel Hill, NC 27514
Abingdon Press, 201 Eighth Ave., S., Nashville, TN 37202
Acre Press, Dearborn Heights, MI 48127
Adams Press, 30 W. Washington St., Chicago, IL 60602
Ahsahta Press, Boise State University, English Dept., Boise, ID 83725
Allegany Mountain Press, 111 N. 10th St., Olean, NY 14760
Allyne Co., Santa Cruz, CA 95060
Alpha Centauri Publishers, Highland, NY 12528
Alpha Publishing Co., Blue Bell, PA 19422
American Studies Press, 13511 Palmwood Lane, Tampa, FL 33624
Angelstone Press, 316 Woodland Dr., Birmingham, AL 35209
Ansuda Publications, Box 123, Harris, IA 51345
Anthroposophic Press, South Egremont, MA 01258
Antietam Press, P.O. Box 62, Boonsboro, MD 21713
Apeiron Press, P.O. Box 5930, Chicago, IL 60680
Apple-Wood Press, P.O. Box 2870, Cambridge, MA 02139
Applezaba Press, 333 Orizaba, Long Beach, CA 90814
Ararat Press, 628 Second Ave., New York, NY 10016
Ardis Publishers, 2901 Heatherway Dr., Ann Arbor, MI 48104
Arrow Publishing Co., 1238 Chestnut St., Newton Upper Falls, MA 02164
Arte Publico Press, Gary, IN
Artichoke Press, 3274 Parkhurst Dr., Rancho Palos Verdes, CA 90274
Atheneum Publishers, 122 E. 42nd St., New York, NY 10017
Avon/Bard Books, 959 Eighth Ave., New York, NY 10019

B

A. S. Barnes & Co., Forsgate Dr., Cranbury, NJ 08512
Barnwood Press Cooperative, R.R. 2, Box 110, Daleville, IN 47334
William L. Bauhan, Publisher, Old Country Rd., Dublin, NH 03444
Beacon Press, 25 Beacon St., Boston, MA 02108
Beatitude Press, c/o Serendipity Books, 1790 Shattuck Ave., Berkeley, CA 94709
Beautiful Snow, Willow Springs, MO 65793
Bellevue Press, 60 Schubert St., Binghamton, NY 13905
Benedictine Sisters, 3888 Paducah Dr., San Diego, CA 92117
Berkeley Poets' Workshop and Press, P.O. Box 459, Berkeley, CA 94701
Bits Press, Case Western Reserve University, Dept. of English, Cleveland, OH 44106
Black Moss Press, Windsor, Ontario
Black Oak Press, Lincoln, NE
Black Sparrow Press, P.O. Box 3993, Santa Barbara, CA 93105
Blain Press, Cleveland Heights, OH 44118
John F. Blair, Publisher, 1406 Plaza Dr., Winston-Salem, NC 27103
Blind Beggar Press, Bronx, NY

Block Publishing Co., 915 Broadway, New York, NY 10010
Blue Cloud Quarterly, Blue Cloud Abbey, Marvin, SD 57251
Blue Coot Press, Laurinburg, NC 28352
Blue Leaf Editions, New London, CT 06320
Blue Mornings Press, P.O. Box 411, New York, NY 11357
Blue Mountain Press, 511 Campbell St., Kalamazoo, MI 49007
Blue Oak Press, P.O. Box 27, Sattley, CA 96124
Blue Wind Press, P.O. Box 7175, Berkeley, CA 94707
Boa Editions, 92 Park Ave., Brockport, NY 14420
Boardwell-Kloner Press, 323 S. Franklin, Rm. 804, Chicago, IL 60606
Branden Press, 21 Station St., Boston, MA 02146
Breitenbush Publications, P.O. Box 02137, Portland, OR 97202
Briarpatch Press, P.O. Box 2482, Davidson, NC 28036
Brigham Young University Press, 209 University Press Bldg., Provo, UT 84602
Broadman Press, 127 Ninth Ave., N., Nashville, TN 37234
Bruccoli Clark Books, 1700 Lone Pine, Bloomfield Hills, MI 48013
Burning Deck Press, 71 Elmgrove Ave., Providence, RI 02906
Byron Books, Scranton, PA

C

Calamus Books, P.O. Box 689, Cooper Station, New York, NY 10003
California Street Books, 723 Dwight Way, Berkeley, CA 94710
Calliope Press, 1162 Lincoln Ave., #227, Walnut Creek, CA 94596
Cambridge University Press, 32 E. 57th St., New York, NY 10022
Carnegie-Mellon University Press, Pittsburgh, PA 15213
Carolina Wren Press, 300 Barclay Rd., Chapel Hill, NC 27514
Carroll College Press, 100 North East Ave., Waukesha, WI 53186
Cedar Creek Press, P.O. Box 801, DeKalb, IL 60115
Cedar Rock Press, 1121 Madeline, New Bruanfels, TX 78130
Celestial Arts Publishing Co., 231 Adrian Rd., Millbrae, CA 94030
Celestial Otter Press, 1923 Finchley Court, Schaumburg, IL 60194
Celli Press, New York, NY
Center Publications, 905 S. Normandie Ave., Los Angeles, CA 90006
Charioteer Press, 2475 Virginia Ave., NW, Washington, DC 20037
Chowder Chapbooks, P.O. Box 33, Wollaston, MA 02170
Christian Mother Goose Book Co., Grand Junction, CO 81501
Cider Mill Press, P.O. Box 211, Stratford, CT 06497
Citadel Press, 120 Enterprise Ave., Secaucus, NJ 07094
City Miner Books, P.O. Box 176, Berkeley, CA 94701
Cleveland State University Poetry Center, Cleveland, OH 44115
Cleveland State University Press, Cleveland, OH 44115
Clinton Press, Plattsburgh, NY 12901
Coach House Press, 401 Huron St., Toronto, Ontario M5S 2G5
William Collins Publishers, 2080 W. 117th St., Cleveland, OH 44111
Colorado Associated University Press, Boulder, CO 80309
Columbia University Press, 562 W. 113th St., New York, NY 10025
Confluence Press, Spalding Hall, Lewis & Clark Campus, Lewiston, ID 83501
D. C. Cook Publishing Co., 850 N. Grove Ave., Elgin, IL 60120
Copper Beech Press, Brown University, Providence, RI 02912
Copper Canyon Press, P.O. Box 271, Port Townsend, WA 98368
Coraddi Publications, University of North Carolina, Elliot Center, Rm. 205, Greensboro, NC 27412
Cornell University Press, 124 Roberts Place, Ithaca, NY 14850
Cottonwood Review Press, Box J, Kansas Union, University of Kansas, Lawrence, KS 66044
Countryman Press, Woodstock, VT 05091
Crescent Publications, 5410 Wilshire Blvd., Suite 400, Los Angeles, CA 90036
Croissant Press, P.O. Box 282, Athens, OH 45701
Cross-Cultural Communications, 239 Wynsum Ave., Merrick, NY 11566
The Crossing Press, 17 W. Main St., Trumansburg, NY 14886
Crown Publishers, 1 Park Ave., New York, NY 10016
Curbstone Press, 321 Jackson St., Willimantic, CT 06226

D

Dandelion Press, R.F.D. 2, Box 118, Bedford, NY 10506
Dark Horse Press, P.O. Box 36, Newton Lower Falls, MA 02166
Deerfield Press/Gallery Press, Deerfield, MA 01342
Deluxe Co., Shreveport, LA
DeVorse, Marina del Rey, CA 90291
Dia Books, New York, NY
Dodd, Mead & Co., 79 Madison Ave., New York, NY 10016
$ Publishing, Costa Mesa, CA 92626
Doubleday & Co., 245 Park Ave., New York, NY 10017
Dovetail Press, P.O. Box 1496, Boulder, CO 80306
Downtown Poets, P.O. Box 1720, Brooklyn, NY 11202
Dragon's Teeth Press, El Dorado National Forest, Georgetown, CA 95634
Dryad Press, P.O. Box 29161, Presidio, San Francisco, CA 94129
Dufour Editions, Chester Springs, PA 19425
Dustbooks, P.O. Box 100, Paradise, CA 95969
E. P. Dutton & Co., 2 Park Ave., New York, NY 10016

E

Ecco Press, 1 W. 30th St., New York, NY 10001
Elizabeth Press, 103 Van Etten Blvd., New Rochelle, NY 10804
Elpenor Books, P.O. Box 3152, Merchandise Mart Plaza, Chicago, IL 60654
Everest House, Publishers, 1133 Ave. of the Americas, New York, NY 10036

F

Faber & Faber, 99 Main St., Salem, NH 03079
Fallen Angel Press, 1981 W. McNichols, C-1, Highland Park, MI 48203
Farmington Press, Farmington, MO 63640
Farrar, Straus & Giroux, 19 Union Square. W., New York, NY 10003
Fiddlehead Poetry Books, The Observatory, University of New Brunswick, Fredericton, New Brunswick E3B 5A3
Field, Rice Hall, Oberlin College, Oberlin, OH 44074
The Figures, 2016 Cedar, San Francisco, CA 94709
Fortress Press, 2900 Queen Lane, Philadelphia, PA 19129
Four Zoas Night House, P.O. Box 461, Ware, MA 01082
Free State Press, Annapolis, MD
Friends United Press, 101 Quaker Hill Dr., Richmond, IN 47374

G

Garrard Publishing Co., 1607 N. Market St., Champaign, IL 61820
Gay Sunshine Press, P.O. Box 40397, San Francisco, CA 94140
K. M. Gentile Publishing, St. Louis, MO
Gnomen Press, P.O. Box 106, Frankfort, KY 40601
David R. Godine, Publisher, 306 Dartmouth St., Boston, MA 02116
Golden Quill Press, Francestown, NH 03043
Gondwana Books, Calistoga, CA 94515
Good News Publishers, Westchester, IL 60153
Gotham Book Mart, 41 W. 47th St., New York, NY 10036
Graywolf Press, P.O. Box 142, Port Townsend, WA 98368
Great Raven Press, P.O. Box 813, Fort Kent, ME 04743
Green River Press, University Center, MI 48710
Greenfield Review Press, P.O. Box 80, Greenfield Center, NY 12833
Greenhouse Review Press, 126 Escalona Dr., Santa Cruz, CA 95060
Greenwillow Books, 105 Madison Ave., New York, NY 10016
Grey Fox Press, P.O. Box 159, Bolinas, CA 94924

H

Hanging Loose Press, 231 Wickoff St., Brooklyn, NY 11217
Harcourt Brace Jovanovich, Inc., 757 Third Ave., New York, NY 10017
Hard Cider Press, 38 Lisbon Ave., Buffalo, NY 14214
Harlo Press, 50 Victor, Detroit, MI 48203
Harper & Row, Publishers, 10 E. 53rd St., New York, NY 10022
Harper Square Press, c/o Artcrest Products Co., 401 W. Ontario St., Chicago, IL 60610
Hartmus Press, 23 Lomita Dr., Mill Valley, CA 94941
Harvest Press, P.O. Box 1265, Santa Cruz, CA 95061
Hibiscus Press, P.O. Box 22248, Sacramento, CA 95822
Hobart & William Smith Colleges Press, Geneva, NY 14456
W. D. Hoffstadt & Sons Press, 606 Ulster St., Syracuse, NY 13204
Holiday House, 18 E. 53rd St., New York, NY 10022
Hollow Springs Press, R.D. 1, Bancroft Rd., Chester, MA 01011
Holmgangers Press, 22 Ardith Lane, Alamo, CA 94507
Holt, Rinehart & Winston, Inc., 383 Madison Ave., New York, NY 10017
Holy. Cow! Press, P.O. Box 618, Minneapolis, MN 55440
Houghton Mifflin Co., 1 Beacon St., Boston, MA 02107
Hounslow Press, 124 Parkview, Toronto, Ontario
Howard University Press, 2935 Upton St., NW, Washington, DC 20008
Huntington Press, Huntington, NY 11743

I

Icarus Press, P.O. Box 8, Riderwood, NJ 21139
Illuminati Press, 1147 S. Robertson Blvd., Los Angeles, CA 90035
Imaginery Press, P.O. Box 193, Cambridge, MA 02141
Inland Boat Series (see Porch Publications)
Intermedia Press, P.O. Box 3294, Vancouver, British Columbia V6B 3X9
Ironwood Press, P.O. Box 40907, Tucson, AZ 85717
Ithaca House, 108 E. Plain St., Ithaca, NY 14850

J

Jade Publishing Co., Livermore, CA 94550
Alice James Books, 138 Mt. Auburn St., Cambridge, MA 02138
Jemta Press, 11313 Beech Daly, Redford Township, MI 48239
Johns Hopkins University Press, Baltimore, MD 21218
Judson Press, Valley Forge, PA 19481
Jump River Press, 819 Single Ave., Wausau, WI 54401
Juniper Press, 1310 Shorewood Dr., LaCrosse, WI 54601

K

Kamazu Press, Chicago, IL
Karmic Revenge Laundry Shop Press, P.O. Box 14, Guttenberg, NJ 07093
King and Cowen, 299 Park Ave., 32nd Flr., New York, NY 10017
Alfred A. Knopf, Inc., 201 E. 50th St., New York, NY 10022
Kulchur Foundation, 888 Park Ave., New York, NY 10021

L

Latigo Press, Phoenix, AZ
Laueroc Press, Brooktondale, NY 14817
L'Epervier Press, 1219 E. Laurel, Fort Collins, CO 80521
Lightning Tree, P.O. Box 1837, Santa Fe, NM 87501
Linden Publishers, 27 W. 11th St., New York, NY 10011
Lintel, P.O. Box 34, St. George, NY 10301
Little, Brown & Co., 34 Beacon St., Boston, MA 02106

Liveright Publishing Corp., 500 Fifth Ave., New York, NY 10036
Lotus Press, P.O. Box 21607, College Park Station, Detroit, MI 48221
Louisiana State University Press, University Station, Baton Rouge, LA 70803
Love Street Books, 2176 Allison Lane, #13, Jeffersonville, IN 47130
Lynx House Press, P.O. Box 800, Amherst, MA 01004
Lyra Press, Miami, FL

M

Macmillan Publishing Co., 866 Third Ave., New York, NY 10022
Maelstrom Press, P.O. Box 4261, Long Beach, CA 90804
Malki Museum Press, 11-795 Fields Rd., Morongo Indian Reservation, Banning, CA 92220
Mammoth Press, State University of New York College, Brockport, NY 14420
Richard Marek Publishers, 200 Madison Ave., New York, NY 10016
Mayapple Press, P.O. Box 7508, Liberty Station, Ann Arbor, MI 48107
McClelland and Stewart, Ltd., 25 Hollinger Rd., Toronto, Ontario M4B 3G2
Merging Media, 59 Sandra Circle, A-3, Westfield, NJ 07090
Methuen, Inc., 733 Third Ave., New YOrk, NY 10017
Midnight Sun, New York, NY
Minnesota Review Press, P.O. Box 211, Bloomington, IN 47401
Momentum Press, 512 Hill St., #4, Santa Monica, CA 90405
Montemora Foundation, P.O. Box 336, Cooper Station, New York, NY 10003
Moore Publishing Co., P.O. Box 3036, Durham, NC 27705
More Than Coincidence Press, Brooklyn, NY
William Morrow & Co., 105 Madison Ave., New York, NY 10016
Mosaic Press/Valley Editions, P.O. Box 1032, Oakville, Ontario L6J 5E9
Mudborn Press, 209 W. De la Guerra, Santa Barbara, CA 93101

N

New Directions Publishing Corp., 80 Eighth Ave., New York, NY 10011
New England Press, 45 Tudor City, No. 1903, New York, NY 10017
New House Publishers, Charlotte, NC
New Merrymount Press, New York, NY
New Rivers Press, 1602 Selby Ave., St. Paul, MN 55104
New Wave Press, Iowa City, IA 52240
New York Literary Press, 419 W. 56th St., New York, NY 10019
Nonpareil Books, Boston, MA
North Atlantic Books, 635 Amador St., Richmond, CA 94805
North Point Press, San Francisco, CA
Northwood Institute, Midland, MI 48640
Northwoods Press, P.O. Box 249, Stafford, VA 22554
W. W. Norton & Co., 500 Fifth Ave., New York, NY 10036

O

Oberon Press, 350 Sparks, Ottawa, Ontario
Ohio State University Press, 2070 Neil Ave., Columbus, OH 43210
Ohio University Press, 56 E. Union St., Athens, OH 45701
Omnation Press, 5548 N. Sawyer, Chicago, IL 60625
Open Places, Stephens College, P.O. Box 2085, Columbia, MO 65201
Oregon State University Press, 101 Waldo Hall, Corvallis, OR 97331
Overlook Press, 667 Madison Ave., New York, NY 10021
Owl Creek Press, 520 S. Second, W., Missoula, MT 59801
Oxford University Press, 200 Madison Ave., New York, NY 10016; 70 Wynford Dr., Don Mills, Ontario
Oyez, P.O. Box 5134, Berkeley, CA 94705

P

Pageant-Poseidon Press, 155 W. 15th St., New York, NY 10011

Painted Bride Quarterly Press, 527 South St., Philadelphia, PA 19147
Panjandrum Books, 11321 Irva Ave., Los Angeles, CA 90025
Pantheon Books, 201 E. 50th St., New York, NY 10022
Paulist Press, 1865 Broadway, New York, NY 10023
Paycock Press, P.O. Box 57206, Washington, DC 20037
Penumbra Press, Moonbeam, Ontario
Perivale Press, 13830 Erwin St., Van Nuys, CA 91401
Persea Books, 225 Lafayette St., New York, NY 10012
Petrarch Press, New York, NY
Philosophical Library, 15 E. 40th St., New York, NY 10016
Pinnacle Books, 1 Century Plaza, 2029 Century Park East, Los Angeles, CA 90067
Pocket Books, 1230 Ave. of the Americas, New York, NY 10020
Poetry Gallery Press, 224 W. 29th St., New York, NY 10001
Porch Publications, c/o James Cervantes, Arizona State University, Dept. of English, Tempe, AZ 85281
Porcupine's Quill, 68 Main St., Erin, Ontario NOB 1T0
Prairie Poet Books, P.O. Box 35, 902 10th St., Charleston, IL 61920
Prentice-Hall, Inc., Englewood Cliffs, NJ 07632
Prescott Street Press, 407 Postal Bldg., Portland, OR 97204
Princeton University Press, 41 William St., Princeton, NJ 08540
Printed Editions, P.O. Box 26, West Glover, VT 05875
Pterodactyl Press, San Francisco, CA
Pulmac Enterprises, Middlesex Star Route, Montpelier, VT 05602
Pulp Press, P.O. Box 3868, Main Post Office, Vancouver, British Columbia V6B 3Z3
Pulse-Finger Press, P.O. Box 18105, Philadelphia, PA 19116
Purdue University Press, S. Campus Courts-D, West Lafayette, IN 47907
Pynyon Press, Atlanta, GA

Q

Quarterly Review of Literature, 26 Haslet Ave., Princeton, NJ 08540

R

Random House, Inc., 201 E. 50th St., New York, NY 10022
Red Weather Press, P.O. Box 1104, Eau Claire, WI 54701
Remo Publishers, 1411 Mar Vista Ave., Pasadena, CA 91104
Fleming H. Revell Co., 184 Central Ave., Old Tappan, NJ 07675
Routledge & Kegan Paul, Ltd., 9 Park St., Boston, MA 02108
Ruffled Feathers Publishing Co., Boulder, CO

S

Sackbut Press, 2513 E. Webster Place, Milwaukee, WI 53211
Saint Andrews Press, Saint Andrews Presbyterian College, Laurinburg, NC 28352
St. Luke's Press, 1407 Union Ave., Memphis, TN 38104
Salt Lick Press, P.O. Box 1064, Quincy, IL 62301
Samisdat Press, P.O. Box 231, Richford, VT 05476
San Marcos Press, P.O. Box 53, Cerrillos, NM 87010
Charles Scribner's Sons, 597 Fifth Ave., New York, NY 10017
Seal Press, 533 11th E., Seattle, WA 98102
Seven Search Publications, La Jolla, CA
Seven Woods Press, P.O. Box 32, New York, NY 10014
Shearwater Press, Wellfleet, MA 02667
Sheep Meadow Press, 145 Central Park West, New York, NY 10023
Sibyl-Child Press, P.O. Box 1773, Hyattsville, MD 20783
Sierra Club Books, 530 Bush St., San Francisco, CA 94108
Slough Press, P.O. Box 370, Edgewood, TX 75117
Slow Loris Press, 923 Highview St., Pittsburgh, PA 15206
The Smith Publishers (New York/London), 5 Beekman St., New York, NY 10038
Solo Press, 750 Nipomo, San Luis Obispo, CA 93401
Sombre Reptiles, Berkeley, CA

Sono Nis Press, 1745 Blanshard St., Victoria, British Columbia V8W 2J8
Southern Illinois University Press, P.O. Box 3697, Carbondale, IL 62901
Sparrow Press, c/o Vagrom Publications, 103 Waldron St., West Lafayette, IN 47906
Spoon River Poetry Press, P.O. Box 1443, Peoria, IL 61655
State University of New York Press, Albany, NY 12246
Station Hill Press, Barrytown, NY 12507
Street Fiction Press, 201 E. Liberty St., Ann Arbor, MI 43108
Street Press, P.O. Box 555, Port Jefferson, NY 11777
Studio Press, P.O. Box 361, Upper Darby, PA 19082
Sun, 456 Riverside Dr., Apt. 5B, New York, NY 10027
Sunstone Press, P.O. Box 2321, Santa Fe, NM 87501
Survivors' Manual, 2823 Rockaway Ave., Oceanside, NY 11572
Swallow Press, Scott Quadrangle, Athens, OH 45701
Swift Systems, Sioux Falls, SD
Symposium Press, Los Angeles, CA

T

Tamal Land Press, Fairfax, CA 94930
Telephone Books, P.O. Box 672, Old Chelsea Station, New York, NY 10011
Temple University Press, Broad & Oxford Sts., Philadelphia, PA 19122
Ten Speed Press, P.O. Box 7123, Berkeley, CA 94707
Texas Review Press, Sam Houston State University, Dept. of English, Huntsville, TX 77340
Thistledown Press, 668 East Place, Saskatoon, Saskatchewan S7J 2Z5
Three Rivers Press, Carnegie-Mellon University, P.O. Box 21, Pittsburgh, PA 15213
Three Trees Press, Toronto, Ontario
Ticknor & Fields, 152 Temple St., Rm. 324, New Haven, CT 06510
Times Books, 3 Park Ave., New York, NY 10016
Tombouctou Books, P.O. Box 265, Bolinas, CA 94924
Toothpaste Press, 626 E. Main St., P.O. Box 546, West Branch, IA 52358
Turnstone Press, St. John's College, University of Manitoba, Winnipeg, Manitoba R3T 2M5
Charles E. Tuttle Co., 28 S. Main St., Rutland, VT 05701
Tuumba Press, 2639 Russell St., Berkeley, CA 94705
Two Rivers Press, Aurora, OR 97002

U

E. M. Underwood Co., San Leandro, CA 94577
Frederick Ungar Publishing Co., 250 Park Ave., S., New York, NY 10003
Unicorn Press, P.O. Box 3307, Greensboro, NC 27402
University of Alabama Press, Drawer 2877, University, AL 35486
University of California Press, 2223 Fulton St., Berkeley, CA 94720
University of Chicago Press, 11030 Langley Ave., Chicago, IL 60628
University Presses of Florida, 15 NW 15th St., Gainesville, FL 32603
University of Georgia Press, Waddell Hall, Athens, GA 30602
University Press of Hawaii, 2840 Kolowalu St., Honolulu, HI 96822
University of Illinois Press, 54 E. Gregory Dr., Champaign, IL 61820
University of Massachusetts Press, P.O. Box 429, Amherst, MA 01004
University of Minnesota Press, 2037 University Ave., SE, Minneapolis, MN 55455
University of Missouri Press, 107 Swallow Hall, Columbia, MO 65201
University of Notre Dame Press, Notre Dame, IN 46556
University of Pittsburgh Press, 127 N. Bellefield Ave., Pittsburgh, PA 15260
University of Texas Press, P.O. Box 7819, Austin, TX 78712
University of Utah Press, Salt Lake City, UT 84112
University Press of Virginia, P.O. Box 3608, University Station, Charlottesville, VA 22903
University of Washington Press, Seattle, WA 98105
Upper Room, 1908 Grand Ave., Nashville, TN 37202
Uzzano Press, 511 Sunset Dr., Menomonie, WI 54751

V

Vanguard Books, P.O. Box 3566, Chicago, IL 60654
Vanguard Press, 424 Madison Ave., New York, NY 10017
Vega, 252 N. 16th St., Bloomfield, NJ 07003
Viking Press, 625 Madison Ave., New York, NY 10022

W

Wake Forest University Press, Winston-Salem, NC 27109
Walker & Co., 720 Fifth Ave., New York, NY 10019
Wampeter Press, P.O. Box 512, Green Harbor, MI 02041
Frederick Warne & Co., 2 Park Ave., New York, NY 10016
Warthog Press, West Orange, NJ 07052
Washington Writers' Publishing House, P.O. Box 50068, Washington, DC 20004
Washout Publishing Co., 112 Morningside Ave., Schenectady, NY 12309
Watermark Press, 175 E. Shore Rd., Huntington Bay, NY 11743
Franklin Watts, Inc., 730 Fifth Ave., New York, NY 10019
Weathervane Books, New York, NY
Weed Patch Press, Sedona, AZ 86336
Wesleyan University Press, 55 High St., Middletown, CT 06457
West Coast Poetry Review, 1335 Dartmouth Dr., Reno, NV 89509
West End Press, P.O. Box 697, Cambridge, MA 02139
Western World Press, P.O. Box 366, Sun City, CA 92381
Wesport Press, P.O. Box 277, Los Altos, CA 94022
Westview Press, 5500 Central Ave., Boulder, CO 80301
Whatever Publishing Co., 158 E. Blithedale, Ste. 4, Mill Valley, CA 94941
White Ewe Press, P.O. Box 996, Adelphi, MD 20783
Windflower Press, P.O. Box 82213, Lincoln, NE 68501
Windy Row Press, 43 Grove St., Peterborough, NH 03458
Wingbow Press, 2940 Seventh St., Berkeley, CA 94710
Wings Press, R. 2, Box 325, Belfast, ME 04915
Wolfsong Publications, 509 W. Fulton, Waupaca, WI 54981
Word Books, 4800 W. Waco Dr., Waco, TX 76710
Word Works, P.O. Box 4054, Washington, DC 20015
Writers' Center Press, 6360 N. Guilford Ave., Indianapolis, IN 46220

Y

Yale University Press, 302 Temple St., New Haven, CT 06511
Yellow Press, 2394 Blue Island Ave., Chicago, IL 60608
Yellow Umbrella Press, Lowell, MA
Yiqralo Press, Laurel, MD 20810

Z

Z Press, 104 Greenwich Ave., New York, NY 10011
Ziesing Bros., 768 Main St., Willimantic, CT 06226

Magazines Publishing Poetry

*The following United States and Canadian periodicals publish
original poetry on a regular basis.*

A

A.M.E. Review, 468 Lincoln Dr., NW, Atlanta, GA
30318

ASPO Newsletter, P.O. Box 6112, Albany, CA 94706

A Different Drummer—The Poets Journal, P.O. Box
487x, Toms River, NJ 08753

*A Shout In The Street: A Journal Of Literary And
Visual Art,* English Dept., Queens College,
Flushing, NY 11367

Abba, A Journal Of Prayer, P.O. Box 8516, Austin,
TX 78712

Abbey, 5011-2 Green Mountain Circle, Columbia, MD
21044

Absinthe, Indian Tree Press, Barryville, NY 12719

Abyss, P.O. Box C, Somerville, MA 02143

Acceptance, 230 San Juan, Venice, CA 90291

Acid Switch, 716 Clement Ave., Charlotte, NC 28204

Adirondack Almanack, Box 11-A, RD 2, Corinth, NY
12822

Adventures In Poetry Magazine, 3915 SW Military Dr.,
San Antonio, TX 78211

Advisory Board Record, P.O. Box 2066 or 2204,
Chapel Hill, NC 27514

Aeolian-Harp, 1395 James St., Burton, MI 48529

Aero Sun-Times, 435 Stapleton Bldg., Billings, MT
59101

Against The Wall, P.O. Box 444, Westfield, NJ 07091

The Agni Review, P.O. Box 349, Cambridge, MA
02138

Ahsahta, Boise State University, Dept. of English,
Boise, ID 83725

Aitia, Knapp Hall, Suny-Farmingdale, Farmingdale,
NY 11735

Akwesasne Notes, Mohawk Nation, Roosevelt, NY
13683

Albatross, P.O. Box 2046, Central Sta., East Orange,
NJ 07019

Alberta Poetry News, 6211-94 B Ave., Edmonton,
Alta., Canada T6B 0S5

Albireo Quarterly, P.O. Box 4345, Albuquerque, NM
87106

The Alchemist, Box 123, LaSalle, P.Q., Canada

Alcheringa: Ethnopoetics, 745 Commonwealth Ave.,
Boston, MA 02215

Aldebaran, Roger Williams College, Bristol, RI 02809

Alembic, 1744 Slaterville Rd., Ithaca, NY 14850

Aleph, 7319 Willow Ave., Takoma Park, MD 20012

Alive! For Young Teens, P.O. Box 179, St. Louis, MO
63166

Alive, P.O. Box 1331, Guelph, Ont., Canada

All-Time Favorite Poetry, P.O. Box 2057, North
Babylon, NY 11705

Alpha, P.O. Box 1269, Wolfville, N.S. BOP 1X0,
Canada

The Altadena Review, P.O. Box 212, Altadena, CA
91001

The Alternative Press, 3090 Copeland Rd., Grindstone
City, MI 48467

Alternative Sources of Energy Magazine, Rt. 2, Box
90A, Milaca, MN 56353

America, 106 W. 56th St., New York, NY 10019

The American Atheist, 4408 Medical Pkwy., Austin,
TX 78756

American Dane Magazine, Box 31748, Omaha, NE
68131

American Jewish Times-Outlook, P.O. Box 10674,
Charlotte, NC 28234

American Poetry League Magazine, 3925 SW Military
Dr., San Antonio, TX 78211

American Poetry Review, 1616 Walnut St., Rm. 405,
Philadelphia, PA 19103

The American Scholar, 1811 Q St., NW, Washington,
DC 20009

The American Zionist, 4 E. 34th St., New York, NY
10016

Androgyne, 930 Shields, San Francisco, CA 94132

Anemone, Journal of Poetry And Related Arts, 550
Alta Vista Way, Laguna Beach, CA 92651

Angelstone, 316 Woodland Dr., Birmingham, AL
35209

Anima, 1053 Wilson Ave., Chambersburg, PA 17201

Ann Arbor Review, Washtenaw Community College,
Ann Arbor, MI 48106

Annals Of Sant De Beaupre, Basilica of St. Anne,
Quebec, P.Q. GOA 3C0, Canada

Another Chicago Magazine, 1742 W. Touhy, Chicago,
IL 60626

Antaeus, 1 W. 30th St., New York, NY 10001

Antenna, 2070 Abbott St., San Diego, CA 92107

Anthos, P.O. Box 4789, Sta. E., Ottawa, Ont. K1S
5H9, Canada

The Antigonish Review, St. Francis Xavier University,
Antigonish, Nova Scotia B2G, 1C0, Canada

Antioch Review, P.O. Box 148, Yellow Springs, OH
45387

Apalachee Quarterly, P.O. Box 20106, Tallahassee, FL
32304

Appalachian Heritage, Alice Lloyd College, Pippa
Passes, KY 41844

Applecart, 12201 N. Woodcrest Dr., Dunlap, IL 61525

Aquila, Box 174-B, Petersburg, PA 16669

Ararat, 628 Second Ave., New York, NY 10016

Arc, Dept. of English, Carleton University, Ottawa, Ont., Canada K1S 5B6

The Ardent Saboteur: A Journal of Amnemonics, 716 Clement Ave., Charlotte, NC 28204

Ariel, University of Calgary, Calgary, Alta. T2N 1N4, Canada

Arizona Quarterly, University of Arizona, Tucson, AZ 85721

The Ark River Review, c/o A. G. Sobin, Box 14, Wichita State University, Wichita, KS 67208

Artaud's Elbow, P.O. Box 1139, Berkeley, CA 94701

The Arts Journal, 324 Charlotte St., Asheville, NC 28801

As Is, 6302 Owen Pl., Bethesda, MD 20034

Ascent, English Dept., University of Illinois, Urbana, IL 61801

The Asia Mail, P.O. Box 1044, Alexandria, VA 22313

Aspect, 13 Robinson St., Somerville, MA 02145

Aspen Anthology, P.O. Box 3185, Aspen, CO 81611

Aspire, 1819 E. 14th Ave., Denver, CO 80218

Ataraxia, 291 Pine St., Madison, GA 30650

Athanor, P.O. Box 652, Victoria Sta., Westmount, Que., Canada H3Z 2Y6

The Atlantic Advocate, Gleaner Bldg., Phoenix Square, Fredericton, N.B. E3B 5A2, Canada

The Atlantic Monthly, 8 Arlington St., Boston, MA 02116

Atlantis, Box 294, Acadia University, Wolfville, N.S., Canada

Attention Please, 708 Inglewood Dr., Broderick, CA 95605

August Derleth Society Newsletter, 61 Teecomwas Dr., Uncasville, CT 06382

Auntie Bellum, P.O. Box 3473, Columbia, SC 29230

B

Bachy, 11317 Santa Monica Blvd., Los Angeles, CA 90025

Back Country, P.O. Box 83, Elkins, WV 26241

Back Door, P.O. Box 481, Athens, OH 45701

Back Roads, P.O. Box 543, Cotati, CA 94928

Ball State University Forum, Ball State University, Muncie, IN 47306

Baltic Avenue Poetry, 1027 So. 30th St., Birmingham, AL 35205

The Barat Review, Barat College, Lake Forest, IL 60045

Barataria, P.O. Box 15060, New Orleans, LA 70175

Barbeque Planet, 2513-B Ashwood Ave., Nashville, TN 37212

Bardic Echoes, 1036 Emerald Ave., NE, Grand Rapids, MI 49503

The Beehive, 201 8th Ave., S., Nashville, TN 37203

The Bellingham Review, 412 N. State St., Bellingham, WA 98225

Beloit Poetry Journal, P.O. Box 2, Beloit, WI 53511

Bennington Review, Bennington College, Bennington, VT 05201

Berkeley Barb, P.O. Box 1247, Berkeley, CA 94701

Berkeley Monthly, 2275 Shattuck Ave., Berkeley, CA 94704

Berkeley Poetry Review, c/o Office of Student Activities, 103 Sproul Hall, University of California, Berkeley, CA 94720

Berkeley Poets Cooperative, P.O. Box 459, Berkeley, CA 94701

Best Friends, 29 Montclaire, NE, Albuquerque, NM 87108

Best in Poetry, P.O. Box 2057, North Babylon, NY 11703

Best Poets Of The 20th Century, Drawer J, Babylon, NY 11702

Beyond Baroque, 681 Venice Blvd., Venice, CA 90291

Big Moon, P.O. Box 4731, Modesto, CA 95352

Bird Effort, 25 Mudford Ave., Easthampton, NY 11937

Birthstone, 1319 6th Ave., San Franciso, CA 94122

Bitterroot, Blythebourne Sta., P.O. Box 51, Brooklyn, NY 11219

Bittersweet, 777 Brice St., Lebanon, MO 65536

Black American Literature Forum, Indiana State University, Parsons Hall 237, Terre Haute, IN 47809

The Black Cat, c/o Richard Morgan, English Dept., P.O. Box 22990A, East Tennessee State University, Johnson City, TN 37601

Black Forum, P.O. Box 1090, Bronx, NY 10451

Black Graphics International, P.O. Box 732, Detroit, MI 48206

Black Maria, 815 W. Wrightwood, Chicago, IL 60614

Black Moss, RR 1, Coatsworth, Ont., Canada

The Black Scholar, P.O. Box 908, Sausalito, CA 94965

The Black Warrior Review, University of Alabama, P.O. Box 2936, University, AL 35486

Blackberry, P.O. Box 4757, Albuquerque, NM 81706

Bleb/The Ark, P.O. Box 322, Times Square Sta., New York, NY 10036

Blind Alley, P.O. Box 1296, Edinburg, TX 78539

Bloodroot, P.O. Box 891, Grand Forks, ND 58201

Blue Buildings, 2800 Rutland, Des Moines, IA 50311

The Blue Hotel, P.O. Box 82213, Lincoln, NE 68501

Blue Moon News, c/o English Dept., University of Arizona, Tucson, AZ 85721

Blue Pig, 23 Cedar St., Northampton, MA 01060

Blue Ridge Review, P.O. Box 1425, Charlottesville, VA 22902

Blue Unicorn, 22 Avon Rd., Kensington, CA 94707

The Body Politic-Gay Liberation Journal, P.O. Box 7289, Sta. A, Toronto, Ont. M5W 1X9, Canada

Bombast Poetry Review, P.O. Box 3752, Modesto, CA 95352

Bonsai: A Quarterly Of Haiku, P.O. Box 7211, Phoenix, AZ 85011

Books In Canada, 366 Adelaide St., E., Toronto, Ont., Canada

The Boston Phoenix, 100 Massachusetts Ave., Boston, MA 02115

Boston University Journal, 704 Commonwealth Ave., Boston, MA 02215

Both Sides Now, 1232 Laura St., P.O. Box 13079, Jacksonville, FL 32206

Bottomfish Magazine, 21250 Stevens Creek, Cupertino, CA 95014

Boundary 2, State University of New York, Binghamton, NY 13901

Box 749 Magazine, P.O. Box 749, Old Chelsea Sta., New York, NY 10011

Boxcar, 1001-B Guerrero, San Francisco, CA 94110

Boxspring, Hampshire College, Amherst, MA 01002

Branching Out, P.O. Box 4098, Edmonton, Alta T6E 4T1, Canada

Breakthrough! 2015 S. Broadway, Little Rock, AR 72206

Bridge Magazine, P.O. Box 477, New York, NY 10013

Brilliant Corners: A Magazine Of The Arts, 1372 W. Estes, #2N, Chicago, IL 60626

Buckeye Farm News, 245 N. High St., Columbus, OH 43216

Buckle, English Dept., State University, 1300 Elmwood Ave., Buffalo, NY 14222

Bucks County Panorama Magazine, 57 W. Court St., Doylestown, PA 18901

Buffalo Gnats, P.O. Box 163, Glen Rock, NJ 07452

Buffalo Spree Magazine, 4511 Harlem Rd., Buffalo, NY 14226

The Bulletin Board, 190 E. 21st St., 6D, Brooklyn, NY 11226

Bush League, P.O. Box 67, Angels Camp, CA 95222

C

CQ Contemporary Quarterly: Poetry And Art, P.O. Box 41110, Los Angeles, CA 90041

C.S.P. World News, P.O. Box 2608, Sta. D, Ottawa, Ont. K1P 5W7, Canada

CV-11, 14 Fourth St., Toronto, Ont., Canada M5J 2B1

Cafeteria, P.O. Box 4104, Modesto, CA 95352

The California Quarterly, 100 Sproul Hall, University of California, Davis, CA 95616

Callaloo, English Dept., University of Kentucky, 1249 Patterson Office Tower, Lexington, KY 40506

Calliope, Creative Writing Program, Roger Williams College, Bristol, RI 02809

Calyx, Route 2, Box 118, Corvallis, OR 97330

Campus Ambassador Magazine, 1445 Boonville Ave., Springfield, MO 65802

Campus News, Box 614, Corte Madera, CA 94925

Canadian Author & Bookman, P.O. Box 120, Niagara-On-The-Lake, Ont. LOS 1J0, Canada

Canadian Dimension, 44 Princess St., Suite 801, Winnipeg, Man. R3B 1K2, Canada

The Canadian Forum, 70 The Esplanade, Third Floor, Toronto, Ont. MSE 1R2, Canada

Canadian Literature, University of British Columbia, 2075 Westbrook Mall, Vancouver, B.C., Canada, V6T 1W5

Cannibal, 716 Clement Ave., Charlotte, NC 28204

Canto Review Of The Arts, 11 Bartlet St., Andover, MA 01810

The Cape Rock, English Dept., Southeast Missouri State University, Cape Girardeau, MO 63701

The Capilano Review, 2055 Purcell Way, North Vancouver, B.C. V7J 3H5, Canada

Capper's Weekly, 616 Jefferson St., Topeka, KS 66607

Career World, 501 Lake Forest Ave., Highwood, IL 60040

Carleton Miscellany, Carleton College, Northfield, MN 55057

Carolina Quarterly, Greenlaw Hall 066A, University of North Carolina, Chapel Hill, NC 27514

Carousel Quarterly of Poetry, P.O. Box i11, Mt. Laurel, NJ 08054

Cat Fancy, P.O. Box 4030, San Clemente, CA 92672

Cats Magazine, P.O. Box 4106, Pittsburgh, PA 15202

Cedar Rock, 1121 Madeline, New Braunfels, TX 78130

The Centennial Review, 110 Morrill Hall, Michigan State University, East Lansing, MI 48824

Centering: A Magazine of Poetry, Michigan State University, East Lansing, MI 48824

Channel One, 1229 N. Highland Ave., Los Angeles, CA 90038

Chariton Review, Language & Literature Dept., Northeast Missouri State University, Kirksville, MO 63501

Chelsea, P.O. Box 5880, Grand Central Sta., New York, NY 10017

The Chelsea Journal, 1437 College Dr., Saskatoon, Sask. S7N 0W6, Canada

Chicago Review, University of Chicago, Faculty Exchange, Box C, Chicago, IL 60637

Chomo-Uri, P.O. Box 1057, Amherst, MA 01002

Choomia, P.O. Box 107, Framingham, MA 01701

Chouteau Review, P.O. Box 10016, Kansas City, MO 64111

The Chowder Review, P.O. Box 33, Wollaston, MA 02170

The Christian Athlete, 812 Traders National Bank Bldg., 1125 Grand Ave., Kansas City, MO 64106

The Christian Century, 407 S. Dearborn St., Chicago, IL 60605

Christian Herald, 40 Overlook Dr., Chappaqua, NY 10514

Christian Living, 616 Walnut Ave., Scottsdale, PA 15683

Christianity Today, 465 Gundersen Dr., Carol Stream, IL 60187

Chrysalis, 635 S. Westlake Ave., Los Angeles, CA 90057

The Church Herald, 1324 Lake Dr., SE, Grand Rapids, MI 49506

Cimarron Review, Oklahoma State University, Stillwater, OK 74074

Cincinnati Review, University of Cincinnati, Cincinnati, OH 45202

City Miner, P.O. Box 176, Berkeley, CA 94701

Clifton Magazine, University of Cincinnati, 204 Tangeman University Center, Cincinnati, OH 45221

Climb, 1200 E. Fifth St., Anderson, IN 46011

Clues To The Second Coming, 1719 Eddystone Ave., Columbus, OH 43224

Coast Magazine, 509 N. Fairfax Ave., Ste. 212, Los Angeles, CA 90036

Coastline Magazine, P.O. Box 914, Culver City, CA 90230

Cobblestone, P.O. Box 1128, Los Alamitos, CA 90720

Coe Review, Fiction & Poetry Workshops, Coe College, 1220 First Ave. NE, Cedar Rapids, IA 52402

CoEvolution Quarterly, P.O. Box 428, Sausalito, CA 94965

Coffee Break, P.O. Box 103, Burley, WA 98322

The Coffeehouse, 392 San Jose Ave., San Francisco,

CA 94116

College English, Dept. of English, Indiana University, Bloomington, IN 47401

Colorado-North Review, University Center, Greeley, CO 80639

Colorado Quarterly, Hellems 134E, University of Colorado, Boulder, CO 80309

Columbia: A Magazine Of Poetry And Prose, 404 Dodge, Columbia University, New York, NY 10027

Combinations: A Journal Of Photography, Middle Grove Rd., Greenfield Center, NY 12833

Commonweal, 232 Madison Ave., New York, NY 10016

Communicator, P.O. Box 2140, Springhill, N.S. BOM 1X0, Canada

The Compass, P.O. Box 632, Sub Sta. 11, University of Alberta, Edmonton, Alta., Canada T6G 2E0

Concerning Poetry, English Dept., Western Washington University, Bellingham, WA 98225

Conditions, P.O. Box 56, Van Brunt Sta., Brooklyn, NY 11215

Confrontation, English Dept., Long Island University, Brooklyn, NY 11201

Confrontation/Change Review, 1107 Lexington Ave., Dayton, OH 45407

The Congregationalist, 801 Bushnell, Beloit, WI 53511

Connecticut Fireside And Review Of Books, P.O. Box 5293, Hamden, CT 06518

The Connecticut Quarterly, P.O. Box 68, Enfield, CT 06082

Connections Magazine, Bell Hollow Rd., Putnam Valley, NY 10579

Contact/11: A Bimonthly Poetry Review Magazine, P.O. Box 451, Bowling Green Sta., New York, NY 10004

Contempo, 796 Carlaw Ave., Apt. 32, Toronto, Ont. M4K 3L2, Canada

Contraband Magazine, P.O. Box 4073, Sta. A., Portland, ME 04101

Contrast, Western Maryland College, Westminster, MD 21157

The Copper Country Anthem, P.O. Box 330, Hancock, MI 49930

Core, 200 W. 135th St., New York, NY 10030

Cornfield Review, Ohio State University, 1465 Mt. Vernon Ave., Marion, OH 43302

Cottonwood Review, Box J, Kansas Union, University of Kansas, Lawrence, KS 66045

Country Club Golfer, 2171 Campus Dr., Irvine, CA 92715

Country Women, P.O. Box 208, Albion, CA 95410

Crazy Horse, P.O. Box 552, Murray, KY 42071

Crazy Paper, 160 Avenue of the Americas, New York, NY 10013

Creacion, P.O. Box 111, Estacion 6-UCPR, Ponce, PR 00731

Cream City Review, P.O. Box 413, English Dept., Curtin Hall, University of Wisconsin, Milwaukee, WI 53201

Creative Moment, P.O. Box 391, Sumter, SC 29150

Creative Pittsburgh, P.O. Box 7346, Pittsburgh, PA 15213

Creative Review, 1718 S. Garrison, Carthage, MO 64836

Credences, 150 S. Mantua St., Kent, OH 44240

Cricket, P.O. Box 100, LaSalle, IL 61301

Crime And Social Justice: Issues In Criminology, P.O. Box 4373, Berkeley, CA 94704

The Crisis, 1790 Broadway, New York, NY 10019

The Critical List, 32 Sullivan St., Toronto, Ont. M5T 1B9, Canada

Crosscountry, P.O. Box 21081, Woodhaven, NY 11421

Cruising World, P.O. Box 452, Newport, RI 02840

Cthulhu Calls, Northwest Community College, Powell, WY 82435

Cumberlands, Pikeville College, P.O. Box 2, Pikeville, KY 41501

Cutbank, English Dept., University of Montana, Missoula, MT 59812

D

The D. C. Gazette, 1739 Connecticut Ave., NW, washington, DC 20009

Dacotah Territory, P.O. Box 775, Moorhead, MN 56560

Daily Meditation, P.O. Box 2710, San Antonio, TX 78299

Daily Word, Unity Village, MO 64065

Daimon, P.O. Box 7952, Atlanta, GA 30357

The Dakota Farmer, P.O. Box 1950, Aberdeen, SD 57401

Dalhousie Review, Dalhousie University, Halifax, N.S. B3H 4H8, Canada

Dance Scope, 1619 Broadway, Rm. 603, New York, NY 10019

Dandelion, 922-9th Ave., SE, Calgary, Alta., Canada

Dark Fantasy, P.O. Box 207, Gananoque, Ont. K7G 2T7, Canada

Dark Horse, c/o Margery M. Cuyler, 225 Grove St., Newton, MA 02166

Dark Tower Magazine, University Center, Cleveland State University, Cleveland, OH 44115

Davinci Magazine, P.O. Box 125, Sta. G, Montreal, P.Q. H2W 2M9, Canada

Davka Magazine, L.A. Hillel Council, 900 Hilgard Ave., Los Angeles, CA 90024

December Magazine, 4343 N. Clarendon, Chicago, IL 60613

Decision Magazine, 1300 Harmon Pl., Minneapolis, MN 55403

De Colores (Quarterly Journal of Chicano Expression and Thought), 2633 Granite, NW, Albuquerque, NM 87104

The Dekalb Literary Arts Journal, 555 N. Indian Creek Dr., Clarkston, GA 30021

Delta Scene, Box B-3, Delta State University, Cleveland, MS 38733

The Denver Quarterly, University of Denver, Denver, CO 80210

Descant, English Dept., Texas Christian University, Fort Worth, TX 76129

Descant, P.O. Box 314, Sta. P., Toronto, Ont. M5S 1S8, Canada

The Dickinson Review, Div. of English, Dickinson State College, Dickinson, ND 58601

Dico, P.O. Box 6204, Postal Depot C, Victoria, BC, Canada

Dignity, 3719 6th Ave., Suite F, San Diego, CA 92103
Dimension, University of Texas-Austin, P.O. Box 7939, Austin, TX 78712
The Disciple, P.O. Box 179, St. Louis, MO 63166
Discoveries, 6401 The Paseo, Kansas City, MO 64131
Discovery, 999 College Ave., Winona Lake, IN 46590
Dogsoldier, E. 2933 Queen, Spokane, WA 99207
Dragonfly: A Quarterly of Haiku, 4102 NE 130th Pl., Portland, OR 97230
Dreamworks, 72 Fifth Ave., New York, NY 10011

E

Earth's Daughters, 944 Kensington Ave., Buffalo, NY 14215
East River Review, 128 E. 4th St., New York, NY 10003
East West Journal, 233 Harvard St., Brookline, MA 02146
Ebony Jr.!, 820 S. Michigan Ave., Chicago, IL 60605
Eclipse, 456 Picadilly St., London, Ont., Canada N5Y 3G3
Edcentric Magazine, P.O. Box 10085, Eugene, OR 97440
The Edge On Christian Education, 6401 The Paseo, Kansas City, MO 64131
Educational Studies, 331 De Garmo Hall, Illinois State University, Normal, IL 61761
Ego, P.O. Box 31312, San Francisco, CA 94131
El Coqui, P.O. Box E, Carolina, PR 00630
El Nahuatzen, P.O. Box 2134, Iowa City, IA 52444
El Viento, 348 7th St., Huntington, WV 25701
Elbow Drums, 140 2nd Ave., SW, Calgary, Alta T2P 0B9, Canada
Electrum, 34061 Violet Lantern, Dana Point, CA 92629
Eleven, 340 Calkins Hall, Hofstra University, Hempstead, NY 11550
Ellipse, Arts Faculty, University of Sherbrook, Sherbrook, Que., Canada J1K 2R1
The Emissary, P.O. Box 328, Loveland, CO 80537
En Passant / Poetry, 4612 Sylvanus Dr., Wilmington, DE 19803
Encore: A Quarterly Of Verse And Poetic Arts, 1121 Major Ave., NW, Albuquerque, NM 87107
Enduring World Adult Teacher, 6401 The Paseo, Kansas City, MO 64131
Endymion, 562 West End Ave., Apt. 6A, New York, NY 10024
Epoch: A Magazine Of Contemporary Literature, 245 Goldwin Smith Hall, Cornell University, Ithaca, NY 14853
Epos, Dept. of English, Troy State University, Troy, AL 36081
Etc: A Review Of General Semantics, University of Wyoming, Laramie, WY 82070
Etcetera, 2988 Wilson School Lane, Sinking Spring, PA 19608
Eureka Review, Dept. of English, University of Cincinnati, Cincinnati, OH 45221
Euterpe, 417 W. 56th St., New York, NY 10019
Evangel, 999 College Ave., Winona Lake, IN 46590
The Evangelical Beacon, 1515 E. 66th St., Minneapolis, MN 55423
Event, Douglas College, P.O. Box 2503, New Westminster, B.C. V3L 5B2, Canada
Exile, Box 546, Downsview, Ont., Canada
Exit, 50 Inglewood Dr., Rochester, NY 14619
Expanding Horizons (for older poets only), 93-05 68th Ave., Forest Hills, NY 11375
Explorer, 538 W. Grove St., Mishawaka, IN 46544
Expressive Arts Review, P.O. Box 444, Brentwood, NY 11717

F

Face-To-Face, 201 8th Ave., S., Nashville, TN 37202
The Falcon, Mansfield State College, Mansfield, PA 16933
Fantasy Crossroads, P.O. Box 12428, Shawnee Mission, KS 66212
Far West, 2949 Century Pl., Costa Mesa, CA 92626
Farm Wife News, 733 N. Van Buren, Milwaukee, WI 53202
The Fault, 33513 6th St., Union City, CA 94587
Feminary, P.O. Box 954, Chapel Hill, NC 27514
Feminist Studies, c/o Women's Studies Program, University of Maryland, College Park, MD 20742
The Fiddlehead, The Observatory, University of New Brunswick, Fredericton, N.B. E3B 5A3, Canada
Field, Rice Hall, Oberlin College, Oberlin, OH 44074
Fifth Sun, 1134-B Chelsea Ave., Santa Monica, CA 90403
Film Culture, G.P.O. Box 1499, New York, NY 10001
Fireweed, P.O. Box 279, Sta. B, Toronto, Ont., Canada, MST 2W2
Firelands Arts Review, Firelands Campus, Huron, OH 44839
First World: An International Journal Of Black Thought, 1580 Avon Ave., S.W. Atlanta, GA 30311
Fit, 524 Linden Rd., University Park, PA 16802
The Florida Arts Gazette, P.O. Box 397, Fort Lauderdale, FL 33302
Florida Fiesta, P.O. Box 820, Boca Raton, FL 33432
Floral Underawl Gazette, P.O. Box 2066 or 2204, Chapel Hill, NC 27514
Focus: A Journal For Gay Women, Room 323, 419 Boylston St., Boston, MA 02116
Focus/Midwest, 928a N. McKnight, St. Louis, MO 63132
Folio, 2207 Shattuck Ave., Berkeley, CA 94704
Follies, P.O. Box 5231, Pasadena, CA 91107
The Foolkiller: A Journal Of Popular People's Culture, 2 W. 39th St., Kansas City, MO 64111
The Foothill Quarterly, 12345 El Monte Rd., Los Altos Hills, CA 94022
Footprint Magazine, 150 W. Summit St., Somerville, NJ 08876
Forge, 47 Murray St., New York, NY 10007
Forms, 79 W. Goepp St., Bethlehem, PA 18017
Fortune News, 229 Park Ave. So., New York, NY 10003
Forum On The Jewish People, Zionism and Israel, 515 Park Ave., New York, NY 10022
4 Elements, 504 Inverness Ct., St. Simons Island, GA 31522

Four Quarters, La Salle College, Olney Ave. at 20th St., Philadelphia, PA 19141

Fragments, P.O. Box 1128, Los Alamitos, CA 90720

Free Lance: A Magazine Of Poetry And Prose, 6005 Grand Ave., Cleveland, OH 44104

Freedomways, 799 Broadway, New York, NY 10003

The Friend, 50 East North Temple, Salt Lake City, UT 84150

Friday Forum (Of The Jewish Exponent), 226 S. 16th St., Philadelphia, PA 19102

The Front, P.O. Box 1355, Kingston, Ont. K7L 5C6, Canada

Front Street Trolley, 2125 Acklen Ave., Nashville, TN 37212

Frontiers: A Journal Of Women Studies, Hillside Court 104, University of Colorado, Boulder, CO 80309

Frozen Waffles, 321 N. Indiana, Bloomington, IN 47401

The Further Range, 27 Oval Rd., Millburn, NJ 07041

G

G.P.U. News, P.O. Box 92203, Milwaukee, WI 53202

Galileo, 339 Newbury St., Boston, MA 02115

Gargoyle, 160 Boylston St., No. 3, Jamaica Plain, MA 02130

Gargoyle, P.O. Box 57206, Washington, DC 20037

Gay Sunshine: A Journal Of Gay Liberation, P.O. Box 40397, San Francisco, CA 94140

Gay Tide, P.O. Box 14638, Sta. A, Vancouver, B.C. V5L 1X5, Canada

The Georgia Review, University of Georgia, Athens, GA 30602

Germination, P.O. Box 40, River Hebert, N.S., Canada NOL 1G0

Gesar-Buddhist Perspectives, 5856 Doyle St., Emeryville, CA 94608

Ghost Dance: The International Quarterly Of Experimental Poetry, 526 Forest, East Lansing, MI 48823

Glassworks, P.O. Box 163, Rosebank Sta., Staten Island, NY 10305

Gnostica Magazine, Box 3383, St. Paul, MN 55165

Golf Magazine, 380 Madison Avenue, New York, NY 10017

The Goliards, 3515 18th St., Bellingham, WA 98225

Good Housekeeping, 959 Eighth Ave., New York, NY 10019

Gourmet, 777 Third Ave., New York, NY 10017

Graffiti, English Dept., Box 418, Lenoir Rhyne College, Hickory, NC 28601

Graham House Review, Box 489, Englewood, NJ 07631

Grain, P.O. Box 1185, Saskatoon, Sask., Canada

The Gramercy Review, P.O. Box 15362, Los Angeles, CA 90015

Granite, P.O. Box 1367, Southampton, NY 11968

Grass Roots Forum, P.O. Box 472, San Gabriel, CA 91778

Gravida, P.O. Box 76, Hartsdale, NY 10530

Gray Day, 2830 Napier Ave., Macon, GA 31204

Great Circumpolar Bear Cult, P.O. Box 468, Ashland, WI 54806

The Great Lakes Review, Northeastern Illinois University, Chicago, IL 60625

Great River Review, 211 W. Wabasha, Winona, MN 55987

Green Mountain Quarterly, 460 N. Main St., Oshkosh, WI 54901

Green River Review, SVSC Box 56, University Center, MI 48710

The Greenfield Review, P.O. Box 80, Greenfield Center, NY 12833

Greenhouse Review, 126 Escalona Dr., Santa Cruz, CA 95060

Green's Magazine, P.O. Box 313, Detroit, MI 48231

Greensboro Review, Dept. of English, North Carolina University, Greensboro, NC 27412

Grist, 195 Lakeview Ave., Cambridge, MA 02138

Grit, 208 W. Third St., Williamsport, PA 17701

Grub Street, P.O. Box 91, Bellmore, NY 11710

Gryphon, College of Arts & Sciences, Room 370, The University of South Florida, Tampa, FL 33620

Guide, 6856 Eastern Ave., Washington, DC 20012

H

Haight Ashbury Literary Quarterly, 1997 Oak St., San Francisco, CA 94117

Hampden-Sydney Poetry Review, P.O. Box 126, Hampden-Sydney, VA 23943

Hand Book, 184 NW Broadway, Columbus, OH 43214

Hang Gliding, P.O. Box 66306, 11312½ Venice Blvd., Los Angeles, CA 90066

Hanging Loose, 231 Wyckoff St., Brooklyn, NY 11217

Happiness Holding Tank, 1790 Grand River, Okemos, MI 48864

Happy Times, 3558 S. Jefferson Ave., St. Louis, MO 63118

Hard Pressed, P.O. Box 161915, Sacramento, CA 95816

Harlequin, 240 Duncan Mill Rd., Don Mills, Ont. M3B 1Z4, Canada

Harmony, M.U.B. Rm. 153, University of New Hampshire, Durham, NH 03824

Harper's Magazine, 2 Park Ave., Room 1809, New York, NY 10016

Harpoon, P.O. Box 2581, Anchorage, AK 99510

The Harvard Advocate, 21 South St., Cambridge, MA 02138

Harvest, P.O. Box 78, Farmington, CT 06032

Harvest, 22 Fifeshire Rd. So., Willowdale, Ont., Canada M2L 2G5

Harvest Quarterly, 907 Santa Barbara St., Santa Barbara, CA 93101

Hawaii Review, Dept. of English, University of Hawaii, Honolulu, HI 96822

Heirs, 657 Mission St., San Francisco, CA 94105

The Helen Review, 3215 Ave. H, Brooklyn, NY 11210

The Herald, SPO 11, Asbury Theological Seminary, Wilmore, KY 40390

Heresies: A Feminist Publication On Art And Politics, 225 Lafayette St., Rm. 1008, New York, NY 10013

Hh Magazine, 5355 Walkley, No. 40, Montreal, P.Q., Canada

Higginson Journal Of Poetry, 4508 38th St., Brentwood, MD 20722

High/Coo: A Quarterly Of Short Poetry, 26-11 Hilltop Dr., West Lafayette, IN 47906

Hill And Valley, 4512 Lancaster, Charleston, WV 25304

Hills, 1220 Folsom, San Francisco, CA 94183

Hiram Poetry Review, P.O. Box 162, Hiram, OH 44234

His, 5206 Main St., Downers Grove, IL 60515

Hodmandod, 610 35th Ave., San Francisco, CA 94121

The Hollins Critic, P.O. Box 9538, Hollins College, VA 24020

Hollow Spring Review Of Poetry, P.O. Box 76, Berkshire, MA 01224

Horseman: The Magazine Of Western Riding, 5314 Bingle Rd., Houston, TX 77092

Hot Water Review, 42 W. Washington Lane, Philadelphia, PA 19144

Houston Scene Magazine, 3600 Yoakum, Houston, TX 77006

The Hudson Review, 65 E. 55th St., New York, NY 10022

Huerfano, P.O. Box 49155, University Sta., Tucson, AZ 85717

The Humanist, 923 Kensington Ave., Buffalo, NY 14215

Humanist In Canada, P.O. Box 157, Victoria, B.C. V8W 2M6, Canada

Humpty Dumpty's Magazine, 52 Vanderbilt Ave., New York, NY 10017

Huron Review, 423 S. Franklin Ave., Flint, MI 48503

Hyperion: A Poetry Journal, c/o Hogan/Chase Park 2-D, Chapel Hill, NC 27514

I

Icarus, P.O. Box 8, Riderwood, MD 21139

Iconomatrix, P.O. Box 2, Postal Sta. A, Fredericton, N.B. E3B 4Y2, Canada

Ideals, 11315 Watertown Plank Rd., Milwaukee, WI 53201

Identity, 420 Madison Ave., New York, NY 10017

Illinois Quarterly, Illinois State University, Normal, IL 61761

Illuminations, 1900 9th St., No. 8, Berkeley, CA 94710

Illyrian Revue, P.O. Box 450, Saddle Brook, NJ 07662

Image Magazine, P.O. Box 28048, St. Louis, MO 63119

Images, English Dept., Wright State University, Dayton, OH 45435

Impact: An International Quarterly Of Contemporary Poetry, P.O. Box 61297, Sunnyvale, CA 94088

Impressions, P.O. Box 5, Sta. B, Toronto, Ont. M5T 2T2, Canada

Impulse, P.O. Box 901, Sta. Q, Toronto, Ont., Canada

In A Nutshell, P.O. Box 22248, Sacramento, CA 95822

In Stride (poems about running, bicycling, raquetball, kayaking, etc.), 407 Jasmine Ave., Corona del Mar, CA 92625

In Touch, P.O. Box 2000, Marion, IN 46952

Indiana Writes, 321 Goodbody Hall, Bloomington, IN 47401

Inlet, Virginia Wesleyan College, Norfolk, VA 23502

Insight, 6856 Eastern Ave., Washington, DC 20012

Insight: A Quarterly Of Gay Catholic Opinion, P.O. Box 5110, Grand Central Sta., New York, NY 10017

The Insurgent Sociologist Magazine, c/o Dept. of Sociology, University of Oregon, Eugene, OR 97403

Integrity: Gay Episcopal Forum, 701 Orange St., No. 6, Fort Valley, GA 31030

Interaction, 3558 S. Jefferson, St. Louis, MO 63118

Intermedia, P.O. Box 31-464, San Francisco, CA 94131

Intermedia, Century Club Educational Arts Project, 10508 W. Pico Blvd., Los Angeles, CA 90026

The International New Age Newsletter, P.O. Box 1137, Harrison, AR 72601

International Poetry Review, SVSC Box 56, University Center, MI 48710

The International University Poetry Quarterly, 501 E. Armour Blvd., Kansas City, MO 64109

Interstate, P.O. Box 7068, University Sta., Austin, TX 78712

Intrepid, P.O. Box 1423, Buffalo, NY 14214

Intrinsic, P.O. Box 485, Sta. P, London, Ont., Canada M5S 2T1

Intro, P.O. Box 501, Sta. S, Toronto, Ont. M5M 3L8, Canada

Invisible City, 6 San Gabriel Dr., Fairfax, CA 94930

The Iowa Review, EPB 321, University of Iowa, Iowa City, IA 53342

Ironwood, P.O. Box 40907, Tucson, AZ 85717

It's Our World, 800 Allegheny Ave., Pittsburgh, PA 15233

J

Jacksonville Poetry Quarterly, 5340 Weller Ave., Jacksonville, FL 32211

Jam To-day, P.O. Box 249, Northfield, VT 05663

Japanophile, P.O. Box 223, Okemos, MI 48864

Jeopardy, Western Washington University, Humanities 346, Bellingham, WA 98225

Jewish Currents, 22 E. 17th St., New York, NY 10003

The Jewish Spectator, P.O. Box 2016, Santa Monica, CA 90406

"Joint" Conference (material written by prison inmates), P.O. Box 19332, Washington, DC 20036

Journal Of The Hellenic Diaspora, 461 Eighth Ave., New York, NY 10001

Journal Of Irish Literature, P.O. Box 361, Newark, DE 19711

Journal Of New Jersey Poets, English Dept., Fairleigh Dickinson University, 285 Madison Ave., Madison, NJ 07940

Journal Of Reading: The Reading Teacher, 600 Barksdale Rd., Newark, DE 19711

Journal Of World Education, 530 E. 86th St., New York, NY 10028

Jubilee (Canadian material only), 332 Minnic St., Wingham, Ont. NOG 2W0, Canada

Juice, 5402 Ygnacio, Oakland, CA 94601

Jump River Review, 819 Single Ave., Wausau, WI 54401

K

Kaldron, 441 N. 6th St., Grover City, CA 93433

Kansas Quarterly, Denison Hall, Kansas State University, Manhattan, KS 66506

Karaki, 831 Kelvin St., Coquitlam, B.C., Canada

Karamu, English Dept., Eastern Illinois University, Charleston, IL 61920

Kayak, 325 Ocean View, Santa Cruz, CA 95062

The Kenyon Review, Kenyon College, Gambier, OH 43022

The Kindergartner, 201 Eighth Ave., S., Nashville, TN 37202

Konglomerati, 5719 29th Ave., S., Gulfport, FL 33707

Kontaki, 121 Walmer Rd., Toronto, Ont., Canada M5R 2X8

Kosmos, 130 Eureka, San Francisco, CA 94114

Kudzu, P.O. Box 865, Cayce, SC 29033

Kuksu: Journal Of Backcountry Writing, P.O. Box 980, Alleghany State Route, Nevada City, CA 95959

Kyriokos, 25 Beacon St., Boston, MA 02108

L

La-Bas: A Newsletter Of Experimental Poetry & Poetics, P.O. Box 431, College Park, MD 20740

The Ladder, P.O. Box 5025, Washington Sta., Reno, NV 89503

Lady-Unique-Inclination-Of-The-Night, P.O. Box 803, New Brunswick, NJ 08903

The Lake Superior Review, P.O. Box 724, Ironwood, MI 49938

Lakes & Prairies: A Journal Of Writings, P.O. Box A-3454, Chicago, IL 60690

The Lamb, 2352 Rice Blvd., Houston, TX 77005

Language, 464 Amsterdam Ave., New York, N.Y. 10024

Laomedon Review, 3359 Mississauga Rd., Mississauga, Ont. L5L 1C6, Canada

Lapis Lazuli: An International Quarterly, 712 NW 4th St., Corvallis, OR 97330

Latin-American Literary Review, Dept. of Modern Languages, Carnegie-Mellon University, Pittsburgh, PA 15213

Laughing Bear, P.O. Box 14, Woodinville, WA 98072

The Laurel Review, West Virginia Wesleyan College, Buckhannon, WV 26201

Leatherneck, P.O. Box 1775, Quantico, VA 22134

The Lesbian Tide, 8855 Cattaragus Ave., Los Angeles, CA 90034

Lesbian Voices, 330 S. 3rd, Suite B, San Jose, CA 95112

Letters, P.O. Box 82, Stonington, ME 04681

Liberation, 186 Hampshire St., Cambridge, MA 02139

Life And Health, 6856 Eastern Ave., NW, Washington, DC 20012

Light: A Poetry Review, P.O. Box 1298, Stuyvesant Sta., New York, NY 10009

The Limberlost Review, c/o Dept. of English, Idaho State University, Pocatello, ID 83209

Listen Magazine, 6830 Laurel St., NW, Washington, DC 20012

The Literary Monitor, 1070 Noriega Ave., No. 7, Sunnyvale, CA 94086

Literary Review, Fairleigh Dickinson University, 285 Madison Ave., Madison, NJ 07940

The Little Around Journal, P.O. Box 541, Mentone, IN 46539

Little Caesar, 3373 Overland Ave., No. 2, Los Angeles, CA 90034

The Little Magazine, P.O. Box 207, Cathedral Sta., New York, NY 10025

The Little Review, English Dept., Marshall University, Huntington, WV 25701

Live, 1445 Boonville Ave., Springfield, MO 65802

The Living Wilderness, 1901 Pennsylvania Ave., NW, Washington, DC 20006

Logos Journal, 201 Church St., Plainfield, NJ 07060

Long Island Review, 360 W. 21st St., New York, NY 10011

Long Pond Review, English Dept., Suffolk Community College, Selden, NY 11784

Look Quick, P.O. Box 4434, Boulder, CO 80306

The Lookout, 15 State St., New York, NY 10004

Loon, P.O. Box 11633, Santa Rosa, CA 95406

Loremaster, 897 Gramercy Turn, Boubonnais, IL 60904

Lost And Found Times, 137 Leland Ave., Columbus, OH 43214

Lowlands Review, 8204 Maple, No. 1, New Orleans, LA 70118

Lucille, 5 Kern Ramble, Austin, TX 78722

Lunch, 220 Montross Ave., Rutherford, NJ 07070

The Lutheran Journal, 7317 Cahill Rd., Edina, MN 55435

The Lutheran Standard, 426 S. 5th St., Minneapolis, MN 55415

Lutheran Women, 2900 Queen Lane, Philadelphia, PA 19129

The Lyric, 307 Dunton Dr., SW, Blacksburg, VA 24060

M

Mademoiselle, 350 Madison Ave., New York, NY 10017

Madrona, 4730 Latona, NE, Seattle, WA 98105

Maelstrom Review, P.O. Box 4261, Long Beach, CA 90804

Magook, 254 Bartley Dr., Toronto, Ont., Canada M4A 1G1

Maine Edition, 22 Bridge St., Topsham, ME 04086

Maine Magazine, P.O. Box 494, Ellsworth, ME 04605

The Mainstreeter, Dept. of English, University of Wisconsin, Stevens Point, WI 54481

Maize, P.O. Box 8251, San Diego, CA 92102

Makara, 1101 Commercial Dr., Vancouver, B.C. V5L 3X1, Canada

The Malahat Review, P.O. Box 1700, Victoria, B.C. V8W 2Y2, Canada

Mamashee, R. R. 1, Inwood, Ont. NON 1KO, Canada

Many Smokes, P.O. Box 9167, Spokane, WA 99209

The Massachusetts Review, Memorial Hall, University of Massachusetts, Amherst, MA 01002

Mati, 5548 N. Sawyer, Chicago, IL 60625

Matrix, Dept. of English, Champlain Regional College,

Lennoxville, St. Lambert, Que., Canada J4P 3P2

Mature Living, 127 9th Ave., N., Nashville, TN 37234

Maybe Mombasa, c/o Ralph La Charity, #701-LAMC, San Francisco, CA 94129

Magazine, Pima College, 2202 W. Anklam Rd., Tucson, AZ 85709

The Mennonite, 600 Shaftesbury Blvd., Winnipeg, Man. R3P 0M4, Canada

Meridian, 506 W. 113th St., New York, NY 10025

Merlin Papers, P.O. Box 5602, San Jose, CA 95150

The Message Magazine, P.O. Box 59, Nashville, TN 37202

Metamorphosis, Rumford, ME 04276

Miami Magazine, 3361 SW Third Ave., Miami, FL 33145

Michigan Quarterly Review, 3032 Rackham Bldg., University of Michigan, Ann Arbor, MI 48109

The Mickle Street Review, 330 Mickle St., Camden, NJ 08103

Micromegas, 84 High Point Dr., Amherst, MA 01002

The Midatlantic Review, P.O. Box 398, Baldwin Place, NY 10505

Midstream, 515 Park Ave., New York, NY 10022

Midwest Chaparral, 5508 Osage, Kansas City, KS 66106

The Midwest Quarterly, Pittsburg State University, Pittsburg, KS 66762

Mikrokosmos, Box 14, Dept. of English, Wichita State University, Wichita, KS 67208

Milk Quarterly, 2394 Blue Island Ave., Chicago, IL 60608

Milkweed Chronicle, P.O. Box 24303, Edmina, MN 55424

The Mill, P.O. Box 996, Adelphi, MD 20783

Mill Street Journal, P.O. Box 10562, Eugene, OR 97401

Mini Review, P.O. Box 4261, Long Beach, CA 90804

The Minnesota Review, P.O. Box 211, Bloomington, IN 47401

Minotaur, 2131 Shelter Island Dr., San Diego, CA 92106

The Miraculous Medal, 475 E. Chelten Ave., Philadelphia, PA 19144

The Mississippi Mud, 3125 SE Van Water, Portland, OR 97202

Mississippi Review, Center for Writers, University of Southern Mississippi, P.O. Box 37, Southern Sta., Hattiesburg, MS 39401

Mississippi Valley Review, Dept. of English, Western Illinois University, Macomb, IL 61455

The Missouri Review, Dept. of English, 231 Arts & Science, University of Missouri, Columbia, MO 65211

Mr. Cogito, Box 627, Pacific University, Forest Grove, OR 97116

Mix, 1300 Elmwood Ave., Buffalo, NY 14222

Mixed Breed, 1275 N. Swinton Ave., Delray Beach, FL 33444

Mixed Voices, 163 W. 17th St., New York, NY 10011

Modern Bride, 1 Park Ave., New York, NY 10017

Modern Haiku, 260 Vista Marina, San Clemente, CA 92672

Modern Liturgy, P.O. Box 444, Saratoga, CA 95070

Modern Maturity, 215 Long Beach Blvd., Long Beach, CA 90801

The Modern Woodmen, 1701 1st Ave., Rock Island, IL 61201

The Modularist Review, 65-45 Yellowstone Blvd., Forest Hills, NY 11375

Moment Magazine (Jewish oriented), 462 Boylston St., Suite 301, Boston, MA 02116

Montemora, P.O. Box 336, Cooper Sta., New York, NY 10003

Montreal Writer's Forum, P.O. Box 333, Morin Heights, Que., Canada J0R 1H0

Moondance, 720 Shotwell, Memphis, TN 38111

Moons And Lion Tailes, P.O. Box 8434, Lake St. Sta., Minneapolis, MN 55408

The Moonshine Review, c/o Tom Liner, Rt. 2, Box 488, Flowery Branch, GA 30542

The Moosehead Review, P.O. Box 287, Waterville, P.Q., Canada

Mother's Manual Magazine, 176 Cleveland Dr., Croton-on-Hudson, NY 10520

Mountain Gazette, 2025 York St., Denver, CO 80205

Mountain Review, P.O. Box 660, Whitesburg, KY 41858

Mountain Summer, "Glen Antrim," Sewanee, TN 37375

The Mountain Thought Review, 612 E. Georgia, No. 8, Gunnison, CO 81230

Moving Out, Wayne State University, 4866 3rd, Detroit, MI 48202

Ms. Magazine, 570 Lexington Ave., New York, NY 10017

Mundus Artium: A Journal Of International Literature And The Arts, University of Texas, Box 688, Richardson, TX 75080

N

Nantucket Review, P.O. Box 1444, Nantucket, MA 02554

Natchez Trace Literary Review, P.O. Box 6945, Jackson, MS 39212

The Nation, 333 Ave. of the Americas, New York, NY 10014

National Forum, Box 19420A, East Tennessee University, Johnson City, TN 37601

Nebula, 970 Copeland St., North Bay, Ont. P1B 3E4, Canada

Nethula Journal Of Contemporary Literature, P.O. Box 50638, Washington, DC 20004

New America: A Review, Humanities Rm. 324, University of New Mexico, Albuquerque, NM 87131

New Boston Review, 77 Sacramento St , Somerville, MA 02143

New Catholic World, 1865 Broadway, New York, NY 10023

New Collage Magazine, 5700 North Trail, Sarasota, FL 33580

New Directions, Dept. of Human Relations and Publications, Howard University, Washington, DC 20059

New Directions For Women, 223 Old Hook Rd., Westwood, NJ 07675

New Earth Review, P.O. Box 83, Murfreesboro, NC 27855

The New Earth Review, 58 St. Marks Pl., New York,

NY 10003

The New England Journal Of Medicine, 10 Shattuck St., Boston, MA 02115

New England Review, P.O. Box 170, Hanover, NH 03755

New England Sampler, RFD 1, Box M119, Brooke, ME 04921

New England Senior Citizen/Senior American News, 470 Boston Post Rd., Weston, MA 02193

The New Era, 50 E. North Temple, Salt Lake City, UT 84150

The New Infinity Review, P.O. Box 412, South Point, OH 45680

New Jersey Poetry Monthly, P.O. Box 824, Saddle Brook, NJ 07662

The New Kent Quarterly, 239 Student Center, Kent State University, Kent, OH 44240

The New Laurel Review, P.O. Box 1083, Chalmette, LA 70044

New Letters, University of Missouri, 5346 Charlotte, Kansas City, MO 64110

New Literature & Ideology, P.O. Box 727, Adelaide Sta., Toronto, Ont., Canada

The New Magazine, P.O. Box 12, Boyes Hot Springs, CA 95416

New Mexico Humanities Review, Box A, New Mexico Tech, Socorro, NM 87801

The New Moon, 2147 Oakland Dr., Kalamazoo, MI 49008

New Orleans Review, Loyola University, New Orleans, LA 70118

The New Renaissance, 9 Heath Rd., Arlington, MA 02174

The New Republic, 1220 19th St., NW, Washington, DC 20036

New Voices, P.O. Box 308, Clintondale, NY 12515

New World Journal, 2845 Buena Vista Way, Berkeley, CA 94708

New York Arts Journal, 560 Riverside Dr., New York, NY 10027

The New York Culture Review, 128 E. 4th St., New York, NY 10003

New York Quarterly, P.O. Box 2415, Grand Central Sta., New York, NY 10017

The New York Smith, 5 Beekman St., New York, NY 10038

The New Yorker, 25 W. 43rd St., New York, NY 10036

NeWest ReView, 11441 84th St., Edmonton, Alta. T5B 3B5, Canada

Newsart, 5 Beekman St., New York, NY 10038

Neworld, 6331 Hollywood Blvd., Los Angeles, CA 90028

The Niagara Magazine, 195 Hicks St., Apt. 3B, Brooklyn, NY 11201

Nicotine Soup, P.O. Box 22613, San Francisco, CA 94122

Nimbus, 7 Foxwarren Dr., Willowdale, Ont., Canada M2K 1L1

Nimrod, University of Tulsa, 600 S. College, Tulsa, OK 74104

Nit And Wit, 1908 W. Oakdale, Chicago, IL 60657

Nitty-Gritty, 331 W. Bonneville, Pasco, WA 99301

North American Mentor Magazine, 1745 Madison St., Fennimore, WI 53809

The North American Review, University of Northern Iowa, Cedar Falls, IA 50613

The North Carolina Review, 3329 Granville Dr., Raleigh, NC 27609

North Coast Poetry, P.O. Box 56, East Machias, ME 04630

North County, Dept. of English, University of North Dakota, Grand Forks, ND 58201

North Country Anvil, P.O. Box 37, Millville, MN 55957

North Stone Review, P.O. Box 14098, University Sta., Minneapolis, MN 55414

Northeast, 1310 Shorewood Dr., LaCrosse, WI 54601

Northeast Journal, P.O. Box 235, Annex Sta., Providence, RI 02901

Northern Light, University of Manitoba, 605 Fletcher Argue Bldg., Winnipeg, Man. R3J 2E4, Canada

Northern New England Review, P.O. Box 825, Franklin Pierce College, Rindge, NH 03461

Northwest America, P.O. Box 9365, Boise, ID 83707

Northwest Magazine, The Sunday Oregonian, Portland, OR 97201

Northwest Review, 369 P.L.C., University of Oregon, Eugene, OR 97405

Northwood Journal, P.O. Box 340, Moonbeam, Ont., Canada, POL 929

Northwoods Journal, R.D. No. 1, Meadows of Dan, VA 24120

Nostoc, 101 Nehoiden Rd., Waban, MA 02168

Not Man Apart, 124 Spear St., San Francisco, CA 94105

The Notebook & Other Reviews, P.O. Box 180, Birmingham, MI 48012

Nous: A Journal Of Arts And Ideas, 716 Clement Ave., Charlotte, NC 28204

Nursery Days, 201 8th Ave., S., Nashville, TN 37202

O

Obras, 681 Venice Blvd., Venice, CA 90291

Occident, University of California-Berkeley, 103 Sproul Hall, Berkeley, CA 90291

The Ohio Journal, Dept. of English, Ohio State University, 164 W. 17th Ave., Columbus, OH 43210

Ohio Motorist, P.O. Box 6150, Cleveland, OH 44101

The Ohio Review, Ellis Hall, Ohio University, Athens, OH 45701

Oink! 7021 Sheridan, Chicago, IL 60626

Omega, 145 E. Main St., Cambridge, NY 12816

On The Line, 616 Walnut Ave., Scottdale, PA 15683

Ontario Review, 6000 Riverside Dr., E., Windsor, Ont. N8S 1B6, Canada

The Ontario Review, 9 Honey Brook Dr., Princeton, NJ 08540

Open Places, Box 2085, Stephens College, Columbia, MO 65201

Opinion, P.O. Box 1885, Rockford, IL 61110

The Orchard, 500 26th Ave., Santa Cruz, CA 95062

Oregon Times Magazine, 1000 SW 3rd Ave., Portland, OR 97204

Origins, P.O. Box 5072, Sta. E, Hamilton, Ont. L8S 4K9, Canada

Orpheus, 1147 S. Robertson Blvd., Los Angeles, CA 90035

Osiris, P.O. Box 297, Deerfield, MA 01342

Other Islands, 28 So. First Ave., Highland Park, NJ 08904

Other Press Poetry Review, 2503 Douglas College, New Westminster, B.C., Canada

Our Family, Box 249, Battleford, Sask. SOM OEO, Canada

Our Little Friend; Primary Treasure, 1350 Villa St., Mountain View, CA 94042

Out There Magazine, 552 25th Ave., San Francisco, CA 94121

Outerbridge, The College of Staten Island, English Dept., 715 Ocean Terr., Staten Island, NY 10301

Oxymoron: Journal Of Convulsive Beauty, P.O. Box 3424, Charlottesville, VA 22903

P

Pacific Northwest Review Of Books, P.O. Box 21566, Seattle, WA 98111

Pacific Poetry And Fiction Review, English Office, San Diego State University, San Diego, CA 92182

The Pacifica Review, P.O. Box 1034, Pacifica, CA 94044

Padan Aram, 52 Dunster St., Harvard University, Cambridge, MA 02138

Paintbrush, Dept. of English, Northeastern University, Boston, MA 02115

Painted Bride Quarterly, 527 South St., Philadelphia, PA 19147

Pan American Review, 1101 Tori Lane, Edinburg, TX 78539

Panache, P.O. Box 77, Sunderland, MA 01375

The Panhandler, Writers Workshop, English Dept., University of West Florida, Pensacola, FL 32504

Panjandrum Poetry Journal, 99 Sanchez St., San Francisco, CA 94114

Parabola, 150 Fifth Ave., New York, NY 10011

The Paris Review, 45-39 171st Place, Flushing, NY 11358

Parnassus: Poetry In Review, 205 W. 89th St., New York, NY 10024

Partisan Review, Boston University, 128 Bay State Rd., Boston, MA 02215

Pass-Age: A Futures Journal, 431 S. 45th St., Philadelphia, PA 19104

The Passage, 40 Pleasant St., Portsmouth, NH 03801

Passages North, Wm. Boniface Fine Arts Center, Escanaba, MI 49829

Paunch, 123 Woodward Ave., Buffalo, NY 14214

The Pawn Review, P.O. Box 29250, Dallas, TX 75229

Pebble, 118 S. Boswell, Crete, NE 68333

Pembroke Magazine, P.O. Box 756, Pembroke, NC 28372

The Pen Woman Magazine, 1300 17th St., NW, Washington, DC 20036

Pennsylvania Black Observer, P.O. Box 72, Reading, PA 19603

The Penny Dreadful, Dept. of English, Bowling Green State University, Bowling Green, OH 43403

Pentecostal Evangel, 1445 Boonville, Springfield, MO 65802

Pequod, P.O. Box 491, Forest Knolls, CA 94933

Periodical Of Art In Nebraska, University of Nebraska at Omaha, P.A.N., U.N.O., Annex 21, Box 688, Omaha, NE 68101

Permafrost Magazine, University of Alaska, Fairbanks, AK 99701

Perspectives, English Dept., West Virginia University, Morgantown, WV 26506

Phantasm, P.O. Box 3404, Chico, CA 95927

Phoebe, 4400 University Dr., Fairfax, VA 22030

The Phoenix, Morning Star Farm, RFD, Haydenville, MA 01039

Photo Insight, Suite 2, 91-24 168th St., Jamaica, NY 11432

Piedmont Literary Review, P.O. Box 3656, Danville, VA 24541

Pierian Spring, Brandon University Press, Brandon, Man. R7A 6A9, Canada

Pigiron, P.O. Box 237, Youngstown, OH 44501

The Pikestaff Forum, P.O. Box 127, Normal, IL 61761

Pivot, 221 S. Barnard, State College, PA 16801

Plainsong, Box U245, Bowling Green, KY 42101

Plainswoman, P.O. Box 8027, Grand Forks, ND 58202

Plexus, 2600 Dwight Way, 209, Berkeley, CA 94704

Ploughshares, P.O. Box 529, Cambridge, MA 02139

Plum, 549 W. 113th St., New York, NY 10025

Plumbers Ink, 780 Amana St., No. 1606, Honolulu, HI 96814

Poem, P.O. Box 1247, West Sta., Huntsville, AL 35807

Poet, 208 W. Latimer Ave., Campbell, CA 95008

The Poet, 2314 W. 6th St., Mishawaka, IN 46544

Poet & Critic, English Dept., Iowa State University, 203 Ross Hall, Ames, IA 50011

Poet Lore, 4000 Albemarle St., NW, Suite 504, Washington, DC 20016

Poet Papers, P.O. Box 528, Topanga, CA 90290

The Poetic Hardware Press, 1815 Riverside Dr., 4K, New York, NY 10034

Poetic License, P.O. Box 3810, Postal Sta. B, Calgary, Alta., Canada T2N 4N6

Poetry, 601 S. Morgan St., P.O. Box 4348, Chicago, IL 60680

Poetry Canada Poesie, P.O. Box 1280, Sta. "A," Toronto, Ont. M5W 1G7, Canada

Poetry Canada Review, P.O. Box 277, Sta. "F," Toronto, Ont. M4Y 2L7, Canada

Poetry &, P.O. Box A3298, Chicago, IL 60690

Poetry East, 530 Riverside Dr., New York, NY 10027

The Poetry Memo Of Brentwood, 783 Old Hickory Blvd., Brentwood, TN 37027

The Poetry Miscellany, P.O. Box 165, Signal Mountain, TN 37377

Poetry Newsletter, Dept. of English, Temple University, Philadelphia, PA 19122

Poetry Northwest, 4045 Brooklyn, NE, University of Washington, Seattle, WA 98195

Poetry Northwest Magazine, The Oregonian, Portland, OR 97201

Poetry Now, 3118 K St., Eureka, CA 95501

Poetry Society of America Bulletin, 15 Gramercy Park, New York, NY 10003

Poetry Texas, Div. of Humanities, College of the Mainland, Texas City, TX 77590

Poetry Toronto, 43 Eglinton Ave. E., Toronto, Ont., Canada M4P 1A2

Poetry Venture, 2135-49 1st Ave. S., St. Petersburg, FL 33712

Poetry View, 1125 Valley Rd., Menasha, WI 54952

Poetry-Windsor-Poesie, P.O. Box 7186, Sandwich P.O., Windsor, Ont. N9C 3Z1, Canada

Poets' League Of Greater Cleveland Newsletter, P.O. Box 6055, Cleveland, OH 44101

Poets On:, P.O. Box 255, Chaplin, CT 06235

Point Of Contact, 110 Bleecker St., 16B, New York, NY 10012

Pontchartrain Review, P.O. Box 1065, Chalmette, LA 70044

Porch, Dept. of English, Arizona State University, Tempe, AZ 85281

Porch, 1422 37th Ave., Seattle, WA 98122

Portico, Sheridan College, Trafalgar Rd., Oakville, Ont., Canada L6H 2L1

Portland Review, P.O. Box 751, Portland, OR 97207

Prairie Schooner, 201 Andrews Hall, University of Nebraska, Lincoln, NE 68588

Praxis: A Journal Of Radical Perspectives On The Arts, P.O. Box 207, Goleta, CA 93017

Prelude To Fantasy, Rt. 3, Box 193, Richland Center, WI 53703

Presbyterian Record, 50 Wynford Dr., Don Mills, Ont., Canada M3C 1J7

Present Tense (Jewish oriented), 165 E. 56th St., New York, NY 10022

Pre-Vue, P.O. Box 20768, Billings, MT 59104

Primavera, Ida Noyes Hall, University of Chicago, Chicago, IL 60637

Primipara (contributors restricted to Wisconsin residents), P.O. Box 171, Oconto, WI 54153

Princeton Spectrum, P.O. Box 3005, Princeton, NJ 08540

Prism International, Dept. of Creative Writing, University of British Columbia, Vancouver, B.C. V6T 1W5, Canada

Progressive Labor Magazine, GPO Box 808, Brooklyn, NY 11201

Proteus, 1004 N. Jefferson St., Arlington, VA 22205

Pteranodon, P.O. Box 229, Bourbonnais, IL 60914

Ptolemy, P.O. Box 6915-A Press Ave., Browns Mills, NJ 08015

The Pub, P.O. Box 123, Harris, IA 51345

Puddingstone, P.O. Box 8800, University Sta., Knoxville, TN 37916

Puerto Del Sol, P.O. Box 3E, Las Cruces, NM 88003

Pulp, c/o Sage, 720 Greenwich St., 4H, New York, NY 10014

Pulp: Fiction & Poetry, P.O. Box 243, Narragansett, RI 02882

Purpose, 616 Walnut Ave., Scottdale, PA 15683

Q

Quarry, P.O. Box 1061, Kingston, Ont. K7L 4Y5, Canada

Quarry West, College V, University of California, Santa Cruz, CA 95064

Quarterly Review Of Literature, 26 Haslet Ave., Princeton, NJ 08540

Quarterly West, 312 Olpin Union, University of Utah, Salt Lake City, UT 84112

Queen, 40 S. Saxon Ave., Bay Shore, NY 11706

Queen's Quarterly: A Canadian Review, Queen's University, Kingston, Ont. K7L 3N6, Canada

Quercus, P.O. Box 25-4502, Sacramento, CA 95825

Quest, 1133 Ave. of the Americas, New York, NY 10036

Quoin, 1226 W. Talmage, Springfield, MO 65803

R

R.T.: A Journal Of Radical Therapy, P.O. Box 89, West Somerville, MA 02144

Raccoon, 561 Ellsworth, Apt. 1, Memphis, TN 38111

Radcliffe Quarterly, 10 Garden St., Cambridge, MA 02138

The Rag, 850 Reynard St., SE, Grand Rapids, MI 49507

Ragged Claw, 20 College St., Toronto, Ont., Canada, M5G 1K2

Rainbow, American Baptist Board of Educational Ministries, Valley Forge, PA 19481

Raincoast Chronicles, P.O. Box 119, Madeira Park, BC, Canada V0N 2H0

Raintree, 4043 Morningside Dr., Bloomington, IN 47401

Ram: The Letter Box, 430 4th St., Brooklyn, NY 11215

Realities Library, 2480 Escaloma Court, San Jose, CA 95121

Reconstructionist, 432 Park Ave., S., New York, NY 10016

Red Cedar Review, 325 Morrill, Dept. of English, Michigan State University, East Lansing, MI 48824

Red Fox Review, Mohegan Community College, Norwich, CT 06360

Red Weather, P.O. Box 1104, Eau Claire, WI 54701

The Remington Review, 505 Westfield Ave., Elizabeth, NJ 07208

Repository, R. R. 7, Buckhorn Rd., Prince George, B.C., Canada

Response: A Contemporary Jewish Review, 523 W. 113th St., New York, NY 10025

Review, Center for Inter-American Relations, 680 Park Ave., New York, NY 10021

Revista Chicano-Riquena, Indiana University Northwest, 3400 Broadway, Gary, IN 46408

Revista/Review Interamericana, G.P.O. Box 3255, San Juan, PR 00936

Rhino, 77 Lakewood Pl., Highland Park, IL 60035

Rikka, P.O. Box 6031, Sta. A, Toronto, Ont. M5W 1P4, Canada

Ripples, 718 Watersedge, Ann Arbor, MI 48105

River Styx, 7420 Cornell Ave., St. Louis, MO 63130

Riversedge, P.O. Box 1547, Edinburg, TX 78539

Riverside Quarterly, P.O. Box 14451, University Sta., Gainesville, FL 32604

Road Apple Review, 3263 Shorewood Dr., Oshkosh, WI 54901

Road/House, 99 W. 9th St., Belvidere, IL 61008

Rockbottom, 209 W. De La Guerra, Santa Barbara, CA 93101

Rocky Mountain Review, English Dept., Arizona State University, Tempe, AZ 85281

The Romantist, 3610 Meadowbrook Ave., Nashville,

TN 37205

Roof Magazine, 300 Bowery, New York, NY 10012

Room Magazine, P.O. Box 40610, San Francisco, CA 94140

Room Of One's Own (Feminist), 1918 Waterloo St., Vancouver, B.C. V6R 3G6, Canada

Round Notes, P.O. Box N, Boulder Creek, CA 95006

Roundtable, 170 S. Hobart, Los Angeles, CA 90004

Rufus, P.O. Box 16, Pasadena, CA 91102

Ruhtra, P.O. Box 12, Boyes Hot Springs, CA 95416

Rune, 81 St. Mary's St., Box 299, Michael's College, Toronto, Ont. M5S 1J4, Canada

Rural Electric Missourian, 2722 E. McCarty St., Jefferson City, MO 65101

S

Sackbut Review, 2513 E. Webster, Milwaukee, WI 53211

Sagebloom, P.O. Box 79464, Houston, TX 77079

St. Andrews Review, St. Andrews College, Laurinberg, NC 28352

St. Joseph's Messenger & Advocate Of The Blind, St. Joseph's Home, P.O. Box 288, Jersey City, NJ 07303

Saint Louis Literary Supplement, 3523 Itaska St., St. Louis, MO 63111

Salmagundi, Skidmore College, Saratoga Springs, NY 12866

Salome: A Literary Dance Magazine, 5548 N. Sawyer, Chicago, IL 60625

Salt, 1119 13th Ave., NW, Moose Jaw, Sask. S6H 4N5, Canada

The Salt Cedar, Route 3, Box 652, Fort Collins, CO 80521

Salt Lick Press, P.O. Box 1064, Quincy, IL 62301

Salthouse, 1562 Jones Dr., Ann Arbor, MI 48105

Sam Houston Literary Review, English Dept., Sam Houston State University, Huntsville, TX 77340

Samisdat, P.O. Box 231, Richford, VT 05476

San Jose Studies, San Jose State University, San Jose, CA 95192

San Marcos Review, P.O. Box 4368, Albuquerque, NM 87106

Sandlapper: The Magazine Of South Carolina, P.O. Box 1668, Columbia, SC 29202

Sands, 17302 Club Hill Dr., Dallax, TX 75248

Sandscript, P.O. Box 333, Cummaquid, MA 02637

The Saturday Evening Post, 1100 Waterway Blvd., Indianapolis, IN 46202

Scandinavian Review, 127 E. 73rd St., New York, NY 10021

Scholia Satyrica, Dept. of English, University of South Florida, Tampa, FL 33620

Scimitar And Song, P.O. Box 151, Edgewater, MD 21037

Scope, 426 S. Fifth St., Minneapolis, MN 55415

The Seattle Review, Padelford Hall GN-30, University of Washington, Seattle, WA 98195

Second Coming, P.O. Box 31249, San Francisco, CA 94131

Second Growth, Dept. of English, East Tennessee State University, Johnson City, TN 37601

The Second Wave, P.O. Box 344, Cambridge A., Cambridge, MA 02139

Secrets, Macfadden Women's Group, 205 E. 42nd St., New York, NY 10017

The Seeker Newsletter, P.O. Box 7601, San Diego, CA 92107

Seems, Dept. of English, University of Northern Iowa, Cedar Falls, IA 50613

Seems 13, Lakeland College, Sheboygan, WI 53081

Seneca Review, Hobart & William Smith Colleges, Geneva, NY 14456

Sequoia, Storke Publications Bldg., Stanford, CA 94305

Seriatum: A Journal Of Ectopia, 122 Carmel, El Cerrito, CA 94530

Serpent's Egg, P.O. Drawer 2850, La Jolla, CA 92038

Seven, 3630 NW 2, Oklahoma City, OK

Seven Stars Poetry, P.O. Box 33512, San Diego, CA 92103

Seventeen, 850 Third Ave., New York, NY 10022

Sewanee Review, University of the South, Sewanee, TN 37375

Shabda Poetry Journal, 217 W. Julian St., San Jose, CA 95110

Shadowgraph, P.O. Box 177, Bedford, MA 01730

Shakespeare Newsletter, University of Illinois, Chicago Circle, Chicago, IL 60680

Shameless Hussy Review, P.O. Box 424, San Lorenzo, CA 94580

Shantih, P.O. Box 125, Bay Ridge Sta., Brooklyn, N.Y. 11220

Shelly's, 6560 Tower St., Ravenna, OH 44266

Shenandoah, P.O. Box 722, Lexington, VA 24450

Sibyl-Child: A Woman's Arts & Culture Journal, P.O. Box 1773, Hyattsville, MD 20783

Silver Vain, P.O. Box 2366, Park City, UT 84060

Sisters Today, St. John's Abbey, Collegeville, MD 56321

Sketch Book, 4625 E. Broadway, Tucson, AZ 85711

Skywriting, 511 Campbell St., Kalamazoo, MI 49007

Slackwater Review, Confluence Press, Lewis-Clark Campus. Lewiston, ID 83501

Slick Press, 5336 S. Drexel, Chicago, IL 60615

Slit Wrist, 333 E. 30th St., New York, NY 10016

The Slough, 184 Q St. (2), University of Utah, Salt Lake City, UT 84103

Slow Loris Reader, 923 Highview St., Pittsburgh, PA 15206

The Small Farm, P.O. Box 563, Jefferson City, TN 37760

Small Moon, 52½ Dimick St., Somerville, MA 02143

The Small Pond Magazine of Literature, 10 Overland Dr., Stratford, CT 06497

The Smith, 5 Beekman St., New York, NY 10038

The Smudge, P.O. Box 19276, Detroit, MI 48219

Snakeroots, Pratt Institute, Liberal Arts & Sciences, Brooklyn, NY 11205

Snowy Egret, 205 S. Ninth St., Williamsburg, KY 40769

So & So, 1730 Carleton, Berkeley, CA 94703

The Socialist Republic, P.O. Box 80, Madison Square Sta., New York, NY 10010

Solana (women writers only), 5712 Pennsylvania, St. Louis, MO 63111

The Sole Proprietor, 2770 NW 32nd Ave., Miami, FL 33142

Soma-Haoma, P.O. Box 649, Dennis, MA 02638

Some, 309 W. 104th St., Apt. 9D, New York, NY 10025

Some Friends, P.O. Box 6395, Tyler, TX 75701

Song, 808 Illinois, Stevens Point, WI 54481

So's Your Old Lady, 3149 Fremont Ave., S., Minneapolis, MN 55408

Soulbook, P.O. Box 61213, Los Angeles, CA 90059

Soundings/East, English Dept., Salem State College, Salem, MA 01970

Source, Queens Council on the Arts, 161-04 Jamaica Ave., New York, NY 11432

South Atlantic Quarterly, P.O. Box 6697, College Sta., Durham, NC 27708

South Carolina Review, English Dept., Clemson University, Clemson, SC 29631

South Dakota Review, Box 111, University Exchange, Vermillion, SD 57069

South Shore, P.O. Box 95, Au Train, MI 49806

South & West, P.O. Box 446, Fort Smith, AR 72901

South Western Ontario Poetry, 396 Berkshire Drive, London, Ont., Canada N6J 3S1

Southern Erotique, P.O. Box 2303, Baton Rouge, LA 70821

Southern Exposure, P.O. Box 230, Chapel Hill, NC 27514

Southern Fried Turnip Greens, P.O. Box 5003, Greensboro, NC 27403

Southern Humanities Review, 9090 Haley Center, Auburn University, Auburn, AL 36830

Southern Poetry Review, Dept. of English, University of North Carolina, UNCC Sta., Charlotte, NC 28223

The Southern Review, Drawer D, University Sta., Baton Rouge, LA 70893

Southwest Review, Southern Methodist University, Dallas, TX 75275

Sou'wester, Dept. of English, Southern Illinois University, Edwardsville, IL 62025

Speak Out, P.O. Box 737, Stamford, CT 06904

The Spirit, 601 Market St., St. Genevieve, MO 63670

The Spirit That Moves Us, P.O. Box 1585, Iowa City, IA 52240

The Spoon River Quarterly, Bradley University, Peoria, IL 61606

Spring Rain Press, P.O. Box 15319, Seattle, WA 98115

The Squatchberry Journal, Box 205, Geraldton, Ont. POT 1MO, Canada

Stand, 16 Forest St., Norwell, MA

Star West, P.O. Box 731, Sausalito, CA 94965

Stardancer, P.O. Box 128, Athens, OH 45701

Star-Web Paper, All This & Less Publishers, La Mesilla, NM 88046

Starwind, P.O. Box 3346, Columbus, OH 43210

Stone Country, 20 Lorraine Rd., Madison, NJ 07940

Stone Mountain Review, 857 N. Broadway, Massapequa, NY 11758

Stonecloud, 1906 Parnell Ave., Los Angeles, CA 90025

Stony Hills, P.O. Box 715, Newburyport, MA 01950

Story Friends, 616 Walnut Ave., Scottdale, PA 15683

Street Cries, 33 Edi Ave., Plainview, NY 11803

Street Magazine, P.O. Box 555, Port Jefferson, NY 11777

The Student, 127 9th Ave., N., Nashville, TN 37234

Studia Mystica, California State University, Sacramento, CA 95819

Studies In Poetry: A Graduate Journal, Dept. of English, Texas Tech University, Lubbock, TX 79409

Stuffed Crocodile, 764 Dalkeith Ave., London, Ont. N5X 1R8, Canada

Sulfur: A Literary Tri-Quarterly of the Whole Art, Box 228-77 California Institute of Technology, Pasadena, CA 91125

The Sun: A Magazine Of Ideas, 412 W. Rosemary St., Chapel Hill, NC 27514

Sun & Moon: A Journal Of Literature And Art, 4330 Hartwick Rd., No. 418, College Park, MD 20740

Sun Tracks: An American Indian Literary Magazine, Dept. of English, University of Arizona, Tucson, AZ 85721

Sunbury, P.O. Box 274, Jerome Ave. Sta., Bronx, NY 10468

Sunday Digest, 850 N. Grove Ave., Elgin, IL 60120

Sunshine, P.O. Box J, Babylon, NY 11702

The Sunstone Review, P.O. Box 2321, Santa Fe, NM 87501

Surfside Poetry Review, P.O. Box 289, Surfside, CA 90743

Survivor, 50 Inglewood Dr., Rochester, NY 14619

Swallowing The Poison, P.O. Box 911, W. T. Sta., Canyon, TX 79016

T

Tailings, Hancock, MI 49930

Tamarack, 909 Westcott St., Syracuse, NY 13210

Tamarisk, 188 Forest Ave., Ramsey, NJ 07446

Tar River Poetry, Dept. of English, East Carolina University, Austin Bldg., Greenville, NC 27834

Tawte: Texas Artists And Thinkers In Exile, 2311-C Woolsey, Berkeley, CA 94705

Teens Today, 6401 The Paseo, Kansas City, MO 64131

Telephone, P.O. Box 672, Old Chelsea Sta., New York, NY 10011

10 Point 5, P.O. Box 124, Eugene, OR 97440

Tendril, P.O. Box 512, Green Harbor, MA 02041

The Texas Arts Journal, P.O. Box 7458, Dallas, TX 75209

Texas Country Magazine, P.O. Box 966, Alief, TX 77411

The Texas Methodist/United Methodist Reporter, P.O. Box 1076, Dallas, TX 75221

Texas Quarterly, P.O. Box 7517, University Sta., Austin, TX 78712

The Texas Review, English Dept., Sam Houston State University, Huntsville, TX 77341

Text, 552 Broadway (6th Flr.), New York, NY 10012

Third Eye, 250 Mill St., Williamsville, NY 14221

13th Moon, P.O. Box 3, Inwood Sta., New York, NY 10034

This, 326 Connecticut St., San Francisco, CA 94107

Thistle: A Magazine Of Contemporary Writing, P.O. Box 144, Ruffs Dale, PA 15679

Thoreau Journal Quarterly, 304 English-Math Bldg., University of Maine, Orono, ME 04473

Thought: The Quarterly Of Fordham University, Box

L, Fordham University, Bronx, NY 10458

Three Cent Pulp, P.O. Box 48806, Sta. Bental, Vancouver, B.C., Canada

Three Rivers Poetry Journal, P.O. Box 21, Carnegie-Mellon University, Pittsburgh, PA 15213

Three Sisters, P.O. Box 969, Hoya Sta., Washington, DC 20057

The Threepenny Review, P.O. Box 335, Berkeley, CA 94701

Thunder Mountain Review, P.O. Box 11126, Birmingham, AL 35202

Tightrope, 300 Main St., Oneonta, NY 13820

Tinderbox, 334 Molasses Lane, Mt. Pleasant (Charleston), SC 29464

Titmouse, 720 W. 19th Ave., Vancouver, B.C., Canada

Total Lifestyle: The Magazine Of Natural Living, P.O. Box 1137, Harrison, AR 72601

Touch, P.O. Box 7244, Grand Rapids, MI 49510

Touchstone, Drawer 42331, Houston, TX 77042

Tower Poetry Magazine, c/o Dundas Public Library, 18 Ogilvie St., Dundas, Ont., Canada L9H 2S2

Town And Country Journal, 101½ Mill St., Coudersport, PA 16915

Tracks: A Journal Of Artists' Writings, P.O. Box 557, Old Chelsea Sta., New York, NY 10011

Translation, 307A Mathematics, Columbia University, New York, NY 10027

Trellis, P.O. Box 656, Morgantown, WV 26505

Triquarterly, Northwestern University, University Hall 101, Evanston, IL 60201

Truck, 1645 Portland Ave., St. Paul, MN 55104

True Experience, Macfadden Women's Group, 205 E. 42nd St., New York, NY 10017

True Romance, Macfadden Women's Group, 205 E. 42nd St., New York, NY 10017

Two Steps In, P.O. Box 11425-A, Palo Alto, CA 94301

U

US1 Worksheets, 21 Lake Dr., Roosevelt, NJ 08555

UT Review, University of Tampa, Tampa, FL 33606

Ululatus, P.O. Box 397, Fort Smith, AR 72902

Umbral: A Quarterly of Spectual Poetry, 2330 Irving St., Denver, CO 80211

Unicorn, 4501 N. Charles St., Baltimore, MD 21210

Unicorn: A Miscellaneous Journal, 345 Harvard St., 3B, Cambridge, MA 02138

Unitarian Universalist Christian, 5701 So. Woodlawn Ave., Chicago, IL 60637

Unity Magazine, Unity Village, MO 64065

University Of Windsor Review, University of Windsor, Windsor, Ont. N9B 3P4, Canada

The Unlimited, 1806 Bonita, Berkeley, CA 94709

Unmuzzled Ox, P.O. Box 840, Canal St. Sta., New York, NY 10013

The Unrealist, P.O. Box 53, Prince, WV 25907

The Unspeakable Visions Of The Individual, P.O. Box 439, California, PA 15419

Upcountry: The Magazine Of New England Living, 33 Eagle St., Pittsfield, MA 01201

Uroboros, 111 N. 10th St., Olean, NY 14760

Urthkin, P.O. Box 67485, Los Angeles, CA 90067

Uzzano, P.O. Box 169, Mount Carroll, IL 61053

V

Vagabond, 1610 N. Water, Ellensburg, WA 98926

Valhalla 5, 1719 13th Ave., S., Birmingham, AL 35205

Valley Views Magazine, P.O. Box 39096, Solon, OH 44139

Vanderbilt Poetry Review, c/o Rochester Routes, 50 Inglewood Dr., Rochester, NY 14619

Vanguard, 229 College St., Toronto, Ont. M5T 1R4, Canada

Vantage Point, Centre College, Danville, KY 40422

Vector Magazine, c/o Ball State News, Ball State University, Muncie, IN 47306

Velvet Wings, 1228 Oxford St., Berkeley, CA 94709

Victimology: An International Journal, P.O. Box 39045, Washington, DC 20016

View From The Silver Bridge, 1928 Nunns Rd., Campbell River, B.C. V9W 1H2, Canada

Village Idiot, 209 W. De la Guerra, Santa Barbara, CA 93101

The Villager, 135 Midland Ave., Bronxville, NY 10708

The Vine, 201 Eighth Ave., S., Nashville, TN 37203

The Virginia Quarterly Review, 1 West Range, Charlottesville, VA 22903

Vista, P.O. Box 2000, Marion, IN 46952

Voices International, 1115 Gillette Dr., Little Rock, AR 72207

Vortex, P.O. Box 2471, Sta. M, Calgary, Alta., Canada T2P 3CI

W

The Walrus Said, P.O. Box 5904, St. Louis, MO 63134

Waluna: The Soho Review, 72 Wooster St., New York, NY 10012

Wascana Review, University of Regina, Regina, Sask., Canada

Washington Review, 802 F St., NW, Washington, DC 20004

The Washingtonian Magazine, 1828 L St., NW, Washington, DC 20036

Washout Review, P.O. Box 2752, Schenectady, NY 12309

Waters Journal Of The Arts, Box 19341, Cincinnati, OH 45219

Waves, 79 Denham Dr., Thornhill, Ont., Canada L4J 1P2

Waves: Two, Rt 2.2, Shepherd, MI 48883

The Wayah Review, Macon County Cultural Arts Council, Franklin, NC 28734

Wayside Quarterly, P.O. Box 475, Cottonwood, AZ 86326

Webster Review, Webster College, Webster Groves, MO 63119

Wee Wisdom, Unity Village, MO 64065

Weekly Bible Reader, 8121 Hamilton Ave., Cincinnati, OH 45231

Weid: The Sensibility Revue, P.O. Box 1409, Homestead, FL 33030

West Branch, Dept. of English, Bucknell University, Lewisburg, PA 17837

West Coast Poetry Review, 1335 Dartmouth Dr., Reno, NV 89509

West Coast Review, English Dept., Simon Fraser University, Burnaby, B.C. V5A 1S6, Canada

West End Magazine, P.O. Box 354, Jerome Ave. Sta., Bronx, NY 10468

West Hills Review, Walt Whitman Birthplace Association, 246 Walt Whitman Rd., Huntington Station, NY 11746

Westbere Review, 2504 E. 4th St., Tulsa, OK 74104

The Westerly Review, 229 Post Rd., Westerly, RI 02891

The Western Critic, P.O. Box 591, Boise, ID 83701

Western Humanities Review, University of Utah, Salt Lake City, UT 84112

The Western Reserve Magazine, P.O. Box 243, Garrettsville, OH 44231

Westways, P.O. Box 2890, Terminal Annex, Los Angeles, CA 90051

Whetstone, P.O. Box 226, Bisbee, AZ 85603

Whiskey Island Quarterly, University Center, Rm. 7, Cleveland State University, Cleveland, OH 44115

Wild Fennel, 2510 48th St., Bellingham, WA 98225

Willmore City, P.O. Box 1601, Carlsbad, CA 92008

Willow Springs Magazine, Eastern Washington University, P.O. Box 1063, Cheney, WA 99004

Win Magazine, 503 Atlantic Ave., 5th Flr., Brooklyn, NY 11217

Wind, P.O. Box 2000, Marion, IN 46952

Wind Literary Journal, RFD Rt. 1, Box 809K, Pikeville, KY 41501

The Windless Orchard, Indiana University, English Dept., Fort Wayne, IN 46805

Window, 7005 Westmoreland Ave., Takoma Park, MD 20012

Wip, c/o English Dept., Box 1852, Brown University, Providence, RI 02912

Wisconsin Review, Box 245, Dempsey Hall, University of Oshkosh, Oshkosh, WI 54901

Wisconsin Trillium, P.O. Box 213, Shawano, WI 54166

Wolfsong, P.O. Box 252, Iola, WI 54945

Woman Spirit (women contributors only), P.O. Box 263, Wolf Creek, OR 97497

Women: A Journal of Liberation (women contributors only), 3028 Greenmount Ave., Baltimore, MD 21218

Women Talking, Women Listening, P.O. Box 2414, Dublin, CA 94566

Women's Circle Home Cooking, P.O. Box 338, Chester, MA 01011

Wonder Time, 6401 The Paseo, Kansas City, MO 64131

Woodrose, 524 Larson St., Waupaca, WI 54981

The Woodstock Review, 27 Oriole Dr., Woodstock, NY 12498

Word Garden, 225 Norton St., Long Beach, CA 90805

Working Cultures, 2039 New Hampshire Ave., NW (#702), Washington, DC 20009

World Literature Today, 630 Parrington Oval, Room 110, Norman, OK 73019

World Of Poetry, 2431 Stockton Blvd., Sacramento, CA 95817

The World Of Rodeo, P.O. Box 660, Billings, MT 59103

The Wormwood Review, P.O. Box 8840, Stockton, CA 95204

WOT, 657 Ardmore Dr., R. R. 2, Sidney, BC, Canada V8L 3S1

Wow, American Baptist Board of Educational Ministries, Valley Forge, PA 19481

Wree-View, 130 E. 16th St., New York, NY 10003

Writ, 2 Sussex Ave., Toronto, Ont. M5S 1J5, Canada

Writer's Digest, 9933 Alliance Rd., Cincinnati, OH 45242

Writers In Residence, P.O. Box 393, Tiffin, OH 44883

Writers News Manitoba, 304 Parkview St., Winnipeg, Man., Canada

Writing, 9231 Molly Woods Ave., La Mesa, CA 92041

X

X: A Journal Of The Arts, P.O. Box 2648, Harrisburg, PA 17105

Xanadu, Box 773, Huntington, NY 11743

Y

The Yale Literary Magazine, Box 243-A, Yale Station, New Haven, CT 06520

The Yale Review, 1902A Yale Sta., New Haven, CT 06520

Yankee, Dublin, NH 03444

Yellow Brick Road, P.O. Box 40814, Tucson, AZ 85717

Young Judean, 817 Broadway, New York, NY 10003

Young World, P.O. Box 567B, Indianapolis, IN 46206

Youth Alive! 1445 Boonville Ave., Springfield, MO 65802

Z

Z, Poets Corner, Calais, VT 05648

Zahir, P.O. Box 715, Newburyport, MA 01950

Zeugma, 25 Jeanette Ave., Belmont, MA 02178

Zone, P.O. Box 194, Bay Sta., Brooklyn, NY 11235

Poetry Associations, Organizations and Clubs

This directory lists organizations in the United States and Canada devoted to poetry. An asterisk (*) denotes affiliation with the National Federation of State Poetry Societies.

ALABAMA
Alabama State Poetry Society*, c/o Dr. Frances T. Carter, 2561 Rocky Ridge Road, Birmingham, AL 35243

ARIZONA
Arizona State Poetry Society*, c/o Dorothy Lykes, 5318 E. Arcadia Lane, Phoenix, AZ 85108
First Friday Poets, c/o Changing Hands Bookstore, 414 Mill Ave., Tempe, AZ 85281
University of Arizona Poetry Center, c/o Lois Shelton, 1086 N. Highland, Tucson, AZ 85721

ARKANSAS
Poets Roundtable of Arkansas*, c/o Helene Stallcup, 110 Shamrock, Conway, AR 72032

CALIFORNIA
Alchemedias Poets Circle, c/o Stephanie Buffington, 1005 Buena Vista St., South Pasadena, CA 91030
California Federation of Chaparral Poets, 1422 Ashland Ave., Claremont, CA 91711
California Poetry Reading Circuit, c/o James McMichael, University of California, Dept. of English, Irvine, CA 92664
California Poets-in-the-Schools, c/o J. O. Simon, San Francisco State University, 1600 Holloway (HLL Bldg.), San Francisco, CA 94132
California State Poetry Society*, c/o Ward Fulcher, 2925 Roanoke Court, Bakersfield, CA 93306
College of San Mateo Poetry Center, c/o Jean Pumphrey, 1700 W. Hillsdale Blvd., San Mateo, CA 94402
The Grand Piano Poetry Readings, c/o Steve Benson and Carla Harryman, 1607 Haight St., San Francisco, CA 94117
Intersection Poets and Writers Series, c/o Jim Hartz, 756 Union St., San Francisco, CA 94133
New College Modern American Poetry and Poetics Program, c/o Louis Patler, 777 Valencia St., San Francisco, CA 94110
The Poetry Center, San Francisco State University, 1600 Holloway Ave., San Francisco, CA 94132
Poetry Organization for Women, P.O. Box 2414, Dublin, CA 94566
The Poets Place, c/o Beverly Michaels-Cohn, Hyperion Theatre, 1835 Hyperion Ave., Los Angeles, CA 90027
World Order of Narrative Poets, P.O. Box 2085, Walnut Creek, CA 94596
World Poetry Society, c/o E. A. Falkowski, 208 W. Latimer Ave., Campbell, CA 95008
Yuki Teikei Haiku Society, c/o Haiku Journal, Kiyoshi Tokutomi, 1020 S. 8th St., San Jose, CA 95112

COLORADO
Columbine Poets, c/o Veda Steadman, 631 S. Grant Ave., Fort Collins, CO 80521
Poetry Society of Colorado*, c/o Vera M. Graham, 2235 Newport St., Denver, CO 80207

CONNECTICUT
Connecticut Poetry Circuit, c/o Jean Maynard, The Honors College, Wesleyan University, Middletown, CT 06457
Connecticut Poetry Society*, c/o Ann Yarmel, P.O. Box 583, Stamford, CT 06904
Golden Eagle Poetry Club, P.O. Box 1314, New Milford, CT 06776

DELAWARE
First State Writers*, c/o E. Jean Lanyou, 4 E. Cleveland Ave., Newark, DE 19711

DISTRICT OF COLUMBIA
Federal Poets of Washington*, c/o Betty Wollaston, 5321 Willard Ave., Chevy Chase, MD 20015

FLORIDA
Florida State Poet's Association*, c/o Robert DeWitt, P.O. Box 608, Green Cove Springs, FL 32043
National Poetry Day Committee, 1110 N. Venetian Dr., Miami Beach, FL 33139

GEORGIA
Atlanta Poetry Society, c/o Robert Manns, 1105-E N. Jamestown Road, Decatur, GA 30033
Georgia State Poetry Society*, c/o Edward Davin Vickers, Peachtree Commons, #A-8, 2222 Peachtree Road NW., Atlanta, GA 30309
Poetry at Callanwolde, c/o Gene Ellis, 980 Briarcliff Road, NE, Atlanta, GA 30306

HAWAII
Hawaii Writers Club*, c/o Louise Martin, 1634 Makiki St., Honolulu, HI 96822

IDAHO
Idaho Poets-in-the-Schools, c/o Keith Browning, Lewis & Clark State College, Dept. of English, Lewiston, ID 83501
Idaho State Poetry Society*, c/o Margaret Ward Dodson, 3883 Northbridge Way, Boise, ID 83706

ILLINOIS
Apocalypse Poetry Association, c/o Rose Lesniak, Creative Writing Center, 3307 Bryn Mawr, Chicago, IL 60625
Illinois State Poetry Society*, c/o Dr. Edwina B. Doran, Rte. 3, Box 47, Eureka, IL 61503
Modern Poetry Association, 1228 N. Dearborn Pkwy., Chicago, IL 61610
The Poetry Center, c/o Paul Hoover, Museum of Contemporary Art, 237 E. Ontario, Chicago, IL 60611
Poets Club of Chicago, c/o Nolan Boiler Co., 8531 S. Vincennes Ave., Chicago, IL 60620
Poets and Patrons of Chicago, c/o Mary Mathison, 13924 Keeler Ave., Crestwood, IL 60445

INDIANA
Indiana State Federation of Poetry Clubs*, c/o Kay Kinnamon, Rte. 3, Alexandria, IN 46001
Poets' Study Club of Terre Haute, 826 S. Center St., Terre Haute, IN 47807

IOWA
Ellsworth Poetry Project, c/o Daniel M. McGuiness, Ellsworth College, 1100 College Ave., Iowa Falls, IA 50126
Iowa Poetry Association*, c/o Will C. Jumper, 111 Lynn Ave., Apt. 408, Ames, IA 50010

KENTUCKY
Kentucky State Poetry Society*, c/o James W. Proctor, 505 Southland Blvd., Louisville, KY 40214

LOUISIANA
Louisiana State Poetry Society*, c/o Claire C. Mears, 6629 Fleur de Lis, New Orleans, LA 70124
New Orleans Poetry Forum, c/o Garland Strother, 76 Marcia Dr., Luling, LA 70070

MAINE
Maine Poetry and Writers Guild*, c/o Warren L. Elder, 57 River Road, Westbrook, ME 04092

MARYLAND
Howard County Poetry and Literature Society, c/o Ellen C. Kennedy, 10446 Waterfowl Terrace, Columbia, MD 21044
Maryland State Poetry Society*, c/o B. Floyd Flickinger, 300 St. Dunstans Road, Baltimore, MD 21212

MASSACHUSETTS
Blacksmith House Poetry Program, c/o Gail Mazur, 5 Walnut Ave., Cambridge, MA 02140
Massachusetts State Poetry Society*, c/o Jeanette Maes, 64 Harrison Ave., Lynn, MA 01905
New England Poetry Club, c/o Diana Der Hovanessian, 2 Farrar St., Cambridge, MA 02138

MICHIGAN
Miles Modern Poetry Committee, c/o Steve Tudor, Wayne State University, Dept. of English, Detroit, MI 48202
Poetry Resource Center, c/o Lori Eason, Thomas Jefferson College/Grand Valley State Colleges, Lake Huron Hall, Allendale, MI 49401
Poetry Society of Michigan*, c/o Joye S. Giroux, 825 Cherry Ave., Big Rapids, MI 49307
Rhyme Space and West Park Poetry Series, c/o Carolyn Holmes Gregory, 709 W. Huron, Ann Arbor, MI 48103

MINNESOTA
Hungry Mind Poetry Series, c/o Jim Sitter, Hungry Mind Bookstore, 1648 Grand Ave., St. Paul, MN 55105
League of Minnesota Poets*, c/o Elvira R. Johnson, 4425 W. Seventh St., Duluth, MN 55807
University Poets' Exchange of Minnesota, c/o William Elliott, Bemidji State University, Dept. of English, Bemidji, MN 56601

MISSISSIPPI
Mississippi State Poetry Society*, c/o Charlene V. Barr, 943 Carlisle St., Jackson, MS 39202

MISSOURI
American Poets Series and Poetry Programs, c/o Gloria Goodfriend, Jewish Community Center of Kansas City, 8201 Holmes Road, Kansas City, MO 64131
St. Louis Poetry Center, c/o Leslie Konnyu, 5410 Kerth Road, St. Louis, MO 63128

NEBRASKA
Nebraska Poets' Association*, c/o Charles I. Bryant, 5509 Camden, Omaha, NE 68104

NEVADA
Nevada Poetry Society*, c/o Sister Margaret McCarran, McCarran Ranch, via Sparks, NV 89431

NEW HAMPSHIRE
The Frost Place, c/o Donald Sheehan, Ridge Road, Box 74, Franconia, NH 03580
Poetry Society of New Hampshire*, c/o Robert Pralle, Box 371, Wolfeboro Falls, NH 03896

NEW JERSEY
Kilmer House Poetry Center, c/o Robert Truscott, 88 Guilden St., New Brunswick, NJ 08901
New Jersey Poetry Society*, c/o Vivian M. Meyer, 6 Park Ave., Mine Hill, Dover, NJ 07801
Poets & Writers of New Jersey, P.O. Box 852, Upper Montclair, NJ 07043
Walt Whitman International Poetry Center, c/o Frederick W. Missimer, 2nd and Cooper Sts., Camden, NJ 08102

NEW MEXICO
National Federation of State Poetry Societies, c/o Alice Briley, 1121 Major Ave., Albuquerque, NM 87107
New Mexico State Poetry Society*, c/o Latayne C. Scott, Star Rte. #109F, Tijeras, NM 85059

NEW YORK
Academy of American Poets, 177 E. 87th St., New York, NY 10028
Bronx Poets and Writers Alliance, 5800 Arlington Ave., Bronx, NY 10471
Columbia Street Poets, c/o Emilie Glen, 77 Barrow St., New York, NY 10014
Haiku Society of America, Japan House, 333 E. 47th St., New York, NY 10017
Ithaca Community Poets, c/o Katharyn Machan Aal, 431-B E. Seneca St., Ithaca, NY 14850
New York Poetry Forum*, c/o Dorothea Neale, 3064 Albany Crescent, Apt. 54, Bronx, NY 10436
New York State Poets-in-the-Schools, c/o Myra Klahr, 24 N. Greeley Ave., Chappaqua, NY 10514
Noho for the Arts Poetry Forum, c/o Palmer Hasty, 542 La Guardia Place, New York, NY 10012
Nuyorican Poet's Cafe, c/o Miguel Algarin, 524 E. 6th St., New York, NY 10003
Outriders Poetry Program, c/o Max A. Wickert, 182 Colvin Ave., Buffalo, NY 14216
Poetry Center, c/o Grace Schulman, 92nd St. YM-YWHA, 1395 Lexington Ave., New York, NY 10028
Poetry Society of America, 15 Gramercy Park, New York, NY 10003
Poets Union, c/o Lester Von Losberg, Jr., 315 Sixth Ave., Brooklyn, NY 11215
Poets & Writers, Inc., 201 W. 54th St., New York, NY 10019
C. W. Post Poetry Center, Dept. of English, C. W. Post Center, Long Island University, Greenvale, NY 11548
Rochester Poetry Central, c/o Jim LaVilla-Havelin, 322 Brooks Ave., Rochester, NY 14619
Rochester Poetry Society, c/o Dale Davis, 155 S. Main St., Fairport, NY 14450
St. Mark's Poetry Project, c/o Maureen Owen or Paul Violi, Second Ave. and 10th St., New York, NY 10003
Shelley Society of New York, c/o Annette B. Feldmann, 144-20 41st Ave., Apt. 322, Flushing, NY 11355

NORTH CAROLINA
North Carolina Poetry Society*, c/o Ruby Shackleford, Rt. 5, Box 407, Wilson, NC 27893

OHIO
Cleveland State University Poetry Center, c/o Alberta T. Turner, Euclid at 24th St., Cleveland, OH 44115
Kenyon Poetry Society, c/o George C. Nelson, Kenyon College, Gambier, OH 43011
Ohio Poetry Day Committee, c/o Evan Lodge, 1506 Prospect Road, Hudson, OH 44236
Poetry Circuit of Ohio, c/o R. W. Daniel, P.O. Box 247, Gambier, OH 43022
Poets League of Greater Cleveland, P.O. Box 6055, Cleveland, OH 44101
Toledo Poets Center, c/o Joze Lipman, UH-507-C, University of Toledo, Toledo, OH 43606
Verse Writers' Guild of Ohio*, c/o Amy Jo Zook, 3520 State Rte. 56, Mechanicsburg, OH 43044
Yellow Pages Poets, c/o Jack Roth, P.O. Box 8041, Columbus, OH 43201

OKLAHOMA
Poetry Society of Oklahoma*, c/o Helen Downing, 2309 NW 47th, Oklahoma City, OK 73122

OREGON
Oregon State Poetry Association*, c/o Anita M. Hamm, 15505 SE Arista, Milwaukie, OR 97222
Western World Haiku Society, 40102 NE 130th Place, Portland, OR 97230

PENNSYLVANIA
Homewood Poetry Forum, Inner City Services, Homewood Branch, Carnegie Library, 7101 Hamilton Ave., Pittsburgh, PA 15206
International Poetry Forum, c/o Dr. Samuel Hazo, 4400 Forbes Ave., Pittsburgh, PA 15213
Pennsylvania Poetry Society*, c/o Cecilia Parsons Miller, 264 Walton St., Lemoyne, PA 17043
Y Poetry Center/Workshop, c/o Anne-Sue Hirshorn, YM-YWHA Branch of JYC, Broad & Pine Sts., Philadelphia, PA 19147

RHODE ISLAND
Rhode Island State Poetry Society*, c/o Mary Bramante, 878 West St., Appleboro, MA 02703

SOUTH DAKOTA
South Dakota State Poetry Society*, c/o Robert G. Vessey, 2313 Western, Yankton, SD 57078

TENNESSEE
Poetry Society of Tennessee*, c/o Chester Rider, 254 Buena Vista, Memphis, TN 38112
Tennessee Poetry Circuit, c/o Paul Ramsey, University of Tennessee, Chattanooga, TN 37405

TEXAS
American Poetry League, 3915 SW Military Dr., San Antonio, TX 79601
Hyde Park Poets, c/o Albert Huffstickler, 609 E. 45th St., Austin, TX 78751
Poetry Society of Texas*, c/o Pat Stodghill, 1424 Highland Road, Dallas, TX 75218
Stella Woodall Poetry Society, P.O. Box 253, Junction, TX 76849

UTAH
Utah State Poetry Society*, c/o Maxine Jennings, 3985 Orchard Dr., Ogden, UT 84403

VIRGINIA
Pause for Poetry, c/o Margaret T. Rudd, 6925 Columbia Pike, Annandale, VA 22003

WASHINGTON
Poetry League of America, 5603 239th Place, SW, Mountain Terrace, WA 98043

WEST VIRGINIA
Morgantown Poetry Society, 673 Bellaire Dr., Morgantown, WV 26505
West Virginia Poetry Society*, c/o Dr. Kathleen Rousseau, 239 Hoffman St., Morgantown, WV 26505

WISCONSIN
Wisconsin Fellowship of Poets*, c/o Marjorie Pettit, 2243 Woodview Court, #8, Madison, WI 53718

WYOMING
Poetry Programs of Wyoming, c/o David J. Fraher, P.O. Box 3033, Casper, WY 82602
Poets of Wyoming Writers*, c/o Gene Nowlin, Box 884, Dubois, WY 82513

CANADA
League of Canadian Poets, 175 Carlton, Toronto, Ont. M5A 2K3

Poets Laureate

Numerous states recognize the excellence and stature of particular poets residing within their borders by officially designating a state poet laureate. Although the specifics of the appointment vary somewhat among the states, the title is usually bestowed by the Governor and is frequently for the life of the poet. The following list is correct for 1980.

ALABAMA: William Young Elliott
ALASKA: Sheila Nickerson
ARIZONA: None
ARKANSAS: Lily Peter
CALIFORNIA: Charles B. Garrigus
COLORADO: Thomas Hornsby Ferril
CONNECTICUT: None
DELAWARE: E. Jean Lanyon
FLORIDA: Edmund Skellings
GEORGIA: John Ransom Lewis, Jr.
HAWAII: None
IDAHO: Sudie Stuart Hager
ILLINOIS: Gwendolyn Brooks
INDIANA: Franklin Arthur Mapes
IOWA: None
KANSAS: None
KENTUCKY: Jesse Stuart; Lillie Chaffin; Agnes O'Rear
LOUISIANA: Henry Thomas Voltz
MAINE: None
MARYLAND: Lucille Clifton
MASSACHUSETTS: None
MICHIGAN: None
MINNESOTA: None
MISSISSIPPI: Winifred Hamrick Farrar (bestowed by Mississippi State Poetry Society)
MISSOURI: None
MONTANA: None
NEBRASKA: John G. Neihardt
NEVADA: Norman Kaye
NEW HAMPSHIRE: Richard Eberhart
NEW JERSEY: None
NEW MEXICO: None
NEW YORK: None
NORTH CAROLINA: James Larkin Pearson
NORTH DAKOTA: Henry R. Martinson; Lydia Jackson
OHIO: None
OKLAHOMA: Maggie Culver Fry
OREGON: None
PENNSYLVANIA: None
RHODE ISLAND: None
SOUTH CAROLINA: Helen von Kolnitz Hyer
SOUTH DAKOTA: Audrae E. Visser

TENNESSEE: Pek Gunn
TEXAS Weems S. Dykes
UTAH: None
VERMONT: None
VIRGINIA: None
WASHINGTON: None
WEST VIRGINIA: Louise McNeill
WISCONSIN: None
WYOMING: None

Awards and Prizes for Poetry /
The 1980 Winners

For the purpose of this list, 1980 winners are those announced during the calendar year 1980; they are arranged alphabetically by name of sponsor.

Academy of American Poets
177 E. 87th St.
New York, NY 10028
    The Fellowship: Mark Strand.
    Walt Whitman Award: Jared Carter, for "Work, For The Night Is Coming."
    Lamont Poetry Selection: Michael Van Walleghen, for "More Trouble With The Obvious."
    Harold Morton Landon Award: Edmund Keeley, for "Ritsos In Parenthesis"; Saralyn R. Daly, for "The Book Of True Love."

American Poetry Review
1616 Walnut St., Rm. 405
Philadelphia, PA 19103
    American Poetry Review Prizes: First—Frederick Seidel, for "Sunrise" and Other Poems; Second—Judy Grahn, for "A Woman Is Talking To Death."

Artists Foundation, Inc.
100 Boylston St.
Boston, MA 02116
    Writing Fellowships (poetry): Catherine E. Anderson; Frank Bidart; Christopher Gilbert; Lewis Hyde; John Owen Maloney; Michael Milburn; Bruce Smith; Chase Twichell.

Associated Writing Programs
Old Dominion University
Norfolk, VA 23508
    Series In Contemporary Poetry: William Carpenter, for "The Hours Of Morning."

Association of American Publishers
1 Park Ave.
New York, NY 10017
    National Book Award (poetry): Philip Levine, for "Ashes."

Association for Poetry Therapy
Casriel Institutes
47 E. 51st St.
New York, NY 10022
    Poetry Therapy Competition: Samuel G. Gilburt, for "Polyphonic Case-Histories; Carl Grasso, for "Lonely Are The Brave." Honorable Mention—Jack Rose, for "Prescription For Insomnia."

Bitterroot Magazine
Blythebourne Station
P.O. Box 51
Brooklyn, NY 11219

Gustave Kaitz Award: First—Marjorie Touzjian, for "Donor"; Second—Caroline Patterson, for "The Bitterroot''; Third—Jeannette Barnes, for "Beulah."
William Kushner Annual Award: First—Charles Sabukewicz, for "The Old Men"; Second—Nancy Davies, for "Circe's Poem"; Third—Gloria G. Murray, for "Asylums."

Black Warrior Review
P.O. Box 2936
University, AL 35486
    Black Warrior Review Literary Award (poetry): Mary Ruefle, for poems in Fall/79 issue.

California Federation of Chapparal Poets
1422 Ashland Ave.
Claremont, CA 91711
    Theme Poem: Gloria Springer Oberg, for "Wedding Polka."
    Dramatic Monologue: First—Ben Sweeney, for "Voice From Donner Pass"; Second—Nathalie Cole-Johnson, for "Prayer For A Water Buffalo"; Third—Helen Mar Cook, for "Jefferson Invites Thomas Paine."
    Light Or Humorous: First—Henry Schwartz, for "Grate Mate"; Second—Mary F. Lindsley, for "Literary Limerick"; Third—Gloria Buckner, for "Ode To The Fiery Diary."
    Sonnet: First—Ruth Hammond, for "Greek Temples"; Second—M. Michael Black, for "A Sonnet For Mr. S."; Third—Beth Martin Haas, for "Inborn Surges."
    Nature (the Desert): First—M. Michael Black, for "Death Valley Winter"; Second—B. Jo Kinnick, for "Sirocco"; Third—Mary F. Lindsley, for "Desert Ballet."
    8 Lines or Less: First—Beth Martin Haas, for "Spring Preludes"; Second—Grace Holliday Scott, for "The Brave Explorer"; Third—Nicholas, for "A Bare Tree."
    Haiku or Senryu: First—Norma Calderone, for "shoulder to shoulder"; Second—Miriam C. Maloy, for "Sunset clouds windswept"; Third—Marie Maestro Dean, for "Mirage."
    Maud O'Neil Memorial Contest: First—Leah Briggs, for "San Francisco Fog"; Second—Claire J. Baker, for "Belle Of Amherst"; Third—Nelle Fertig, for "Nebraska Driftwood."

5 Line Poem: First—Ian Wolfe, for "Scented Memories"; Second—Ben Sweeney, for "P.O.W."; Third—Mary M. Pronovost, for "Sun-Filled Morning."

Quatrain: First—Helen V. Malkerson, for "Flowering Quince"; Second—Jeanne Bonnette, for "Tearing Off A Page"; Third—Corinne Aitken, for "Graveyard."

Narrative Ballad: First—Mary F. Lindsley, for "Cabin Boys—1912"; Second—Steve Eng, for "The Pioneer Waltz"; Third—Marie Maestro Dean, for "Of Beggars And Kings."

Callanwolde Arts Center
980 Briarcliffe Road, NE
Atlanta, GA 30306
Poets' and Writers' Workshop Poetry Award: Nancy Simpson

Canada Council
P.O. Box 1047
Ottawa, Ont. K1P 5V8
Canada
Governor General's Literary Awards (poetry): English language—Michael Ondaatje, for "There's A Trick With A Knife I'm Learning To Do"; French language—Robert Melancon, for "Peinture Aveugle."

Canadian Broadcasting Corporation
1400 Dorchester E.
Montreal, P.Q.
Canada
CBC Radio Competition for Writers (poetry): First—Mary Di Michele, for "Mimosa"; Second—Bill Bissett, for "birds"; Third—Robert Currie, for "Brother."

Carolina Quarterly
Greenlaw Hall 066A
University of North Carolina
Chapel Hill, NC 27514
Contest in Fiction and Poetry (poetry winners): First—Richard Kenney, for "Misrule (A Pantomime)"; Second—David Stark, for "Whale Watch—St. Lawrence Island, Alaska"; Third—Mary Ann Daly, for "In An Artist's Backyard"; Honorable Mention—Nick Bozanic, for "The Crane's Ascent."

Columbia University
Advisory Board on Pulitzer Prizes
New York, NY 10027
Pulitzer Prize in Poetry: Donald Rodney Justice, for "Selected Poems." Also nominated—Richard Hugo, for "Selected Poems"; Dave Smith, for "Goshawk, Antelope."

CutBank Magazine
English Dept.
University of Montana
Missoula, MT 59812
Poetry Prize: Daniel Simko, for translations of two Slavik poets (Milan Rufus and Stefan Strazay).

George Elliston Poetry Foundation
University of Cincinnati
Cincinnati, OH 45221
Elliston Book Award: Mary Barnard, for "Collected Poems."

Great Lakes Colleges Association
220 Collingwood, Suite 240

Ann Arbor, MI 48103
New Writer's Award (poetry): Robert Bohm, for "In The Americas."

Grolier Book Shop
6 Plympton St.
Cambridge, MA 02138
Grolier Poetry Prize: John Hodgen, Camille Norton and Diane Wald.

Gusto Magazine
2960 Philip Ave.
Bronx, NY 10465
Poetry Prize: Ruth Wildes Schuler, for "An American Entering The Age Of Aquarius."
Haiku Contest: Jim Handlin, for "Where The Picture Book Ends."
Driftwood East Contest: Edna Janes Kayser, for "Magic Moments."
Best of Issue Contests: Rita Rosenfeld, for "Early Harvest"; Annette Wexler, for "Illusions"; Denise Sobilio, for "Growing Up, Grim"; Thelma Paddock Hope, for "You Have To Love Lizards"; Marguerite Stanley.

Houghton Mifflin Company
666 Third Ave.
New York, NY 10017
Houghton Mifflin New Poetry Series: James McMichael, for "Four Good Things."

Illinois Arts Council
111 N. Wabash Ave.
Chicago, IL 60602
Annual Literary Awards (for poetry): Mark Perlberg; Paul Breslin; Jim Elledge; Margo Maxwell; Lisel Mueller; Pamela Miller; Sterling Plumpp.

Imprimatur Magazine
Box 4
Upper Jay, NY 12987
Harry Steiner Memorial Poetry Contest: First—Linda Maloney, for "Untitled," "Any Night Now," "Nobody Knows Why, One Day He Just," "I Think, I Do Not Like," "This Is What Happens," "September," "Everything" and "Enough"; Sherrie Parks, for "A Drama," "Barriers," "Deception" and "Bitterness." Second—Marilyn Carmer, for "I Shall Will My Books To You" and "To The Black Child At 6th And Division Street"; Laurie Strobles, for "How To Read A Man Like A Book," "Contributor's Note," "Silver Spring Diner" and "What Do Poets Look Like?"; C. M. Eagle, for "The Meal," "My Mother's Tablecloth" and "No."

International Platform Association
2564 Berkshire Rd.
Cleveland Heights, OH 44106
Carl Sandburg Award: John Ciardi.

International Poetry Review
P.O. Box 3161
Princeton, NJ 08540
Annual Contest: (Poetry in English) First—Barbara Jordan, for "Real Places"; Second—John Barr, for "War Zone." (Translation) First—Lyn Coffin, for group by Jiri Orten (from Czech); Second—Nadia Christensen, for group by Henrik Nordbrandt (from Danish); Special translation prize—Michael Mott, for ballads of Francois Villon (from French).

Islands and Continents
P.O. Box 25
Setauket, NY 11733
Translation Award: Teresa de Jesus, for "All Of A Sudden" (translated from the Spanish by Maria A. Proser, Arlene Scully and James Scully; Takis Sinopoulos, for "Landscape Of Death" (translated from the Greek by Kimon Friar.

Kansas Quarterly
Dept. of English
Denison Hall
Kansas State University
Manhattan, KS 66506
Kansas Quarterly/Kansas Arts Commission Poetry Awards: First—Jonathan Holden, for "God"; Second—Ted Schaefer, for "The Estuary"; Third—Jeanine Hathaway, for "Mercey"; Honorable Mention—Robert Leitz, for "Bad Child" and Susan Fromberg, for "Letter To Albuquerque."
Seaton Awards (poetry): First—Helen Sorrells, for "The Lost Child"; Second—Jeanine Hathaway, for "The Hermit Woman"; Third—Shirley Buettner, for "Home Brew"; Fourth—George Bascom, for "August Dawn For M. R." and Roger Stamp, for "Fear."

Los Angeles Times
Times Mirror Square
Los Angeles, CA 90053
Los Angeles Times Book Prize (poetry): Robert Kelly, for "Kill The Messenger."

Louisiana State Poetry Society
c/o Golda F. Walker, Contest Chairman
915 Aberdeen Ave.
Baton Rouge, LA 70808
National Poetry Contest—
Grand Prix: First—W. Lea Pennington, for "Climbing Jacob's Ladder"; Second—Alice Morrey Bailey, for "Crumb Of Earth"; Third—Verna Lee Hinegardner, for "He Heard The Music."
Leo Horan Award: First—Vivian Smallwood, for "Cave Woman"; Second—Agnes Gray Ronald, for "Watchers Of The Sky" and Lois Stevens, for "The Waxwings Came For Lunch"; Third—Eva Braden Hatchett, for "Sonnet For My Someone."
Book Review: First—Helen Toye; Second—Margaret Ann Marston; Third—James W. Proctor.
2-Page Prose Poem: First—Ruth Shaver Means, for "Blessed Art Thou Among Nations."
Portrait of a Black Woman: First—Donna Dickey Guyer, for "Plight Of A Young Black Artist"; Second—Ruth Shaver Means, for "La Forza Del Destino".
Love: First—Alice Mackenzie Swaim, for "In A Different World"; Second—Harry B. Sheftel, for "Ballast"; Third—Alice M. Ermlich, for "With Love."
Narrative Poem: First—Margarette Parker, for "Now Is Lilac Time"; Second—Lola Beall Graham, for "Delayed Adventure"; Third—Helena C. Defenbaugh, for "And There Was . . . Something."
Lyric Poem: First—Vesta P. Crawford, for "Look For A Small Lamb"; Second—Alice Mackenzie

Swaim, for "A Falstaff Face"; Third—Gwen Casilli, for "Wonder Flower."
Inspirational: First—Glenna Holloway, for "The Enlightened One"; Second—Christine Young, for "This Day"; Third—Margaret Ward Moreland, for "Something Springs Green."
General Sonnet: First—Violette Newton, for "To Bring Me Back From Lost"; Second—Wilma Dean Williams, for "Roads"; Third—Ida Crane Walker, for "Sounds Of Music."
Gems: First—Margaret Ward Moreland, for "Jadeshine"; Second—Elaine Carreon Hollows, for "The Quest"; Third—Owen Casilli, for "Opal Essence."
Religious: First—Maryon Wood Harper, for "Donkey At Midnight"; Second—Ralph D. Eberly, for "My Dearest Friend"; Third—Margaret Ward Moreland, for "Carol Of The Cool Cat Shepherd" and Nancy Sweetland, for "Lament Of The Prodigal's Brother."
Petrarchan Sonnet: First—Antoinette Adam, for "The Open Spiral: Sign Of The Infinite"; Second—Isabel D. Howard, for "In Memorium C.W.D."; Third—Alice Mackenzie Swaim, for "Island Of Innocence."
Nostalgia: First—Nancy Sweetland. for "Running Ten"; Second—Verna Lee Hinegardner, for "Easter Glory"; Third—Louise Lamar, for "Go Merrily Round."
Philosophical About Walking/Graveyards: First—Violette Newton, for "Your Name Cut In Stone"; Second—Jack Fenwick, for "Elegy For The Living"; Third—Gwen Casilli, for "Remains."
Infinite Within Commonplace: First—Vesta P. Crawford, for "A Place For Dorian"; Second—Margaret Ward Moreland, for "Last Sunday Morning The Grackles"; Third—James W. Proctor, for "Legends."
Humorous Light Verse: First—Wanda B. Blaisdel, for "How To Catch A Cloudburst"; Second—Evelyn Amuedo Wade, for "To Each His Own"; Third—Irene Warsaw, for "High Ride, Forced Landing."
Living Is So Daily—Coping: First—Maxine R. Jennings, for "The Longing"; Second—Helena Cheney Defenbaugh, for "Tumbleweeds And Lilac Sprays"; Third—Sally Eyre, for "We Stop For Coffee."
Golda Design: First—Jessica Gonsoulin, for "Water Sculptures"; Second—Clarence P. Socwell, for "The Pulse I Feel"; Third—Sybil Nichols Gutkowski, for "Mt. St. Helens."
Haiku: First—Gloria Buckner; Second—Bohumila Falkowski; Third—Margaret Whitis.
Villanelle: First—Ruth Van Ness Blair, for "Sweet Eve"; Second—Esther M. Leiper, for "Song For Celina"; Third—Vivian Smallwood, for "February Warning."
Swamp Scene: First—Vivian Smallwood, for "'Nobody Walks Too Softly . . .'"; Second—Edward Davin Vickers, for "Oaks From Acorns (Saint Simons Island, Georgia)"; Third—Esther M. Leiper, for "A Haunting Of Swamp Mist."
Free Verse: First—James W. Proctor, for "The Thorn Garden"; Second—Nadine Neubig, for

"Winter"; Third—Melinda Ellen Gorham, for "Madonna."

About Children: Janet McCann, for "C-A-T (For Stephanie)" and Melissa Fike, for "Anyone But You (For Ritchie At 4)."

Folklore: First—Margaret Ann Marston, for "Anything At All"; Second—LeRoy Burke Meagher, for "The Aromatic Cure"; Third—Selma Youngdahl, for "Ready For Another Success."

Rockingchair Scene: First—Norma Weathersby Blank, for "Not Enough"; Second—Margaret Ann Marston, for "Telltale Evidence."

The Lyric
307 Dunton Dr., S.W.
Blacksburg, VA 24060

Lyric Memorial Prize: Donna Dickey Guyer, for "On Re-reading A Diary."

Nathan Haskell Dole Prize: John Robert Quinn, for "Stranger."

Roberts Memorial Prize: Gail White, for "The Midas Touch."

Leitch Memorial Prize: Dorothy Arlene Bates Kirk, for "Days Of Wine And Apples."

Virginia Prize: Amanda Benjamin Hall, for "Italian Nobility."

New England Prize: Tom Galt, for "Here Where We Are."

Panola Prize: Marie Daerr Boehringer, for "Mystery."

Fluvanna Prize: George Brandon Saul, for "Weatherwise."

Quarterly Awards: Winter—Diana Der Hovanessian, for "Armenian Needlework"; Spring—Helen Bryant, for "The Pharaoh Visits His Tomb"; Summer—Kay Wissinger, for "New Moon"; Fall—Doreen Gandy, for "Running Out Of Days."

Collegiate Poetry Contest: First—Francine Toft, for "Lines For A Rainy Night"; Second—George C. Fillingham, for "Something In Myself"; Third—James R. Lord, for "Eden Everlasting."

National Federation of State Poetry Societies
Amy Jo Zook, Contest Chairman
3520 State Rte. 56
Mechanicsburg, OH 43044

NFSPS Prize: First—Norma Calderone, for "Parade"; Second—David W. Parsley, for "Passer In The Storm"; Third—Geraldine C. Little, for "Meditation And Celebration For Rainer Maria Rilke."

Agnes Brothers Award: First—Marion Brimm Rewey, for "A Study In Silver"; Second—Nancy Sweetland, for "Letter To My Sister"; Third—Kay Ellison, for "Homecoming."

John A. Lubbe Memorial Award: First—M. Michael Black, for "Somewhere In Between"; Second—Norma Calderone, for "Mea Culpa"; Third—Ernestine Hoff Emrick, for "Yesterday's River."

Patriotism Award: First—Marion Brimm Rewey, for "The Unforgiven"; Second—Norma Calderone, for "Basics"; Third—Verna Lee Hinegardner, for "Picture Window Patriot."

Poetry Society of Texas Award: First—Jaye Giammarino, for "Prevision"; Second—Marion Brimm Rewey, for "Southern Gothic"; Third—Violette

Newton, for "Old Trinity County Graveyard."

Mason Sonnet Award: First—Virginia Moran Evans, for "Portrait Of My Irish Grandmother"; Second—Sheila C. Forsyth, for "Pale Gardens"; Third—Gwendolyn Niles, for "Impromptu."

Christian Poetry Award: First—John Murray, for "De Profundis"; Second—Jacqueline Swann, for "He Is Not Here"; Third—Joye S. Giroux, for "He Chose A Cross."

Music Award: First—Marion Brimm Rewey, for "Music For Healing"; Second—Elinor J. George, for "Concerto"; Third—Alice Briley, for "Universe Of Song."

Alabama State Poetry Society Award: First—Glenna Holloway, for "Long Night Homeside"; Second—Lois Beebe Hayna, for "Since Then"; Third—Evelyn Corry Appelbee, for "Objects."

Indiana Award: First—Glenna Holloway, for "Cat-Walk"; Second—Lael W. Hill, for "Dirge, On A Bonny Sunday"; Third—Mildred Crabtree Speer, for "On Witnessing Extinction."

Random Rhyme Award: First—Pauline Shortridge, for "Inferences"; Second—Sister M. Ricarda McGuire, for "Encounter"; Third—Jean M. La-Rocco, for "Vain Regret."

Amelia Reynolds Long Award: First—Maureen Cannon, for "Watching The Bird-Watchers"; Second—Lael W. Hill, for "If The Shoe Fits"; Third—Dorothy Lee Richardson, for "Through A Glass Brightly."

Mary Lee Hite Memorial Award: First—Vivian Smallwood, for "Elizabeth And The Changeling"; Second—Esther M. Leiper, for "The Shaman Answers"; Third—Tab France, for "Twining."

Mary Ellen Riddell Award: First—Jeanie Dolan Carter, for "Halloween Masquerade"; Second—Helen Mar Cook, for "Visit With Aunt Sara"; Third—Barbara Peters, for "The Old Woman Speaks."

California State Poetry Society Award: First—Sister Helene, for "Night Bus West"; Second—Pat Stodghill, for "Inner Core"; Third—Lois Beebe Hayna, for "In Answer To Your Query."

Arkansas Award: First—Ernestine Hoff Emrick, for "Video Void"; Second—Julia Hurd Strong, for "Victim"; Third—Ada Betty Reynolds, for "Great Day."

Florida State Poet's Association Award: First—Sylvia Rosenbaum, for "Climbing To Masada"; Second—Helen McMillin, for "Riverpark '79"; Third—Sister M. Ricarda McGuire, for "Mea Culpa."

Oklahoma State Poetry Society Award: First—Otta Louise Chase, for "Desert Sunset"; Second—Gordon MacIntyre, for "Cliff-Cities"; Third—Lora Dewey Finley, for "Measles And Snow."

Our American Indian Heritage Award: First—Verna R. Hollinger, for "Woven Memories"; Second—Helen Lair, for "Liberation"; Third—Tharin Williamson, for "Carolina Clay."

South Dakota Poetry Society Award: First—Ida Crane Walker, for "Ballad Of Big Foot Bend"; Second—Lael W. Hill, for "Approach To Stars"; Third—Maribel Coleman Haskin, for "Harriet."

Manningham Award: First—Marge Killilea, for "Young At Heart"; Second—Beatrice Mayer, for "Cruel And Unusual Punishment"; Third—David Andrews, for "I Heard Two Mules."

Poet Laureate Emeritus of Louisiana Award: First—Hervey Caton, for "Eternal Flame"; Second—Louise Hajek, for "Fool's Choice"; Third—Otta Louise Chase, for "Hurricane."

Humorous Poetry Award: First—A. T. Roy, for "Going To Print"; Second—Margaret Ricks, for "Ode To A Pocket Calculator"; Third—Claire Cooperstein, for "Dirty Trick."

Olive McHugh Memorial Award: First—Carlee Swann, for "My Brother"; Second—Margaret Brekke, for "Crossing The I"; Third—Lucile D. Nitzkowski, for "The Human Spirit."

Bible Award: First—Geraldine R. Pratt, for "The Singing Stones"; Second—Kitty Yeager, for "A Wedding In Cada"; Third—Alice Morrey Bailey, for "The Fourth Day."

Clement Hoyt Memorial Haiku Award: First—Ana Barton, for "Discarding Old Toys"; Second—Genevieve Sargent, for "Old Wooden Fence Rail"; Third—Winnie E. Fitzpatrick, for "Bright Summer Morning."

Beymorlin Sonnet Award: First—Glenna Holloway, for "The Winners"; Second—Carlee Swann, for "How Do You Prove A Brownie?"; Third—Margaret Ricks, for "Banding The Geese."

Evans Spencer Wall Memorial Award: First—Evelyn Corry Appelbee, for "Beach Violinist"; Second—Lois Beebe Hayna, for "Meditations On A Beanstock"; Third—Susan Adair Khan, for "The Painting Of The Shell."

Modern Award: First—Evelyn Corry Appelbee, for "Mexico, A Foreign Country"; Second—Esther Whitehead, for "The River View"; Third—Lael W. Hill, for "Fallen To Green."

Traditional Award: First—Carol A. Roberts, for "Hostages"; Second—Norma Calderone, for "Cry The Splendored Dark"; Third—Marion Brimm Rewey, for "Threshold Words For A Sunset House."

Arizona State Poetry Society Award: First—Marilee L. Pallant, for "Sleeping Positions"; Second—Max Golightly, for "Change Of Heart"; Third—Bayla Winters, for "Jannie At 4."

Maryland Award: First—Jack E. Murphy, for "The Hotel Near The End Of The Road"; Second—Esther M. Leiper, for "The Witch And The Unicorn"; Third—Wilma Dean Williams, for "And We Saw That Geysers Were Very Good."

Spoon River Award: First—Marion Brimm Rewey, for "Anne Boleyn"; Second—Ben Pierce, for "Min's Panegyric"; Third—Lucinda Oakland Morken, for "Lucy Locket."

Louisiana State Poetry Society Award: First—Georgia Earnest Klipple, for "Matagorda"; Second—Joe Shaffer, for "Between The Covers"; Third—Bettie M. Sellers, for "Revelation."

Utah State Award: First—Suzie Siegel, for "Waiting"; Second—Marilee L. Pallant, for "Song Long I've Harbored Granite"; Third—LeRoy Nurke Meagher, for "Visiting Hour."

Wichita Falls Texas Poetry Society Award: First—Benny McAdams, for "Hymn To The Heart Of Gladness"; Second—Helen B. Harary, for "Stasha Serafin"; Third—Marilyn Eynon Scott, for "Spring Song For Winter."

Wisconsin Poetry Award: First—LeRoy Burke Meagher, for "April Legacy"; Second—Alfhild Wallen, for "Rival—A Portrait In Watercolor"; Third—Marilyn McComas, for "A New Intimacy."

VerseWriters' Guild of Ohio Award: First—Bonnie Hearn, for "After 'Julia' "; Second—Esther Whitehead, for "Used-Angel Lot"; Third—Marcella Siegel, for "I Wonder If You Ever Got To Colorado."

Poet Laureate of Texas Award: First—Mickey Huffstutler, for "The Traveler Through The Dusty Earth"; Second—Elinor J. George, for "Genesis"; Third—David Chorlton, for "No Guns On Whiskey Row."

Leona Lloyd Memorial Award: First—Rita Norwood, for "The Stallion's Name"; Second—Mary Cogar, for "The Mirror"; Third—Edith E. Leavitt, for "The Flower Letter."

Ozarks Writers & Artists Guild Award: First—Hervey Caton, for "The Frolic At Fairbanks"; Second—Gertrude Ryder Bennett, for "Wynant Bennet's Kitchen"; Third—LeRoy Burke Meagher, for "Wild Horse Chase."

Poetry Society of Tennessee Award: First—Benny McAdams, for "Echoes And Mirrors"; Second—John Dickson, for "American Gothic"; Third—Zinita Fowler, for "Hide And Seek."

Pteranodon Award: First—Reba Terry, for "Land Fill"; Second—Alice Briley, for "On Rainy Evenings"; Third—David Chorlton, for "In Vino Veritas."

West Virginia Poetry Society Award: First—Linda G. Bunner, for "Indian Eyes"; Second—Annette Burr Stowman, for "Harper's Ferry"; Third—LeRoy Burke Meagher, for "Stars Over Grave Creek Mound."

Vivian Laramore Rader Memorial Award: First—Myrtle Marmaduke, for "As The Leaf Falls"; Second—Esther Whitehead, for "The Pharoah/The Architect"; Third—Frances Sydnor Tehie, for "Afternoon At The Louvre."

Perryman-Visser Award: First—Dorothy W. Wright, for "Seashore Symphony"; Second—Bernice Larson Webb, for "Design And Redesign"; Third—Madelyn Eastlund, for "A Constant Sign."

Nevada State Award: First—William Howard Cohen, for "For Alexander Solzhenitsyn"; Second—Normajean MacLeod, for "The Passing Of Our Time"; Third—Ida Fasel, for "Report On The 70s."

Massachusetts State Poetry Society Award: First—Lucille Gripp Maharry, for "Visit To Concord"; Second—Verna Lee Hinegardner, for "Those Bold, Bold Patriots"; Third—Virginia Moran Evans, for "The Ghost Of Rebecca Nurse Comes To Salem."

Philip E. Bartlett Memorial Award: First—Emma S. McLaughlin, for "Requiem For A Bird Watcher"; Second—Marilyn McComas, for "The Journey Over"; Third—M. Michael Black, for "First Flight From Crete."

Youth Award: First—Susan Gilbert, for "The Fire"; Second—John Shaw, for "The Bells Of Creation"; Third—Laura Margolis, for "Le Petit Chapeau Rouge."

National League of American Pen Women
Alexandria Branch
c/o Evelyn A. Wade
P.O. Box 398
Annandale, VA 22003
Annual Poetry Contest—
Sonnet: First—Evelyn Ritchie, for "Hayfever Season"; Second—Sarah Singer, for "Neanderthal"; Third—Esther M. Leiper, for "October Nicklaus."
Traditional: First—Olivia Wendy Holmes, for "Aubade"; Second—Gladys Moon Cook, for "Ebb Tide"; Third—Viette C. Sandbank, for "Rest In Peace."
Free Verse: First—Holt Fairfield, for "The Spirit Jar"; Second—Barbara Bass, for "Bon Voyage"; Third—Gonny Van den Broek, for "The Floating Market—Bangkok."
Light Verse, Rhymed: First—Virginia P. Oren, for "Sew-So"; Second—Mae Z. Scanlan, for "Stopping By A Gas Station On The Turnpike"; Third—Constance M. Ellison, for "Hang-Ups Ad Infinitum."
Light Verse, Free: First—Nedda Davis, for "Multiple Me"; Second—Ellen Anderson, for "Talisman"; Third—Pat Parnell, for "Peripatetic Author."
Lyric Verse (Swearingen Award): First—Barbara Bennet, for "Loss"; Second—Kristen Deming, for "Jerusalem"; Third—Margaret Weaver, for "Wake For A Dying Year."
Haiku: First—Dave Scott, for "The corn has grown old"; Second—Jeanne Bonnette, for "The lemonade days"; Third—Catherine K. Limperis, for "Brushing up against."

National Magazine Awards Foundation
1240 Bay St., Suite 300
Toronto, Ont. M5R 2A7
Canada
du Maurier Awards for Poetry: Gold—Michael Ondaatje, for "Campion: Sri Lanka" *(Canadian Forum);* Silver—Earle Birney, for "Deer Hunt" *(Toronto Life);* Honorable Mentions—Tom Wayman, for "Teething" *(Saturday Night),* Erin Moure, for "Post-Modern Literature" *(This Magazine),* and Florence McNeil, for "Bakerville Poems" *(Event).*

National Poetry Series
284 Fifth Ave.
New York,, NY 10001
National Poetry Series (winning manuscripts): "Gumbo," by George Barlow; "In That Part Of The City," by Robert Peterson; "In Winter," by Michael Ryan; "The Dollmaker's Ghost," by Larry Levis; "So This Is The Map," by Reg Saner.

New England Poetry Club
2 Farrar St.
Cambridge, MA 02138
Golden Rose Award: William Jay Smith.
Daniel Varoujan Award: Michael Akillian.

New Hope Foundation
430 Park Ave.
New York, NY 10022

Lenore Marshall Poetry Prize: Stanley Kunitz, for "The Poems Of Stanley Kunitz 1928-1978."

New Letters Magazine
5346 Charlotte
University of Missouri
Kansas City, MO 64110
William Carlos Williams Prize for Poetry: Diane Wakoski, for "Learning To Swim."

New York Quarterly
80 8th Ave.
New York, NY 10011
Poetry Day Award: Richard Eberhart.

Nimrod Magazine
Arts and Humanities Council of Tulsa
2210 S. Main
Tulsa, OK 74114
Pablo Neruda Prize for Poetry: First—Don Welch, for "The Rarer Game"; Second—Judith McCombs, for four poems from a sequence entitled "After The Surveyor's Death."

North American Mentor Magazine
P.O. Drawer 69
Fennimore, WI 53809
Annual Poetry Contest: First—William (Haywood) Jackson, for "There Is A Backyard"; Second—Bruce St. John, for "St. George's Harbour."

North Carolina Literary and Historical Association
109 E. Jones St.
Raleigh, NC 27611
Roanoke-Chowan Poetry Cup: Fred Chappell, for "Wind Mountain."

Ohio Poetry Day Association
c/o Evan Lodge
1506 Prospect Rd.
Hudson, OH 44236
Poet of the Year: (co-winners this year) Daisy Lee Donaldson, for "Surface Fragments"; Avonelle Mary Oliver, for "Twelve Moons."

Pacific Northwest Writers Conference
1811 NE 199th
Seattle, WA 98155
Pacific Northwest Writers Conference Poetry Contest: First Prize—Eugene Schlossberger, for "Three Runesongs" ("Last Song," "Instruction," "Seventh Ancient Scroll").

P.E.N. American Center
47 Fifth Ave.
New York, NY 10003
P.E.N. Translation Prize: Charles Simic, for his translation of "Homage To The Lame Wolf," by Vasco Popa.
American-Scandinavian/P.E.N. Translation Prize: Anselm Hollo, for his translation of the Finnish poet, Pentti Saarikoski.
P.E.N. Writing Awards for Prisoners (poetry): First—Michael Knoll, for "An Overture"; Second—D. L. Klauck, for "Myths"; Third—Joyce DeVillez, for "Cells."

Poetry Canada Review
P.O. Box 1280, Sta. A
Toronto, Ont. M5W 1G7
Canada

Editor's Prizes—
Mainstream Prize: Francis Sparshott, for "Impromptu For Voice And Woodwind."
Experimental Prize: Diane Schoemperlen, for "The Witchey House."
New Voices Prize: Kenneth Radu, for "Old Fort: Coteau Du Lac, Quebec."

The Poetry Center
92nd St. YM-YWHA
1395 Lexington Ave.
New York, NY 10028
*Discovery/*The Nation *Poetry Contest:* Dan Bogan, for "Election Day, 1989"; Michael McFee, for "Allhallows"; Rosanna Warren, for "Escape By Sea"; Stephen Yenser, for "Domestic."

Poetry Magazine
P.O. Box 4348
Chicago, IL 60680
Levinson Prize: Marilyn Hacker, for poems in Dec./79 and June/80 issues.
Oscar Blumenthal Prize: Robert Beverley Ray, for poems in Aug./80 issue.
Eunice Tietjens Memorial Prize: Sandra M. Gilbert, for poems in Jan./80 and July/80 issues.
Bess Hokin Prize: Gerald Stern, for poems in Dec./79 and June/80 issues.
Jacob Glatstein Memorial Prize: Lisel Mueller, for translations of Kaschnitz in Sept./80 issue.
English-Speaking Union Prize: David Wagoner, for poems in Jan./80 issue.

Poetry Society of America
15 Gramercy Park
New York, NY 10003
Elias Lieberman Student Poetry Award: Laura B. Margolis, for "Baking Bread."
Emily Dickinson Award: Virginnia Linton, for "The Sense Of An Alien Presence."
Bernice Ames Memorial Award: Patricia Hooper, for "At The Cemetery Near Mendon, 1976."
Gordon Barber Memorial Award: Myra Sklarew, for "Somnambulist."
Alfred Kreymborg Memorial Award: L. L. Zeiger, for "Silent Letters."
Consuelo Ford Award: Phyllis Janowitz, for "The Fisherman's Wife."
Gertrude B. Claytor Memorial Award: Marlene Rosen Fine, for "The Other Aunt."
Charles and Celia B. Wagner Award: Phyllis Janowitz, for "Electronic Capriccio For Solo Electron."
Mary Carolyn Davies Memorial Award: Ralph Robin, for "Swearing By Wildflowers."
Cecil Hemley Memorial Award: L. L. Zeiger, for "On Pack Monadnock."
Gustav Davidson Memorial Award: Willis Barnstone, for "The Good Beasts," "Eve," and "Tongues Of The Deep."
Lucille Medwick Memorial Award: Florence Grossman, for "Biblioteca Ambrosiana"; Gary Miranda, for "Visibilities."
John Masefield Memorial Award: Ellery Akers, for "Letters To Anna, 1846-54."
Melville Cane Award: Richard Hugo, for "Selected Poems."
Witter Bynner Poetry Translation Prize: John and

Bogdana Carpenter, for "Selected Poems" of Zbigniew Herbert.
Witter Bynner Grant-in-Aid: Charles Guenther: Anselm Hollo.
William Carlos Williams Award: David Ray, for "The Tramp's Cup"; Honorable Mention: William Dickey, for "The Rainbow Grocery."
Shelley Memorial Award: Julia Randall, for "Maryland."

Poetry Society of Oklahoma
c/o Clara Laster, Contest Chairman
204 E. 45th Pl.
Tulsa, OK 74105
Donors Award: Clara Laster, for "Definitions."
Non-Member Award: Doll Gardner, for "People To The Mountain Born."
Oliver Award: Dianne Moore, for "Machu Picchu."
Poet Laureate Award: Carol Hamilton, for "You Can, Too, Thomas Wolfe."
Green Award: Leroy Meagher, for "Epilogue."
Stealey Award: Wilma D. Williams, for "Under The Spreading Cottonwood."
Agnew Award: Clara Laster, for "The Twilight Hour."
Anonymous Award: Onette Rhodes, for "The 'Ec' And I."
Bennett Award: Winona Nation, for "The Silence."
Capps Award: Effa Roseboom, for "The Redbud."
Chapman Award: Carol Hamilton, for "Arapaho Measure."
Clay Award: Reba Terry, for "Houseguest."
Dougherty Award: Ray J. Davis, for "Speak To Me."
Hill Award: Clara Laster, for "The Wild Honey Of Scotland Heather."
Johnston Award: Gretelle LeGron, for "One Living Spray."
Kolbe Award: Emma Crobaugh, for "He Gathered Husks."
Laster Award: Ray J. Davis, for "We Met."
Lilly Award: Violet Amy Davis, for "More Than A Bug Catch."
Lucy Award: Robert Carson, for "The Guiding Past."
McMahan Award: Maggie Smith, for "Imagination Is A Culture."
McRill Award: Jerald J. Daly, for "Reunion."
Rider Award: Winona Nation, for "Longer Than Love."
Skaggs Award: Reba Terry, for "Scene From A Portrait: Mirror Image."
Smith Award: Winona Nation, for "Words For My Mother."
Thomason Award: Carol Hamilton, for "Pope John XXIII."
Wurtzbaugh Award: Reba Terry, for "To A Regular Contributor Of A.L. Magazine."

Poets Club of Chicago
Anne Nolan, Chairman
c/o Nolan Boiler Co.
8531 S. Vincennes Ave.
Chicago, IL 60620
National Shakespearean Sonnet Contest: First— Marie Daerr Boehringer, for "Intruder"; Second—

Ettie Hunter, for "This Is A Winter Thing"; Third—Nan E. R. Hagland, for "The Portrait And The Man."

Poets & Patrons, Inc.
c/o Mary Mathison, Contest Chairman
13924 Keller Ave.
Crestwood, IL 60445

International Narrative Contest: First—Evelyn Amuedo Wade, for "Wild Boer Escaped"; Second—Ellis, Atkisson McDonald, for "Excerpt From Great-Aunt Sarah's Diary"; First Honorable Mention—Delova S. Durnford, for "Any Rags, Any Bottles"; Second Honorable Mention—Alice Morrey Bailey, for "Mary Queen Of Scots."

Post Poetry Center
C. W. Post College
Greenvale, NY 11548

Winthrop Palmer Prize: Karen Treanor, for "The Voice Of Water."

Post Poetry Center Awards: Graduate—Terrence Cunningham, for "On Yeats' Cathleen Ni Houlihan"; Alumni—Glenn Schmidt, for "After The Bible Recital"; Third—Marcia Epstein, for "Communication."

Post Library Association Community Awards: First—Susan Astor, for "Child Of The Year"; Second—David Axelrod, for "The Vandal"; Honorable Mention—Sarah Singer, for "From Beacon Hill To Kansas—1890" and Robyn Spraner, for "The Crock."

Floyd and Dorothy Lyon Award: Ellen Ackerman, for "Sketch."

Prairie Schooner Magazine
201 Andrews Hall
University of Nebraska-Lincoln
Lincoln, NE 68588

Prairie Schooner Prize for Poetry: Dave Smith, for "Suburban Flight," "Red-Headed Woodpecker: Ben's Church, Virginia," "Cabin, Ruined, Uncoming Night" and "Reading The Books Our Children Have Written."

Flora Strousse Award: Lynn Emanuel, for "The Artists," "Dracula" and "What I Know About The End Of The Second World War."

Primapara Magazine
P.O. Box 371
Oconto, WI 54153

Susan Jansen Memorial Award: First—Carolyn Pettit, for "The Princess Breaks Out"; Second—Jean Ross, for "Tiger Lilies"; Third—Lita DiSalvo, for "The Lodger" and Joan Rohr Myers, for "Mrs. Johnson's Night Out"; Honorable Mention—Virginia Coonen, for "The Remodeling."

Dora Babka Kamke Memorial Award: First—Virginia Coonen; Second—Iris Day; Third—Michaelle Deakin Schall.

Waunette Tangen Memorial Award: First—Carolyn Pettit, for "Good Morning Heartache"; Second—Estella Lauter, for "To The Amazon Within"; Third—Carolyn Muentner, for "Denouement."

Pteranodon Magazine
P.O. Box 229
Bourbonnais, IL 60914

Fourth Pteranodon Poetry Contest: First—Emma

Dimit, for "Last Chance"; Second—Verna Lee Hinegardner, for "Love In Braille"; Third—Mary A. Gaumond, for "Dragon Slayer."

Fifth Pteranodon Poetry Contest: First—Nancy G. Westerfield, for "A Poet In The Schools"; Second—Jennifer Groce, for "Spell Cast For Michael"; Third—Jennifer Groce, for "Sunday Morning."

Religious Arts Guild
25 Beacon St.
Boston, MA 02108

Dorothy Rosenberg Annual Poetry Award: First Prize (two winners)—Bonnie Hearn, for "On Wanting To Open A Chinese Restaurant," and Betty Lowry, for "The Realist"; Honorable Mentions—Nancy Andrews, for "Arthur Comes To The Nursing Home," Vincent Canizaro, Jr., for "One Day At Red's Coney Island," Michael Knoll, for "From A Cell In Isolation: An Overture," Philip Golabuk, for "Courage In The Country," Sandia Belgrade, for "An Optional History," Nereo E. Condini, for "Haggadahs," and Marianne Andrea, for "Four Letters."

St. Louis Poetry Center
c/o Leslie Konnyu
5410 Kerth Rd.
St. Louis, MO 63128

Poets of Merit: Judith Saul Stix; Ms. Weisenberg.

San Francisco Foundation
425 California St.
San Francisco, CA 94104

Joseph Henry Jackson Literary Award (this year awarded to a poet): Wendy Bishop, for poems from two partially completed collections, "Island Seas" and "Scenarios." An Honorable Mention was granted to a poet, Ernest Albert Benck, Jr., for a partially completed collection, "A Stone's Throw."

James D. Phelan Literary Award (this year awarded to a poet): David Marshall St. John, for a collection of poems, "The Shore."

Saxifrage Prize
36C Stratford Hills
Chapel Hill, NC 27514

Saxifrage Prize (poetry); Robert Pinsky, for "An Explanation Of America."

Seven Magazine
3630 NW 22
Oklahoma City, OK 73107

Jesse Stuart Contest: First—Louise Derby, for "Aunt Missouri Watched The Sun Come Up." Second—Dorothy Foltz-Gray, for "Drought"; Rennie McQuilkin, for "Nesting." Third—Rennie McQuilkin, for "Baptism"; Alice Mackenzie Swaim, for "In The Silence Listening"; Esther N. Leiper, for "Roland Hall." Fourth—Ruth Joy Smith, for "A Desert In The Ozarks"; Louise Derby, for "Grace Note"; Rennie McQuilkin, for "The Vision."

South Western Ontario Poetry
396 Berkshire Dr.
London, Ont. N6J 3S1
Canada

Poetry Contest: (General) First—Ron Clarke; Second–Keitha K. MacIntosh; Third–S. D. Neill. (Short Poem) First–Gladys Nolan; Second–Mary Hoy Schmidt; Third–Bea Wallace. (Humorous) Lloyd Bloom. (Juvenile) Robin Tessier, Carolyn Hogarth, Robert Baker.

Southwest Review
Southern Methodist University
Dallas, TX 75275
Elizabeth Matchett Stover Memorial Award: L. M. Rosenberg, for "Saint Guthlac."

Stanford University
Creative Writing Center
Dept. of English
Stanford, CA 94305
Wallace E. Stegner Fellowships (in poetry): Barbara Thomsen; Michael Ramsey-Perez.

Stella Woodall Poetry Society
P.O. Box 253
Junction, TX 76849
Thanksgiving Theme: Catharine Albright Waldraff, for "Thanksgiving Wisdom."

Stone Country Magazine
20 Lorraine Rd.
Madison, NJ 07940
Phillips Poetry Award: Patrick Worth Gray, for "The Longest Journey"; Judith McPheron, for "In The Swaying Field"; Joan Colby, for "The North Wife's Pillow."

Syracuse University
Dept. of English
Syracuse, NY 13210
Delmore Schwartz Prize: Ron Block, for "My Feral Child."
Loring Williams Prize: Brooks Haxton, for group of poems including "Breakfast Ex Amino" and "Easter Mass For Little John."
Whiffin Prize: Andrew Abrahamson, for "Five Places With Rob And Hannes."

Triton College
2000 Fifth Ave.
River Grove, IL 60171
All Nations Poetry Contest: (Experience) Michael Gude, for "One Of Us Only, Pure Prose"; Debra Hines, for "At Mexico Gravel"; L. A. Jacobs, for "The Wasp"; Janet Krauss, for "To David, Spring, 1979"; Norman Leer, for "The Candlestick"; Curtis Nelson, for "Transplantation"; Marion Helz Perry, for "To My Student Eight Years Later"; Larry Rubin, for "The Nazi In The Dock, At Sixty"; Peter Sharpe, for "Failures"; Bill Silverman, for "As A Child." (Success) Feroz Ahmed-Ud-Din, for "Home"; Susan Baumann, for "Contagious Magic"; Muhammed Enamul Huque, for "A Full Magazine"; Jessie Kachmar, for "The Dropout's Revenge"; Daud Kamal, for "An Archway Of Stairs"; Donna Lane, for "I Want My Hand In This Poem"; Jeffery Skeate, for "Rhapsody"; Nena Yvonne Smiddy, for "No Drums Or Trumpets"; Pat Smith, for "At Minimum Wage"; Stephen Roberts, for "Grandfather From Whales." (Evil)

Katharyn Machan Aal, for "Little Bear Is Dead"; Gary Fincke, for "The Sniper Who Does Not Shoot"; David Gersshator, for Untitled; Norman Leer, for "Hotel Uterus"; Robert J. Levy, for "The Enlightenment Of Revolving Doors"; Thomas McNamee, for "White Nude"; Carol Artman Montgomery, for "Knife In The Window"; Janice Townley Moore, for "Reunion At Vengeance Creek Church"; Stephen Roberts, for "Escalation"; Heather Stewart, for "Cast Off."

University of Chicago
Division of Humanities
1010 E. 59th St.
Chicago, IL 60637
Harriet Monroe Poetry Award: Charles Simic.

University of Massachusetts Press
P.O. Box 429
Amherst, MA 01102
Juniper Prize: Lucille Clifton, for "Two-Headed Woman."

University of Missouri-Kansas City
Dept. of English
Kansas City, MO 64110
Barbara Storck Award (poetry): Mary Ruth Herzon

University of Western Ontario
1151 Richmond St., N.
London, Ont. N6A 3K7
Canada
President's Medal for Canadian Literature (poetry): Elizabeth Brewster, for "The Hoop."

Virginia Quarterly Review
1 West Range
Charlottesville, VA 22903
Emily Clark Award for Poetry: Cynthia Huntington, for "No One."

Wilory Farm
Route 1
Quemado, TX 78877
Wilory Farm Poetry Contest: First–Vivian Smallwood, for "Brief Encounter With A Blackbird"; Second–Suzanne Howes, for "Milking The Goat"; Third–Wesley McNair, for "Country People."

Writer's Digest
9933 Alliance Rd.
Cincinnati, OH 45242
Writing Competition (Grand Prize, poetry): Ken Duffin, for "Estrangement In Black And Gray."

Yale University Press
92A, Yale Sta.
New Haven, CT 06520
Yale Series of Younger Poets: John Bensko, for "Green Soldiers."

Yankee Magazine
Dublin, NH 03444
Annual Poetry Contest: First–Lawrence P. Spingarn, for "Vignette-1922."

Acknowledgments

The publisher expresses appreciation to the authors represented in this anthology for graciously permitting the inclusion of their poetry.

In addition, credit has been given to all magazines where material in this volume was originally published, with their names appearing after each respective poem.

In individual instances where authors, magazines or publishers required special acknowledgments or credit lines for copyrights they control, such recognition is hereby given as follows:

"Cock," by Aharon Amir, appears in *Modern Hebrew Poetry,* published by University of Iowa Press.

"The Road The Crows Own," by Susan Astor, appears in her book, *Dame,* published by The University of Georgia, and is reprinted by permission.

"The New Formalists," by Marvin Bell, first appeared in *Antaeus.* Copyright © by Marvin Bell. Reprinted by permission.

"The Copperhead," by David Bottoms, is copyright © 1980 by The Atlantic Monthly Company, Boston, Mass. Reprinted with permission.

"Wine From The Cape," by Turner Cassity, is copyright © 1980 by Turner Cassity. Reprinted by permission of *The Southern Review.*

"Braille," by Gerald Costanzo, first appeared in *The Missouri Review,* Vol. III, No. 3, Summer, 1980.

"Three Sunrises From Amtrack," by Florence Dolgorukov, is reprinted by permission from *The Christian Science Monitor.* Copyright © 1980, The Christian Science Publishing Society.

"Indian," by Jeanne Doriot, first appeared in *America.* Reprinted with permission of America, Inc., 106 West 56th Street, New York, N. Y. 10010. Copyright © 1980. All rights reserved.

"Nantucket's Widows," by Richard Foerster, first appeared in *Nantucket Review.* Reprinted by permission of the Author. All rights reserved.

"Dana Point," by Brewster Ghiselin, first appeared in *The Blue Hotel,* and is in his book, *Windrose: Poems 1929-1980.* Copyright © by Brewster Ghiselin. Reprinted by permission.

"On The Hazards Of Smoking," by Leah Goldberg, appears in *Modern Hebrew Poetry,* published by University of Iowa Press.

"Reading Faust," by Judah Goldin, is reprinted from *The American Scholar,* Vol. 49, No. 2, Spring, 1980. Copyright © 1980 by Judah Goldin. By permission of the publishers.

"The Wreck Of The Great Northern," by Robert Hedin, appears in his book, *At The Home-Altar,* published by Copper Canyon Press.

"Factories" and "Little Political Poem," by Edward Hirsch, will appear in 1981 in a book of poems by the author (as yet untitled), to be published by Alfred A. Knopf, Inc. Reprinted with permission of Alfred A. Knopf, Inc.

"Letter To Garber From Skye," by Richard Hugo, is reprinted from *The Right Madness On Skye,* poems by Richard Hugo, with permission of the author and the publisher, W. W. Norton & Company, Inc., New York, N. Y. Copyright © 1980 by Richard Hugo.

"Case," by Phyllis Janowitz, first appeared in *The New Yorker.* Copyright © 1980 by *The New Yorker Magazine.* Reprinted with permission.

"Skin," by Philip K. Jason, appears in his book, *Thawing Out,* published by Dryad Press.

"Old Men Pitching Horseshoes," by X. J. Kennedy, is reprinted by permission of the author.

"J'Accuse," by Peter Klappert, appears in his book, *The Idiot Of The Last Dynasty: The Apocryphal Monologues Of Doctor Matthew O'Connor,* published by Alfred A. Knopf, Inc. Reprinted by permission.

"News Of The World" and "My Angel," by Philip Levine, first appeared in *Antaeus.* Copyright © by *Antaeus.* Reprinted by permission.

"Starship," by David McAleavey, appears in his book, *Shrine, Shelter, Cave,* published by Ithaca House. Reprinted by permission.

"The Judge," by Kenneth A. McClane, first appeared in *Freedomways Magazine,* 799 Broadway, New York, N. Y. 10003. Vol. 20, No. 1, 1980.

"My Mother's Life," by William Meredith, appears in his book, *The Cheer,* published by Alfred A. Knopf, Inc. Copyright © by Alfred A. Knopf, Inc. Reprinted with permission.

"Alexander," by Frederick Morgan, first appeared in *"The American Scholar.* Copyright © by Frederick Morgan. Reprinted by permission.

"Castle Rock," by Frederick Morgan, first appeared in *Harper's Magazine.* Copyright © by Frederick Morgan. Reprinted by permission.

"The Choice," by Frederick Morgan, first appeared in *The New Republic.* Copyright © 1980 by Frederick Morgan. Reprinted by permission.

"Telling The Cousins," by Les A. Murray, appears in his book, *The Boys Who Stole The Funeral,* published by Angus & Robertson, Sydney, Australia, August, 1980. Reprinted by permission.

"My Best Clothes," by Eli Netzer, appears in *Modern Hebrew Poetry,* published by University of Iowa Press.

"Hide And Seek," by Dan Pages, appears in *Modern Hebrew Poetry,* published by University of Iowa Press.

"Ethics," by Linda Pastan, first appeared in *Poetry.* Copyright © 1980 by The Modern Poetry Association. Reprinted by permission of the Editor of *Poetry.* "Ethics" also appears in the author's book, *Waiting For My Life,* published by W. W. Norton & Company, Inc.

"To Robert Lowell And Osip Mandelstam," by Frederick Seidel, appears in his book, *Sunrise,* published by Viking Penguin, Inc. Copyright © 1964, 1966, 1967, 1968, 1969, 1971, 1972, 1978, 1979, 1980 by Frederick Seidel. Reprinted by permission of Viking Penguin, Inc.

"No Such Thing," by Marcia Southwick, appears in her book, *The Night Won't Save Anyone,* published by The University of Georgia Press. Reprinted by permission of The University of Georgia Press. Copyright © 1980 by The University of Georgia Press.

"Geological Faults," by Barbara Unger, first appeared in *The Nation.* Copyright © 1980 by The Nation Associates. Reprinted by permission.

"His Sleep," by Constance Urdang, appears in her book, *The Lone Woman And Others,* published by The University of Pittsburgh Press.

"Virgin Pictured In Profile," by Rosanna Warren, appeared originally in *The Atlantic Monthly.* Copyright © 1980 by The Atlantic Monthly Company, Boston, Mass. Reprinted with permission.

"The Grown-Up Sons," by Miller Williams, is copyright © 1979 by Miller Williams.

The following poems first appeared in *Kansas Quarterly:* "At The Spa," by James H. Bowden; "Bonner's Ferry Beggar," by Duane Clark; "Cousins," by Paula B. Cullen; "Armstrong Spring Creek," by Lloyd Davis; "Afternoon At Cannes," by Paul Davis; "The Undreamed," by Elaine V. Emans; "Dichterliebe," by Robert Klein Engler; "A July Storm: Johnson, Nehama County, Nebraska," by Steve Hahn; "Washing My Son," by Jonathan Holden; "The Hairdresser," by David Hopes; "Expecting," by Daniel J. Langton; "High Plains Harvest," by Bruce Morton; "Yahrzeit Candle," by Jean Nordhaus; "False Prophet," by Sr. Emanuela O'Malley; "At Times I Feel Like A Quince Tree," by John Robert Quinn; "June Song," by Abby Rosenthal; "When You Are Gone," by Nance Van Winckel; "Tenant Farmer," by Robert Ward; "The Limits Of Equitation," by Barbara Winder; "The Linebacker At Forty," by Jon Wallace; "Sparrows In College Ivy," by Edgar Wolfe. Copyright © 1979 / 1980 by *Kansas Quarterly.* Reprinted by permission of *Kansas Quarterly* and by the individual authors.

The following poems first appeared in *Poetry.* Copyright © 1980 by The Modern Poetry Association. Reprinted by permission of the Editor of *Poetry:* "Winter In Another Country," by AI; "Books," by William Baer; "The Old Biograph Girl," by Margaret Benbow; "The Flirtation," by Michael C. Blumenthal; "Oedepus, Pentheus," by David Bromwich; "Summer Visitors," bv Stephen Clark; "Roses, Revisited, In A Paradoxical

Autumn," by J. W. Cullum; "Oatmeal Deluxe," by Stephen Dobyns; "The Visit," by Jim Gauer; "Rissem," by Sandra M. Gilbert; "Back Road," by Bruce Guernsey; "At The Smithsonian," by Vanessa Haley; "Late," by Daniel Halpern; "Gull Lake Reunion," by Kelly Ivie; "The Children's Hour," by Don Johnson; "Oxford Commination," by Paris Leary; "Ode" and "In Praise Of Robert Penn Warren," by David Lehman; "To A Wall Of Flame In A Steel Mill, Syracuse New York, 1969," by Larry Levis; "Saying One Thing," by Robert Long; "Leaving One Of The State Parks After A Family Outing," by Elizabeth Macklin; "The Bald Spot," by Wesley McNair; "My Mother's Life," by William Meredith; "The Kiss," by Robert Pack; "Ethics," by Linda Pastan; "The Water Tower" by James Paul; "Dying," by Robert Pinsky; "Riverside Drive, November Fifth," by Katha Pollitt; "A Jerusalem Notebook," by Harvey Shapiro; "Partial Draft," by Robert B. Shaw; "His Side" and "Her Side," by Jeffrey Skinner; "Tide Pools," by Dave Smith; "Static," by Barton Sutter; "Feeling For Fish," by Leonard Trawick; "Under The Sign Of Mother," by David Wagoner; "Love In Brooklyn," by John Wakeman; "Moose," by Robert Wiljer; "Porcupines," by Robley Wilson, Jr.; "Venice," by James Wright; "To An Estranged Wife," by Gary Young; "Lilly's Song," by Evan Zimroth.

The following poems first appeared in *The Yale Review*. Copyright © by Yale University. Reprinted with permission: "An Unseen Fire," by Michael G. Cooke; "Developers At Crystal River," by James Merrill; "Masks," by Brian Swann.

The following poems first appeared in *Yankee*. Reprinted with permission of Yankee, Inc., and by the individual authors: "Windfall," by Joel Arsenault; "Homing," by P. C. Bowman; "Song For A Lost Art," by Virginia Brasier; "How Stars And Hearts Grow In Apples," by Virginia Elson; "Nothing Gold Can Stay," by Norma Farber; "A Farewell" and "Moonsong," by Hildegarde Flanner; "Pause Between Clock Ticks," by James Hearst; "Two Birds," by Kathleen Linnell; "Tree Man," by Rennie McQuilkin; "These Magicians," by Sarah Provost; "Fat Cat," by John Ronan; "Telephone," by Robin Shectman; "Breathe On The Glass," by Raymond Stineford.